CREATING EXPERT SYSTEMS FOR BUSINESS AND INDUSTRY

Related titles of interest from Wiley:

EXPERT SYSTEMS: ARTIFICIAL INTELLIGENCE IN BUSINESS
Harmon and King

EXPERT SYSTEMS TOOLS AND APPLICATIONS
Harmon, Maus, and Morrissey

PUTTING ARTIFICIAL INTELLIGENCE TO WORK: EVALUATING AND IMPLEMENTING BUSINESS APPLICATIONS
Schoen and Sykes

ARTIFICIAL INTELLIGENCE PROGRAMMING WITH TURBO PROLOG
Weiskamp and Hengl

DESIGNING INTELLIGENT FRONT ENDS FOR BUSINESS SOFTWARE
Shafer

PROGRAMMING EXPERT SYSTEMS IN PASCAL
Sawyer and Foster

CREATING EXPERT SYSTEMS FOR BUSINESS AND INDUSTRY

PAUL HARMON
BRIAN SAWYER

John Wiley & Sons, Inc.
New York • Chichester • Brisbane • Toronto • Singapore

Editor: Therese A. Zak
Managing Editor: Ruth Greif
Editing, Design, & Production: G&H Soho, Ltd.

This publication is designed to provide accurate and authoritative information in regard to the subject matter covered. It is sold with the understanding that the publisher is not engaged in rendering legal, accounting, or other professional service. If legal advice or other expert assistance is required, the services of a competent professional person should be sought. FROM A DECLARATION OF PRINCIPLES JOINTLY ADOPTED BY A COMMITTEE OF THE AMERICAN BAR ASSOCIATION AND A COMMITTEE OF PUBLISHERS.

Copyright © 1990 by John Wiley & Sons, Inc.

All rights reserved. Published simultaneously in Canada.

Reproduction or translation of any part of this work beyond that permitted by section 107 or 108 of the 1976 United States Copyright Act without the permission of the copyright owner is unlawful. Requests for permission or further information should be addressed to the Permission Department, John Wiley & Sons, Inc.

Library of Congress Cataloging-in-Publication Data

Harmon, Paul.
   Creating expert systems for business and industry / Paul Harmon, Brian Sawyer.
      p.   cm.
   Bibliography: p.
   Includes index.
   ISBN 0-471-61495-5. — ISBN 0-471-61496-3 (pbk.)
   1. Business—Data processing. 2. Industrial management—Data processing. 3. Expert systems (Computer science) I. Sawyer, Brian. II. Title.
HF5548.2.H366 1989
651.8—dc20   89-14834
                                                                           CIP

Printed in the United States of America

90 91 10 9 8 7 6 5 4 3 2 1

To
Thomas F. Gilbert
and
Geary A. Rummler

Trademarks

1st-CLASS is a registered trademark of 1st-CLASS Expert Systems, Inc.

AION is a registered trademark of AION Corporation.

APEX Client Profiling is a trademark of Applied Expert Systems, Inc.

Apollo is a registered trademark of Apollo Computers, Inc.

Application Expert is a trademark of Cullinet Software, Inc.

Arborist, Business-Pro, Explorer, Images, microExplorer, Personal Consultant Easy, Procedure Consultant, TestBench, TestBuilder, TestBridge, and TestView are trademarks of Texas Instruments Incorporated.

ART is a trademark of Inference Corp.

ASK DAN is a copyrighted product of Legal Knowledge Systems, Inc.

CATS-1 is a trademark of General Electric Corp.

DASD Advisor and DASD Monitor are trademarks of Boole and Babbage.

DB2, IBM, IBM PC/AT, and KnowledgeTool are registered trademarks of International Business Machines, Inc.

dBASE III is a registered trademark of Ashton-Tate.

DEC, PDP-11, VAX, VAX Decision Expert, VMS, XCON, and XSEL are trademarks of Digital Equipment Corporation.

EnForm is a trademark of Mind Path Technologies, Inc.

ExperTax is a trademark of Coopers & Lybrand.

Expert-Ease is a product of Intelligent Terminals Limited.

Exsys is a trademark of Exsys, Inc.

G2 is a trademark of Gensym.

Golden Common Lisp, Golden Connection, GoldWorks, and GoldWorks AXLE are trademarks of Gold Hill Computers, Inc.

GURU is a trademark of Micro Data Base Systems, Inc.

I-CAT is a trademark of Automated Reasoning Corporation.

KBMS is a registered trademark of AICorp Inc.

KEE and KEEconnection are trademarks of Intellicorp, Inc.

KES is a trademark of Software Architecture and Engineering, Inc.

Knowledge Craft is a registered trademark of Carnegie Group, Inc.

Lending Advisor is a trademark of Syntelligence, Inc.

LEVEL5 is a trademark of Information Builders, Inc.

Lotus 1-2-3 is a registered trademark of Lotus Development Corp.

M.1. and S.1. are patented software of Cimflex-Teknowledge, Inc.

Nexpert Object and Nextra are trademarks of Neuron Data, Inc.

OPS/83 is a trademark of Production Systems Technologies, Inc.

OS/2 is a trademark of MicroSoft Corporation.

Scheme is a trademark of M.I.T. Artificial Intelligence Laboratory.

Smalltalk 80 and Xerox Star are trademarks of Xerox Corporation.

SPARC is a trademark of Sun Microsystems, Inc.

UNIX is a trademark of AT&T.

VP-Expert is a trademark of Paperback Software International.

Contents

Foreword xiii
Preface xv

Section One. Basic Concepts   1

     1. **Expert Systems Today**   3
         What Is Artificial Intelligence? What Are Expert Systems? *3*
         What Is the State of the Expert Systems Market? *3*
         What Are the Problems Standing in the Way of Wider Use? *8*
         The Future *10*

     2. **Basic Expert Systems Techniques**   12
         Overview *12*
         Key Concepts in AI and Expert Systems *12*
         Induction Systems *20*
         Rule-Based Systems *24*
         Hybrid Systems *41*
         Symbolic Language Techniques *47*

Section Two. Identifying Opportunities   49

     3. **Identifying and Scoping Potential Applications—Part 1**   51
         Overview *51*
         Step 1. Choosing an Overall Corporate Strategy *51*
         Step 2. Developing a List of Potential Applications *58*
         Step 3. Checking Key Expert Systems Criteria *63*

     4. **Identifying and Scoping Potential Applications—Part 2**   75
         Step 4. Identifying the Basic Cognitive Structure of the Problem *75*
         Step 5. Considering User, Cost, and Management Issues *83*
         Summary *88*

Section Three. Knowledge Acquisition and System Design   89

     5. **Analyzing a Consultation**   91
         Introduction *91*
         Human Performance Analysis *92*
         Dataflow Analysis *99*
         Summary: Creating a Scenario *105*

6. Cognitive Analysis — 109
Introduction *109*
Some Cognitive Assumptions *110*
The Object-Attribute-Value Model *120*
Knowledge Mapping Notation *124*
Developing a Knowledge Map *133*
Summary *135*

7. Knowledge Acquisition — 137
Introduction *137*
Knowledge Acquisition Problems *138*
Interviewing *142*
Summary *149*

Section Four. Program Development — 151

8. Creating Small Rule-Based Systems — 153
Introduction *153*
Phase 1. Defining the Problem *153*
Phase 2. Developing an Initial Set of Rules *155*
Phase 3. Enhancing the Rules *159*
Phase 4. Customizing Inference *167*
Summary *169*

9. Creating Forward Chaining Systems — 171
Introduction *171*
Phase 1. Defining the Problem *174*
Phase 2. Writing Code to Obtain Facts *176*
Phase 3. Writing an Initial Set of Rules *177*
Phase 4. Giving the System a Way to Stop *179*
Phase 5. Controlling the Execution of Rules *180*
Phase 6. Further Development *184*
Additional Considerations *185*

10. Creating Systems with Context Trees — 189
Introduction *189*
Phase 1. Deciding What Contexts Signify *191*
Phase 2. Creating an Initial Context Tree *194*
Phase 3. Implementing the Context Tree *195*
Phase 4. Expanding and Revising the Context Tree *201*
Summary *202*

11. Creating Hybrid Systems — 203
Introduction *203*
Phase 1. Defining the Problem *205*
Phase 2. Defining Frames *206*
Phase 3. Defining Instances *210*
Phase 4. Defining Screen Objects (or the User Interface) *212*

Phase 5. Adding Rules *212*
Phase 6. Adding Demons *215*
Phase 7. Adding Message-Passing *216*
Inference and Control *218*
Summary *220*

12. **Procedural Considerations** 221
    Introduction *221*
    Incorporating Some Procedural Code into a Knowledge Base *222*
    Combining Conventional Programs with an Expert System *226*
    Converting a Symbolic Language-Based Expert System to a Conventional Language *229*
    Converting a Conventional Application into an Expert System *230*
    Summary *234*

13. **Database Considerations** 235
    Introduction *235*
    Integrating Expert Systems and Databases *235*
    Object-Oriented Databases *245*
    Spreadsheet Access *245*
    Summary *246*

14. **Interface Considerations** 248
    Introduction *248*
    The Interface for the User *248*
    Summary *263*

Section Five. **Managing the Development of Expert Systems** 265

15. **Managing an Expert Systems Development Effort** 267
    Introduction *267*
    Phase 1. Front End Analysis *267*
    Phase 2. Analysis and Design *271*
    Phase 3. Prototype Development *273*
    Phase 4. Systems Development *277*
    Phase 5. Testing and Implementation *281*
    Phase 6. Maintenance *283*

Appendices 287

Appendix I:
A List of Expert Systems Building Tools *289*

Appendix II:
Glossary *305*

References and Notes 315
Index 319

Foreword

This book describes the technology behind an emerging revolution in software—the expert systems revolution. Computer practitioners may wonder: Why call this software revolutionary? Is it not part of a steady evolution of computer capabilities?

The term "revolution," when applied to a technology, means that the technology induces an order of magnitude change in the use for which it is targeted. The automobile revolutionized our way of life by making an order of magnitude change in the speed of personal travel, from the four or five miles per hour of walking to the 40 or 50 miles per hour of driving. The jet plane made another order of magnitude change, transporting us at 500 miles per hour. Each order of magnitude makes a revolutionary change in what is possible.

Expert systems are power tools for knowledge work—for knowledge access and reasoning. They are almost always used as assistants, as aids for human professional and semi-professional endeavor. The most impressive effect of their use is that they speed up human work by at least an order of magnitude, sometimes two orders of magnitude or more! Following are typical results of expert systems in industry:

- A manufacturing planning task that took hours to do is now done in 15 minutes.
- A scheduling activity that once took eight man weeks is done in half a man day.
- A design task that once took a month of work is done in two days.
- A product configuration task that normally takes a manufacturing engineer three hours is done in half a minute.

The order of magnitude effect is seen in dollar savings as well, measured as internal rate of return on the investment in the expert system. One company, with 500 expert systems deployed, reports internal rates of return of up to 1,500 percent. A typical excellent IRR on a new technology is a mere 40 percent.

Putting expert knowledge and systematic search and reasoning skills at the fingertips of the average performer significantly improves the quality of that performer's work. There's plenty of "room at the top" between expert performance and average performance (about a factor of 50 in productivity), so an order of magnitude effect on quality of work is possible by distributing a company's expertise to its average performers.

These and other major economic and organizational effects of the use of expert systems are surveyed and discussed in a recent book of case studies, *The Rise of the Expert Company*, that I co-authored with H. Penny Nii and Pamela McCorduck.

Paul Harmon, with his various collaborators, has been a champion, a shaper, and a chronicler of this revolution. Things move fast in a new technology, and the story must be told accurately, clearly, and in a timely manner. The industry has come to rely on Paul Harmon's newsletter (*Expert Systems Strategies*), his lectures, and his books for up-to-date technical information on tools, applications, and trends. Insight and clarity are the hallmarks of his contribution.

This book extends the range of his coverage of the expert systems technology. Here, Paul Harmon and Brian Sawyer make an important move from the what-for to the how-to. The book is of remarkable scope. It begins with a discussion of the market but quickly moves to strategic considerations. An important chapter deals with proper scoping of the expert system—the vital front-end work that I like to call "planning for success."

Section Three uncovers details of analysis and design. What's in a consultation? How is the knowledge to be structured? How is it to be acquired?

Section Four provides the necessary underpinning at the programming level. It contains all the major how-to topics of a good course for knowledge engineers. The field is moving toward an integration with conventional computing languages and database systems, so the inclusion of Chapters 12 and 13, dealing with these topics, is refreshing and important.

All of this fuel, for what fire? The fire burning in the expert systems revolution is productivity enhancement. National wealth is built with natural resources and gains in the productivity of its workers.

The Japanese, with few natural resources, have become a world-class economic power through productivity gains alone. On the other hand, an article in *Science* magazine a few years ago posed the question of the U.S. economy in its title: What ever happened to productivity gains? Productivity gains in the manufacturing sectors have been all right (average), but productivity gains among knowledge and information workers have been dismal.

Technology can make a difference, as it did during the agricultural and industrial revolutions. Expert systems technology, and its underlying science of artificial intelligence, will make a difference in boosting the sagging productivity of "thinking work." And it seems to be having an important effect also on manufacturing—"doing work"—since two-thirds of the manufacturing dollar is spent on information handling and knowledge work (planning, scheduling, decision making, etc.).

A fanning of the productivity fire is seen in the well-planned projects of the Japanese government (Fifth-Generation Project) and the European Economic Community (ESPRIT). The United States eschews national planning for information technology outside of the defense context. So the task devolves upon individuals—corporate CEOs charged with having strategic vision, engineers and computer professionals on the firing line, and most of all the middle managers with day-to-day decision-making authority—to plan and act.

All are well served by this book. Harmon and Sawyer have made their jobs easier, and their list of excuses shorter.

EDWARD A. FEIGENBAUM
Stanford, California
June 12, 1989

Preface

In 1984, we published *Expert Systems: Artificial Intelligence in Business*. In 1986, *Expert Systems: Tools and Applications* was completed. Now, in early 1989, we are wrapping up *Creating Expert Systems*. Each of these books has a slightly different focus, although each has the same central theme: providing you, the reader, with a basic overview of the techniques and methodologies that constitute expert systems.

We believe that this book will ultimately replace *Expert Systems: Artificial Intelligence in Business*. It provides a clearer overview of the basic concepts underlying the technology than was possible in 1984. And, at the same time, it presents detailed information about how to actually design, develop, and manage the creation of expert systems.

We don't expect this book to replace *Expert Systems: Tools and Applications*. That book contains information about specific tools and applications that is omitted from this book. We expect instead to revise *Expert Systems: Tools and Applications* to expand and update its coverage of expert systems building tools and its catalog of fielded expert systems applications. For example, new tools that incorporate domain-specific knowledge, natural language components, and neural networks are about to become available, and anyone considering expert systems tools should certainly know about them. We also expect to update *Creating Expert Systems* as companies build more systems and developmental methodologies become more formalized. We hope that this book and *Tools and Applications* together will provide a good solid introduction to the concepts, tools, applications, and methodologies that constitute commercial expert systems.

With this end in mind, we have focused this book on two things: the basic concepts and techniques involved in the development of expert systems, and the methodologies that are being used to analyze, design, develop, and manage the creation of expert systems. We do not focus on tools and we provide only a little information about specific applications. We urge anyone who wants such information to consult *Expert Systems: Tools and Applications*.

We have divided *Creating Expert Systems* into five sections. The first section provides a brief overview of the expert systems market and a good introduction to the concepts and techniques that are used to encode knowledge and make inferences about such knowledge.

We devote the second section to identifying appropriate opportunities to use expert systems. We begin by discussing the various strategies different organizations have adopted and then move on to specific techniques for identifying and scoping potential applications.

The third section focuses on the problems of analyzing tasks, acquiring knowledge, and formalizing that knowledge in a way that facilitates knowledge base development. The fourth section considers the actual steps involved in developing various types of expert systems. We suggest ways to go about developing small rule-based systems, forward chaining systems. In addition, we discuss how expert systems can be integrated into conventional data processing environments by combining conventional programs and databases with expert systems, and how developer and user interfaces can affect the final application.

Throughout Sections Two, Three, and Four, we provide information about how to go about analyzing, designing, and developing an expert system. In Section Five, we summarize what we have said by providing systematic recommendations for someone who is asked to manage the development of an expert system.

We have hardly solved all the problems or answered all the questions that challenge the developers of expert systems. Indeed, we are keenly aware that new people are rapidly discovering new ways to create and manage expert systems development; this book has to be regarded as a snapshot of a rapidly changing technology. We believe, however, that *Creating Expert Systems* summarizes the best of the current practices and identifies the pitfalls that should be avoided. We hope that this book will provide you with a comprehensive basic approach to use when you set out to create an expert system.

To make this book flow as smoothly as possible, we have avoided footnotes and references. Annotated citations are collected in the References and Notes section at the end of the book. We have limited our references to commonly available books or magazine articles. This is consistent with our goal of providing a broad overview for business readers. If you want more depth you can check the references at the back of the book. Most of the books listed there provide citations that will lead to the extensive technical literature.

There are many ways to read this book, depending on your needs. If you want a general introduction to the field, then beginning at the beginning and going through the chapters systematically is your best strategy. On the other hand, if you understand the basics and want help with analysis and design, you could begin at Chapter 3, 4, or 5. If you know which general type of tool you want to use and simply want an overview of how to use such a tool in a systematic development effort, you should turn to Section Four and read the chapter devoted to the approach you are interested in. If you are a manager, you might want to begin by reading Section Five, and then read other chapters as you see fit. If you skip around, you may encounter terms that you don't know. We have included a Glossary that should help those of you who take an unconventional route.

A book that surveys a rapidly changing field is possible only because of the help and cooperation of many different people. At the risk of offending people who are inadvertently omitted, we must try to acknowledge some of those who have helped make this book possible.

To provide a consistent thread of reality throughout the book, we discuss three expert systems in many different chapters. We owe a special acknowledgment to the people who developed those systems and shared the details of their work with us, including Yehudah Freunlich, Andrea Rudenko, Jack van Kinsbergen, and John Kees. Steven Schur, Robert Hink, Stuart Froman, and Terry Schussler each provided helpful suggestions.

Early in the development of this book, Avron Barr shared many insights with us. Some of Avron's insights into the expert systems development process are preserved here and we gratefully acknowledge Avron's help.

Many other people have helped us keep up with the field. Each time we interact with one of them, we come away with new insights about what is happening and what is about to happen. An inadequate, short list includes Jan Aikens, K.C. Branscomb, Jerry Baker, Denny Brown, Ester Dyson, Dan Easterlin, Ed Feigenbaum, Mark Fox, Tommy Fox, Aaron Goodman, Tom Grubb, Steve Hardy, Larry Harris, Peter Hart, Carl Hewitt, Alex Jacobson, Tom Kehler, John Landry, Mark Linesch, Tod Loofbourrow, Frank Lynch, Tom Martin, Claudia Mazzetti, Ed Mahler, DeJean Melancon, Bonnie Merritt, Jim Miller, Bill Morrissey, Makato Nagao, Harvey Nequest, Penny Nii, Peter O'Farrel, Ron Ogg, Adam Osborne, Bill Paulk, Ed Payne, Jeffrey Perione, Jean-Claude Rault, Elaine Rich, Koji Sasaki, Dan Schafer, Tom Schwartz, George Schussel, Karl and Henry Seiler, Harry Tennet, Peter Van Cuylenburg, Gene Wang, Karl Wiig, Mike Williams, Celia Wolf, and Carl Wolf.

There are other people who are unknown in the expert systems community whom we have worked with for many years. They taught us how to analyze human performance and communications problems and develop solutions that would work in business settings. This book draws a number of key insights from the work of these mentors, and we predict that the relevance of Thomas F. Gilbert, Geary A. Rummler, Joe Harless, James L. Evans, and Donald T. Tosti will come to influence the analysis and design of knowledge systems in the same way that it currently influences work in the design and development of instructional systems.

We also want to thank Curtis Hall, who created most of the graphics, and Paul Heidt and Nikki Grubb, whose research efforts helped assemble the information that is presented in this book.

Finally, of course, we must express our appreciation to our families and office associates, as well as to Allison Kohrs and Bruce Ito. We would also like to thank our editors, Therese Zak and Ellen Greenberg, and their associates at John Wiley & Sons, who have been both helpful and supportive.

PAUL HARMON
BRIAN SAWYER
San Francisco, California
May 1989

CREATING EXPERT SYSTEMS FOR BUSINESS AND INDUSTRY

Section One

BASIC CONCEPTS

In this section, we consider the nature of the expert systems market and review the basic concepts and techniques that are used in expert systems. These concepts and techniques are fundamental and powerful and will increasingly find their way into all aspects of commercial programming.

1.
Expert Systems Today

WHAT IS ARTIFICIAL INTELLIGENCE? WHAT ARE EXPERT SYSTEMS?

If you read computer-related newspapers or magazines, you've been encountering articles about artificial intelligence (AI) and expert systems since about 1984. The early articles suggested that AI was going to transform the world of computing by introducing new hardware and a completely new way of developing software. Later, other articles suggested that there were many unresolved problems involved in using AI and that the results were not as exciting as many had been led to expect. Now, having gone through the early "hype" phase and having survived the ensuing "letdown," AI and expert systems are being considered in a more realistic light.

Expert systems can be defined narrowly or broadly. Narrowly, expert systems techniques make computer programming easier and more effective. Broadly, they represent the first step in a process that will transform computing by moving programming technology beyond numerical programming into the realm of logical, symbolic programming. Construed narrowly, expert systems have accumulated a rather impressive record of achievement. Considered broadly, of course, the existing techniques and the resulting applications constitute only a first step.

This book is written for managers and programmers in business, industry, and government who are concerned with how they can use the concepts and techniques that are commercially available right now. Accordingly, we take the more narrow view of expert systems and focus on how currently available techniques can be used effectively to create useful and valuable commercial software applications.

We do not focus on expert systems as an isolated technology, however, but rather as a set of techniques to be integrated with conventional programming techniques. We stress the analysis, design, development, and programming techniques that expert systems developers use much more than the specific applications that result from the use of these techniques. Expert systems applications do not constitute a distinct, well-defined class of applications. Instead, they are a fuzzy set of software applications produced in whole or in part by the application of techniques developed in AI laboratories. We hope to convince you that these techniques can be used in most software development efforts.

WHAT IS THE STATE OF THE EXPERT SYSTEMS MARKET?

From a broad historical perspective, the 1980s and 1990s will prove to be amazing decades. The world economy is being integrated in a way and at a pace that nobody foresaw in the 1970s. At the same time, large corporations are decentralizing and small firms are being created at a rapid rate to provide the flexibility and innovation that are required for sharply increased domestic and international competition.

The collection, analysis, and distribution of data are keys to this worldwide economic integration, corporate decentralization, and innovation. Computer technology is therefore becoming increasingly important, which, in turn, creates tremendous demand and incentives for computer companies to keep changing and improving in order to achieve the right mix of hardware and software necessary for the rapidly changing world economic situation.

Within the computer world itself, we are witnessing a continuing revolution that is almost impossible to comprehend. It is happening too fast to be termed an evolutionary process; the only thing to compare it to is the Industrial Revolution, when steam engines changed the world between about 1775 and 1850.

Mainframe computers are not going to go away, but their relative importance is being undermined by personal computers and workstations. This shift, in turn, is changing the way people make decisions within corporations. The centralized departments that have controlled computers in most companies (Corporate MIS) are rapidly losing control over budgets and decisions, while departmental management information systems (MIS) groups are acquiring it. Significant power struggles are going on within many corporations that have little to do with rational business planning.

Established hardware vendors have been trying to resist the trend toward open systems, systems that allow users to assemble their own computer networks. Their resistance is proving hopeless, though, and they are now beginning to tumble over each other to get into the open systems game. Digital Equipment Corporation (DEC), for example, just announced a RISC-based UNIX machine, thus breaking with their decade-old commitment to their proprietary VMS system. Even IBM and DEC are working to develop a new, open UNIX standard.

It is still too early to tell what approaches will ultimately prove the most successful, but at the moment, the obvious winner is UNIX. In the next few years, workstations will become more and more important: They can function as standalone engines for powerful decision support applications, as nodes in networks of PCs, and as links to mainframes that will increasingly serve as file servers. New companies and new approaches will compete to make the best use of these workstations, which will soon become the center of corporate computing.

We say all this to emphasize that AI and expert systems came on the commercial scene just as the computer world was convulsed in battles over hardware and software standards. And these struggles may go on for another 10 years. For most companies, trying to choose an operating system or a hardware package is a major decision. Do you stay with DOS, or move to OS/2 or UNIX? Do you try to link Apple and DEC hardware, or stay with IBM?

Trying to decide if and when the company should begin to explore symbolic processing and expert systems is a smaller concern. Symbolic computing and expert systems may transform the whole world of computing by the year 2000, but in the meantime, companies have to approve budgets and buy hardware, and a wrong hardware decision can cost millions and affect MIS careers.

Thus, expert systems vendors and expert systems advocates within corporations find themselves positioning their products and projects to facilitate one or another major trend without particular regard to more rational considerations. It can't be any other way, but it makes the analysis of the expert systems market difficult, since enthusiasm for expert systems technology is often held captive to considerations about staying with mainframes, shifting to UNIX, or buying 386 machines. Everything about computers is changing simultaneously and will continue to do so for several years. Therefore, developing a clear explanation of what is happening in any one market within the interconnected network of computer markets is difficult. And developing a clear picture of the entire computer market is quite impossible. We try here to provide an overview of what is happening in expert systems, but we caution you to keep in mind that we are describing a very small part of a large, complex, and dynamic whole.

A Brief History of Expert Systems

The first commercial expert system, DEC's XCON, was put into use in 1981. Expert systems building tools (VAX, OPS5, Expert Ease, KEE, and S.1) were first offered for sale around 1983. The years 1985 and 1986 were very hot years for expert systems, but 1987 and 1988 were rather slow, as companies tried to absorb and evaluate what they had acquired in the previous years. The years 1989 and 1990 mark the beginning of a more mature expert systems market. The early 1990s should witness the widespread ac-

Expert Systems Today

ceptance and use of expert systems to transform the way companies develop software and use computers.

First-generation tools written in LISP are now being replaced by more sophisticated tools designed for complete integration with existing commercial hardware and software. Development procedures that were based on standalone systems running on specialized hardware are being replaced by new methodologies that combine conventional and new analysis and design techniques.

Figure 1.1 illustrates three waves of interest that have driven the U.S. expert systems market. The first wave was driven by R & D groups that wanted to learn more about the new technology. The second wave was driven by leading-edge companies that had the interest and the resources to move quickly to take advantage of the new technology. These companies were willing to try expert systems before the technology was mature, and they have, in fact, contributed a great deal to the maturation and sophistication of the current market. The most successful of these second wave companies have now fielded large, valuable applications and are moving rapidly to take strategic advantage of what they have learned about expert systems.

The third wave, which is just beginning to grow now, involves the majority of large U.S. companies. The companies that are just beginning to become interested in expert systems are companies that have waited for the technology to mature, for prices to come down, and for hardware and implementation issues to be solved.

We are writing this book while the market is in transition from the second to the third wave of interest. Some companies are still focusing on large, LISP-based, standalone applications while others are focusing on integrating inference techniques and small amounts of knowledge into large conventional

Figure 1.1 The waves of expert systems adaptation.

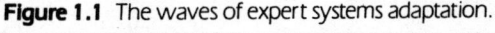

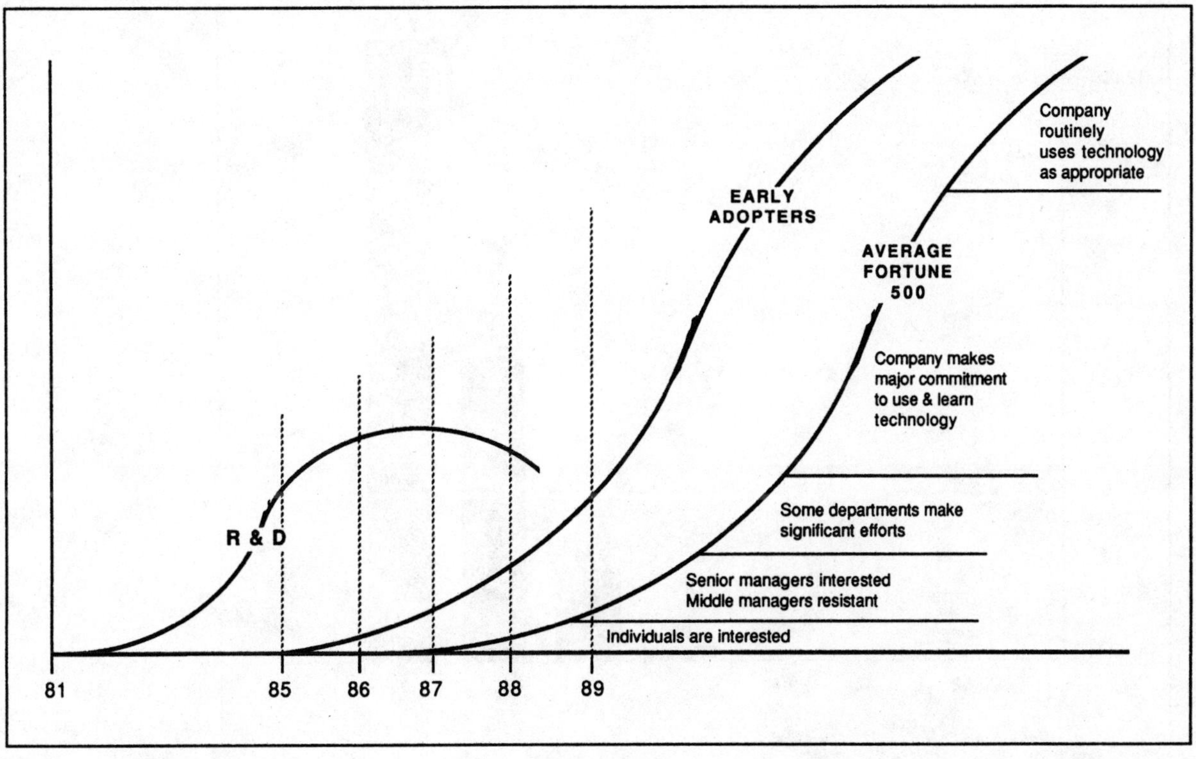

mainframe applications in order to facilitate more efficient transaction processing.

Some companies have set up independent expert systems development groups while others have integrated their expert systems development efforts into their conventional MIS groups. The use of expert systems techniques and the approaches different groups take to manage and develop projects vary widely. Clearly, business, industry, and government are still in the early stages of learning how best to develop and integrate expert systems techniques with conventional MIS practices. The confusion and the variety of different approaches are necessarily reflected in this book. We would like to be able to present a single, systematic approach to building expert systems. Unfortunately, there is no such thing,
so we are, instead, explaining a number of different approaches that are each producing effective results.

In 10 years, with clear hindsight, we will no doubt be able to identify the really valuable techniques offered by expert systems and explain how they were most effectively combined with existing techniques to produce the programming practices common in the year 2000. In the meantime, we can only chronicle what has been tried in the last few years, guess which of the practices will prove most useful, and hint at the integration that will come in the next several years.

What we can say with certainty at this time is that a growing number of people are using expert systems techniques to develop useful applications. Figure 1.2 illustrates the way the number of applications has

Figure 1.2 Total fielded expert systems applications.

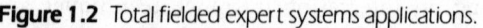

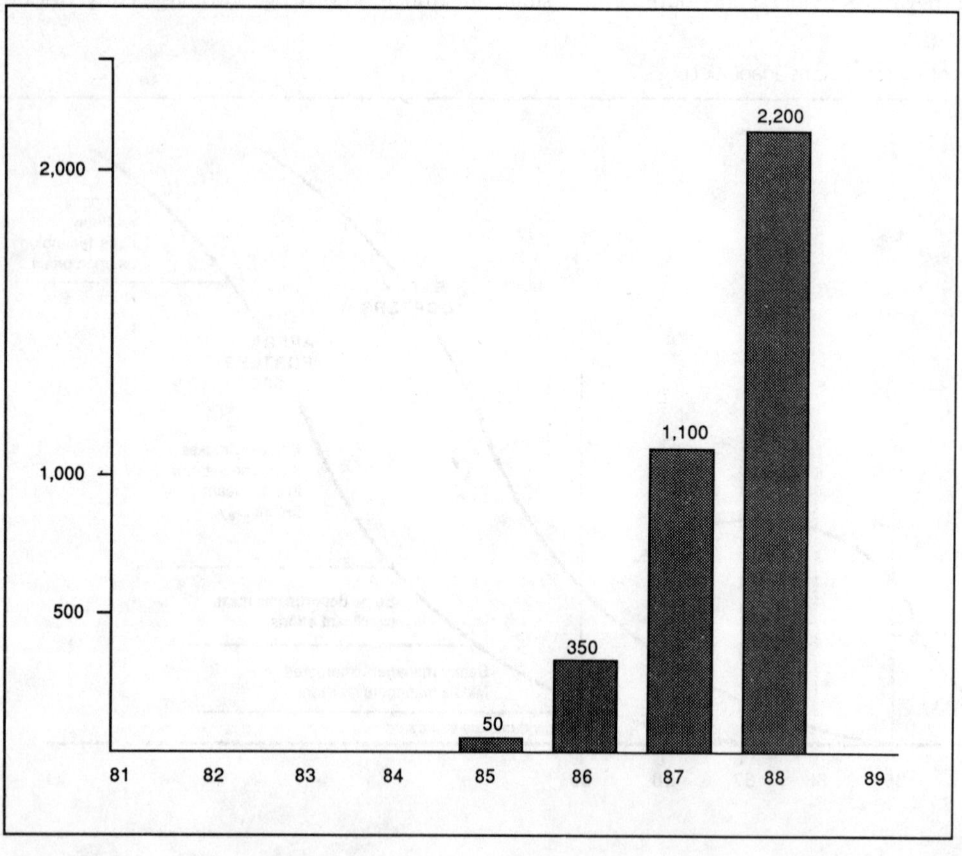

Expert Systems Today

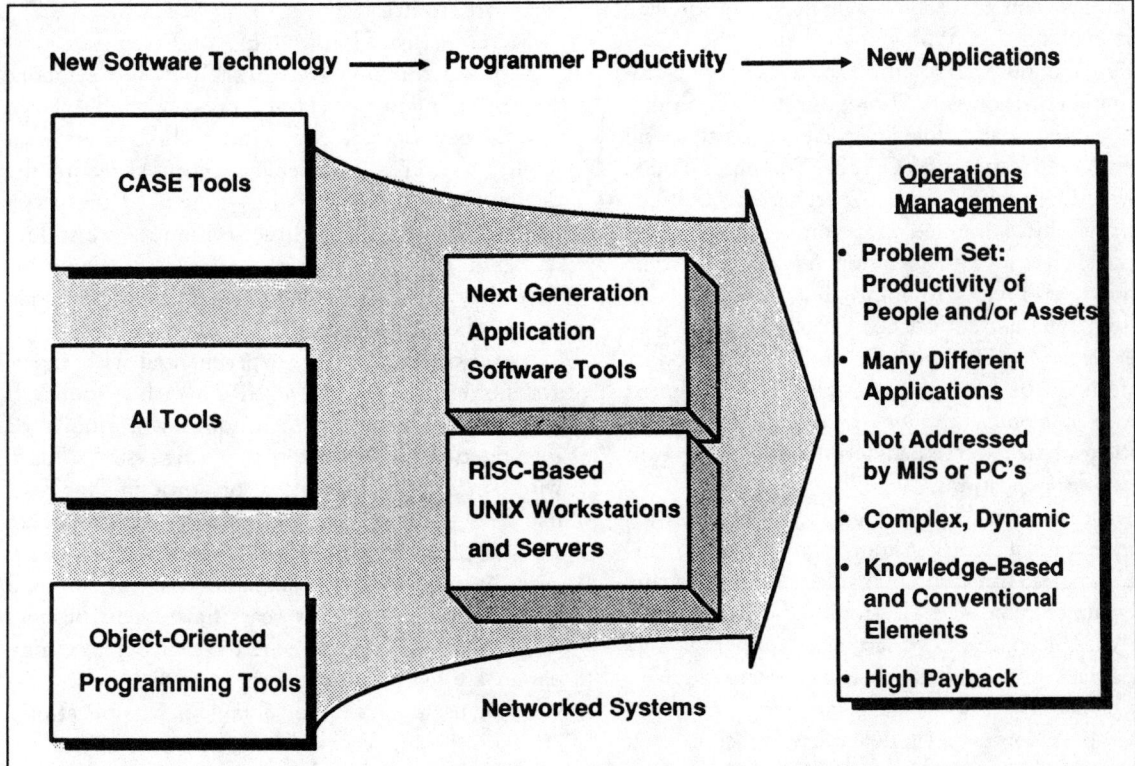

Figure 1.3 Texas Instruments' strategy for the 1990s. © 1989 Texas Instruments.

grown throughout the 1980s. We fully expect the number of applications to double for a couple more years and then begin to level off as it becomes impossible to distinguish between expert systems and other software applications that contain expert systems techniques.

One Company's Strategy

A nice illustration of the coming evolution of the expert systems market was provided during a press briefing held in early 1989. The speaker was Peter Van Cuylenburg, the head of Texas Instruments Data Systems Group. Mr. Van Cuylenburg had called the press conference to provide analysts with an outline of TI's strategy for the rest of the 1980s and 1990s. In a nutshell, TI regards the Explorer, its Mac co-processor (the MicroExplorer), and its LISP-based generic tools, including Personal Consultant Easy and Personal Consultant Plus, as "mature products." They will be supported and maintained, but TI clearly intends to put its main emphasis on new products.

Figure 1.3 provides an overview of TI's announced strategy for the 1990s. In effect, TI proposes to continue selling its LISP chip products and its PC-based expert systems building tools. In the course of the next two to five years, however, it proposes to shift both the hardware base and the software that it uses for expert systems development and deployment.

Initially, TI will shift toward using RISC-based UNIX machines for AI. TI has an agreement with Sun Microsystems to help develop the next generation of the SPARC chip, and it proposes to build dynamic data typing capabilities into that chip. This, in turn, means that the company will be able to create an environment that runs on top of the UNIX operating system and allows higher levels of software to use dynamic data typing and other symbolic processing techniques. In addition to this symbolic programming environment, TI proposes to field a number of problem- and domain-specific tools that will combine the features of CASE (Computer Aided Software Engineering) tools, expert systems building tools, and object-oriented programming (OOP) tools.

TestBench is a first-generation version of the type of tool that TI has in mind, but its soon-to-be-released "symbolic spreadsheet" tool will be an even better example. The symbolic spreadsheet product will probably be marketed jointly by TI and United Airline's computer division. It will be a domain-specific tool designed to help airlines quickly develop scheduling applications.

At the moment, TI has identified four areas for which it wants to develop tools: transportation (airlines, airports, trucking companies), manufacturing (aerospace, automobiles, electronics), health care (patient care, laboratories, pharmacies, and radiology companies), and dealerships (cars, trucks, agriculture). Since TI's knowledge engineering group has already been doing a great deal of custom consulting work with these vertical markets, the company is prepared to tailor tools for the specific needs found in each of these industries.

We've reviewed TI's announced strategy simply because TI has been such a strong advocate of LISP hardware and software in recent years and because TI was so explicit in explaining how it intends to modify its strategy for the 1990s. In fact, what TI has proposed is very similar to the strategy that both IBM and Apple have advocated. Each of these vendors proposes to build a symbolic environment that will run on top of a conventional operating environment to facilitate the use of symbolic programming techniques. IBM calls its symbolic processing environment the Knowledge Processing Environment (KPE) and Apple's John Sculley refers to it as the Knowledge Navigator. In effect, many of the expert systems techniques, like forward and backward chaining and rule-based knowledge representation, are going to be incorporated into the generation of operating systems that will begin to emerge in the next three to five years.

Moreover, like TI, IBM, DEC, and Apple are moving toward combining CASE, OOP, and symbolic processing into a new class of tools designed to facilitate the development of specific, high-value end-user applications. The commercial use of AI techniques during the last few years has convinced the major hardware vendors that those techniques are so fundamental and important to the future of computing that they should be incorporated into their computers' operating systems.

Many companies have experimented with expert systems techniques and liked what they found. It isn't certain how the techniques will finally be integrated—as tools, within operating systems, hardwired on chips, via modified conventional languages like C++—but it is certain that these techniques are going to play a major role in the future of computing.

In the meantime, the companies that have profited most during the last few years have been the ones that have been creating expert systems. These companies are learning to use the new techniques, developing useful and often valuable new applications, and positioning themselves to take advantage of whatever happens in the coming decade.

WHAT ARE THE PROBLEMS STANDING IN THE WAY OF WIDER USE?

Having described what will make the future of expert systems exciting, if unpredictable, we come to specific reasons for writing this book at this time. What are the problems that managers and expert systems developers face right now? What has been learned that may save others from difficulties? What problems need to be solved in the next few years by developers who will necessarily be working in today's environment with today's tools?

There are several problems that recur in discussions with people who are engaged in the creation of commercial expert systems. We have written this book to document the practical problems and the tentative solutions that have emerged out of the first few years of experimentation with expert systems techniques.

Management Interest

One recurring concern involves engaging the interest of management in the development of expert systems. Part of the problem has already been suggested: The whole world of business and computing is convulsed with change. Managers are being asked to make very complex, expensive, and risky decisions. Deciding when and how to explore and integrate a new software technology into an already turbulent environment often doesn't seem as pressing as deciding how to maintain critical existing applications or purchase costly new hardware.

Managers know that the world keeps changing and that we have to change with it, but when we are in the midst of a storm of change, most of us would rather put off any unnecessary change. During the early 1980s, AI techniques and expert systems were new and unproven. They constituted the sort of change that prudent managers could put off. That time is now past. There are now enough valuable applications to prove that the benefits of expert systems techniques outweigh the costs and risks of exploring yet another new technology. The fact that the computer companies are moving toward integrating these techniques into the core of their operating systems suggests that everyone involved in commercial computing needs to understand exactly what these techniques are and how they are likely to affect MIS operations in the years ahead.

Recent polls of MIS executives suggest that the tide has indeed turned and that increasing numbers of MIS managers have decided that they need to learn about, incorporate, and manage these new techniques.

Choosing the Right Strategy

As soon as executives decide that they want to use expert systems technology in their organizations, they are forced to think about how they should go about introducing expert systems in their companies. Should they set up an AI group, or simply train conventional programmers to develop expert systems? Should they consider buying new hardware, or can they get the benefits by using tools that run on mainframes or on PCs?

If waste and duplication is to be avoided, a company needs to develop an explicit strategy for using expert systems. Different strategies seem to work best for different industries and for the specific companies within those industries. We document some of those strategies and discuss what sorts of things have contributed to their successes and failures.

Choosing and Scoping Applications

One of the key factors that contributes to the success or failure of expert systems development projects is the selection of problems. You must not only select a suitable problem, but also often place a number of boundaries around the problem to guarantee that a workable expert system will result from the effort.

One commentator remarked that AI gurus always begin by talking about how hard it is to acquire and refine knowledge. Then, they shift their ground and talk about how to choose problems that avoid those difficulties. There's more than a little truth in this observation. Much depends on the hardware and tools that you plan to use. Some tools can, in fact, tackle very difficult problems that could not be handled by conventional techniques. More often, the currently available tools have significant limitations and need to be used only within rather narrow constraints. This doesn't mean that the tools and techniques aren't useful; it simply means that the company and the project manager must consider the costs and risks of various strategies and then adjust expectations to the strategy and the tools that are chosen. Learning to choose appropriate problems and tools is a very important key to success.

Project Management

Once a problem is chosen, someone needs to organize the effort to develop an application that will solve the problem. In the past few years, several projects have failed because they lacked good managers. Early AI advocates often wrapped the technology in mystery and suggested that it couldn't be managed by conventional managers or by means of conventional managerial techniques. In fact, successful projects result from good management. And, increasingly, managers are using conventional structured management techniques to organize the development and integration of expert systems. Expert systems techniques offer certain advantages over more traditional techniques, and a smart manager will want to understand and take advantage of the differences. On the other hand, where conventional organizational techniques are appropriate, they should and indeed must be used to assure that projects are done on time and within budget.

No company should undertake the development of a software application that will not pay for itself and provide more to its developers than alternative expenditures would. Expert systems can meet these criteria, and they must be required to do so. In fact, companies that have learned how to choose appropriate projects and manage the ensuing development process routinely find that expert systems applications meet cost/benefit tests much better than conventional applications.

Knowledge Acquisition

The good news is that expert systems techniques allow developers to capture and encode human knowledge that could not be captured by conventional approaches. The world of computing is gradually expanding beyond its early focus on numerical analysis to incorporate logical analysis techniques. This, in turn, makes it possible to reason about whole new classes of problems. Expert systems are now routinely using knowledge to analyze and diagnose problems and recommend solutions, to design or configure complex entities, and to monitor, plan, and schedule very complex operations.

The bad news, temporarily, is that new techniques have to be used to acquire and encode the knowledge that is needed to analyze and reason about these new classes of problems. Knowledge acquisition is not necessarily difficult, but it is based on a new way of conceptualizing the knowledge that a computer program must incorporate and it involves new skills that developers must master.

We examine the concepts underlying knowledge acquisition and the skills required to accomplish it in a systematic manner.

Systems Integration

Finally, we consider how expert systems can be integrated with other programs, and with databases. Knowledge about how and when to integrate expert systems techniques will grow rapidly in the years ahead, and we provide only an initial report about what has been happening in the last few years. Hopefully, it will allow some developers to avoid mistakes and suggest fruitful opportunities to others.

As we have stressed, the appropriate use of expert systems techniques is evolving very quickly, and it is not likely to slow down in the near future. This book presents the basic concepts and techniques underlying expert systems, provides heuristics that others have found useful, and points to the new techniques and the more integrated applications that you, the reader, may very well help to create in the years ahead.

THE FUTURE

Beyond the concepts and techniques discussed in this book, there are other AI techniques that are just beginning to be explored by the R & D departments of leading-edge companies. Techniques like neural networks and new ways of developing and using natural language interfaces are in the works. Ways to integrate expert systems into larger knowledge networks and new computers that exploit parallel processing techniques will follow in about 5 to 10 years. We have not covered these topics here because we wanted to stay focused on those aspects of expert systems that are of current commercial value. The future holds many new and exciting ideas that will continue to expand what can be done with computers.

Those who figure out how to incorporate and manage expert systems techniques will be ready for the next generation of AI technology, while those who wait will face an increasingly steep learning curve and eventually, like industries stuck with out-of-date factories, will find that their information systems and their companies will be too inflexible to be saved.

At the moment, expert systems are ready to be used. Companies that move quickly and decisively are going to find that they can significantly increase their productivity, flexibility, and effectiveness. Expert systems represent a unique and important opportunity for business, industry, and government which managers and organizations cannot afford to ignore.

2.
Basic Expert Systems Techniques

OVERVIEW
This chapter defines the basic concepts and techniques that are used in the development of expert systems. If you are already familiar with the basics, you may need only to skim this chapter. If you are new to the field, however, you should read the chapter carefully, since all later chapters assume that you know the basic concepts and the vocabulary introduced here.

KEY CONCEPTS IN AI AND EXPERT SYSTEMS
Discussions of artificial intelligence and expert systems often seem to assume that everyone understands the meaning of the words *knowledge* and *intelligence*. They are key concepts in AI and expert systems and they are often used in vague ways. We will begin by defining the functional uses of these terms in AI, and then consider how they are embodied in the techniques that are used to develop "intelligent, knowledge-based systems."

Knowledge
Knowledge involves relationships between things. Knowledge is active. *Data*, on the other hand, is passive. You might have a database with information about employees that included their educational history, the jobs they had held, their performance on different tasks, and so on. If you wanted to choose one employee for a new job, you could examine the data to see who was best qualified for the job. The data about the employees is passive—it just sits there—but the knowledge you bring to the examination of the data is active. You think of the skills the new job will require, you consider the type of historical performance that would qualify someone for such a job, and you sort through the data on the various employees, applying your criteria in order to select the best employee for the new job.

There are different kinds of knowledge. One kind involves knowing that you can follow a specific set of steps to achieve a particular result. Another kind of knowledge involves knowing that two terms are logically related; they are equivalent, or one is a part of another, and so forth. Still another kind of knowledge is comprised of the hunches and rules of thumb that you have learned from experience with similar problems.

Procedural versus declarative knowledge. A *procedure* is a step-by-step method for obtaining some specific result. For example, to find the average of a set of numbers, you add all the numbers together and then divide by the number of numbers in the set. A well-defined procedure for a computer is often called an *algorithm*.

Declarative knowledge is concerned with logical or empirical relationships between terms. For example, to say that a "well-defined procedure" is often called an "algorithm" is also to say that the two terms equal each other. This, in turn, means that you can substitute "well-defined procedure" for "algorithm." The two terms are equivalent, by definition.

In conventional data processing, you tend to think of procedural knowledge as a *program* and declarative knowledge as *data* in a database. Thus, you might have a procedure that went to a database file and retrieved specific addresses and printed them on envelopes. The declarative relationship involved would be between a variable called "address" and a whole series of specific addresses that were known to be equivalent to (or acceptable values for) that variable.

When you analyze the knowledge that humans use in complex analytic and judgmental problem solving, you need to mix procedures and declarative knowledge in more complex ways. This is necessary in order to adequately represent and manipulate the knowledge needed to solve problems. Some procedures must incorporate declarative knowledge and some data must include procedures. For example, an expert system might go to a database looking for a specific piece of data (a value) and find, instead, a set of rules that can be used to determine the value it needs.

Some other basic terms. A *statement* establishes a relationship between two terms. In general, terms are noun phrases and the relationship is established by an operator or connector, which is a verb phrase. Thus, the statement "Shawn Smith is 65 years old" asserts that two terms, "Shawn Smith" and "65 years old," are connected by an "is" relationship, which asserts that they are equal. Some statements are logical tautologies, like 2 + 2 = 4, but most relationships are empirically established and depend on scientific evidence.

Definitional relationships are defined (or declared) by common agreement about how words are to be used. If someone sets up a database and declares that the city of Austin (or a particular zip code) is in Texas, then, when you find out that a specific individual lives in Austin, you can also be sure that that person lives in Texas.

Some definitional relationships are relatively stable while others change constantly and cannot be known in advance. Austin will always be in Texas. On the other hand, the only way to find out if Shawn Smith lives in Austin is to ask.

In the worst case, you may not be able to determine for sure that Shawn Smith lives in Austin. You may have to use other information to make a guess about Shawn's address. You may know, for example, that she teaches at the University of Texas at Austin, and assume that she probably also lives in Austin.

A *heuristic* is a rule of thumb that allows you to assign a value to a variable that would otherwise be uncertain. Heuristics are rules for good guessing. The likelihood that someone lives in the same town that they work in is a heuristic; it is not always true, but it is true often enough to be useful in some situations.

In any complex problem-solving task, the decision maker usually employs both heuristic statements and definitional statements to reach a decision. Declarative knowledge refers to both definitional and heuristic knowledge.

In the world of expert systems, people tend to describe things by using three categories: *objects*, *attributes*, or *values*. Any particular situation is broken down into objects. *Objects* can be concrete things or they can be concepts. Most objects have sub-objects, or "children." Where you draw the boundaries to create objects in a particular situation is arbitrary, depending on your purposes and the nature of the problem you face.

Objects have attributes. (See Figure 2.1). *Attributes* can take on different values. Some of the attributes of an object describe its relationship with other objects. Objects can be related in a number of different ways: One object may be a part or a subspecies of another, or two objects may share the same parent, or they may represent two phases in a process.

Most of the attributes and values of objects are definitional. For example, if you are dealing with a bird, as in Figure 2.1, it will have wings and it will lay eggs. (If it doesn't, it isn't a bird—by definition.) The values of some definitional attributes may be empirical. In this case, the assigned value will serve as a default value that can be overridden by specific data. A specific bird, for example, may be too old to lay eggs, or it may be a stuffed bird with only one wing.

One of the hardest parts of complex knowledge engineering efforts is deciding how knowledge should be encoded. First, you need to define the elements of the problem using one or more levels of abstraction. Then, you must group elements into objects and decide what attributes each object should have.

Figure 2.1 Objects have attributes which can have values. Objects are related in various ways.

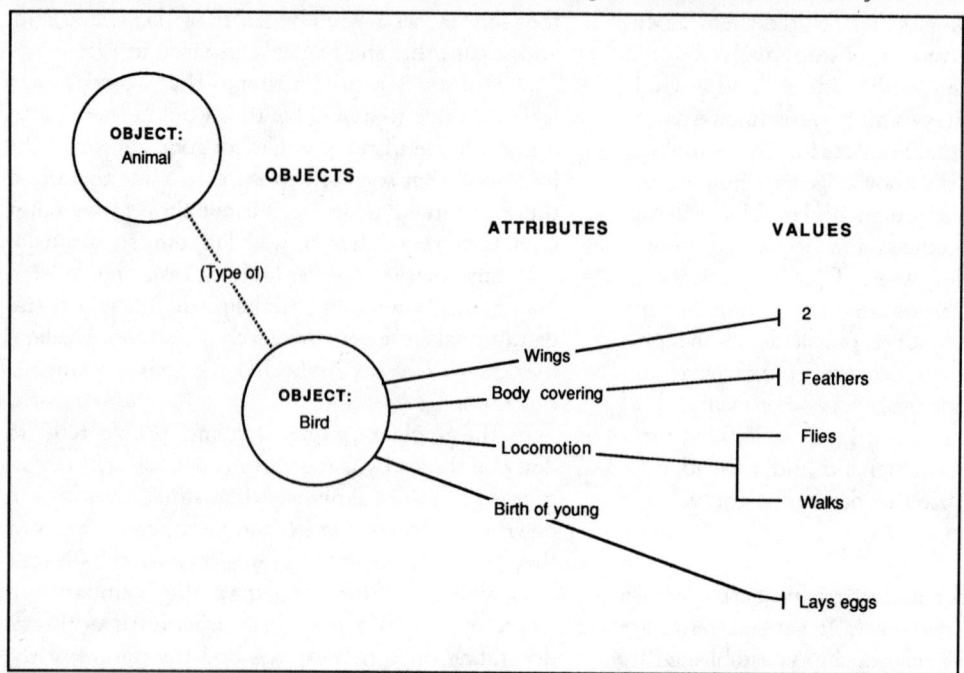

Knowledge of a step-by-step procedure is usually pretty easy to define. This is what programmers do all the time when they develop an algorithm or decision tree to describe a task.

More complex decision making is characterized by the use of *inference*. The most common way of establishing inferential relationships is to state a rule, as shown below.

Rule 1

IF   animal_lays_eggs = true AND
          animal_has_feathers = true
THEN animal = bird.

Using the logical principle called *modus ponens*, if you declare that Rule 1 is correct and then, in a specific instance, determine that a particular animal lays eggs and has feathers, you can infer that the animal is a bird.

Heuristics are rules of thumb that deal with judgments that are not completely certain. Thus, if you know the animal lays eggs and flies, you can be reasonably certain that it's a bird. Since there are a few flying reptiles that lay eggs, you can't be absolutely certain that it's a bird, but you can make the inference with a high degree of confidence. You might write a rule to describe this heuristic as follows:

Rule 2

IF   animal_lays_eggs = true AND
          animal_flies = true
THEN animal = bird (confidence = 95).

People rely on both procedural and inferential knowledge when they solve problems.

Intelligence

"Intelligence" is harder to define than "knowledge." When people in AI talk about intelligence, they commonly use the word to suggest that their software is more flexible, more readable, and easier to use than other software.

There is no useful sense in which artificial intelligence can be compared to human intelligence. Instead, "intelligent software" is simply more flexible than conventional software; it can respond in more complex ways and can deliver highly tailored recommendations. But the software had to be written by a programmer.

An intelligent machine fault diagnosis system, for example, might tell the user:

- I am not certain what is causing the machine to accelerate.
- I think it might be circuit board R345 that is malfunctioning (with a confidence of 80%).
- It might also be circuit board M321 that is malfunctioning (with a confidence of 70%).
- Since it is much easier and much less expensive to change M321, and it has a reasonable chance of solving the problem, I recommend you change M321 first and see if that solves the problem.

Leaving aside the anthropomorphic phrases that some programmer inserted (e.g., "I," "I think," "I recommend"), the system demonstrates that it can provide multiple answers with different degrees of certainty and thereby provide the maintenance person with multiple options.

Another way to think about intelligence is to consider what a person does when trying to solve a problem. Figure 2.2 presents the basics of a game called Nickels and Dimes. The game is played on a strip of paper that is divided into five spaces. When the game begins, two nickels are placed on the left two spaces and two dimes are placed on the right two spaces. There are two kinds of moves that can be made: slide and hop. The object of the game is to reverse the nickels and dimes using only the two legal

Figure 2.2 The nickel and dime problem.

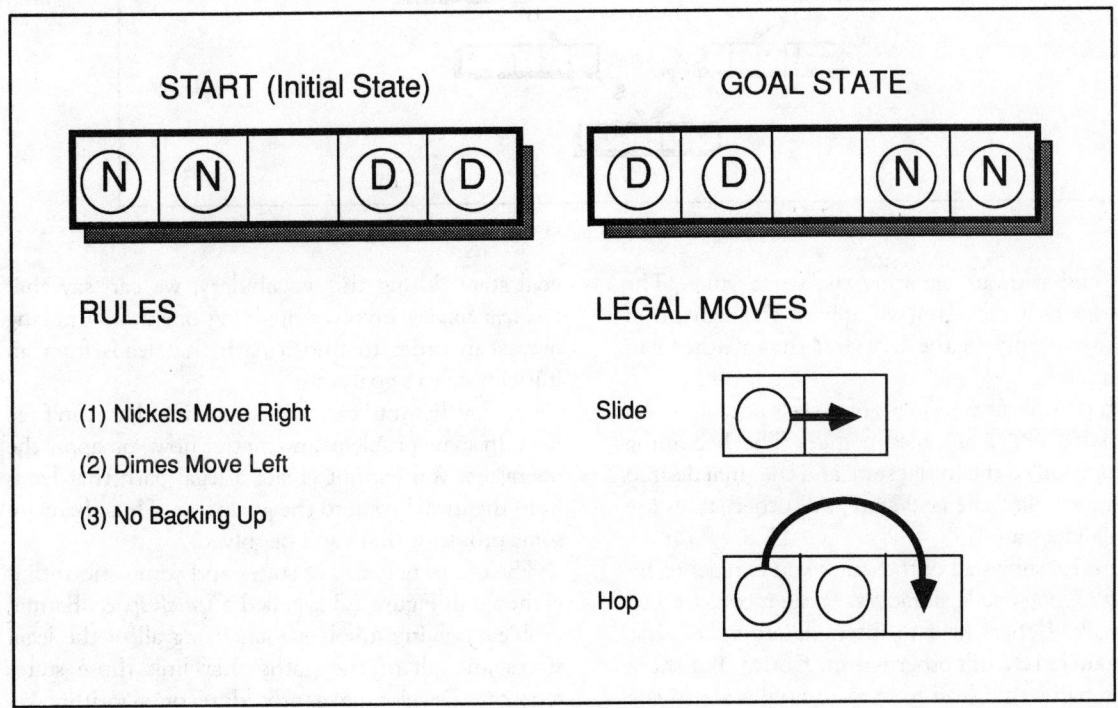

Figure 2.3 The nickel and dime search space.

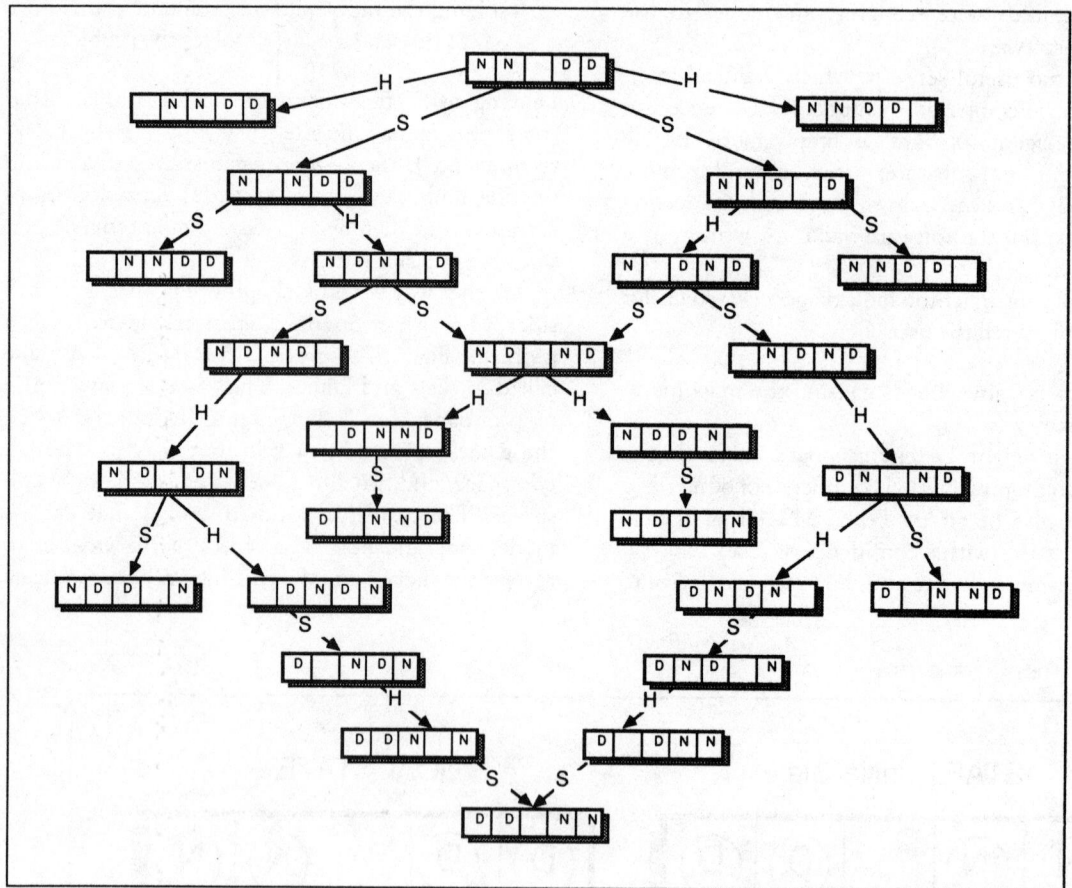

moves and without violating the three rules. The rules state that nickels move only to the right, that dimes move only to the left, and that neither can back up.

Each possible arrangement of nickels and dimes on the playing board is called a *state*. The beginning position is called the initial state and the final desired outcome is called the goal state. All other states are intermediate states.

Figure 2.3 shows all of the states you can get to by making all possible legal moves. Some moves lead to dead ends. Others lead to intermediate states that can be altered by still other moves. Notice that there are two paths that lead from the initial state to the goal state. Using this vocabulary, we can say that *problem solving* involves applying operators (making moves) in order to find a path that leads from an initial state to a goal state.

Obviously, you can define games that can't be won. In some problems, no matter how you apply the operators, you cannot create a legal path that leads from the initial state to the goal state. Thus there are some problems that can't be solved.

The entire network of states and connections that is shown in Figure 2.3 is called a *search space*. Formal problem solving involves identifying all of the legal states and all of the paths that link those states together. Developing a procedure or algorithm involves solving a problem by identifying one or more legal paths from the initial state to the goal state.

Search Spaces and Decision Trees

Another way of thinking about a search space is to conceptualize it as a decision tree. If you do, you can determine the size of the search space by determining the number of nodes in the decision tree. Figure 2.4 shows a hypothetical decision tree. From the point at the top of the triangle, 10 lines extend to 10 different nodes, or states. (Our choice of the number 10 is arbitrary.) From each of those nodes 10 more lines extend to 10 different nodes. This process is repeated 20 times. The result is a huge decision tree that has 10^{20} nodes. The time and effort required to search such a large decision tree is beyond the capabilities of existing computers.

You can use knowledge to simplify large search problems by reducing the search space. Consider a practical example: Suppose someone told you he was going from Los Angeles to New York, and asked what you thought it would cost. If he only told you the beginning and ending points of his trip, you would be hard pressed to help. Would he be flying or driving or cycling? Would he be going alone, or taking his family? Did he need to stop at any particular place along the way? There are so many alternatives that unless you have more knowledge, you can't even begin to guess the price.

If he tells you that he is going alone, that he has to stop in St. Louis, Chicago, and Washington along the way, and that he must complete the trip within three days, the problem becomes much easier. He will have to travel by plane to make the journey within three days. (This is heuristic knowledge that you have because you know about the speed of different modes of transportation.) You can check the

Figure 2.4 Hypothetical search space represented as a decision tree.

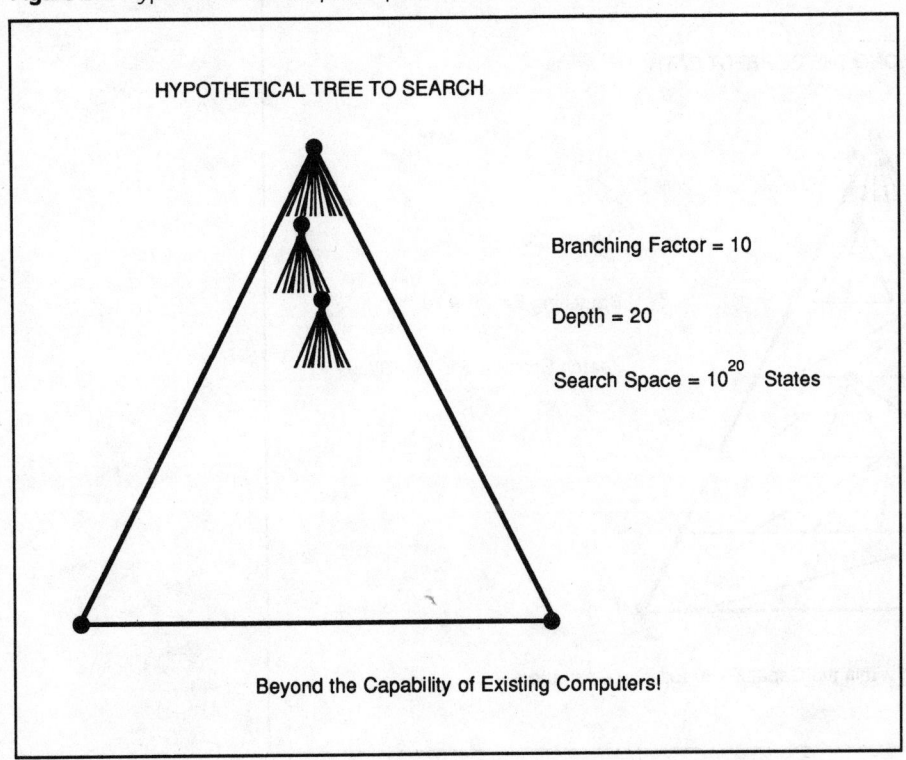

HYPOTHETICAL TREE TO SEARCH

Branching Factor = 10

Depth = 20

Search Space = 10^{20} States

Beyond the Capability of Existing Computers!

airplane flights between the stops along the way and come up with perhaps 50 possible schedules and determine an average price. Having the additional information makes the problem tractable by reducing the number of options you have to consider.

Figure 2.5 shows how knowledge can reduce the search space in the previous decision tree. If you have five landmarks (points you know you have to reach), each distributed 20 percent further through the hypothetical search tree, you can cut the search space down to 5×10^4 states, which is well within the capability of existing computers.

In the 1960s, AI researchers focused on trying to develop powerful general problem-solving strategies that would be able to search large search spaces. They were not very successful. In the 1970s, they switched to creating expert systems, systems that contained relatively weak search strategies that could handle hard problems. The expert systems could handle such problems because they contained a great deal of very specific knowledge about the particular type of problem the system was tailored to solve. The success of expert systems lies in their ability to identify and store domain-specific knowledge and heuristics and encode them in a way that enables them to search large problem spaces in a reasonable time.

Consider another example of a complex decision-making problem: the game of chess. Chess is played on a board of 64 squares; there are 16 pieces per side, many with different legal moves. Different pieces can move in different ways. The number of states in the chess search space is 10^{120}. That's a very large search space. In fact, those are more states than there are atoms in the known universe. That means that no one is ever going to examine the search space and determine all of the ways a chess game could be won or lost.

When people play chess they use heuristics. For

Figure 2.5 Hypothetical decision tree with five landmarks.

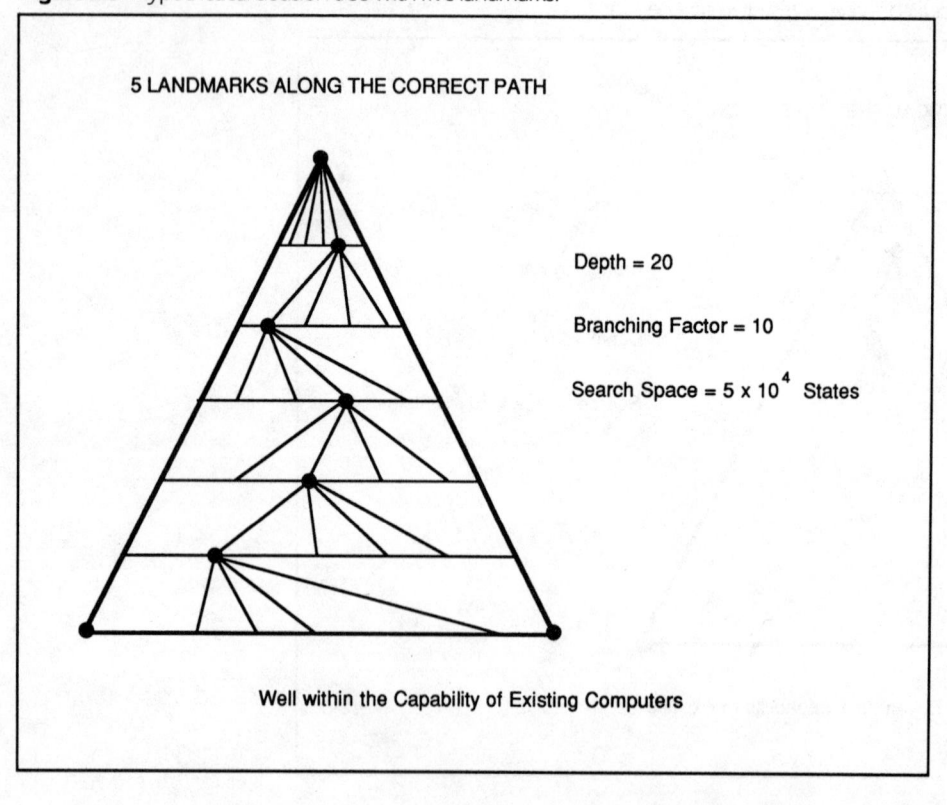

5 LANDMARKS ALONG THE CORRECT PATH

Depth = 20

Branching Factor = 10

Search Space = 5×10^4 States

Well within the Capability of Existing Computers

example, the objective for the early part of the game is to gain control of the center of the board. This heuristic doesn't prescribe a specific set of moves, but it guides the player's overall strategy. In effect, players use heuristics to decide which possible moves to examine in detail and which to ignore. They use heuristics to prune an unmanageably large search space into a space they can search. In the process, they lose the possibility of being certain that they haven't overlooked some fruitful move. But, if the search space is too big to search every state and you have to make a decision, limiting the search is the only practical option you have.

As hard as chess may seem, however, it is still a relatively easy problem. At least you know all of the pieces and all of the legal moves. At any point in the game you can draw up a finite list of all of the moves that you could make at that point in the game and assign a rating to each possible move.

Consider an even more complex problem: making a loan to a medium-sized foreign company. The bank officer facing this problem does not necessarily know all of the players or all of the legal moves. The U.S. Federal Reserve Bank could change the rules of the game at any point, just as the foreign country could change its laws. A third country might take action that would change the currency exchange rate of one or both countries involved in the loan. A key manager of the foreign company might die or an unknown individual might buy a controlling interest in either the bank or the foreign company and dictate new policies. The business the company is involved in might seem very prosperous when the loan is considered but then take a turn for the worse in a few years. The human decision maker must make a decision without knowing all of the factors that will affect the outcome. No one could develop a procedural algorithm to solve such a middle-market loan analysis problem. However, a program that used heuristics to make reasonable guesses based on a number of key variables could assist a manager in making a loan decision. Moreover, it could offer the manager several alternative recommendations.

The ability to handle large, complex, and uncertain decisions like loan analysis is another way in which expert systems are said to be intelligent. They can help people deal with complex and vaguely defined problems that conventional programs cannot handle.

Separating Knowledge from Inference

In addition to providing ways of representing knowledge, making inferences about uncertain information, and deciding how to search large and complex problem spaces, AI has contributed a major new approach to developing software programs. Expert systems typically separate the declarative knowledge from the code that controls the inference and search procedures that are contained in a system. The declarative knowledge is kept in a *knowledge base* while the control knowledge is kept in a separate area called an *inference engine*. In effect, an inference engine is an algorithm that dynamically directs or controls the system when it searches its knowledge base. (See Figure 2.6.)

When you begin a consultation with an expert system, the inference engine initiates a search of the knowledge in the knowledge base to see if it can develop a recommendation. The path the inference engine will follow is not determined in advance; it depends on the goal you set for the system and the answers you provide to the questions that the system generates.

The separation of knowledge and inference does two things. First, it guarantees that the system can respond in a more flexible manner.

Second, it means that the developer can focus on the specification of the declarative knowledge that goes in the knowledge base and leave the development of a specific search strategy to the inference engine. This, in turn, makes it possible for developers to create much more complex programs than they could if they had to not only capture the expert's knowledge but also simultaneously assemble it into a step-by-step decision process. Most experts can define their terms and specify the heuristic rules they use to analyze problems. They usually can't lay out all their knowledge at one sitting. In fact, they usually provide it by discussing specific problems or cases

Figure 2.6 Architecture of an expert system.

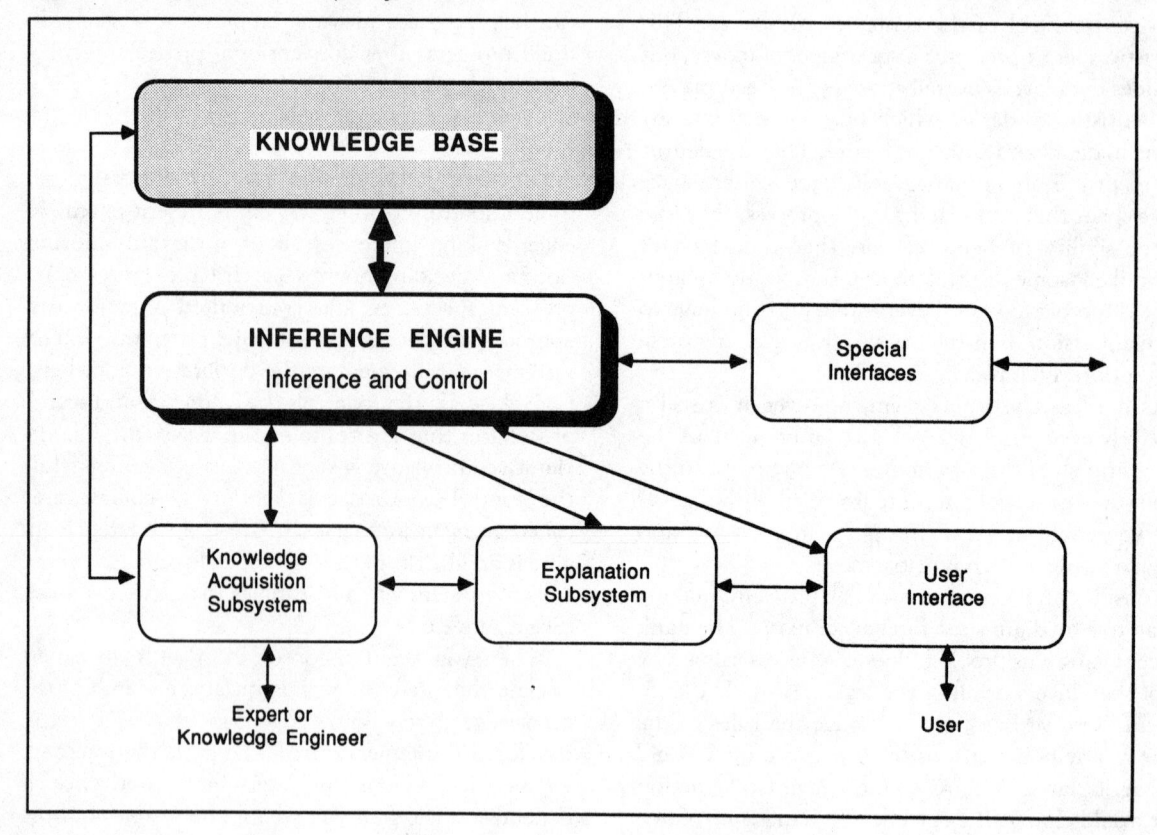

they have solved. The separation of knowledge and inference frees the developer to work with the experts to describe their knowledge as it comes to them, in unconnected pieces, instead of requiring them to provide it in the form of a complete, step-by-step procedure.

Given these underlying concepts and techniques, we now turn to some of the specific ways we can represent knowledge and manage inference and control in expert systems. There are a number of different ways of representing knowledge and manipulating it using various inference and control techniques. Some systems involve a mix of all of the different techniques, but most systems use a specific set of knowledge representation and inference techniques. We will consider three typical combinations of knowledge and inference and control:

- *Induction systems*, which use examples and the induction algorithm
- *Rule-based systems*, which use facts, rules, and either forward or backward chaining
- *Hybrid systems*, which add objects, inheritance, and message passing to rule-based systems

INDUCTION SYSTEMS

One simple way of constructing a small expert system is to represent the experts' knowledge in a table of attributes and values and use an induction algorithm to convert the experts' knowledge into a decision tree. The induction algorithm is simply an inference technique that derives a decision tree from a table of attributes and values.

In order to use induction, you must first be able to produce a matrix that lists all of the possible attributes of a problem, as well as some examples of decisions made under various circumstances.

Consider the problem of choosing a printer for your computer. You could begin by thinking of all the attributes (or characteristics or variables) that might go into your decision. Then you should consider what values each attribute might take.

In practice, you could do this in one of three ways.

You could consider printers in the abstract (top down), you could compare several specific printers to see what their common characteristics are (bottom up), or you could shift back and forth, alternately considering specific and generic printers. Most people follow the last course.

Figure 2.7 presents one possible approach to analyzing the printer selection problem. Depicted here is a generic printer with its attributes and their values at the top, and beneath it are the attributes and

Figure 2.7 Printer object-attribute-value characteristics.

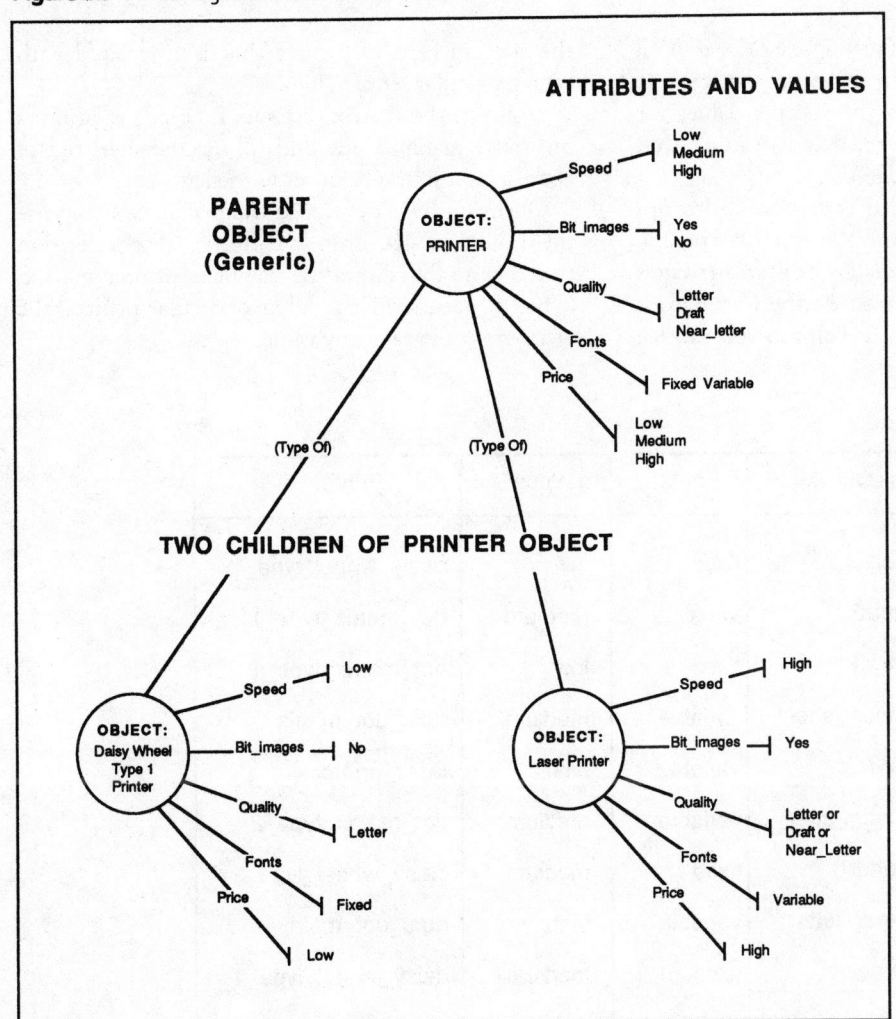

ATTRIBUTES AND VALUES

PARENT OBJECT (Generic)

OBJECT: PRINTER
- Speed — Low, Medium, High
- Bit_images — Yes, No
- Quality — Letter, Draft, Near_letter
- Fonts — Fixed, Variable
- Price — Low, Medium, High

(Type Of) (Type Of)

TWO CHILDREN OF PRINTER OBJECT

OBJECT: Daisy Wheel Type 1 Printer
- Speed — Low
- Bit_images — No
- Quality — Letter
- Fonts — Fixed
- Price — Low

OBJECT: Laser Printer
- Speed — High
- Bit_images — Yes
- Quality — Letter or Draft or Near_Letter
- Fonts — Variable
- Price — High

Figure 2.8 Top of printer matrix.

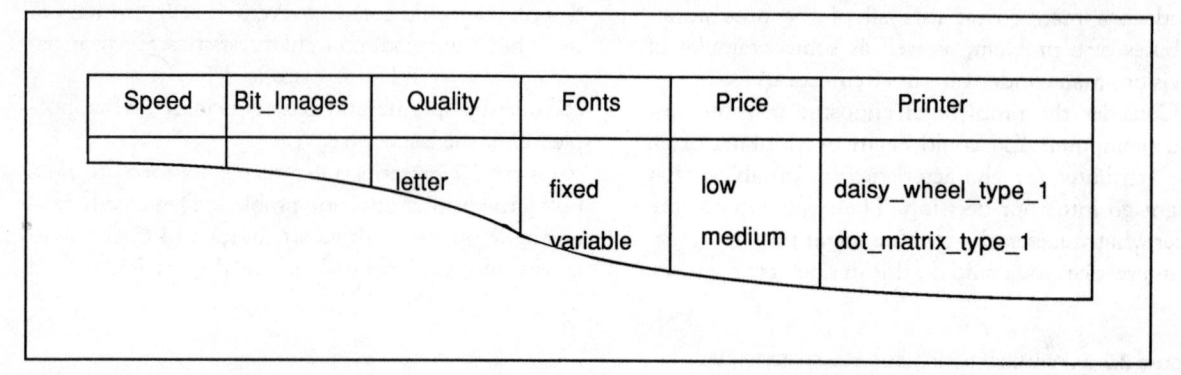

Speed	Bit_Images	Quality	Fonts	Price	Printer
		letter	fixed	low	daisy_wheel_type_1
			variable	medium	dot_matrix_type_1

values of two specific types of printers. Notice that all possible values for each attribute of the generic printer are listed, as well as the specific values for each particular type of printer. (Keep in mind that this is all declarative knowledge.)

Once you are satisfied with your overall description of printers, you can create a matrix like the one shown in Figure 2.8. Each of the printer attributes is listed at the top of the matrix. At the very right is a sixth heading, printer; in this column you can list the specific type of printer that is associated with each particular set of values.

To fill in the matrix, list specific types of printers on the right-hand side and fill in characteristics of each printer in the columns to the left.

Once you have developed the matrix, you can use the induction algorithm to convert it into a decision tree. Figure 2.9 shows the complete printer matrix. (The "*" means that for that particular printer, the attribute could take any value.)

Figure 2.9 Printer selection matrix.

Speed	Bit_Images	Quality	Fonts	Price	Printer
low	no	letter	fixed	low	daisy_wheel_type_1
low	yes	draft	variable	medium	dot_matrix_type_1
medium	yes	draft	fixed	low	dot_matrix_type_1
medium	yes	near_letter	variable	medium	dual_dot_matrix
high	yes	*	variable	high	laser_printer
high	yes	near_letter	variable	medium	dot_matrix_type_2
high	no	letter	fixed	medium	daisy_wheel_type_2
low	yes	near_letter	variable	high	dual_dot_matrix
*	no	letter	fixed	medium	daisy_wheel_type_2

Using an expert systems building tool called 1st-Class, which is specifically designed to handle induction, you can convert the matrix to the decision tree shown in Figure 2.10.

Notice that the induction algorithm has reordered the attributes into the most efficient sequence for reaching a specific recommendation. In some cases, you have to ask only two questions to determine which printer is best, while in others, you must ask three. No decision requires you to ask for the values of all five attributes. In fact, by simply knowing about the user's price, quality, and speed requirements, you can reach a recommendation without ever having to ask about bit images or fonts. This is one strength of induction: Many companies have found that they can use induction tools to quickly improve the efficiency of their troubleshooting by eliminating unnecessary hardware checks, questions, or recordkeeping.

Notice that some paths in the decision tree lead to "no data." Thus, for example, if a user requests a low-priced printer that will print near letter quality output, you are forced to say that there is no printer available that meets those requirements. In effect, the existence of "no data" paths means that the initial matrix was incomplete. But you were still able to arrive at a useful decision tree without exhaustively examining the entire printer selection problem space.

Typically, in expert systems development, an expert will describe her overall approach to a problem and the knowledge engineer who develops the system will take notes and derive a model of the attributes of the problem. Then, when the expert discusses a specific case, the developer will note what new attributes are introduced that the expert may have forgotten to mention when discussing the problem in the abstract. In addition, after working with the

Figure 2.10 Printer decision tree (printer selection matrix as optimized in 1st class).

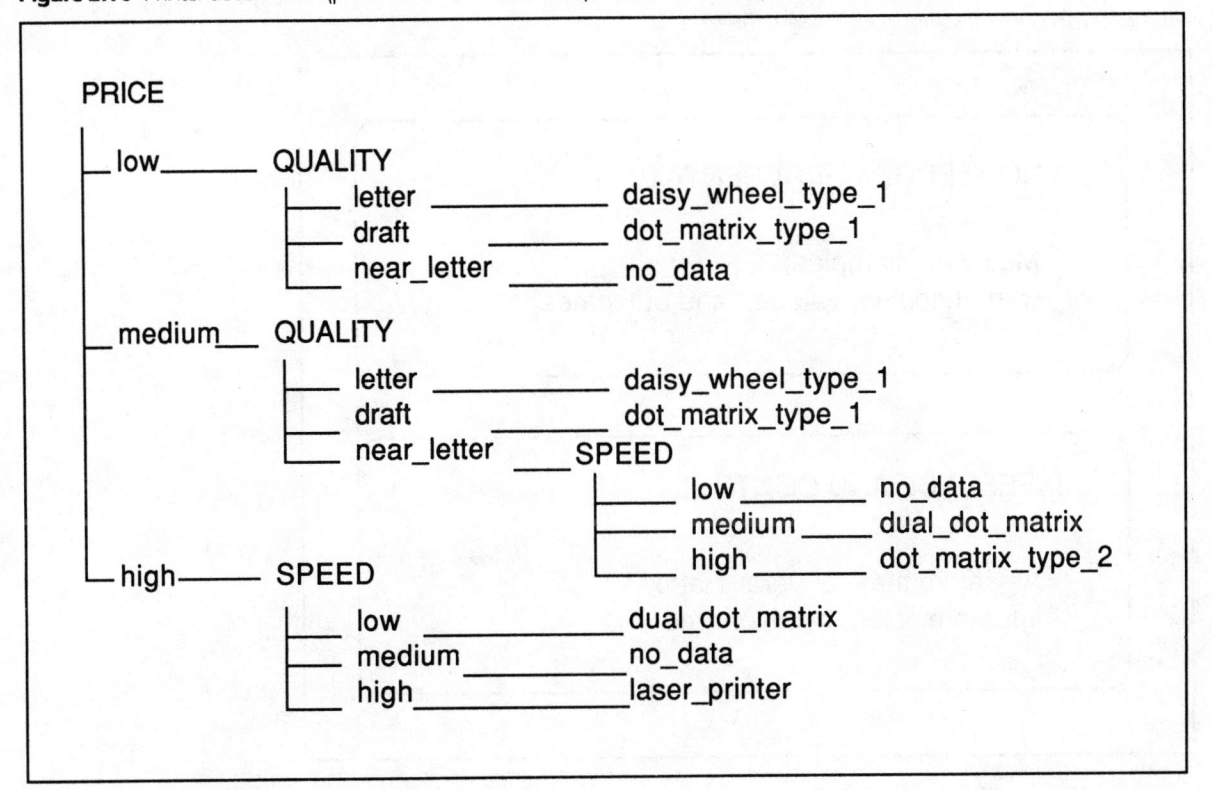

```
PRICE
  ├─ low ──────── QUALITY
  │                 ├─ letter ──────── daisy_wheel_type_1
  │                 ├─ draft ────────── dot_matrix_type_1
  │                 └─ near_letter ──── no_data
  │
  ├─ medium ────── QUALITY
  │                 ├─ letter ──────── daisy_wheel_type_1
  │                 ├─ draft ────────── dot_matrix_type_1
  │                 └─ near_letter ─── SPEED
  │                                      ├─ low ──────── no_data
  │                                      ├─ medium ──── dual_dot_matrix
  │                                      └─ high ─────── dot_matrix_type_2
  │
  └─ high ──────── SPEED
                    ├─ low ──────── dual_dot_matrix
                    ├─ medium ──── no_data
                    └─ high ──────── laser_printer
```

problem for a while, the developer may realize that the expert mentioned some attributes of the problem that are not, in fact, ever used in actual problem-solving situations.

Using 1st-Class, the expert systems developer can create a matrix and convert the matrix to a decision tree with a single command. With one more command, the developer can convert the decision tree to an application that will ask a user a set of multiple choice questions and then recommend a printer. The developer doesn't have to worry about the actual development of the decision tree or the development of the application that asks the questions; these things are done automatically. All the developer has to focus on is identifying the attributes and values involved in the problem and providing an adequate number of examples. If the developer fails to cover all of the reasonable possibilities, or if a new type of printer is introduced, all the developer has to do to modify the application is to change the matrix and then use the induction algorithm to generate an updated version of the application.

Figure 2.11 is a representation of an induction system in the generic expert systems format. The matrix, with its attributes, values, and recommendations, constitutes the knowledge base, while the induction algorithm constitutes the inference engine.

RULE-BASED SYSTEMS

The second and most common way of representing knowledge and handling inference and control is found in rule-based systems.

This approach represents knowledge as statements and rules and uses forward or backward chaining to handle the inference and control. Rule-based systems come in two varieties. The simpler rule-based systems group all the rules together in one set and then examine them all at once. The more complex or structured rule-based systems divide the rules into

Figure 2.11 Architecture of an induction system.

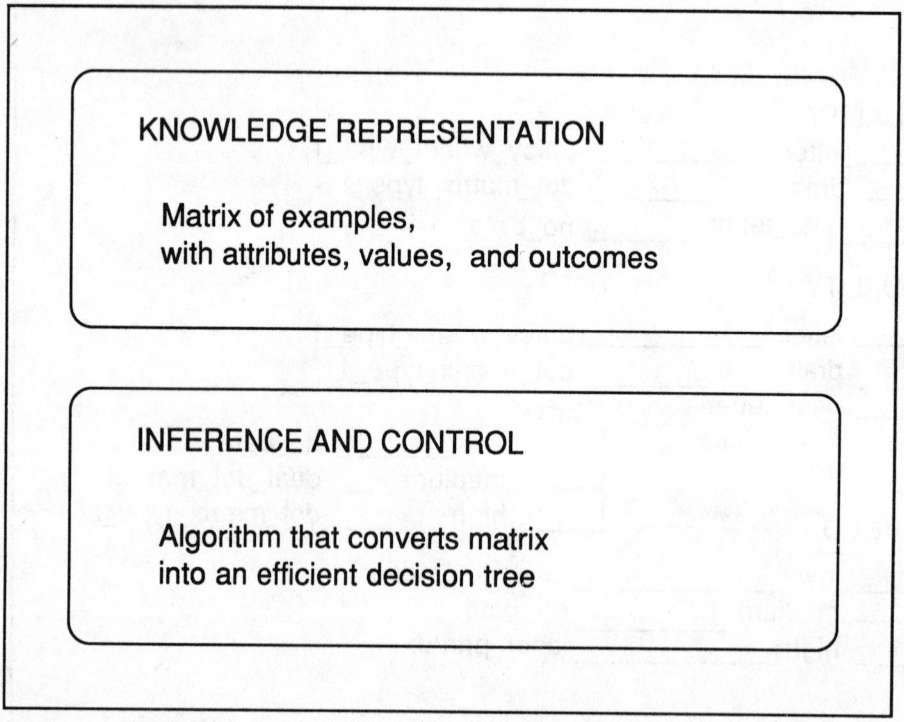

```
┌─────────────────────────────────────────────────┐
│   ╭─────────────────────────────────────────╮   │
│   │                                         │   │
│   │   KNOWLEDGE REPRESENTATION              │   │
│   │                                         │   │
│   │   Matrix of examples,                   │   │
│   │   with attributes, values, and outcomes │   │
│   │                                         │   │
│   ╰─────────────────────────────────────────╯   │
│                                                 │
│   ╭─────────────────────────────────────────╮   │
│   │                                         │   │
│   │   INFERENCE AND CONTROL                 │   │
│   │                                         │   │
│   │   Algorithm that converts matrix        │   │
│   │   into an efficient decision tree       │   │
│   │                                         │   │
│   ╰─────────────────────────────────────────╯   │
└─────────────────────────────────────────────────┘
```

subsets, arrange the subsets into a tree, and then examine them according to some search strategy. We consider the vocabulary and the techniques involved in each type, starting with a simple rule system.

Rules

A rule is an If-Then construct that links statements together in order to facilitate inference. A rule is made up of If-statements and Then-statements (or If-clauses and Then-clauses). In effect, a rule asserts that IF the If-statements are true, THEN the Then-statements can be inferred to be true. Consider Rule 3.

Rule 3

```
IF      speed = low AND
        bit_images = no AND
        quality = letter AND
        fonts = fixed AND
        price = low
THEN    printer = daisy_wheel_type_1.
```

Rule 3 is made up of five If-statements and one Then-statement. Each of the statements in turn is made up of an attribute and a value. Thus, the first If-statement can be read: If the attribute "speed" takes the value "low." This rule defines what you mean by a daisy wheel type 1 printer. If you ask a user about his needs and it turns out that they match the statements in the IF-part of the rule, then you can infer that the user can use a daisy wheel type 1 printer.

You can formally represent a generic rule as follows:

Rule

```
IF      <attribute> = <value>
THEN    <attribute> = <value>.
```

Different systems allow the developer to use different connectors and to use different types of values. Most systems allow the developer to connect statements with AND and OR. Some also allow the use of ELSE, and some even allow ELSEIF. Systems commonly allow the use of <, >, <=, >=, and < >, or NOT. Most systems provide four types of values:

yes/no (or T/F), a number, a literal value, or a list. Thus, a rule could easily look like this:

Rule

```
IF      <attribute> = <literal value> AND
        <attribute> >- <numerical value>
        OR
        <attribute> = <one of a list of values>
THEN    <attribute> = <literal value> AND
        <attribute> = <literal value>
ELSE    <attribute> = <false>.
```

More sophisticated systems allow you to substitute a "pointer" in place of a value in a rule. When the rule is evaluated, the system uses the pointer to find a procedure that it can use to obtain the value. In this case, the value would be a variable that would be filled in when the program was run. Even more sophisticated systems allow both the attributes and the values to be variables. (We consider rules that incorporate variables as attributes or values in a later chapter.)

Two Types of Rules

Inference occurs between the If-statements and the Then-statements. In effect, there are two general types of rules:

1. *Definitional rules*, where the inference establishes a relationship between terms
2. *Heuristic rules*, where the inference is based on incomplete evidence

Thus, Rule 4 is a definitional rule:

Rule 4

```
IF      home_town = Austin
THEN    home_state = Texas.
```

And Rule 5 is a heuristic rule:

Rule 5

```
IF      home_state = Texas AND
        sex = male
THEN    footwear = boots (confidence = 35).
```

26 BASIC CONCEPTS

Rule 4 is true because a class-subclass relationship between Texas and Austin has been defined; this rule will be true whenever an individual lives in Austin. Rule 5 may or may not be true in any particular situation. You can only be sure in any specific case by checking an individual male Texan. Rule 5 says, in effect, that if you are forced to guess about what a male Texan might wear, lacking specific knowledge, you could assume that about one-third of them might be wearing boots.

Most rule-based systems are comprised of many definitional rules and a few heuristic rules.

Simple and Structured Rule Systems

In simple rule-based systems, all of the rules are placed together in one set and then examined as a whole. This approach would be fine for a rule base that was going to help a user identify a printer. Table 2.1, for example, illustrates a rule base with rules about printer selection. Notice that it includes one rule for each line that occurred in the matrix in Figure 2.9. Thus, the same analysis effort used for developing a matrix for induction can also be used to identify rules.

In some expert systems building tools, you begin by constructing a matrix of examples, which the system automatically converts into a set of rules instead of a decision tree. This provides the developer with a valuable knowledge acquisition aid for addressing simple problems.

Now imagine that you developed your printer knowledge base, tested it with users, and then decided that what you really wanted to do was to create a system that would include much more knowledge about computer hardware and connections and would allow a user to define the computer needs of an entire office.

You would need to develop rules about how to select computers, terminals, modems, and how to connect all of these things together. Just to facilitate the analysis effort, you would probably want to keep the knowledge about printer selection separate from the knowledge about computer and terminal selection. There are ways to do this with a simple rule

Table 2.1 Printer Rule Base (Created in VP-Expert).

GOAL : PRINTER

RULE 1
IF
    SPEED = LOW AND
    BIT_IMAGES = NO AND
    QUALITY = LETTER AND
    FONTS = FIXED AND
    PRICE = LOW
THEN
    PRINTER = DAISY_WHEEL_TYPE_1 CNF 80;

RULE 2
IF
    SPEED = LOW AND
    BIT_IMAGES = YES AND
    FONTS = VARIABLE AND
    QUALITY = DRAFT AND
    PRICE = MEDIUM
THEN
    PRINTER = DOT_MATRIX_TYPE_1 CNF 75;

RULE 3
IF
    SPEED = MEDIUM AND
    BIT_IMAGES = YES AND
    QUALITY = DRAFT AND
    FONTS = FIXED AND
    PRICE = LOW
THEN
    PRINTER = DOT_MATRIX_TYPE_1 CNF 50;

RULE 4
IF
    SPEED = MEDIUM AND
    BIT_IMAGES = YES AND
    FONTS = VARIABLE AND
    QUALITY = NEAR_LETTER AND
    PRICE = MEDIUM
THEN
    PRINTER = DUAL_DOT_MATRIX CNF 90;

RULE 5
IF
    SPEED = HIGH AND
    BIT_IMAGES = YES AND
    FONTS = VARIABLE AND
    PRICE = HIGH
THEN
    PRINTER = LASER_PRINTER CNF 100;

RULE 6
IF
    SPEED = HIGH AND
    BIT_IMAGES = YES AND
    FONTS = VARIABLE AND

	QUALITY = NEAR_LETTER AND
	PRICE = MEDIUM
THEN	PRINTER = DOT_MATRIX_TYPE_2 CNF 100;
RULE 7	
IF	SPEED = HIGH AND
	BIT_IMAGES = NO AND
	QUALITY = LETTER AND
	FONTS = FIXED AND
	PRICE = MEDIUM
THEN	PRINTER = DAISY_WHEEL_TYPE_2 CNF 75;
RULE 8	
IF	SPEED = LOW AND
	BIT_IMAGES = YES AND
	FONTS = VARIABLE AND
	QUALITY = NEAR_LETTER AND
	PRICE = HIGH
THEN	PRINTER = DUAL_DOT_MATRIX CNF 60;
RULE 9	
IF	BIT_IMAGES = NO AND
	QUALITY = LETTER AND
	FONTS = FIXED AND
	PRICE = MEDIUM
THEN	PRINTER = DAISY_WHEEL_TYPE_2 CNF 90;

ASK SPEED: "What is the value of SPEED?" ;
CHOICES SPEED: LOW, MEDIUM, HIGH ;

ASK BIT IMAGES: "What is the value of BIT IMAGES?" ;
CHOICES BIT IMAGES: NO, YES;

ASK QUALITY: "What is the value of QUALITY?" ;
CHOICES QUALITY: LETTER, DRAFT, NEAR LETTER ;

ASK FONTS: "What is the value of FONTS?" ;
CHOICES FONTS: FIXED, VARIABLE ;

ASK PRICE: "What is the value of PRICE?" ;
CHOICES PRICE: LOW, MEDIUM, HIGH :

system, but ideally, when faced with this problem, it is best to switch to a structured rule system that allows you to partition your rules into groups.

Structured rule systems allow the developer to create a tree structure. Each node is called a *context*, and the whole thing is called a *context tree*. Structured rule systems and context-tree-based systems are one and the same.

Here, as everywhere else in the world of expert systems vocabulary, people differ on their use of these terms. We are using "context" because we think it is clear and commonly used. Others prefer "object," or "frame," or something else.

Figure 2.12 illustrates a context tree you might use if you were trying to develop a system to help users select computer equipment for their office. The top context, or *root context*, would contain facts or rules about the general characteristics of the office relevant to every part of the problem. Thus, it might contain rules to determine how many people were in the office, if they each needed computers or could share, and the total amount of money the office could afford to spend.

Notice that the rules on printer selection have been placed in a printer selection subcontext. If rules in the root context determined that the office needed only dumb terminals to connect to a mainframe and that all printing would be done elsewhere, the system would avoid examining the rules in the printer subcontext. This makes the system more efficient.

You could also use the system to recommend several different printers, or recommend a printer that could handle the needs of several different people, each with his own printing requirements. To facilitate this, structured rule systems allow the rules in a subcontext to be used more than once. Moreover, since they save what they learn during each execution, rules can reason using information based on the results of several executions.

Thus, you might have a consultation in which Nikki, Curt, and Paul were working together to determine the needs of their office. During the initial questions, which are generated by the rules in the root context, the system learns that three workers will share the office and that they will need one or more printers. When the system moves from the root context to the printer subcontext, it creates an *instantiation*, or a working copy of the subcontext. It uses all of the rules in the subcontext once, to ask

Figure 2.12 Office computer equipment advisor context tree (static context tree).

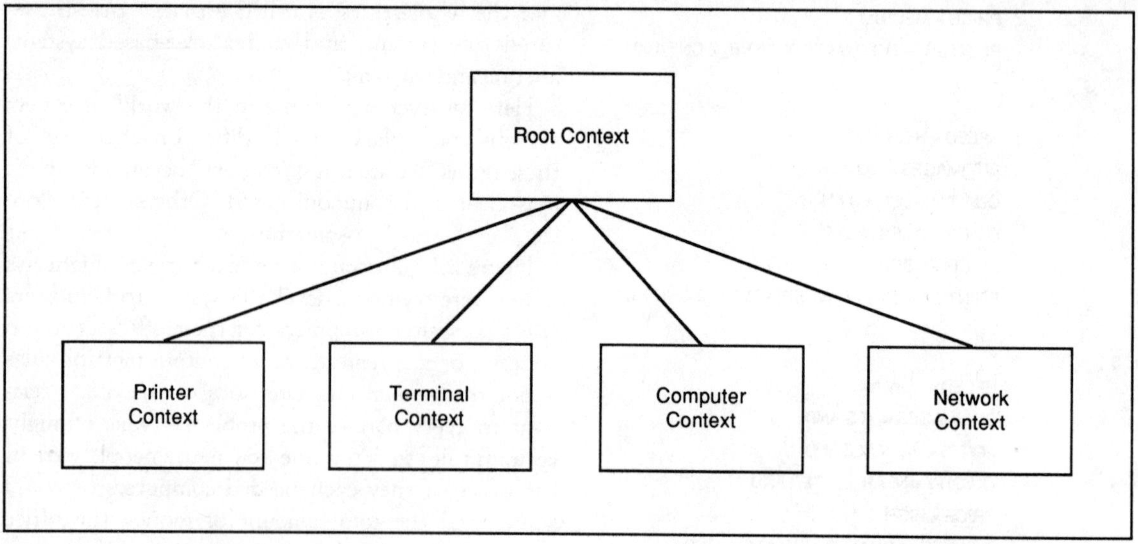

Nikki about her needs. It will then reinstantiate the rules in the subcontext and ask Curt about his needs. It will reinstantiate the rules a third time to ask Paul about his needs. Assuming that it determines that Nikki and Curt can share a printer but that Paul needs his own printer, the system will recommend one printer for Paul, based on his needs, and another printer for Nikki and Curt, based on their common needs.

Figure 2.13 shows how you typically represent a context tree when a subcontext has reinstantiated three times. A generic context tree, like the one shown in Figure 2.12, is referred to as a *static context tree*; it simply shows the contexts that make up a particular context tree. The context tree shown in Figure 2.13, on the other hand, is called a *dynamic context tree*, since it shows how many times a specific context was examined during a particular consultation.

To enable rules to be used within a context structure, you have to add an additional term to each attribute name to show where its value will reside. This third term is usually called the *context* or the *object*. (The use of the term "object" here is very common and is derived from the initial analysis in which we said that the printer object had certain attributes. Later, however, when we introduce the object-oriented programming concepts and vocabulary that occur in hybrid systems, this use of the term object can become quite confusing, so we recommend using the word "context" to avoid confusion.) All this means that the statements that are used in structured rule systems have three terms, as illustrated in Rule 6:

Rule 6

IF   context_printer_1/speed = low AND
context_printer_1/bit_images = no AND
context_printer_1/quality = letter AND
context_printer_1/fonts = fixed AND
context_printer_1/price = low
THEN context_printer_1/printer = daisy_wheel _type_1.

Notice that context names, attribute names, and value names of more than one word are connected by underscores. The context name is separated from the attribute name by means of a slash. This syntax is arbitrary and differs with each language and tool.

When you use this rule in an actual structured rule consultation, one or more specific values are substituted for context_printer_1. Thus, once the system found out, in response to some question that was asked while it used rules in the root context, that three people, named Nikki, Curt, and Paul, would be using printers, it would know that it needed to create and run three versions of the rules residing in the Printer subcontext. The first set of rules it instantiates would be used to ask about Nikki's needs, and the term "Nikki" would be substituted in place of context_printer_1. The second instantiation of the rule set would incorporate Curt's name, and the third set would use Paul's. This allows the system to associate specific attributes and values with specific people, and thus facilitates subsequent use of the context-attribute-value statements in rules that seek to determine a common printer for Nikki and Curt.

Thus, there are simple rule systems that use rules made up of attribute-value statements. These systems keep the rules in a single set, and process them during one pass. And there are structured rule or context-tree-based systems that use rules composed of context-attribute-value statements, subdivide the rules into contexts that are placed in a context tree, and reuse sets of rules as necessary.

Inference and Control

Inference. As we already noted, inference, in rule-based systems, is based on an ancient common sense principle of logic called *modus ponens*. Modus ponens asserts that if you declare If $A + B$ Then C, and you subsequently find in a particular situation that A and B are, in fact, true, then you are justified in inferring that C is also true.

The real work of the inference engine is done by techniques that implement various search or control strategies. The two common control strategies used in rule-based systems are called backward chaining and forward chaining. Some systems use a combination of the two strategies. In addition, some systems allow rules that incorporate confidence or probability or use other search strategies.

Figure 2.13 Office computer equipment advisor context tree that has evaluated Curt, Nikki, and Paul's need for a printer (dynamic context tree).

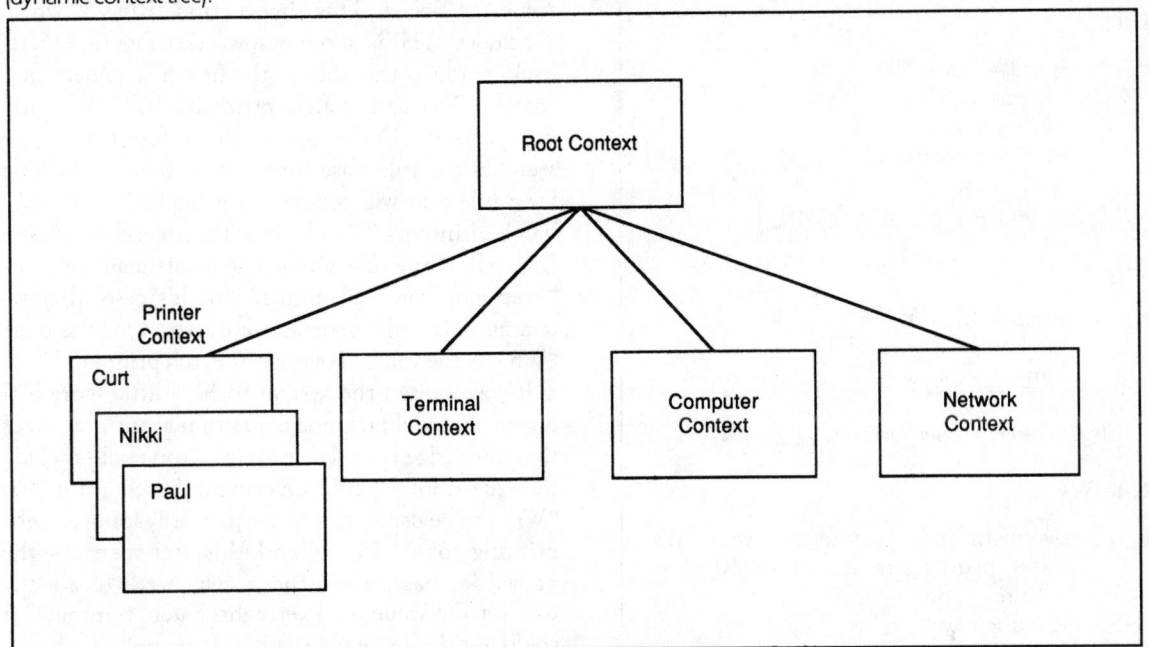

Control by backward chaining. *Backward chaining* is by far the most common strategy used in the simple rule systems. A backward chaining system starts with one or more goals. A *goal* is an attribute for which the system is trying to establish a value. The backward chaining inference engine proceeds to examine the knowledge base to see if it can establish a value for the goal attribute.

Let's consider an example in detail to show how backward chaining works. We'll use a modified version of the printer selection knowledge base, which is reproduced in Table 2.2. Notice that at the top of the list of rules there is a goal, which is to establish a value for printer. In addition, notice the addition of a new rule to define low printer speed.

Figure 2.14 provides another picture of the expert systems architecture, with two changes. We have added a small box to the right of the knowledge base to represent working memory. When the user indicates that she wants to run a printer selection consultation, the expert system loads the printer knowledge base (a file) into active memory (RAM). It also creates a cache, a special section of active memory in which it stores conclusions that are reached during the consultation. This cache is usually called *working memory*.

Notice that the system has placed "Printer =?" in working memory. That is the goal of the consultation. Having identified a goal, a backward chaining inference engine begins at the top of the list of rules and examines each one to determine if any of them has a THEN statement that provides a value for printer. In this particular example, the first rule has a conclusion that provides a value for printer (i.e., THEN printer = daisy_wheel_type_1). The inference engine then backs through Rule 1 to the first IF-clause and sets that attribute as a new intermediate goal. Thus, the second item entered in working memory is: "Speed =?".

The inference engine then repeats its search process, starting at the top again, and searches the rules for a rule that has a THEN-clause that provides a value for Speed. This time it finds Rule 3, which concludes "THEN speed = low." (See Figure 2.15.) It backs through this rule to the first If-statement and enters "Overnight_batch_printouts =?" into working memory. Once again, the inference engine searches the rule base from top to bottom, looking for a rule that will conclude a value for "overnight_batch_printouts." This time the inference engine fails to find any rule whose Then-statement concerns "overnight_batch_printouts." In this case, the system automatically generates a question for the user: "What is the value of overnight batch printouts?"

If you wanted the system to be a little more eloquent, you could include a question at the bottom of the knowledge base. For example, you could include the question: "ASK: Overnight_batch_printouts: "Will you be using the printer primarily for overnight printing jobs?" If you add this statement to the knowledge base, when the system needs to ask the user for the value of "overnight_batch_printouts" it could put this more polished question on the screen.

Table 2.2 The Printer Selection Knowledge Base Set Up for Use with a Backward Chaining System.

Goal: Printer

Rule 1

IF   speed = low AND
          bit_images = no AND
          quality = letter AND
          fonts = fixed AND
          price = low
THEN printer = daisy_wheel_type_1.

Rule 2

IF   speed = high AND
          bit_images = yes AND
          fonts = variable AND
          price = high
THEN printer = laser_printer.

Rule 3

IF   overnight_batch_printouts = yes AND
          letter_printing_in_less_than_10_minutes = no
THEN speed = low.

Figure 2.14 Expert systems architecture ready to run a forward chaining consultation.

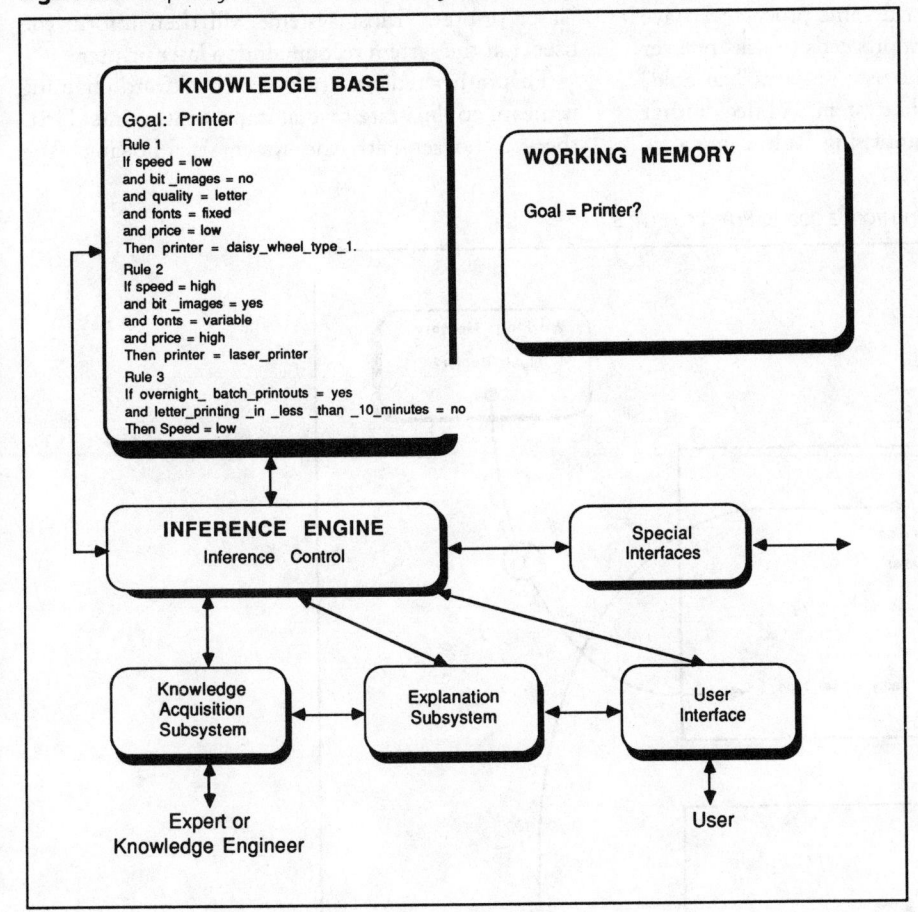

```
KNOWLEDGE BASE
Goal: Printer
Rule 1
If speed = low
and bit _images = no
and quality = letter
and fonts = fixed
and price = low
Then printer = daisy_wheel_type_1.
Rule 2
If speed = high
and bit _images = yes
and fonts = variable
and price = high
Then printer = laser_printer
Rule 3
If overnight_ batch_printouts = yes
and letter_printing _in _less _than _10_minutes = no
Then Speed = low
```

```
WORKING MEMORY
Goal = Printer?
```

INFERENCE ENGINE
Inference Control

Special Interfaces

Knowledge Acquisition Subsystem

Explanation Subsystem

User Interface

Expert or Knowledge Engineer

User

Once a question appears on the screen, it is up to the user to provide a value. In this case, assume the user answers "no." First, the system records the value "no" in working memory: "overnight_batch_printouts =no." Then, it decides that Rule 3 cannot be true (see Figure 2.16), so it stops considering Rule 3 and pops back to its efforts to find the value for "Speed." It searches the rule base for any other rule that concludes about "Speed," and finding none, it automatically generates another question for the user: "What is the value for speed?"

Let's assume that the user answers "high." The inference engine enters this value in working memory, "speed=high," and then decides that Rule 1 must fail. (See Figure 2.17.) It then resumes its effort to find a value for "printer" and searches the rule base from the point where it left off, at Rule 1, seeking another rule that concludes with a value for "printer." It finds Rule 2. (See Figure 2.18.) It backs up to the first If-statement in Rule 2 and finds that it has this value in working memory: "speed =high." So far, Rule 2 is viable, so the inference engine moves to the second If-statement and places the attribute "bit_images =?" in working memory. It then searches for a rule that will conclude about "bit_images." It doesn't find such a rule, so it generates a question:

32 BASIC CONCEPTS

"What is the value of bit-images?" Let's assume that the user says "yes." Using the same process we have been describing, the system proceeds to ask the user about fonts and price. If the user answers "variable" and "high," respectively, the system will decide that all of the If-statements comprising Rule 2 are true and it will then infer that one value for printer is "laser printer." Most systems will then inform the user that the system recommends a laser printer.

This rather tedious analysis of backward chaining is meant to illustrate several important points. First, there is no set path the system is following. The

Figure 2.15 Backward chaining from a goal to Rule 1 to Rule 3.

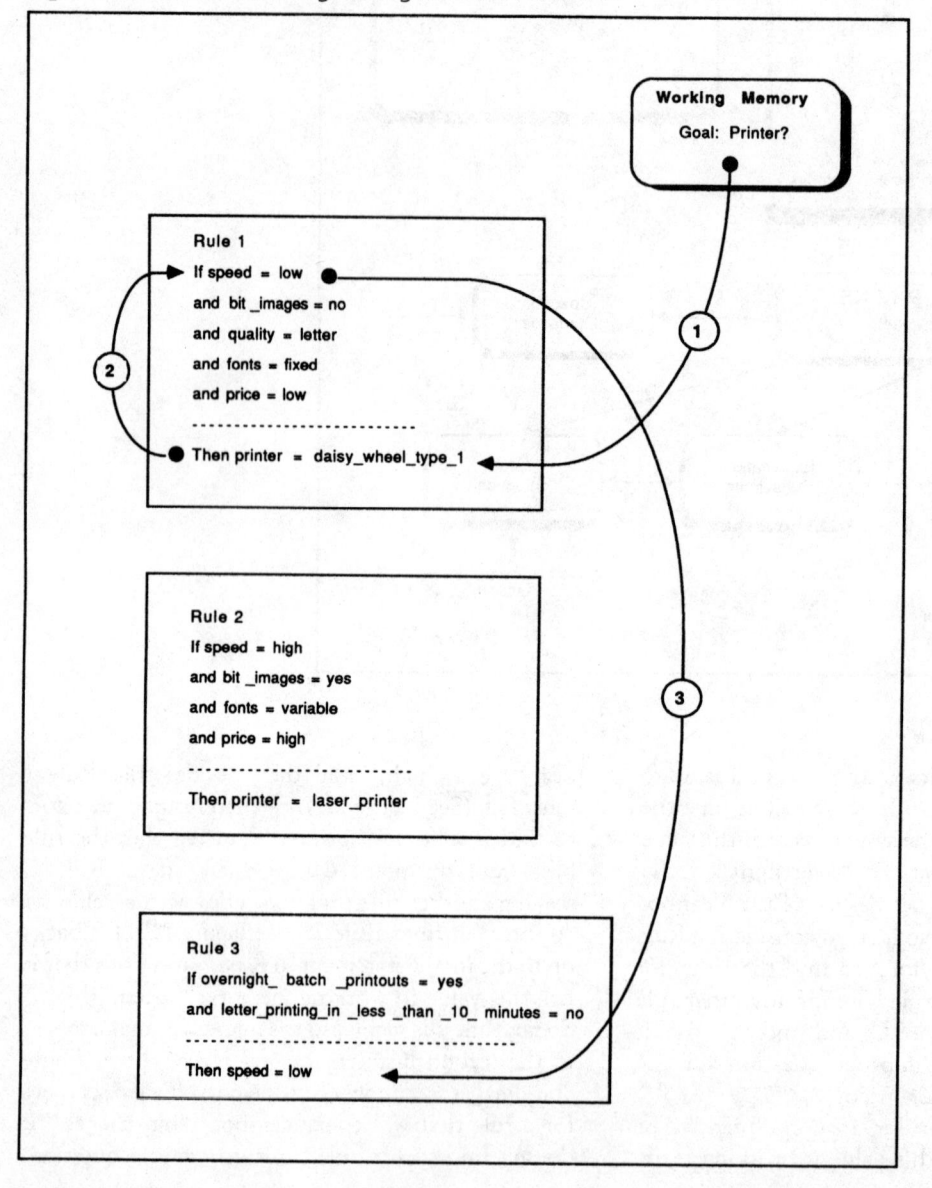

```
Working Memory
Goal: Printer?
```

Rule 1
If speed = low
and bit_images = no
and quality = letter
and fonts = fixed
and price = low
- -
Then printer = daisy_wheel_type_1

Rule 2
If speed = high
and bit_images = yes
and fonts = variable
and price = high
- -
Then printer = laser_printer

Rule 3
If overnight_batch_printouts = yes
and letter_printing_in_less_than_10_minutes = no
- -
Then speed = low

Figure 2.16 Backward chaining to a question and determining that Rule 3 will fail.

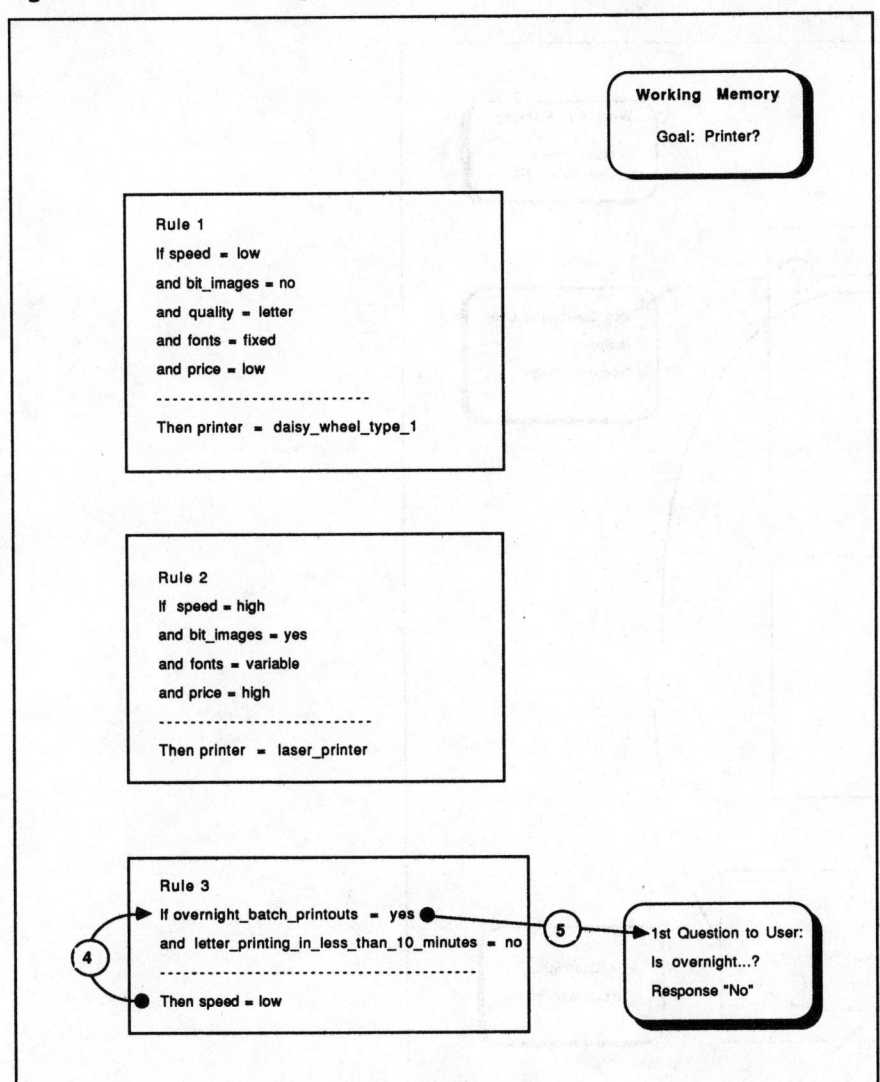

```
                                    ┌─────────────────────┐
                                    │  Working  Memory    │
                                    │                     │
                                    │  Goal: Printer?     │
                                    └─────────────────────┘

   ┌──────────────────────────────────┐
   │ Rule 1                           │
   │ If speed = low                   │
   │ and bit_images = no              │
   │ and quality = letter             │
   │ and fonts = fixed                │
   │ and price = low                  │
   │ -------------------------------  │
   │ Then printer = daisy_wheel_type_1│
   └──────────────────────────────────┘

   ┌──────────────────────────────────┐
   │ Rule 2                           │
   │ If speed = high                  │
   │ and bit_images = yes             │
   │ and fonts = variable             │
   │ and price = high                 │
   │ -------------------------------  │
   │ Then printer = laser_printer     │
   └──────────────────────────────────┘

   ┌──────────────────────────────────┐         ┌─────────────────────┐
   │ Rule 3                           │         │ 1st Question to User:│
   │ If overnight_batch_printouts = yes●───⑤───▶│ Is overnight...?    │
   │ and letter_printing_in_less_than_10_minutes = no │ Response "No" │
 ④ │ -------------------------------  │         └─────────────────────┘
   │ Then speed = low                 │
   └──────────────────────────────────┘
```

inference engine creates a decision tree as it obtains answers, and then it selects new rules to try. Whenever it determines that any one of the If-statements of a rule is false, it knows that the rule cannot be correct, it stops processing that rule, and it never asks questions about other If-statements in the rule. Thus, it is impossible to know in advance which rules will be examined in any particular consultation, because the next step is always determined by the answers the user provides.

Moreover, given this strategy, it makes no logical difference what the order of the rules is. If you inverted the rule base so that Rule 3 is at the top and Rule 1 is at the bottom, the system will still reach exactly the same recommendation. The inference engine will develop a different path through the rule

34 BASIC CONCEPTS

Figure 2.17 Popping up to Rule 1, and finding no other way to determine Speed, the inference engine asks the user. The user's response guarantees that Rule 1 will fail.

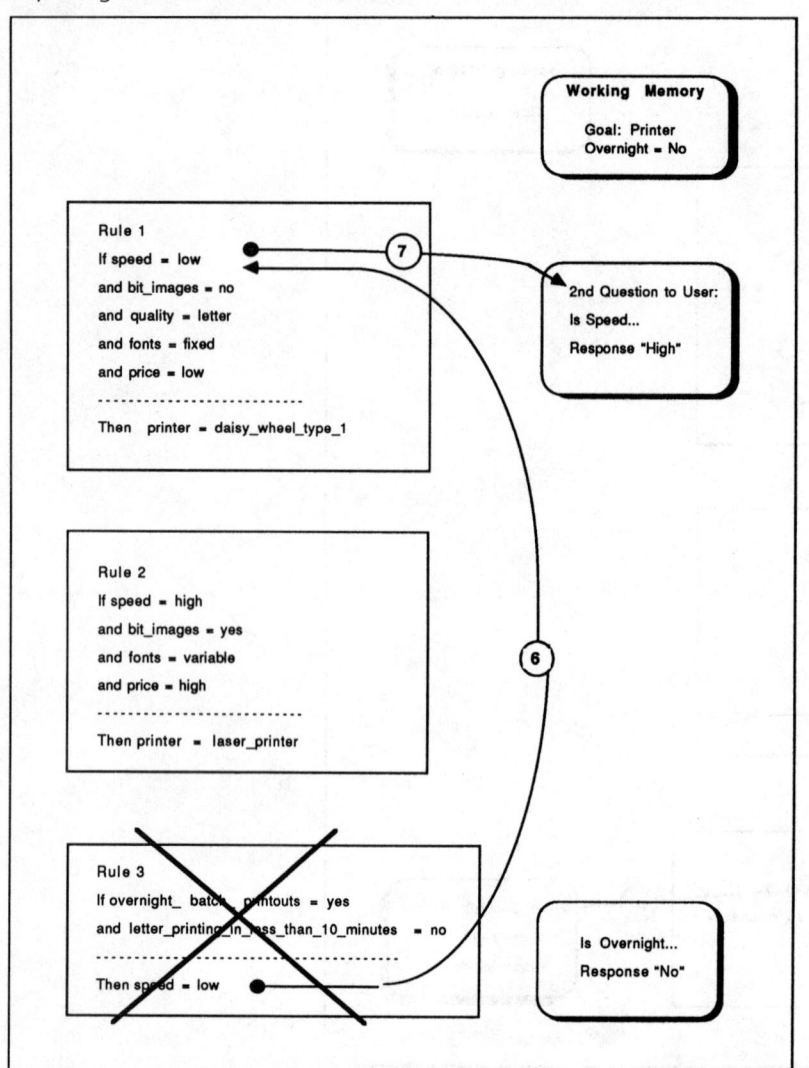

Working Memory
Goal: Printer
Overnight = No

Rule 1
If speed = low
and bit_images = no
and quality = letter
and fonts = fixed
and price = low

Then printer = daisy_wheel_type_1

2nd Question to User:
Is Speed...
Response "High"

Rule 2
If speed = high
and bit_images = yes
and fonts = variable
and price = high

Then printer = laser_printer

Rule 3
If overnight_batch_printouts = yes
and letter_printing_in_less_than_10_minutes = no

Then speed = low

Is Overnight...
Response "No"

base and ask the questions in a different order, but it will still reach the same conclusion. In this case, when the inference engine searches for a rule that concludes with a value for printer, it will skip Rule 3 and stop at Rule 2. It will back up to the first If-statement in Rule 2 and set Speed as its first subgoal. It will then search for a rule that concludes about speed, find Rule 3 right on the top, back up to the first If-clause, and set "overnight_batch_printing" as its second subgoal. It will look for a rule that provides a value for overnight batch printing, not find one, and generate a question. Assuming the user still answers "no," the system will discard Rule 3, pop back to Speed, and ask the user about speed. If the user says she wants high speed, the system will proceed to the second If-clause in Rule 2, and so on.

More sophisticated inference engines allow the developer to assign priorities to rules to help order the

Basic Expert Systems Techniques   35

inference engine's search and thus the order in which questions are asked. But the fundamental fact remains: By using the backward chaining search strategy, an inference engine will find and investigate every possible way to establish a true value for the goal, no matter what the order of the If-statements or the order of the rules in the rule base is. This provides the developer with a great deal of flexibility when he is developing the knowledge base. Rules can be added or rearranged at any time, and the system will always provide any logical answer that can be inferred from any given set of rules.

Finally, the knowledge in a knowledge base is independent of any particular goal. You might create a knowledge base to help with selecting printers and later decide that you wanted to set a different goal for

Figure 2.18 The user's answer to the second question means that the rule fails. Still seeking a way to determine the value for printer, the inference engine moves on to Rule 2, determines that the first IF-statement is true (from working memory), and proceeds to ask the user about "bit images."

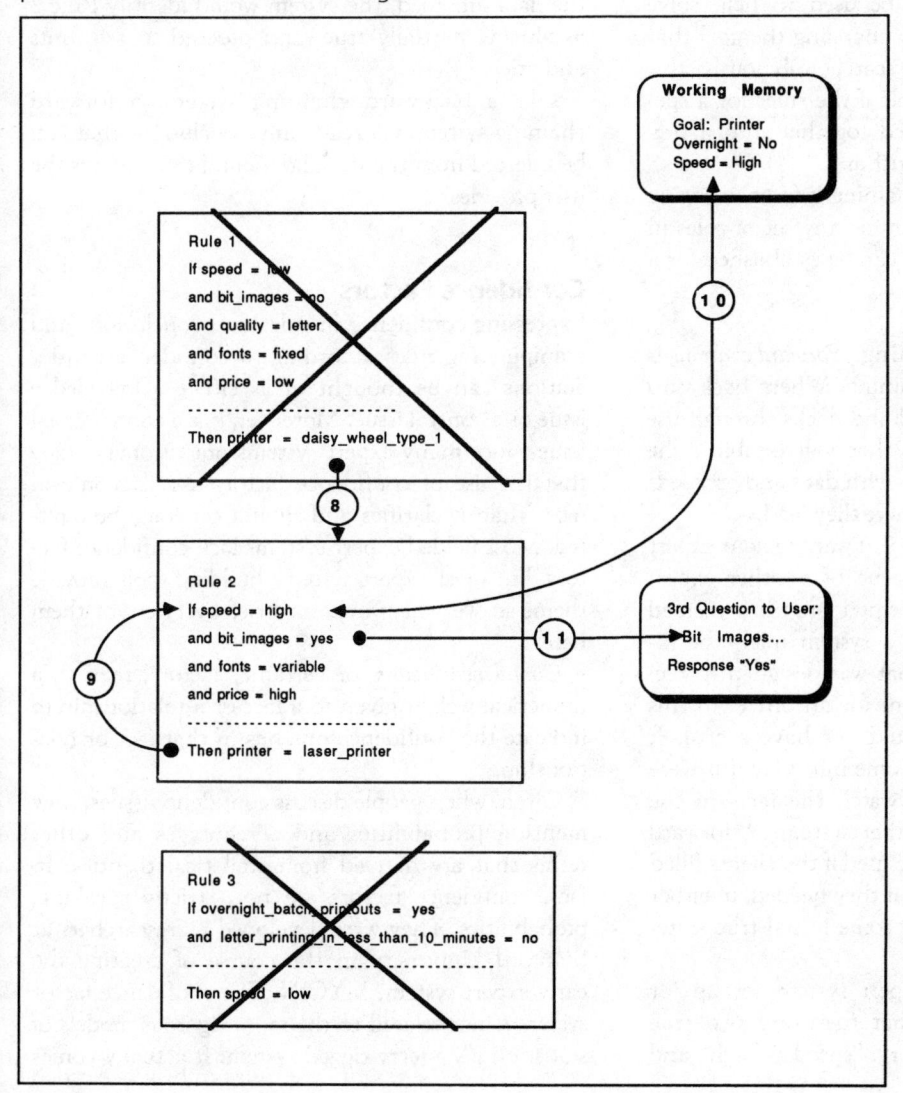

a consultation. Using the same inference strategy, the system would examine the rules in the same way in an effort to establish a value for some other goal.

The knowledge base here is too simple to provide a very interesting illustration of this, but consider that if you started a consultation and set the goal as Speed, the inference engine would still search the three rules, find only one rule that would apply, back up to "batch_processing_overnight," and ask the user a question. This would be silly in the context of this rudimentary knowledge base, but it means that large knowledge bases can be used to help solve different problems simply by changing the goal that starts the inference engine's search. Obviously, this flexibility would be impossible if the rules for a specific consultation were linked together into a predetermined sequence or algorithm.

In effect, the backward chaining inference engine is an algorithm that will examine any set of rules in order to determine if a value can be established for a given goal.

Control by forward chaining. *Forward chaining* is the reverse of backward chaining. Where backward chaining starts with the goal and backs through the rules looking first for rules that will establish the goal, forward chaining begins with data and proceeds to fire rules in order to see where they lead.

Imagine, for example, that you wanted your expert system to monitor the dialogue of another expert system, and recommend a printer only if it seemed the user needed one. Such a system might be attached to another system that was designed to recommend computer equipment for an office. In this case, the printer system would not have a goal. It would simply be waiting to come into play if it were needed. It would wait and watch the facts in the working memory of some other system. A forward chaining system could also be used if the clients filled out a form that indicated what they needed. In either case, the system would need some initial true statements before it could begin.

Figure 2.19 shows an expert system set up for forward chaining. Notice that there are two true statements in working memory: "speed = high" and "bit_images = yes." Also notice that there is no goal for the system.

When an inference engine uses a forward chaining strategy, it begins by examining the facts in working memory and then going to the rule base and searching for rules whose If-clauses will be satisfied by the data it has. Because this example is so small, the inference engine will not find any rules that can be established. It will determine that Rule 1 and Rule 3 cannot be true. If you set the system to generate questions from any rules that might be true based on the data provided, the system would identify Rule 2 as already partially true, and proceed to ask fonts and price.

Like a backward chaining system, a forward chaining system will reach any conclusions that can be inferred from the initial data and the answers the user provides.

Confidence Factors

Expressing confidence in rules and conclusions and manipulating rules according to confidence considerations can be thought of as either a knowledge issue or a control issue. Moreover, it is a controversial issue, since many expert systems practitioners argue that the use of confidence factors usually confuses more than it clarifies and should generally be omitted. Most fielded expert systems lack confidence factors, but most expert systems building tools provide them, so we will provide a brief overview of them here.

Confidence factors, or certainty factors, refer to a numerical weight given to a fact or a relationship to indicate the confidence one has in that fact or relationship.

Often, when people discuss confidence issues, they mention probabilities and percentages and other terms that are derived from statistical theories. In fact, confidence factors are not, strictly speaking, probabilities. They were developed by researchers at Stanford University in the course of creating the early expert system, MYCIN. The confidence factor system is not related to the more rigorous models of statistics; it's a jerry-rigged system. It actually comes

Figure 2.19 Expert Systems architecture ready to run a forward chaining consultation.

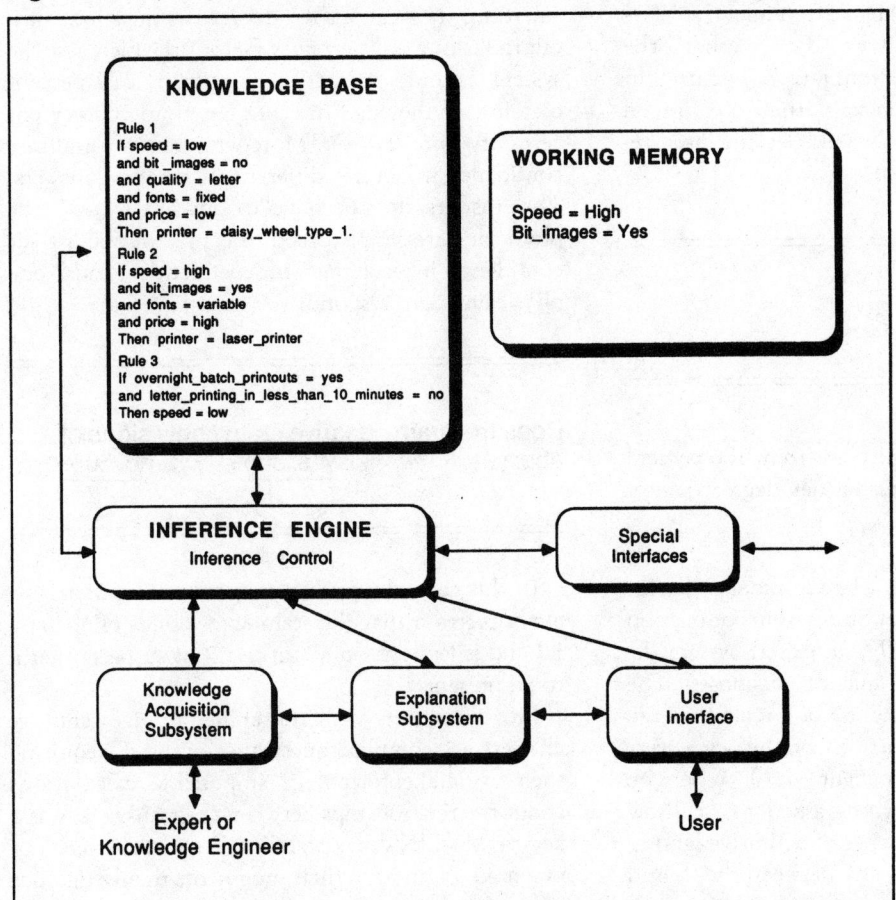

```
KNOWLEDGE BASE

Rule 1
If speed = low
and bit_images = no
and quality = letter
and fonts = fixed
and price = low
Then printer = daisy_wheel_type_1.
Rule 2
If speed = high
and bit_images = yes
and fonts = variable
and price = high
Then printer = laser_printer
Rule 3
If overnight_batch_printouts = yes
and letter_printing_in_less_than_10_minutes = no
Then speed = low
```

```
WORKING MEMORY

Speed = High
Bit_images = Yes
```

INFERENCE ENGINE
Inference Control

Special Interfaces

Knowledge Acquisition Subsystem

Explanation Subsystem

User Interface

Expert or Knowledge Engineer

User

closer to the thinking of human experts in many cases, but it lacks the rigorous underpinnings of a well thought-out mathematical theory and therefore must be used with considerable caution. We'll first define the two kinds of confidence that exist and then explain the Stanford approach to confidence factors, which most expert systems developers use.

Two kinds of confidence. There are two kinds of confidence: *expert confidence*, the confidence that an expert feels when suggesting a rule and *user confidence*, the confidence that a user feels when answering a question. Consider the earlier rule about birds that lay eggs and fly.

Rule 2

IF   animal_lays_eggs = true AND
          animal_flies = true
THEN animal = bird (confidence = 95).

Assuming you are working with a biologist to develop these rules, you could ask the biologist how confident she is in predicting that an animal that lays eggs and flies is a bird. If the expert says that, lacking any other evidence, she would almost always assume that it was a bird, you might assign 95 percent confidence to the relationship stated in Rule 2. The 95 represents the expert's confidence that the If-statements will typically lead to the Then-statement.

Now assume that you use this rule during a consultation and ask the user: "Did the animal fly?" The user may not be certain; it was dark, perhaps the animal simply glided down from a tree. The user, in effect, says: "I'm almost certain that the animal flew." Most expert systems would let the user respond to the question as follows.

Did the animal fly?: yes, 80%.

In providing an answer with less than 100 percent certainty, the user is expressing her degree of user confidence.

How confidence works. The Confidence Factor (CF) system was developed at Stanford in connection with the creation of MYCIN, an expert system devised to aid physicians in making diagnoses. The initial approach involved the use of a scale that ran from -1.00 to $+1.00$. Portions of the scale were given names, as shown in Figure 2.20. When an expert provided a rule, he was asked to say how confident he was, in the absence of definitive laboratory data, that an empirical link between the If- and Then-statements would turn out to be true. Specifically, he was asked to use one of the terms shown in Figure 2.20. The expert was not asked to give a number, since experts generally don't think of their knowledge in terms of numerical relations.

Each rule was considered independently. Thus, some rules might provide evidence for the presence of a specific bacteria, while other rules might provide evidence against that bacteria being present. Likewise, the same evidence might be used in several different rules to support the presence of different bacteria, and so on. The expert was not asked to develop a systematic "theory" of how difference was to be weighted, he was simply asked about the confidence he normally associated with any particular rule.

Separately, when physicians run a MYCIN consultation, they can either answer the question without indicating any certainty factor (in which case the system assumes that the physician is 100 percent certain), or they can indicate less than 100 percent certainty in an answer. Moreover, they can indicate confidence in several different alternative answers. The answers do not have to add up to 100; the physicians are simply asked to comment about their confidence in each fact independently. Thus, one physician might respond:

Does the gram negative stain show signs of abc: yes, 80%   **jkl:** yes, 80%   **xyz:** no, 50%.

In this case, the physician is indicating that he is almost certain that the stain shows signs of abc and jkl and is less certain about xyz, but suspects that it too is present.

Providing users with the ability to give tentative answers to complex questions, without requiring them to make formal or impossible calculations about the relationships between their answers, was a key to MYCIN's acceptability. Physicians were not prepared to quantify their judgments in any rigorous way, but they were used to talking to colleagues about hunches and judgments about which they were "almost certain," or felt were "very unlikely."

To calculate the final confidence the system has in any recommendation, the confidence factor system has to do two things. It needs to know how to adjust the expert's confidence in a rule when the user (or another rule) suggests that some of the If-statements in that rule are less than certain. It also needs some way of consolidating the confidence associated with various rules to reach a single confidence factor. Consider Rule n:

Rule n

   IF $A = b$
   THEN $C = d$ (confidence = 80).

Figure 2.20 Mycin confidence factor or certainty factor scale.

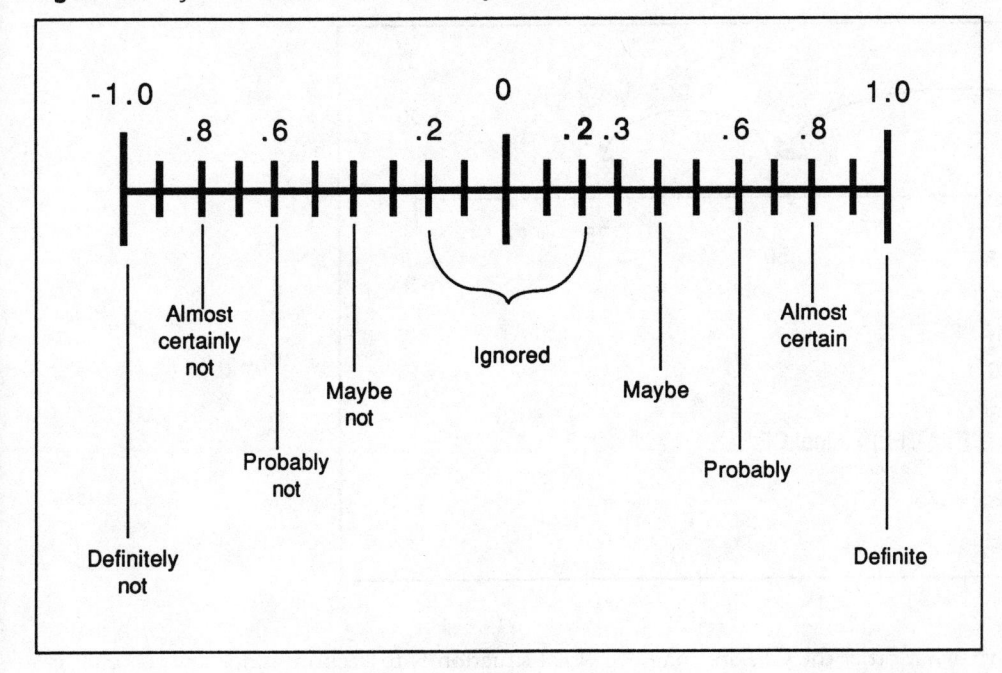

```
-1.0              0                    1.0
   .8  .6    .2      .2 .3      .6  .8
├──┼──┼──┼──┼──┼──┼──┼──┼──┼──┼──┤

    Almost                        Almost
    certainly                     certain
    not
          Maybe         Maybe
          not
       Probably              Probably
       not
Definitely                          Definite
not
```

                        Ignored

If you assume that this rule is used in a consultation and the user says that the value of $A = b$, and that he is 50 percent confident of that, then the system would take the 50 associated with $A = b$ and multiply it by the 80 associated with the rule's conclusion, divide by 100, and enter $C = d$ in working memory with a confidence of 40.

If there were more than one If-statement connected by AND, and if they had different confidence factors associated with them, the system would use the lowest confidence factor associated with any of the If-statements, multiply it by the confidence associated with the Then-statement, divide by 100, and enter the resulting confidence with the Then-statement in working memory.

If the If-statements were connected by OR, the rule would be treated as if it were two or more separate rules.

If the system pursued different rules associated with different lines of reasoning, the working memory could contain several different values for the same statement. Thus, for example, working memory could contain the following facts:

$C = d$ CF 50
$C = d$ CF 50
$C = d$ CF $-$ 20

The system would combine the positives and the negatives and then subtract and assign the resulting CF (confidence factor) to C. To combine all the positives (or negatives), the system uses the following formula:

$$CF1 + CFn - (CF1 \times CFn) = \text{Final CF}$$

The effect of this, in the case of our example, is to move a pointer 50 percent of the way from 0 to 1.00, and then move it 50 percent of the remaining distance. (See Figure 2.21.) To handle the negative confidence, the system would subtract 20 from 75 and assign a final confidence of 55 to $C = d$.

If you use this approach, you're guaranteed that (1)

Figure 2.21 CF calculations.

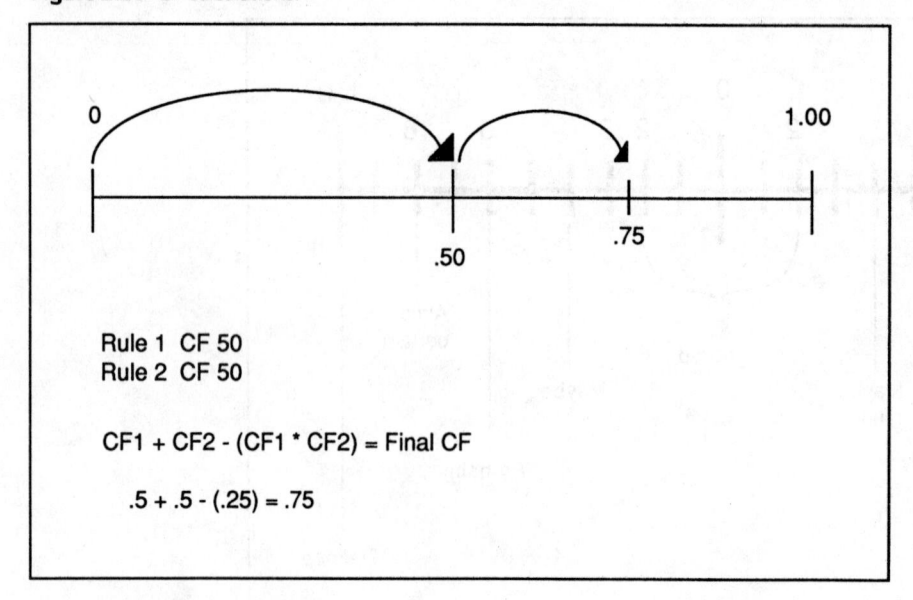

```
0 ─────────────────► .50 ──────► .75            1.00
├──────────────────────┼──────────┼──────────────┤
                      .50        .75
```

Rule 1 CF 50
Rule 2 CF 50

CF1 + CF2 - (CF1 * CF2) = Final CF

.5 + .5 - (.25) = .75

---

it makes no difference what order the CFs are combined, and (2) no number of positive CFs, each of which is less than certain, can sum to 100 percent certainty.

This approach seems to approximate what human experts intuitively feel about how they reason about uncertain evidence. As we have already noted, this is not a rigorous statistical approach. Normal statistical systems could not handle different evidence from different, independent sources. Those who favor a more rigorous approach prefer Bayesian statistics, but the Bayesian approach requires that experts commit themselves to assumptions that are much more rigorous and formal than what they are generally willing to accept. (For example, following the Bayesian approach, if an expert asserts that If $A = b$, Then $C = d$, and that she is 80 percent confident of this relation, then she automatically asserts that If A does not equal b, she is 20 percent certain that C does not equal d. When you consider that most experts don't associate numbers with their judgments in the first place, you realize that they will find it difficult to agree to such a rigorous approach.)

The important thing in using confidence in a practical situation is to keep in mind how the end user will interpret the results. Let's assume that after running a consultation, a user is told the following by a system:

I believe that the cause of your malfunction is:
part A   80% confidence
part B   75% confidence
part C   45% confidence
part D   5% confidence

The user will decide that either part A or part B is the most likely cause. He will consider part C seriously only if replacing part A and part B fails to solve the problem, and he will turn to part D only if the other three fail. If the system could be refined to raise the confidence in part A by 2 percent and reduce the confidence in part C by 3 percent, it wouldn't make any difference in the user's behavior. The user relies on confidence only as an indication that the system is not certain what the answer to the problem is and for a rough ranking of the possible answers.

The use of the confidence factors proved vitally important to getting physicians to accept MYCIN's suggestions. They knew that on the basis of the evidence that MYCIN had, it could not be certain of a particular diagnosis any more than a human physician would be in a similar situation. They considered MYCIN's suggestions in the same way they would a colleague's statement of "I'm not certain of course, but it sounds like it's either organism A or organism B. On the other hand, it could be organism C. I don't think it's organism D, but because of the tissue stain evidence, I might check it, if treating the other three doesn't eliminate the problem." If you face a situation in which an expert might typically provide such advice, you might want to consider using confidence factors. Otherwise, it's probably best to avoid them, as most of the people who have developed expert systems have decided to do.

HYBRID SYSTEMS

Combining Rules and Objects

We have now considered the techniques involved in inductive and rule-based systems. The third popular combination of techniques results in a class of tools generally called *hybrid systems*. A hybrid system combines object-oriented programming techniques with rules and context trees to facilitate the development of the most complex expert systems.

Object-oriented programming gives you the ability to easily define and store large numbers of facts and relationships without having to incorporate the facts into rules. In effect, the statements that make up declarative rules are stored as statements within objects, while the heuristic knowledge is kept in rules.

Before we discuss object-oriented programming in any detail, it's important to consider one semantic difficulty. Some expert systems people use the term "frame" while others use the term "object." Frame comes out of a long AI tradition. A *frame* is a chunk of knowledge. The term was developed without specific reference to programming to refer to the way experts group their knowledge into conceptual units. Thus, a businessperson has a financial statement frame that includes all of the terms and numbers she associates with a financial statement. If she is analytical, her frame probably includes certain formulas that can be used to calculate financial statement ratios, along with the information necessary to decide what is indicated by ratios that fall in different ranges, and so on.

The term *object* originated as a programming concept. An object is an entity that includes facts, rules, pointers, and procedures. When AI people want to develop a software system that implements a knowledge base organized around frames of knowledge, they use object-oriented programming techniques. Thus, a frame is essentially descriptive in nature, while an object is functional in nature. At this point, most people use the terms interchangeably. We tend here to use the term "object." If we are talking about an object as a unit of domain knowledge, however, you can substitute the word "frame" if you wish.

We will briefly describe the key object-oriented programming techniques, and then consider how these techniques can be combined with the rule-based techniques that we have already discussed.

Object-Oriented Programming

Object-oriented programming is an exciting new way to think about organizing data and procedural code when you develop an application. There are programming languages that are especially designed for object-oriented programming, including Smalltalk and C++. Object-oriented programming can also be implemented in LISP. Hybrid expert systems building tools, no matter what language they are written in, include utilities for the development and use of object-oriented systems. We begin by considering object-oriented programming as an independent way of programming, defining it the way a Smalltalk programmer might. Then we consider how we would modify a pure object-oriented system to make it a component of an expert systems building tool.

There are three fundamental concepts that underlie object-oriented programming: (1) encapsulation, (2) inheritance, and (3) message passing. Each of these concepts includes subconcepts and techniques. We consider each of the three major concepts and their subconcepts in turn.

Encapsulation. The fundamental module in an object-oriented system is the object. The term *encapsulation* refers to the fact that an object is a block of code that is more or less independent of any other block of code within an object-oriented application. An object can store both data and procedures.

For example, you might create a Printer object. In addition to having a name, the Printer object would contain attributes that are typically associated with printers and procedures to determine their values. An object can also contain methods, ways for the object to respond to requests for information or action. One way to represent an object is by means of a matrix. Figure 2.22 illustrates a more graphic representation of a Printer object.

Inheritance. *Inheritance* refers to the way in which objects can acquire or inherit information from other objects that they are linked to.

Each object has a "unique part," data or procedures that belong specifically to that object, and a separate part that contains pointers to one or more parents that contain data or procedures that the specific object can access, if necessary. When an object receives a "message" that requests it to provide data about itself, it begins by checking for the necessary data within its "unique part." If it fails to find it there, it then checks with its inherited part, thus turning to its parents to see if they contain the data.

Figure 2.22 Graphic representation of a printer object.

OBJECT: PRINTER	
(Slot Name)	(Possible Values or Constraints)
Parent	Computer Hardware
Attribute: Speed	(Low, Medium, High)
Attribute: Bit_Images	(Yes, No)
Attribute: Quality	(Letter, Draft, Near_letter)
Attribute: Fonts	(Fixed, Variable)
Attribute: Price	(Low, Medium, High)
Children	Daisy_wheel_Type_1 Printer, Laser_Printer (etc.)

SLOTS

FACETS

Figure 2.23 Inheritance in object-oriented systems.

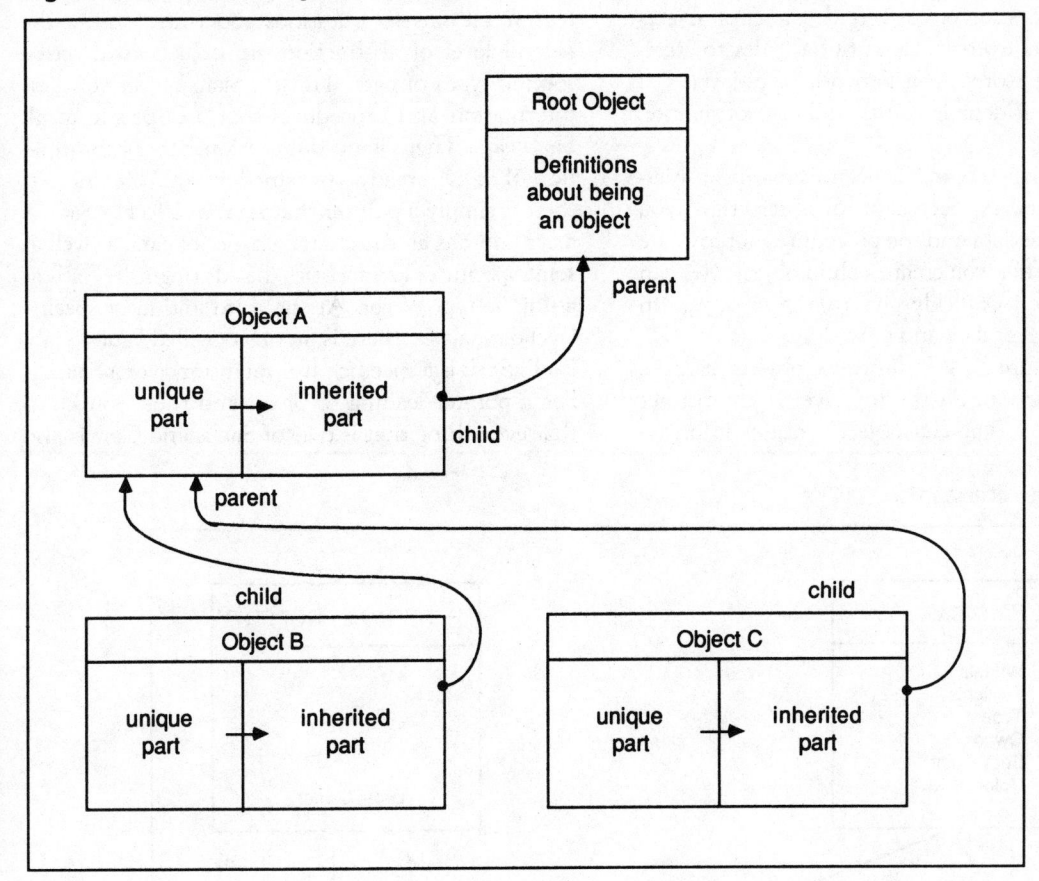

[Diagram: Root Object (Definitions about being an object) at top; Object A below it labeled as child/parent relationship, with unique part → inherited part; Object B and Object C are children of Object A, each with unique part → inherited part.]

Obviously, this process can be repeated at the next higher level. The parent begins by checking its "unique part" to see if it has the data the child needs. If it doesn't, it then turns to its parents in order to obtain the information, and so on. (See Figure 2.23.)

Message passing. A *message* is a request from one object to another, or from a user. A message is not a procedure, but simply a name or symbol to which the object responds. When an object receives a message, it checks within its own data and procedures to determine how it should respond. Thus, each object (or its parents or their parents) must contain procedures that will decode, interpret, and act on any messages the object might receive. Its actions will typically include procedures that generate messages to other objects or to a user.

The Uses of Object-Oriented Programming

Given this brief description, you might ask why anyone would want to create an object-oriented system. Object-oriented systems are a much simpler and more natural way of clustering procedures and data than those used in either conventional programming languages or databases. They are also a powerful way to modularize code so that it can be used without modification in different applications. Any program that can be written in a conventional language can also be written in an object-oriented language like

Smalltalk. More important for our purposes, any collection of rules can be converted to a set of objects and rules. By converting definitional rules to statements that are stored in a network of objects, you can achieve considerable clarity and ease of maintenance.

The key to this approach lies in creating a hierarchy of objects. At each level of abstraction, you describe just the data and the procedures appropriate at that level. When you create a child object, you can use inheritance to quickly give that new object an impressive range of data and procedures.

Consider Figure 2.24. It illustrates objects at three levels of abstraction. At the top level is an abstract entity called Car. The Car object contains information that is true about all cars and procedures to reason and answer questions about any car. At the second level of abstraction are objects to describe specific types of cars. Thus, a Saab object contains information and procedures that are specific to all Saab cars. There is no duplication here of information that is already contained in the Car object; there is simply a pointer that says, in effect, a Saab is a car and has all the characteristics of cars, as well as some specific characteristics that distinguish Saabs as a unique type of car. At the third and most specific level of analysis, there is an object called Paul's Saab. Paul's Saab is a specific physical instance of a Saab. It has a pointer leading to Saab, and thus, you know that everything that is true of Saabs and Cars is also

Figure 2.24 Levels of abstraction.

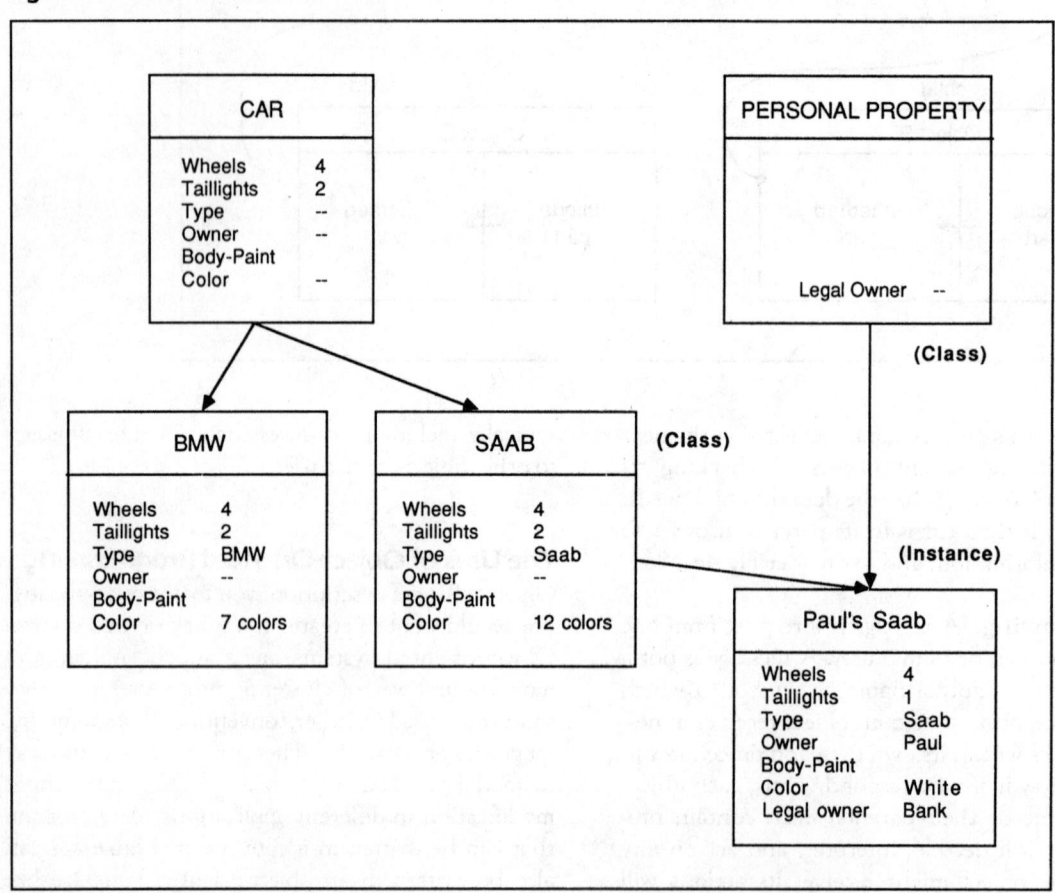

true of Paul's Saab. This means that you can create Paul's Saab without writing much code and still have an application that can provide a user with all kinds of information about Paul's Saab. A user might ask if Paul's Saab has four wheels. Paul's Saab would then respond to the question (a message) by checking Saab, which would, in turn, check Car to determine that all cars, and thus Paul's Saab, have four wheels.

There might be something abnormal about Paul's Saab. It might have a broken taillight, for example. That information would be stored in the "unique part" of Paul's Saab, along with the object's name. Thus, if a user sent a message asking how many working taillights Paul's Saab has, the object would respond with one, rather than two, because it would find that information in its unique part and thus would not check with the Saab object, which would otherwise provide the value two.

Notice also that Paul's Saab has a second parent, Personal Property. This object has information about legal contracts and financing. If someone asked who owned Paul's Saab, the object might respond "Paul," but if someone asked, "How much does Paul still owe to the bank?", the object might go to the Personal Property parent object in order to find what payments are remaining and to calculate how long it will be before Paul "really" owns Paul's Saab.

Object-oriented programming techniques are especially helpful in handling graphics. Indeed, the entire Macintosh operating system is based on object-oriented principles, as are some windowing packages and graphics software like CAD-CAM and drawing programs.

Combining Object-Oriented Systems with Rule-Based Systems

People have used object-oriented techniques for years to build windowing systems, to handle complex graphics, and even to create operating systems for machines like the Xerox Star and the Macintosh. Thus, you can think of object-oriented programming languages as a separate and independent part of computer science. They are related to AI in the sense that they are descriptive languages that are concerned with symbolic processing, but they have their own history in simulation, graphics, and interface design. For our purposes, though, object-oriented programming techniques can also play a very important role in expert systems development.

The key to the development of an expert system is a description of the knowledge an expert uses to solve a problem. If the expert naturally thinks in terms of If-Then procedures, then rule-based systems may be a natural and adequate way of capturing and encoding the expert's problem-solving knowledge. If, on the other hand, the expert thinks in terms of diagrams, models, and complex relationships between parts and components or phases, the expert's knowledge may require an object-oriented approach to knowledge representation.

Using an object-oriented approach, a developer can create complex models that capture volumes of statements and complex hierarchical relationships between things that would be very hard and time consuming to represent as rules. Moreover, the synthesis of rule-based techniques, inference and control, and the object-oriented approach results in a very powerful programming environment.

Let's now briefly review what we have said about objects, hierarchies, and message passing, with an emphasis on expert systems development.

Suppose you have to represent an expert's knowledge. You begin by determining the objects (i.e., frames, concepts, physical objects) in the expert's world. At any particular level of abstraction, the objects are related to other objects. Moving from one level of abstraction to another, you find that objects are related in networks, and that some objects are parents or children of other objects.

Figure 2.22 illustrates the Printer object. Expert systems developers tend to draw a network of objects as a set of boxes connected by lines representing the relationships between the objects. Within each box there is a matrix. The rows are called *slots* and the columns are called *facets*. At a minimum, an object has attributes. In many cases, an object has defaults, which are values to be associated with particular attributes if there are no other means of obtaining a value.

In addition to an attribute and value slot, there is typically a slot containing information about possible (legal) values, the type of value, and how to determine the value. A conventional object-oriented system would rely on methods (i.e., procedural code) to obtain values. By adding expert systems techniques, however, you can introduce the use of rules, inference, and search (heuristic knowledge) as an additional way to obtain a desired value. Thus, a hybrid system can support slots with procedures to calculate the value or obtain it from a database, questions to ask a user, and rules that can be used with either a forward or backward chaining system to obtain a needed value.

All object-oriented languages support inheritance from parent objects to their children. More complex systems typically support multiple inheritance. In that case, the system needs to allow the developer to determine which slot is to inherit its value from which parent. It quickly becomes complex when you start adding procedures to determine that a particular slot will inherit from a particular parent only when some complex set of criteria is met.

Some objects contain statements and relationships that could be used in different consultations. We refer to these more or less permanent objects as *classes*. Thus, in Figure 2.23, Car, BMW, Saab, and Personal Property are classes. Other objects are created only in the context of a particular consultation. In effect, these objects hold the facts that are inherited or established during the course of the consultation. These objects are called *instances*. In Figure 2.24, Paul's Saab is an instance of the Saab object.

As we have already suggested, in object-oriented systems used in hybrid tools, messages can trigger or be triggered by either messages or rules.

A sample hybrid system. Let's consider how to create a small system to handle printer selection. Normally, we would never use a hybrid tool for such a simple task, but we will use it here to illustrate the concepts we have been discussing.

Figure 2.25 illustrates an overview of the object system we have developed to capture the basic facts about printers. The most abstract object describes printers in general. This object has a slot for specific types of printers, which lists a number of children. Each of the children describes (defines) a specific type of printer, and each has default values that describe the type.

In addition to the printer network, there are two other objects: "Preferences," which houses the qualities the user wants in a printer, and "Recommended Printer," in which the system stores information about the printer that it ultimately recommends.

When a consultation starts, the system creates (instantiates) an instance of "preferences." It then asks the user for information about what kind of printer he wants and records this information into slots in "Preferences." Once it has all of the information, the system seeks to find a value for recommendation. In this case, the system determines the value by using a general rule that is applied to each instance of the Printer object, checking to see if its values fit the values in the "Preferences" object.

If one of the rules representing a specific printer fires, then the system recommends that printer to the user.

As we noted earlier, this approach would be too complex for a simple problem like printer selection, but it might be very useful if you added instances of specific brands of printers. If you were dealing with 100 kinds of printers, 30 computers, 12 modems, 30 monitors, and so forth, the advantages of an object-oriented approach to representing the basic descriptive information associated with all of these pieces of hardware would become more apparent.

There are two types of inference in hybrid systems. One type occurs via rules; the other type occurs via inheritance. In effect, we say that IF- object b is a child of object a, THEN- object b has the attributes of object a. An object-oriented knowledge base could always be rewritten as rules; the advantage of using objects is that you can work much more intuitively with them, they clarify the relationships between various levels of conceptual abstraction, and they are much easier to edit and maintain.

By combining the power of object-oriented programming with an inference engine and the use of

Figure 2.25 Architecture of a hybrid printer system.

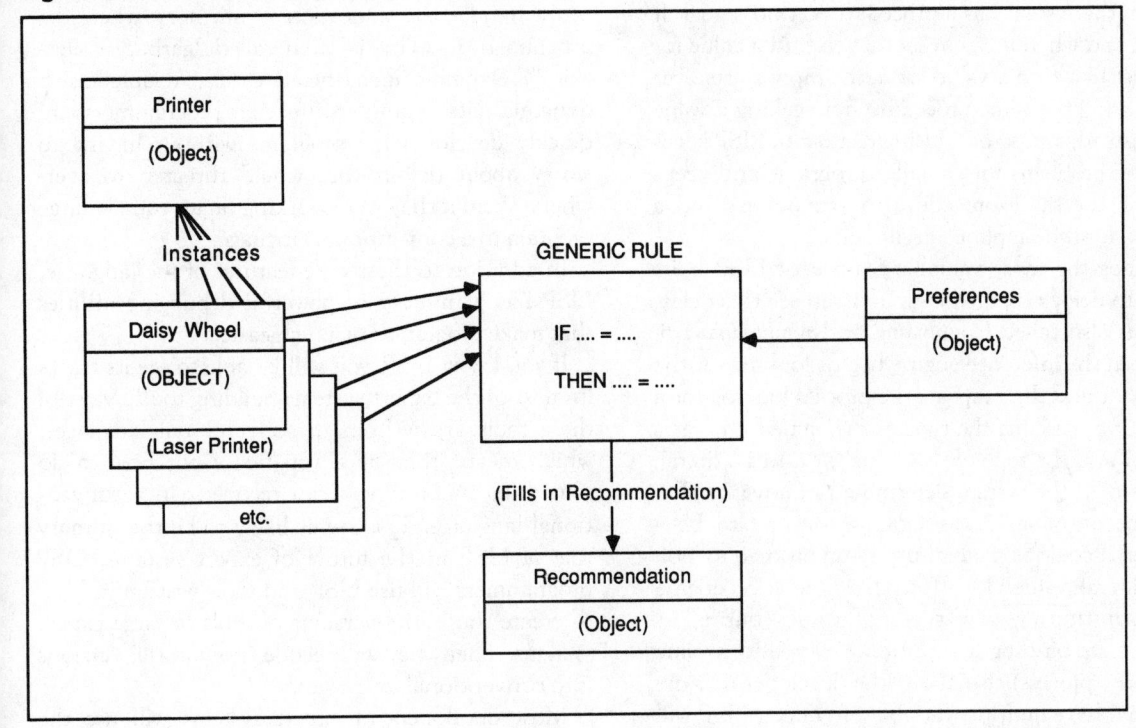

```
    Printer
    (Object)
       |
   Instances
       |
   Daisy Wheel  ─────►  GENERIC RULE  ◄─────  Preferences
    (OBJECT)            IF .... = ....          (Object)
    (Laser Printer)     THEN .... = ....
       etc.                  |
                      (Fills in Recommendation)
                             ▼
                       Recommendation
                          (Object)
```

both rules and procedures as messages, you get the most flexible environment possible for systems development. In subsequent chapters, we consider where each of the different knowledge representation and inference and control techniques can be most effectively used.

SYMBOLIC LANGUAGE TECHNIQUES

We need to consider one more set of techniques to make our discussion of AI and expert systems techniques complete—those techniques found in the symbolic languages like LISP and PROLOG. We consider only LISP in this chapter, and do so only briefly at that.

LISP has played a long and important role in the development of AI, and all of the initial expert systems were written in LISP. LISP stands for LISt Processing. The language was created to facilitate the use of logic and symbols. Since both logical operators and symbols are more generic, abstract concepts than numbers or numerical operators, LISP is a more abstract and more flexible language than most of the conventional programming languages. Although LISP has some 200 fundamental operators, it is easy to define additional operators whenever they are needed. This makes LISP an ideal language in which to write other languages. Thus, most modern LISP environments include object-oriented programming environments within the LISP language.

LISP makes no distinction between data and programs, so LISP programs can use other LISP programs as data. LISP is also highly interactive; in essence, any LISP statement always seeks to evaluate itself and return an answer to the user.

LISP relies heavily on *recursion* (while conventional languages tend to rely on iteration). Recursion is a powerful way of handling search problems. (The example of backward chaining described earlier could just as well be used as an example of recursion. In essence, the system has a procedure to find a goal. It begins, and when it discovers that to find a value for c it must first find a value for a, it simply starts over again, using the same procedure but seeking a value for a instead, and so on.) Using recursion, LISP keeps breaking problems into smaller programs and keeps recalling the same procedure to attempt to find a solution for the simplified arguments.

Perhaps the most valuable feature of LISP is its ability to delay typing values. You can see this delay, which is also called *late binding* or *dynamic data typing*, when the inference engine begins looking for the value for c and then repeats the process looking for a value for a. Assume the type of the value for c was a number and the type of the value for a was a literal, like "red." If the system determined in advance that the type of value it was looking for had to be a number, it could not substitute a and proceed to look for a literal value. In effect, the inference engine keeps substituting new types of values during its search. Late binding (i.e., binding a type to a value late in the process) also allows the developer to write rules that have multiple variables. In effect, LISP will look through many different tables for any set of values that matches the abstract pattern of the rule. This same approach also allows developers to write programs that can modify lines of its own code while the program runs.

Still another feature of LISP is its ability to dynamically handle the allocation of memory when the program runs. (This is often called "garbage collection.") Dynamic memory allocation, coupled with dynamic data typing, means that programmers can quickly develop large programs without having to worry about details that would threaten to overwhelm them if they were working on an equally large program in a conventional language.

In addition to these core features of the language, LISP has a number of powerful debugging utilities that make programming much easier.

If you know LISP, you will be able to see its traces in most of the expert systems building tools. Most of these tools are written in conventional languages, which means that once you figure out how to do something in LISP, you can recode it in a conventional language. This seems likely to be the primary role of LISP in the future of expert systems. LISP programmers will use LISP and tools written in LISP to create the initial versions of tools or large expert systems. Then they will recode those initial versions into conventional languages.

Most developers of expert systems will use the recoded tools and never need to learn LISP. We will not consider it further in this book. If you really want to understand techniques like dynamic data typing and recursion, however, you should consider learning LISP.

Section Two

IDENTIFYING OPPORTUNITIES

In the first section of this book, we discussed the basic concept and vocabulary that people use when they talk about commercial artificial intelligence and expert systems. In this section, we consider how you go about identifying potential expert systems applications.

Although people approach the selection of potential expert systems applications in many different ways, we present a single systematic approach here. You can use this approach as a model, and then adopt it as you need for your particular circumstances.

Ideally, the selection of an application should take about five steps, as described below, but you can vary the emphasis as you wish.

1. *Choose an Overall Corporate Strategy.* You should begin by identifying the overall type of application you want to develop. Some people, for example, are interested only in small PC-based applications, while others want to consider only mid-size applications that can be developed and delivered on a mainframe. Some companies have developed corporate strategies that dictate what sort of application the company wants to invest its effort in, while other companies do not have an overall strategy and leave the decision up to the individual developer.
2. *Develop a List of Potential Applications.* Once you know what general class of application you are interested in, you should develop a list of potential applications. Some people do this in a more or less informal way, while others systematically analyze departmental workflows to pick potential applications. We discuss both the informal and the systematic approaches to developing a list of potential applications.

3. *Check Key Expert Systems Criteria.* Once you have a list, you should check each potential application for signs that it can be successfully developed to solve the problem. The first step is to apply a number of key criteria that can eliminate potential applications that will prove difficult or impossible to develop for your needs.
4. *Identify the Basic Cognitive Structure of the Problem.* Next, you should consider the basic nature of the task involved in each potential application. Some problems are much easier to solve than others, and you should develop a good idea of the potential difficulty and the software development implications of each of the basic problems that can be solved by expert systems techniques.
5. *Consider User, Cost, and Management Issues.* Finally, you should consider the user, cost, and management issues associated with expert systems development.

In some cases, the criteria we consider here should allow you to eliminate potential applications. In all cases, it should help you develop a better understanding of each specific application you are examining so that you can choose a problem that can most likely be solved. When you have selected an application to develop, you should prepare a proposal for the development of your expert system.

3.
Identifying and Scoping Potential Applications—Part 1

OVERVIEW

In the introduction to this section, we said that we would present a systematic approach to identifying and selecting appropriate applications for expert systems. We suggested that an ideal way to handle the selection problem involved a five-step process.

1. Choosing an Overall Corporate Strategy
2. Developing a List of Potential Applications
3. Checking Key Expert Systems Criteria
4. Identifying the Basic Cognitive Structure of the Problem
5. Considering User, Cost, and Management Issues

The first three steps will be discussed in this chapter, the final two in Chapter 4.

STEP 1. CHOOSING AN OVERALL CORPORATE STRATEGY

Several of the early expert systems were developed by individuals to see if the technology could help them solve a specific problem. In such a situation, strategy was irrelevant, since the individual developer simply selected the hardware and software that was available. Increasingly, however, companies are being more systematic about their use of expert systems technology. Departments or groups within companies are being assigned responsibility for directing the corporate expert systems effort. Once such a group is established, a more systematic effort to identify appropriate problems, select software, and budget for development projects usually evolves. One of the key steps any expert systems group usually takes is to determine an overall strategy to guide its efforts.

A survey of many companies actively involved in developing expert systems suggests that there are five common corporate strategies. Each strategy focuses on developing expert systems to serve a specific function and typically emphasizes a particular hardware platform as well. The five most common strategies are as follows:

1. Use small expert systems designed to function as intelligent job aids and to be fielded on PCs or Macintoshes (Macs).
2. Use mid-size expert systems designed to serve as advisors and to be fielded on PCs or workstations.
3. Use mid-size expert systems designed to serve as advisors and to be fielded on mainframes.
4. Use large strategic systems generally developed in LISP and fielded on either LISP machines or on workstations running in LISP.
5. Use embedded expert systems to enhance the development or maintenance of mainframe applications.

We will briefly consider some of the advantages and disadvantages of each of these approaches (see Table 3.1 for a summary of these five strategies).

Table 3.1 Corporate strategies for expert systems development.

	Intelligent Job Aids	Mid-Size Workstation Advisors	Mid-Size Mainframe Advisors	Large LISP Systems	Embedded Systems
Benefits	Leverage valuable technical & managerial personnel. Cost savings. Nonprogrammer programming.	Medium returns. Leverage existing databases and applications. Create valuable new applications.	High returns by leveraging existing applications. Income productivity. Reduce maintenance costs.	High returns. Competitive advantage. New sources of income.	Medium to high returns. Leverage existing applications. Improve existing hardware and software.
Costs	Low costs. Primarily training and support.	Medium costs. Software and training. Some new hardware.	Medium costs. New software and training.	High costs. New hardware, expensive software. LISP programmers.	Medium costs. New software and training.
Hardware/ Personnel	PCs. Managers and technical personnel. Nonprogrammers.	PCs, workstations and VAX's. Application programmers.	Mainframes. Mainframe application programmers.	LISP configured computers and knowledge engineers.	Mainframes, workstations. Special hardware. Regular application programmers.
Risks	Low. Users know their problems. Some risk of poor tool choices.	Medium to low. Some problems with choosing and scoping applications.	Low. Problems known and most applications save money.	High. Hard to choose applications. Steep learning curve. May involve corporate reorganization.	Low. Problems known and most applications improve performance and save money.
Technology/ Results	Technology becoming available. Results in 6 months.	Technology available. Results in 6-18 months.	Technology becoming available. Results in 6-12 months.	Maybe. Depends on application. Results in 1-5 years.	Technology becoming available. Results available in 6 months.
Good example of company using this strategy	Du Pont Eastman Kodak	Texas Instruments Pacific Bell	Boole & Babbage	DEC Schlumberger	–
Good example of tools for this approach	VP-Expert KnowledgePro 1st-Class	Personal Consultant Level5 Nexpert Object	AION KBMS ESE	KEE GoldWorks ART	–
Good example of system being sold for this purpose	Oracle Credit Advisor	Client Profiling ASEA Maintenance Adv.	DASD Advisor DEFT	Lending Advisor Service Bay Diagnostic FRESH	–

Intelligent Job Aids (PCs or Macs)

The strategy. An *intelligent job aid* is a small expert system that an individual can use during the actual performance of some task.

We've all used the more common job aids: An address book or telephone book helps us find a phone number when we need it. A step-by-step checklist helps us assemble a new toy or install a new card in our computer. A manual ensures that we follow company procedures in hiring a new employee. Documentation or a call to a hotline service gets us diagnostic help when we can't get new hardware or software to function correctly.

Some expert systems are good at analyzing problems and offering advice; they can serve as a new type of job aid that is computer-based and more flexible than the paper-based job aids that are in common use.

Although intelligent job aids are beginning to appear on multi-user mainframe systems, most job aids are small expert systems that are fielded on PCs or Macs. If your company places its emphasis on developing intelligent job aids for PCs or Macs, then you are, in effect, committed to a small systems approach. This approach can be very cost-effective, but it depends on having end users, managers, and valuable technical people develop their own systems. This, in turn, suggests that your effort will depend on easy-to-use PC-based expert systems building tools and a small support group. That support group can offer training and some assistance with the more complex problems involved in developing interfaces, accessing data, or perhaps developing a small procedural program that the system can call to handle some number-crunching portion of the task.

Who's using a small systems strategy? All kinds of companies, both large and small, have adopted the small systems approach. Within companies, training departments and equipment maintenance groups are especially prone to embrace this approach. Since this approach emphasizes off-the-shelf tools, end user development (i.e., nonprogrammer development), and PCs and Macintoshes for development and delivery, it is especially popular among individuals who are undertaking their own expert systems development efforts.

Du Pont is probably the best known large company that is publicly pursuing this strategy. Their MIS group encourages managers to develop their own systems using any small tool the manager chooses. (Du Pont has negotiated site-license agreements with vendors to keep costs down.) The MIS group provides training courses and supports user groups to encourage people to share their experiences throughout the company.

Du Pont claims to have fielded about 100 systems, with another 200 in progress. The company has found that these small applications cost about $30,000 to $50,000 apiece to develop and claims to be getting around $250,000 back in increased productivity from each one.

Using existing hardware and small tools, Du Pont's individual managers have been able to identify many small problems that can be solved with expert systems. Ed Mahler, the head of Du Pont's expert systems efforts, refers to this strategy as "rabbit hunting." He says the idea is to send everyone out with small arms to shoot rabbits (i.e., to ask end users to identify their own problems and then try to build a little expert system to solve each one). Every so often, he says, someone ends up shooting an elephant in the knee; they try to tackle a problem that is too big for the resources of the small tools they are using. The hunter calls in the experts to decide if it's worth hiring outsiders to try to skin the elephant. The answer may be no, but at least a big problem has been identified that may be worth tackling at a later date with more resources and more highly trained knowledge engineers.

If you are going to succeed with expert systems, you must be able to accurately evaluate potential applications as to suitability to expert systems technology, development time and cost, and system size. To use the "rabbit hunting" strategy, you must have a clear idea of what is meant by small systems and tools.

Costs and risks. The costs and risks of developing intelligent job aids are very low. The developer is typically the end user, who is familiar with the problem. Moreover, the same individual usually maintains the system. The software typically costs from $200 to $1,000 and the hardware is usually a PC that was already in use. Even if you buy the hardware and software and figure the developer's cost as two months, you have an expense of only some $30,000. That's a very small amount of money to spend for the development and fielding of a useful application. It's less than most companies spend on the development and printing of a procedures manual or documentation, and it's much easier and less expensive to revise and update.

One of the major problems people encounter when they begin to develop expert systems is picking a good task for development. By allowing end users to select tasks, you normally assure that good, small tasks will be selected. In the worst case, if a manager or engineer bites off more than he can handle, the company is probably out only a week or two of salary and the costs of the software; hence, the risks are very low.

Benefits. In addition to replacing many paper job aids, memos, and phone calls with small expert systems, the small systems approach assures that a large number of managerial and technical people within your company will benefit. They will learn about expert systems techniques and how they can use the technology to create and modify small computer applications on their own. In effect, you can combine corporate-wide training in the use of expert systems technology with the development of many intelligent job aids.

Du Pont claims that it is making about $250,000 per system, mostly through saving time and eliminating scrap and other by-products of incorrect decisions. Other studies have indicated that intelligent job aids typically improve the speed of performance by an order of magnitude (10x). That means that fewer people can do the same amount of work, or that one individual can produce much more.

Mid-Size Advisors for PCs or Workstations

The strategy. A second strategy for using expert systems focuses on developing mid-size PC and workstation applications whose primary function is to advise the people actually making the decisions. It's easy to think of advisory systems as just more sophisticated job aids. If there is any difference, it's that the mid-size systems tend to be larger and to perform a significant part of someone's job; they provide advice and alternatives rather than simply suggest how to act.

The mid-size workstation-based advisory systems run on hardware like Sun, Apollo, VAX, HP, or on Mac II workstations or 386-based PCs. The people who use these systems usually already have some experience with both conventional programming and expert systems.

Who's using it? Most companies have decided to begin exploring expert systems with these mid-size advisors. This approach emphasizes using existing programming personnel and mid-size tools to try to tackle some challenging applications. In most cases, MIS groups within the various operating divisions of the companies have set up an expert systems task force to organize the initial effort.

The most active companies pursuing this strategy have been manufacturing companies that are willing to develop and field systems on standalone 386 machines, workstations, or VAXes. They have commonly tackled equipment diagnosis problems first and then moved on to process problems and sales support applications.

General Motors, Ford, Pacific Bell, and Texas Instruments are good examples of companies that have major mid-size expert systems development efforts underway.

Costs and risks. The costs of mid-size system development are modest, but not to be undertaken lightly. Most mid-size systems are developed by individuals who have some programming experience; these individuals are often micro support programmers or applications programmers from MIS groups located within company operating divisions. Thus, personnel costs rise as professional programmers must schedule time to work with domain experts to acquire the knowledge that goes into the systems. In addition, these systems often require special hardware and necessitate handcrafted connections with other company hardware and software. The tools available for the development of mid-size workstation-based systems tend to cost from $2,500 to $10,000. Thus, a small mid-size project that required six months of a programmer's time, and two to three months of a domain expert's time, a $5,000 software package, and a $20,000 computer, could easily end up costing your company $100,000 (without any overhead costs). That's not much money to spend to develop a useful software application, but given opportunity costs, it's not a project to be undertaken without some initial planning and budgeting effort.

As for the risks, the people involved are probably well situated to select a reasonable project, but they can also probably use help to assure that they pick good projects early on, when they are first learning about the technology. Moreover, the tools are just complex enough that the developers will need some training and a learning period to determine how to use them most effectively. In other words, the development of mid-size systems involve moderate risks and require the sort of planning your company would normally put into a project costing from $100,000 to $500,000.

Benefits. The major benefits of mid-size workstation-based systems are similar to the benefits of small systems. In most cases, applications programmers can develop these systems much faster than they could if they tried to use a conventional programming language. Hence, they don't cost much to develop, and they usually result in large savings in labor and material while significantly reducing the time required to accomplish the task.

Mid-Sized Advisors for Mainframes

The strategy. The overall strategy behind the mid-size advisors for mainframes is the same as the strategy driving the mid-size workstation advisors, except that the developers want to field the applications on a mainframe so they can be accessed via dumb terminals and used by several users at once. In addition to the desire to offer access to expert systems via existing mainframe-hosted systems, the developers are often concerned about the security of knowledge bases that contain valuable corporate secrets. They feel they can better guarantee that security within a mainframe operating environment than they can on decentralized workstations.

There are, in fact, two ways to look at expert systems on mainframes. One views mainframes as a way of delivering a system to many users via terminals or downloading to PCs. This perspective is compatible with the mid-size workstation-based advisory approach because the mainframe is essentially used only as a delivery vehicle.

A second perspective focuses on ways to speed the development and maintenance of large, conventional mainframe applications and to make existing mainframe applications more flexible. The objective is to embed expert systems into large-scale production programs or to build expert front ends to make complicated mainframe programs more efficient and easier to set up and use. We consider this second approach when we discuss the fifth strategy, embedded expert systems.

Who's using it? This mid-size mainframe-based approach is primarily being used by corporate and departmental MIS groups. Their reason for using this strategy is quite similar to the reasoning of those developing systems for workstations, except that they want to be able to field the resulting applications on mainframes. In some cases, they want the systems to be available to multiple users via dumb terminals, but they are also interested in developing applications that can augment existing applications by serving as front or back ends. They also want to develop applications that can be used in transaction processing environments. This is a very active part of the current expert systems market, with new tools and new applications being announced every day. IBM has developed about 100 internal applications to study the problems of mainframe development and delivery and to provide demonstrations of its effectiveness. Most of the mainframe software houses have expert systems applications underway, and a significant number of Fortune 500 MIS shops are studying how they can use expert systems technology to improve the production and maintenance of key corporate applications.

Costs and risks. The costs and risks of mid-size expert systems development for the mainframe environment primarily involve opportunity costs. Most mainframe programming shops have plenty to keep them busy. For such a group to try something new and different, with the accompanying risk of failure, results in a natural conservatism. In most cases, companies have decided to try a mainframe approach either because someone within the company learned about expert systems and waged a heroic struggle to get the other members of the organization to give it a try, or because the group learned that some other company had achieved significant results by using the technology and feared falling behind the competition. IBM's active interest in the market and its promotion of its own successes with expert systems has done a great deal to open up this market niche.

The actual costs and risks of a well-chosen mainframe project are usually well below what a conventional approach to the same project would cost. Moreover, the early projects suggest that the payback can be quite remarkable.

Benefits. The main benefit of fielding an expert system on a mainframe is that the mainframe is already in place and can be accessed by users throughout the company. Companies that have emphasized actual expert systems development on the mainframe have tended to select applications that involve significant judgmental components. Thus, they are using the technology to develop applications that would be difficult to develop by conventional means.

Large Strategic Systems (Workstations or LISP Machines)

The strategy. For companies with sufficient R & D resources, a strategy aimed at large LISP-based systems is an option. LISP machines afford the greatest heuristic processing power AI technology currently has to offer. At the Department of Defense (DOD) and at universities, AI scientists use LISP machines to tackle the larger and more challenging tasks of simulating human decision making with computers. The large medical diagnosis system, MYCIN, is an example of the kind of LISP-based system that approaches doing the entire job of an expert.

Such ambitious applications have the potential to change the basic strategy or very nature of a company. Potential savings are enormous, but the corresponding risks are also great. LISP machines are very expensive and the development time of such systems can run for a couple of years. If an inappropriate problem domain is chosen, a company can end up investing a lot of money for a nonviable solution.

Who's using it? The R & D departments of Fortune 500 companies and aerospace companies that are contracting with NASA and DOD are generally the ones using large strategic systems. A few companies that have experimented with these systems have also decided that they could make significant profits by developing large applications that change the way they do business.

Costs and risks. Both the costs and the risks are high if you adopt this approach. It involves acquiring new hardware and software and hiring programmers with new skills. Moreover, if you adopt this approach in an attempt to develop a major strategic system, you will spend a considerable amount of time and money trying to achieve that goal. Some companies have been very successful at it, and the results they have obtained suggest that it's a viable strategy. Other companies have invested a lot in this approach, however, and have very little to show for it, so a significant initial analysis and design effort is warranted.

Benefits. The application of expert systems techniques can allow companies to create large, complex applications that can change the cost structure of their business or allow them to enter new businesses altogether. The payback for a success in this area can be quite remarkable.

AI as a Prototype/Maintenance Aid

The strategy. As we mentioned earlier, some companies have decided that expert systems techniques are more appropriate as aids in the development of prototype applications or to facilitate improving or maintaining existing applications than for developing standalone expert systems. Some of the mainframe and CASE tool vendors have been especially active in advocating this approach.

In many cases, the difference between a standalone expert system and an expert system designed to serve as a front end or to mediate between the user and an existing application may seem subtle. In other cases, however, when the developer embeds an inference engine within an existing COBOL application and uses the inference engine only to process a few rules that reflect changing conditions, the "expert system" is clearly functioning more like a utility than an application.

A small system, for instance, might be embedded in a COBOL transaction processing program that handles a bank's nightly account reconciliations. An inference engine and knowledge base may come into play only when the account reconciliation application encounters exceptions (e.g., checking accounts that don't balance). Currently, most systems kick these accounts out on an exceptions list that is, in turn, submitted to human bank officers to process. In the future, a branch manager might simply maintain a database of customers who are acceptable risks for overdrafts of certain amounts. When the batch application encounters such an exception, it would call on the expert system to check this list, decide whether or not to pay the check, and automatically initiate an overdraft notice.

Any embedded utility that can keep large routine production programs running at top speed while adding a new dimension of judgment could have big payoffs for MIS/data processing tasks. But you can expect hesitancy and resistance to experimenting with large production programs because of the heavy responsibilities on these departments. For instance, a large investment goes into keeping payroll systems running accurately and timely, and no one in a corporate MIS organization wants to be the person to tell senior executives that the payroll isn't ready because of an error by some fancy new expert systems utility.

More readily acceptable mainframe applications are front ends that make expensive programs more accessible and/or efficient. An example is an expert system that IBM developed for the oil industry. IBM had already installed a Fortran analysis package on a mainframe for a major oil company to help engineers with explorations. The problem was that the engineers couldn't easily set up the Fortran program to do what they wanted, so they simply weren't using it. IBM wrote a front end expert system that asks about 20 questions and then automatically sets the parameters for the Fortran run. According to the developer, the expert system takes up about 15 percent of the CPU cycles while the grinding away of the Fortran cycle uses the rest. The value of the expert system is that the Fortran package wasn't being used at all before.

In addition to embedding expert systems technology within existing applications, some vendors are using expert systems techniques to develop tools that users can employ without being aware that they are using AI. Thus, several CASE vendors are using expert systems techniques to develop tools that help COBOL programmers generate or modify COBOL applications.

Who's using it? At the moment, the companies who see the advantages of using expert systems techniques to improve MIS productivity are either computer companies or software developers. Most MIS organizations will consider this new approach only after these companies have demonstrated that the new techniques can result in superior products at reduced costs.

Costs and risks. The costs and risks of using expert systems techniques to develop and maintain mainframe applications are just beginning to be explored. The cost of the tools is modest, by mainframe standards, and the hardware and programmers are already in place. The real costs, however, are opportunity costs. Every large MIS shop is already very busy. Moreover, MIS shops are conservative and cautious about trying new technologies on their machines until they are sure that the benefit will outweigh any risk. The use of expert systems techniques is currently being evaluated against fourth-generation language tools (4GLs) and CASE tools as companies look for ways to improve MIS productivity. To minimize the risks, most companies are currently experimenting with expert systems tools that run on PCs and that can be ported to the mainframe only when they have proved valuable.

Benefits. Many organizations are becoming increasingly concerned about the problems of developing and maintaining large computer applications. The backlog of desired applications and the problems of keeping existing applications up to date are common problems at most MIS shops. These organizations have already tried fourth-generation languages and they are increasingly turning to CASE tools for help. While some people are incorporating expert systems techniques into 4GLs and CASE tools to make those products more flexible and effective, other expert systems vendors advocate that well-designed expert systems building tools that are modular and embeddable will be more useful to MIS people than either the 4GLs or the CASE tools. The correct approach will emerge only over time and will probably involve some mix of methods. Clearly, however, any technology that can accelerate the development of new applications or ease the burdens of updating and maintaining large existing applications will have great value.

Summary

We have tried to suggest some of the advantages and disadvantages of each of the major strategies that companies are pursuing as they incorporate expert systems techniques into their computing environments. Obviously, we have drawn the lines more sharply than they are in reality. Most companies are mixing various strategies and many companies do not draw any sharp distinction between the small and mid-size PC-based systems.

There is no one correct strategy—each has its place, depending upon the broader goals of your company and the position of the group that is advocating expert systems development in your organization. What's important is that your company have a clear idea about which strategy or strategies it wants to pursue.

STEP 2. DEVELOPING A LIST OF POTENTIAL APPLICATIONS

Once you have decided what general sort of application you are interested in attempting, you should next generate a list of possible applications, examine the list, and apply the criteria that we discuss in this chapter. As a result of your examination, you should be able to focus on one application to try first.

To date, most expert systems development efforts have come about from an initial list of potential applications. Once you have created such a list (usually from people just volunteering that various problems might be solved by an expert system), you need to think about how to narrow the list. As you investigate each of the likely possibilities and finally settle on one to try, you are, in effect, attempting to *scope* each potential application.

In order to scope an application, you need to develop an overall description of what's involved in each potential application and then match that against the resources your organization has available, your chances of success, and so on. As you find out more about each potential application, you will discard some as being too large or difficult or risky. You may eliminate others because they are too small and won't make the impact necessary to establish expert systems within your organization.

As you remove some applications from your list, you will be able to spend more time learning about those that remain. In the end, you should be able to narrow down your list to the application that is best suited to an expert system.

In the material that follows, we offer some heuristics and models that you can use to help you scope applications.

Approaches to Developing a List of Potential Applications

There are basically two ways to begin developing a list of potential applications. The top-down approach emphasizes taking a broad overview of your company's needs and activities. It usually involves a search for strategic systems that will significantly improve the way your company operates.

At the opposite extreme is the bottom-up approach. Companies following this approach usually provide their employees with general information about the uses and benefits of expert systems, offer training in the use of specific tools, and encourage employees to try to develop their own applications.

The top-down approach usually involves some sort of formal workflow analysis. The idea is to describe how different jobs and tasks interact and then identify which jobs or tasks wait until they obtain knowledge from others. One analyst suggested that you should just look at the office floor after the people had left for the day and check to see which desk had the most footprints leading back and forth from it. Presumably, the person sitting at that desk knew or had something that many other people needed in order to do their work. If some or all of that key person's knowledge could be captured and distributed, then the organization would presumably be more productive.

In classic schedule management systems (e.g., PERT systems), bottlenecks can occur because inventory becomes scarce, too few people are available to do the job, and so on. At that point, you can use expert systems to analyze problems and make recommendations. Thus, when you look for potential expert systems applications, you are primarily concerned with knowledge or decision bottlenecks. You are looking for situations in which action is delayed or errors occur because people lack sufficient knowledge or because the person qualified to do the analysis, create the proper design, or make the appropriate recommendation was unavailable.

You should be especially watchful for knowledge bottlenecks, situations in which many tasks or information flows converge on one person or at one time. Following are some characteristics of knowledge bottlenecks to help you recognize them.

- People wait for someone else to make a decision.
- People have to stop what they are doing to look up or search for information needed to make a decision. (If several people have to share the same reference resources, that is a particularly noteworthy.)
- Items pile up because decisions "can't be made" regarding them (e.g., the decision is complex and it takes several different people to consider it to be sure all of the angles are covered).

Another way of describing what you are looking for when you seek tasks that would be appropriate for an expert system is to list some of the typical functions of different expert systems. To make this a little easier to apply, consider next some typical applications relative to the size or class of expert system.

Typical small expert systems designed to function as intelligent job aids and to be fielded on PCs or Macs. Most small expert systems are designed to assist with small procedural or diagnostic tasks. They typically help someone who needs information or help in analyzing a situation and making a decision. In most cases, these systems do not replace an "expert" but replace, instead, a senior technician, engineer, or experienced senior clerk. They provide information or help that the performer would otherwise need to ask the other person to provide. Some systems ensure that the performer would do as well as the more experienced person would, if that experienced person were available to analyze the problem and make the required decision. For example, consider the Oracle Credit Advisor. Oracle Electronics & Trading Company wholesales surplus electronics parts and supplies. The company claims an advantage over its competitors by shipping orders the same day they are received. This practice requires order processing and customer credit verification to be done within a few hours after an order is placed. Prior to the development of the expert system, the credit evaluation process had been automated for routine transactions, but cases where the customer's credit was questionable were handled manually. Oracle is small enough that the CEO is familiar with all the customers and their credit histories. In fact, the CEO himself was personally deciding potentially high-risk transactions, which occur on average about six times a day at Oracle. Of course, a CEO's time represents an obvious opportunity cost for any company. Oracle decided that shifting this responsibility to others would clearly be an advantage.

Some of the information on nonroutine orders was available in Customer, Accounts Receivable, and Invoice Line Item dBASE III files. In deciding to grant or deny credit, the CEO used this information in addition to his own knowledge of special factors such as the customer's history with the company. The CEO was the only person at Oracle with the knowledge and experience to make the high-risk credit decisions. If this knowledge could be captured and distributed to less experienced people, the CEO would be free to concentrate on more strategic problems.

In order to expand the automation of order processing to include most of the nonroutine cases, Oracle contracted with Paperback Software to build an expert system to capture the CEO's knowledge and transfer it to the accounting department. The tool chosen for the job was Paperback Software's VP-Expert, a small rule-based expert systems shell. A knowledge engineer from Paperback Software designed a system that accesses the data available from the Customer and Accounting databases and then applies the heuristic rules of the CEO to come up with a recommendation to grant or deny credit for a given order.

With the old method, the CEO would solve about 90 percent of the problem orders, thus avoiding losses from unpaid bills or missed sales opportunities. Achieving 80 percent of this performance level with an expert system should be more than adequate to justify transferring the credit evaluation function from the CEO to the accountant.

In most cases, small systems do not replace a human; instead, they handle 75 to 80 percent of the problems and refer the performer to the human expert whenever really complex, tricky, or infrequently performed tasks are encountered. Small expert systems have been commonly employed to assist performers in the following situations:

- To provide information for special cases when the performer would otherwise have to consult a senior technician, clerk, or procedures manual.
- To assist people who answer hotline calls.
- To help people use hardware or software. In some cases, the expert system is a standalone system, but sometimes it is embedded in the software as intelligent help.
- To provide a readily available source of product or service information.
- To provide guidance in the repair or maintenance of equipment.
- To assist people in completing forms (e.g., income tax forms) or applications or providing data entry.

Most small expert systems have been developed by the person who has the expertise in question. And, in most cases, that person is not a programmer.

Typical mid-size expert systems designed to serve as advisors and to be fielded on PCs or workstations. Most mid-size systems for PCs, workstations, and minis (e.g., VAXes) have been developed to assist users with diagnostic tasks, but some have been developed to assist with monitoring, configuration, or scheduling tasks. As a generalization, mid-size systems are more likely than not to be integrated into the overall computer operations of the organization, but many of them do stand alone. Small systems are commonly used as intelligent job aids to facilitate office automation, while mid-size systems are more likely to be used to facilitate factory or departmental operations.

Mid-size systems are often developed by a knowledge engineer or programmer working with one or more experts. In the cases where the expert is able to write his own system, a programmer usually still needs to be called in to help integrate it into the existing computer operations of the company. The programmer often has to write links so that the expert system can obtain information from existing databases, or work in conjunction with other existing software.

Typical mid-size workstation-based systems are used to replace or partially replace experts or senior technicians. They assist other technicians or managers in the performance of complex analysis work, they make it easy to obtain information or reports, and they provide what-if assistance when the performer wants to explore alternatives in a complex situation.

Typical mid-size expert systems designed to serve as advisors and to be fielded on mainframes. Expert systems are just beginning to be built for and fielded on mainframes. The main interest in mainframe systems is driven by the desire to field expert systems via existing mainframe terminals. The companies that have been most active to date are financial companies that depend on mainframes and want to use expert systems to improve the effectiveness and efficiency of their operational personnel.

In the long run, mainframe-based expert systems will deliver a very broad range of applications, including all of the types of applications we have described under both the small and the mid-size workstation-based systems. Intelligent job aids, hotline systems, advisory systems, and factory automation applications can all be delivered on a mainframe.

While most mainframe applications are diagnostic in nature, small to mid-size monitoring systems are also very popular. These systems usually co-exist in memory while the existing program is running, watch what is happening, and "wake up" and offer advice when they detect certain circumstances. Large configuration and scheduling systems are also being developed for mainframes. Some technical experts are using the friendlier tools to develop their own expert systems, but the majority of the mainframe systems need to be carefully integrated with existing software, and this requires the help of a programmer.

Typical large strategic systems generally developed in LISP and fielded on either LISP machines or on workstations running in LISP. The largest and most sophisticated expert systems have been developed on LISP machines or on workstations running in LISP. In general, these applications require a knowledge engineer who is proficient with LISP. They tend to be systems designed either to capture significant amounts of human expertise and make it widely available throughout the company, or to help supervisors and managers with large, complex planning and scheduling problems. In either case, they are usually large projects and the company needs to carefully analyze them and justify their cost to assure that they will be worth the effort.

Most of these applications have captured the knowledge of people who have significant technical expertise and who must analyze problems or grant approval before work can proceed. Most of the large systems have been advisory in nature (e.g., a loan approval system that helps a loan officer process loans by providing the approval that would otherwise have to come from a loan committee), but some have even surpassed the capabilities of a human expert and are performing better than a human expert could (e.g., DEC's XCON system, which configures all VAX computers).

Typical embedded expert systems used to enhance the development or maintenance of mainframe applications. Some expert systems tools are being used to improve the efficiency or effectiveness with which new programs are developed. In these systems, the technology serves as a kind of intelligent CASE system rather than an application.

In such cases, a systems analyst or a programmer uses an expert systems building tool to facilitate the development of a new application or to enhance existing ones. For example, if a programmer is faced with a task that requires judgment and the experts seem to disagree or be vague about how to make the judgment, the analyst may develop a small rule-based system just to help the experts focus on the exact knowledge needed for the final system. The expert system that results from this effort may be used further or it may be discarded after the required information has been identified and debugged.

In addition, some developers are creating special applications for the mainframe to enhance existing mainframe applications. Some expert systems make it easier for users to request information or to read reports created by existing applications. Expert systems are also being embedded within existing applications to help handle "exceptions" and other judgmental problems that are difficult for existing applications. Further, developers are rewriting some existing applications as expert systems to make their maintenance and future modification easier.

In Chapter 5, we discuss specific methods for analyzing tasks in more detail. At this point, we are giving you only an overview of potential applications. In most cases, to identify a useful application, you should look for people who provide information, analyze, and make judgments. You want to improve the analysis and the judgments they make by providing them with an expert system that can assist them.

Defining the Task in a General Way

Once you think you have a potential expert systems application, describe the current situation and the situation that would result if you developed an expert system. Do this in a rough way, by identifying the current method of solving the problem and treating that as a box or node. Then list the inputs and the outputs of the box. Do this for both the current situation and the situation that would exist if you developed an expert system.

For example, consider the Oracle Credit Advisor system that we introduced earlier. Figure 3.1 provides a picture of the situation before and after the expert system was developed. In the original situation, a customer order generated a credit check. If the credit check suggested problems, the customer order was routed to the CEO for approval or rejection. An expert system was developed that captured the CEO's analysis and judgment process. Now, when a customer order suggests problems, the expert system is used to further evaluate the customer's credit status and determine if credit should be granted or denied.

Though drawing these diagrams may sometimes seem like a trivial exercise, it ensures that you will always be certain of three things:

1. You have an expert (i.e., the person who is currently performing the task).
2. You have a source of input for your system.
3. You have a clear understanding of the advice or recommendations your system will produce.

Figure 3.1 Oracle Credit Advisor overview: Before and after the development of an expert system.

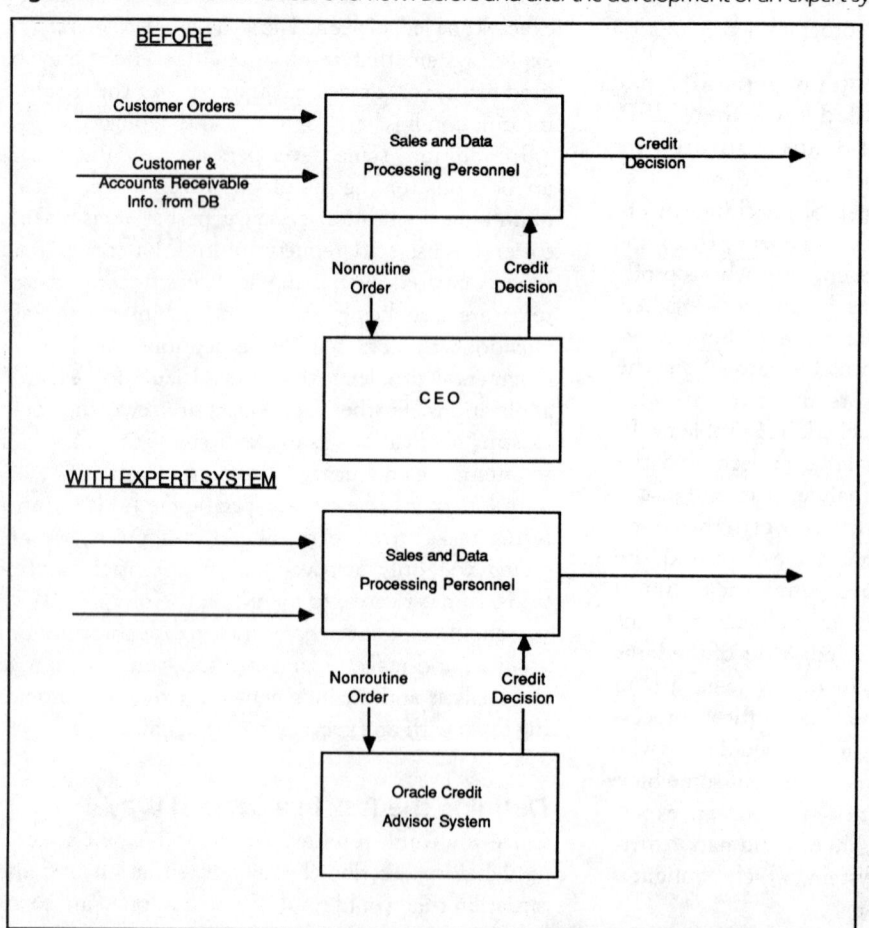

Obviously, whenever you introduce an expert system, you are supplanting the current source of expertise with a computer-based application. Thus, we suggest that you write the type of computer hardware under the box labeled "expert system" to be sure you have a clear idea of what type of hardware will be used to take in information and output recommendations when your expert system is fielded.

Figure 3.2 illustrates a number of different diagrams that you might draw to depict different situations. In general, an expert system can either entirely replace the existing source of expertise, partially replace it, or simply support it. By the same token, expert systems have tended to replace or support humans, computer programs, and documentation or training programs.

Part (a) of Figure 3.2 illustrates a situation in which the expert system completely replaces the human expert. Part (b) illustrates a situation in which the expert system handles part of the tasks that the human expert formerly handled, solves those it can and then passes the hard or unusual cases back to the human expert. Part (c) depicts a situation in which a human expert still interfaces with the users but occasionally uses an expert system to help analyze tricky problems or obscure exceptions. Parts (d), (e), (f), and (g) suggest four ways in which expert systems might be used in conjunction with an existing computer system. In (d), the existing application goes to an expert system for a specific analysis task and in (e), the expert system is embedded within the current application. In (f), the expert system interfaces with the user, asks questions, and then provides the existing application with the input it needs to run. In (g), the expert system takes the output of a conventional application, analyzes it, and makes recommendations to the user. In (h), the expert system replaces the documentation. (It could just as well replace a training program or a paper job aid.)

Using An Application Analysis Worksheet

Figure 3.3 is a worksheet that is designed to let you enter two applications and evaluate them according to the criteria that we are discussing in this chapter.

If you decide to use a worksheet like the one shown, you should use as many as needed to analyze all of the potential applications you are considering. On the other hand, you may want to think of it as a checklist and just check each application against the criteria listed on the worksheet.

The first row of the worksheet asks for a description of the general type of system you are considering. These overall strategies for expert systems development were discussed earlier in this chapter. The next portion of the worksheet asks you to describe the basic input and output of the task as it is currently performed and as it will be performed if you develop and field an expert system. The third portion of the form allows you to check your potential application against certain key criteria that we now consider.

STEP 3. CHECKING KEY EXPERT SYSTEMS CRITERIA

There are a number of criteria for the successful development of an expert system that you ought to check whenever you consider a potential application. They are listed on the Application Analysis Worksheet (Figure 3.3) and described below.

A Human Expert Is Needed

The development of any expert system, from a 50-rule job aid to a 1,000-object system that rivals skilled physicians, depends on the availability of a human who knows how to analyze and solve a problem. Commercial expert systems lack the ability to learn or improve with use, hence, a human who can specify what knowledge the system should have and when that knowledge should be modified or changed is absolutely crucial.

To put it another way, if a corporate executive asks you to develop an expert system to help people deal with a problem that no one can currently solve, you've been given *two* jobs:

1. Figure out how to solve a problem that no one has been able to solve in the past
2. Build an expert system that will embody the knowledge about how to solve that problem

In effect, you would have to first become the human expert who knew how to solve that problem, and then you would have to be the programmer who encoded that knowledge in a knowledge base.

Someone needs to know how to analyze and solve the problem, and that person must be available to provide the knowledge that is encoded in the knowl-

Figure 3.2 A variety of ways in which expert systems have been used.

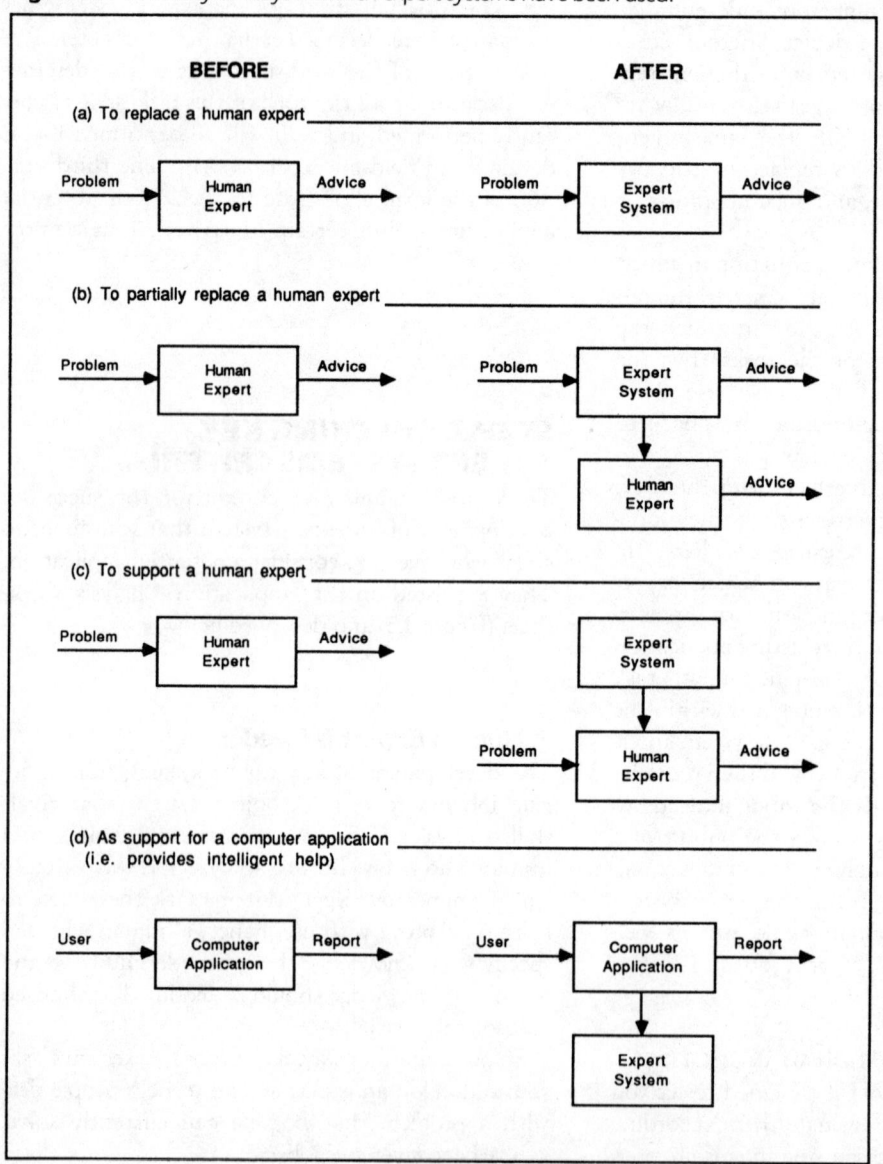

```
                        BEFORE                              AFTER

(a) To replace a human expert

Problem → [Human Expert] → Advice        Problem → [Expert System] → Advice


(b) To partially replace a human expert

Problem → [Human Expert] → Advice        Problem → [Expert System] → Advice
                                                          ↓
                                                   [Human Expert] → Advice


(c) To support a human expert

Problem → [Human Expert] → Advice                  [Expert System]
                                                          ↓
                                         Problem → [Human Expert] → Advice


(d) As support for a computer application
    (i.e. provides intelligent help)

User → [Computer Application] → Report   User → [Computer Application] → Report
                                                          ↓
                                                   [Expert System]
```

edge base of the expert system. In many cases (more that half the time when you consider small to mid-size systems), the expert and the knowledge engineer are the same person. The more complex the problem and voluminous the knowledge, the harder it is to play both roles, but some individuals who have thought a great deal about how they solve problems manage to do so.

Assume, however, that you are a knowledge engineer and that you will be acquiring the knowledge you need to create an expert system from another person. What characteristics should you look for in a human expert?

Within any profession or technical area, some people are commonly known as *theorists*. (What Donald Schon refers to as "reflective practitioners.") Unlike their more pragmatic associates, they enjoy thinking about how they actually analyze and solve the prob-

Figure 3.2 (Continued).

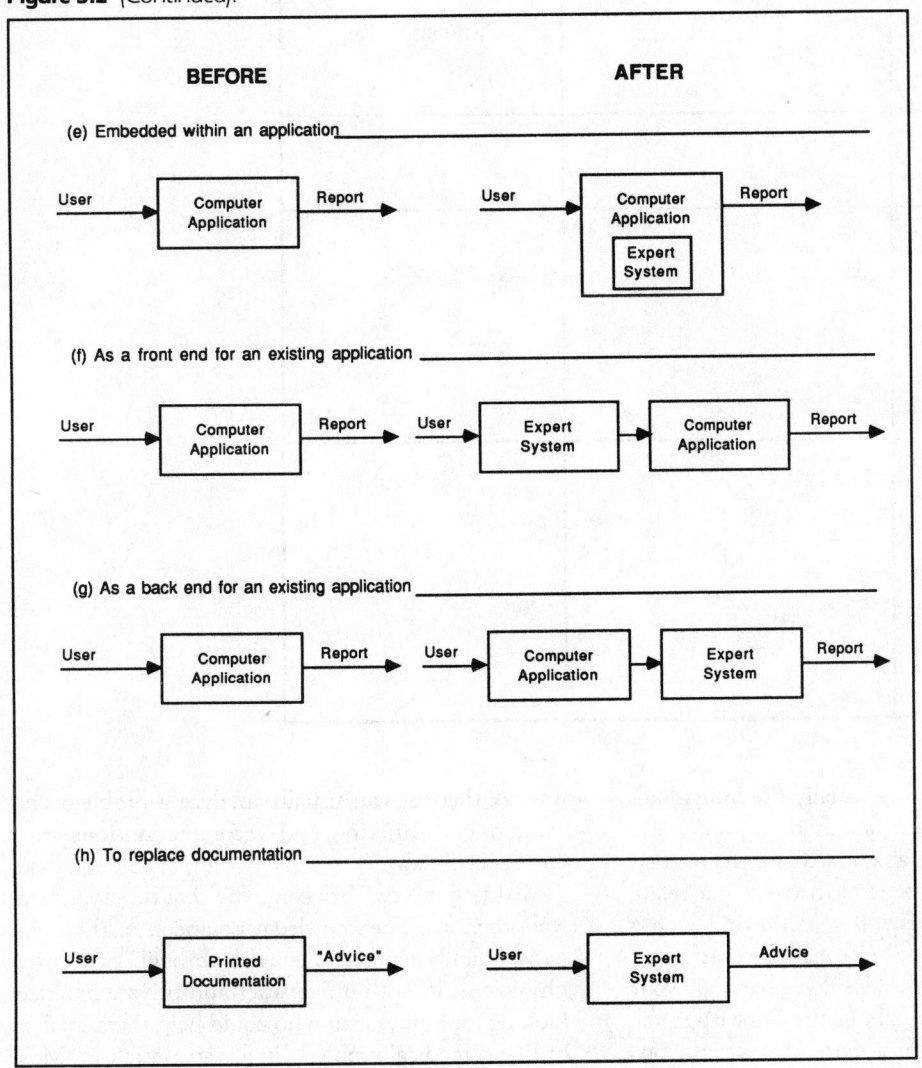

(e) Embedded within an application

(f) As a front end for an existing application

(g) As a back end for an existing application

(h) To replace documentation

Figure 3.3 Application analysis worksheet.

APPLICATION ANALYSIS WORKSHEET		Page 1
Overall Strategy: ☐ Small, PC-based ☐ Mid-Size, PC/Workstation-based ☐ Embedded ☐ Mid-Size, Mainframe-based ☐ Large, LISP-based		
Considerations	Potential Application	Potential Application
Overall description of task the system will perform		
How task is currently accomplished (User → Input → Analysis → Recommendation)		
How task will be accomplished with an expert system		
Key Criteria: ☐ Human Expert Available ☐ Case Data Available ☐ Narrow, Well-Defined Task ☐ Procedural Task ☐ Structured Analysis Task ☐ Verbal Knowledge		
Avoid Tasks Involving: ☐ Common Sense ☐ Reasoning by Analogy ☐ Perceptual Expertise ☐ Very Volatile Expertise ☐ Experts Disagree ☐ Complex Geometric or Spatial Reasoning ☐ Complex Causal or Temporal Relations		

lems they work on. They are usually the individuals who enjoy teaching others about their work, and they are more likely to be able to explain the history, sources of research, and general theories that relate to their specialty. Obviously, if you can find such a theorist, you are likely to have a superior expert.

A theorist will already have done some of your work for you, by thinking about the knowledge she uses for problem solving in a more or less conscious way. A theorist can usually analyze a problem and explain her thinking and recommendations in a fairly specific way.

We know a New York company that develops medical programs. The knowledge engineers at this company literally worked their way through two dozen physicians, in both universities and private practice, looking for a physician who could help them analyze ordinary medical problems in a systematic way. Most

Figure 3.3 (Continued). Page 2

Considerations	Potential Application	Potential Application
Cognitive Structure of Problem: ☐ Procedural ☐ Diagnostic ☐ Monitoring ☐ Configuration (Design) ☐ Planning & Scheduling ☐ Forward Chaining ☐ Backward Chaining		
User Concerns: ☐ Perceived Need ☐ Hardware Available ☐ System Availability ☐ System Speed ☐ Accuracy Acceptable ☐ Explanation Required ☐ Motivation of User ☐ Training of Users		
Management Concerns: ☐ Senior Management Spurns ☐ High/Low Profile ☐ Cultural Impact		
Value of System: ☐ Speeds up Work ☐ Internal Cost Savings ☐ Improves Quality and Consistency of Decison Making ☐ Creates New Products or Services ☐ Captures Company Know-How for: 　☐ Distribution 　☐ Training 　☐ Sales		
Estimated ROI		

physicians ask questions without suggesting what hypotheses or diseases they are considering. The company in question, however, finally found the perfect physician for their purposes. As he conducted a consultation, their "ideal" physician was always verbalizing a decision tree aloud, as if he were talking to himself. He would say: "Well, let's see, if you developed these symptoms during your camping trip, something you encountered on that trip was probably the cause. Let's consider what that could have been. Were you bitten by any insects? Perhaps when you were asleep. Did you wake up with any swollen areas? . . ."

Even if you find a theorist, be aware that she will probably be *case driven*. When you ask her to explain what she does, she will talk in terms of specific cases she has solved in the past. This is natural when you consider that your expert probably has a lot of knowledge and that it is organized in such a way that she can't recall the information in any systematic fashion. Even the theorists who can give you a good overview of the types of problems they deal with, and the kinds of knowledge and reasoning processes they follow, will still lack a good way to enumerate the specific heuristics they use. They will most likely be able to recall specific heuristics only in the context of a specific situation in which they used them.

Here's a good axiom: The best expert is the person the company would least like to give you. Once you've identified the right person, accept no substitutes.

In talking to people about projects that have succeeded, we have typically heard them remark about how important it was that their expert was both knowledgeable and cooperative. In other words, they usually give the expert great credit for making the project a success. By the same token, when we talk to people who have abandoned projects, one of the common reasons they give for their failure is the lack of cooperation or clarity on the part of the expert they tried to work with. A good human expert is extremely important to the success of an expert systems development project.

The interpersonal relationship between the human expert and the knowledge engineer is also an important key to making the project a success. We discuss this matter in more detail when we consider the knowledge acquisition process.

You Need Case Data

Just as any successful project depends upon a human expert, it also depends upon the availability of specific data that you can use to test your system. The ideal situation occurs when you find an expert who can take you to a file drawer where he has stored the dozens or hundreds of cases he has dealt with in the past. More likely, your expert will have some case data, but it won't be as complete or comprehensive as you will need. In the worst case, your expert will not have saved any case data at all. Since the development and the testing of expert systems is driven by test cases, you will need to obtain case data one way or another.

If your expert doesn't have case data, can he create some? (Does the problem you are focusing on occur so frequently that your expert can rapidly accumulate case data?) Or, in the worst case, can your expert create some test cases from memory or imagination? The latter course obviously involves the risk that the expert will forget something, or unconsciously slant the cases he creates to emphasize particular or unusual problems. If your expert is going to create test cases, you should arrange to collect simultaneously any case data you can from end users or from cases that occur while you are working on the problem.

If you explain the importance of case data to the expert systems development process to your expert and he indicates that he either can't develop cases or won't have time to do so, that suggests that you may have made a poor choice of an expert. Such an expert lacks either the time that will be required, or the commitment, or simply has inadequate knowledge or experience in dealing with the problem you want to solve.

The Task Should Be Narrow and Well Defined

It almost sounds like a contradiction to suggest that you should use expert systems techniques to tackle a narrow, well-defined task. After all, when most people think of expert systems applications, they think of fuzzy, complex problems. The fact is that we are just beginning to learn how to use expert systems techniques; we still don't know the best way to approach complex problems and we don't really understand the limits of the technology yet. When you talk with people who worked on projects that were subsequently abandoned, those that were not abandoned because of a poor choice of a human expert were abandoned because the knowledge involved in solving the problem proved to be too voluminous or too complex. In those cases, the knowledge engineers simply quit when they realized that the overall scope of the problem was getting out of hand.

When you consider a potential application, be as precise as you can about exactly what you want the expert system to accomplish. Exclude all of the nice things that are not really part of the core analysis and decision-making process; you can always go back and expand your system.

We discuss techniques for analyzing the specific steps in a task in the next chapter. As a generalization, most of the tasks that you might represent within a single box can, in fact, be subdivided. Two general types of task emerge: procedural tasks and structured analysis tasks.

Procedural tasks. You can subdivide some tasks into steps, which must be taken in sequential order. When you have a task that occurs in steps, consider if it would help to develop an expert system to perform one or a few of the steps in the overall procedure. If so, one way to start is by developing an expert system that will accomplish only one step. In effect, that system will then be your prototype, and you should not plan to go on to the other steps until you are first satisfied with the system that handles the one single step. Another approach is to develop an expert system to handle multiple steps in a shallow way, and then go back later to fill in their details. The danger with this approach is that you may not realize until late in your development if you have bitten off more than you can chew and must narrow your scope to a single step in the process.

The Oracle Credit Advisor system provides a nice example of a procedural task. Figure 3.4 illustrates a dataflow diagram of the task. In effect, Figure 3.4 breaks down the overall view of the Oracle Credit Advisor task originally shown in Figure 3.1 into a series of smaller steps. (We consider the use of dataflow diagrams in the next chapter.) Each circle or node represents a process in which incoming data is changed to produce new data. In effect, each node could be a small expert system. In fact, the data manipulation that occurs in some nodes is much more mechanical or procedural than in others. When faced with a task that can be subdivided into a series of steps, as this one can, you should consider what is involved in each step and then begin with the step that is the most heuristic and judgmental in nature.

Structured analysis tasks. You cannot subdivide some complex tasks into steps. You can, however, subdivide them into a very general decision or fault tree. Each level of the tree represents areas that the expert needs to consider in order to reach an overall conclusion about the nature of the problem and the appropriate recommendation. When you're faced with an analysis task that can be divided into a hierarchy of parts, choose one part, or a subpart to begin with. Create a prototype to accomplish just one branch of the analysis before deciding to expand your system to include the entire analysis effort.

An example of a structured analysis task is the ASEA Maintenance Assistant developed at Ford. Although there is an overall flow to the task, you are considering alternative hypotheses, so the order in which you gather and analyze different information is not so important. Figure 3.5 illustrates the overall structure of the ASEA analysis task. In effect, the task is subdivided into a fault tree. You could choose to begin developing a system at any level of the tree, as long as you include all of the boxes below the box you choose. The larger and more complex the task, the more inclined you should be to choose a single box at the bottom of the fault tree to work with in developing a prototype system.

Another approach to subdividing a task can be used when you are considering developing an expert system that will allow several average performers to perform as well as an expert performer. In effect, you subdivide the expert's effort into steps and then compare, step by step, the differences in how the expert and the average performer accomplish each step. This approach is designed to highlight a fact that seems obvious when it's stated but is often overlooked: Experts are often experts even though they perform only one or a few steps differently than the

Figure 3.4 Oracle Credit Advisor system dataflow diagram.

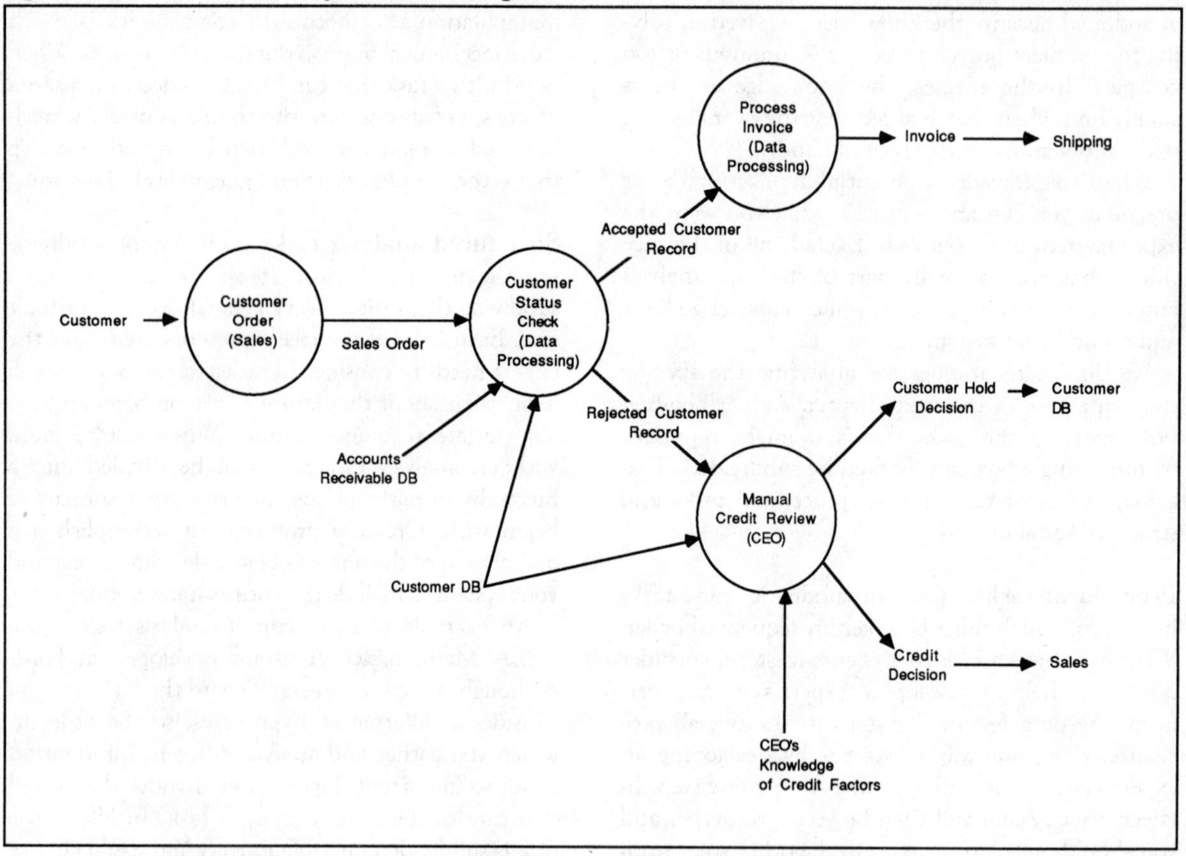

average performer. People sometimes think that because an expert gets much better results than the average performer, the expert must be doing everything an entirely different way than the average performer. This fallacy often results in boring training programs that seek to teach people many things they already know. In fact, most studies indicate that experts are expert because they can handle one or a few steps more effectively than their average coworkers; they perform most parts of a task in the same manner as everyone else.

This insight can be especially valuable when you are faced with a large task and are trying to decide which step to focus on. If you compare average and best performance, you may find that only one or two steps make any significant difference in the outcome. In such a case, if you create an expert system to assist people with just those few steps that really affect the outcome, you will accomplish your goal of improving performance and will have avoided a lot of unnecessary programming.

No matter how large your final system will be, it is relatively easy to develop a small expert system and then later expand it into a larger, more comprehensive system. On the other hand, many failures have resulted from using an expert system to tackle too large a task. Human performers often bring far more knowledge to bear on seemingly small tasks than we realize when we watch them perform the task. Most of their work focuses on the routine cases that they can handle quickly, but when exceptions come up they may rely on vast stores of very specialized knowledge that will prove difficult to capture. It's much safer to start small and then expand; you won't get hurt using that approach. If you try to tackle too much at first, you may find yourself in deep water very quickly.

The Task Should Involve Verbal Knowledge

Most expert systems and the tools that are used to develop them are designed primarily to capture verbal knowledge in the form of rules or hierarchies or networks of descriptive knowledge. This is the kind of knowledge that we can write and talk about, as opposed to highly skilled physical performance or the skilled classification or interpretation of sensory signals. Expert systems can use pictures to describe how to locate or identify items or even use sensory data provided by mechanical sensors, but they are much better at handling information that can be represented in verbal form. Thus, you should choose an expert who can describe rather than demonstrate her knowledge.

One of the best tests for verbal knowledge is the popular "telephone test." If a user can call an expert on the telephone and explain the problem and get a recommendation via phone, you clearly have a problem that is verbal in nature. The expert may ask the user to check for needed information or even make some kind of qualitative evaluation (e.g., Are the headlights bright or dim?). If this can all be done over the phone, you know that the expert can explain the information he needs in words and that the user can understand what the expert wants to know and make any tests and report any results in words. If a task can pass the telephone test, you can render the knowledge in rules and develop an interface to conduct a dialogue with the user.

You should avoid those tasks that require the expert to examine the problem situation personally (e.g., look at the color of the fluid or smell the batch of cookies before agreeing that they are ready to pour). For these tasks, it will prove hard or impossible to represent the knowledge involved in making the recommendation or to develop an interface that can ask the user for the information needed in order to reach a decision.

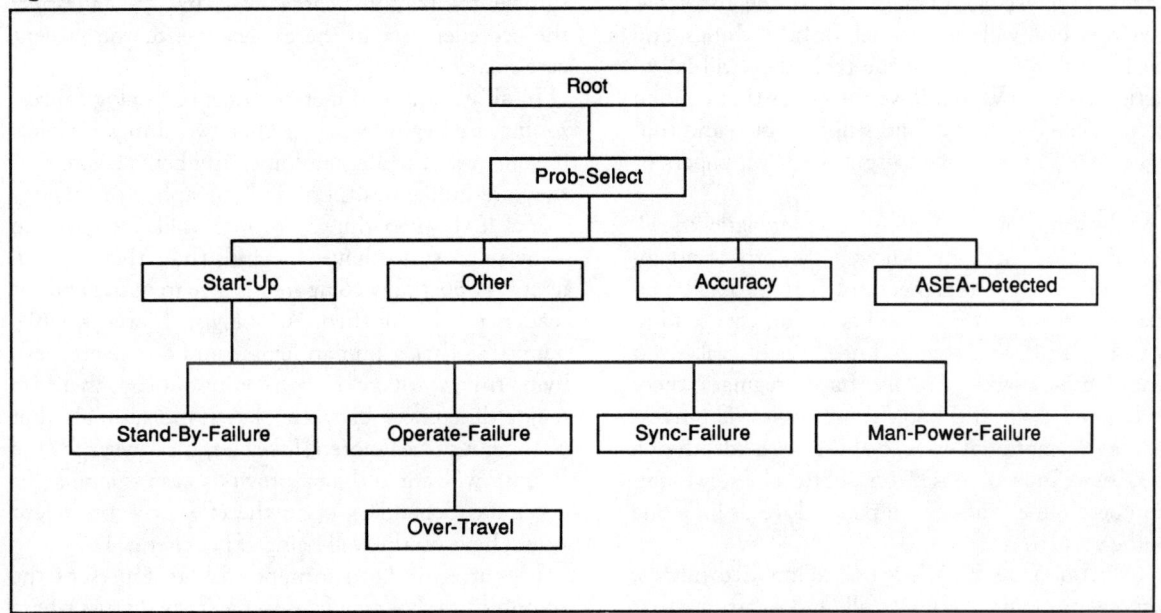

Figure 3.5 ASEA maintenance assistant task subdivided into a fault or context tree.

There are expert systems in the area of process control that use input from sensors, but if you are considering such an application, be sure you have the technology to capture the sensory input before you decide to develop an expert system to interpret sensory data.

The Inverse: Tasks to Avoid

We have discussed some of the key criteria to apply to a potential application to determine if it would be appropriate for expert systems development. If a task fails to meet one or more of these key criteria, you should not consider it very seriously. By the same token, there are certain problems that ought to be avoided. We list signs of tasks to be avoided on the Application Analysis Worksheet (Figure 3.3) and discuss them below.

Avoid tasks involving common sense. When knowledge engineers use the term *common sense*, they refer to the vast amounts of more or less subconscious knowledge that we have all acquired in the process of growing up. We all have, for example, a pragmatic knowledge of physics and chemistry. We know that heat will tend to melt or burn things, and that if we shove things off the table they will fall to the floor. We know that if we turn cups that contain fluids upside down, the fluid will flow out, and that it's normally undesirable to spill fluids on papers or rugs.

By the same token, we all have a pragmatic knowledge of ecology and thus know what sorts of organisms tend to grow together and how various combinations might interact. We know that cats tend to try to kill birds, and that you need "rich" soil if you want to grow flowers. We also have pragmatic theories of psychology and know that people will tend to respond in emotional ways to abuse or the death of a loved one. Indeed, based on subtle clues, we can often determine that certain people love or hate one another, and so on.

Common sense knowledge is common to almost everyone in a culture, and we all tend to assume that "everyone else knows it" whenever we speak and expect to be understood. Expert systems depend upon the developer being able to explicitly specify all the knowledge that the system will employ in analyzing and solving a problem. With a great deal of work, we can explicitly state all the knowledge required for narrow, well-defined tasks like medical diagnoses or factory scheduling, but incorporating common sense knowledge into expert systems is currently well beyond the commercially available technology. We do not understand all of the rich relationships involved in common sense knowledge, and we cannot capture or store the vast amount that even a six year old uses when interacting with playmates or deciding to build a tree fort.

Whenever you are discussing a potential expert systems application and you hear that the expert depends on a lot of common sense, you should consider that the analysis effort would probably be too large and that the application should be avoided.

Avoid tasks involving reasoning by analogy. Reasoning by analogy involves thinking about one thing in terms of another. A judge reasons by analogy when she considers whether a current case is sufficiently like some earlier case that she can apply the precedent set in the earlier case to the present case as well.

In all instances of metaphorical or analogical reasoning, we begin by saying that two things are alike in some ways, while simultaneously being aware that they are unlike in others. The metaphor or analogy works if the two things are more alike, relative to some purpose we have in mind, than they are different. A poet may compare his love to a rose and his reader may be satisfied. A biologist, however, while admitting that a human female and a rose are both living things, will be quick to point out that there are major differences between plants and animals that ought not to be ignored. Likewise, the lawyer for the defense will argue that a previous case is similar or dissimilar depending upon the effect the precedent would have on the well-being of her client.

It's currently hard to impossible to represent the complexities that people use when they discuss where analogies are valid or invalid. If a task involves analogical reasoning, you should avoid it.

Avoid tasks that involve perceptual expertise. This suggestion is just the reverse of saying that tasks should be verbal in nature. If you observe the expert and see that he relies on perceptual or motor skills to make a determination, that's a warning that you should probably avoid the task. An expert who needs to hear how the motor sounds or wants to feel the vibration of the motor as it runs will have trouble communicating his knowledge to you in a way that you can translate into words.

We once had a client who wanted to develop an expert system to duplicate an expert who went into Southern peanut fields in the spring and predicted the yield, in tons, of peanuts to be expected in the fall. The expert was the best person the company had for the task; his estimates, while never perfect, were far better than those of the other people who performed this job. Whatever the expert did, however, it wasn't verbal. He looked at the little green plants, sniffed the soil, made a guess on the weather that the best meteorologist would be afraid to stand behind, and came up with a figure. There was probably a lot of reasoning by analogy in his predictions, but they were analogies that involved sensation and perception and not any kind of verbal reasoning you could capture in rules. The peanut yield expert would never have been able to perform his job over the telephone!

There are many valuable tasks that humans perform that cannot be captured by existing expert systems techniques. Prudent and successful knowledge engineers have a lot of humility about what they can do. They are successful because there are many valuable verbal knowledge-based tasks that can be turned into expert systems, and because they avoid the tasks that are currently beyond what the technology can handle.

Avoid tasks involving very volatile expertise. We have stressed that expert systems can be changed and maintained more easily than conventional programs because the knowledge they contain is modular and easy to inspect and change. This is certainly true, but there are limits. If your expert is constantly working to keep up on the rapidly changing knowledge in her field, then you might want to avoid the task.

We've been asked why we didn't develop an expert system to help other people select expert systems tools or appropriate applications. We have not tried it because the expert systems field is developing and changing so rapidly. Every month new tools and applications are announced. Moreover, existing tools are constantly being enhanced and people are rapidly discovering new uses for expert systems that, in turn, demand tools with new characteristics. It's easy to provide generalities and let people generalize from them, but it's hard to be precise because the technology is so volatile. In a few years, the technology will become more mature, the number of tool vendors will stabilize, and it will make sense to develop an expert system to assist with tool or application selection, but at the moment, it would be a difficult and probably unsatisfactory application.

If the application you are considering is valuable enough to allow you to assign people to full-time maintenance, then you may be able to overcome this objection. XCON, DEC's computer configuration system, is constantly changing as DEC introduces new hardware and modifies existing configuration guidelines. In the course of the last eight years, XCON has grown from a few hundred rules to over 10,000 rules. At a considerable expense, DEC has about 10 knowledge engineers who are constantly modifying and expanding the knowledge contained in XCON. The value of this large system to DEC's operations is so great that it easily covers the cost of having people constantly working on the system and introducing new versions of it each quarter. Only very valuable systems would qualify for this kind of commitment, though.

Avoid situations in which experts disagree. The development of your knowledge base will depend on the knowledge provided by your expert or experts. Moreover, once you have developed your knowledge base, you should test it by having other experts try it. If the experts at a particular task disagree, it could mean one of two things: (1) you don't have real expertise in the domain, or (2) you have political problems and should probably pick another task to focus on.

Expertise is hard to define, but it should be closely related to results. An expert ought to be able to get results consistently, or at least much more commonly than nonexperts attempting the same task. If you have a group of people who are called experts and who frequently disagree and you have no way to choose between them, you probably have pseudo-experts. Some very prestigious people fall into this category. Stock market analysts, for example, are pseudo-experts. They commonly disagree and they will not defer to each other. Moreover, no one analyst's record is that much better than the other leading analysts to allow you to determine who is definitely the best. It's generally best to avoid areas in which there are competing experts. Such areas are usually broad domains that involve common sense and ought to be avoided anyway because you can't identify a sufficiently well-defined, narrow task to focus on in the first place. When you have expertise, other experts usually agree on the criteria and they agree on who knows what they are doing and who doesn't. It's not that different experts might not approach problems in different ways, but they usually agree on who can obtain acceptable results. If you ask a number of physicians in an area who is the best heart specialist or who is really good at some specialized problem, you usually obtain a broad agreement about who you should see. By the same token, engineers and underwriters usually know who is good at handling particular problems.

All this is not to say that you will not encounter problems in which you need the combined judgment of several experts to reach a reasonable conclusion. A loan committee, for example, usually combines several individuals who each focus on different aspects of the loan. One might focus on the financial strength of the company that wants the loan, while another might focus on the managers who run the company. Still another might focus on the overall market for the products the company produces. It's not that they disagree, they just ask different questions because they bring different perspectives to the analysis effort. Many expert systems have been developed that combine the judgments of multiple experts. Building a system that combines multiple perspectives, however, is entirely different from trying to build a system that combines the opinions of people who disagree with each other on the basics.

Obviously, if you have experts who are seemingly competent but have interpersonal disagreements, you should avoid trying to develop an expert system with one of them. If it's likely that other experts will disparage the resulting system, you probably won't have a successful project.

The ideal project is built about one well-recognized expert, or a team of experts who work well together. You should avoid situations in which experts disagree.

Avoid tasks that involve complicated geometric or spacial reasoning, and avoid tasks involving complex causal or temporal relations. Tasks in which experts perform complex geometric or spacial reasoning or deal with complex temporal or causal relationships involve types of knowledge that are difficult or impossible to represent effectively. Projects that involve these types of tasks are better left to research groups. The current crop of expert systems building tools doesn't offer the facilities to handle difficult problems of this nature.

As you consider a potential application, review each of these positive and negative criteria very carefully. You might bend one of the criteria, but if you really ignore them, you are probably letting yourself in for problems.

4.
Identifying and Scoping Potential Applications—Part 2

We continue the application selection process by now moving to Step 4.

STEP 4. IDENTIFYING THE BASIC COGNITIVE STRUCTURE OF THE PROBLEM

When we first considered potential applications, we drew input/output diagrams to help you picture the overall situation the expert system would have to function in (see Figures 3.1 and 3.2). We ignored the actual nature of the analysis task that the human or system performed. In discussing how to divide and narrow problems, we considered you might identify steps within the overall task and thus restrict the size of the system you begin with. Now, we want to consider, in a very general way, how you might classify the cognitive nature of a task or task step. In other words, what sort of cognitive analysis or judgmental process is going on when an expert actually accomplishes a given task or step? Even a very general classification of the cognitive nature of a task can be extremely useful, since some cognitive tasks are much more difficult than others and require a much greater effort.

We will consider five general classes of knowledge-based problems:

1. Procedural Problems
2. Diagnostic Problems
3. Monitoring Problems
4. Configuration or Design Problems
5. Planning and Scheduling Problems

In addition, we will consider some of the signs that suggest either a forward or a backward chaining strategy. Then, we will summarize by providing an estimate of the relative difficulty of each type of problem and the types of tools and efforts that each type of problem suggests.

Procedural Problems

The simplest problems are those that capture the knowledge required to execute a simple procedure. The procedure usually involves applying a few rules or working your way through a decision tree. You can often handle this sort of problem by providing the performer with some kind of printed instructions or documentation (e.g., a printed memo that explains how employee vacation days are calculated).

You know you are faced with a procedural problem if you can write out a step-by-step description of the expert's work or if you can represent the expert's analysis with a decision tree.

Clearly, a problem that is procedural in nature can be programmed in a conventional computer language like BASIC, COBOL, or PASCAL. There are three reasons you might select an expert systems tool to develop a system to handle a procedural problem:

1. You want to develop the system very quickly or incrementally.
2. You know the program will need to be modified frequently.
3. The developer or the people who will modify and maintain the program do not know how to program in a conventional language.

If any of these conditions apply, then you can consider using a small to mid-size expert systems building tool to develop a procedural system.

Diagnostic Problems

Diagnostic problems involve choosing one or more of several recommendations, based on deductions drawn from some set of observations. Physicians use diagnosis when they observe, ask questions, and then decide what drug or treatment to recommend. Auto mechanics use diagnosis when they ask questions, make observations, and then decide what treatment to apply to a malfunctioning car. Clerks use diagnosis when they examine an insurance application and decide that it is complete and can be processed, or that it is incomplete and must be rejected.

Diagnostic problems are more complex than procedural problems either because the number of rules needed to reach a recommendation are so numerous and complex that you can't create a decision tree, or because the rules are fuzzy and involve uncertainty or probability considerations. In other words, diagnostic problems involve the analysis of search spaces that are too large or fuzzy to be analyzed by conventional means. Since conventional means will not work, you must approach the problem by incrementally accumulating the rules or heuristics that the expert uses when he sorts through such problems.

Diagnostic problems are very common and come in many varieties, but the essential characteristics can be observed in almost all cases:

1. The expert depends on observations or answers to questions (in effect, the observations of others).
2. The expert selects one or more actions from a well-established list of treatment options.

Figure 4.1 illustrates a typical diagnosis problem space.

You can handle most diagnostic problems with rule-based systems. Indeed, most of the small expert systems that function as intelligent job aids are rule-based systems that are designed to handle procedural or simple diagnostic problems.

Complex diagnostic problems usually require that the developer keep track of several levels of abstraction. For example, in an animal classification system, you might want to keep track of features of classes of animals like birds and fish; features of families of animals like hawks, ducks, and sparrows; and features of specific species like field sparrows, song sparrows, and marsh sparrows. Trying to keep track of different levels of abstraction via rules can get very complex. In a similar way, more complex diagnostic problems often require that the developer create a model involving abstraction.

At the very high end of the range of diagnosis problems, you encounter situations with so many facts and so much abstraction that a rule-based approach becomes less and less effective. If you know about the various options and tools available, you may want to use an object-oriented approach to make it easier to organize and specify the facts at various levels of abstraction. In effect, you should use an object-oriented approach to create a static or dynamic model of the underlying mechanism.

Monitoring Problems

Monitoring problems are those in which the expert system can watch a process or check values when they are determined and go into action when a particular pattern is observed. The nature of the task is usually very much like a diagnostic task in the sense that the monitoring system typically provides a warning or offers advice by choosing from a limited set of recommendations. The main difference is that most monitoring systems rely on some initial data to begin their work. This, in turn, suggests a data-driven or forward chaining system, in contrast with the typical diagnostic system that is goal driven and uses backward chaining. Moreover, monitoring systems normally respond to data input while diagnostic systems must ask the user questions to get the data they need in order to make recommendations.

We have more to say about monitoring systems after we consider forward and backward chaining,

Figure 4.1 Typical diagnosis problem space.

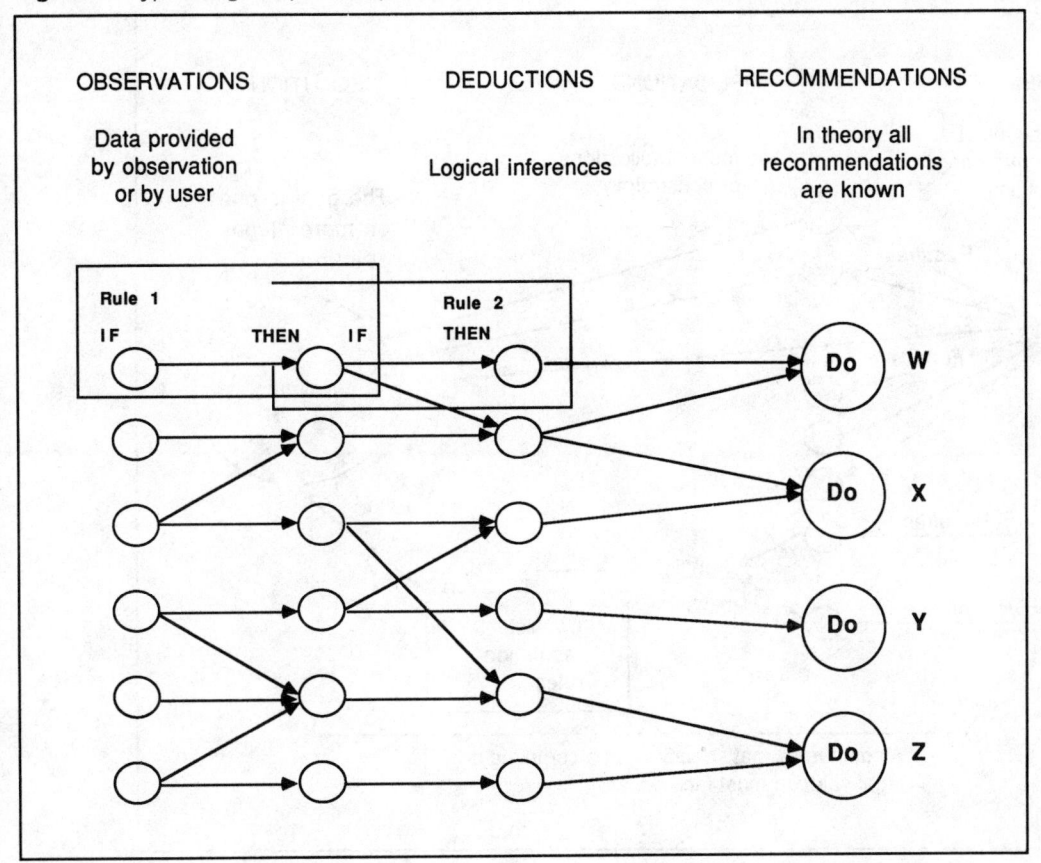

OBSERVATIONS — Data provided by observation or by user

DEDUCTIONS — Logical inferences

RECOMMENDATIONS — In theory all recommendations are known

Rule 1: IF ... THEN
Rule 2: IF ... THEN

Do W
Do X
Do Y
Do Z

which we will delay until after we have defined the five major types of cognitive problems.

Configuration or Design Problems

In a *configuration* or *design problem*, there is no well-established list of all possible outcomes. Instead, the system creates a recommendation, depending upon observations and users' needs. In fact, configuration or design problems can come in two forms:

1. Constrained or Structured Configuration or Design Problems
2. Open-Ended or Creative Configuration or Design Problems

At this point in time, expert systems techniques can't effectively be used to handle the latter case (those problems involve too much common sense!). What expert systems can handle very effectively are constrained or structured configuration or design problems. Thus, if you want to determine the best way to configure a computer given a well-known set of parts and a set of user specifications, you can develop an expert system. If you want to let a user "create" a truck to match his particular needs, you can let him do it using an expert system that provides the user options from a predefined set of parts and assembly relationships.

Figure 4.2 provides an overview of a configuration problem. Notice that the user has needs and the system has options. Some options require or preclude the selection of other options. Thus, once a

Figure 4.2 The typical configuration or design problem space.

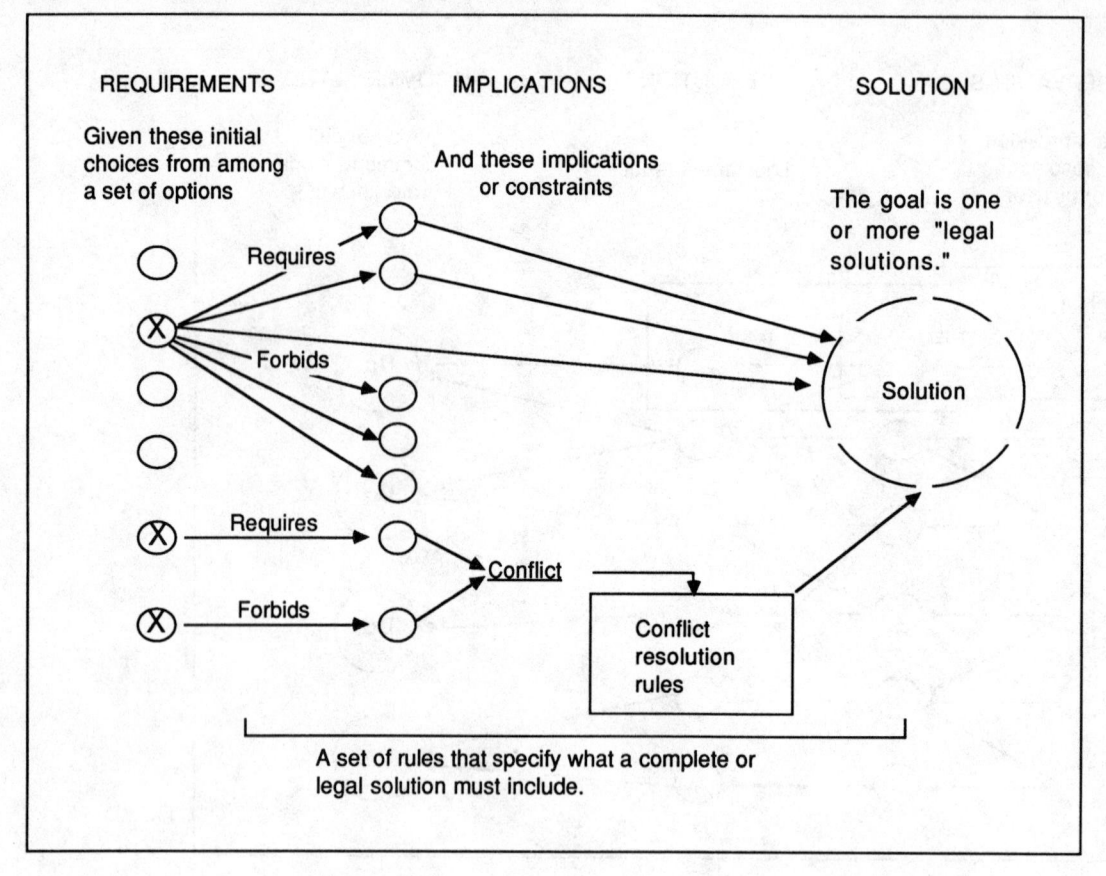

user decides he wants to "create" a truck with three axles, he is thereafter precluded from assuming any arrangement that requires more or less that three axles. By the same token, once the user decides on three axles, he must also select six, ten, or twelve wheels (since wheels must be assigned to axles in pairs and there must be at least one pair per axle). Options that limit or require subsequent choices are called *constraints*. Configuration or design problems typically involve identifying many constraints.

All of the more complex structured configuration or design problems involve situations in which one selection entails a constraint that is in conflict with another constraint resulting from some other decision. A good system has to be able to resolve the conflict created by these incompatible constraints. This is often called a *conflict resolution problem*. For example, if you decide that you want to create a truck with three axles, then there is an upper limit in the weight the truck can bear. If you independently specify that you want a truck that can carry eight tons, you have a conflict, since the system knows that an eight-ton load calls for at least six axles and you have already said you want only three. In some cases, the system can apply rules that will fix the problem without the user's involvement (e.g., more tires might be added to each axle), but in other cases, the user must be confronted with the contradiction and asked to change one or more of his original specifications.

Planning and Scheduling Problems

Planning and scheduling problems are very much like structured configuration problems, except that they include time considerations, which make them more complex. Like configuration problems, planning and scheduling problems that the current generation of expert systems techniques can handle must be based on a structured selection from a prespecified set of people, materials, machines, and job orders. You can't use the current technology to deal with open-ended planning or scheduling problems.

In a typical configuration problem, you are normally concerned with the fact that if you have one part, you can't have another, and so on. In planning or scheduling, you are concerned with combining goals, people, and materials in a way that a series of events can occur in a specific temporal order. You are not as concerned with a particular goal (e.g., a correctly assembled computer) as you are with multiple, simultaneous goals (e.g., assembling the maximum number of correctly assembled computers, given a set of people, materials, and orders).

Moreover, you want the program to be as "smart" as possible and not ask you for data that it should remember or could calculate itself. See Figure 4.3 for an illustration of the typical planning or scheduling problem space.

The five cognitive problems we have described here are hardly exhaustive, but they are by far the most common and the best understood. If you encounter a problem that cannot be classified into one of these five categories, you should be very careful;

Figure 4.3 *The typical planning and scheduling problem space.*

INPUTS	IMPLICATIONS	SOLUTION
Needs		
Job A	Rules that determine a sequence	
Job B	of events that will lead to the	
	satisfaction of all needs and	
Resources	constraints within some time	
People	frame	
Inventory		
Equipment		Plan or Schedule
Constraints		
Time		
Resources		
Alternative		
Options		

Critical constraint is time.

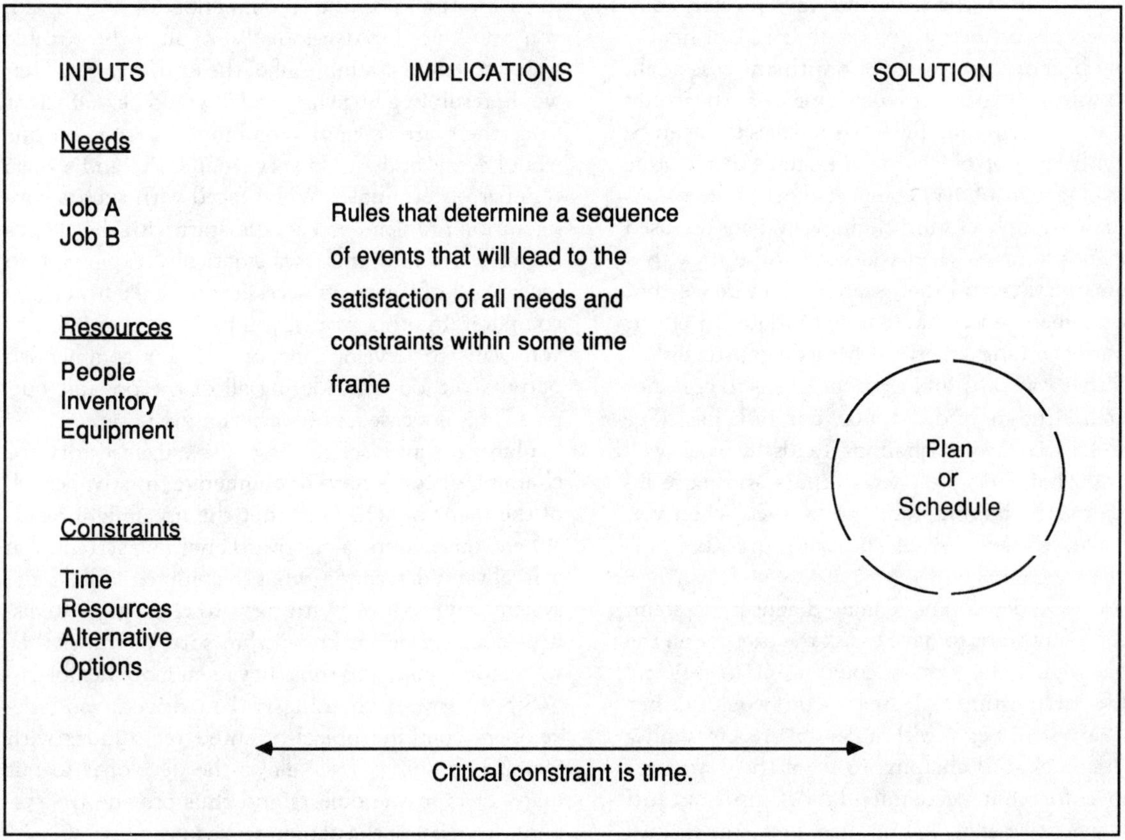

you may be about to undertake knowledge engineering *research*, which can be costly and may not lead to commercial success. If you want to be reasonably sure of success with your expert systems development efforts, at least initially, you should try to stick to the types of problems that we have just described.

A Brief Review of Inference and Control

In Chapter 2, we considered the general characteristics of induction and forward and backward chaining. At this point, we simply want to review some of the implications of the three approaches.

Induction depends on a matrix of examples for its input and it produces a decision table as its output. Induction systems are getting better all the time, but they are still primarily used for procedural and simple diagnostic tasks. Induction systems simply lack the flexibility to allow the developer to represent complex levels of abstractions or multiple sets of heuristics that bear on a single decision with any ease at all.

Backward and forward chaining, on the other hand, are powerful and flexible strategies that can be used with rule- or object-based systems to facilitate the development of very complex expert systems. As a generalization, backward chaining systems are used for diagnostic tasks when you want to begin with a recommendation and then search for evidence that the recommendation may be appropriate. In effect, backward chaining almost defines a diagnostic task.

Another way of thinking about this is to consider how many inputs and outputs your task has. (See Figure 4.4.) Backward chaining tends to work well when you have relatively few outputs and more inputs. Forward chaining tends to be used when you have relatively few inputs and many possible outputs.

If you were developing a small diagnostic system, you would not want to have to ask the user for all the possible inputs the system could want under any possible circumstance. Instead, you would rather have the system begin with a possible recommendation, use backward chaining to see if there was any evidence for that recommendation, and cut off search whenever it was clear that there was insufficient evidence. A backward chaining system tends to ask fewer questions and to create dialogues that sound more conversational.

If you are to use a backward chaining system, however, you must be able to identify all of the possible recommendations the system might make. In this sense, backward chaining is the more rigid of the two chaining strategies, and it often seems much closer to procedural programming than forward chaining.

Imagine that you wanted to develop a configuration system to determine all of the parts you would need to create a workable VAX computer. You would start with a list of the client's requirements (e.g., parts or functionality that implies parts). From this initial list, you should determine all of the additional parts you need to assemble a working computer system. Obviously, you don't want to begin by developing a list of all possible recommendations. To do so, you would need to develop a list of all of the possible ways you could assemble all of the known parts. That would result in a huge list, and it would be inefficient since there are so many combinations that no one would ever want (e.g., a very small CPU and a huge number of terminals). When faced with such a configuration problem, you should start with the client's list of parts and then systematically expand it to include all of the parts necessary to make a working computer. In other words, you have a few inputs and you want to develop one or a few recommended outputs without considering all of the possible outputs. This is a case for forward chaining.

Planning and scheduling also suggest forward chaining since it's hard to enumerate, in advance, all of the plans or schedules that the user might want. When you examine a backward chaining system, you can always determine what recommendations the system can produce. With forward chaining systems, it is much harder to know what sorts of things they will recommend, and thus they seem more flexible.

Since forward chaining is data driven, most developers combine object-oriented techniques with forward chaining. This allows the developer to put many facts in the objects and thus provide the system with most of the data it needs to run.

Figure 4.4 Forward and backward chaining.

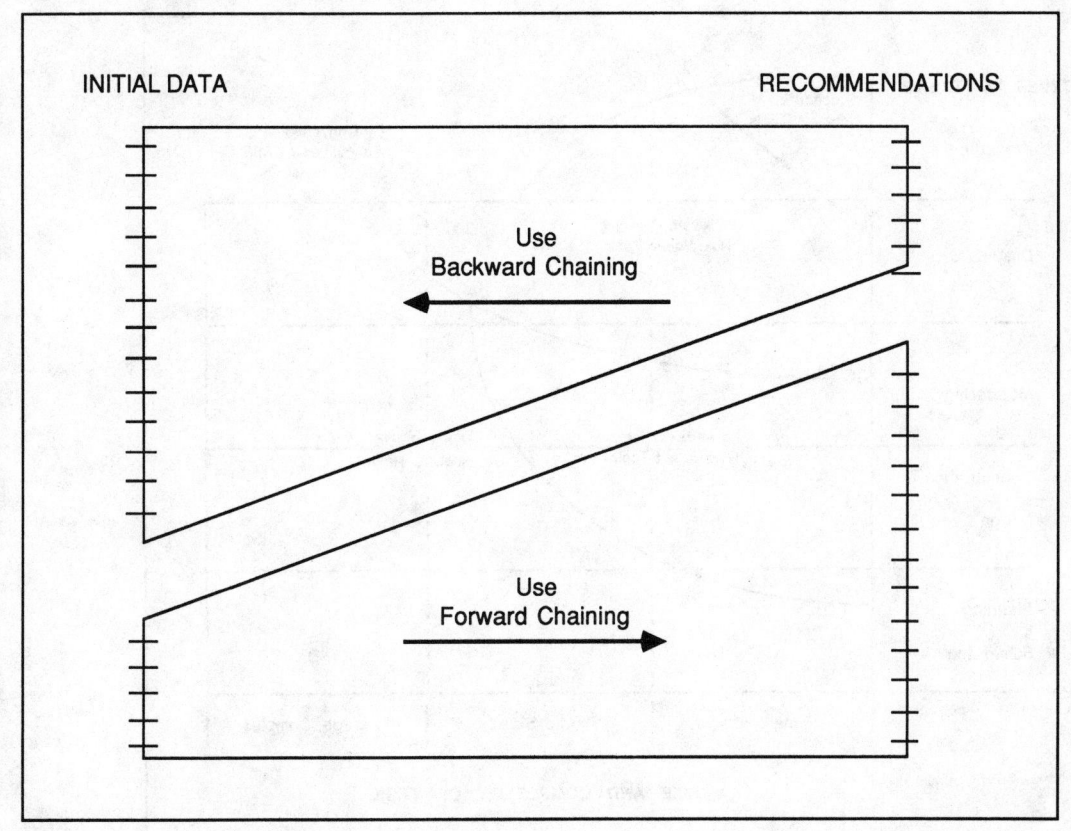

INITIAL DATA   RECOMMENDATIONS

Use Backward Chaining ←

Use Forward Chaining →

The most complex expert systems usually combine forward and backward chaining. For these, the developer attaches rules to objects and specifies if the rules are to be used in a backward or forward manner. Even when this approach is used, however, the system's overall strategy is usually a forward chaining strategy.

The Implications of the Different Types of Cognitive Tasks

Figure 4.5 provides a summary of the implications of the remarks we have just made. On the vertical axis, we show the different classes of knowledge problems. We place procedural problems at the top and move down as the problems become more complex, fuzzy, and difficult. In other words, planning and scheduling problems are the hardest problems to handle, while configuration problems are about halfway between planning and procedural problems. On the horizontal axis, we indicate the overall difficulty and size of the task, independent of the nature of the cognitive nature of the task. Notice that we considered only procedural situations that involve simple and some mid-size problems. We have argued that most people use expert systems for procedural problems simply because they cannot program and the expert systems techniques make it fast and easy to develop a small procedural system. If a procedural problem gets really complex or difficult, however, you should use conventional programming techniques to develop the application. Hence, there are no large expert systems designed to handle procedural problems.

82 IDENTIFYING OPPORTUNITIES

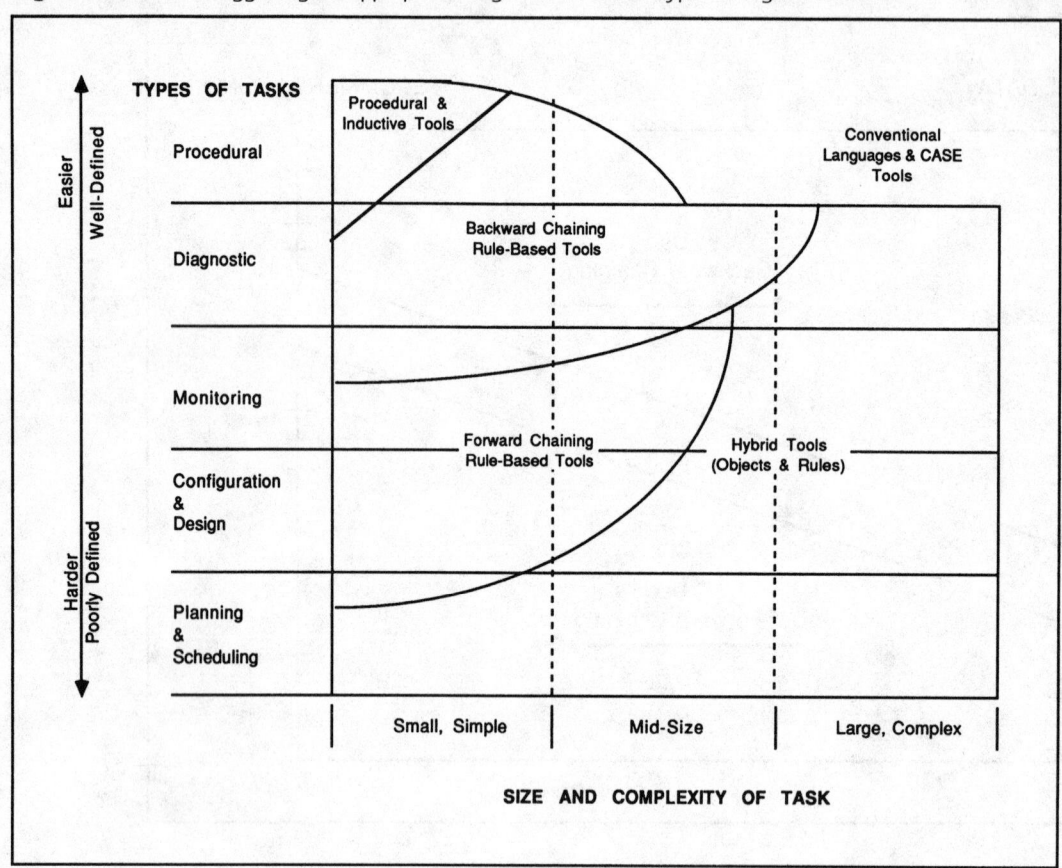

Figure 4.5 A matrix suggesting the appropriate range of the different types of cognitive tasks.

We suggest techniques within the matrix shown in Figure 4.5. Induction is good for small procedural and diagnostic problems. Backward chaining rule-based systems are good for small to mid-size diagnostic problems and a few monitoring and configuration problems. Forward chaining rule-based systems (e.g., OPS5) are good for the small to mid-size monitoring tasks and for some configuration systems. The most complex diagnostic and monitoring tasks, most configuration, and almost all planning and scheduling tasks suggest tools that combine object-oriented programming and forward chaining or bidirectional rule-based techniques.

If you consider what overall strategy you have chosen, you will see what types of problems you should focus on. Developers of small PC-based systems should normally look for procedural and diagnostic tasks. Mid-size system developers using backward chaining rule-based tools should limit themselves to procedural, diagnostic, and the simpler configuration tasks. Mid-size system developers who are using forward chaining rule-based tools should focus on monitoring and configuration tasks. Only those who plan to use an object-oriented tool should try to tackle the more complex diagnostic, configuration, or planning and scheduling problems. The LISP-based tools are most effectively used for the large configuration and the planning and scheduling problems. Those who are interested in embedding systems are often interested in some kind of monitoring system and should consider forward chaining tools, although intelligent help is typically a diagnostic problem, and that suggests backward chaining.

Most expert systems are being developed with tools, and the techniques available in a particular tool should limit your choice of potential applications. One way to fail is to try to use a small backward chaining rule-based tool for a mid-size configuration or scheduling problem. By the same token, a good way to waste money is to buy a large LISP tool to undertake small to mid-size diagnostic problems.

STEP 5. CONSIDERING USER, COST, AND MANAGEMENT ISSUES

If you have developed a list of potential applications and narrowed the list by choosing applications that meet all the key criteria and involve a narrowly defined cognitive task that is appropriate for the strategy, effort, and tool you intend to use, then you should have a pretty good list. The final step in narrowing the list is to consider some practical issues that involve users, management, and cost. We briefly describe some of these concerns in this final section.

User Concerns

So far, we have talked about ways of deciding if an expert system *can* be successfully developed. Our viewpoint has primarily been that of the developer. Now we want to consider if the expert system *should* be developed. Will it be used if it is developed? Will the development and use of the system make your organization money or will it cost more to develop than it will ever earn? The place to start considering these matters is by taking a hard, cold look at the people who will ultimately have to use the system and the environment in which the system will be used if it is successfully deployed. The only way to answer these questions is to look and ask questions. It seems obvious, but many expert systems efforts have floundered when the developers found out that the intended user didn't want the expert system and would not use it once it was delivered. The days when developers could "throw applications over the wall" and expect the users to be grateful for anything they got is long past. From a user's perspective, an expert system is just another computer application. The application either makes the user's job easier and makes the user more effective, or it's just another computer application that will never be used.

The list of items discussed below is hardly exhaustive, but it does suggest a number of things that you should consider before deciding to proceed with the development of any potential expert systems application.

Perceived need. Do the people who would use the expert system, if it was developed, perceive any need for assistance? If they do, you can involve them in the project. If they don't see the need for an expert system, then your first job is to sell them on the value of an expert system. In discussions with users, be sure to talk to them about each of the issues discussed in this section to be sure that the system will, in fact, be useful to them. In the long run, the success of the system depends on the users; they have to use it and they have to help maintain it. If you can't sell the users on the value of an application, you should probably move on to another application. If you can't do that, for whatever reason, then you need to be particularly careful to involve the users at each step of the development process. In effect, you have to use the time while the system is being developed to sell the system and get users to begin to feel that it is, after all, their system. If you fail with the users, chances are the system will never be effectively used and will never deliver its value to the company.

Hardware. What hardware will the system be delivered on? Do the users already have the hardware? It sounds silly, but at least a couple of companies have developed systems without answering this question first. They have developed systems and then found that the hardware running in the user environment was incapable of running the expert systems application. This issue isn't anything new to expert systems development, but it is just as important as it's always been. You need a clear plan for how you will field the system, and that plan needs to take the user's hardware into account.

Availability. How will the users access the expert system? If the expert system is being developed for a PC and everyone in the department has a PC on his or her desk, then obviously access will not be an issue. If, on the other hand, you expect to run the expert system on a workstation and there will be only one in the department, then you may have a problem.

Review your analysis of the inputs and outputs of the task you are seeking to automate. When does the task occur? How urgent is it? Is it reasonable to expect that performers will leave their desks and move to a workstation to use the expert system? Will the system be used during training but then ignored once the person starts working on the job and is under pressure to make decisions quickly?

Some jobs are organized in such a way that a performer can save certain important decisions until a slow period and then move to a workstation to enter data, answer questions, and receive recommendations, and others aren't. You need a clear plan that anticipates when and where the user will access the expert system and specifies what the demand for system access will be at any point in time. No matter how valuable a system is, if the users can't get access to it when they need to make a decision, the system won't be used.

Speed. The question of speed is really just a variation on access: How long will it take the expert system to run and how fast will the expert system's questions and recommendations occur? The system needs to function fast enough to fit into the pace and demands of the user's job. Some jobs are batch jobs in the sense that certain decisions can be delayed and then made systematically with the help of the computer. Other jobs require that the performer make decisions while customers are waiting or during certain specific time periods. Expert systems can handle these "real-time" requirements, but it takes careful advanced planning to assure that it happens.

We would like to provide you with a good method for calculating how fast a given system will run, but it's quite impossible. It depends on the size of the system, which is hard to estimate before you develop the prototype and find out just how much knowledge the expert is really bringing to bear on a portion of the task. And it depends on the tool you use and the hardware you run it on. It's obviously the case that, other things being equal, large systems run slower than small systems, but "other things" are never equal. The steady introduction of powerful tools written in conventional languages and designed to run on 386 PCs and mainframes should go a long way toward resolving the speed problems that many have encountered when they tried to field mid- to large-size systems.

Accuracy. How accurate do the expert system's recommendations need to be? Can the system offer several different options and attach a confidence to each recommendation, or must it provide a single answer and be certain that answer is right? In general, the system will not be as comprehensive as an existing human expert. In most cases, developers have elected to develop systems that were 75 or 85 percent as comprehensive as the expert, relying on the users to ask the human expert when the system failed to make a recommendation. On the other hand, once the systems have been on the job for a while and have been enhanced to handle a large case load, they tend to be about as accurate as the human expert.

You need to examine the performance environment carefully to determine just what degree of accuracy is really required. Keep in mind that most people assume that computer systems, once the initial bugs have been removed, don't make mistakes. They accept the fact that a human expert operating in a complex area like loan approvals or chemical analysis might make "the best decision under the circumstances" and still occasionally be wrong. Unless they are carefully coached, however, they may not expect the same performance from an expert system.

Explanations. Most expert systems tools make it possible for the system to provide users with explanations of why a question is asked or how a specific recommendation was reached. Some users find this capability very important and others never use it. As a generalization, more sophisticated users who expect multiple recommendations and expect to consider the expert's advice and then make their own decisions demand explanations of an expert system just as they expect to be able to ask questions of a human expert before making up their mind. Users who just want specific advice that they will apply without further consideration usually don't expect an explanation facility and don't use it.

Examine what's happening in the user environment right now and then plan your expert system accordingly. Explanations can be offered, if needed.

Motivation. Ask yourself: What will happen if the users actually use the expert system? Will it make their jobs easier and more interesting, or will it put them under pressure to make more decisions per minute with less idea of what they are recommending? Ask yourself a second question: Even if you think it will make their jobs easier, how are they likely to perceive the news that an expert system is being developed to "improve decision making" in their department?

As a very strong generalization, people don't like to change what they already understand and can somehow handle. They don't like to be asked to do things that they don't consider to be part of their jobs. Moreover, they tend to resist doing things that will result in more work or in unpleasant consequences. This all sounds obvious, and it is. You can't afford to overlook it if you want your project to succeed.

Begin with a very clear idea of how the proposed expert system will change the way the users do their jobs. If you've considered the issues we've discussed, you'll have a good idea of how the users will access the system, when the system will be used, how long its use will take, and so on. If the system will make the users' jobs more complex or difficult, then there's a strong likelihood they will not use the system when it's completed.

If the system will simplify the users' jobs by freeing them from unwanted responsibilities or distracting routine questions, then you have a reasonable chance of success. The next step is to get the users together and explain exactly how you expect the expert system to function and how you expect it to improve their situation. The worst possible scenario is for users to be told nothing and then hear rumors that an expert system is being developed that will replace them. You can avoid most motivation problems by providing information and numerous opportunities for users to experiment with the expert system as it is developed.

Training. The use of an expert system often requires that users be trained. In some cases, expert systems primarily serve as training tools. In any case, you need to think about what will be involved in training the users to use the expert system and then develop a plan to facilitate that process. Training is especially important with an expert system because the odds are great that when the system is first tested in the field it will have numerous problems that will require correction.

Management Concerns

We have mentioned some of the issues that users worry about when confronted with an expert system. Now we turn to some of the issues that managers worry about when they consider allowing someone to undertake an expert systems development effort. In effect, the expert systems developer, like any successful innovator, is caught between the two extremes and must sell his effort both "up" and "down."

Career enhancement. Most of the early expert systems development efforts have happened because someone was willing to put a great deal of personal effort into the project. In some cases, this "sponsor" was the manager or developer who actually created the system. In other cases, the developer worked with someone in senior management who believed that the company should explore the possibilities of expert systems use.

In either case, enthusiasm, drive, and the support

of senior management are important ingredients of most successful early expert systems development efforts. Thus, just as you must sell users on the value of an expert system, you must also sell your management. If you are looking for an opportunity and, other things being equal, one department manager is more excited about having a system in her department than another, you should probably go with the enthusiastic manager.

You are, after all, trying to introduce change and, as we noted, people are inclined to avoid change whenever possible. Managers are especially inclined to avoid change since they are usually evaluated on short-term criteria over which they have considerable control. They may be less certain that they will be able to control things after an expert system has been introduced into their department. You need to sell them on the idea that an expert system will make their department and hence them look better. In other words, you need to convince them that sponsoring the introduction of an expert system will be a career enhancing move for them. To do that, you will typically need to convince them that it will eliminate a problem they have, reduce their costs, or increase their productivity. We discuss some of the ways you can measure the cost/benefits of expert systems in a bit, but the important thing now is to be sure you express the benefits of an expert system in terms that they can use when they explain the project to their manager.

You must also determine what kind of exposure the manager is willing to assume. Some managers get enthusiastic about expert systems, decide to sponsor a system, and want to undertake a project that will "make a big splash." They decide that only a mid-size system that will save really significant amounts of money will be worth the risk and hassle involved in their supporting and funding the development effort. Other managers decide they want to introduce expert systems in a very gradual, low-profile way. They do not want to take big risks; they want to test expert systems out on a small scale until they are convinced that the technology is really viable and useful. In talking with the managers who would be involved in any particular application development effort, you need to determine the manager's interests and concerns and be sure they match the effort you have in mind. It's better to reject a potential project than to try to push the project on a management team that really doesn't want to experiment with expert systems at the moment.

You should undertake your first effort in an environment where you can rely on strong management support. Ideally, you should identify an application for a department with a manager who is enthusiastic about expert systems and will help sell the system to other managers and promote the value of expert systems within your organization.

Cultural impact. Some organizations want to be involved in expert systems simply because it is a "cutting edge, high-tech" technology that they think the organization should know about. Other organizations are concerned that employees will be worried about their job security if they hear that the company is exploring expert systems. As with any new technology, a little mystery and glamour is an acceptable thing and helps motivate people to overcome their old habits and give it a try. But too much hype or mystery can get in the way. In general, it's best to position expert systems as a relatively logical extension of what is already being done in the organization and as an aid to help improve operations in some well-defined areas. Properly understood, expert systems have no mystery about them, just a lot of jargon and two very poorly chosen names (i.e., artificial intelligence and expert systems).

You should probably organize some meetings within your organization to let people know what expert systems are and how they can be useful. If you don't oversell the initial systems, you'll be much better off in the long run. Expert systems are, in fact, beginning to deliver quite impressive results. But, like other new technologies, there are going to be some failures and some less than exciting applications before people determine how to best use expert systems in their particular organization. Ideally, you should sell the potential payback and the willingness to experiment and learn without promising huge immediate gains or raising fears of vast organizational change.

The effective introduction of expert systems within an organization depends, in part, on the culture of the organization. You need to choose initial applications that will educate members of your organization without raising fears that can overwhelm your efforts before you even get your first system developed. A well-placed manager or "sponsor" who can talk to other managers, sell the value of expert systems, and head off problems before they develop can be a huge help to you in developing your first application.

Cost/benefit analysis. Early expert systems were often developed by R & D groups that were more interested in proving that an expert system could solve a problem than in actually solving the problem itself. Recent expert systems, however, have proved that expert systems can be efficient and cost effective. The best study of the economic benefits of expert systems is reported in Feigenbaum, McCorduck, and Nii's book, *The Rise of the Expert Company*. This book provides detailed case studies of many different systems and documents their economic benefits. It's the best book to give to senior managers who are skeptical about expert systems.

The dimensions of economic gain offered by the systems that Feigenbaum et al. studied include the following:

- Expert systems speed up professional and semi-professional work.

Using an expert system, one person can make decisions faster than before, thereby increasing the productivity of individuals and decreasing the demand for additional employees. In general, Feigenbaum observed improvements ranging from 10 to 100 times. In other words, expert systems result in productivity increases ranging from 1 to 2 orders of magnitude! Those are extraordinary numbers; economists are usually very happy to hear about productivity improvements of 3 to 7 percent. If this pattern holds, and we expect that it will, expert systems should soon fulfill the long cherished goal of computer advocates and revolutionize the productivity of offices.

When you consider an application, examine how the task is done now and how long it takes to do. Then calculate how long it might take to do if the person doing the task were using an expert system. Expect gains of 5 to 20 times and reject applications that speed up work less, unless they provide overwhelming cost savings in other areas. If you choose the right tasks, you should significantly improve the company's productivity.

- Expert systems result in internal cost savings.

Most companies that use expert systems report that they can plan better, can analyze the exact source of problems, and can develop more efficient designs. These efficiencies result in lower inventories and less wastage. Fewer errors and less scrap lead to significant savings. Also, since hardware can be diagnosed and repaired more quickly with expert systems, and decisions and plans can be made more quickly, there is much less human downtime.

- Expert systems improve the quality and the consistency of decision making.

Some companies value the increased quality and consistency of decision making that results from the use of expert systems because it reduces their exposure to lawsuits, regulatory problems, or customer complaints. Equally important is the fact that if employees make better decisions the company usually saves money. Better credit decisions reduce the company's losses. Better purchasing decisions lead to more cost-effective operations.

- Expert systems result in new products and services.

Other companies are using expert systems to create new business opportunities. Some expert systems allow companies to offer customers more options, while still others allow companies to rapidly simulate a variety of solutions to problems that can help their engineers and designers create new products more rapidly. By capturing and distributing expertise, expert systems can create new business opportunities that would otherwise come about only if the company could afford to hire large numbers of creative human experts and spread them throughout the company. The cost of the automated expertise is so low, however, that it can be used in many "trivial" ways that could hardly justify a human expert. And those "trivial" uses add up; they lead to better product designs, better service advice, and new ways of handling many small problems more efficiently and effectively.

- Expert systems capture organizational know-how and make it available for sale or for internal consulting.

In effect, expert systems are a new and more effective way of "publishing" knowledge. An expert system can package company expertise in a form that allows for its sale. In the past, an expert might have spent time writing a procedures manual or elaborate instructions; now that same expert can develop an expert system that is much more efficient and effective in communicating information to users.

Many consulting companies are now using expert systems to package the knowledge of their experts to assist their own staff or their clients in solving problems.

- Return on Investment (ROI)

Feigenbaum's book reports that most expert systems more than pay back the investment the companies spent in building them. One good example are the many PC-based systems that have been built by technicians at Du Pont. By the summer of 1988, Du Pont had fielded some 100 systems. The typical system took about two months to build and runs on a conventional PC or VAX. The investment, on the average, was about $25,000. The typical system saves Du Pont from $100,000 to $200,000 per year. Different companies use different methods to calculate ROI, but any way you do it, Du Pont's small expert systems are paying off handsomely.

SUMMARY

After reading these two chapters, you should be able to select an appropriate application for your expert systems development. You can use the Application Analysis Worksheet provided in Figure 3.3 to help you evaluate each potential application. Companies like Du Pont, Texas Instruments, IBM, and Northrop have found hundreds of useful applications for expert systems. The trick is to choose your early applications well so that you can gain experience about what works best at your company.

Section Three

KNOWLEDGE ACQUISITION AND SYSTEM DESIGN

In Section Two of this book, we discussed how to identify expert systems opportunities. In this section, we focus on the concepts and processes involved in acquiring knowledge and designing expert systems applications. You can use many of the concepts discussed here in different phases of expert systems development. In developing a small, simple expert system, you might want to gather data and consider aspects of a potential application during an initial interview, while for a larger application, you might choose to put off such knowledge acquisition until a later phase of the development effort. For example, in mid- to large-size projects, where the role of the human expert or experts is very important and often entirely separate from the role of the knowledge engineer, extensive discussions between the knowledge engineer and the expert(s) may occur at several different points during the analysis and design of the potential application. On the other hand, in the case of many small to mid-size applications, the developer and the human expert are the same person, and formal interviews between the expert and the knowledge engineer simply don't occur.

We begin our discussion of the basic concepts of knowledge acquisition and design in Chapter 5, with an examination of how to analyze a specific task. In Section Two, we discussed the types of problems that might yield to an expert systems approach. In this section, we aim to be more concrete. Once you have identified a potential application, you need to gather information and study that application in considerable detail to be sure that it will in fact be cost-effective. This process is sometimes called *scoping the problem*. Others refer to this detailed study of a potential application as a *front end analysis*. This effort occurs before you begin to enter knowledge into the computer, and it consists of asking all of the smart questions you can in order to define the exact scope and nature of your expert system before you actually commit to the development effort. We consider here the various concepts and techniques that people use when they choose and scope potential applications.

In Chapter 5 we will consider how one scopes the overall flow of a task. A detailed study of how people perform a task is generally called a task analysis. We will also consider how you can use data flow diagrams to document the overall structure of a task.

In Chapter 6, we move beyond task analysis and consider how to describe the cognitive content of a problem-solving task. This analysis should guide your overall understanding of the knowledge you need to include in your system and the inference and control strategies you might use to manipulate that knowledge.

Chapter 7 introduces the process of knowledge acquisition. Here we will consider the procedures and techniques that you will need to use to obtain information from a human expert.

5.
Analyzing a Consultation

INTRODUCTION

This chapter discusses some of the concepts and techniques that a knowledge engineer can use to define the particular nature of a problem or opportunity. *Task analysis* is concerned with scoping and defining a problem based on observation and interviews with an expert. The goal of a task analysis is to be able to describe the activities that surround the expert: the inputs the expert receives, the outputs the expert makes, when the expert asks questions or turns to a database for additional information, the success of typical recommendations, and so on. It is not concerned with the actual knowledge that the expert uses in reasoning about a problem and deciding on a solution.

In effect, a task analysis is concerned with the environment that surrounds the expert. In the next chapter, we consider how to analyze the knowledge and the cognitive processes that the expert uses in solving a problem. In psychological terms, a task analysis is concerned with the observable behaviors that occur in the environment when the task is performed, while a cognitive analysis is concerned with the knowledge and covert reasoning processes that occur inside the expert's head.

We have already considered the basic input/output (I/O) diagram. The basic concept is that at the highest or most abstract level of analysis, you can conceptualize the human expert or the problem-solving procedure as a "black box." You cannot observe what goes on inside the box, but you can see when people make requests for help and when the expert makes a recommendation.

The essence of knowledge engineering is figuring out what goes on inside the black box and encoding it using knowledge structures and inference strategies. But before we turn to the analysis of knowledge and inference, we want to be sure you completely understand the observable nature of the task and that you are, in fact, defining or selecting a task that will be worth analyzing.

If you are concerned with a classic "expert systems" problem, where there is one human expert whom people call up when they need help solving very complex problems, then you could probably skip this chapter and go right to Chapter 6, where we discuss how to analyze the knowledge that your expert uses in solving problems. Most of you, however, will be less involved in capturing the knowledge possessed by well-known experts. Instead, you will be looking for opportunities to capture a portion of the knowledge possessed by managers and technicians. This makes task analysis more difficult; it is easier simply to set out to capture all or most of the knowledge a single individual has in a particular domain.

You will need to identify the opportunities for smaller expert systems and the specific tasks within jobs that would benefit most from a small to mid-size system. This chapter is designed to help you analyze an overall organization in order to identify "knowledge bottlenecks" and other expert systems opportunities. Moreover, it should help you develop a good description of the environmental requirements that must be met if you are to develop a successful small to mid-size system.

We will consider two ways to analyze the environment in which problem-solving tasks occur.

1. Examine why people have trouble performing these tasks. You must be sure to focus on knowledge-based tasks and not on motivational problems.

2. Consider how a conventional dataflow analysis will help to analyze these tasks. When you run into difficulties with a dataflow approach, it is time to turn from task analysis to the knowledge-based approach we discuss in Chapter 6.

To summarize what we discuss in this chapter, we return at the end of the chapter to our basic I/O model and provide you with a set of questions that you should be able to answer about the flow of any task you are considering as a potential expert system.

HUMAN PERFORMANCE ANALYSIS

We considered a number of human performance issues in Chapters 3 and 4 that we want to return to briefly here. We want to review a few heuristics that psychologists have developed to predict what sort of interventions will be effective under what circumstances.

Consider Figure 5.1. This diagram provides an overview of all the key components that affect a performer as he tries to do his job. To simplify things, assume that you are analyzing a job performed entirely by one individual. Moreover, assume that the individual performs only a single job. For example, you can examine a senior officer in a securities firm. This individual is responsible for checking a certain type of contract to be sure that it is complete and accurate.

You can now use a model to analyze this hypothetical example.

1. *Situation.* The situation is the arrival of a contract.
2. *Performer.* The performer is the individual who checks the contracts. That individual, presumably, uses knowledge and problem-solving skills in examining the contract.
3. *Work Environment.* The work environment includes all of the tools and materials available to the performer as he performs the task. Figure 5.1 suggests that the performer here has a telephone, a computer, and the ability to check with an expert when he encounters special problems. (The individual might also have a procedures manual and law books that define the contract, relevant laws, and company policies regarding complex cases.)
4. *Feedback.* Feedback is a special part of the performer's work environment. It refers to information that the performer receives about the quality and quantity of previous work (Output). Feedback serves to motivate the performer and to allow him to improve by avoiding certain previous errors or by doing things that are being reinforced.
5. *Output.* Output refers to the products that result from the performer's effort. In this example, the output would be "approved contracts."
6. *Results.* The results refer to the consequences that occur as a result of the performer's output. If the approved contracts are all correctly approved and the consequences of funding the approved contracts are all positive, the results are desirable. Information about the correctness of the work and the nature of the consequences resulting from the work, when given to the performer, constitutes feedback.

You can use this basic overview of a human performance system if you are faced with human performance problems and you want to determine what might be causing them. You simply work through the entire performance system, asking questions about each component. The following sections provide a good idea of the types of problems that can occur in each portion of the system and give you specific questions to ask for each problem.

Situation

Problems caused by some abnormality in the situation result when the performer is unable to determine when it is appropriate to begin action. A performer might receive several memos, for example, and be uncertain which required further action and which should simply be noted and filed. A machine operator might not know what signs to look for to determine if periodic maintenance was indicated. Or,

Figure 5.1 The human performance system. The major components of the performer's environment should be examined before deciding if an expert system should be developed.

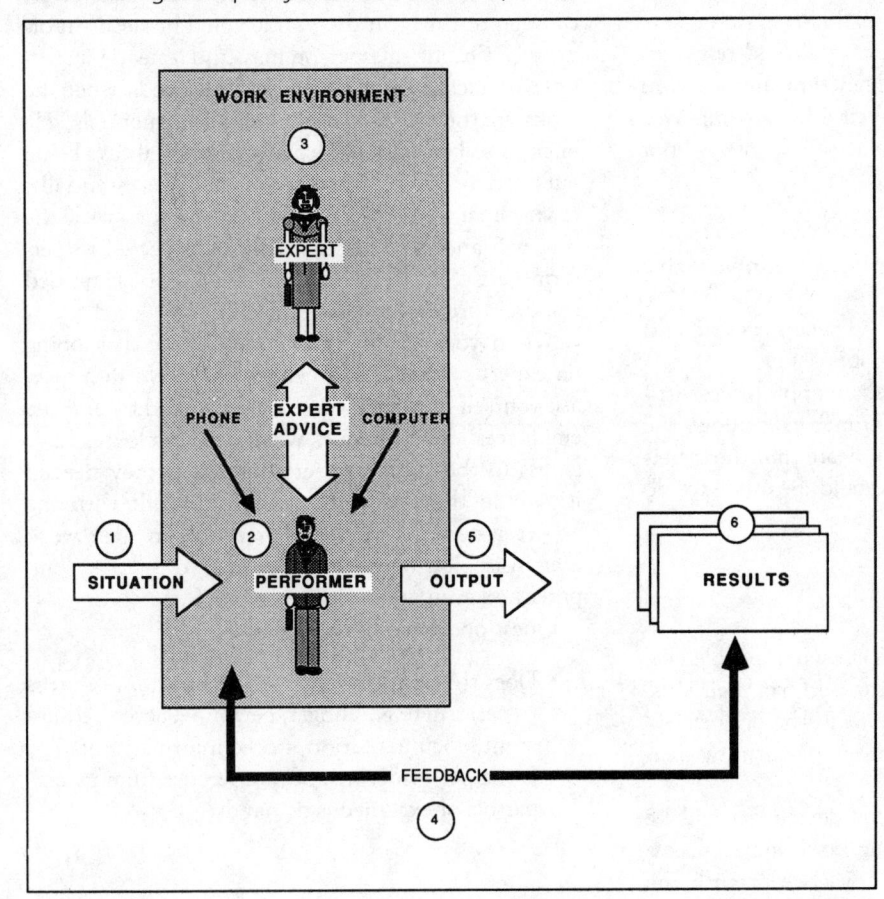

in the case of a nuclear power plant operator faced with 80 blinking lights, the situation might simply be overwhelming.

Questions to ask:

- Is the need for performance recognized by the performer?
- Does the performer know which stimulus to respond to in what order?

Performer

Performer problems occur when the performer is mismatched to the job, when the performer lacks the skill or the knowledge to perform correctly, or when the performer's attitude is inappropriate. Some jobs have physical requirements. Most jobs require that the performer know or acquire specific knowledge and particular skills. Most skill/knowledge problems are caused by a lack of training, a lack of practice or previous experience, or a lack of information necessary to perform appropriately.

Computers present performers with a host of special problems. In most cases, for example, a performer needs typing skills to be able to use a computer. The performer also needs to understand how the computer's operating system works and to have some concept of the architecture of the programs being used.

Problems caused by an inappropriate attitude or deficient self-image normally manifest themselves as skill/knowledge problems. They involve statements by employees that they cannot, or should not, perform in a particular manner. They typically show up in the way people talk about their jobs; an employee may simply assert that some part of the task is "not what I was hired to do."

Questions to ask:

- Is the performer physically and emotionally able to perform?
- Does the performer have the necessary skill and knowledge to perform the job?
- Does the performer have an appropriate attitude? (e.g., Does the performer talk about the job in positive terms and indicate that the task is one that she can and should be able to do correctly?)

The Work Environment

Work environment problems occur when people lack the necessary tools or resources to perform their jobs. They are also caused when events in the performers' environment prevent them from performing correctly or on time.

In most cases, expert systems developers will be considering the problems arising from limited access to someone with specialized knowledge or with the inefficiency or inadequacy of documentation or existing computer programs that the performer is expected to use. Access to databases or information stored on other computers is a common environmental problem faced by many performers.

For example, imagine a situation in which a salesperson is expected to handle customer questions about products the company sells. If there is only one phone line and one salesperson, there may be complaints about never being able to gain access to the person for information. Assuming the salesperson is constantly on the phone, then it is hardly the salesperson's fault; it simply stems from a lack of resources to do the job right. On the other hand, the salesperson may have to get information from other product managers in order to answer certain questions, and he may find that he can never locate them or get through to them on the phone when he needs information. Or, the salesperson may find it nearly impossible to locate the information he needs when he looks in the product documentation manuals. He might also be frustrated by the manuals always being out of date. All of these problems are, essentially, environmental problems. The salesperson, with the best will and effort, can hardly be expected to perform very well in an environment in which needed resources are unavailable.

When you consider the possibility of developing an expert system to help employees perform a task, ask yourself how the expert system would fit into the employees' environment. Would the employees have access to the computer terminal when they needed it? Would they have the time to consult with the expert system, or would other people in their work area insist that they "do something" before the computer had even arrived at an answer?

Questions to ask:

- Does the performer have the necessary resources to perform (e.g., budget, personnel access, equipment, documentation, stored information)?
- Is the performer free of interference from incompatible or extraneous demands?

Feedback

Feedback problems take two general forms. In one, the individual may not get information about the adequacy of her performance. For example, our contract evaluation officer may approve and disapprove contracts and never be told if his performance is always correct or only occasionally correct. The other general problem is when performance-related feedback is saved for quarterly or semi-annual performance appraisals, which is usually far too late to help the individual improve her performance. Immediate feedback is the key to helping people improve at their jobs. If you don't know when the work you are doing is good or bad, it is obviously hard to improve.

To increase the motivational value of feedback,

you can couple it with rewards and punishments designed to support appropriate performance. Problems occur when there is a lack of positive consequences after correct performance or negative consequences following correct performance. Positive consequences following incorrect performance, or poor timing of any kind of consequences can also affect how people perform their jobs. For example, assume our contract officer, Jones, is doing a good job. His boss recognizes that he is doing a good job but doesn't bother to tell him, since good work, after all, is what's expected. What the boss does do, however, is to give Jones more work, since he is doing it correctly, while reducing the work given to another employee, Smith, who seems to be having trouble. In effect, the only thing that Jones gets for doing good work is more work. Smith, on the other hand, is rewarded for poor work by having his workload reduced. Obviously, there may occasionally be some need for this kind of work redistribution, but it must be associated with clear feedback about why it is occurring. Jones needs to be told that he is doing good work and asked to take on some additional work while the boss tries to straighten out Smith. Smith needs to be told that his work reduction is not in fact a reward but an effort to help him come up to standards, failing which he will be demoted or fired. Many problems that seem to be related to skill or knowledge may in fact be related to the effects flowing from the consequences of a performer's work.

Another way of thinking about motivational problems is to contrast them to skill/knowledge problems. Motivational problems arise when the individual knows how to perform, but doesn't. Dr. Thomas F. Gilbert, the best-known human performance engineering theorist, suggests a thought experiment to help distinguish motivational problems from skill/knowledge problems. When you face a situation in which a performer is not doing a task, you need to determine if the performer is failing to perform because she doesn't know how to do the task or because she lacks motivation. Dr. Gilbert suggests you ask yourself: If the employee's life depended upon it, would she be able to do the task? If, under such threatening circumstances the performer could manage to do the task correctly, you then have a motivational problem. If she couldn't do the task even if her life depended on it, then you have a skill/knowledge problem. This is certainly a dramatic way of stating it, but the point is clearly to convince you that there are many motivational problems in the world of business, and expert systems can't fix them. The major way to change a person's motivation is to change the feedback or consequences that follow the performance of the job or task.

Questions to ask:

- Is the performer provided with frequent and relevant feedback as to how well, or how poorly, the job is being performed?
- Does the performer receive any feedback or rewards for correct or incorrect performance?

Output

Output describes the work that the performer produces. It may be a telephone call to tell someone to go ahead with a project, initials on a document submitted for approval, several forms generated by the employee, or a report. In all cases, there are two ways that output is judged. It may be judged by standards developed by a manager, or it may be judged by the person who actually benefits from the work (results). A manager might check an employee's output to determine if enough units were produced during a given period, if the work looked "neatly done," if the output was complete, and so on.

Questions to ask:

- What standards does the department impose on the performer?
- Does the performer know how his output is judged? (Does the performer know how to differentiate between adequate and inadequate output?)

Results

Results occur when a performer's output is given to someone else who reacts to the output with either happiness or dismay. If the output arrives on someone else's desk and the recipient doesn't know where the product or service came from, the performer will probably not get adequate feedback. The individual who will "consume" the product or service is the only one who can realistically evaluate its value. If work is simply passed on without evaluation, the performer will tend to stray off target and may decide that the work isn't very important. Important work results in consequences that can be easily evaluated. Salespeople are almost always given goals and told how well they are doing. Many valuable technical and staff people, however, do work that is never evaluated, at least as far as the performer knows. Our contract evaluation officer, for example, may or may not know if his effort to eliminate bad contracts is really saving the company any money.

Ideally, there should be a close connection between the criteria that management uses to evaluate output and the real value of the results to the consumer. If managers are checking for neatly prepared reports and the consumers of the reports don't care about neatness but want the raw data sooner, then you clearly have a discrepancy that needs to be straightened out.

Questions to ask:

- Are the results of the performer's output recorded and evaluated?
- Does the performer get feedback about the results of her effort?
- Is there a reasonable match between the criteria that management uses to check the performer's output and the value of the performer's results?

Summary of Performance Variables

We have discussed these different performance variables to suggest that a perceived performance problem or inadequate result may or may not be the result of a knowledge problem that could be solved by an expert system.

Perhaps the most important heuristic to take away from this discussion is that knowledge or training will almost never change a problem that results from a motivational deficiency. If people are punished, directly or indirectly, for producing the right results, they will tend to avoid producing the desired results no matter what knowledge or training they are offered.

On the other hand, many problems arise from situations that exist in the performer's environment. Many of these problems are associated with inadequate communication, the difficulty of finding the right people at the right time, or inadequate documentation or procedures. The most sophisticated approach to analyzing entire organizations and combining workflow and performance analysis is illustrated by Dr. Geary Rummler's work in organizational analysis. Using a top-down approach, Dr. Rummler works with companies to identify all of the flows of resources, information, and feedback within an organization. This approach takes time, but it is a highly effective way to identify all of the knowledge bottlenecks in an organization while simultaneously assuring that you are, in fact, focused on knowledge problems and not motivational or other environmental problems. Figure 5.2 is a reproduction of an initial organizational flow plan that Dr. Rummler did for a corporation. He went on to identify all of the various flows within a particular department.

Memorization versus Job Aids

Human performance analysts make another useful distinction when they are faced with skill/knowledge problems. A skill/knowledge problem occurs when you must provide a performer with the knowledge he needs to analyze and solve a problem. There are basically two approaches: You can help the performer memorize the information he needs to perform the task, or you can provide the employee with some kind of job aid that he can use when he needs to solve the problem.

Most organizations tend to treat human performance problems as training problems. If the employee can't do the job, you train him to do it. This usually means that you put the employee in a classroom where he is told how to do the task and then, in the best cases, allowed to practice doing the task until he demonstrates that he has, in effect, memorized how

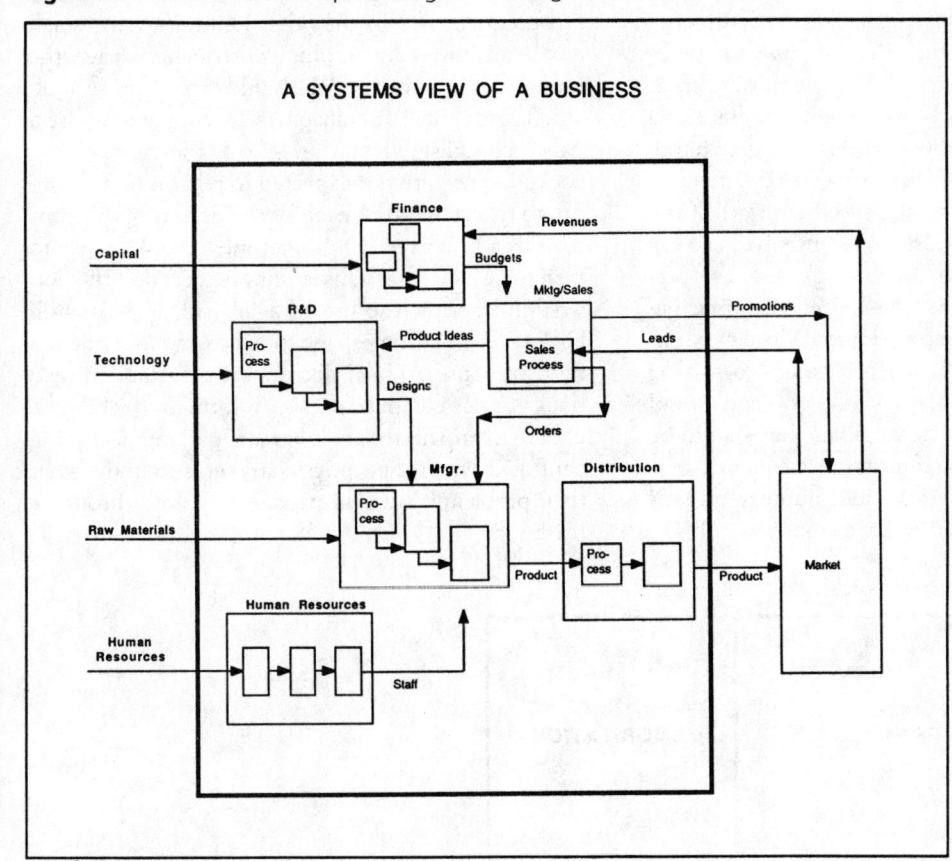

Figure 5.2 A Rummler-Brache top-level diagram of an organization.

to do it. The problem with memorization is that people forget, especially if much time passes between when they are taught the task and when they are asked to actually perform the task.

The alternative is to provide the individual with some kind of job or performance aid that will help him perform when he attempts to do the task. If you assign a person a new home telephone number, you expect that he will memorize it. If you train someone to use a word processing program, you expect that he will memorize the commands he needs to know to start up the computer, load the program, and use it to create text files. Additionally, you can expect that he will have learned how to type (memorize which keys cause which letters to appear on the screen). In a sense, if you memorize something, you make it into habitual behavior.

On the other hand, if you asked a person to give you the telephone number for a local hospital, you would expect her to look it up in a telephone book. There are too many telephone numbers to memorize; it's simply more efficient to use a job aid, like the telephone book, to get specific numbers when they are needed. Likewise, when an individual uses an expert system to help analyze a particular situation, the expert system is really a sophisticated job aid. The individual does not need to memorize all of the knowledge in the expert system, only enough to use the system to help get the answer.

Table 5.1 provides some criteria to help you decide

whether memorization or job aids are appropriate for the performance of a particular task. If response speed is very important, then the responses will probably need to be memorized. You wouldn't expect heart surgeons or fullbacks to consult a job aid at a critical moment in their work. (On the other hand, fighter pilots may soon depend on expert systems to assist them in flying very high-speed aircraft). If the task is infrequently performed or involves a very complex decision-making process, job aids are preferred. People forget, and the longer the time between practice, the more they forget. Moreover, human beings are very poor when it comes to solving complex problems with many variables. People tend to forget one or more of the variables that should be taken into consideration. If tasks are frequently performed and involve only a limited number of variables, then they can usually be memorized. This is especially true if the results of a small error are inconsequential. On the other hand, if even a small error can have catastrophic consequences, then the human performing the job should probably use a job aid. (Commercial aircraft pilots are supposed to use a paper checklist when they check the dials in the cockpit. They are not expected to rely on their memory to determine that each of the dozens of different dials reads correctly.) Sometimes people have to memorize their responses simply because the job wouldn't permit the use of a job aid, like our fullback. At other times, job prestige requires memorized responses. Thus, doctors are reluctant to read books or use computers to get information while the patient is in the room. Likewise, patients feel more confident when their physician seems to know what their problem is without pausing to search through a textbook.

Table 5.1 Choosing between Memorization and Job Aids.

IF	THEN
• Response speed is very important (more important than accuracy). • Small errors won't have large consequences. • Task is frequently performed. • Reading instructions or using a computer would interfere with performance. • Job prestige requires a memorized response.	Choose **MEMORIZATION**
• Response speed isn't as important as accuracy (small errors have large consequences). • Tasks are infrequently performed. • Tasks involve many steps. • Tasks involve complex decision-making process. • Reading instructions or using a computer won't interfere with performance.	Choose **JOB AIDS**

Some expert systems have been built to help people learn memorized responses. These systems take the form of simulators that allow users to practice making responses and evaluating results until they have memorized the correct way to respond.

Most small to mid-size expert systems function as intelligent job aids; they provide advice while the person is actually engaged in performing her job.

Expert systems can be effectively used to solve knowledge-based problems in the following ways:

1. To help a performer obtain information from the environment—in this sense, they completely or partially eliminate the need to call a human expert
2. To provide a more effective source of documentation or policy information
3. To capture some of the performer's own knowledge and thus automate a part of the job
4. To answer questions the expert would otherwise have to answer, thus avoiding frequent disturbances
5. To train an employee to memorize responses to complex situations that will arise on the job

In all of these cases, expert systems can help improve the effectiveness and efficiency of an employee.

Remember always to be certain that it's really a knowledge problem you are focused on. Expert systems can't compensate for poor motivation or inadequate feedback.

DATAFLOW ANALYSIS

Dataflow analysis and the diagrams that result from it are usually thought of as a part of structured programming, a top-down approach to designing conventional computer applications. Dataflow analysis is a very effective way to analyze small and mid-size problems to determine their overall structure. It is especially effective when the problem has a procedural or step-by-step cast to it. Dataflow techniques are less effective as problems grow more complex or take on a more judgmental cast. In those cases, you should probably turn to an object-oriented analysis of the problem, which we discuss in Chapter 6. Even if the problem suggests an object-oriented approach, however, you should still subdivide the overall problem as far as you can, and a dataflow analysis can help do that.

The basic idea behind dataflow analysis is to divide a problem into discrete activities, processes, or computations and show the data that is passed from one activity to another. A dataflow diagram represents processes as circles and the data that is passed between one process and another (a dataflow) as an arrow. In effect, processes are the verbs and data are the nouns of a dataflow diagram. We recommend following Tom DeMarco's suggestion that processes should always be described with active names. (DeMarco's work comes as close to being the standard work on dataflow analysis as anyone's, and we have tried to use his definitions here for consistency with other works on dataflow.)

In addition to processes and dataflows, there are data sources (initial inputs), data stores (databases) that accept dataflows, and a destination that receives the system's output. In addition, dataflow diagrams include data dictionary entries that define the nature of the data that makes up the dataflow. (See Figure 5.3)

To start dataflow analysis, you begin with the highest, most abstract view of a dataflow system, which is usually labeled the *0-level* view and is comprised of a system with only one or a very few processes. In fact, the top-level diagram is usually just like the I/O diagrams we have already considered. (See Figure 5.4.) The top-level diagram identifies the source of input, the end user of the expert system, and any major data stores that the expert system accesses.

The next step in the analysis is to break out the details of the top-level diagram into a more elaborate description of the processes (analysis and decision steps) and dataflows that comprise the expert system. The trick in doing this is to keep the logical level of the processes and the dataflows consistent from one level to another.

Figure 5.5 illustrates a second-level dataflow diagram that describes a hypothetical knowledge base for a site assessment system. This example is drawn

100 KNOWLEDGE ACQUISITION

Figure 5.3 Basic vocabulary of a dataflow diagram.

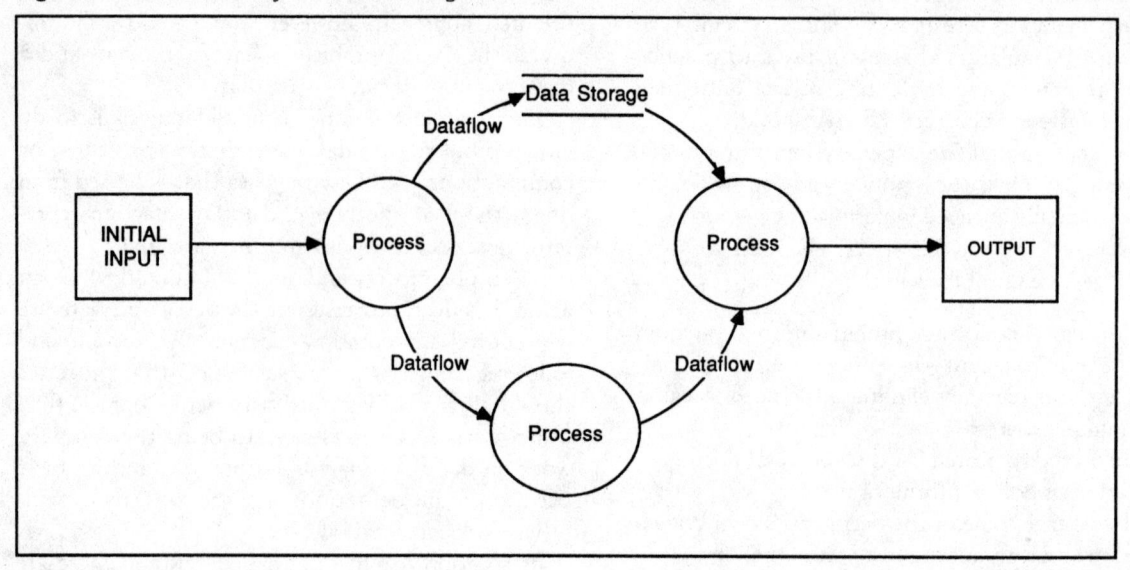

from an article written by Richard Duda and others from Syntelligence to illustrate their use of a dataflow approach in developing expert systems for banking and insurance applications.

Figure 5.6 is a third-level diagram of a portion of the hypothetical site selection system, showing only the processes and dataflows that occur within the overall Assess Physical Facility module of the second-level diagram. Obviously, you would not want to combine modules from the level-three diagram with the more abstract modules of the level-two diagram. There is no hard and fast method for assuring that each level considers modules of more or less the same level of abstraction. It's a problem that requires some trial and error efforts; you try one cut, look at it, then try another, and so on.

The site selection system is a large system that is primarily focused on analyzing a large amount of initial data. Hence, there are no data stores, and each of the processes can be thought of as a small

Figure 5.4 Top-level dataflow diagram for Oracle Credit Advisor.

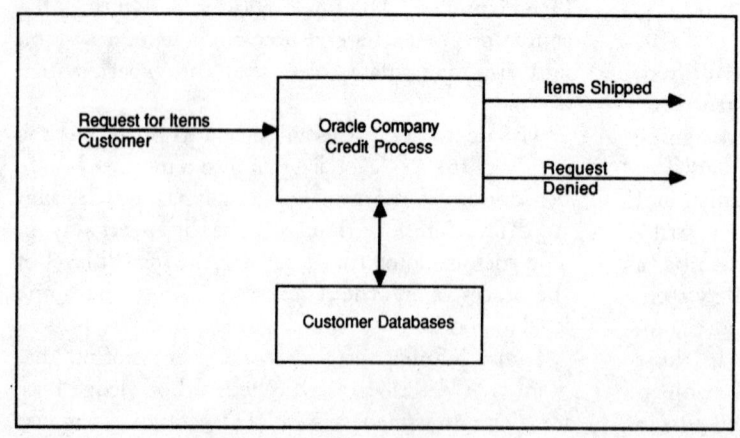

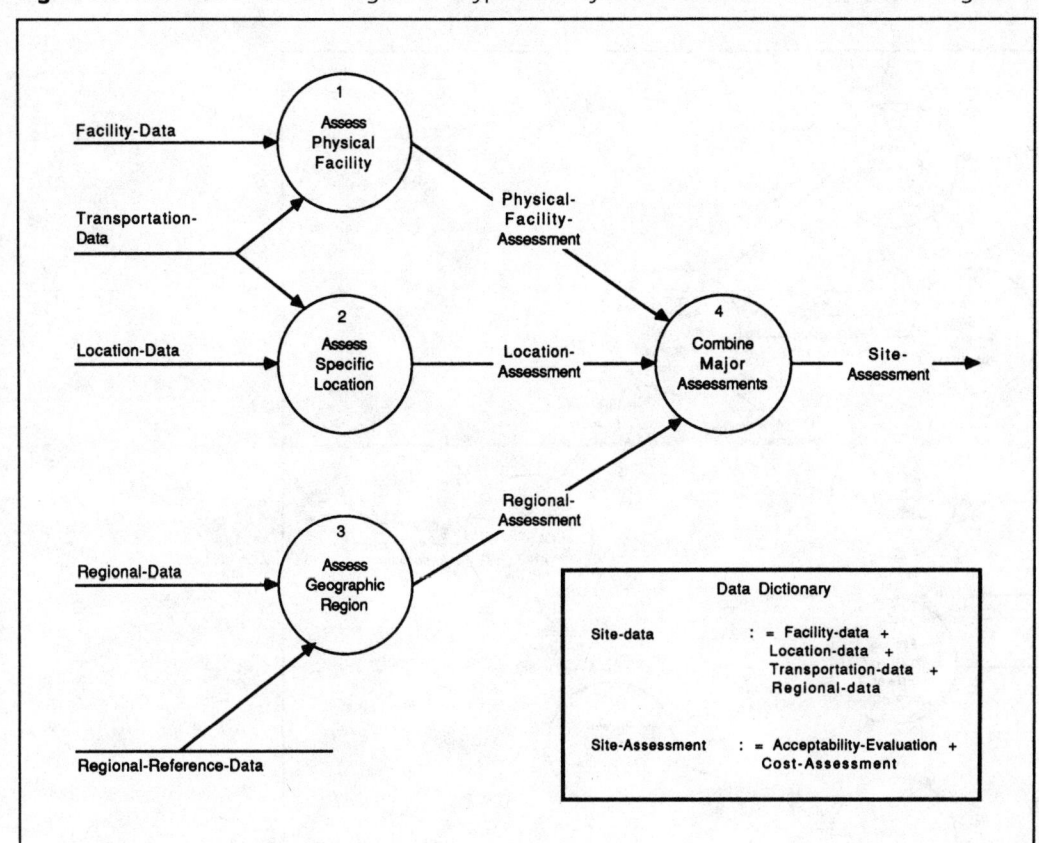

Figure 5.5 Second-level dataflow diagram of a hypothetical system to assist a commercial real estate agent in site assessment.

expert system that analyzes the data and makes a recommendation that it passes on to subsequent nodes.

Oracle Credit Advisor is a better example of a typical small system. Figure 5.7 illustrates the second-level dataflow diagram of Oracle. This diagram has already appeared in Chapter 4, where we used it to illustrate a task that could be broken down into several steps.

Notice in Figure 5.7 that there are several different types of processes involved, and several different databases accessed to get information for the credit evaluation process. The first node, for example, involves taking a customer order. There might be some problem solving involved in this process, such as checking to be sure that all of the needed information is complete and consistent. More likely, however, this process simply involves data entry. By the same token, the nodes for checking customer status and processing an invoice are essentially procedural tasks. You might use an expert system to help accomplish them, especially if the application were small or if you thought the procedures used knowledge that would change frequently in the future. If you were a programmer, however, it's more likely you would program these processes using a conventional language. The one process shown on the dataflow diagram in Figure 5.7 that really suggests an expert system is the Manual Credit Review that the CEO performs on rejected customer records. Here, clearly,

Figure 5.6 A third-level diagram of the site selection system. The diagram shows only the process and dataflows in the Assess Physical Facility module of Figure 5.5.

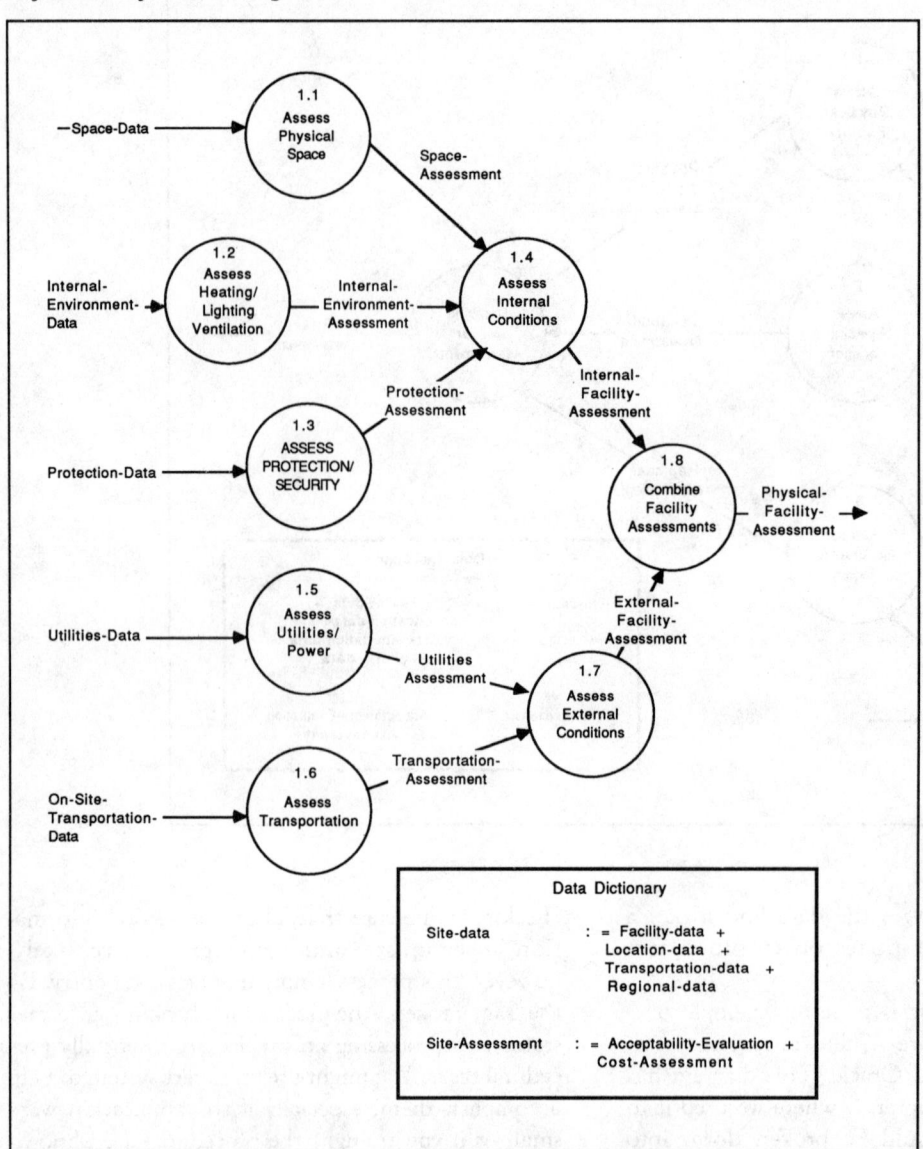

judgment is called for and heuristics are probably used. Hence, only one node of this overall task is an obvious candidate for an expert system.

The process of carefully laying out the whole operation and then identifying the step or steps that are best suited for an expert system is very important.

Frequently, when you carefully document a current operation, as shown in Figure 5.7, you will see opportunities to reorganize the entire operation. You should carefully consider these opportunities before you move on to your expert systems development effort, because any change in the structure of the operation could easily affect the system's requirements.

In a situation like the one faced by Oracle, for example, insertion of the expert system might not change the overall structure of the operation at all; the expert system might be used by someone in the CEO's suite to check rejected customer records. On the other hand, it might make sense to put the expert system in the sales or data processing departments so they could quickly determine if the applicant was eligible for credit. It would certainly improve customer satisfaction if borderline cases could be told, while waiting on the phone, "yes, we can grant you credit," or vice versa.

If you decide to combine an expert system with a conventional program that could check the customer status, and you wanted to place the entire system in the sales offices, you would need to consider if there were computers in the sales offices, if the salespeople would have the time and motivation to use the system, and other factors affecting deployment.

Expert systems often depend on information from users to keep them up to date. Thus, there are often good reasons to rearrange the current way an operation is performed in order to place the decision-making power that expert systems provide in the hands of users, rather than in the back offices or in the hands of a manager or staff expert.

When you consider developing an expert system, you should do a comprehensive analysis to see if it is appropriate to restructure an operation in order to take full advantage of the power of an expert system.

Figure 5.7 Second-level dataflow diagram of Oracle Credit Advisor.

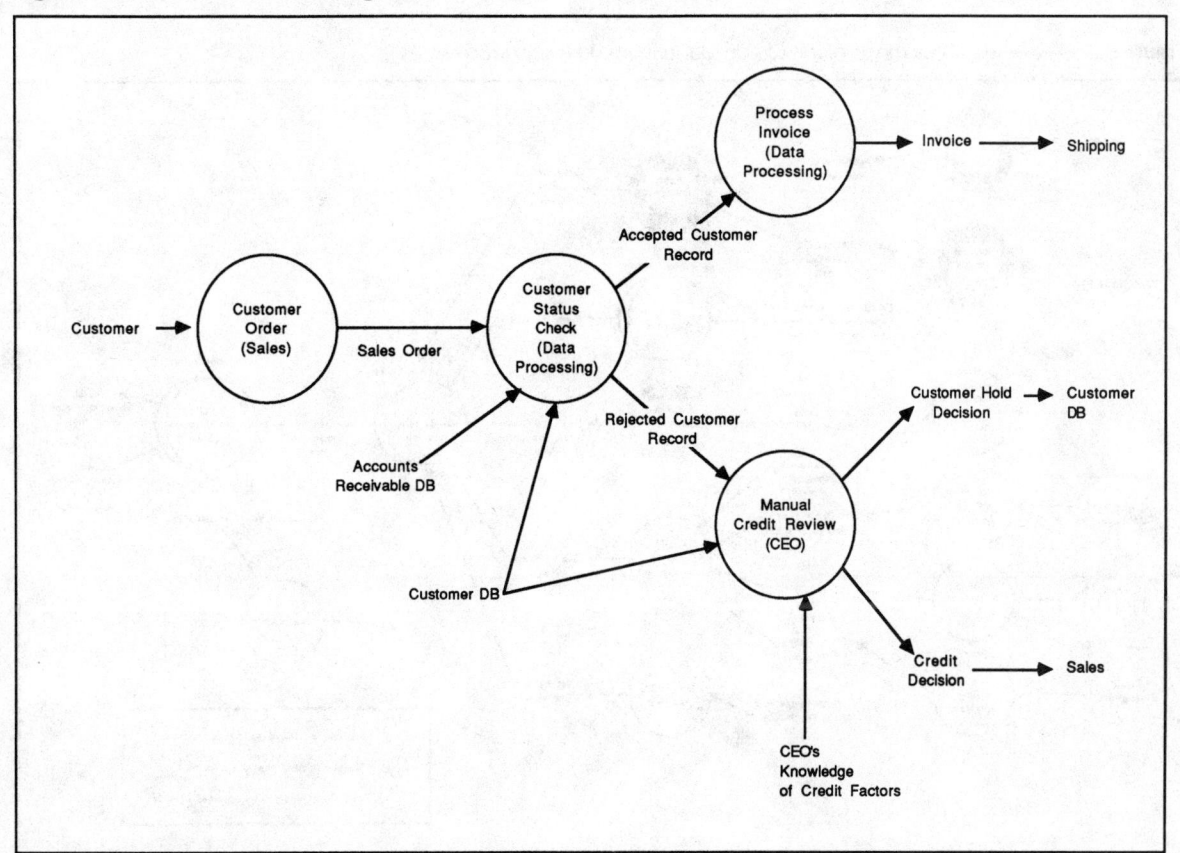

104 KNOWLEDGE ACQUISITION

Smaller, more streamlined organizations are usually more productive organizations. Expert systems provide organizations with techniques that can be used not only to capture expertise but also to redesign the organizations to facilitate more distributed, end-user analysis and decision making.

No matter where you decide to locate the Oracle Credit Advisor system, you would need to analyze the Manual Credit Review process in more detail, both in order to understand the analysis effort that occurs and to determine if there is a portion of the task that you could capture during your prototype development effort.

Figure 5.8 provides a detailed dataflow model of the Manual Credit Review process. Notice that all the flows have been labeled to indicate if they involve data derived from a database (db) or if they involve a judgment (infer). As you examine the various nodes of the detailed dataflow model, you might think that some processes could be accomplished by an algorithm while others might involve the use of heuristics. Volume Value Analysis, for example, is probably an algorithmic task, while Credit History Risk Analysis probably involves some vague judgment calls that will be better handled with heuristic rules. Obviously, you will have to discuss each process with the expert (in this case, the Oracle CEO) to determine what is involved in that part of the overall operation.

You should also consider exactly what information is drawn from each database identified on your dataflow chart. You need to know where the data resides and what would be involved in obtaining it. For example, is the data extracted from a database by electronic means, or is it read from a report that might contain extraneous data? Is the data absolutely

Figure 5.8 Detailed dataflow model of the Oracle Manual Credit Review Process.

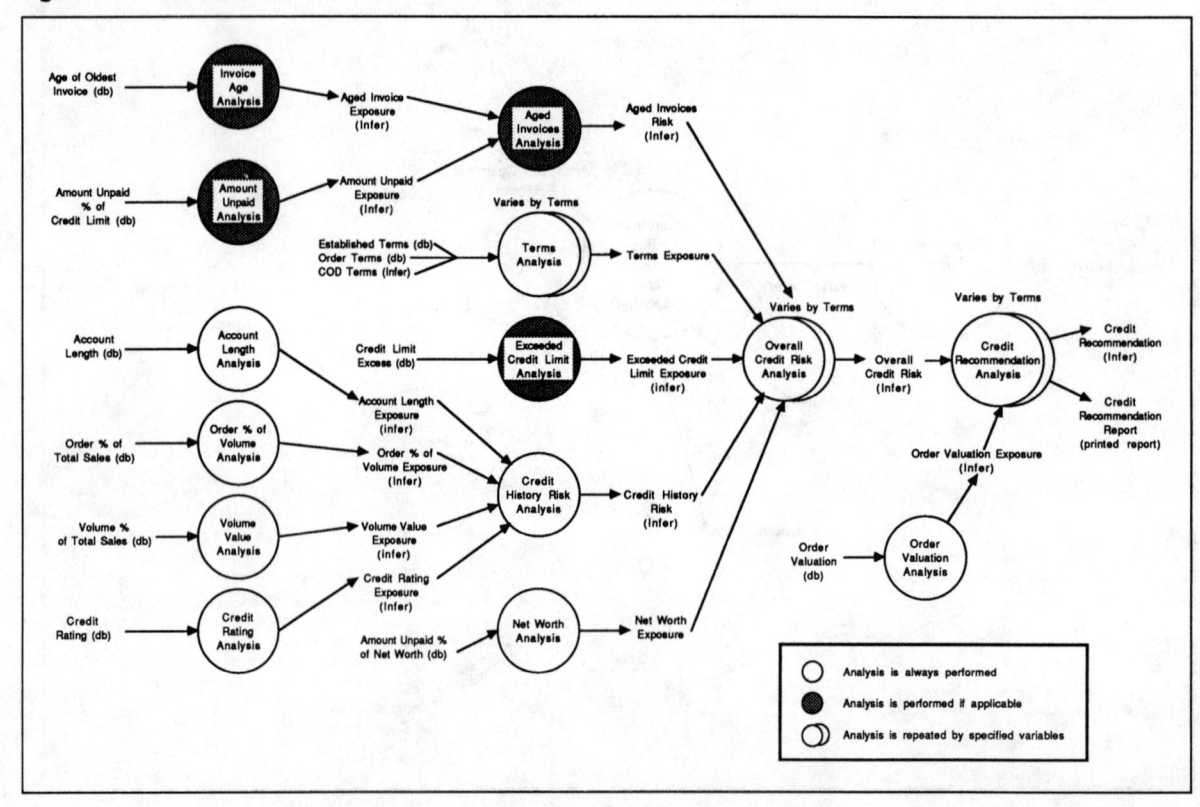

reliable, or does the expert sometimes weigh data by applying heuristics to correct for problems previously encountered when using the data? Different tools and different procedures are involved, depending on how the data is named, grouped, and stored. (We discuss these matters in more detail in Chapter 13.) You need to anticipate problems by answering basic questions about any data the expert system might need to use before you can move on to an analysis of the cognitive content of the decision-making task.

A good dataflow analysis of an operation guarantees that you have examined the overall nature of the task in the detail you should. You need to do so before you can begin to focus on the knowledge and inference processes involved in the heuristic decision-making portions of the task. In effect, you should use task analysis techniques to continue to take apart the steps and decisions in the task until you arrive at an analysis that separates all of the environmental, database, and algorithmic elements of the task from the nodes or processes that involve heuristic analysis and decision making. Then, you should apply the analysis techniques that we discuss in Chapter 6 and the knowledge acquisition techniques we discuss in Chapter 7 to the actual capture of the knowledge contained in the nodes that represent heuristic processes.

SUMMARY: CREATING A SCENARIO

When we began this chapter, we suggested that the highest level of analysis was the I/O diagram. We expanded that a little when we discussed performance and dataflow models to include a user, results, and feedback.

When you begin to consider a potential problem, ask questions and make observations until you are confident that you have a good picture of (1) how the overall operation is performed now, and (2) how it will be performed if an expert system is installed to replace, partially replace, or support the existing decision-making person or mechanism.

When you consider the overview model, ask a number of performance and cost-related questions of each component of the model. These questions are summarized in Figure 5.9 and presented in more detail below.

Users Recognize the Problem

Talk with and observe the people who will use the expert system. Find out what they are doing now and how they will operate after an expert system is installed. Be sure you can answer the following questions about the users:

- WHO will use the system? Who will the users be? How are they accomplishing the task now?
- WHAT will they use the system for? What will the system do: Help someone make a decision? Prompt task performance? Provide a recommendation?
- WHERE will they use the system? How will the users access the system? Will new hardware need to be installed? At what cost?
- WHEN will they use the system? Will the users consult with the system while they are actually performing their job? Will the use of the system decrease the speed of the users' performance? Will it increase the quality of the users' performance?
- WHY will they use the system? As a very strong rule of thumb, employees will not do things that make their jobs or their lives harder rather than easier. There is one exception: People are generally rather conservative; they will stick with a less efficient way of doing a task rather than switch to a new method unless they are convinced that the new way is much easier or more pleasant than the method they are currently using.

It's conceivable that small expert systems will be built to make life easier for experts. Thus, to avoid being interrupted while working on other tasks or being awakened in the middle of the night, an expert technician might develop an expert system that will help junior technicians diagnose and repair a piece of equipment. What if the system is fielded on a computer that is located some distance from the equipment,

106 KNOWLEDGE ACQUISITION

Figure 5.9 Detailed review of questions to ask at each step in the consultation process.

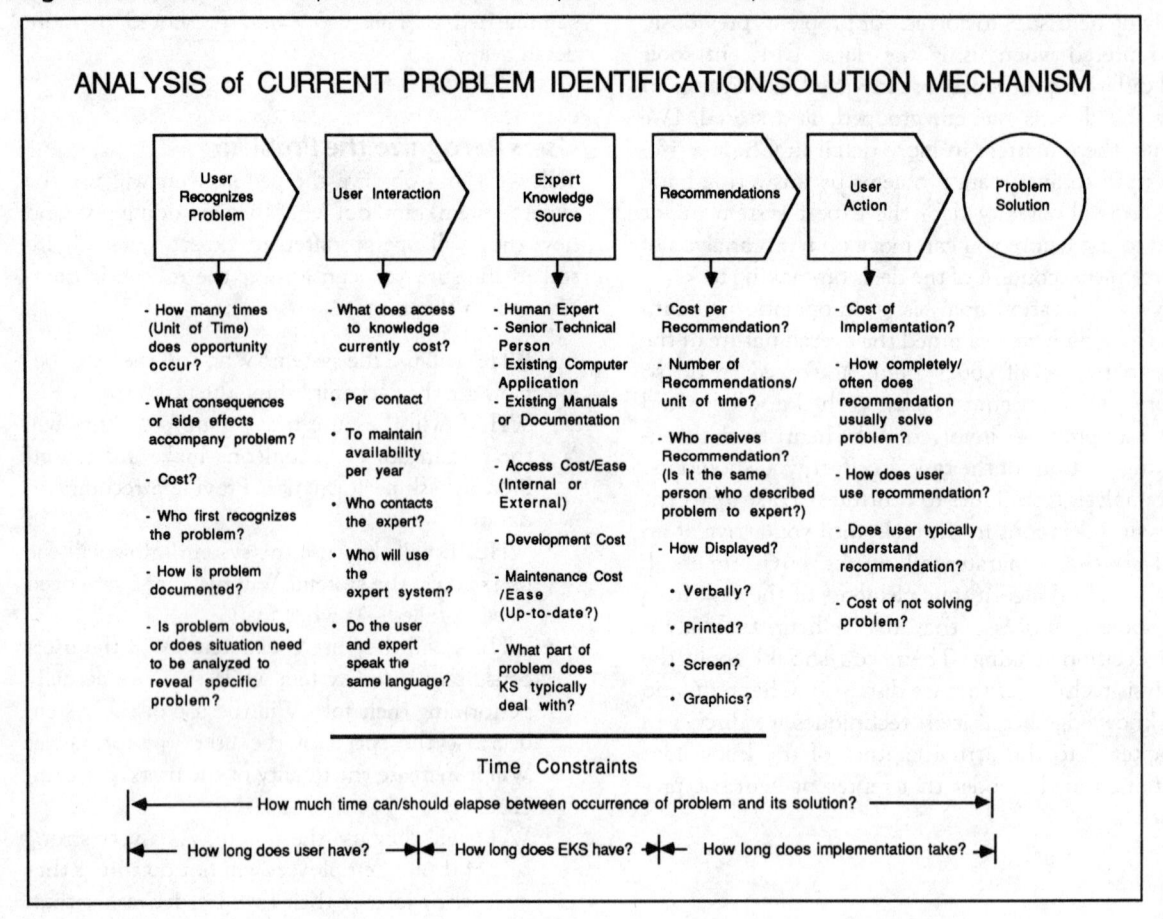

ANALYSIS of CURRENT PROBLEM IDENTIFICATION/SOLUTION MECHANISM

User Recognizes Problem	User Interaction	Expert Knowledge Source	Recommendations	User Action	Problem Solution
- How many times (Unit of Time) does opportunity occur? - What consequences or side effects accompany problem? - Cost? - Who first recognizes the problem? - How is problem documented? - Is problem obvious, or does situation need to be analyzed to reveal specific problem?	- What does access to knowledge currently cost? • Per contact • To maintain availability per year • Who contacts the expert? • Who will use the expert system? • Do the user and expert speak the same language?	- Human Expert - Senior Technical Person - Existing Computer Application - Existing Manuals or Documentation - Access Cost/Ease (Internal or External) - Development Cost - Maintenance Cost /Ease (Up-to-date?) - What part of problem does KS typically deal with?	- Cost per Recommendation? - Number of Recommendations/ unit of time? - Who receives Recommendation? (Is it the same person who described problem to expert?) - How Displayed? • Verbally? • Printed? • Screen? • Graphics?	- Cost of Implementation? - How completely/ often does recommendation usually solve problem? - How does user use recommendation? - Does user typically understand recommendation? - Cost of not solving problem?	

Time Constraints

|←———— How much time can/should elapse between occurrence of problem and its solution? ————→|

|←— How long does user have? —→|←— How long does EKS have? —→|←— How long does implementation take? —→|

and the computer is used by other employees? The junior technicians may find themselves walking back and forth from the equipment to the computer and often waiting for someone else to finish using the computer before they can run their consultation. In such a circumstance, no matter how good the system is, the junior technicians will probably go right on calling the expert technician whenever they need help. They won't use the expert system because it will make their job harder, not easier! When considering why the users will consult with a system, be sure you can state how the use of the system will make the users' job easier or more pleasant. If you can't state why the user might want to use your expert system, you should reconsider whether it's really worth developing in the first place.

When you look at how a problem is solved, you look at the behavioral pattern. First, there is a problem that someone recognizes. Somebody then interacts with a source of expert knowledge which can be a human expert, a written manual, or a piece of software. From the knowledge source come recommendations, and then somebody takes actions, and hopefully the problem is solved. If you are going to write a proposal to build a system, you should walk through each one of the steps in the process.

It is extremely important to analyze how the problem is currently solved and to understand the consequences of *not* using an expert system. For example, if users can always pick up the phone and call Joe, and Joe always gave the answers in the past and will still continue to give the answers, they may never sit down and use the computer. If you ask around your organization and find that there is no way that you can prevent Joe from answering the phone when it rings and that Joe is prepared to answer the questions over the phone, then there is no point in building an expert system. The contingencies aren't there to make people use the system.

Cost considerations in relation to users include the following: What does access to the source of expertise currently cost in both fees and downtime? Is an expert maintained to help solve infrequent problems? What do errors cost? How effective is the expert in reducing errors?

User Interaction

How do users currently access expertise when they need it? Do they use computers? If not, is there any indication that they would like to?

Is the current source of expertise a person? If so, does the person speak the same language as the user, or does the expert ask questions and then conceptualize and calculate a solution in a very different manner? How long does the user have to wait to access the expert? What would the expert be doing if he were not consulting with the user? If the expertise is contained in a manual, is it easy to use? If the expertise is contained in a computer program, how easy is it to access the computer program and get the program to provide the needed responses and suggestions?

What happens while the user is interacting with the system? What does it cost the user to interact with the expert? What do input errors cost?

Expert Knowledge Source

When you consider the current source of expertise, you want to ask a number of questions about how effective and efficient it is. What part of the problem does the current expert typically solve? (100% accuracy 100% of the time, 80% accuracy 100% of the time, 100% accuracy 80% of the time, etc.) How acceptable is the current performance?

How long does it take an expert to solve a typical problem? What special equipment does the expert use? Does the expert use conventional computer programs or access databases?

How often is the existing source of expertise updated? Does the expert attend conferences to learn new approaches? Does the expert rely on feedback from existing cases to prepare for future cases?

What does the expert cost? Are there costs associated with moving the expert to the site with the problem? Does it cost money to have the expert switch from one task to another in order to help solve the problem? What would the expert be doing, at what rate of return to the company, if she didn't have to help the user solve problems? If expertise comes from a computer program, what did it cost to develop and what does it cost to maintain? If recommendations are derived from a manual or other documentation, what did it cost to develop and what is involved in maintaining it?

Recommendations and User Actions

In what form do the users currently get recommendations from the expert (e.g., advice over the phone, a report, physical assistance)? Does the user need any further help in interpreting the expert's advice? Are diagrams, charts, or graphics involved in the recommendations? Do the users need to ask the expert for clarification or further help once they get the recommendations? Is the recommendation typically complete?

Are the experts' recommendations usable in their initial form, or does it take additional time and money to convert the recommendations to specific actions? What do errors in interpreting the recommendations cost? What is a successful solution to the problem worth? What does it cost if a recommendation is tried and fails to solve the problem?

108 KNOWLEDGE ACQUISITION

Figure 5.10 Scenario analysis of a potential expert systems application.

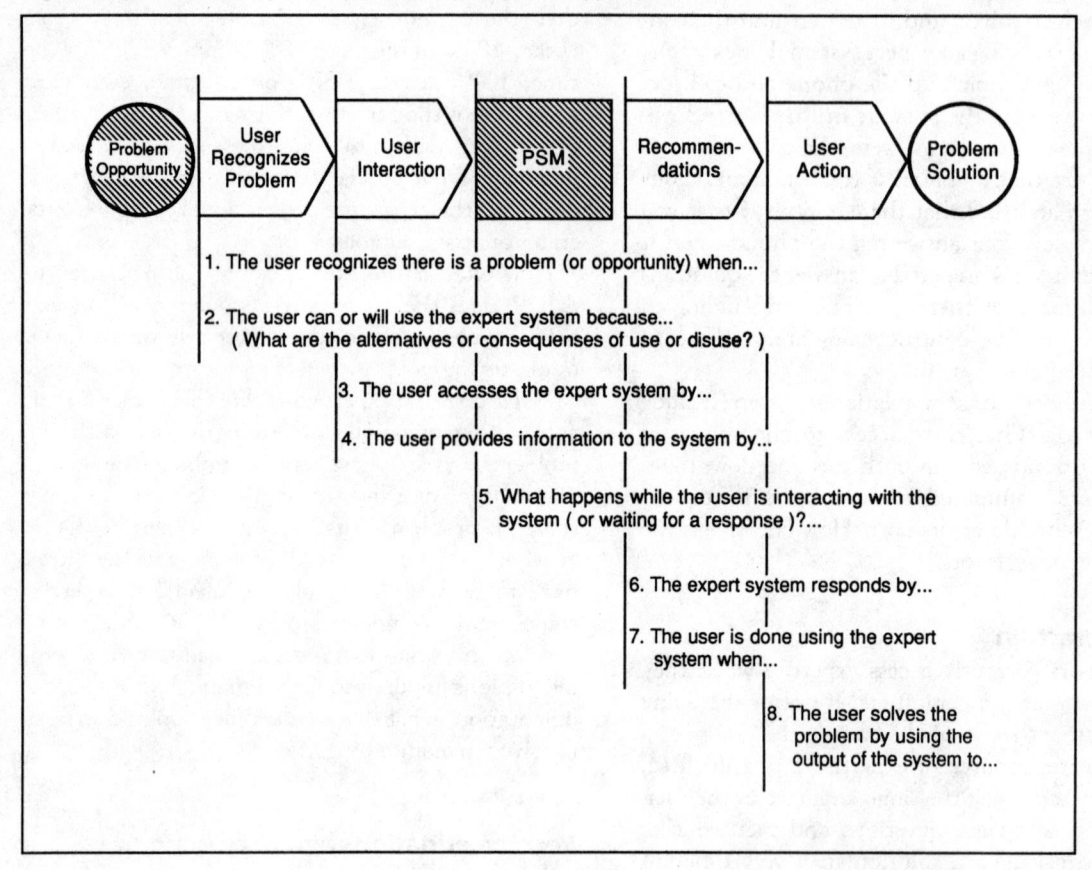

```
Problem  →  User        →  User         →  PSM  →  Recommen-  →  User    →  Problem
Opportunity  Recognizes    Interaction              dations       Action     Solution
             Problem
```

1. The user recognizes there is a problem (or opportunity) when...

2. The user can or will use the expert system because...
   (What are the alternatives or consequenses of use or disuse?)

3. The user accesses the expert system by...

4. The user provides information to the system by...

5. What happens while the user is interacting with the system (or waiting for a response)?...

6. The expert system responds by...

7. The user is done using the expert system when...

8. The user solves the problem by using the output of the system to...

Constructing a Scenario

Once you are confident you have the answers to these overall questions, or perhaps in order to obtain the needed answers, you can turn to the performance, analysis and dataflow approaches we have described earlier in this chapter. When you are satisfied that you understand the task and want to go ahead and propose developing an expert system to perform it, you should compile your findings by writing a short "script" or "scenario" to summarize your understanding.

Actually, you should write two brief scripts: one to describe how the task is handled now and a second to describe how you expect the application to be handled once an expert system is installed. The questions you should answer are outlined in Figure 5.10. Answer them first for the current operation and then answer them again for the operation as it will be performed using an expert system. If you can do this, it means you understand the potential application and should be in a good position to proceed with the project, if it seems worthwhile.

6.
Cognitive Analysis

INTRODUCTION

Cognitive analysis is the heart of knowledge engineering. Once you get beyond small systems, expert systems development involves capturing expert knowledge. That, in turn, involves working with a human expert and figuring out what he knows and how he relates different facts together to reason about the problems he solves.

The interesting things experts do, they do inside their heads. It isn't observable to someone who is simply watching their behavior; if it were, you could rely solely on task analysis. Experts think. They reason. They form hypotheses and then they ask questions to confirm or reject them.

Cognitive analysis is the process by which you figure out what experts know and how they reason about specific tasks. It's an imperfect process; it's frequently more art than engineering. Luckily, there is an empirical method you can use to refine the knowledge you get during the cognitive analysis effort. You can encode the knowledge you obtain in a knowledge base and then sit with the human expert and watch the expert system try to solve cases. As you review each case in turn, you can refine and improve the knowledge in your system until it really does approximate the human expert's knowledge.

When creating small systems, developers often simply encode some knowledge and then move immediately to the trial and error refinement process. This straightforward approach often works with simple systems. If the expert has a lot of knowledge, however, it is better to try to develop a good overview before you begin to write code. To paraphrase one expert, an ounce of analysis is worth a pound of rules. Hence, this chapter is designed to introduce you to the cognitive analysis process.

In the discussion that follows, we assume that you are considering the development of a mid- to large-size expert system of some complexity. Thus, we assume you will be using a hybrid tool that will allow you to use both object networks and rules to represent your expert's knowledge.

Figure 6.1 provides an overview of knowledge engineering. To develop a knowledge-based system, you must obtain and encode knowledge. Someone must already have that knowledge—that person is referred to as the expert or *subject matter expert (SME)*. You must then extract and formalize the knowledge in some manner. That formal representation of knowledge is known as a *knowledge map*. Once you are satisfied with the knowledge contained in the knowledge map, you must encode it in a computer usable form. The process of acquiring the knowledge is generally called *knowledge acquisition*.

The first product of a knowledge acquisition effort is a knowledge map that provides an overview of the expert's knowledge. You can then use the information contained in the knowledge map to develop a knowledge base that can actually be executed. Once you have entered the initial knowledge into a system, you can run test cases through it. Depending on how the system performs, you then modify, refine, and expand the knowledge until the system's performance reaches some predetermined level of expertise. The entire process is called *knowledge engineering*.

You can compare this process to a conventional program development effort. Knowledge acquisition is akin to what conventional software analysts call

110 KNOWLEDGE ACQUISITION

Figure 6.1 The knowledge engineering process.

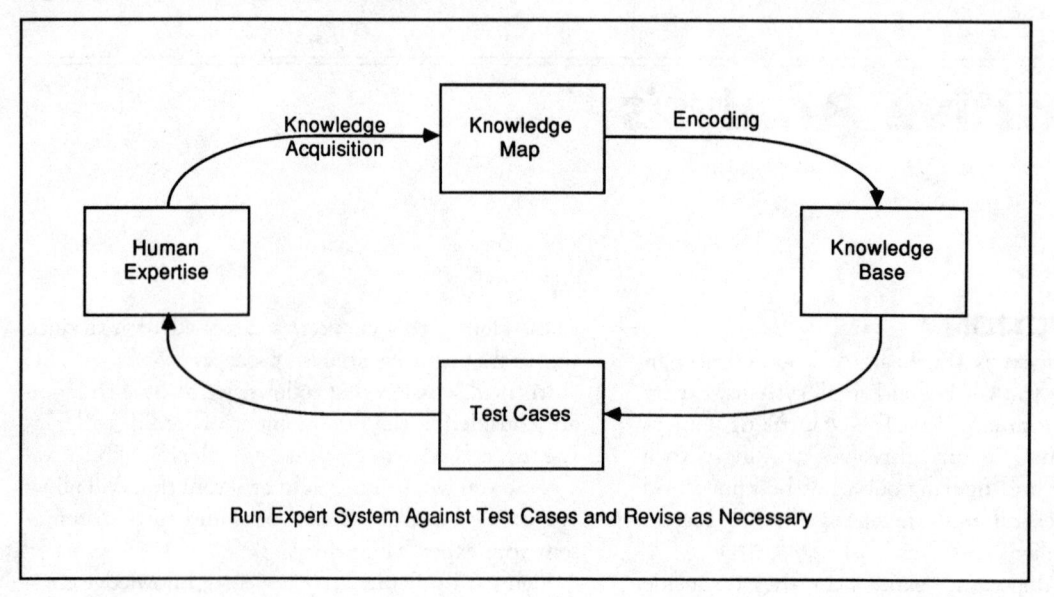

```
Human Expertise --Knowledge Acquisition--> Knowledge Map --Encoding--> Knowledge Base --> Test Cases --> Human Expertise
```

Run Expert System Against Test Cases and Revise as Necessary

the Initial Software Requirements Analysis, and the development of a knowledge map is similar to what they call a Structured Specification. But there are important differences. If the knowledge being captured is complex, conventional representational techniques would be hard-pressed to adequately model the entire network of highly interrelated and heuristic information. Equally important, once a conventional programmer has developed a structured specification, she then begins the process of changing it into a design specification that typically looks nothing like the original structured specification. In developing an expert system, you capture the initial knowledge in a knowledge map that will be very similar to the actual knowledge base that you will then create. Obviously, you must introduce syntax when you encode your knowledge map, but in most cases, the knowledge engineer will be able to point to each item on the knowledge map and identify its code counterpart in the knowledge base.

The experience of the last few years indicates that conventional programmers don't have any trouble learning how to encode information into the knowledge base of an expert systems tool. If they have trouble, it comes when they try to acquire knowledge and produce a declarative or logical description of what the expert knows, rather than a procedural description (e.g. a dataflow model or an algorithm) of what the expert does.

This chapter focuses on the psychological assumptions underlying knowledge mapping and presents a notation system that you can use to represent an expert's knowledge. The next chapter focuses on knowledge acquisition, the actual process of getting the expert to provide the knowledge that you then arrange into a knowledge map. The conventions we discuss are very general. If we knew what tool you were going to be using, we could tailor the vocabulary and the notation so that it would be even closer to the actual code that you write when you create your knowledge base. For our purposes, however, a generic vocabulary is probably best.

SOME COGNITIVE ASSUMPTIONS

Cognitive analysis is based on research that cognitive scientists have undertaken during the past 30 years. We will not go into that research in detail, but you should be acquainted with a few of the basic assumptions that cognitive scientists routinely make when they approach the knowledge engineering task.

Heuristic Knowledge, Domain Knowledge, and Deep Knowledge

There are many ways to classify knowledge. One approach classifies knowledge into three categories:

1. Heuristic or surface knowledge
2. Domain knowledge
3. Deep or theoretical knowledge

(Procedural models, like algorithms, fall under domain knowledge.) Figure 6.2 illustrates these three types or levels of knowledge.

To illustrate this classification, consider how someone might go about trying to get a TV set to work. If someone found that his TV didn't turn on, he'd begin by checking to see if it was plugged in. Assuming it was, he'd lightly shake the cord going into the set and switch all of the obvious knobs on and off a couple of times. If all this failed, he'd decide that he needed to get the TV repaired or he'd think about buying a new TV. Observing this behavior, you might assume that this person is ignorant of how a TV works, and you'd be correct. This person has a few heuristics that he applies to TVs, computers, toasters, and assorted other electrical devices. But beyond using these basic, rather limited and superficial heuristics, he knows he's licked.

Assuming your TV was broken and you took it to a repair shop, you'd expect to find someone with much more knowledge of TVs than you have. Still, you would assume the person at the repair shop probably had a domain-level knowledge of TVs. You wouldn't expect to find someone who had an advanced degree in electronics or really understood the physics of TVs. You would expect that the TV repairperson would have a domain or procedural knowledge of TVs and TV repair that would guide that person in the systematic diagnosis of your TV set and in selecting an appropriate repair strategy. You would be happy to find someone who knew how to apply many more heuristics than you did, in a more systematic way, and, hopefully, arrive at a way to fix your TV.

A domain model would tell the repairperson what the major parts of the TV were and how they worked together. It would include many heuristics about how a malfunction in one part of a unit might induce symptoms elsewhere. A procedural model would provide the repairperson with a step-by-step approach to troubleshooting the TV. The repairperson would probably draw on both models in trying to fix your TV.

If it ever came to it, you could probably find someone in an engineering department of a university who really understood how your TV worked. (You wouldn't necessarily assume that she could fix your TV, but you would assume that she could design a TV from scratch, if necessary.) In other words, you assume that a professor of electrical engineering would probably have the underlying or deep knowledge of physics and electronics that would enable her to create a device that would function as a TV.

Figure 6.2 The three levels of knowledge.

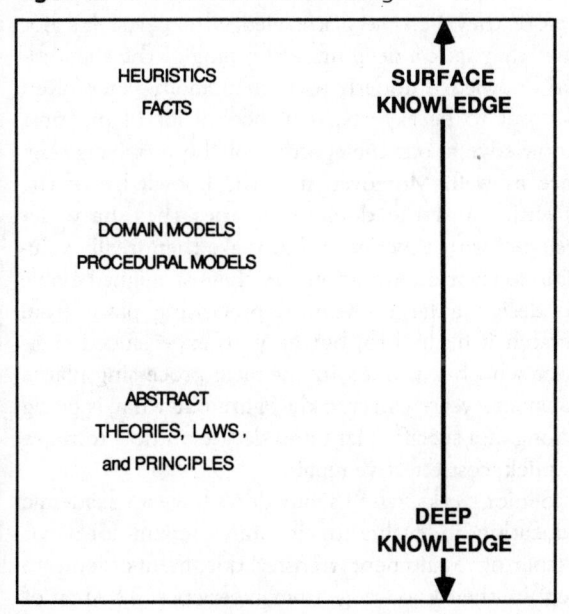

```
HEURISTICS              SURFACE
FACTS                   KNOWLEDGE


DOMAIN MODELS
PROCEDURAL MODELS


ABSTRACT
THEORIES, LAWS,
and PRINCIPLES
                        DEEP
                        KNOWLEDGE
```

KNOWLEDGE ACQUISITION

Figure 6.3 General pattern of professional development.

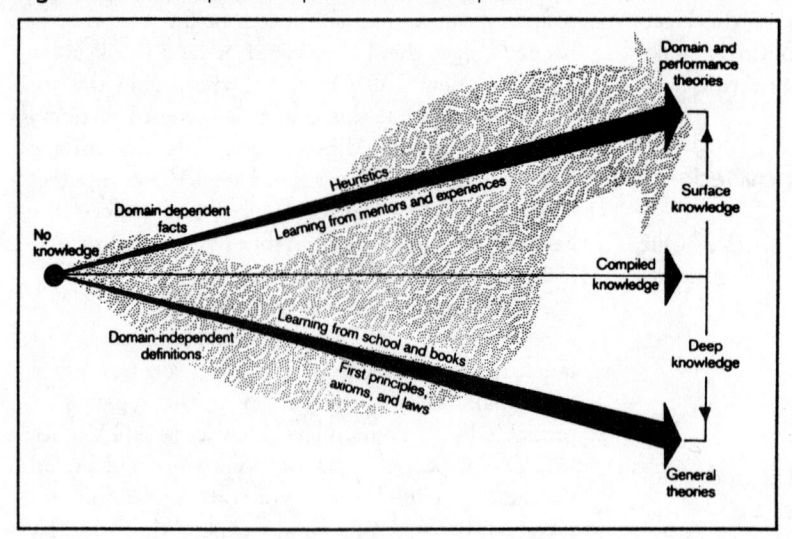

Figure 6.3 illustrates how people acquire knowledge. Everyone is born without knowledge and begins to acquire it by trial and error experience. Your parents help by arranging your experiences so that you will learn certain things and by teaching you the names of objects in your environment, and so on. As you progress through life, you continue to acquire some of your knowledge from experience and other knowledge from instruction.

A "domain" simply refers to any relatively circumscribed set of activities. Thus, baseball, accounting, and playing the cello are all domains. Given the limitations of expert systems, knowledge engineers are primarily concerned with intellectual or cognitive domains like auditing, diagnosing auto failures, scheduling factory operations, and deciding whether or not to make a loan to a mid-size corporation.

Schools tend to teach more or less domain-independent knowledge. They teach mathematics rather than auditing or making loans. They teach physics rather that the specifics of bridge building. Even when schools do teach applied subjects, it is assumed that a graduate will need to work at a job for a while before "really" knowing how to function as an engineer or an accountant.

Actually, working within a particular domain provides you with heuristic and practical ways of approaching problems that differ from the rules and theories you learned in school. In effect, most people have to "recompile" their knowledge when they move from school to the workplace.

Most human experts in organizations have worked within the same domain for some 10 to 15 years before they become acknowledged experts. It's not that they lack a deep understanding of the theoretical knowledge underlying their domain—they often do, but to be experts, they need a lot of practical knowledge about the specifics of the problems they face as well. Moreover, it is the knowledge of the specifics and the domain theories they have developed with experience that make them really valuable to their organizations. A chemist might be able to design a large chemical processing plant from scratch if he had to, but only an experienced engineer who has worked in chemical processing plants for many years can quickly figure out what is going wrong at a specific plant and decide on how to make a quick, cost-effective repair.

Senior clerks, who usually don't have an academic education in evaluating insurance claim forms or preparing equipment transfer documents, tend to acquire their knowledge from experience. The best of

Cognitive Analysis

these technical experts have also worked at their jobs for many years and have an amazing amount of highly specialized knowledge about their companies and the specific problems associated with their jobs.

The technology involved in expert systems design does not include the ability to create and use deep models. You can't put the laws and principles of physics into an expert system and then expect it to be able to design bridges or aircraft. The current techniques can be used to capture either heuristic knowledge or, at most, domain and procedural models. The simple rule-based systems use facts and rules and aim at replicating expert performance in situations in which experts use surface knowledge. (Keep in mind that very interesting expert systems, like MYCIN, contain only surface knowledge.)

The more sophisticated hybrid tools allow the knowledge engineer to create domain or procedural models and are capable of solving a wider range of problems. (As we have already noted, most of the mid- to large-size design, planning, and scheduling systems rely on some kind of domain or procedural model.)

The Hierarchical Structure of Memory

Without examining how the human mind actually stores information, we do know that the effect is to organize knowledge in a hierarchical manner. Figure 6.4 provides a nice illustration of this. The box on the lower right side of the figure illustrates empirical data that two cognitive scientists, Collins and

Figure 6.4 The relationship between human recall time and hierarchical storage. Note that recall times increase as the subject must "move up" in the hierarchy to locate values.

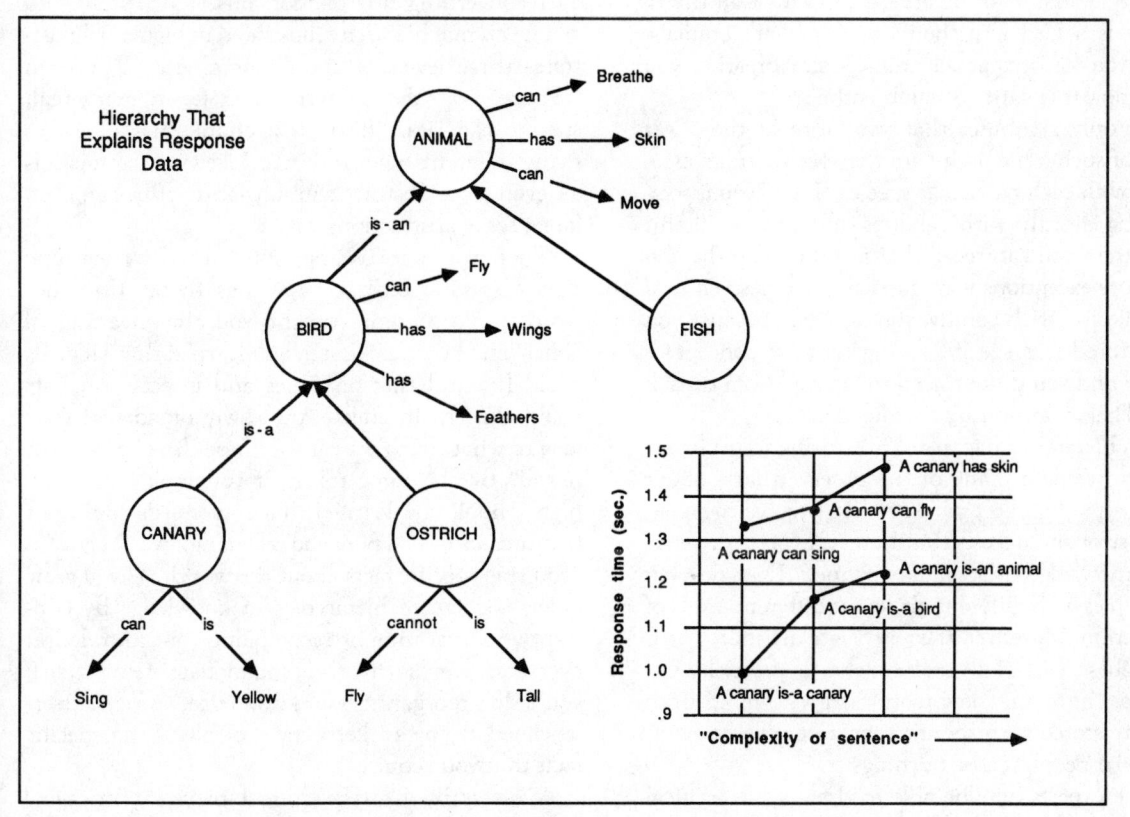

Quillian, gathered. They asked students questions about different types of relationships. Thus, for example, a student might have been asked: "Is a canary a bird?", "Can a canary sing?", "Can a canary fly?", and so on. As obvious as these questions seem, careful studies show that it takes students longer to respond that a canary can fly than it takes them to answer that a canary can sing.

Collins and Quillian explain the differences by arguing that people must store information at the most abstract level possible. This concept is illustrated by the animal object-attribute-value hierarchy shown in Figure 6.4. Rather than trying to remember that canaries fly and that robins fly and that sparrows fly, you simply remember that they are all birds and that birds fly and have feathers and lay eggs, and so on. Likewise, you store even more general traits, such as eating and breathing, with a still more abstract category or object—animals. Thus, to determine if a canary can breathe, you first recall that a canary is a bird and then that birds are animals. Since you know that all animals can breathe, you then know that canaries can breathe.

The only attributes that you store at the lower levels of such a hierarchy are the specific traits associated with each particular species. Thus, you associate song directly with canaries and can recall this faster than you can recall that a canary can fly. You also store exceptions with particular species. Thus, if asked if an ostrich can fly, you say "no" because you have stored this specific fact with your concept of ostrich and you do not need to "move" from ostrich to bird before answering the question.

This hierarchical approach to storing information seems to explain many of the observed facts about how people handle problems that involve memory, and it strongly suggests that human experts organize their knowledge in a similar manner. They develop hierarchies with different objects at different levels of abstraction. Moreover, they associate attributes with the highest level of abstraction that is practical. Exceptions, however, come more readily to mind since they are stored with specific, concrete objects—with particular people, cases, or things.

Some experts may be able to draw a hierarchical chart of the various concepts in their domain. They may begin by subdividing a TV into four major subunits and then subdivide those subunits, and so on. Most experts, however, use a hierarchy without being especially conscious of it. (Their expertise consists in their ability to *solve* problems, not to *explain* how they solve them.) As long as you are aware that a hierarchy lies hidden behind an expert's ability to store and recall the large amounts of specific detail that he uses, you can start helping the expert specify the nature of that hierarchy.

Conceptual Chunking and the Problem-Solving Space

Psychologists use the term "chunking" to describe the process by which people group objects together into some higher-level, more abstract object. Human memory is made up of many different hierarchies, each concerning different domains.

The animal hierarchy illustrated in Figure 6.4 illustrates three levels of chunks or objects. The term "canary" is an abstract term that refers to many real, specific canaries. "Bird" is a chunk that describes many different types of birds. Likewise, "animal" is an even more abstract chunk that describes an even larger set of abstractions.

When you were young, you started by learning that a specific bird you saw was flying. (In other words, your parents taught you the meaning of "bird" and "flying.") Later, you learned that all birds could fly, and that airplanes and insects and bats could also fly. In effect, you slowly broadened your idea of what flying was. It was more than "how birds move." By the same token, if you took biology in high school, you learned that some birds could not fly, and so on. When you're young, you begin by acquiring specific facts about the world. As you grow older, you create hierarchies of knowledge by constantly reorganizing or recompiling your knowledge, over and over again, to accommodate new facts. If you didn't reorganize your knowledge, you'd be overwhelmed trying to keep track of all of the specific facts that you acquire.

A hierarchy like the animal hierarchy contains

more or less straightforward concepts. "Bird," after all, is simply a generic term that refers to any and all specific birds, while "animal" is an even more general concept that refers to anything that moves and eats plants or other animals.

Experts often have elaborate classification hierarchies, like the animal hierarchy, to organize the knowledge in their area of expertise. For example, they can have a hierarchy that refers to the various parts of a machine, or to the types of chemicals used in various industrial processes.

It gets much more complex, however, when experts start using abstraction hierarchies that are more conceptual in nature. Consider what is meant by "speed" (or velocity). Speed isn't a thing you can point to, like a robin. It is a ratio that expresses a relationship between two other things: distance and time. (See Figure 6.5.) In other words, the idea or concept of "speed" emerges from your understanding of how movement can be described as a set of points that results from the interaction of two independent sets of points that occur on scales that measure time and distance.

You can create an even more abstract concept by taking the set of points that emerge for "speed" and placing them on one axis of a matrix that has "time" on the other axis. The interaction of these two concepts results in a still more abstract concept—acceleration. (A concrete way of talking about acceleration is to say that it refers to distance divided by time, divided by time—e.g., miles per hour per hour.) The idea that there is a thing called "acceleration" is misleading. In fact, there is a concept called "acceleration" that really represents a set of points resulting from the division of one set of points by another, divided by still another set. This example illustrates just how complex hierarchies of abstract concepts can become. Most experts in technical areas use concepts like "acceleration" without thinking twice about the complexities involved in such an abstraction. The expert has chunked the underlying concepts and operations together into a single term that refers to all of the underlying measurements and calculations.

Statisticians use a similar concept when they say that a number is "significant." Their use of the word significant implies the use of measurements and calculations. As an average person, you may use the

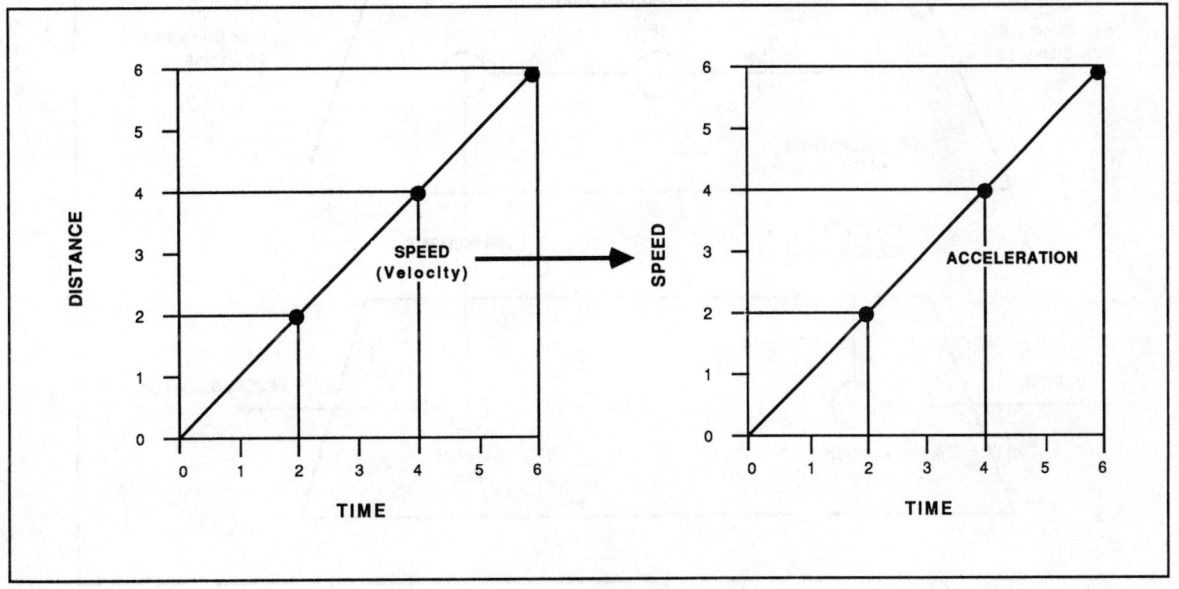

Figure 6.5 Two variables and an emergent concept (speed), and then another (acceleration).

word significant without thinking much about its technical meaning, but once you use it in a statistical context, you must understand the calculations involved in order to use the word (i.e., the concept) correctly.

Cognitive scientists assume that people naturally chunk lower-level concepts together to form more abstract concepts. Most problem solving involves observing some specific data, considering that piece of data as an instance of a higher-level concept, and then reasoning at the more abstract level to determine the meaning of the data. Once the meaning of the data is determined, the problem solver may then descend from abstract considerations to concrete instances by predicting specific events to expect. (See Figure 6.6.)

In trying to figure out how experts solve problems, it's useful to have some general idea about the number of abstract concepts or high-level chunks a person might be considering at any given moment. Cognitive scientists approach this problem the same way they approach the problem of how large a program a computer can process. To process information, a system must be able to keep track of specific items (data) and operators that are to be applied to each piece of data. Using this approach, cognitive scientists hypothesize that people have some kind of working or short-term memory comprised of space (registers) in which they store information that they need to keep in mind while they are thinking about a problem.

Limits on chunking capabilities. There has been much research on the limits of human short-term memory. Initial experiments by G. A. Miller suggested that human short-term memory capacity was 7 ± 2 chunks. Miller derived this conclusion from a number of different experiments. One example should suffice to explain the concept.

Figure 6.6 The process of reasoning about concrete events with abstract concepts. Specific instances establish which abstract objects should be considered. Abstract heuristics determine which classes of solutions are appropriate. Then solutions are refined to specific recommendations.

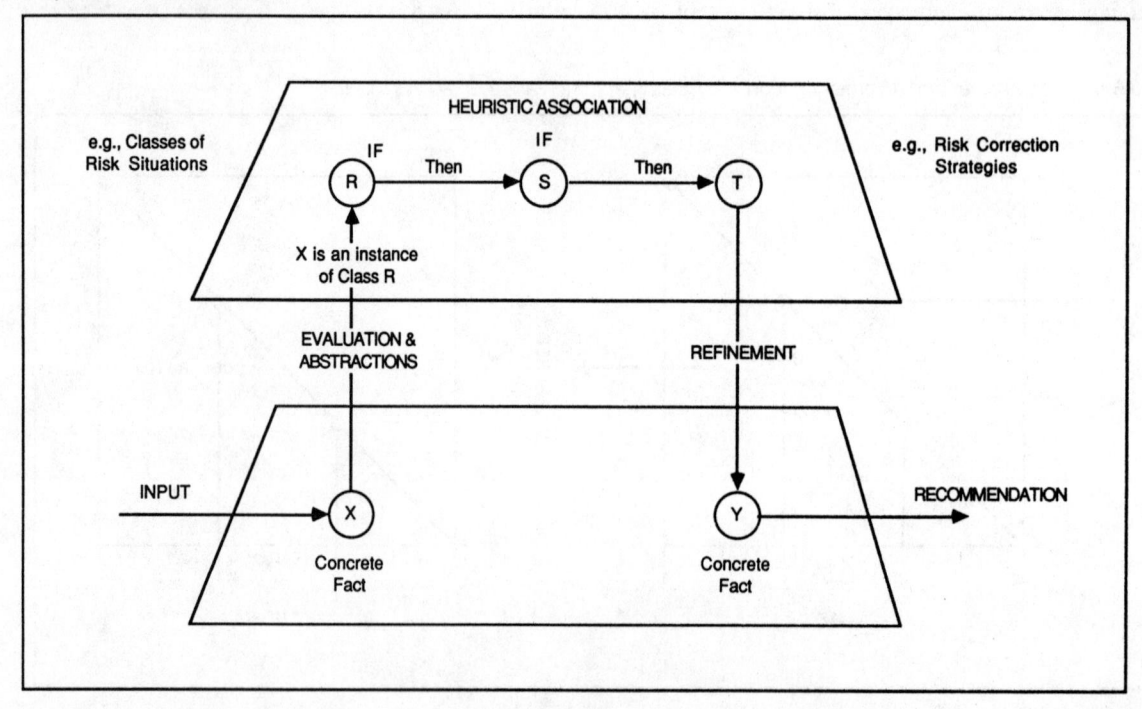

Figure 6.7 Multiplying a two-digit number by a single-digit number.

```
Step 1      Step 2      Step 3      Step 4      Step 5      Step 6

 87          87          87          87                       35
x 5         x 5         x 5         x 5                      +40
                        ---         ---                      ---
                         35          35          35          435

              7                       8
             x5                      x5
             ---                     ---
              35                      40          40
```

If you ask people to multiply two single-digit numbers in their head, say 5 × 8, most people will immediately say 40. You assume that they have memorized that answer and did not do any mental calculation. If you think of people as using a number of "memory registers" to keep track of the numbers involved, they would need three: one for the 5, one for the 8, and then one for the 40.

Now, imagine that you ask someone to multiply a single-digit number by a two-digit number, say 5 × 87. In this case, most people will not be able to answer immediately. They will need to do a mental calculation. We have reproduced the calculation in Figure 6.7 and assigned numbers to each step in the process.

In Step 1, the person has two things in memory: 87 and 5. At Step 2, the person has the original numbers in mind and has also multiplied 7 by 5 to obtain the first subproduct, 35. At this point, there are five items in memory. In Step 3, the person discards the 7 and the 5 and simply retains the original problem and the subproduct; thus in Step 3, the person has three items in memory.

In Step 4, the person does the second multiplication. At this point, she must have six items in active memory simultaneously: the original two numbers, the first subproduct, the two numbers she is multiplying, and the second subproduct. In Step 5, the person can reduce her memory load to two items, the two subproducts. In Step 6 she adds the two subproducts and obtains the answer.

While the memory load varied throughout the problem-solving process, at the high point, the person had six items in memory at the same time. Most people can carry out this mental calculation if they concentrate a bit.

If you ask people to multiply two two-digit numbers, say 54 × 86, most people find that this kind of effort is just at their limit or a little beyond it. If you walked through the process step by step, you would find that the memory load in Steps 4, 7, and 10 would involve six items each and the memory load for Step 9 would be seven items.

Hardly anyone can multiply a three-digit by a two-digit number in their head. Obviously, the problem is one of memory capacity and not mental ability, since most people can easily solve these problems if you allow them to use paper and pencil. In effect, the paper substitutes for memory registers. Using paper and pencil, most people can easily solve a problem like 67 × 875.

These experiments led Miller to suggest that human beings can only process problems that involve keeping from five to nine items in mind simultaneously. Other psychologists have tried to explore this limitation using more verbal or conceptual examples, and they have found that human capacities are even lower than Miller suggested. Indeed, instead

118 KNOWLEDGE ACQUISITION

of 7 ± 2 chunks, human capacities for more complex problems are probably closer to 4 ± 1 chunk.

Charts and graphs help people understand complex interactions by showing how three or four variables interact. By looking at a good graph, you can get a quick overview of the nature of an interaction.

Most cognitive scientists assume that an expert, without the use of graphic devices, can probably consider the simultaneous interaction of only three to seven variables or chunks. Given the complexity of the problems that most human experts work on, this means that they must have chunked a vast amount of information into a few very high-level concepts that they can use when they think about a problem.

An engineer might say something like, "Well, if you think about it, it's really just a matter of force, resistance, and time." That may make sense to the engineer who said it, but it won't make sense to anyone outside that person's specialty, because the concepts the engineer has invoked are so abstract. You would have to ask the engineer exactly what she meant by "force" and "resistance" and "time" and how she had judged them. Chances are the engineer would define "force" in terms of two or three interacting variables. Pressed further, she might define each of those variables in some less abstract terms, and so on.

In other words, if you assume that human working memory is rather limited, as the evidence seems to

Figure 6.8 A diagram of an expert's knowledge hierarchy with the items mentioned during a knowledge acquisition session highlighted.

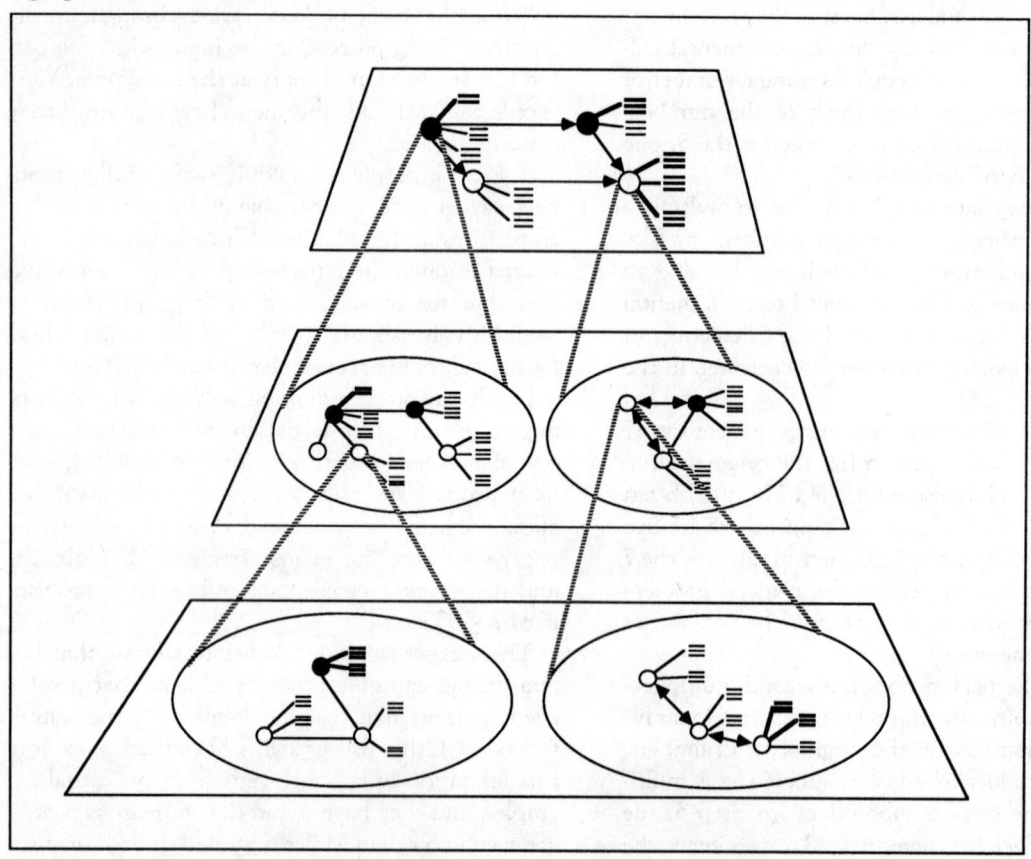

Figure 6.9 A domain theory is something derived from more than one deep theory.

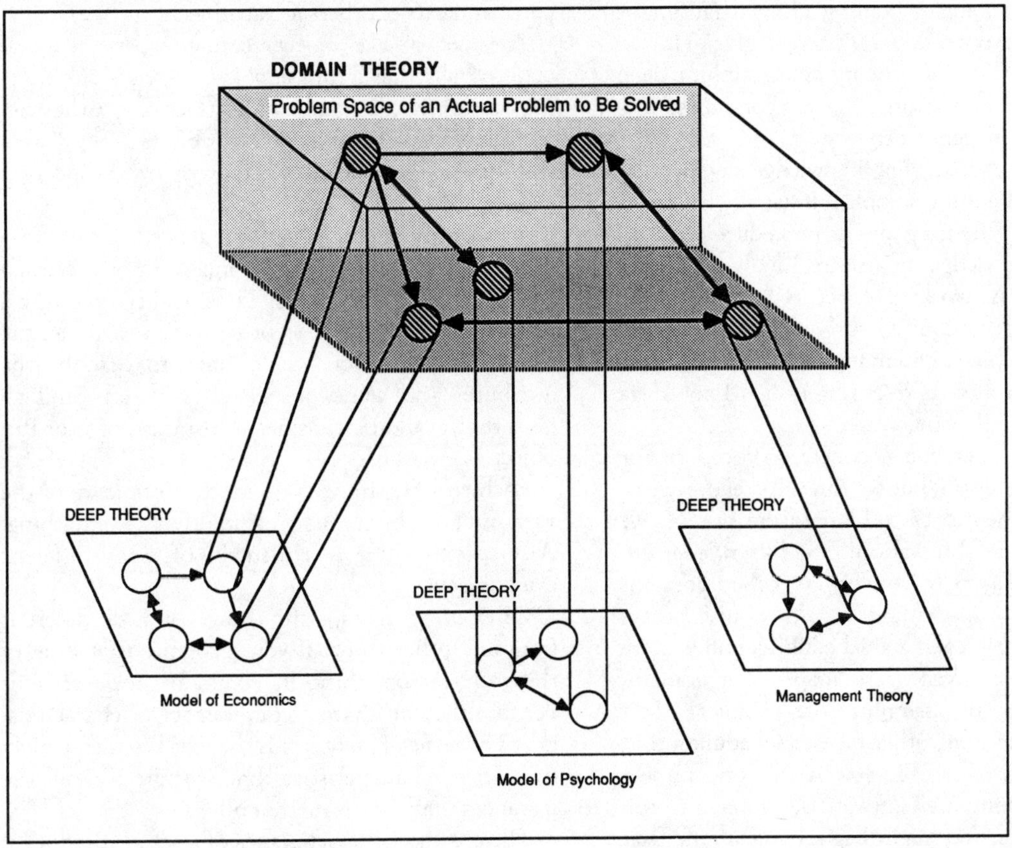

suggest, then you must also assume that humans develop many deep, multilayered hierarchies. It is only by carefully chunking things over and over again that an expert can manage to reduce the complexity of the world to a few variables. That, in turn, allows the expert to quickly analyze the cause of a problem and arrive at a solution strategy.

One of the key challenges the knowledge engineer faces is unchunking an expert's knowledge structure. Unfortunately, when you talk with an expert about a problem, your expert will probably provide you with information at several different levels of his domain hierarchy at the same time. Figure 6.8 provides you with a diagrammatic representation of an expert's domain hierarchy. This is just a diagram, because a real expert could easily have from 250 to 100,000 chunks of information on a multitude of different levels.

To make matters worse, many knowledge engineers assume that the high-level objects that make up a domain theory are the top of a single hierarchy. In other words, they assume that there is only one deep theory that underlies an expert's domain model. In fact, many experts use domain models that are derived from more than one deep theory. (See Figure 6.9.) A bank loan officer, for example, is concerned with a number of factors, such as the financial condition of the company that wants to borrow money, how the company is managed, how the principals get along with each other, how they get along with their employees, and so forth. The same loan officer is also thinking about the market that the would-be borrower is in. Who are the company's competitors? Are there new technologies coming along that might make the company's product uncompetitive? Thus, a good middle-market loan theory must combine deep knowledge from accounting, macro-economics, psychology, and management theory.

All of this suggests that knowledge engineering can sometimes be quite complex. It usually isn't simply a matter of figuring out a procedure that an expert uses. Knowledge engineering involves defining a multilayered network of concepts and heuristics that an expert has acquired and assembled over the course of many years. Disentangling all this interacting information and representing it as a knowledge map is a truly challenging job.

We'd like to offer you a concrete procedure for knowledge acquisition, but we can't. Instead, we can offer you some heuristics and a notation system. We can also offer one observation: Good knowledge engineers often reason by analogy to other domains that they already understand. Thus, if your expert is a specialist in chemical plant scheduling, and you are trying to develop a knowledge map of her domain, you might begin by assuming that chemical plant scheduling is like some other type of scheduling that you know more about. If you have done project scheduling for computer software development projects, for example, you might begin by assuming that your expert must consider the same general variables that you consider when you schedule software development. In fact, of course, she may not, but it provides you with a place to begin. This explains why "Renaissance men and women" make good knowledge engineers; they already tend to understand a number of different domain theories and thus are in a better position to find some domain theory that is similar to the one their expert has.

THE OBJECT-ATTRIBUTE-VALUE MODEL

Anything in the world that can be distinguished from other things can be thought of as an *object*. Thus you, your pet, your pen, your car, and the pets, pens, and cars of others are all objects.

Any set of like objects can be abstracted and conceptualized as a *class of objects*. A class of objects (or class-object) is simply an abstract object that can include several more concrete objects. "Bird" is a class-object that includes hundreds of specific bird objects.

To identify a class-object, you need to specify a boundary, or some criteria for including or excluding specific objects in the class. Thus, you could create a class-object for all pens. In order to be able to use the class-object Pen, you would have to describe the attributes and values associated with any and all pens that would be considered instances of your Pen object.

Each specific thing is, in effect, an *instance* of the various class-objects that include that specific thing. Any specific thing is a member of many different class-objects.

Obviously, each specific thing is a little different from any other thing. If you recognize that a set of things have something in common, however, it is because they all share a common set of characteristics. The *name* of an object is the word that you apply to a set of characteristics that is shared by all the instances that constitute that object.

The common characteristics of a set of things that you abstract into an object can, themselves, become the attributes of that object. An *attribute* is the name given to the abstraction of a single characteristic that each instance of an object possesses. All of the attributes of an object must be independent of each other.

A specific set of values is associated with each attribute. Class-objects can have specific values associated with them, but, in general, we only associate sets of values with the attributes of class-objects.

Figure 6.10 shows that the word "bird" can be a class-object that represents all of the specific instances of birds. Some of the characteristics that birds have in common are wings, feet, and beaks. Each of these characteristics can be thought of as an attribute of the Bird object. Birds, as a class, have some unique attributes and values. For example,

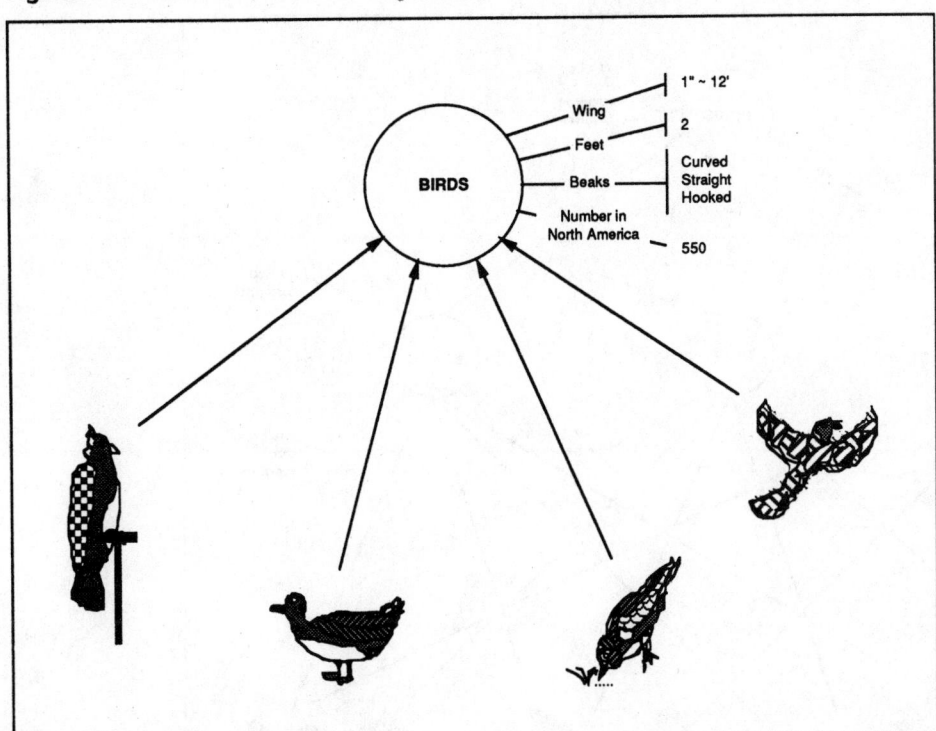

Figure 6.10 The derivation of the class-object "birds" from a number of real instances of birds.

there are about 1000 different species of birds that live in North America. Most of the attributes you associate with birds as a class, however, lack specific values. Birds, in general, don't have a specific wing length, a particular type of feet, or a specific type of beak. Only actual instances of the abstraction called birds have these specific values.

Attributes can become objects in their own right, with attributes of their own. (See Figure 6.11.) It's simply a matter of how much detail you want to capture in your model. For example, you might decide to make bird a higher-level class-object and create independent class-objects for wings, feet, and beaks, each with its own attributes and values. The instances—specific birds—would remain constant, although you would be observing more and more of their characteristics, and in more detail, as you defined more attributes and values.

By providing more detail, you can erect a hierarchy of class-objects, with each higher level focusing on more abstract attributes. As you add more levels of class-objects, you must be sure to keep track of the types of relationships that exist between the different objects. The simplest relationship is the one existing between lower-level class-objects and specific instances of that class-object. Thus, a specific robin is an instance (or instance-object) of the class (or class-object) robins.

Relationships between different class-objects can become quite complex. There are two general types of hierarchies involved: classification hierarchies and complex relationship hierarchies (or networks).

Classification Hierarchies

Our animal hierarchy (Figure 6.4) is a good example of a classification hierarchy. Each level of the classification hierarchy provides a more abstract way of

122   KNOWLEDGE ACQUISITION

Figure 6.11 Two levels of abstractions about some specific birds.

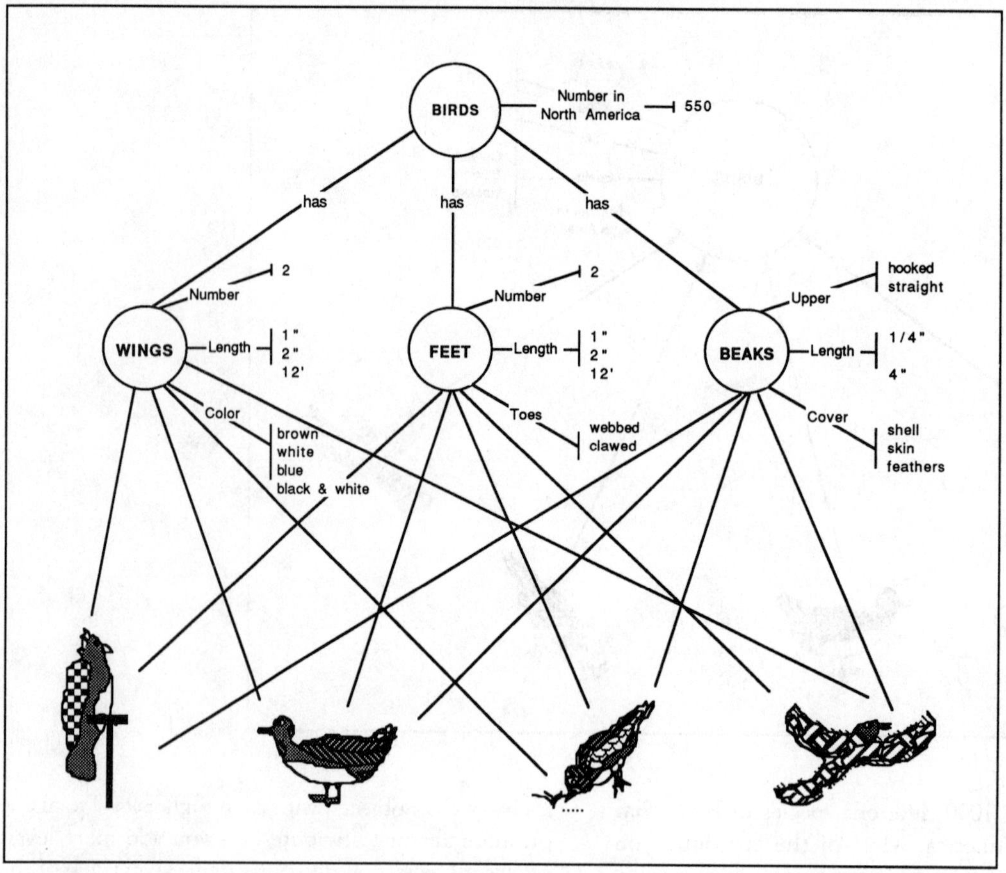

grouping the objects described on the next lower level. The more abstract term is often referred to as a *superset*, while the more specific term is usually called a *subset*. The relationships are all called "IS-A" relationships. A bird IS-A type of animal, and so on. In effect, each lower level of a classification is included in the definition of the next higher level. An animal, properly understood, includes birds and fish and mammals, and so on.

A hierarchy that divides an organization into its component parts is also an example of a classification hierarchy. Figure 6.12 provides a description of a manufacturing organization in the form of a hierarchy. We could just as well have provided an example of a car engine, and then slowly subdivided the engine into its constituent sets of parts and ultimately subdivided it into specific pieces of metal, nuts and bolts, and so on.

Complex Relationship Hierarchies

Complex relationship hierarchies are often called *networks*. Some hierarchies use many different relationship labels to describe the specific relationships between objects. These hierarchies are usually represented as networks and they can become quite complex.

Figure 6.13 illustrates a complex relationship hierarchy as opposed to a classification hierarchy. Notice that the relationship lines in the complex relationship hierarchy can be labeled to indicate the relationship, depending upon which way the relationship line is traversed. Thus robin and worm have a relationship, such that the worm is eaten by the robin, while the robin eats worms.

A classification hierarchy groups concepts together so that each layer of objects is a subclass of the level above. A network represents both objects and attributes as nodes and labels the links between them. This approach is sometimes more flexible than a classification hierarchy, but it is often more confusing. We recommend that you begin any project by trying to represent your expert's knowledge in a classification hierarchy and move to a network only when you find that the simpler approach fails to capture important aspects of your expert's knowledge.

The hierarchies we have been considering have all been static, as if the objects were always unchanging. In fact, most objects change in the course of time. A bird, for example, has a life cycle. It begins as an embryo in an egg. It hatches and becomes a chick. Later it matures and behaves as an adult bird. Later still, it dies. When an object changes from time to time, any particular phase in its life cycle is called a *state*.

If an object changes state, that fact is usually represented as an attribute of the object. In such a case, one of the object's attributes specifies the state it is in at any point in time. Other attributes of the object can take different values, depending upon the state of the object. Thus, our Bird object has a life cycle. The class-object, bird, has an attribute, "state." The value that the state attribute takes, in

Figure 6.12 A classification hierarchy for a manufacturing organization.

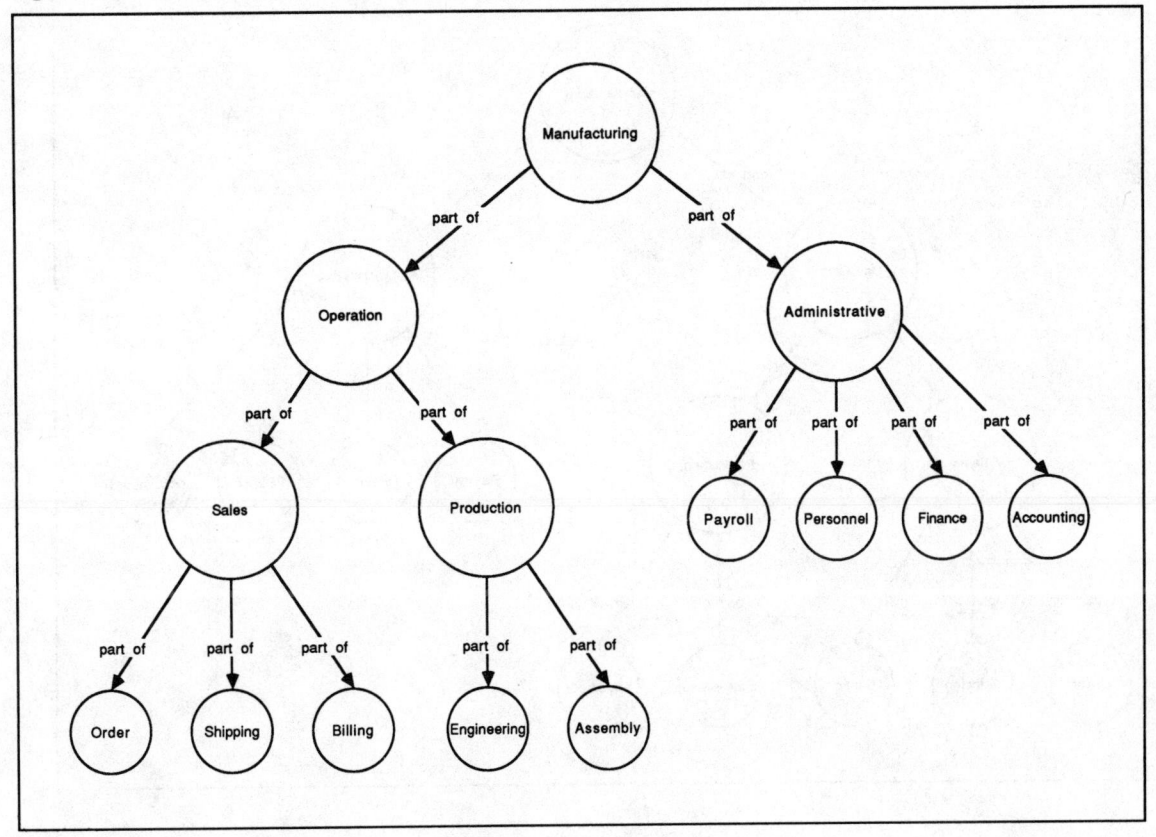

turn, determines the values of other state-related attributes that are associated with the Bird object. (See Figure 6.14.)

Sometimes a change in an object's state can have such a sweeping impact on its attributes that a completely separate object is needed to describe the new state. For example, the attributes that describe a caterpillar would be considerably different after the caterpillar emerged from its chrysalis as a butterfly.

You can build expert systems that will handle the complexities involved in state changes, but you need to use various approaches, including demons and multiple hierarchy systems.

KNOWLEDGE MAPPING NOTATION

In this section, we provide you with a notation system that you can use to record the knowledge you obtain from your expert. We suggest a minimal approach, which you can expand as needed, to handle any particular body of knowledge you wish to represent.

Describing a Hierarchy

The place to begin developing a description of a body of knowledge is with a hierarchy or network of objects.

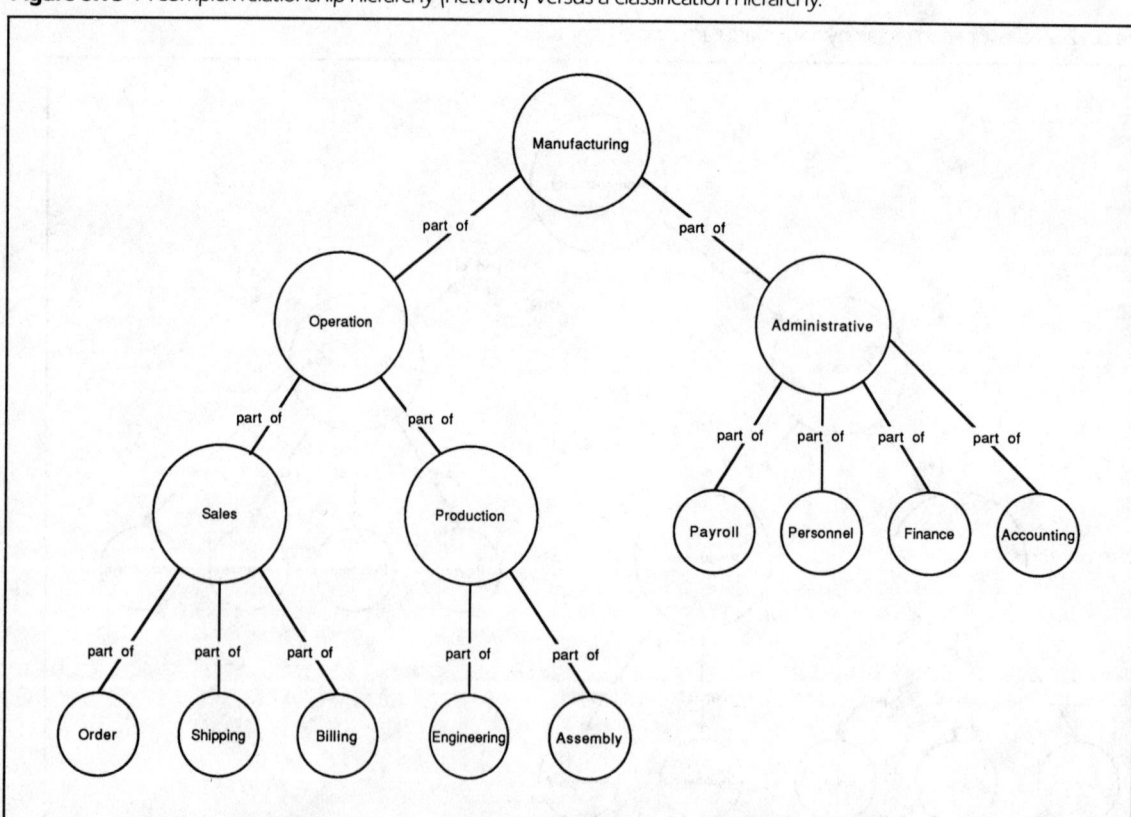

Figure 6.13 A complex relationship hierarchy (network) versus a classification hierarchy.

Figure 6.14 An object that has several states. Constraints or demons can be used to assure that state changes occur in the proper order (e.g., from chick to adult).

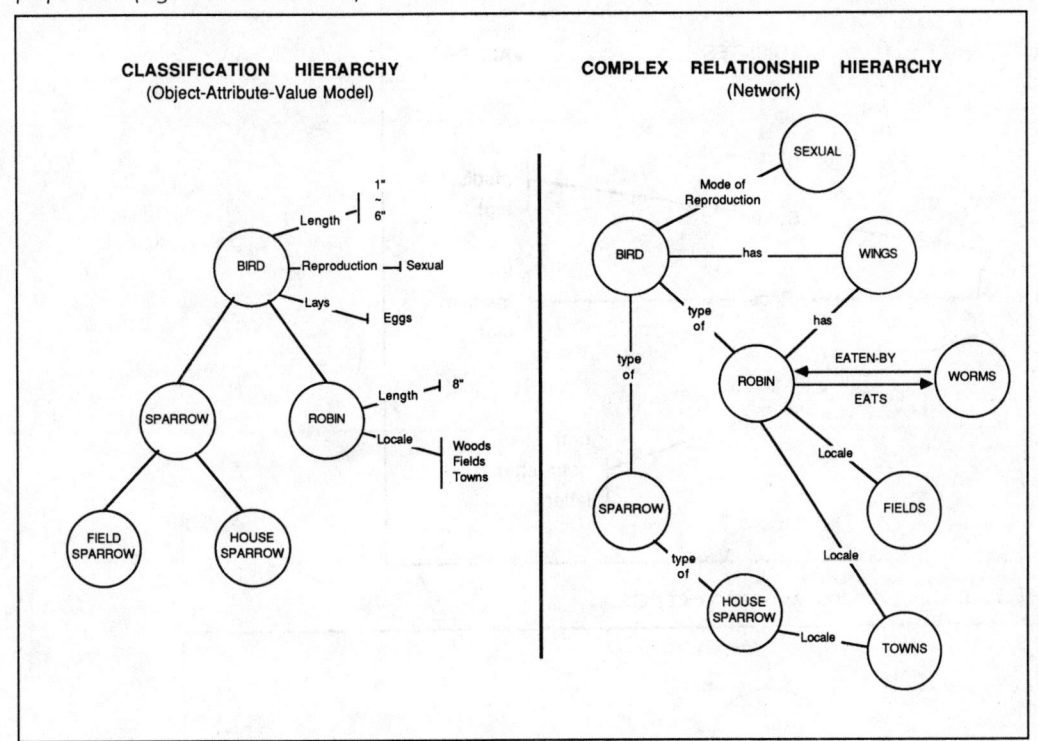

```
CLASSIFICATION HIERARCHY          COMPLEX RELATIONSHIP HIERARCHY
(Object-Attribute-Value Model)             (Network)
```

If you face a simple problem, you can probably represent all of the information in a single diagram. Figure 6.15 illustrates an overview of a single object with three attributes, each with its range of associated values. In this example, the object is a printer. We show three attributes of printers: speed, price, and quality. For each attribute, we list three possible values.

This printer system is a very simple system. If you were building a small rule system to help someone choose a printer, you might not bother to create a diagram like this one. If you were building a system to help people choose a whole collection of computer equipment and thought your knowledge might become complex, you should diagram the basic knowledge, starting, in this example, with a printer. Our Printer object is a class-object. Specific printers would be instances of the Printer class-object. Each instance would take specific values and have its own name. Figure 6.16 shows two instances of the Printer object. We have changed the lower left instance into a rule to show how the instances of this simple analysis could just as well have been represented in terms of rules. (We discuss this in detail in Chapter 8, when we talk about developing simple rule systems.)

Notice that we have represented the class-instance relationship between the Printer object and the instances with a dashed line. The instance-objects themselves are represented as circles with shadow circles behind them to remind you that they are instances. Instances may or may not exist in the knowledge base of an object-oriented system. In any case, when a consultation is in progress, it is the instances that are entered in working memory. Nor-

Figure 6.15 An object with attributes and values.

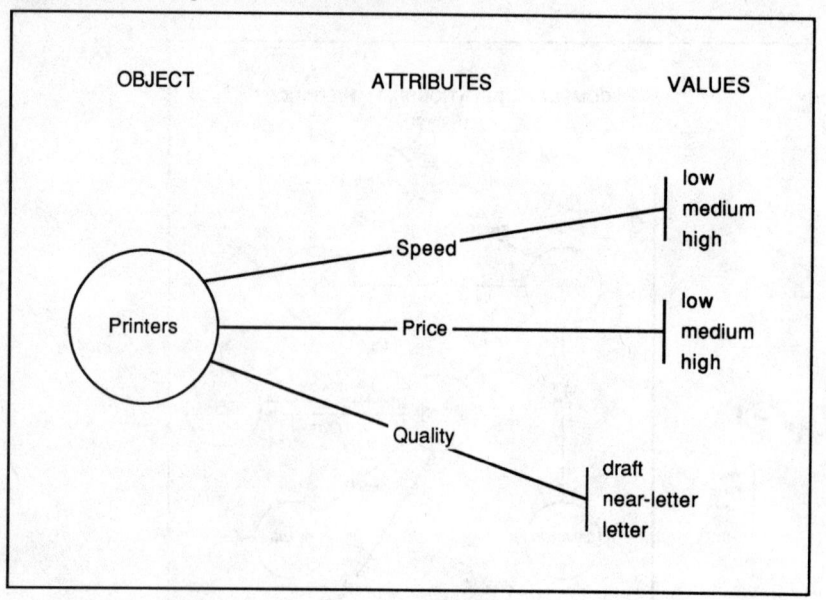

Figure 6.16 The Printer class-object and two instance-objects.

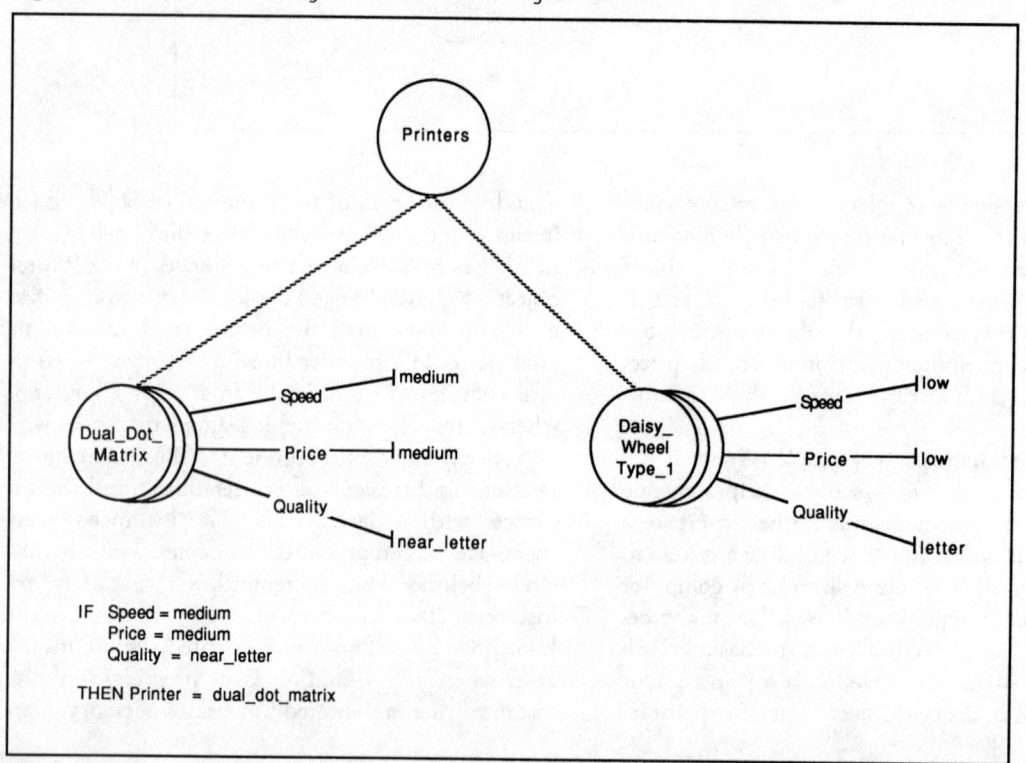

```
IF  Speed = medium
    Price = medium
    Quality = near_letter

THEN Printer = dual_dot_matrix
```

mally, you can create as many instances of a class-object as you need during a particular consultation.

The minute you move beyond small systems, the class hierarchies start to become complex and the ... object can increase dramat-
... are analyzing the
... uctured rule sys-
... uld shift to the

... are all represented
... resented by circles
... icate that they can
... gain. Relationships
... nted by solid lines,
... class-objects and
... by dashed lines.
... bject" and "instance-
... We are using them at

... twork of objects.

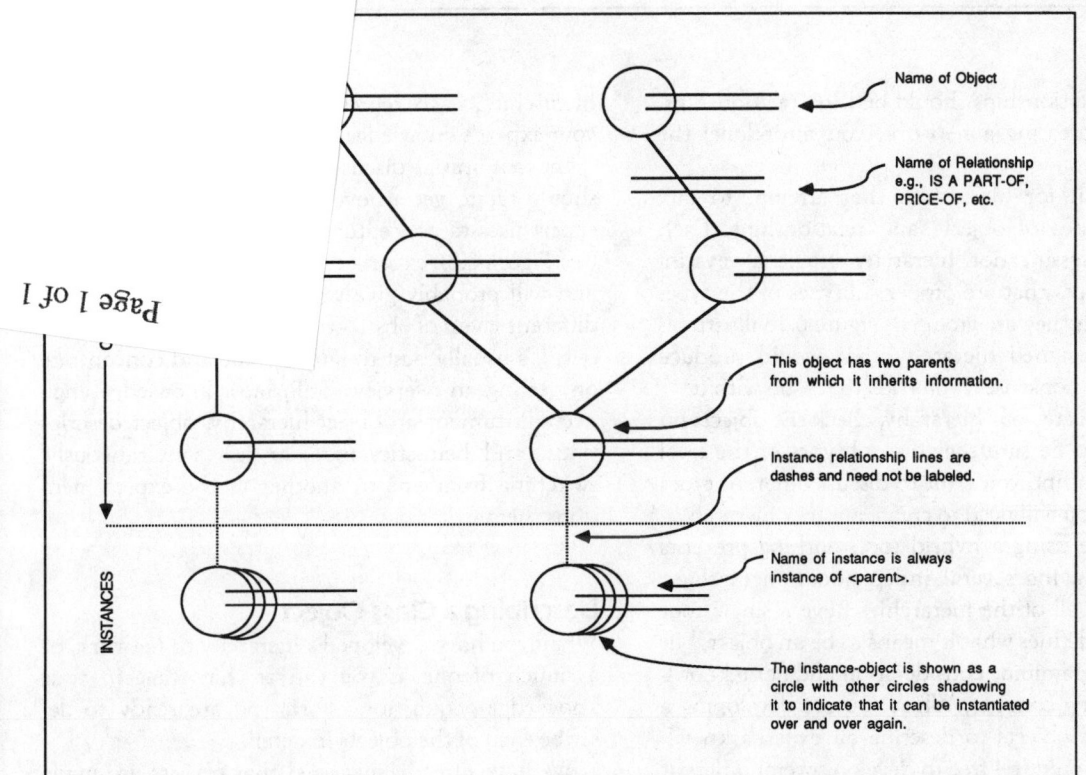

this time simply to be sure you see the difference between the two types of objects. We'll gradually just refer to them all as objects. But keep the distinction in mind. When you look at tools, different vendors will use different terms. Some will call class-objects "units" or "schema" or "classes." Others will distinguish between "objects," by which they mean class-objects and "instances." But when talking casually, nearly everyone uses "object" to refer to almost anything, and hence a lot of confusion arises. No matter what they are called, the important distinction is that class-objects are templates (i.e., sets of attributes without specific values) while instance-objects have specific values associated with their attributes during a specific consultation, and these attribute-value pairs are then placed in working memory.

If you are dealing with a classification hierarchy,

- Name of Object
- Name of Relationship e.g., IS A PART-OF, PRICE-OF, etc.
- This object has two parents from which it inherits information.
- Instance relationship lines are dashes and need not be labeled.
- Name of instance is always instance of <parent>.
- The instance-object is shown as a circle with other circles shadowing it to indicate that it can be instantiated over and over again.

INSTANCES

128 KNOWLEDGE ACQUISITION

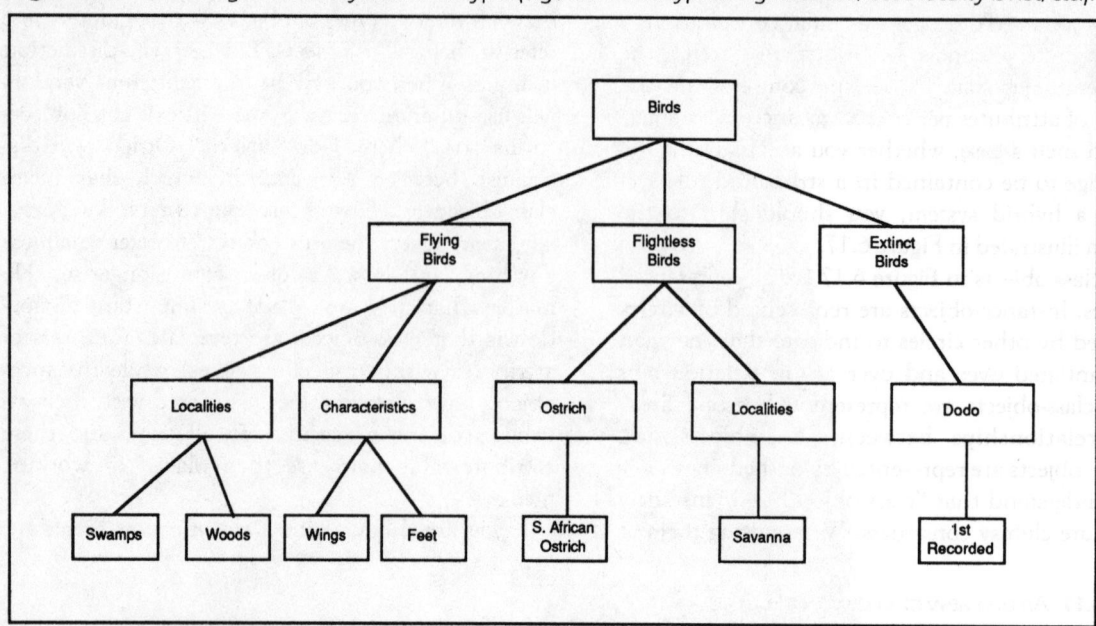

Figure 6.18 A meaningless hierarchy that mixes types (e.g., ostrich is a type of flightless bird, but a locality is not, etc.).

all of the relationships should be IS-A relationships. If you are creating a network, you must label the relationships.

Watch out for hierarchies that attempt to mix different types of objects and relationships. Each level of a classification hierarchy should always include concepts that are proper subtypes of the types under which they are grouped. Figure 6.18 illustrates a poorly designed hierarchy that would produce nothing but nonsense if you tried to reason with it.

As you create your hierarchy, check the objects on each level to be sure they are subtypes of the level above. If you find you want to discuss different types of objects, you will need to create another hierarchy.

If you are using a hybrid tool, nothing prevents you from having several independent hierarchies. Technically, all of the hierarchies have a single root object that defines what it means to be an object, but this is a programming consideration and not a knowledge mapping concern. When you are developing a hierarchy of objects to describe an expert's knowledge, you should feel free to develop several different hierarchies, each representing a different aspect of your expert's knowledge.

In your initial discussions with your expert, you should try to get an overview of the knowledge the expert uses to conceptualize problems. As we noted (see Figure 6.8), experts tend to be very case-oriented and will probably give you different information at different levels of abstraction. You will need to sort it out; it's usually best to ignore some and concentrate on getting an overview. Still, most knowledge engineers document an object hierarchy, object descriptions, and heuristics more or less simultaneously, switching from one to another as the expert mentions them.

Describing a Class-Object

When you have developed a hierarchy or network, or as much of one as you can at that stage in your knowledge acquisition effort, you are ready to describe each of the objects in detail.

We have already suggested that objects are made

up of attributes and values. Figure 6.19 illustrates a worksheet that you can use to describe an object. There is a blank for the object's name and a space to indicate its parent object(s). Below that there are a number of rows or slots. You should enter each attribute associated with the object in a slot.

We have divided each slot or row into four columns (or facets), each for a specific type of information. In Column 1, you should enter the name of the attribute. In Column 2, you should enter information about the possible values associated with each attribute. In Column 3, you should enter information about how the system will obtain the value of the attribute. Finally, in Column 4, you should enter any information about what the system might do if it actually created an instance and obtained a value for a particular attribute.

Attribute names. As a general rule, you should keep your attribute names as simple and short as possible. If you need to store much information to remind you of the exact definition of an attribute, you should write a question that you might ask a user to determine that value. For example, in an auto diagnosis system, you might have an attribute called "spark" and a question associated with it that read: "If you take your key and scratch a lead to your battery, do you see a spark?" The question clarifies

Figure 6.19 An Object Description Worksheet.

	OBJECT WORKSHEET			
System:				
Object Name:				
Parent(s):				

Slot	ATTRIBUTES	VALUES/CONSTRAINTS	SOURCE(S) OF VALUE(S)	WHEN MODIFIED
1.		e.g., possible values 　type of values 　　-default 　　-single/multiple value 　　-inherited by children (yes/no)	e.g., inheritance (from object) -database lookup rule(s) -Procedure/Sensor method	e.g., Demon(s) -when created -when modified -when deleted
2.				
3.				
4.				
5.				
6.				

the meaning of the more cryptic name "spark." We have not provided room for questions on the object worksheet. At first, if you need to write out questions, you should put the information on the back of the object worksheet.

Values/constraints. Although the attributes of most class-objects will not have specific values associated with them, they normally have a set of possible values. In effect, these values constrain the possible values that any instance could take. For example, a light bulb could have an attribute referring to whether the bulb was lit or not. The values that "lit" could take would be "on," "off," and perhaps "broken." You might want to indicate that one of these possible values was more likely than the others (a default value that should be assigned to any child, or instance of the object, when no other information is available). You might decide that "off" should be the default value for light bulbs. Some attributes might take only a single value while others might take several values. Thus, while light bulbs take either "on" or "off," someone's favorite colors might include "red," "orange," and "violet."

The attribute of a class-object might be unique to the class-object, or it might be inherited by lower-level class-objects or instances (children).

Source(s) of value(s). In the third column, you should enter information about how the expert normally determines the value(s) that should be associated with an attribute. The source of a value might be inheritance from a parent object, it might be looked up in a database, or a user might be asked for the value. Likewise, the system might obtain the data from a sensor reading, or he might use rules of thumb to provide a value for the attribute.

Obviously, in a complex object hierarchy, many of the class-objects obtain values from their parent class-objects. In such a case you should indicate "inherited from <parent object>" in the third column.

When modified. In the final column, you should indicate any relationships between attributes and values associated with different objects. For example, if you know that a change in the value of one attribute will lead to a change in the value of some other attribute's value, you should indicate this in the last column. In most tools, you will use this information to write demons or procedures that will make the necessary adjustments when the system is being used. (We discuss these issues in detail in Chapter 11 when we consider how hybrid systems are actually constructed.)

Modified information is critical when you are dealing with objects that assume different states. In effect, a modification is a state change.

Completing the worksheet and the diagram. You should work back and forth between your object worksheets and your object hierarchy diagram until you are satisfied that you have a good overview of your expert's knowledge. Each object on your network chart should have an accompanying object worksheet that defines the attributes, values, and methods of obtaining and modifying those values.

Describing Rules and Specifying a Procedural Model

As you define the objects and attributes in your expert's knowledge base, you should also record the heuristics that your expert uses to reason about her knowledge. In effect, your expert's object-attribute network or domain model is like a database; the object diagrams are the knowledge engineer's equivalent of database structures (e.g., entity-relationship diagrams). In addition to a domain model that describes the objects and attributes in your expert's world, you will usually have to create a procedural model that describes the sets of heuristics that your expert uses to solve problems and the order in which the various sets of heuristics are used. In structured rule systems, the procedural model is called a context tree, while in hybrid systems, it is generally called a procedural model. The procedural model is equivalent to a high-level structured dataflow model. In effect, it is comprised of sequenced sets of rules that can be used to solve a problem. (See Figure 6.20.)

Cognitive Analysis   131

Figure 6.20 The relationship between domain and procedural models and more conventional analysis concepts.

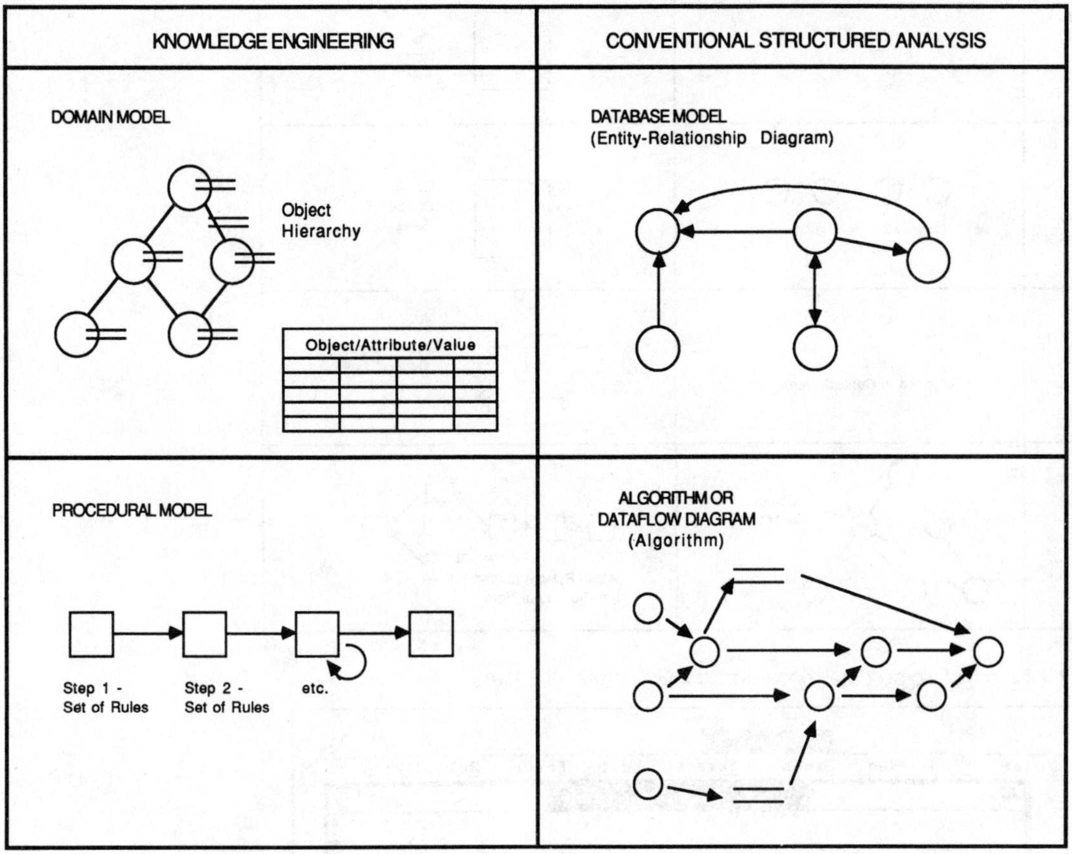

KNOWLEDGE ENGINEERING	CONVENTIONAL STRUCTURED ANALYSIS
DOMAIN MODEL — Object Hierarchy; Object/Attribute/Value	DATABASE MODEL (Entity-Relationship Diagram)
PROCEDURAL MODEL — Step 1 - Set of Rules, Step 2 - Set of Rules, etc.	ALGORITHM OR DATAFLOW DIAGRAM (Algorithm)

In very simple systems, the entire knowledge base consists of a single set of rules. It is a very simple procedural model that says, in effect, that to solve a problem you should consider the rules in the knowledge base.

More complex knowledge bases have domain knowledge organized into object hierarchies and procedural models that consist of several sets of rules that should be tried in some specific order. In some sophisticated systems, the domain and procedural models are integrated within the object-oriented framework (e.g., in KEE, rules are objects within their own "rule hierarchy"). Figure 6.21 illustrates some of the patterns that you find in typical expert systems building tools.

A procedural model for a complex system consists of a number of sets of rules arranged in a step-by-step pattern. To diagram a procedural model, you should begin by simply creating a box for each step that an expert goes through. Then you should begin to write the rules that you want to include in each set. In some cases, your expert will give you rules without necessarily describing any way to cluster them. In such a case, you should write down the rules as you learn about them, and then cluster them later. Most of the sophisticated expert systems building tools make it easy to enter rules directly into the system as you learn about them. Then, the system presents you with a diagram that shows how the rules are related to each other. (See Figure 6.22.) We consider the

Figure 6.21 Some declarative and procedural models typical of expert systems building tools.

	DECLARATIVE MODEL	PROCEDURAL MODEL
Simple Backward Chaining Rule-Based Tools	None	One Set of Rules
Simple Forward Chaining Rule-Based Tools (OPS5)	Simple Objects - No Class Hierarchy	One Set of Rules
Structured Rule-Based Systems	None (Contained in Context Tree)	Rules Arranged in Context Tree
Hybrid Systems	Object Hierarchy	Sets of Rules Arranged in a Procedural Model

Figure 6.22 Diagram of a procedural model from the GoldWorks program.

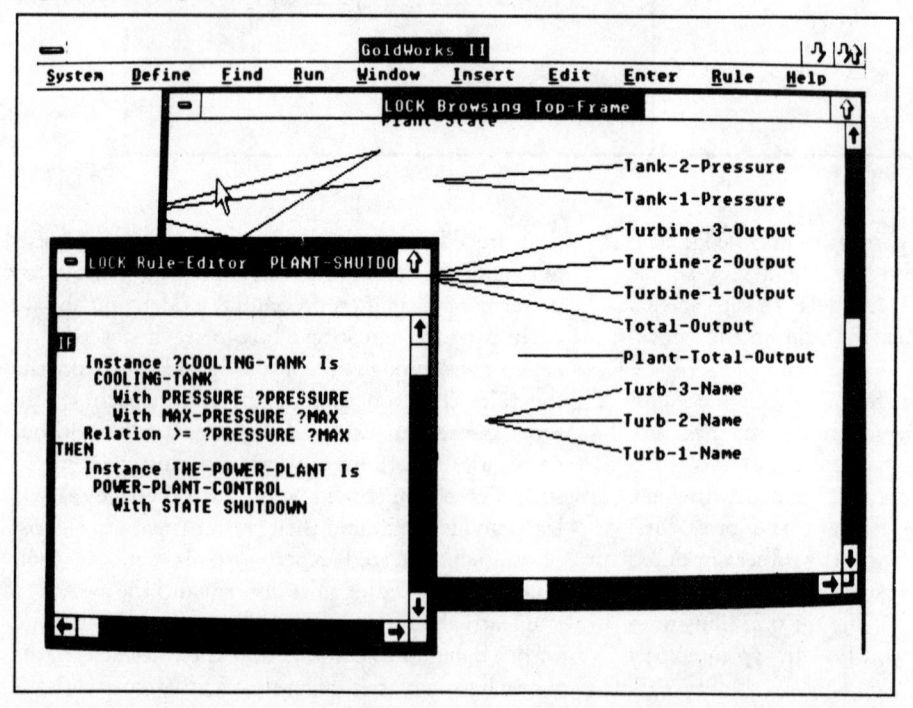

process of writing rules and clustering them in Chapters 8 through 11.

DEVELOPING A KNOWLEDGE MAP

To make these concepts more concrete, let's consider a knowledge map that describes the knowledge contained in Data General's Automated Transfer Pricing System (ATP). (This map was not developed by the actual developers of ATP; we have created it after the fact simply to illustrate how our notation conventions would represent an actual system.)

ATP (Automated Transfer Pricing System)

ATP is a system used by salespeople at Data General to quickly determine the price of parts that are being shipped to the company's overseas subsidiaries. The system first determines the type of part transfer taking place, and then implements the pricing policy that covers that type of transfer.

Data General wanted to assist its salespeople in picking prices, so they wouldn't have to consult the Data General manual on pricing policies for each order that came in. Originally, this was done with a COBOL program, but it was just too cumbersome to maintain and keep current. Data General saw the possibility of a much cleaner solution to the problem by using an expert system. ATP was built with Gold-Works, a hybrid tool, and now is easy to use and maintain.

Figure 6.23 illustrates ATP's object hierarchy. Notice that there are three separate hierarchies used in ATP. One describes the organizational unit that is ordering the part, another describes the part, and the third describes the pricing policy that governs the transfer of the part from the United States to the

Figure 6.23 Data General's ATP object hierarchies. These are three independent small object hierarchies that contain the knowledge of the transfer operation.

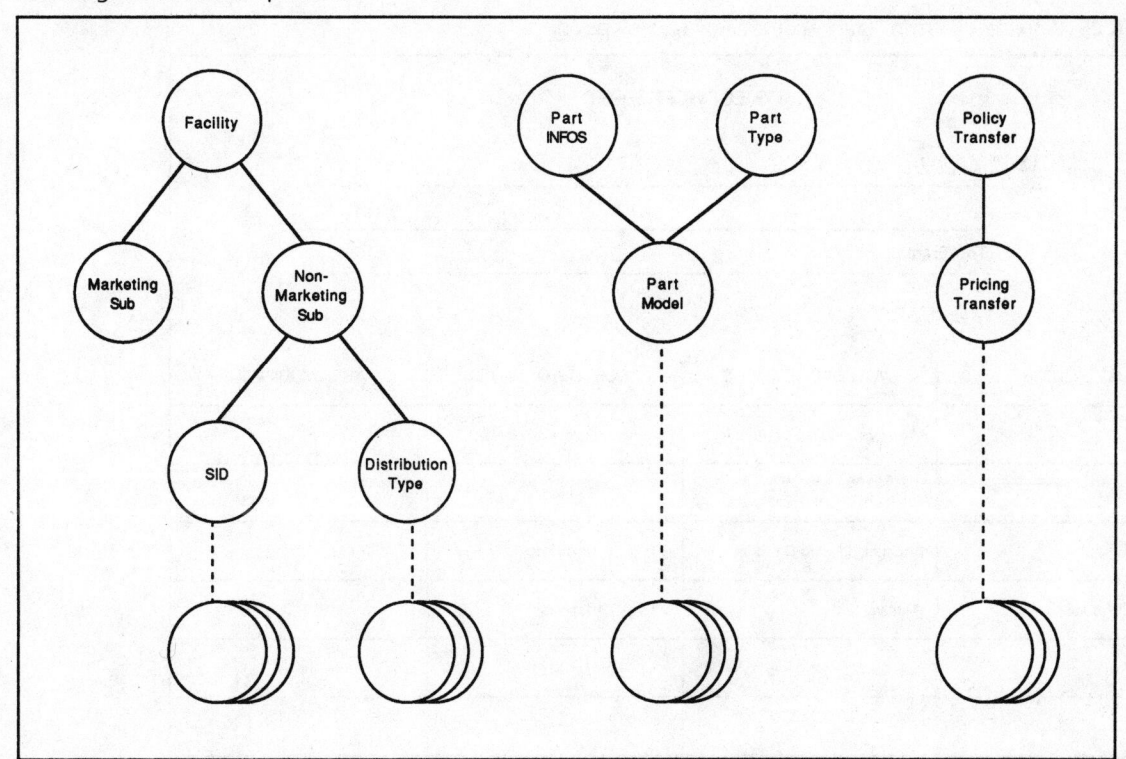

Figure 6.24 An Object-Attribute Worksheet for ATP's Part-Type object.

```
OBJECT WORKSHEET

System:       Data General's ATP
Object Name:  Part-Type
Parents:      (Top-Frame)
```

ATTRIBUTES	VALUES/CONSTRAINTS	SOURCE(S) OF VALUES	WHEN MODIFIED
Built-By	Manufactured/Vendor Purchased	Database	
Type	(Hardware, Software, Literature, Services)	Database	
Discountability	Discount, Limited-Discount	Database	
Special-Products	(Multivalue)	Database	

Figure 6.25 Worksheet with an instance of the Distribution-Type object.

```
OBJECT WORKSHEET

System:       Data General's ATP
Object Name:  Part-Type
Parents:      (Top-Frame)
```

ATTRIBUTES	VALUES/CONSTRAINTS	SOURCE(S) OF VALUES	WHEN MODIFIED
Built-By	Manufactured/Vendor Purchased	Database	
Type	(Hardware, Software, Literature, Services)	Database	
Discountability	Discount, Limited-Discount	Database	
Special-Products	(Multivalued)	Database	

organizational unit that is ordering it. We have not given names to instances here, but each of the lower-level class-objects could have one or more instances during any actual consultation.

Figure 6.24 illustrates the attributes and values associated with the Part-Type object. The BUILT-BY attribute can have one of two possible values: MANUFACTURED or VENDOR-PURCHASED. The TYPE attribute describes the type of part that is being shipped, and the DISCOUNTABILITY attribute states whether or not the part is discountable. Notice that the SPECIAL-PRODUCTS attribute needs to be multivalued (i.e., able to be associated with more than one value at the same time).

Figure 6.25 shows a specific instance of the Distribution-Type object. The instance is called NDG, which is an abbreviation for Nippon Data General. Notice that we have filled in values for each of the attributes in the object worksheet. We have given the CUSTOMER-NUMBER attribute, which is multivalued, a series of numbers that correspond to the identification code that can be used to refer to Nippon Data General. The CUSTOMER-DESCRIPTION and LOCATION attributes are used to store other ways of referring to Nippon Data General. Other attributes hold numerical values that are used in calculating the price for shipping parts to Nippon Data General.

Figure 6.26 illustrates the procedural model used in ATP. In effect, we divided the rules into three sets. Each set was used in succession. The first set of rules, inquiry rules, recognize the kind of parts to be shipped. The next set of rules, recognition rules, identify the destination of the part shipment. Finally, the transfer rules decide the actual price that should be charged for the shipment.

SUMMARY

We have tried to provide you with an overview of the object-attribute-value vocabulary that cognitive scientists typically use when they try to analyze and map the cognitive knowledge that experts use to conceptualize and solve problems.

We have suggested a general approach to creating a knowledge map of an expert's domain and procedural knowledge. This approach will help you gain an overview of the knowledge that is used in a task before you begin to encode it into a specific knowledge base.

When you think about it broadly, a knowledge engineer has three sets of tools to use in analyzing cognitive tasks.

1. *Intellectual tools.* You know that experts tend to store their knowledge in hierarchies that are ultimately chunked into a few very general, abstract objects. Thus, you know that knowledge engineering involves breaking down these chunks of an expert's knowledge. You also know that knowledge engineers develop domain models by thinking of analogous models that they already have in order to get an overview of the general structure of the model the expert must be using.

Figure 6.26 A procedural model for ATP.

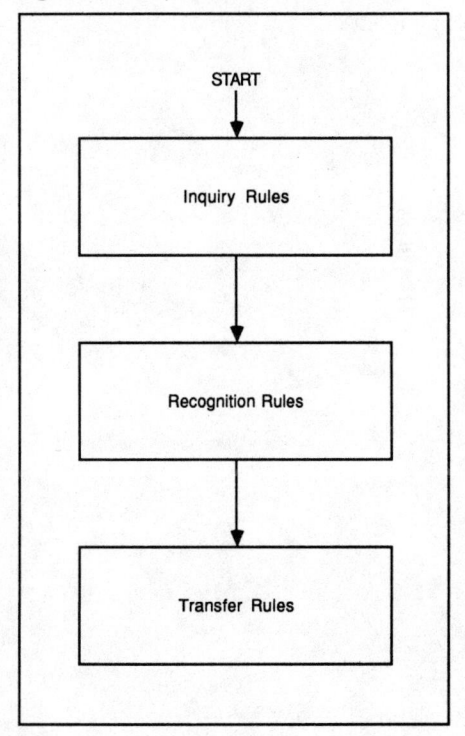

2. *Notation tools.* You have a basic vocabulary that describes the expert's knowledge in terms of objects, attributes, values, and relationships. You also have a notation convention that allows you to represent an object hierarchy and procedural models.
3. *Empirical tools.* The first two tools are limited; they only get you started. Once you have developed a domain model and a set of rules to describe your expert's knowledge, you need to encode that knowledge and try it out on a number of real cases. The system will work in some cases and fail to make the correct recommendations in other cases. Your most important tool is this empirical method. You can keep testing and revising your knowledge base and heuristic rules until you have a system that will solve all of the cases to the satisfaction of your expert. The code in your final system is, in effect, your real cognitive analysis of the knowledge and heuristics that your expert uses to solve problems.

7.
Knowledge Acquisition

INTRODUCTION

Knowledge acquisition is a complex process. In the narrowest sense, it involves obtaining the knowledge that goes into an expert system. In a broader sense, it involves the entire knowledge engineering process, including interviewing the expert, developing a knowledge map and encoding that knowledge into a knowledge base, and then testing and revising the knowledge with the expert and with the users until the system is ready to field. In this chapter, we limit our discussion to the process of obtaining information from an expert, with a few minor remarks on the problems involved in working with the expert and users during the testing and revision. Figure 7.1, which first appeared in Chapter 6, is reproduced here to highlight the position we assign to knowledge acquisition. In effect, as we define "knowledge acquisition," it involves gathering the knowledge necessary to facilitate the development of a knowledge map.

Knowledge acquisition, even using our limited definition, offers many challenges. Some knowledge engineers serve as their own experts. Others obtain all the knowledge they need from one expert, while still others work with several experts. We try to comment on the special problems raised by each of these different approaches to knowledge acquisition.

We begin with a general discussion of some of the

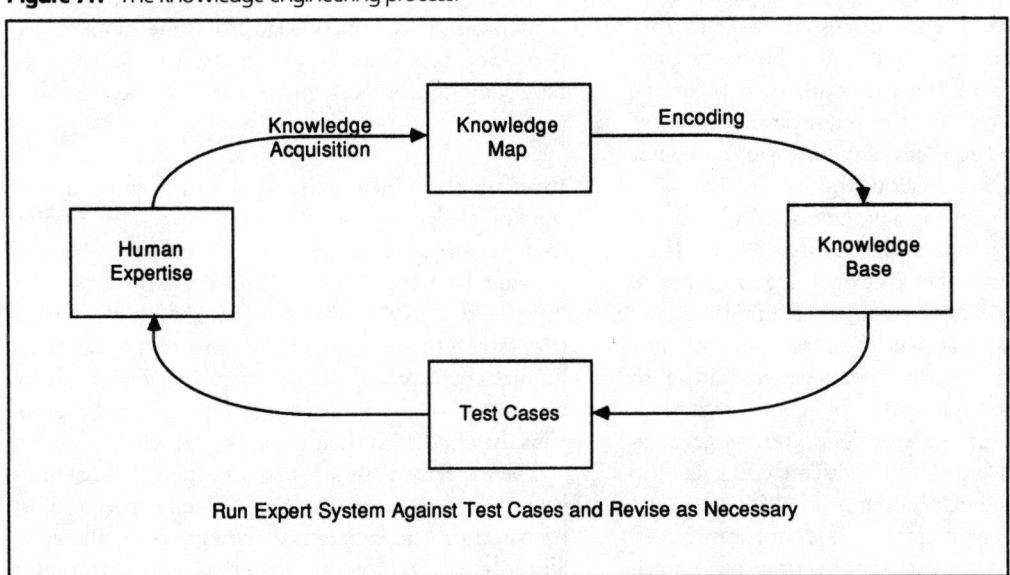

Figure 7.1 The knowledge engineering process.

problems associated with knowledge acquisition. Then we move to the actual procedures involved in setting up interviews, asking questions, and so on.

KNOWLEDGE ACQUISITION PROBLEMS

Being Your Own Expert

Many expert systems have been developed by people who served as their own experts. While this approach is most common among those developing small PC- and Macintosh-based systems, it also occurs during the development of mid-size systems designed to run on workstations or mainframes. It is most common for engineering problems of a diagnostic nature, where the expert may have already thought of his work in terms of rules, and thus is prepared to develop a system without the aid of a knowledge engineer.

The advantages of being your own expert are obvious: You don't have to worry about motivation, scheduling, or interpersonal problems. There are some significant problems, however. You will need to think very hard and objectively about what you know and how you actually go about analyzing a problem. We have already discussed the fact that humans chunk information into elaborate hierarchies. Most experts have to work to explain the hierarchies they rely on; they often developed these hierarchies so long ago that they forget exactly what assumptions they built in along the way.

If you are interviewing another person, you can usually spot the jumps and gaps in their explanations. A causal statement that makes good sense to an expert (who knows about many assumptions and exceptions but doesn't bother to state them) may seem like an outrageously broad generalization to someone who doesn't share the expert's implicit knowledge base. An independent knowledge engineer is in a good position to notice these gaps and probe further. It's much harder to identify your own jumps and gaps, but it can be done. You can gain a certain amount of perspective by putting your knowledge into a knowledge base, running a consultation, and checking to see if the system asks the right questions and reaches the proper conclusions.

If you develop your own system, you can usually sketch a knowledge map without too much trouble, but you may end up revising it more than a map developed by someone else. An outside person will ask more questions before deciding how to arrange the objects, attributes, and values that make up the map.

The safest bet is to stick as close as you can to your actual problem-solving process. Don't try to develop a broad theoretical model of your knowledge too quickly. Begin by reviewing several recent problems you have solved, one at a time, in considerable detail. Exactly what did you ask? Precisely what did the user say or show you?, and so on. All of the advice that we give to knowledge engineers working with experts applies to developers who are going to be their own expert. You have advantages if you thoroughly understand the subject matter, but you have to avoid trying to move too quickly and making too many assumptions.

Working with an Expert

Assuming that you will be developing an expert system that requires knowledge from one or more experts, you face a variety of challenges. We consider here some of the most important elements, one at a time.

Finding the right expert. If you have to obtain the knowledge you need from someone else, finding that person is your first task. When we talk with people who have developed successful projects, they invariably remark about how important the expert they worked with was. By the same token, when we inquire about projects that were unsuccessful, a large percentage of the interviewees remark on the problems they had with their expert or experts.

The experts or subject matter experts (SME) must know how to solve the problem. Their expertise must be based on the experience they gained while actually solving the problem. (In other words, you must avoid being assigned an expert who is fresh out of school or who hasn't been in the field in several years.) You must base your system on practical experience, not theoretical knowledge.

If you have a choice, you should select the best expert the company has; this is the person all of the other experts will defer to in the really tricky cases. In many situations, you will find that you will be offered a "junior expert" who can be more easily spared than the "best expert." That may have to suffice, but it will make your job much harder, and you should avoid it if you possibly can.

On the other hand, no matter how good your expert is, it won't help you if your expert isn't willing to cooperate. Indeed, what you really want is an expert who is highly motivated to help you develop an expert system, and that kind of expert is difficult to find.

The place to start in finding the best expert is when you first begin to interview experts and discuss developing a particular expert system. You need to decide exactly what the expert system will do (e.g., Will it replace the expert at an onerous task or replace the expert entirely? Will it assist people in performing the task or actually perform the task without human assistance?). Then you need to ask yourself: What's in it for the human expert? You should be trying to develop an expert system that will make the human expert's job easier. It may, for example, relieve the expert from boring, routine questions or repetitious tasks. (Remember, many experts have developed expert systems precisely because they wanted to make their jobs easier.) At a minimum, you should make the project intellectually interesting to the expert. It will give the expert a chance to reflect on his knowledge. Many experts report that they understand their work much better after having gone through the process of working with a knowledge engineer to develop an expert system.

Some experts are professionals and will help with the effort simply because the company asks them to do it. Others may agree to do it because they are told to, but they will actually resist the effort. Since the development of a useful system depends on the expert's cooperation, you must avoid, at all costs, getting into a situation in which you are trying to acquire knowledge from an expert who doesn't want to provide it. Luckily, most expert systems benefit the expert and most companies have more than one expert, so that you can find at least one who is interested or will cooperate with the effort. If you can't, you are better off canceling the project and looking for another expert systems opportunity than trying to force an expert to work with you against her inclination.

It will help your effort if you can provide your expert with a clear explanation of what you are trying to do and what the function of the final system will be. For example, meeting with your expert and building a five-rule system is a good idea; it makes the whole process much more concrete and less intimidating.

In one organization, the knowledge engineers talked about knowledge acquisition as "brain draining." What kind of human expert would be inclined to submit to or cooperate with such a process? Make it clear right from the start that AI and expert systems technology is not all that mysterious, and that the development of an expert system absolutely depends on a human expert who has acquired knowledge over a period of years. Most experts are proud of their achievements in mastering a complex problem-solving technology. It doesn't hurt to tell them how impressed you are with their expertise and how grateful you are that they are consenting to help you develop your system. Tact and explicit appreciation will always help facilitate knowledge acquisition, just as they make most other human undertakings go more smoothly.

Scheduling and management support. If your human expert is involved in important and critical company work, then scheduling time with the expert can be a major problem. If you have senior management support and your expert system is perceived to be of strategic importance to the company, you may be able to get significant blocks of your expert's time. Much more commonly, you will need to adjust your schedule to fit the expert's schedule. When a crisis comes up, accept the fact that your expert will be unavailable. If too many crises come up, however, you will have to determine how serious management is about your effort. You will have to be able to meet with your expert for a few hours every few weeks—depending on the size of your effort—if you are to develop and test your system. If that becomes impossible, you need another expert or another project.

Experts and users. If you are working on a typical diagnostic problem, there is an expert who knows how to solve the problem and there are users who need to get advice from the expert. The expert system you develop will allow the users to obtain recommendations from the system rather than getting advice from the human expert. Hence, you have two sources of knowledge about the problem: You have the users, who know when the problem occurs, the various types of problems they face, and the sorts of information the expert typically requires, and you have the expert, who knows how to analyze the problem and recommend a solution.

In some cases, users may be junior maintenance personnel or clerical workers, but in a large number of cases, users are sophisticated technicians or professional people who can contribute a great deal to your analysis of the knowledge that must be included in your system. Moreover, they are usually more qualified than the expert to tell you about what interface would be most useful and what specific tasks they would like the expert system to perform. Too many expert systems efforts have initially focused entirely on the expert and turned to the users only when the system was ready for a field test. In most cases, this proved to be a mistake that resulted in a poorer system or required that the knowledge engineer make significant changes in the system to accommodate the actual needs of the people who were going to use the expert system.

When you first begin to consider developing an expert system, you need to identify an expert and you also need to meet with users and discuss exactly how they would use an expert system, if you were to develop one. In most cases, the users can help you design a narrower, better focused system. Users, for example, may be satisfied with a system that is 80 percent accurate. Your expert, on the other hand, may feel that you want him to tell you everything he knows. Working with both users and experts helps you define your effort more narrowly and more functionally. This, in turn, makes it more likely that the project will be completed and fielded.

Coopers & Lybrand has an expert system called ExperTax. The system incorporates the knowledge of 40 top partners of the firm. ExperTax replaces a written questionnaire (that could run up to 200 pages) that junior auditors formerly completed and submitted to senior tax experts for analysis. The expert system now allows the junior auditors to make the analysis with ExperTax and make the resulting recommendations available much more quickly. In the process of developing ExperTax, which took some 7,000 hours, Coopers & Lybrand knowledge engineers developed a very useful technique for acquiring knowledge. They used a large table that was divided in the middle by a partition. The firm's tax experts sat on one side and junior auditors sat on the other. The junior auditor would explain what she was looking at, and the experts, who could not see the materials, would ask questions.

The partition assured that the tax experts would not make assumptions that the knowledge engineer wouldn't know about. If the expert could look over the junior auditor's shoulder, he might glance at the form and then ask a question that depended on knowledge he had just gained by seeing the information on the form. Without being able to see the form, the experts were forced to ask much more elaborate questions. They asked the junior auditor to read them various numbers. In some cases, they heard the results and then said "never mind." This provided the knowledge engineer with an opportunity to ask why the experts were asking the questions. The knowledge engineer could also ask what the expert would have recommended if the answers had been different. This technique of making experts ask for all of the information they need before reaching any conclusions makes knowledge acquisition much more efficient.

The Coopers & Lybrand approach emphasizes two things. First, it provides a nice example of how users and experts can work together to develop an expert system. Second, it illustrates one of the problems involved in developing an expert system while serving as the expert. Before they started using the partitioned table, Coopers & Lybrand experts, with the best of intentions, were saying things like, "If the company is facing an xyz inventory problem, as they are, then you should consider B." Only when probed would they explain how they determined that the company was, in fact, running an xyz inventory problem. They had glanced at information on the form, noted certain specifics, and automatically assumed that the company was running an inventory deficit. It was so obvious to them that they didn't think to explain how they knew it, until they were forced to by the partition. Before recommending B, they had to ask for certain information to know if the company was running an inventory deficit. If asked, they might not have even realized they were obtaining the information. After years of evaluating forms and questionnaires, they just "automatically" checked forcertain conditions and assumed that everyone else would, too.

In developing a small system, you should plan to spend almost as much time with the users as with the expert. They may not know how the expert conceptualizes and thinks about the problem, but they can certainly help you design and edit the input and output requirements of the system. And they can often help by providing cases and participating in trials. Users have knowledge just as experts do, and a successful knowledge acquisition effort will involve identifying and capturing all of the relevant knowledge from both parties.

Single versus multiple experts. The classic description of an expert systems development effort always assumes a single expert and a single knowledge engineer. In fact, many systems have been developed by someone who was both the knowledge engineer and the expert. Of the remaining systems, at least as many have involved multiple experts as single experts. (In other words, the "classic model" is just what most classic models are: an ideal that is only occasionally realized.)

It's certainly easier to work with one expert than with several. It's easier to develop a relationship with one person than with several, and it's easier to schedule and plan. Most important, if you have only one expert, she can provide you with a single view of the domain and can name the objects and attributes of the domain in whatever manner she prefers. If you are working with several experts, you will necessarily spend some time arguing about what certain things should be called, or if a specific entity or concept should be an object or simply an attribute of some other object.

If you have to work with multiple experts, you should try, when possible, to work with the group to develop a broad overview and then subdivide the effort and work with different experts on different subtasks. This is often a successful strategy. Indeed, one reason projects use multiple experts is because each expert is an expert in only part of the task.

If you have three experts who all share exactly the same knowledge and you are forced to work with all three for "political" reasons, you must simply resign yourself to listening to some disagreements among your experts. In many cases, one attribute name would do as well as another, but one must be chosen and, once chosen, used consistently thereafter. If your experts disagree on what word to use, there is only so much you can do to resolve the problem.

Human communication problems. Whether you deal with one expert or several, people occasionally misspeak themselves. And people occasionally hear one thing and write down another. Some knowledge engineering studies in which everything has been tape recorded and then cross-checked reveal that these errors occur just as commonly in knowledge engineering efforts as anywhere else. We discuss documentation techniques later, but assuming that you are recording a session by taking notes, it's a good idea to keep the sessions short and review the notes at the end of each session. You should also give the expert the rules to edit as soon as possible. Most important, you should expect some mistakes to creep in and then be as good natured as possible in dealing with these problems. It ultimately doesn't make any difference whether the expert mistakenly said something he didn't really mean to say or whether you were mistaken when you wrote down what you thought the expert said. Both cases will occur, and the only thing to do is to use editing and cross-checking procedures to identify and eliminate mistakes with as little fuss or blame as possible.

We have already mentioned that experts often fail to recognize just what they know. Most experts underestimate the extent of their knowledge. They know of the high-level concepts and procedures that they bring to bear, but they often fail to appreciate all of the many lower-level concepts and assumptions that you must identify and understand in order to create an adequate and functional map of their knowledge.

Some experts are very good at explaining their knowledge in an orderly way and others are not. When asked to explain their decision processes, those experts who have not thought about what they do in a systematic way will often fall back on approaches they have read in books. These explanations are typically too neat and tidy. The touchstone of all explanations is their ability to account for the actual steps the expert takes in specific cases, the questions the expert asks, and the predictions the expert makes. Experts often rely on heuristics that they find difficult to verbalize. The heuristics may even seem silly or unrelated to the theories that the experts believe should explain their actions. The best way to deal with these problems is to rely on the careful review of cases and on the relationship that you develop with the expert. In effect, the knowledge engineer should encourage the experts to have confidence in their own expertise. This, in turn, should help experts to ignore the theories of others and focus on exactly how they think about a particular problem.

INTERVIEWING

If you are going to be your own expert, then you will have to ask yourself how you actually solve the task you want to turn into an expert system. In all other cases, the knowledge engineer must meet with the expert to obtain the knowledge needed to develop the expert system. Interviewing is the heart of the knowledge acquisition process, and there are many different ways to go about it. We consider one general strategy here, but also provide information on some of the other ways people approach this task.

Figure 7.2 gives you an overview of the entire process. In general, we suggest that knowledge acquisition takes place in four different phases:

Phase 1. Initial Task Analysis and Expert Selection
Phase 2. Prepare for Knowledge Acquisition Interviewing
Phase 3. Conduct Initial Knowledge Acquisition Interviews
Phase 4. Conduct Case Review Interviews

We consider each phase in turn.

Phase 1. Initial Task Analysis and Expert Selection

During the first phase of knowledge acquisition, you, as the developer, should meet with managers, experts, and users in order to select an appropriate task and to identify one or more experts whom you can work with to develop a system.

During this initial period, you're not concerned with knowledge acquisition as such, but you are in a good position to get an overview of the nature of the task, its inputs and outputs, and the overall problem-solving methodology used by the expert or experts. This information not only allows you to decide if an expert system is feasible, but it also enables you to learn about the nature and scope of the knowledge you will need to acquire from the expert. If possible, you should get one or two sets of case data and references to books and articles that you can study before the next phase.

This first phase also gives you a chance to get to know the expert or experts and to choose an expert to work with if there are options available. Initially, of course, you must satisfy yourself that there is an expert and that the expert would be willing to cooperate in developing an expert system. If the initial

Figure 7.2 An Overview of the Knowledge Acquisition Process.

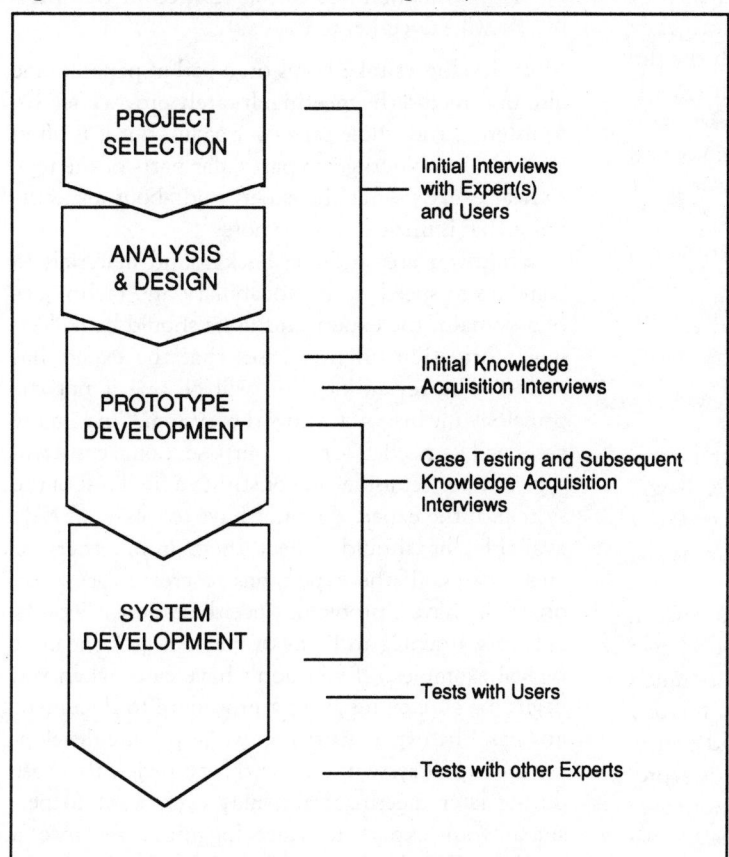

```
PROJECT SELECTION ─────┐
                       ├── Initial Interviews with Expert(s) and Users
ANALYSIS & DESIGN ─────┘

PROTOTYPE DEVELOPMENT ──── Initial Knowledge Acquisition Interviews
                      ──── Case Testing and Subsequent Knowledge Acquisition Interviews

SYSTEM DEVELOPMENT
                      ──── Tests with Users
                      ──── Tests with other Experts
```

phase of the project fails to identify an appropriate expert, you should conclude that the project is unfeasible and proceed to the consideration of another task.

Phase 2. Prepare for Knowledge Acquisition Interviewing

Once you have selected a project and identified one or more experts to work with, you should spend some time preparing for the knowledge acquisition task.

Although it will vary from project to project, experts will normally prefer to speak with someone who has at least some knowledge of their field. If they sense that they are going to have to teach you the basics of their field, they may decide the effort will take too much time. Further, if you are asking experts to talk about the procedures they use in analyzing and solving problems, they will be most comfortable doing so if they can use the technical language of their specialty. All of this suggests that you should make an effort to learn as much as possible about a domain before you begin to interview the expert.

If possible, you should consider reading an introductory textbook in the domain, or some technical papers recommended by the expert. If you do read technical papers and encounter many concepts and terms that are unfamiliar, you should probably seek out more basic texts to familiarize yourself with those concepts and terms.

Most people who want to develop an expert system begin with a system in a domain in which they are already familiar. This reduces the effort they must expend in acquainting themselves with the domain before they begin interacting with an expert. Individuals who enjoy developing expert systems in different domains are typically people who enjoy and are good at learning about a new subject in a short period of time.

In addition to becoming familiar with the domain, you should develop an overall interviewing strategy. Things to consider when developing a strategy include the following questions.

- How often and how long will the interviews be?

In most cases, the frequency and length of the interviews will depend on the expert's schedule. If you have to travel to reach the expert, however, you may also have to impose constraints on the time or frequency of the meetings.

If possible, three- to five-hour meetings once a week will probably be the most productive. These shorter meetings are easier to arrange and are much less of a strain on the participants than full-day conferences. After each meeting, you should review what you have learned and experiment with representing the knowledge on paper and in a knowledge base. If you meet with the expert for three to five hours on Monday, you can usually collect enough information to keep busy throughout the rest of the week.

- How many developers will participate in the interview?

Some knowledge engineers prefer to interview experts alone. Others prefer to work in pairs. In general, the larger the project, the more useful it will be to double up. Two developers, working together, can divide the work. One can ask questions while the other takes notes. Then, when the one asking questions has exhausted a line of questioning, the developers can switch roles.

Having two developers at each interview is especially useful if you are forced to schedule longer, less frequent meetings with the expert.

- How will the information learned in the interview be documented?

Most developers take notes on a pad of paper. Some also tape record the meeting. It rarely proves effective to listen to the whole tape over again, but it is often useful to be able to go to particular parts of the tape to hear exactly what the expert said about a specific point that is unclear in your notes.

While you are studying background materials to come up to speed in the vocabulary and techniques of a domain, the expert and users should be collecting information on past cases that the expert has solved. The review of cases will be one if not the principal means of testing the system, and many cases will be needed for this purpose. Some cases will typically be "set aside" to constitute a final test of the system. If the expert does not have test cases already available, he should collect them from others or create cases. (If the expert has to create cases, you obviously have a problem, since the expert will probably forget details and may or may not pick the most typical examples.) If you don't have cases when you begin, be sure to institute a procedure to document any case the expert works on while you are developing the expert system so that you can review that case during later meetings. You may even want to persuade your expert to start logging cases into a database. The database can be used when the system is ready for testing, provided your tool has the ability to interface with it. Figure 7.3 provides an overview of the various stages of interviewing and when test cases are used.

Figure 7.4 provides some rough estimates of the time required for the development of various size systems, and the number of cases that can be used to develop each type of system. These estimates are necessarily only approximations and vary widely. We haven't even tried to estimate times for the large systems since they vary so much.

Phase 3. Conduct Initial Knowledge Acquisition Interviews

After you have prepared for the interviews, you should arrange for the first serious knowledge

Figure 7.3 The use of test cases.

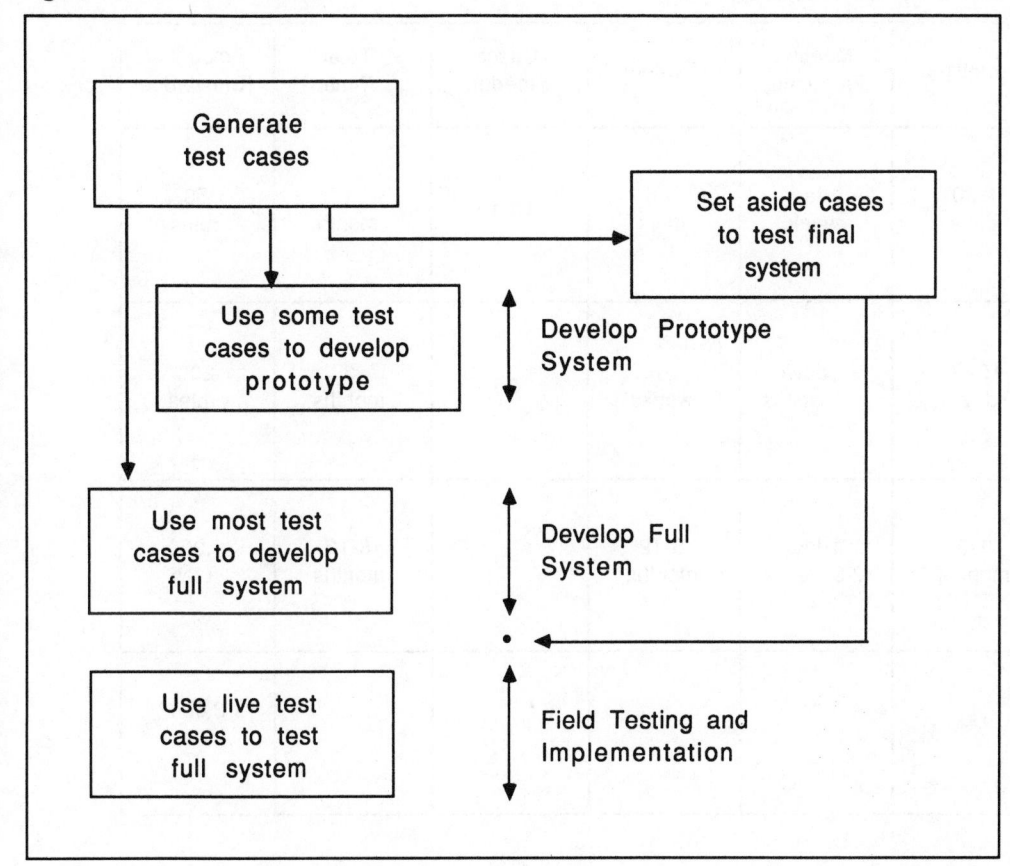

```
┌─────────────────┐
│  Generate       │
│  test cases     │
└─────────────────┘
        │           ┌──────────────────┐
        ├──────────→│  Set aside cases │
        ↓           │  to test final   │
┌─────────────────┐ │  system          │
│  Use some test  │ └──────────────────┘
│  cases to develop│    ↕  Develop Prototype
│  prototype      │       System
└─────────────────┘
        │
        ↓
┌─────────────────┐
│  Use most test  │    ↕  Develop Full
│  cases to develop│      System
│  full system    │←──────────┘
└─────────────────┘
        
┌─────────────────┐
│  Use live test  │    ↕  Field Testing and
│  cases to test  │       Implementation
│  full system    │
└─────────────────┘
```

gathering session with the expert. During this session, you should review the expert systems development process, arrange to see the expert work with users, if possible, review the cases the expert has gathered, and begin a formal discussion of the basic concepts and relationships that define the expert's domain of expertise.

As a general rule, you should spend the first two or three interviews trying to get a clear understanding of the overall analysis and decision-making process used by the expert. In effect, you are trying to get to the point where you can draw a procedural model, an object network, or a context tree to describe the major objects or variables the expert considers and the various steps or conceptual topics into which the expert divides the task.

If you have not already observed the expert interacting with users, and you can arrange to do it, you should. It's invaluable to actually see how a consultation between an expert and a user typically proceeds.

If it is feasible, you should arrange to observe several expert/user sessions and take notes. In effect, this should be a natural extension of the task analysis effort in which you first studied the problem to see if it was suitable for expert systems development. In some cases, it makes sense always to interview the expert in the context of an expert/user consultation. In effect, the consultation is a case, and you watch, listen, and then ask questions to determine what the expert thought and why she asked the questions she did. If you intend to observe expert/user consultations, it probably makes good sense to arrange to

Figure 7.4 Some rough estimates of time and case needs.

	Prototype	Meeting Frequency	System	Cases Needed	Total Time	Amount of Knowledge
Very Small System	2-30 days	1 day/ week	3-6 days	10-12	1 month	50 rules
Small System	15-60 days	1 day/ 1-2 weeks	6 weeks	30	3 months	200 rules
Mid-Size System	1-3 months	1 day/ 2-3 weeks	6-12 months	50	6-12 months	1,200 rules
Large System						3,000 rules

tape record the sessions so you can review selected portions of the dialogue at a later time.

If your expert's task is difficult to observe, or if it's a task that doesn't involve direct user contact, then you can use a technique called *protocol analysis* to "observe" your expert's thoughts. Protocol analysis involves asking your expert to verbalize his thoughts as he works on a problem. Some experts are much better at this than others, but most can do it with a little support and encouragement. You can prompt them with questions like: "What do you see?" "Does that suggest anything to you?" "What do you think of next?" and so on. In the best situation, your expert will be able to talk aloud as he works through an elaborate analysis and decision-making sequence and provide you with a very good overview of all of the steps and concepts that he is relying upon as he solves the problem. If you decide to ask your expert to talk through several problems, you should tape record the process so that you can review it in detail later.

Once you have a good overview of how your expert solves problems (or even before you have it, if it proves difficult to obtain), you should review some cases to be sure the general model you are developing actually fits with specific cases the expert has solved.

The typical interview should run from one to three hours. If you are to get the information you require in that time, you should work to keep the meeting focused on the topics you are interested in.

Experts can usually discuss the application of their knowledge most easily in the context of a specific case. This is good, because it keeps the discussion practical rather than allowing it to get too theoretical. On the other hand, experts sometimes elaborate discussions of their cases with amusing anecdotes or interesting but extraneous information. You will have to work out your own techniques to keep the meeting focused. Moreover, you will have to tailor these techniques to the individual expert and the occasion. Usually, assuming that you are taking notes as the expert talks, you will know you have lost your focus when you find that you are no longer bothering to take notes.

The initial knowledge acquisition interviews should be guided by your need to develop a knowledge map that you can then translate into a knowledge base. At some point, you will want to focus on the broad view and at other times, you will want to focus on specific details. It's usually best to start with a broad view and work with the expert to sketch out an object hierarchy of the key objects and their relationships. Once you have an overview, you should then test it by considering a case and working through it in detail to be sure that you can use the knowledge you have to solve the problem. The general acquisition interviews should conclude as soon as you are confident that you can develop a prototype system that will be able to solve from one to three typical cases.

If the problem is very complex, you may want to begin encoding the knowledge as soon as you are satisifed that you have enough knowledge to provide a general solution for one typical case. Once you have a knowledge base and begin running the system and trying to use it to solve cases, it will be much easier for both you and the expert to see what kind of additional knowledge will be needed to improve the system.

Don't expect that the first prototype you develop will become the basis for your final system. It's much more likely that you will develop a simple prototype, play with it, try a case or two, and then decide that you want to rearrange your knowledge map and entirely recode your knowledge base. Indeed, you may go through this process several times before you are satisfied that you have an initial knowledge base that you can systematically expand simply by adding new rules as you try new cases.

Phase 4. Conduct Case Review Interviews

After the interviews of Phase 3, you can create a knowledge map that describes a portion of the critical knowledge possessed by the expert. The ideal knowledge map should contain not only the objects, relationships, and attributes necessary to provide the overall structure for a knowledge base, but also enough specific information to solve two or three actual cases. This mix of general and very specific information helps assure that the knowledge base will be ordered in both a comprehensive and a pragmatic manner.

As soon as you are confident in your initial knowledge map, you should begin to develop a knowledge base. Some experienced knowledge engineers develop a minimal map and then move quickly to developing the knowledge base, while others prefer to work on the knowledge map until they are relatively confident in it, before moving to the encoding phase. The size and the nature of the knowledge undoubtedly influence these decisions. A larger and more complex body of expert knowledge suggests more initial analysis, while a smaller and better organized body of expertise leads you to begin coding sooner. In some cases, you may find that the knowledge map keeps growing larger and more complex and seems to include knowledge that doesn't seem like it will be useful in solving actual cases. Whenever you feel that the expert is primarily adding "nice to know" information rather than "need to know" information, you should shift toward gathering information on specific cases and then start coding a prototype to test the relevance of the knowledge you have been collecting.

In any case, you must sooner or later test your understanding of the expert's knowledge by developing a knowledge base. Once even the most tentative knowledge base is developed, you can begin running one or two cases to determine if the system can obtain the correct results. As soon as you are reasonably happy with the first version of the knowledge base (i.e., the first prototype expert system), you should arrange to sit down with the expert and run several cases through the system to see what it recommends. Running cases, examining recommendations, and tracing the flow of the system's reasoning is the best possible way to focus the expert on the primary nature of the expert systems development task. After working with the first prototype, experts typically start providing much better and more focused information.

After the expert has seen the first prototype, you need to make a decision. In some cases, it may be useful to return to a general discussion of the problem-solving task. If so, you will, in effect, be working on revising the knowledge map. In other cases, it will be more useful to take up specific cases and develop the knowledge base directly, by adding specific knowledge.

Assuming the initial session with the expert goes reasonably well, you should arrange to show the initial prototype to the potential end users. You should warn these end users that they are seeing a very early version of the system, but encourage them nevertheless to work through one or two cases, following a script if necessary. Such test cases will help the users determine if you are on the right track. This is a very important part of the early development effort. The users need not know what the knowledge base contains or how it works, but they will know if the system's input and output is useful to them.

If the system asks for information the potential users don't have, it's a sign that you will have to develop rules to help the system obtain the more specific information that the users are capable of giving and infer the higher-level inputs the expert has described. (This is exactly the problem that the Coopers & Lybrand developers encountered, and it is why they introduced the partition between the experts and the users.) On the other hand, the system may currently make recommendations that the users don't know how to interpret. This suggests that you will have to put more effort into defining the specific goals or conclusions the system makes. (A physician, for example, might start developing a system that would identify the diseases the patient could have. The nurses that will use the system are less interested in the diseases themselves than in the specific drugs and dosages they should give when specific diseases are present.)

An effective expert system is always a combination of expert knowledge and input and output that is tailored for the end user. The good expert typically provides both, but sometimes fails to explain to the developer what sorts of techniques or questions she uses to gather data and make useful recommendations. The expert's "interface" knowledge is just as important as her "problem-solving" knowledge, and they both affect system design. Hence, as soon as possible, you should get a good idea of how the two types of knowledge can be combined in a specific expert systems design.

The typical prototype review session should include the following steps:

1. Set the stage by explaining to the expert and users what the session should accomplish.
2. Run the current version of the system, discussing any problems that you encountered while trying to encode the knowledge acquired during your last interview or review session.
3. Have the expert run the current version of the system, focusing on the problems (cases) that have been discussed to date. If the expert is unhappy with the system's questions or the recommendations, determine what should be changed to overcome the expert's objections.
4. Take up a new case and discuss it with the expert. Why is this case different than ones previously considered? Does the expert assume that the system will be able to handle this case, or does he expect you will have to add more knowledge to the system first?
5. Run the system and see if it can handle the new case. Discuss any failures or inappropriate questions as they arise during the consultation. If appropriate and time allows, work with the expert to edit specific rules (usually on paper) to be sure you understand the nature of the changes that will be required.
6. Summarize the session. State, if possible, all of the following:
    - Errors in knowledge representation that need to be corrected

- Inconsistencies that need to be eliminated
- Missing or inadequate knowledge or functionality
- User interface difficulties

7. Schedule the next meeting. Agree on what everyone will do by that time and propose a general agenda for that meeting.

SUMMARY

Knowledge acquisition is still more of an art than a technology. It requires the ability to work with experts to help them identify their knowledge, and it involves figuring out how to effectively and efficiently model that knowledge in a knowledge base. In the near future, there will be a wide variety of new tools and techniques to help knowledge engineers with knowledge acquisition, but at the moment, we are still learning about the process. We have tried to offer some heuristics that can help you avoid some of the pitfalls, but in the end, given the current state of the art, it all comes down to good communication skills and a healthy dose of common sense.

Section Four

PROGRAM DEVELOPMENT

In this section, we look at how systems are actually built. In Chapter 8, we consider how to develop a small, backward chaining rule-based system. In Chapter 9, we consider the development of a forward chaining rule-based system. Chapter 10 is concerned with the problems of developing rule-based systems that incorporate context trees, while Chapter 11 is devoted to the special problems involved in developing hybrid systems.

Later in this section, we examine other aspects of expert systems construction, including database integration, designing the user interface, and integrating procedural code into a knowledge base. The order of these chapters should not suggest a sequence of tasks to be addressed. Frequently, user interface and database issues need to be dealt with from the very outset, even before the first rule is written.

This section assumes you are familiar with the fundamental expert systems techniques that we introduced in Chapter 2. If you are uncertain about these fundamentals, you may want to review Chapter 2 before starting this section.

8.
Creating Small Rule-Based Systems

INTRODUCTION

In this chapter, we consider the phases that a developer goes through in order to build a small expert system. To simplify our discussion, we assume that most small rule-based systems are developed to handle diagnostic, classification, or selection problems. Thus, they will generally be backward chaining systems in which rules are used in order to determine appropriate values for a goal. To illustrate the process involved in developing a small expert system, we consider how you might create a small, backward chaining rule-based diagnosis system to recommend which VCR a customer might purchase.

Experienced programmers may be struck by the simplicity of these small systems. The AI techniques they use are fairly basic. Many small systems can be developed using conventional languages like C or PASCAL. Some can even be implemented in a database package. What makes expert systems tools desirable for these tasks is the ease with which a nonprogrammer can use them. Since the knowledge base is readable, maintenance and debugging are also much easier using an expert system than a conventional programming language.

There are four phases to the procedure of developing a small, backward chaining system:

1. Define the problem
2. Develop an initial set of rules
3. Enhance the rules
4. Customize inference and control

An actual development project is almost always an iterative process. You follow the prescribed steps to create an initial knowledge base, and then repeat them over and over again, as you expand and refine the knowledge base. We consider next some of the typical activities that occur in each phase.

PHASE 1. DEFINING THE PROBLEM

You begin a small system development effort by examining the problem. A typical small expert system will function as a kind of intelligent job aid; it will help someone (or some other program) solve some problem. We assume that there is an expert, technician, or manager who can currently solve the problem. Thus, the developer's goal is to get the necessary knowledge from a current "expert" and put it into a system so that others can access that knowledge when they want to solve similar problems.

The particular example we have chosen is VCR selection. In the video section of an electronics store, one wall is usually lined with different VCRs. Curious shoppers are greeted by an array of twinkling lights, digital displays, and colored buttons. To help customers sort through these mysterious features, salespeople are available to talk with them and recommend an appropriate machine.

Suppose that you have been asked to develop an expert system to help customers select VCRs. You have access to a salesperson who now performs this task by asking customers about their preferences and making recommendations. Thus, you will want to develop a system that will automate the consultation process that a customer would normally go through in talking with an expert VCR salesperson.

If you observe the VCR salesperson consulting with a customer, you can see that the consultation begins with the customer indicating that she wants to buy a VCR. The salesperson asks the customer a number of questions about her needs and resources, and then makes a recommendation. In addition to recommending one or more VCRs that will fit the customer's needs, the salesperson offers an explanation of why the VCRs that are being recommended will successfully satisfy the customer's stated preferences.

Figure 8.1 summarizes the analysis of the task. The input to the system is data on customer preferences. The problem analysis is performed by the expert applying rules and asking questions. The output, or goal, of the system is to recommend VCRs.

Next, you should look at the factors that the expert considers when he determines what VCR might be desirable or undesirable. Assume that your discussions with the expert lead you to believe that VCRs have five main characteristics:

1. Their type (VHS or Beta)
2. Their cost
3. The number of heads they have
4. Whether or not they have a freeze frame ability
5. Whether or not they have a search ability

For such a simple problem, you might not go to the trouble of drawing a diagram, but to illustrate the process, we've created a diagram that shows a VCR as an object with attributes and potential values. (See Figure 8.2.)

You can obtain the information about the attributes and values in various ways. You could begin by asking the expert salesperson about the questions he typically asks customers. You could also look at VCR sales brochures or reports comparing VCRs. The purpose is to develop a comprehensive list of all of the attributes that describe and discriminate between the various VCRs that might be recommended.

Once you have settled on the factors relevant to VCR selection, you need to decide how to describe them in the knowledge base. You need to give each one a name that you can reference when you want to refer to that attribute in rules and other statements. Names should be long enough to make the attribute readable, without being verbose. Tools vary on the maximum length they allow for attribute names, but most systems provide for names that are from 20 to 30 characters long.

For this VCR system, we named the attributes FREEZE_FRAME, SEARCH, PRICE, TYPE, and HEADS. Notice that we use an underscore to meld together the words "freeze" and "frame." This emphasizes that the words refer to a single attribute.

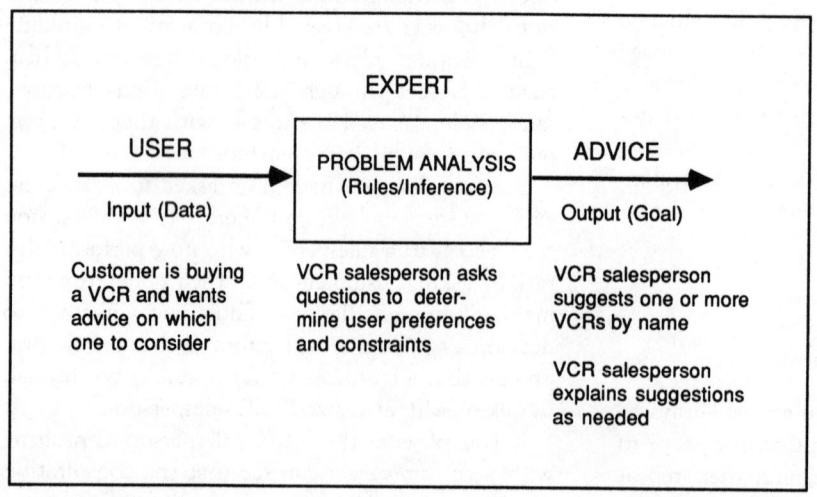

Figure 8.1 Overall analysis of VCR recommendation task.

Figure 8.2 VCR system's object-attribute-value characteristics.

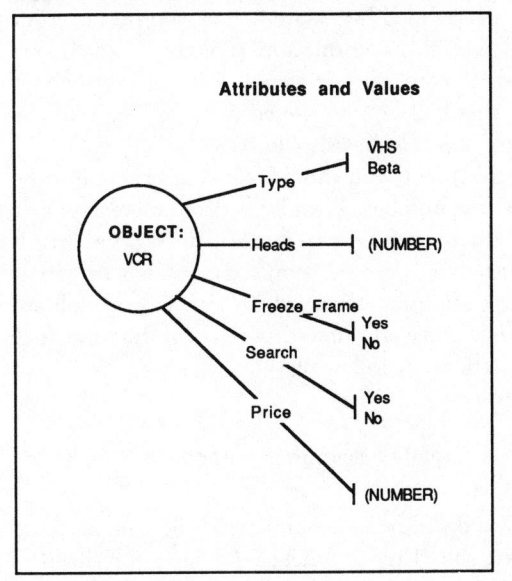

You also need an attribute to represent the system's goal, to pick a VCR. We use the attribute named RECOMMENDATION for that purpose.

PHASE 2. DEVELOPING AN INITIAL SET OF RULES

Once you have a good overview of the knowledge involved in the task, you can begin writing specific rules.

Developing Some Initial Rules

The first rules you write should apply directly to your goal, RECOMMENDATION. Begin by focusing on one machine discussed by the expert, called a VCX_1000. This is a VHS machine, with four recording heads. It has freeze frame and search abilities, and it sells for a relatively low price. Given this information, you can write the following rule:

Rule 1

IF   type = VHS AND
heads = 4 AND
freeze_frame = yes AND
search = yes AND
price = low
THEN recommendation = VCX_1000.

This rule is shown exactly as it might be written in a text editor and entered into the knowledge base of a small expert systems building tool. Figure 8.3 shows this same rule in a slightly different graphic format. In the figure, the five If-clauses, or premises, are shown on the left leading to a conclusion on the right. Since the conclusion is the goal-attribute RECOMMENDATION, the arrow simply points to one value that would be assigned to RECOMMENDATION, if all five of the premises proved true.

If you construct a small system with four rules and all of the rules conclude with a value for the goal-attribute RECOMMENDATION, your system would have only one level of depth. Such a simple system would not employ much expert knowledge.

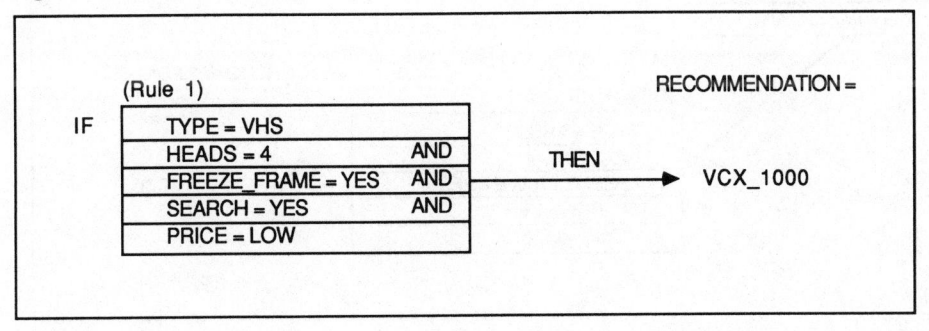

Figure 8.3 A rule to recommend a VCR.

Users would answer questions about the premises of the rules and the system would provide a recommendation. For all practical purposes, it would act just like a database. It would take in customer preferences and fire the rule that matches them.

In order to take your system beyond this simple stage, you have to add some abstraction to your knowledge base. Abstraction is manifested by intermediate rules that actually make inferences (reason) about the users' input. The addition of intermediate rules allows the system to reason with concepts at a higher level than the specific features of VCRs. Ideally, customers should be able to choose a VCR by answering questions about their needs and resources, rather than being asked if they want some specific technical VCR feature. In order to do this, you have to acquire some more rules from the expert about how a customer's needs and desires are related to the specific features of the various VCRs.

As you add each VCR rule, you need to check if there are opportunities to add abstraction to the knowledge base. You have to look at each attribute in the premise of the rule and ask yourself if its value could be provided by the customer. Some attributes, like "price," can easily be supplied; most people who are shopping for a machine have a price range in mind. Other attributes, however, may be unknown to the customers. For example, customers may have absolutely no idea how many video heads they need to have in their VCR. Indeed, they may not even know what video heads are. Thus, you do not want to ask for this information directly. Instead, you should develop rules that will ask the users about needs that can be interpreted or translated into the number of heads they should have.

At this point, you should ask your expert how he decides the number of heads needed for a machine. It turns out that the expert has a heuristic for this: If the customer is a perfectionist and insists on noise-free tape scanning, then at least four video heads are essential. You can enter this new information into the system as the following rule:

Rule 2

    IF   quality_scanning = important
    THEN heads = > 4.

Figure 8.4 shows how this new rule complements the first rule. Rule 2 concludes a value for "heads," and thus provides the value for one of the premises of Rule 1. By adding this rule, you give a second layer to the system. Now, instead of having all the rules conclude with a value for the systems' overall goal, RECOMMENDATION, you have one rule that applies to a subgoal, HEADS. When the system is trying to find if all of Rule 1's premises are true, it will first ask users if they want a Beta or VHS system. If they say they want a VHS, then the system will back up to Rule 2 in order to find the value of "heads."

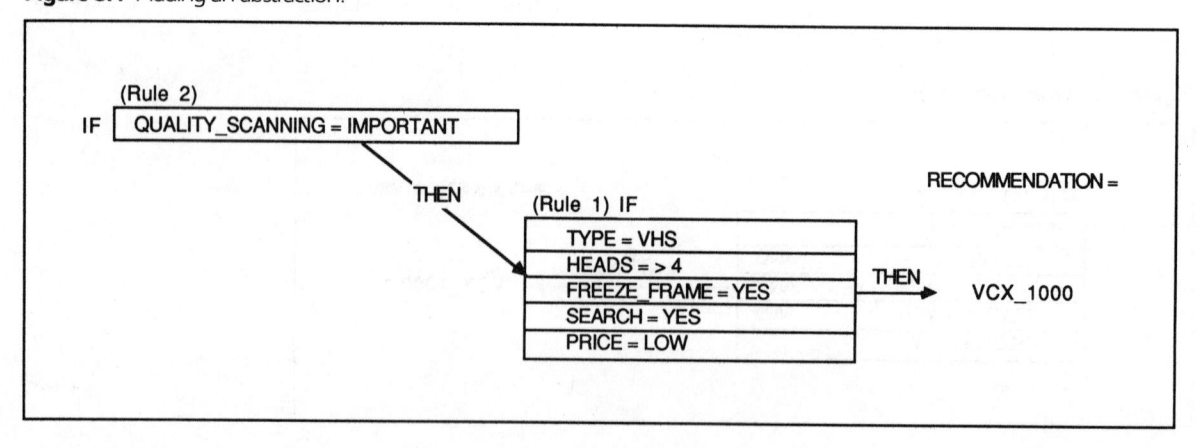

Figure 8.4 Adding an abstraction.

Figure 8.5 Adding three new rules.

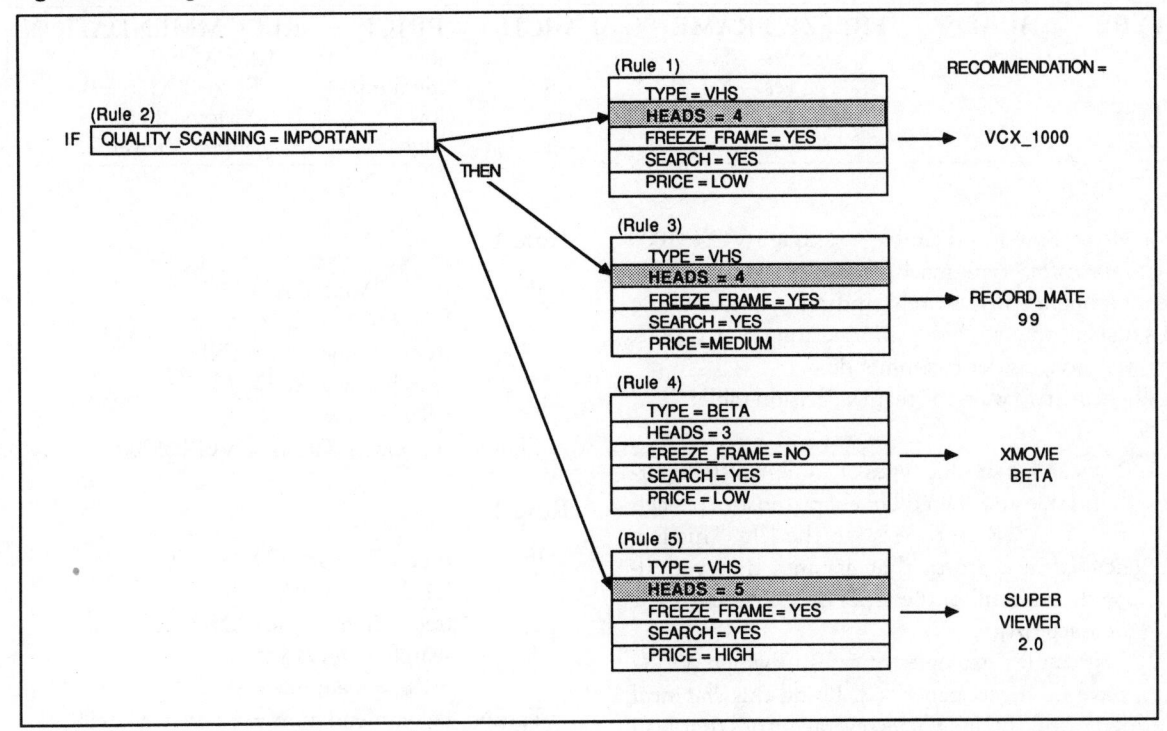

```
                                    (Rule 1)
                                   ┌─────────────────────┐      RECOMMENDATION =
                                   │ TYPE = VHS          │
          (Rule 2)                 │ HEADS = 4           │
   IF  ┌──QUALITY_SCANNING = IMPORTANT──┐ FREEZE_FRAME = YES  │ ───► VCX_1000
                                   │ SEARCH = YES        │
                          THEN     │ PRICE = LOW         │
                                   └─────────────────────┘

                                    (Rule 3)
                                   ┌─────────────────────┐
                                   │ TYPE = VHS          │
                                   │ HEADS = 4           │
                                   │ FREEZE_FRAME = YES  │ ───► RECORD_MATE
                                   │ SEARCH = YES        │        99
                                   │ PRICE = MEDIUM      │
                                   └─────────────────────┘

                                    (Rule 4)
                                   ┌─────────────────────┐
                                   │ TYPE = BETA         │
                                   │ HEADS = 3           │
                                   │ FREEZE_FRAME = NO   │ ───► XMOVIE
                                   │ SEARCH = YES        │       BETA
                                   │ PRICE = LOW         │
                                   └─────────────────────┘

                                    (Rule 5)
                                   ┌─────────────────────┐
                                   │ TYPE = VHS          │
                                   │ HEADS = 5           │
                                   │ FREEZE_FRAME = YES  │ ───► SUPER
                                   │ SEARCH = YES        │      VIEWER
                                   │ PRICE = HIGH        │       2.0
                                   └─────────────────────┘
```

You continue development by examining the rest of the attributes in Rule 1: FREEZE_FRAME, SEARCH, and PRICE. You assume that the customer can easily provide values for each of these attributes, without assistance from the expert. Later in development, you may want to add rules to help find these facts with expert knowledge, but for now, two layers of depth are sufficient.

You can now resume writing rules that recommend VCRs. Figure 8.5 shows three new rules to recommend three additional VCRs: RECORD_MATE_ 99, XMOVIE-BETA, and SUPER_VIEWER_2.0.

Developing Rules from a Decision Table

When you're faced with a small, simple problem, like the VCR Advisor, another way to begin developing your initial knowledge base is to create a *decision table*. This gives you an orderly way to quickly arrive at the first set of rules.

You build a decision table by listing all of the attributes you are interested in across the top of the table. The attribute on the top right should always be your goal-attribute. You then list various sets of possible values in the rows below, each concluding with a specific recommendation (i.e., a value for your goal-attribute).

Decision tables are helpful only for certain problems, where each potential recommendation is evaluated by checking the same set of attributes. If the expert looks at one set of factors while considering one recommendation, and different factors for another, then there is no way to unify the recommendations within a single table.

Recall that in the sample VCR system, the expert picks a VCR based on the values of five attributes: type, price, search, freeze frame, and heads. Every possible VCR is described in terms of these five attributes. Thus, you could list them in a decision table, like the one shown in Table 8.1.

Table 8.1 A Decision Table for VCR Selection.

TYPE	HEADS	FREEZE_FRAME	SEARCH	PRICE	RECOMMENDATION
VHS	4	yes	yes	low	VCX_1000
VHS	4	yes	yes	medium	Record_Mate99
Beta	3	no	yes	low	XMovie_Beta
VHS	5	yes	yes	high	Super_Viewer_2.0

In effect, Row 1 of the table says that a VCX_1000 VCR is a VHS-type machine with four heads, the freeze frame feature, search, and a low price. Using this matrix, you can enter information on any VCR you want to consider recommending.

There are two ways to create a decision table:

1. You can list specific types of VCRs on the right-hand side and then fill in characteristics of each type of VCR in the row to the left. This is a *descriptive approach* that assumes that you already know all of the types of VCRs and their characteristics.
2. You can list examples of cases in which VCRs have been recommended. Using this *empirical approach*, you may have several entries that lead to the same type of VCR. Many companies have records of equipment failures in which they list all of the observed conditions of the failure and what turned out to be the problem. Other companies maintain hotline records that describe each call they get, the answers to the questions that they ask, and the recommendation they make. In such cases, the developer can quickly set up a matrix using the examples to dictate the attributes and filling in the right-hand column to indicate the recommendations that were given in each case.

Tools that use induction can take a decision table and convert it to a set of rules. If you use a tool that does not support induction, you can manually convert your table to rules. Each row in the decision table shown in Table 8.1 can easily be translated into a rule, as follows.

Rule 1

IF   type = VHS AND
       heads = 4 AND
       freeze_frame = yes AND
       search = yes AND
       price = low
THEN recommendation = VCX_1000.

Rule 2

IF   type = VHS AND
       heads = 4 AND
       freeze_frame = yes AND
       search = yes AND
       price = medium
THEN recommendation = Record_Mate99.

Rule 3

IF   type = Beta AND
       heads = 3 AND
       freeze_frame = no AND
       search = yes AND
       price = low
THEN recommendation = XMovie_Beta.

Rule 4

IF   type = VHS AND
       heads = 5 AND
       freeze_frame = yes AND
       search = yes AND
       price = high
THEN recommendation = Super_Viewer_2.0.

Converting decision tables to rules isn't always this simple. For example, it would be more difficult if the decision table included duplicate rows (this might occur if the decision table were based on case data in which the same scenario occurred several times). A decision table might also have multiple rows with different values that lead to the same recommendation. In these cases, there isn't a simple correspondence between rows in the table and rules in the knowledge base. You would need to convert multiple rows from the table into a single rule in the knowledge base with OR conditions.

Writing a Goal Statement

We have already mentioned that every backward chaining system needs to have a goal-attribute to get started. In the VCR matrix, we listed the goal-attribute, RECOMMENDATION, on the right-hand side. Most small tools require that you create your knowledge base in a text processor. In such cases, the goal is usually listed at or near the top of the knowledge base. For example, in M.1, the statement "goal = <ATTRIBUTE>" can be written at the top of the knowledge base. When the system starts, it finds the goal-attribute and then immediately backward chains to find the value of the attribute. In M.1, you would list the goal of the VCR system like this:

GOAL = recommendation

A consultation with the system using these four rules would appear as follows.

VCR CONSULTATION

(Note that the underscore indicates the option the customer chose.)

What is the value of type?
    VHS   Beta
What is the value of quality_scanning?
    important   unimportant
What is the value of freeze_frame?
    yes   no
What is the value of search?
    yes   no
What is the value of price?
    low   medium   high
Recommendation = Super_Viewer_2.0

PHASE 3. ENHANCING THE RULES

The VCR expert system still has several blind spots. To begin with, the four rules cover only a limited number of variables. Customers, in fact, have needs that have not been considered. In addition, this system has only four rules that recommend VCRs, while there are in fact dozens of VCRs in any large electronics store. If you were serious about developing a system to recommend a VCR, you would have to add 50 to 100 rules to cover all of the different features and the various machines that are available. To limit this chapter, however, we will keep to these four rules and assume that you are concerned only with recommending one of four machines. But even if you don't expect to add more rules to handle other features and machines, you still have to do a number of things to enhance the overall flow and efficiency of the consultation. We consider six ways you can enhance the rule base of a small system:

1. Ensure that the system makes a recommendation
2. Add text for the questions the system presents to the user
3. Provide for situations in which you want the system to make more than one recommendation
4. Add certainty factors to express your confidence in relationships expressed by the various rules
5. Improve the rules themselves by adding abstraction and by adding rules to do conversions, and so on
6. Consolidate repetitive rules

We discuss each type of enhancement in turn.

Adding Rules to Ensure a Recommendation

In conventional applications, the developer usually analyzes all of the possibilities and creates a system that will always have a recommendation ready. When developing expert systems, however, you develop the knowledge base incrementally and often face situations in which the system will fail to reach any recommendation.

In the case of the VCR system, for example, if the customer wanted a Beta recorder with four heads, none of the rules would fire. Consequently, the system would not give a recommendation. This is unacceptable; you have to provide the system with a way to determine that no rules have fired and to print a message to tell the user that the system cannot provide any advice. You can do this by writing a rule to check if a goal-attribute is unknown. Many tools actually use "unknown" as a special, reserved word that can be written directly into rules to test whether an attribute has a value.

The following rule uses this feature to check if the goal-attribute has been given a value by previous rules. If not, it fires, printing a message to the customer:

Rule 6

IF   recommendation = UNKNOWN
THEN
    DISPLAY "Sorry, but no recommendation is available."
    recommendation = Not_Available.

At first glance, this rule may appear strange, but it makes good sense once you consider how a backward chaining system works. The VCR system is seeking a value for RECOMMENDATION. It finds this rule at the end of the knowledge base with the attribute RECOMMENDATION in its conclusion. It backs into the rule and checks to see if it can determine a value for the If-clause of the rule and then validate the conclusion. The If-clause attribute is also RECOMMENDATION. The system checks working memory to see if it has a value for RECOMMENDATION. If it has any value associated with the attribute RECOMMENDATION, then this clause will fail. On the other hand, if there is no value for RECOMMENDATION in working memory, the If-clause will be confirmed, and the Then-clause of the rule will be considered true. In this case, the system will display "Sorry, but no recommendation is available." and set the value of RECOMMENDATION to "not_available."

Developing Specific Questions

In the sample consultation with the VCR system shown previously, the questions were automatically generated by the system. Most small tools will simply ask for the value of an attribute when they have exhausted their search for rules that can provide a needed value.

This approach works well enough when the developer is initially creating the system, but a question like: "What is the value of . . . ?" is too crude for end users. When you're ready, you can arrange for the system to ask friendlier questions.

To tailor questions, simply add the text for each question the system might want to ask. Most tools allow question text to be attached to attributes, which means the question is produced when the system needs to query the customer for a value. In VP-Expert, for example, you can add questions to the end of the knowledge base. You begin by using the reserved word ASK and then identifying the attribute to be associated with the text.

Most small tools allow you to tailor the system further by providing a list of choices that the user can respond to. This is done by using the reserved word CHOICE, followed by the attribute and the possible values that the attribute could take.

```
ASK type: "What kind of VCR do you need?"
CHOICE type: VHS, Beta
ASK quality_scanning: "How important is scanning quality to you?"
CHOICE quality_scanning: important, unimportant
ASK freeze_frame: "Do you need a freeze frame ability?"
CHOICE freeze_frame: yes, no
ASK search: "Do you need a search ability?"
CHOICE search: yes, no
ASK price: "What price range can you afford?"
CHOICE price: low, medium, high
```

Note that there is no question text for the attribute HEADS, since the customer is not going to be asked to provide this information.

Once you've added question text, the consultation will make much more sense to the user. It would, for example, create the following consultation.

VCR CONSULTATION

(Note that the underscore indicates the option the customer chose.)

What kind of VCR do you need?
    <u>VHS</u>   Beta
How important is scanning quality to you?
    <u>important</u>   unimportant
Do you need a freeze frame ability?
    <u>yes</u>   no
Do you need a search ability?
    <u>yes</u>   no
What price range can you afford?
    low   medium   <u>high</u>
Recommendation = Super_Viewer_2.0

Identifying Multivalued Attributes

As soon as this current system picks a VCR, the goal is satisfied and the system stops, printing its recommendation. However, this isn't how the human expert behaves. He may rattle off two or three possible machines to buy, thereby giving the customer some choice in the matter.

To allow the system to make multiple recommendations, you have to define the goal as *multivalued*. This causes the inference engine to continue trying rules until they run out, no matter how many have passed. When the system finishes, the attribute RECOMMENDATION will have the names of all the appropriate VCRs.

Most small tools allow you to use a reserved word to specify which of the attributes can take more than one value. If you wanted to ensure that the VCR system would make as many recommendations as it could, you would enter a line like the following to the knowledge base:

MULTIVALUED: recommendation

This would guarantee that the system would continue to seek values for RECOMMENDATION until it had exhaustively examined all rules that concluded with a value for it.

Adding Certainty Factors

In their current form, the four VCR rules all have equal weight. In other words, every recommendation is made with the same amount of certainty. However, this is not consistent with how the VCR expert behaves. When he makes recommendations to a customer, he does so with varying degrees of confidence. For example, you might observe that even when the "Super Viewer" perfectly matches all of the customers' stated needs, the salesperson still recommends it with only moderate enthusiasm. Upon inquiry, you might determine that this is because the machine is occasionally unreliable, priced slightly too high, or has a record of customer complaints.

By using certainty factors, you can codify the confidence the expert has in each recommendation. You can add a number from 0 to 100 to the conclusion of each rule to indicate the expert's certainty. If the rule fires, its conclusion is added to the knowledge base with that certainty factor attached to it. The customer can use the certainty factor as a measure of the strength of the system's recommendation. If the system makes multiple recommendations, certainty factors help customers decide which one is best.

We have modified the rule base that follows to include a certainty factor with each rule. Figure 8.6 presents the certainty factors in a more graphic way.

Figure 8.6 Adding certainty factors.

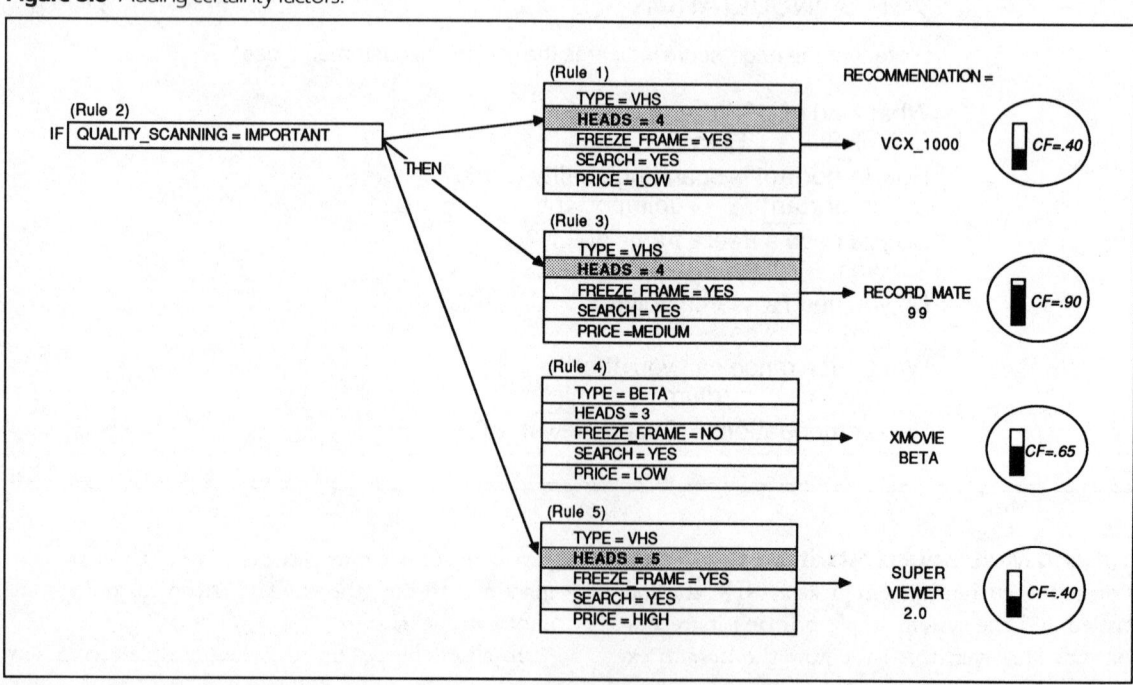

VCR ADVISOR KNOWLEDGE BASE

GOAL = recommendation

Rule 1
IF   type = VHS AND
        heads = 4 AND
        freeze_frame = yes AND
        search = yes AND
        price = low
THEN recommendation = VCX_1000 (CF = 40).

Rule 2
IF   quality_scanning = important
THEN heads = < 4.

Rule 3
IF   type = VHS AND
        heads = 4 AND
        freeze_frame = yes AND
        search = yes AND
        price = medium
THEN recommendation = Record_Mate99 (CF = 90).

Rule 4
IF   type = Beta AND
        heads = 3 AND
        freeze_frame = no AND
        search = yes AND
        price = low
THEN recommendation = XMovie_Beta (CF = 65).

Rule 5
IF   type = VHS AND
        heads = 5 AND
        freeze_frame = yes AND
        search = yes AND
        price = high
THEN recommendation = Super_Viewer_2.0 (CF = 40).

Rule 6
IF   recommendation = UNKNOWN
THEN
        DISPLAY "Sorry, but no recommendation is available."
        recommendation = not_available.

ASK type: "What kind of VCR do you need?"
CHOICE type: VHS, Beta
ASK quality_scanning: "How important is scanning quality to you?"
CHOICE quality_scanning: important, unimportant
ASK freeze_frame: "Do you need a freeze frame ability?"
CHOICE freeze_frame: yes, no

ASK search: "Do you need a search ability?"
CHOICE search: yes, no
ASK price: "What price range can you afford?"
CHOICE price: low, medium, high

MULTIVALUED: recommendation

Certainty factors can also be used by customers to indicate their confidence in the answers they give to the questions they are asked. For example, a customer may prefer freeze frame ability but not think it's really essential. Thus, when the system asked whether freeze frame ability was needed, the customer could answer "yes," with a certainty of 80. The consultation with the new system would be as follows.

What kind of VCR do you need?
    <u>VHS</u>   Beta
How important is scanning quality to you?
    <u>important</u>   unimportant
Do you need a freeze frame ability?
    <u>yes (CF = 80)</u>   no
Do you need a search ability?
    <u>yes</u>   no
What price range can you afford?
    low   medium   <u>high</u>
Recommendation = Super_Viewer_2.0 (CF = 56).

Notice that the customer has requested a freeze frame ability, but only with a certainty of 80, indicating a moderate interest in that feature. When the system presented its final recommendation, its certainty was diminished proportionally.

Improving the Rules Themselves

In addition to adding questions and certainty factors, the developer can often improve the rules themselves by adding rules to introduce more abstraction into the knowledge base.

One way to add abstraction to a knowledge base is to look for clauses in the rules that the customer would not understand. This is what led us to add Rule 2 to find a value for "heads," an attribute that most customers would not know how to evaluate. You should examine your rule base and write rules to convert confusing concepts into more concrete attributes that the user can easily evaluate. Identifying opportunities for adding abstract concepts to a knowledge base is an important part of enhancing the friendliness of your system.

Looking for recurring clauses in rules. Another way to add abstraction to a rule base is to look for sets of attribute-value pairs that occur in several different rules. This usually suggests that you can add a new attribute-value that will replace or describe the entire set of attribute-values. For example, notice in Figure 8.6 that Rules 1, 3, and 5 share a set of attribute-value pairs: FREEZE_FRAME = YES and SEARCH = YES.

You can add a new rule to represent the combination of these two conditions being true:

Rule 7

IF   freeze_frame = yes AND
          search = yes
THEN effects = yes.

In other words, you are saying that EFFECTS = YES is a synonym for FREEZE_FRAME = YES and SEARCH = YES.

This process of substituting a single, more abstract word for a longer, more complex and more concrete phrase is an example of chunking. It is the process by which languages grow and allow people to talk about complex matters without having to go into paragraphs of concrete descriptive words. When you say that someone is "wealthy," you are using an abstract word to describe the fact that the person has lots of money, lives in a mansion, drives a very expensive car, belongs to expensive country clubs, and so on.

One single, abstract word or chunk stands in place of many specific facts. Actually, language is a hierarchy of many levels of abstraction. In developing an expert system, you are often forced to figure out how a portion of that hierarchy works in order to move back and forth from the abstract needs of the user to some underlying set of concrete facts and then back to abstract recommendations. Or, vice versa, you must move from the concrete terms of the user to the abstractions the expert uses to conceptualize the problem, and then back to a concrete recommendation for the user.

Once you have written Rule 7 to assert the following

(FREEZE_FRAME = YES and SEARCH = YES) = (EFFECTS = YES)

you can revise the other rules in the knowledge base as shown in Figure 8.7. In this figure, each occurrence of the original set of attribute-value pairs has

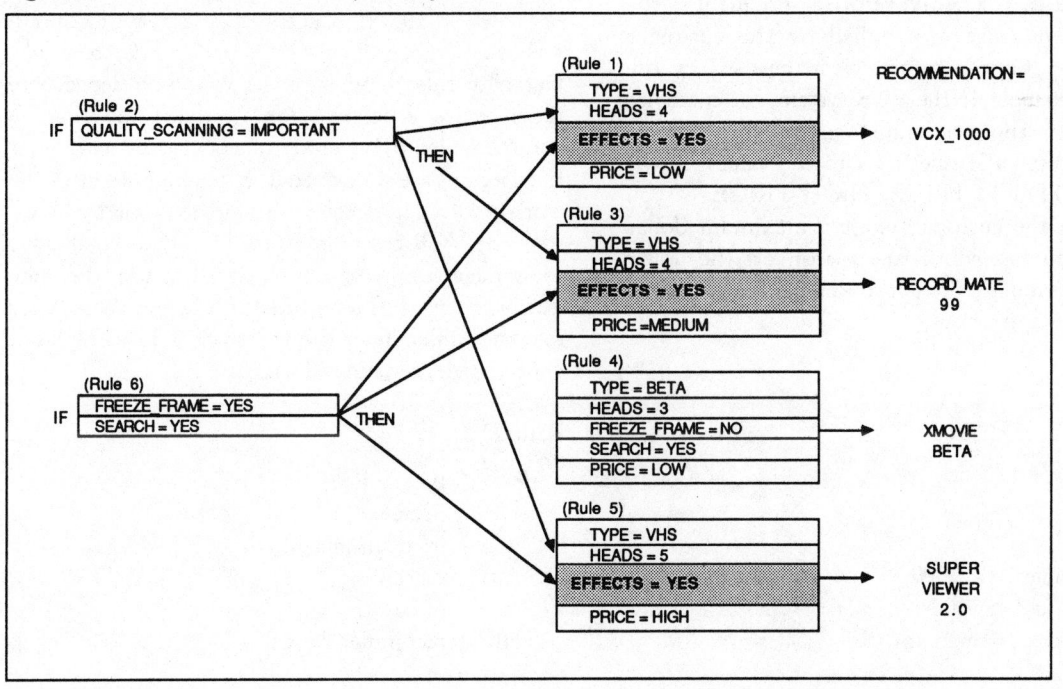

Figure 8.7 Three common clauses replaced by abstraction.

been replaced by the new attribute-value pair EFFECTS = YES.

Abstractions of this kind don't add significant new knowledge to the system, but they do make for much better dialogues. Moreover, they make it much easier to expand and maintain the knowledge base. Since all the rules that recommend VCRs are now one clause shorter, it takes less time for the system to test them. Editing the knowledge base is also easier; if you want to change either of the If-clauses in Rule 7, you can do it in that one rule, rather than having to make a change in each of the rules that previously contained that pair of attribute-values.

Just because an attribute-value clause is shared by a number of rules doesn't always mean that a higher concept can be abstracted from it. For example, notice in the rules in Figure 8.7 that every VHS machine also has a search ability. This turns out to be purely coincidental—the two features are completely unrelated. In this case, it would not be useful to create a new rule to represent this condition.

Adding rules for conversions. Frequently, the format of information supplied by the customer needs to be changed before it can be used by the rules. For example, in the VCR system, the customer should enter the maximum amount that can be spent. However, the rules refer to the values LOW_PRICE, MEDIUM_PRICE, HIGH_PRICE. If you want to let the customer enter a maximum dollar amount, you can add a rule to convert the dollar price the customer enters into one of the values the existing rules can use.

Rule 8

    IF   max < $300
    THEN price = low.

Rule 9

    IF   max >= $300
             max < $600
    THEN price = medium.

Rule 10

    IF   max >= $600
    THEN price = high.

After you enter these rules and some associated questions into the knowledge base, you can present the end user with the following question:

"What is the maximum price (in dollars) that you want to pay?"

The customer can type the exact dollar price she can afford, and the system will then determine if the customer wants a low-, medium-, or high-priced machine.

Consolidating Repetitive Rules

If you find that you are creating many rules that share a similar attribute structure, you should consider consolidating them all into a single, general rule that can access a database table to get different sets of values. A rule that accesses a database to obtain sets of different values is often called a *database rule*. Database rules tend to make your knowledge base much more efficient. You do have to create a database file to be used in association with your knowledge base, but overall, it generally reduces the work involved in developing a large knowledge base.

In the VCR example, Rules 1, 3, 4, and 5 all have the same attribute structure; each one uses the same attributes, in the same order. Only the values they reference differ. They can therefore be easily replaced with a single, generalized database rule:

Rule DB

    IF   type = [   ] AND
             heads = [   ] AND
             freeze_frame = [   ] AND
             search = [   ] AND
             price = [   ]
    THEN recommendation = [   ].

Figure 8.8 Plugging values into a general rule.

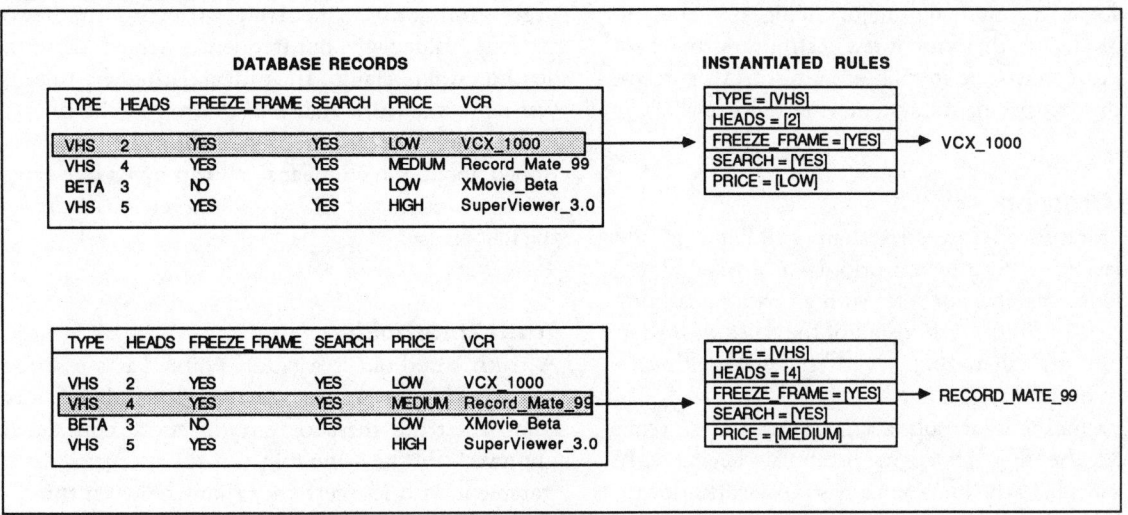

	DATABASE RECORDS						INSTANTIATED RULES	
TYPE	HEADS	FREEZE_FRAME	SEARCH	PRICE	VCR		TYPE = [VHS] HEADS = [2] FREEZE_FRAME = [YES] SEARCH = [YES] PRICE = [LOW]	→ VCX_1000
VHS	2	YES	YES	LOW	VCX_1000	→		
VHS	4	YES	YES	MEDIUM	Record_Mate_99			
BETA	3	NO	YES	LOW	XMovie_Beta			
VHS	5	YES	YES	HIGH	SuperViewer_3.0			

TYPE	HEADS	FREEZE_FRAME	SEARCH	PRICE	VCR		TYPE = [VHS] HEADS = [4] FREEZE_FRAME = [YES] SEARCH = [YES] PRICE = [MEDIUM]	→ RECORD_MATE_99
VHS	2	YES	YES	LOW	VCX_1000			
VHS	4	YES	YES	MEDIUM	Record_Mate_99	→		
BETA	3	NO	YES	LOW	XMovie_Beta			
VHS	5	YES		HIGH	SuperViewer_3.0			

You can now link this database rule to a table of specific values in some database file. The file would contain several sets of values, as follows:

VHS, 2, yes, yes, low, VCX_1000
VHS, 4, yes, yes, medium, Record_Mate99
Beta, 3, no, yes, low, XMovie_Beta
VHS, 5, yes, yes, high, Super_Viewer_2.0

When the expert system is running and the database rule comes up for consideration, the system goes to the database file and retrieves each set of values, one after the other. Each set of values is plugged into empty spaces in the database rule, and the resulting rule is tested. It passes or fails, and the system goes on to the next set of values. This continues until all the sets in the database file have been tested.

Expert systems developers often say that the single database rule is *instantiated* each time a new set of values is tested. In effect, you can think of the database rule as a template of a class, and each of the rules that are created when the template is matched to a set of values is one instance of that template. In the case above, the one database rule would be instantiated four times.

The addition of this database rule doesn't change the behavior of the knowledge base at all. But this one rule does all of the work of the four rules it replaced.

Figure 8.8 shows graphically how values from a database table are plugged into a general rule that picks a VCR. As the system processes the generic database rule, it plugs each entry in the table into the rule. The figure shows two instantiations of the general rule as the system considers the first two records in the table.

PHASE 4. CUSTOMIZING INFERENCE

The built-in backward chaining inference engine that is the heart of most of the small expert systems building tools is usually sufficient for modest applications. It may look at a few extraneous rules during a consultation, but it can still solve the problem in a reasonably short time. The built-in inference engine works well enough to assure that the developer will not have to worry about changing it.

Sometimes, however, you need to make changes to

the built-in inference process. While small tools usually don't let you make major changes to the inference engine, there are a few techniques that can be used to fine-tune it: rule ordering, truth thresholds, and expanding the system with multiple goals.

Rule Ordering

More sophisticated expert systems building tools allow developers to attach a priority to a rule. When the system searches for rules with a certain attribute in their conclusion, it finds all of the rules with that attribute and then begins with the rule with the highest priority.

Most inexpensive tools lack a rule priority system. Instead, the inference engine arbitrarily begins with the first rule in the knowledge base and works down, trying the first rule it finds. Knowing this, a developer working with a small system can exert a certain amount of control over the way a consultation will run (and hence the efficiency of the system) by ordering the rules in the knowledge base.

You must realize that the order of the rules in the knowledge base does not usually affect the conclusions the system will reach. A backward chaining system will reach any conclusions that are logically implicit in the knowledge base, regardless of the order of the rules. You would introduce order into the rule base only when you want to control the order in which the rules will fire and, thus, the order in which questions will be put to a user. This, in turn, may result in a more efficient consultation.

You can sometimes increase execution speed by keeping rules that are likely to pass at the top of the file. This reduces the chance that the system will have to consider a number of failing rules before it finds one that passes. By the same token, if you place rules that are more likely to succeed or fail with 100 percent certainty before less certain rules, you can often reduce the amount of search the system undertakes before it reaches an answer.

In small systems, the clauses within a rule are also taken in order. Thus, you can also switch the order of the attribute-value pairs to improve efficiency. Imagine, for example, that you had a rule with four If-clauses. Reviewing consultations, you find that users commonly concurred with the first two attribute-value pairs, but frequently denied the third attribute-value clause, thus invalidating the rule. If you move the third clause to the top of the rule, it will be the first attribute that the user will be questioned about, which means you can avoid questions about the other two clauses whenever a user denies the first clause.

Truth Thresholds

A truth threshold is a cutoff point. Facts asserted into working memory that have a level of certainty below the truth threshold are, in effect, considered unproved. By the same token, if the user provides a statement with less certainty than the truth threshold setting, it is as if the user asserted that the statement was false.

Most tools have a reserved word that allows the developer to assert the truth threshold that is to be used in evaluating a particular knowledge base. For example, in Level5, you can set the truth threshold as follows:

THRESHOLD = 30

Figure 8.9 shows how the truth threshold behaves in the VCR system. When it is set at .2, three rules pass, recommending three machines: the Record_Mate_99, the VCX_1000, and the Super_Viewer_2.0. If the threshold were raised to .6, however, only two VCRs would be recommended since Super_Viewer_2.0 would now fall below the threshold.

You can use truth thresholds for problems that demand highly accurate solutions. You can also use them to limit systems that produce an inconveniently large number of solutions. Imposing a stringent standard for certainty can reduce the search space considerably. When the certainty of a rule falls under the truth threshold and fails, it may prevent dozens of other rules from being considered through backward chaining. But you must remember, if the threshold is set too high, then all potential recommendations are submerged beneath it and no solution is reached.

Figure 8.9 Truth Threshold Set to .2.

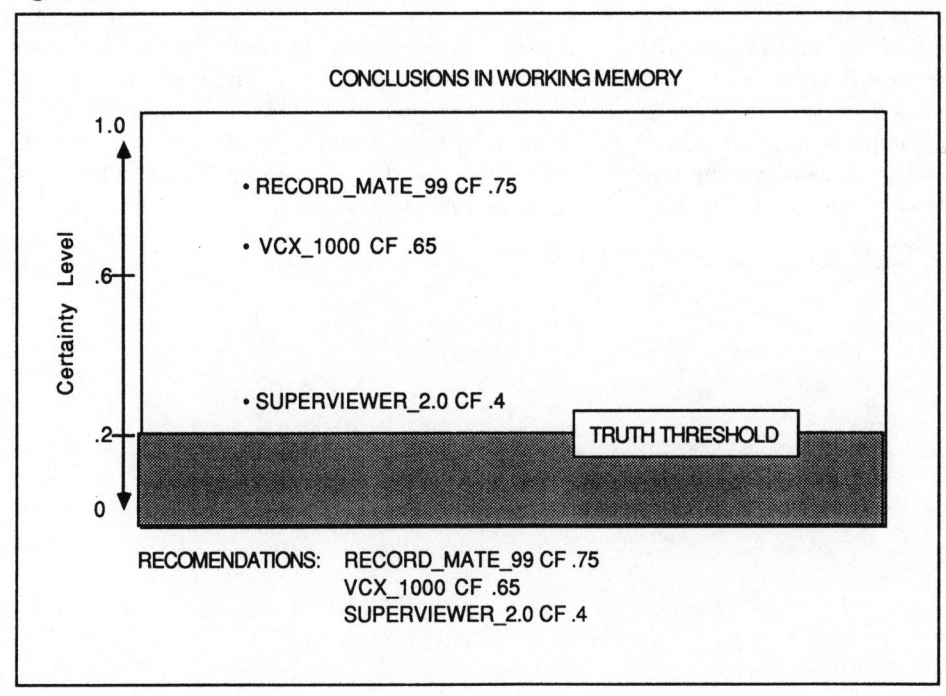

```
                    CONCLUSIONS IN WORKING MEMORY
    1.0

              • RECORD_MATE_99 CF .75

              • VCX_1000 CF .65
     .6
Certainty Level

              • SUPERVIEWER_2.0 CF .4
                                          TRUTH THRESHOLD
     .2

      0

     RECOMENDATIONS:   RECORD_MATE_99 CF .75
                       VCX_1000 CF .65
                       SUPERVIEWER_2.0 CF .4
```

Expanding the System with Multiple Goals

Once your system has been developed to a point where it solves one goal, you may want to broaden its scope by adding additional goals. For instance, you could expand the scope of the VCR Advisor so that it also recommended television sets. The first goal of the system would be to find the best VCR, after which it would pursue a second goal, to find the best television set to go with that VCR.

Most small tools consider goals in the order in which they are listed in the knowledge base. Thus, you can control the system by ordering the goals. For example, in the Oracle Credit Advisor, a simple rule-based application, the system is designed for credit evaluation and the task is divided into stages. Each stage is triggered by a goal that causes the system to go after a value for a different goal-attribute. At each stage, the system backward chains on an attribute, invoking a set of rules that apply to the goal at hand. In VP-Expert, goals are called *FIND statements* and they are ordered in an *ACTIONS block*. Each FIND command in the ACTIONS block invokes backward chaining. The following portion of the Oracle Credit Advisor's knowledge base shows three consecutive FIND commands. Each causes the system to backward chain to find a value for a variable.

ACTIONS

    FIND aged_invoices_display
    FIND credit_limit_exceeded_display
    FIND networth_display
    DISPLAY "-----------------End of Report-----------------"

SUMMARY

We have discussed a number of different ways to improve the VCR knowledge base. In spite of all our efforts, though, it is still far from complete. Before the system can be fielded, it will have to be repeatedly tested and refined. Existing rules need to be fine-tuned, and new rules and attributes need to be added. As each new set of rules is added to the system, all of the considerations we have just discussed would have to be reviewed again.

At certain points in the development of an application, the developer concentrates on adding knowledge just to see what conclusions the new knowledge will allow the system to reach. At other times, the developer concentrates on refining the knowledge in the knowledge base to improve the system's efficiency and to make the user interface friendlier and more effective. There are no hard and fast rules on when to do what, but it all needs to be done, usually over and over again, if you want to create a system that will be useful, easy to use, efficient, and easy to maintain.

9.
Creating Forward Chaining Systems

INTRODUCTION
In this chapter, we consider how to build an expert system that uses a forward chaining inference strategy. Forward chaining is the reverse of backward chaining. Unlike backward chaining, which starts with the goal and backs through the rules looking for facts that will establish the goal, forward chaining begins with facts and proceeds to fire rules to see where they lead.

Backward chaining chooses among pre-existing goals (i.e., solutions). Forward chaining often assembles new solutions. This makes it a useful technique for problems that don't have a fixed set of possible answers. In a diagnosis/selection problem like choosing a VCR, each possible recommendation could be anticipated in advance. The expert system had information about all of the available VCRs and asked questions in order to choose the best VCR for the customer. But consider the problem of developing a factory scheduling system that will create a plan to organize workers, machines, and jobs into an efficient schedule. You could never anticipate all the different possible schedules that might need to be created—there could be millions. Each new schedule might be a unique solution to the problem at hand. Many planning, configuration, and design problems are of this nature. They require a new, creative solution to be assembled for each new case of the problem that comes along.

Of course, forward chaining systems aren't creative the same way that people are. When people come up with unique solutions to problems, they often bring in ideas from other disciplines. Expert systems don't have this ability; their knowledge is limited to a single, narrow domain. Within a narrow domain, however, they can be creative in many modest ways, constructing unique, new solutions to fit the resources and constraints of specific problems. A system to develop factory schedules might take into account a variety of information, such as the workers' skills, union rules, machine capabilities, maintenance requirements, and job requirements in constructing a solution.

In backward chaining systems, the inference engine has a great deal of authority. It dictates most of the system's flow, setting up subgoals, applying rules, and generating queries. The knowledge engineer's main responsibility is to put rules into the system, trusting the inference engine to use them wisely in order to solve an overall goal.

In forward chaining systems, the developer has a greater responsibility for looking after issues of control. This is because forward chaining inference engines behave more unpredictably than backward chaining inference engines, and thus require more supervision. Instead of zeroing in on an overall goal, forward chaining systems are driven by data into uncharted territory. Since rules can fire whenever their conditions become valid, the system may leap to another part of the problem when new data arrives. Faced with such an unpredictable process, the developer often has to put constraints on rules to assure that they are considered at the proper time. Figure 9.1 illustrates the different control issues facing forward and backward chaining systems.

OPS5
We illustrate principles of forward chaining system design with a sample system written in the OPS5

172 PROGRAM DEVELOPMENT

Figure 9.1 Managing control issues in forward and backward chaining systems.

	BACKWARD CHAINING	FORWARD CHAINING
Knowledge Engineer	Writes heuristics with little regard to control	Writes both heuristics and control clauses
Inference Engine	Fires rules that apply to a goal	Fires rules freely

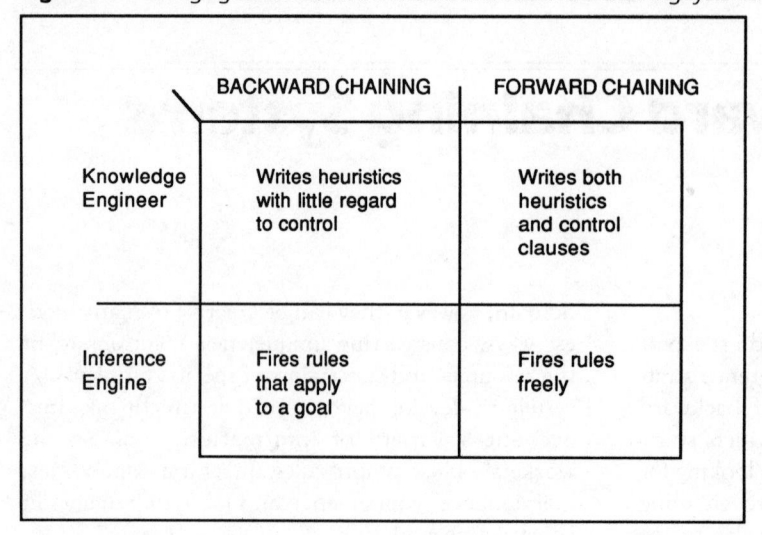

Figure 9.2 Forward chaining inference.

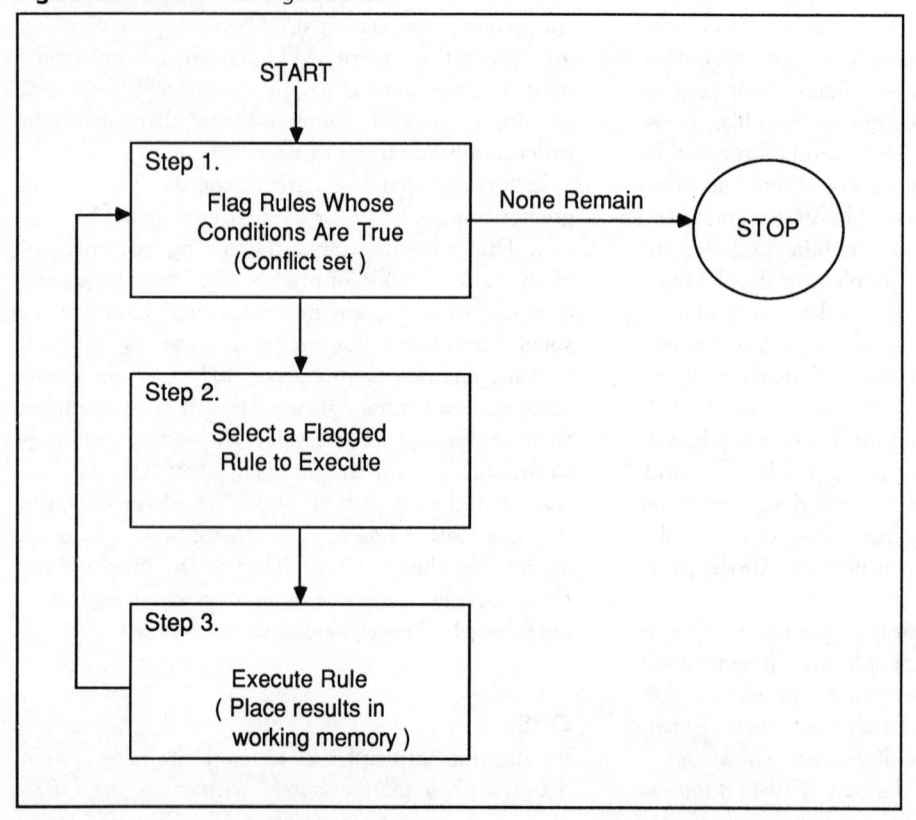

START

Step 1. Flag Rules Whose Conditions Are True (Conflict set) — None Remain → STOP

Step 2. Select a Flagged Rule to Execute

Step 3. Execute Rule (Place results in working memory)

language. OPS5 is an AI programming language commonly used for developing rule-based forward chaining systems. (OPS5 stands for Official Production System 5 for reasons that we're sure its developers would rather forget.) It has been used to develop large, complex systems, including DEC's XCON. OPS5 is probably the most popular development environment for building rule-based forward chaining systems. Though OPS5 is not limited to forward chaining, it is well suited for it.

OPS5 offers a large and flexible set of low-level commands that make it a "language," instead of a "tool." Moreover, most versions lack good developer and user interface utilities. You simply write code with OPS5 and then run it. However, the basic architecture of OPS5 is the same as a backward chaining expert systems building tool. The developer creates a knowledge base, which is processed by an internal inference engine.

The OPS5 Inference Engine

In OPS5, the inference engine operates by repeating a three-step process. First, it looks at any facts that are in working memory. The inference engine finds all the rules whose If-clauses are true, given the facts in working memory. This set of rules is placed into a group called the *conflict set*. The inference engine then evaluates the rules in the conflict set to determine which one to fire first. Once it makes its selection, the rule is fired. The inference engine then goes back to the first phase, checking again to see which rules could now be fired. The system continues this cycle until it finds that there are no longer any unfired rules whose If-clauses are included in working memory. This process is illustrated in Figure 9.2.

There are several methods the inference engine can use for selecting which rule in the conflict set it should execute. A rule might be selected because of its "recency"—those rules that deal with recently discovered information are favored over those that deal with older information. Another consideration is a rule's complexity—complex rules are favored over simpler ones. Or, rules may have priorities attached to them, in which case the rule with the highest priority is chosen. Using these criteria, the inference engine rates all the rules in the conflict set and then selects the one with the best rating as the rule to fire.

Knowledge Representation in OPS5

To create an OPS5 program, you must start by defining one or more objects. A LITERALIZE declaration defines an object and its attributes. For example, the following piece of code creates an object called "Cat" and states that Cats have three characteristics: names, weights, and degrees of finickiness.

```
(literalize cat
    name
    weight
    finickiness
)
```

With this code, whenever an OPS5 consultation is run and a cat is referenced, the inference engine will make an instance of this object and attempt to determine the name, weight, and finickiness of the specific cat being referenced. In other words, LITERALIZE creates a template or class that can later be used to generate instances.

We refer to both classes and instances as objects and use class and instance only when we want to emphasize that a class, in OPS5, is a permanent piece of code that is kept in the knowledge base, while an OPS5 instance is a copy that is created and kept in working memory during a specific consultation. Unlike more sophisticated hybrid systems, OPS5 objects cannot be arranged into hierarchies; each OPS5 object stands alone. Recall that the attributes of an object are called its *slots*. Although "objects" and "slots" are not the terminology used in OPS, we use these terms in our discussion to keep this chapter consistent with other chapters in the book. Thus, the Cat object has three slots: name, weight, and finickiness.

Once you have identified objects, you're ready to create rules. An OPS5 rule that references the Cat objects might look like this:

```
(p food_rec
    (cat ∧ weight high)
    (cat ∧ finickiness extreme)
    - >
    (make food ∧ type dry))
```

Every OPS5 rule begins with the letter p, followed by the rule's name. Its premise is made of a set of conditions enclosed in parentheses. Each condition is in the form (OBJECT ∧ ATTRIBUTE VALUE). The two conditions in the rule above say, in effect, "if a cat is heavy and extremely finicky." This part of the rule is called the antecedent (or left-hand side, LHS).

The —> sign indicates the rule's conclusion. The conclusion contains a "make" command that assigns the value DRY to the TYPE attribute of the Food object. (OPS5 rules can be much more complex, but for our examples we use only this one basic type of rule.)

Even those who like OPS5 will usually admit that OPS5 code is ugly and convoluted. To simplify our discussion, we use a pseudocode that will be easier to read. Our pseudocode rules will be written in standard, If-Then form, similar to the rules in the preceding chapter. Thus, our OPS5 rule given above can be converted into the following form:

Rule Food

    IF   Cat–weight = high AND
             Cat–finickiness = extreme
    THEN Food–type = dry.

We connect objects and their attributes with a dash. For example, the clause CAT-WEIGHT refers to the WEIGHT attribute of a Cat object. We continue to use underscores to connect words that make up attribute or object names. Thus: CAT-EYE_COLOR = GRAY means that the Cat object has an attribute called EYE_COLOR, and that attribute takes the value GRAY.

The Phases in Creating a Forward Chaining System

The actual development of a forward chaining system involves two separate and essentially simultaneous activities. Part of the work involves knowledge acquisition: identifying the objects and rules to be included in the knowledge base. The other part of the effort involves figuring out how to manage the flow of the consultation. To do this, you need to give the system a way to start, constrain the course it follows, and make sure it has a way to finish. (See Figure 9.3.)

When building a real system, you need to address both knowledge and control issues in parallel. However, to make our explanation easier to follow, we divide the development into six phases:

1. Define the problem
2. Write code to obtain facts
3. Write a first set of rules
4. Give the system a way to stop
5. Control rule execution
6. Further development

We illustrate the development of a small, forward chaining rule-based system with a simple example. Suppose the layout editor of a small-town newspaper is going on a vacation. She wants to give her assistants the responsibility of doing layout during her absence. To facilitate this, she decides to have a small expert system developed to give them advice about how to place news stories within the paper.

PHASE 1. DEFINING THE PROBLEM

As with a small, backward chaining system, the first phase in building a forward chaining system is to analyze the task as it is currently solved by the expert. In the case of the newspaper layout system, the expert is the layout editor who takes the day's news stories as input. By applying rules she has developed while working at the job, she decides where each story should be placed within the paper. See Figure 9.4 for an overall analysis of this task.

Once you have an overview of the task, you should interview the expert to determine how she decides where to place stories. It turns out that the editor takes into account such factors as the type of story (whether it is national, local, or a feature), its topic, and whether it is part of a series. She also considers how many stories have already been put on the front page when trying to place a new one.

Creating Forward Chaining Systems 175

Figure 9.3 Parallel approach to knowledge acquisition for forward chaining.

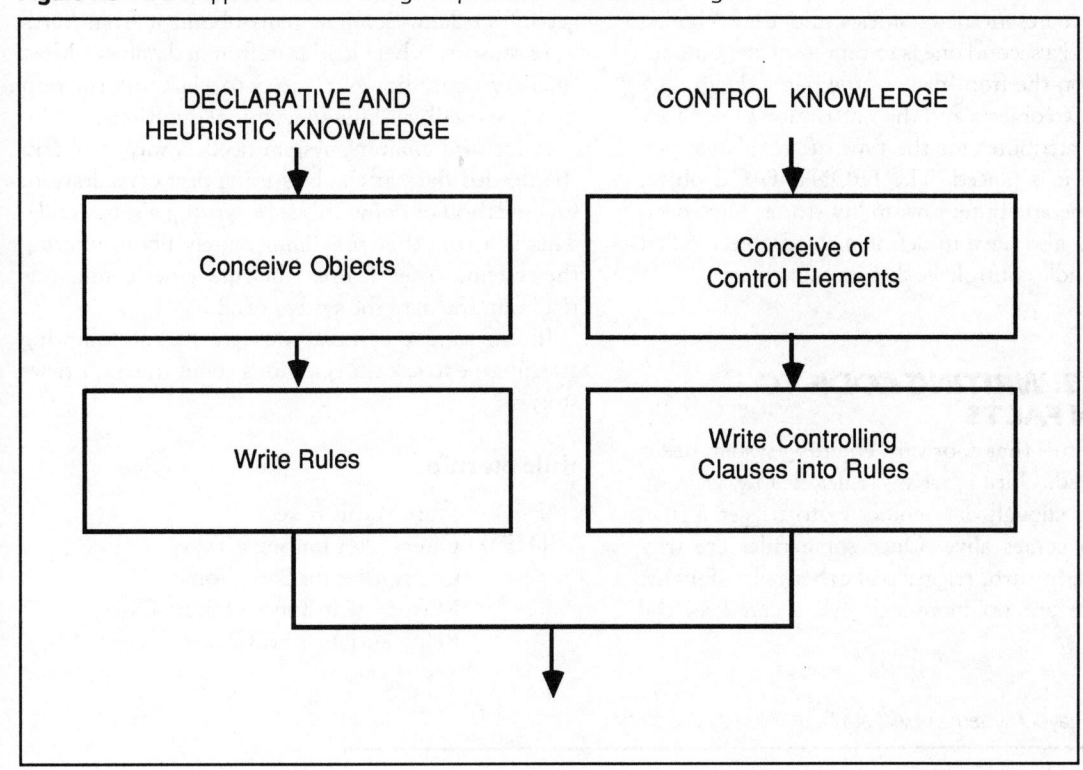

```
DECLARATIVE AND                    CONTROL KNOWLEDGE
HEURISTIC KNOWLEDGE
        ↓                                   ↓
┌─────────────────┐              ┌─────────────────┐
│ Conceive Objects│              │   Conceive of   │
│                 │              │ Control Elements│
└─────────────────┘              └─────────────────┘
        ↓                                   ↓
┌─────────────────┐              ┌─────────────────┐
│   Write Rules   │              │ Write Controlling│
│                 │              │ Clauses into Rules│
└─────────────────┘              └─────────────────┘
              ↓                      ↓
                       ↓
```

Figure 9.4 Overall analysis of news layout task.

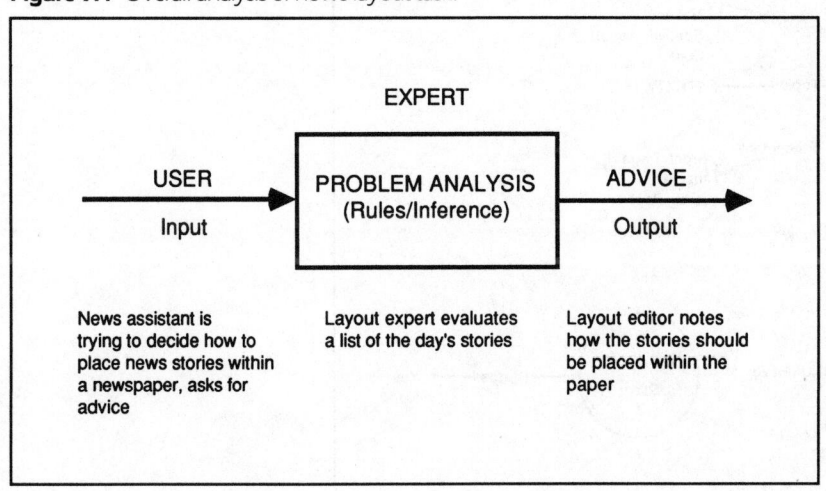

```
                         EXPERT
                  ┌──────────────────┐
     USER         │ PROBLEM ANALYSIS │   ADVICE
    ─────────→   │ (Rules/Inference)│  ─────────→
     Input        └──────────────────┘   Output

News assistant is      Layout expert evaluates   Layout editor notes
trying to decide how to  a list of the day's stories  how the stories should
place news stories within                         be placed within the
a newspaper, asks for                             paper
advice
```

From this initial discussion, two objects emerge: One is to represent news stories and their characteristics, and a second one is to represent the number of articles on the front page of the paper. Figure 9.5 shows the two objects and their attributes. The Story object has attributes for the type of story, its topic, and where it is placed. The FRONT_PAGE object has only one attribute: how many stories have been placed. You also have to define a third object called Start to handle control; we discuss Start later.

PHASE 2. WRITING CODE TO OBTAIN FACTS

Data is the fuel that a forward chaining system needs to get started. Until it arrives, rules sit idly, waiting. As soon as enough data comes in to trigger a rule, the system comes alive. Once some rules are triggered, they, in turn, trigger still other rules. Finally, when there are no more rules that can fire, the system stops.

Every forward chaining system needs a means to get initial data. Some systems obtain it from hardware sensors, others load it in from a database. Most small systems, however, need to elicit information from the user by asking some initial questions.

A forward chaining system needs a way to obtain the needed data at the beginning of a consultation. One method of doing this is by writing a *startup rule*. This is a rule that fires immediately upon entering the system. When it fires, the rule issues commands to obtain the data the system needs.

In our sample system, you can use the following startup rule to ask the questions about the day's news stories:

Rule Startup

IF	Start–status = yes
THEN	Query User for Story Type
	Query User for Story Topic
	Make New Instance of Story Object
	Reinstantiate Start Object.

Figure 9.5 Layout system's object-attribute-value characteristics.

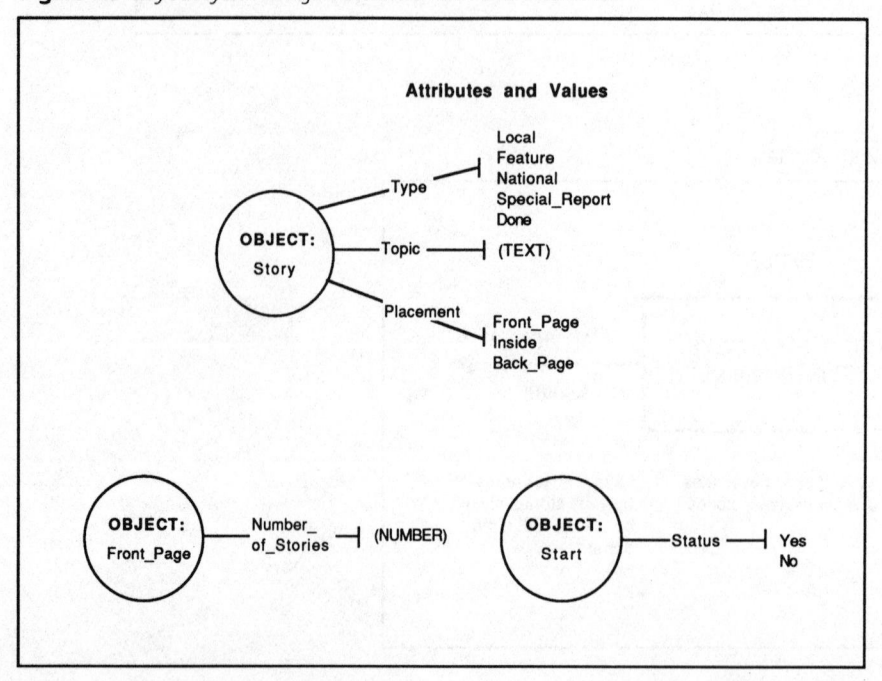

To set the system in motion, the user must first set the status of the Start object to YES. This can be done with a typed command from the OPS5 prompt, causing the startup rule to fire.

When it fires, the startup rule queries the user for the type of story (National, Local, or Feature) and its topic. The rule then creates a new instance of the Story object. It fills in the object's slots, TOPIC and TYPE, with the values provided by the user. Finally, the rule reinstantiates the Start object, thereby refiring the startup rule. This allows the user to enter multiple stories into the system.

PHASE 3. WRITING AN INITIAL SET OF RULES

Once some objects are established, you can create an initial set of rules that reference them. These rules emerge from the initial interview with the expert, in which she gave the following facts: Only four stories can fit on the front page. If the story is a special report, then it should always appear on the front page. Since the paper has a hometown flavor to it, the editor likes the front page to reflect local news. However, there are certain national news topics of great interest to the town. Since more than half the town's residents work at an automotive manufacturing plant, they are especially interested in reading national news stories about automotive and labor issues. From time to time, the paper will run "feature" stories, which focus on a special theme or investigative report. Whenever a new feature is first introduced, it is placed on the front page to attract reader interest.

Based on this information, you can construct the following knowledge base with heuristic rules about story placement.

NEWSPAPER STORY PLACEMENT ADVISOR SYSTEM

LITERALIZE Story
    Type
    Topic
    Placement

LITERALIZE Front_page
    Number_of_stories

Rule Special_report
    IF   Story–type = special_report
    THEN Story–placement = front_page.

Rule Labor
    IF   Story–type = national AND
           Story–topic = labor
    THEN Story–placement = front_page.

Rule Feature
    IF   Story–type = new_feature
    THEN Story–placement = front_page.

Rule Local
    IF   Story–type = local
    THEN Story–placement = front_page.

LITERALIZE Start
    Status

Rule Startup
    IF   Start–status = yes
    THEN Query User for Story Type
             Query User for Story Topic
             Make New Instance of Story Object
             Reinstantiate Start Object.

Running the System

Let's consider what actually happens when these rules are used. The system is turned on when the user creates an instance of the Start object by typing "make start." This causes the startup rule to fire. That rule, in turn, generates two questions about the news story, and then instantiates a Story object. The instance of the Story object has two values filled in with the information supplied by the user.

In reality, instances of objects are placed in working memory. Thus, the first Story object and its two attribute-value pairs (i.e., two facts) are placed in working memory. The inference engine now begins its cycle and identifies any rules whose If-clauses or antecedents are satisfied by the facts in working memory. For example, if the instance of the Story object concerns a local news story, then the local rule fires. After all possible rules have finished firing, the

178   PROGRAM DEVELOPMENT

system re-executes the startup rule and the user can enter another new story.

Another way to look at how the system executes is shown in Figure 9.6. The first column shows user inputs and system outputs. The second column shows the activity of the inference engine—what objects are created, what rules fire, and so on. The third column shows the stories that have been placed on the front page.

Obviously, the consultation illustrated in Figure 9.6 is pretty simple. A startup rule triggers the creation of an instance of the Story object and then asks the user about a story for the newspaper. In effect, each time the user wants to volunteer information about a story, the system creates an instance of the Story object and puts the information in working memory. Then it fires any rules that are appropriate. The conclusion of the rules simply assigns a value to

Figure 9.6 Consultation with the Layout Advisor.

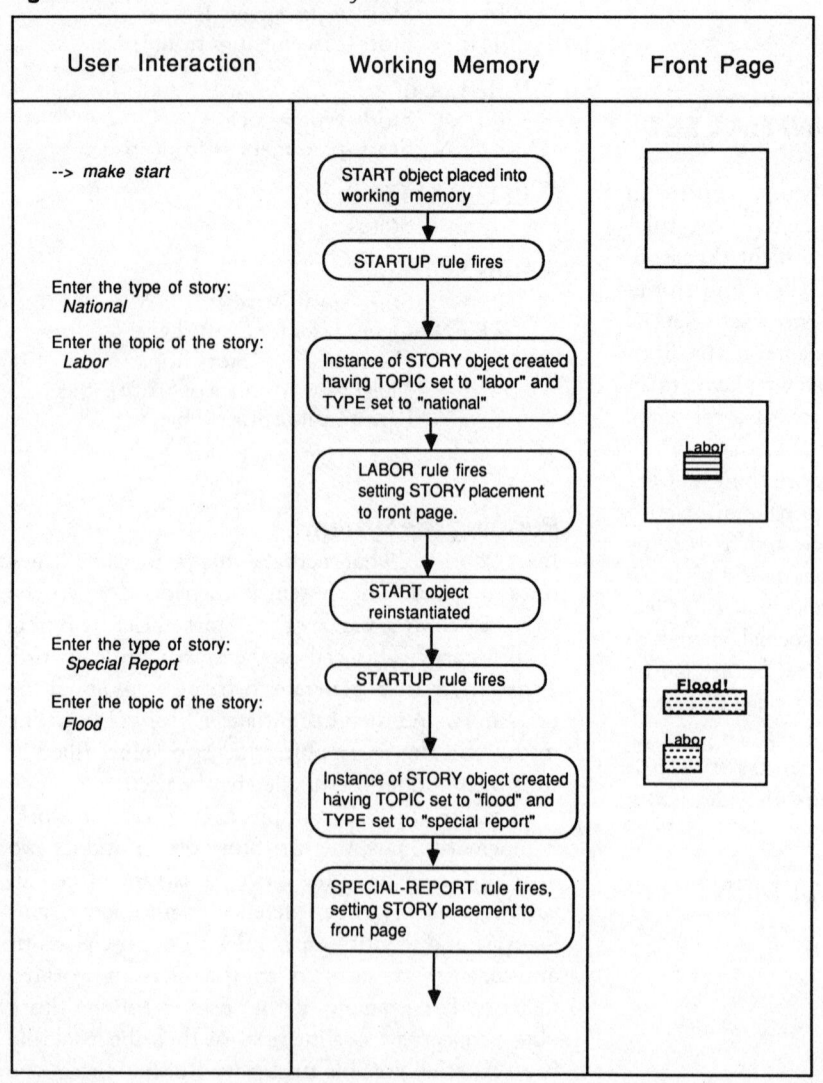

User Interaction	Working Memory	Front Page
--> make start	START object placed into working memory	
	STARTUP rule fires	
Enter the type of story: National		
Enter the topic of the story: Labor	Instance of STORY object created having TOPIC set to "labor" and TYPE set to "national"	
	LABOR rule fires setting STORY placement to front page.	Labor
	START object reinstantiated	
	STARTUP rule fires	Flood! Labor
Enter the type of story: Special Report		
Enter the topic of the story: Flood	Instance of STORY object created having TOPIC set to "flood" and TYPE set to "special report"	
	SPECIAL-REPORT rule fires, setting STORY placement to front page	

one of the attributes of the Story object instance—placement. Although this example assumes that each story is different and thus triggers a different rule, there could just as easily have been three labor stories that fired the labor rule three times in a row, assigning each story to the front page.

PHASE 4. GIVING THE SYSTEM A WAY TO STOP

As we stated earlier, a forward chaining system stops when there are no rules left to fire. This is the most graceful way for the system to conclude, but not always the most desirable. Sometimes you may need to force the system to terminate, even though there are rules left to consider.

Recall that the expert said that only four stories can fit on the front page. So once the system has placed four stories on the front page, you would like it to stop, even if additional rules may be eligible to fire. However, given the current knowledge base, the system would go on and on, allowing more than four stories to be placed on the front page.

You have to write rules to keep track of how many stories have been placed on the front page, and terminate the system once it is full. You have already created a Front_Page object whose single attribute is NUMBER_OF_STORIES. To provide this attribute with a value, you must create two new rules. These

Figure 9.6 (Continued).

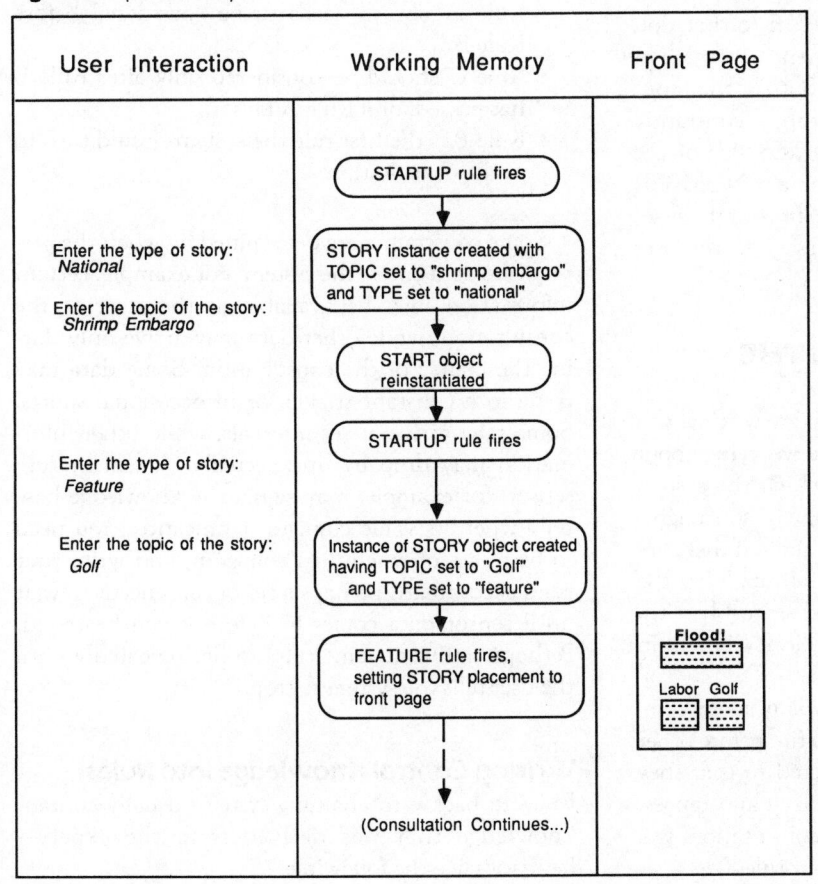

User Interaction	Working Memory	Front Page
	STARTUP rule fires	
Enter the type of story: *National* Enter the topic of the story: *Shrimp Embargo*	STORY instance created with TOPIC set to "shrimp embargo" and TYPE set to "national"	
	START object reinstantiated	
	STARTUP rule fires	
Enter the type of story: *Feature* Enter the topic of the story: *Golf*	Instance of STORY object created having TOPIC set to "Golf" and TYPE set to "feature"	
	FEATURE rule fires, setting STORY placement to front page	Flood! Labor Golf
	(Consultation Continues...)	

rules increment the NUMBER_OF_STORIES attribute of the Front_Page object every time a rule decides to place a story on the front page:

Rule Count

    IF   Story-placement = front_page
    THEN increment the value of the NUMBER_OF_STORIES slot of the Front-Page object.

Rule Stop

    IF   Front_page-number_of_stories = 4
    THEN HALT.

The word HALT is a predefined command in OPS5 that causes the system to end execution. In effect, the Rule Count is constantly watching the PLACEMENT slot of instances of the Story object. If a rule assigns the value FRONT_PAGE to that slot, then the count rule fires and increments the value of the NUMBER_OF_STORIES attribute of the Front_Page object by one. The Rule Stop is constantly watching the NUMBER_OF_STORIES slot of the Front_Page object. Whenever the value of NUMBER_OF_STORIES is 4, the Stop rule fires and causes the system to halt and print a message to the user saying that the front page is full.

PHASE 5. CONTROLLING THE EXECUTION OF RULES

Depending on the type of system you are writing, you will have to spend more or less time worrying about "control issues" like the order in which the system processes the rules. Small systems may be so straightforward that control isn't a concern at all. If there are only a handful of rules, and they all apply to the same object, the system may proceed smoothly without additional control imposed upon it. It will take in data, fire some rules, and stop.

Forward chaining systems are usually more complex. Normally, certain rules need to fire before other rules. Some rules need to be restricted so that they will be considered only under specific circumstances. To guide the system through such a consultation, you need to add control knowledge to your rules.

Get an Overview of Dependencies

To add control, start by thinking of the overall tasks addressed by the system: when it needs to start, when it needs to finish, and the relationships among the tasks that need to be accomplished along the way.

You don't have to lay out the entire flow of the system in advance. In fact, if this were so, conventional programming might be a better way to write the system. In developing an OPS5 system, however, you do need to think about the circumstances under which rules should be applied. In other words, as you add each new rule to your knowledge base, you have to consider the situations in which that rule should be used.

For example, you might have a system with three rules, A, B, and C, and the following constraints:

- Rule A always needs to be considered before Rule B.
- Rule C should be considered only after Rule B has passed, or if Rule A fails.
- Rule B is the first rule the system should turn to in the consultation.

Some constraints are determined by when the prerequisite data enters the system. For example, certain information may be available at the start of the consultation, while other data may arrive only during the course of the consultation. Some data may come in a constant trickle, or in occasional spurts. Some may arrive at set intervals, while other information may drop by unexpectedly. A temperature sensor, for example, may signal the knowledge base only when its value changes significantly. You need to be aware of when data comes in, and write your rules accordingly. Perhaps a set of rules needs to wait until sensor data comes in before it can be tested. Perhaps you want some rules to fire repeatedly until the user tells the system to stop.

Writing Control Knowledge into Rules

Rules in backward chaining systems usually contain knowledge that was derived from the expert—heuristics like the following:

IF   the lights are dim
THEN the battery may be dead.

Forward chaining rules often have an additional component to them. In addition to heuristic knowledge derived from the expert, they also tend to include control knowledge added by the developer. For instance, that same rule rewritten for a forward chaining system might become:

IF   once you have finished checking the fuel system the lights are dim
THEN the battery may be dead.

Control knowledge tells the system when the rule should be used.

Enabling/Disabling Conditions

By adding control knowledge to rules, you limit their use to specific times, when their *enabling conditions* are true. This effectively "locks out" rules from consideration except when appropriate. For example, the following rule is locked out from consideration until another rule enables it by setting the STATUS attribute of the Focus object to ELECTRICAL_SYSTEM.

Rule Battery

IF   Focus–status = electrical_system AND
      Car–lights = dim
THEN Car-problem = battery.

The heuristic knowledge in this rule states that if the car's lights are dim, there may be a problem with the battery. The control portion of the rule states that the rule should be considered only when the system's focus is on the electrical system.

The above rule might be "enabled" by the following rule:

Rule Check_elect

IF   Focus-status = fuel_system AND
      Fuel_system–status = OK
THEN Focus-status = electrical_system.

This rule sets the STATUS attribute of the Focus object to ELECTRICAL_SYSTEM, thereby enabling the battery rule to be considered. We sometimes say that the If-clause

Focus–status = fuel_system

is the *screening clause* of the battery rule.

Control knowledge and heuristic knowledge are not necessarily different. Screening clauses are sometimes used only for control, but at other times they may involve meaningful facts about the problem.

The use of screening clauses is not limited to forward chaining systems. They can also be used by backward chaining systems to prevent the inference engine from using rules under certain circumstances. For example, it makes sense to ask the user for values of PREGNANT or LAST_MENSTRUAL_PERIOD only if the SEX of the patient is female. By including the screening clause SEX = FEMALE in the following rule, questions about the possibility of the patient being pregnant or missing a menstrual period will be asked only if the first condition is known:

Rule 1

IF   Sex = female AND
      Pregnant = yes OR
      Last_menstrual_period = missed
THEN Radiology_procedure = inappropriate.

In general, screening clauses are used in backward chaining systems for efficiency. By placing a screening clause at the start of a rule, you can sometimes prevent the system from asking superfluous questions. In forward chaining systems, on the other hand, screening clauses serve a more critical purpose. They help keep the system "on track," preventing it from embarking on inefficient or erroneous lines of reasoning.

Because you always know your goals in advance in backward chaining systems, the system can never recommend a solution that isn't among your goals. The worst case is that questions will be asked in a strange order. In a forward chaining system, though, the system is assembling the recommendation. If you have rules without appropriate screening clauses, the system can include components in a proposed solution that could or should not be included. In the worst case, if your system is designed to offer only a single recommendation, and it lacks appropriate screening clauses, it could arrive at a recommendation that would be invalid or undesirable.

Putting Control into the Layout Advisor

Let's consider how you might add control to the newspaper layout system. When you run the system developed in Phase 2, certain control problems could arise. Even though all the rules are individually valid, the system still does not always behave properly. This happens because you considered each placement rule separately. You didn't consider how the rules might actually work together as a whole.

Suppose, for example, that the first four stories entered were local news items. As the user entered each story, the local rule would fire, placing the story on the front page. If the fifth story that came in was a special report, it would have to be buried in the paper, since the front page would be full. This is obviously a mistake, since according to the expert, special reports are more important than local stories. This reflects a control problem in the system. Though you have been specific about the knowledge in the rules, you haven't been specific about when they should fire.

To solve this problem, you need some way to force the system to consider special reports before considering local news items. One way to do this is by adding control knowledge to the rules, so that only after all special reports are considered will the system apply rules to process other kinds of stories. This guarantees that the system never buries a special report inside the paper.

To accomplish this, you need to define a new object, called Special_Reports_Placed. This object will control when the rules can be executed. By adding it as a condition to the rules, you will prevent them from being considered until after Special_Reports_Placed has been set to Yes.

LITERALIZE Special_reports_placed
    Status

Rule Labor
    IF   Special_reports_placed-status = yes AND
          Story-type = national AND
          Story-topic = labor
    THEN Story-placement = front_page.

Rule Feature
    IF   Special_reports_placed-status = yes AND
          Story-type = new_feature
    THEN Story-placement = front_page.

Rule Local
    IF   Special_reports_placed-status = yes AND
          Story-type = local
    THEN Story-placement = front_page.

Now, none of the rules will fire until the value of the STATUS attribute of the Special_Reports_Placed object becomes yes. As each story comes in, the only rule that is considered is Special_report, since it lacks the Special_reports_placed clause.

Once the user has entered all the day's news stories into the system, he finishes by typing the word "DONE" when asked for the type of the latest story. This sets the value of the TYPE slot in the Story object to DONE.

At this point, the Special_Report rule has had an opportunity to fire for each story, so you can free up the rest of the rules for consideration. To do this, you have to write a rule to detect when the final story is entered, and then enable Special_reports_placed.

Assume that the user signifies that he has entered the last story by creating an instance of the Story object with TYPE set to DONE. The following rule detects this, releasing the rest of the rules to be considered:

Rule All_stories_in_system
    IF   Story-type = done
    THEN Special_reports_placed-status = yes.

By doing this, you ensure that the system will begin only by considering instances of stories that are special reports.

The complete knowledge base of the Newspaper Layout Advisor is reproduced below.

NEWSPAPER LAYOUT ADVISOR

LITERALIZE Story
    Type
    Topic
    Placement

LITERALIZE Front_page
    Number_of_stories

LITERALIZE Start
    Status

LITERALIZE Special_reports_placed
    Status

Rule Special_report
  IF   Story-type = special_report
  THEN Story-placement = front_page.

Rule Startup
  IF   Start-status = yes
  THEN Query User for Story Type
         Query User for Story Topic
         Make New Instance of Story Object
         Reinstantiate Start Object.

Rule Count
  IF   Story-placement = front_page
  THEN (increment the value of the
         NUMBER_OF_STORIES slot of the
         Front- page object).

Rule Stop
  IF   Front_page-number_of_stories = 4
  THEN HALT.

Rule Labor
  IF   Special_reports_placed-status = yes AND
         Story-type = national AND
         Story-topic = labor
  THEN Story-placement = front_page.

Rule Feature
  IF   Special_reports_placed-status = yes AND
         Story-type = new_feature
  THEN Story-placement = front_page.

Rule Local
  IF   Special_reports_placed-status = yes AND
         Story-type = local
  THEN Story-placement = front_page.

Rule All_stories_in_system
  IF   Story-type = done
  THEN Special_reports_placed-status = yes.

Figure 9.7 shows how constraints are used in the Layout Advisor to eliminate rules from possible use by the inference engine. Originally there were four layout rules available to the inference engine. The addition of the clause Special_reports_placed-status = yes to three of the rules causes them to be eliminated from consideration by the inference engine.

Rule Priorities

We now pause from our example to take a look at another way to control rule execution in a forward chaining system. In Data General's Automated Transfer Pricing System (ATP), *priorities* are used to control the order in which the system forward chains through rules.

Recall that the purpose of ATP is to determine the price to charge for parts shipped to various divisions of Data General. The price to charge for a shipment is calculated by a set of pricing rules. These are divided into two types: general rules, and exceptions to them. General rules deal with broad categories of part transfers. For example, one such rule deals with all shipments of hardware that is manufactured or vendor purchased. Exception rules deal with special cases that override the general rules. For example, parts shipped to Nippon Data General require a special way to set their price.

To make sure the system worked properly, a method was needed to ensure that the system looked at the exception rules before the general rules. In addition, once an exception fired, the general rules had to be kept from firing.

To accomplish this, the developer used rule priorities. These are numbers attached to rules that describe their urgency. When processing a set of

Figure 9.7 Using constraints to eliminate rules from consideration.

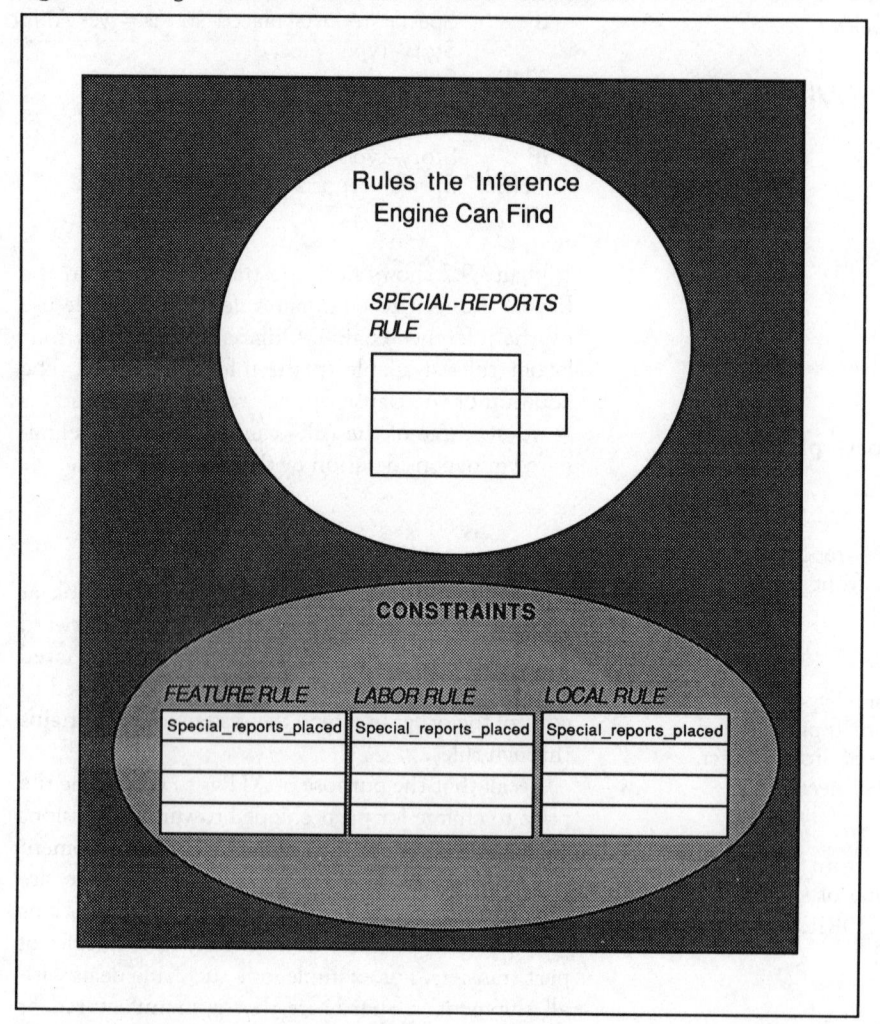

rules, the system considers those with a high priority first.

In ATP, the exception rules were given a higher priority. This made the system consider them first. General rules were given a low priority and were considered later. Special screening clauses were added to general rules to make them fail if an exception rule had already passed. This was done by including the clauses "WITH-UNKNOWN UPLIFT" and "WITH-UNKNOWN DISCOUNT" at the start of every general rule. If an exception had fired, the attributes "DISCOUNT" and "UPLIFT" would be known, so the general rules would fail. Figure 9.8 illustrates these rule priorities.

PHASE 6. FURTHER DEVELOPMENT

As a forward chaining system develops, you may make many of the same kinds of refinements we discussed in Chapter 8. You can consolidate repetitive rules, add certainty factors, and so on.

Recall that one way to refine a backward chaining system is to add abstractions. While forward chaining systems are perfectly capable of reasoning with abstractions, they are refined somewhat differently. In backward chaining systems, abstract rules will be used automatically by the system if they refer to needed values. In forward chaining systems, you need to carefully link abstract rules to existing rules so that they fire at the proper times.

ADDITIONAL CONSIDERATIONS

When you develop an expert system in OPS5, there are two additional considerations that you will want to think about: search strategies and the Rete algorithm.

Figure 9.8 *Priority use in ATP.*

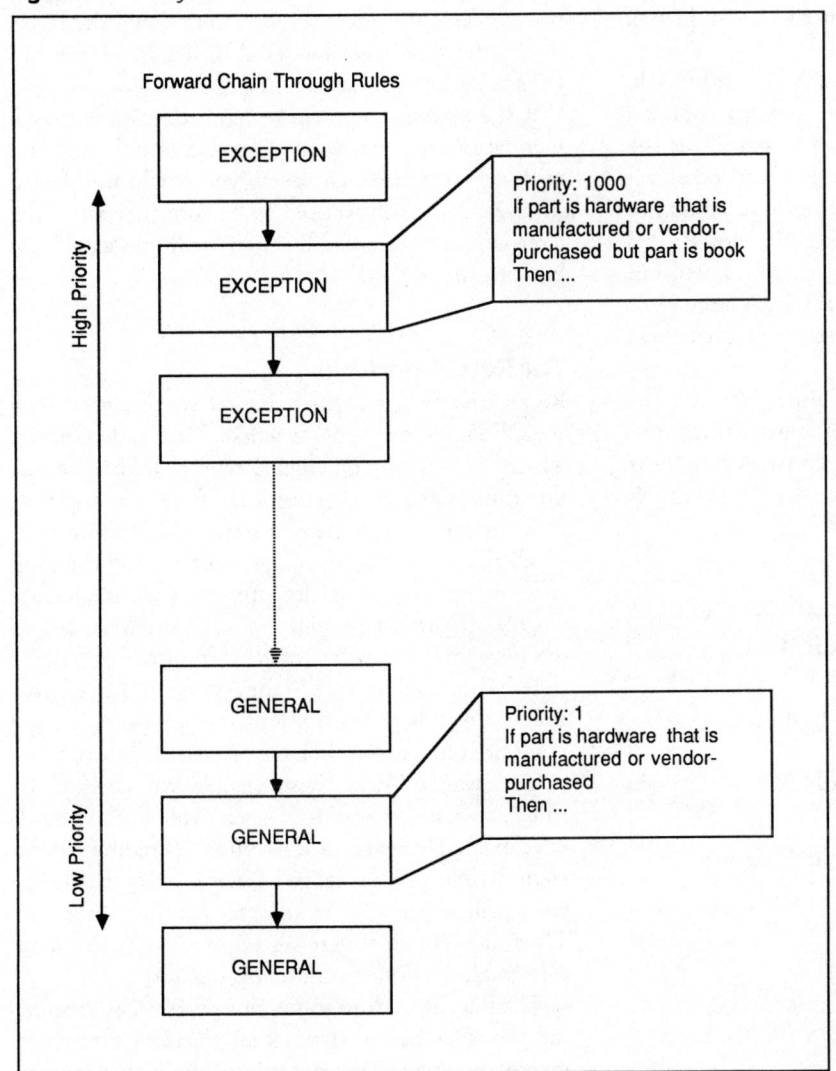

```
Forward Chain Through Rules

High Priority
    EXCEPTION
        ↓
    EXCEPTION  ──── Priority: 1000
        ↓            If part is hardware that is
    EXCEPTION        manufactured or vendor-
        ⋮            purchased but part is book
                     Then ...
    GENERAL
        ↓        ──── Priority: 1
    GENERAL          If part is hardware that is
        ↓            manufactured or vendor-
    GENERAL          purchased
Low Priority         Then ...
```

Depth-First and Breadth-First Search

Once you make the decision to implement your system using forward chaining, you need to examine it in more detail. There are two types of forward chaining methods available: *breadth-first* and *depth-first* search. To make the choice, you need to consider how fast the system needs to run, and whether it will make multiple recommendations.

We illustrate the difference between these two search strategies by considering the rule base listed in Table 9.1. To keep the discussion simple, we have used capital letters to stand for attributes and small letters to stand for values.

Assume that there are two facts, $A = j$ and $B = k$, in working memory and that the forward chaining inference engine has started up. If it started at the top, it would determine that Rule 1 succeeded and it would place $C = 1$ in working memory. It would not have to decide if it should check Rule 2 or Rule 3 next. It would simply work from the top down, but that involves inefficiency if the rule base is large.

Figure 9.9 shows a decision tree that uses these alphabetic rules.

When you use a backward chaining system, the system always follows any path it starts on right to the end, and then backs up and considers the next closest path, and so forth. This search strategy is called depth-first search. All backward chaining systems use depth-first search.

Forward chaining systems, on the other hand, can use either depth-first or breadth-first search. If a forward chaining system were using depth-first search in our alphabetic rule base, it would go from Rule 1 to Rule 3 to Rule 5. But if it were using breadth-first search, it would check all rules that could be checked using the initial data before it checked any rules that depended on facts established by firing those first rules. Moreover, it would repeat this process over and over as it went down the layers of the decision tree. Figure 9.10 illustrates the difference between these two strategies.

If the system could make more than one recommendation, but you were interested in only one and were also interested in speed, you would use depth-first search; if you wanted to be sure that all of the alternatives were carefully examined, you would use breadth-first search.

The Rete Algorithm

Recall that earlier in this chapter we discussed how the OPS5 inference engine works. First, it determines which rules might be eligible to fire. It then selects one rule, based upon a number of criteria, and fires it. It then returns to the first step and finds a new set of eligible rules to fire. The most time-consuming step in this process is determining which rules are eligible to fire when new information is added to working memory. During this phase, sometimes called the "match step," the system finds eligible rules by testing the conditions in their premises. If a rule's premise passes, then that rule is eligible to fire.

One way to find these eligible rules would be simply to test the premise of every rule in the knowledge base. However, this is often incredibly inefficient. In a large knowledge base, it is likely that many rules will share the same tests in their premises. Thus, if every rule were tested separately, the same tests might be done over and over again.

The Rete algorithm solves this problem by examining the rules before the system starts to execute. It creates a network that organizes rules into categories

Table 9.1 An Alphabetic Rule Base

Rule 1		Rule 4	
IF	$A = j$ AND $B = k$	IF	$D = m$
THEN	$C = 1$.	THEN	$F = o$.
Rule 2		**Rule 5**	
IF	$A = j$ AND $B = k$	If	$E = n$
THEN	$D = m$.	THEN	$G = p$.
Rule 3			
IF	$C = 1$		
THEN	$E = n$.		

Creating Forward Chaining Systems 187

Figure 9.9 The alphabetic rule decision tree.

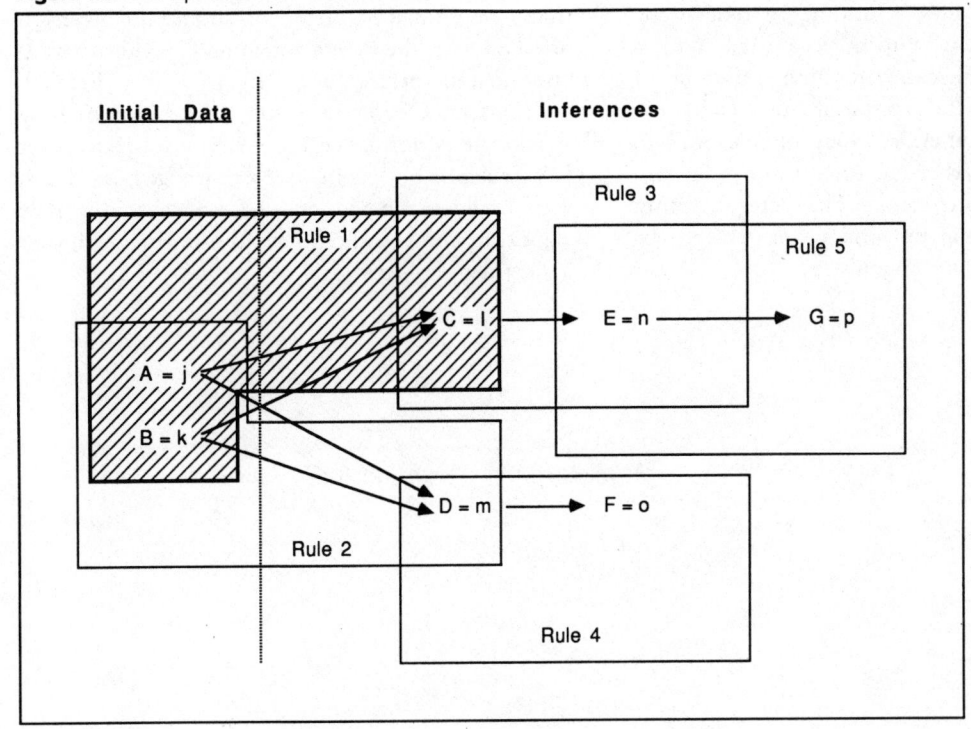

Figure 9.10 Breadth-first and depth-first search strategies.

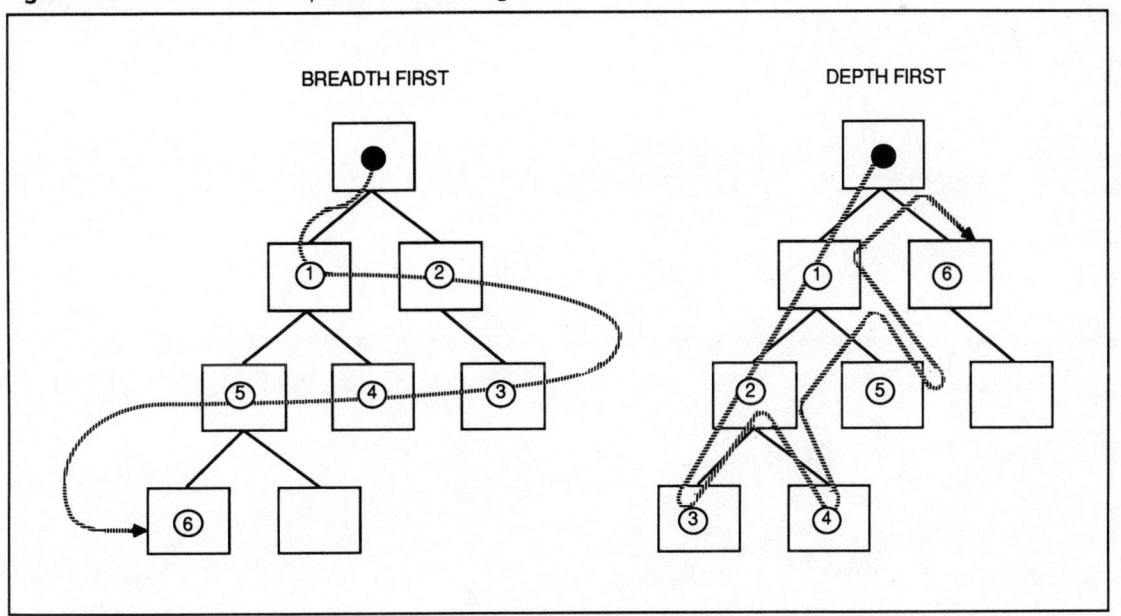

based on conditions their premises share. This network is later used during runtime to reduce the number of tests that need to be performed. With a single test, the system can determine if a group of rules will pass or fail. If the test evaluates to false, the system can ignore the entire group of rules and go on. If the test passes, then the rules in the group can be evaluated in greater detail. The Rete algorithm ensures that the same test will never have to be repeated within the same match step.

If you are going to use OPS5 for anything other than a very small problem, you should use a version of OPS5 with the Rete algorithm. The alternative is poor system performance. Even with a Rete algorithm, an OPS5-type system will begin to have significant performance problems if you have over 5,000 rules or objects in your knowledge base. Thus, you should use a version of OPS5 with the Rete algorithm and you should avoid problems with over 5,000 rules or objects.

10.
Creating Systems with Context Trees

INTRODUCTION

In a small expert system like the VCR Advisor or the Newspaper Layout Advisor, all of the system's rules can be conveniently kept in one set. As you try to develop larger systems, however, the knowledge base becomes increasingly complex, and it becomes necessary to consider alternatives to simple rule systems.

If the knowledge to be encoded is easy to represent in rules, and the task you are faced with is procedural or diagnostic in nature, a backward chaining rule-based system that incorporates context trees may offer the best approach to the problem. In this chapter, we consider how to develop rule-based systems that incorporate context trees. Such systems are often called *structured rule systems* because the rules are subdivided or structured into sets or contexts.

Structured rule systems offer two major advantages over simple rule systems. First, by subdividing rules, you achieve more control over how the system operates. This, in turn, can improve the efficiency with which the system runs. Subdivision also facilitates more efficient development and maintenance. When a simple rule system starts to grow too large, maintenance becomes a laborious task because the developer must consider all of the possible interactions with existing rules before adding a new rule. Tracing facilities get bogged down with many rules, making debugging difficult. Memory runs short because all of the system's knowledge is kept in one big lump. When these problems begin to occur, you should consider subdividing the knowledge base into multiple contexts.

The second benefit of structured or context-based systems is their ability to automatically use the same set of rules over and over again. You can think of a *context* as a kind of object that includes rules. Because you can reinstantiate the context, you can reuse the rules many times during a consultation. For example, suppose a tax advisor system includes a set of rules to find the appropriate deduction for each dependent of the user. If the user has three dependents, the rule set needs to be used three times during the consultation. By keeping this set of rules in a context, you can repeatedly execute them by reinstantiating the context.

Texas Instrument's Personal Consultant Easy and Personal Consultant Plus provide a nice illustration of the relationship between simple and structured rule systems. Personal Consultant Easy is a simple rule tool. It keeps all of its rules in a single knowledge base. When you run a dialogue with Personal Consultant Easy, each rule in its knowledge base is examined once and you are then presented with the results. If you find that your Personal Consultant Easy application is getting too large, you can move it to Personal Consultant Plus, a structured rule system. A Personal Consultant Easy knowledge base is automatically converted into one context within Personal Consultant Plus. (See Figure 10.1.)

If you do not begin developing your knowledge base with a tool like Personal Consultant Easy that has a larger counterpart, it is more difficult to move a simple rule base to a structured rule system. Thus, if you anticipate developing a mid- to large-sized backward chaining rule-based system, you should probably begin by developing your system with a structured rule tool.

How a Context Tree System Works

Systems organized around context trees are usually backward chaining systems. In effect, the system

Figure 10.1 Personal Consultant Easy and Plus.

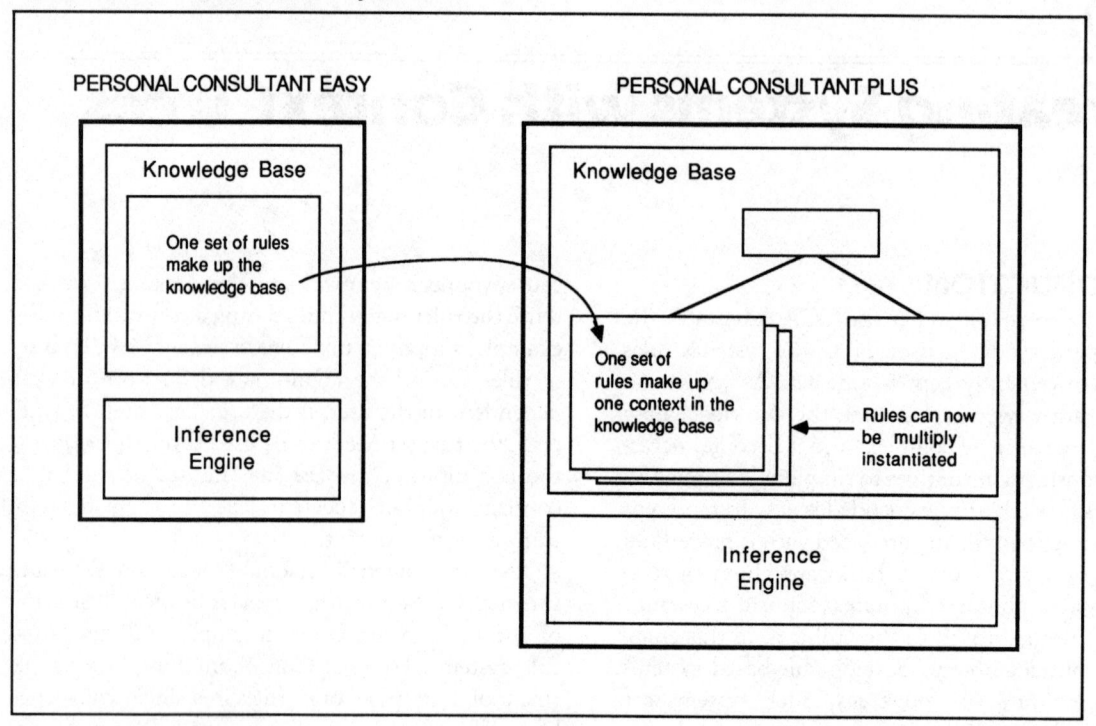

backward chains first on the context tree and then secondarily on the rules within the contexts.

There is a sense in which contexts might be called objects, but in structured rule systems, the context or object is conceptualized primarily as a set of rules. It is thus rather different from the simple objects that are used in OPS5 or the much more complex objects that are found in hybrid systems. It's probably more accurate to think of a context tree as a way of replacing some of the control objects and many of the screening clauses that are used in OPS5.

The first structured rule tool was EMYCIN, the tool that resulted from the initial expert systems development research at Stanford in the mid to late 1970s. EMYCIN was developed after the Stanford researchers developed the expert system MYCIN. MYCIN was an expert system designed to diagnose infectious diseases and recommend an appropriate treatment. After the researchers developed the MYCIN system, they went on to develop the first expert systems building tool by removing the MYCIN knowledge base and just keeping the inference engine and the developer utilities, hence the name, a shortening of "Empty MYCIN."

The developers of EMYCIN used the term "context," and we have retained it since EMYCIN is so well documented in the literature and since commercial vendors have subsequently adopted a confusing variety of alternatives.

Static and Dynamic Contexts

There is a difference between the original context tree that the knowledge engineer creates during development and the context tree that is actually used by the system during runtime. The original version is referred to as the *static context tree*. It comprises the code that defines the structure of the tree with a single copy of each general context. Later, during runtime, the system creates a *dynamic context tree*.

This is a runtime version of the static context tree. During a consultation, contexts are omitted or replicated as they are needed. (In the same sense, when you use a simple rule-based system, there is the static rule base and the specific or dynamic set of rules that are actually tried during a particular consultation.)

Rules, in EMYCIN and in most subsequent context-based systems, are made up of facts comprised of three terms. The first term refers to the context, the second to the attribute, and the third to the value. We reproduce a pseudocode EMYCIN rule below. (The original MYCIN rules were written in LISP.)

```
IF      Organism_Context_1-Gram_stain =
        Gramneg AND
        Organism_Context_1-Morphology =
        Rod AND
        Organism_Context_1-Aerobicity =
        Anaerobic
THEN    Organism_Context_1-Identity = Bacteroides (CF = 60).
```

Notice that each statement begins with the name of the context, ORGANISM_CONTEXT_1, followed by an attribute and then a value.

During runtime, whenever the system reinstantiates a context, it reinstantiates all of the rules associated with that context and automatically changes the number associated with the context of each statement to indicate which instantiation the statements and the rules are associated with. For example, if two versions of the ORGANISM context had been created during runtime, the rules in the second copy of the context would appear as follows:

```
IF      Organism_Context_2-Gram_stain =
        Gramneg AND
        Organism_Context_2-Morphology =
        Rod AND
        Organism_Context_2-Aerobicity =
        Anaerobic
THEN    Organism_Context_2-Identity = Bacteroides (CF = 60).
```

Developing a Structured Rule System

Structured rule systems are usually developed by means of a four-phase process:

1. Decide what contexts signify
2. Create an initial context tree
3. Implement the context tree
4. Expand and revise the context tree and rules as necessary

We consider in turn the activities that occur in each phase.

PHASE 1. DECIDING WHAT CONTEXTS SIGNIFY

In Chapter 5, we noted that tasks that can be subdivided fall into one of two general types of tasks. Some tasks are essentially procedural; the subparts of such tasks form a sequence of steps. Other tasks can be divided into subparts that represent closely related topics that aren't necessarily steps. These tasks are referred to as structured analysis tasks. The first phase in building your context tree is to decide which kind of task you are addressing, and hence what the contexts in your context tree will signify: steps in a process, or related parts of a problem.

When you develop a context tree for a procedural task, each context becomes a step in the process. Each level of the context tree hierarchy represents a set of steps of a similar size. Figure 10.2 illustrates a context tree for a procedural system. The overall diagnosis effort has been subdivided into three major steps. Step 1, in turn, has been subdivided into two steps. Step 2 has been subdivided into three steps, one of which has, in turn, been subdivided into five steps.

When faced with a task that is best represented as a structural analysis task, you need to subdivide the overall subject matter into related clusters of more or less independent information. Figure 10.3 shows the context tree of Ford Motor Companies' ASEA Advisor system. This system helps Ford maintenance people troubleshoot and maintain ASEA robotic devices.

Figure 10.2 A context tree that models a procedural task.

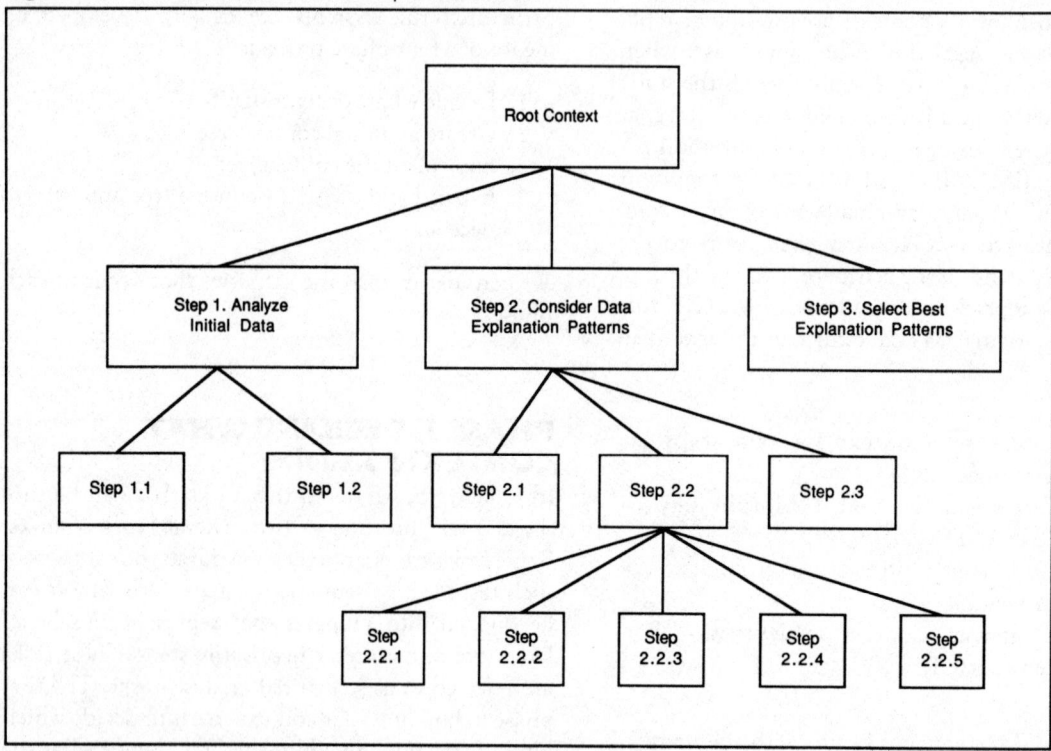

Figure 10.3 Ford's ASEA Advisor context tree.

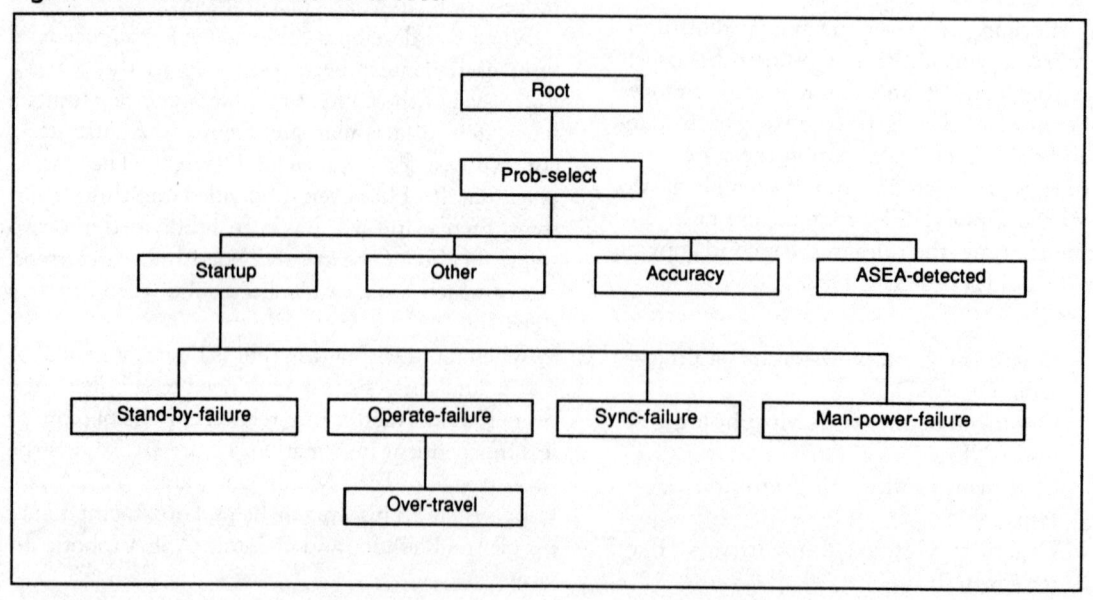

In the case of the ASEA Advisor, you do not have to work through the context tree in a step-by-step manner. Normally, only one condition is causing the problem, and it's a matter of considering one problem area after another, in whatever sequence seems appropriate, in order to find out what is causing the problem. Notice that the third level of the context tree reveals that the Ford developers have considered four general causes of problems: startup problems, accuracy problems, ASEA-detected problems, and other problems. By observing how startup problems have been subdivided, you can deduce either that most problems are startup problems, or that this is a prototype system that is currently developed to deal with startup problems in considerable detail.

Traversing a Context Tree

If you have chosen to implement your contexts as steps in a process, it is up to you to write the code to control the order in which they are used. If, on the other hand, your context tree represents a structured analysis task, then it is up to the inference engine to decide how the context tree will be traversed.

We examine traversal further by comparing two tools that embody these two fundamentally different approaches to contexts: AION's AION Development System (ADS) (Version 4.1), and IBM's Expert System Environment (ESE) (Version 2). Both ADS and ESE support a hierarchy of contexts. ESE refers to contexts as FCBs (Focus Control Blocks), while ADS calls them states. Throughout this chapter, for simplicity, we refer to both as contexts.

ESE, like EMYCIN, moves from one context to another by using the backward chaining mechanism. If a rule in a parent context calls for the value of an attribute that the system locates in a child context, the system moves to the child context attempting to find the attribute's value. The ESE context tree is more or less transparent when the system is being run, and rules access other rules in a backward chaining manner, almost exactly the same way that they do in simple backward chaining systems.

ADS, on the other hand, is controlled by the explicit specification of steps. Each context has an *entry block* in which the developer specifies a sequence of steps the system must follow when it enters that context. Any of the following can be specified as goals: messages, reports, graphs, parameters, rules, functions, processes, or other contexts. In effect, the developer specifies a procedural sequence for the system to follow. That sequence may call for the system to go to another context. If it does, when the system arrives at the new context, there is a test to determine if the system can enter the context. If the test is passed, the system enters the child context; otherwise, it returns to the parent context.

Whenever ADS reinstantiates a context or moves from a child context to a parent context, it automatically clears working memory of all of the facts that it determined while in that context, unless the developer has specified that certain facts should be saved in working memory after the system exits the context. Subsequent reasoning about any facts derived while the system was in the context will be possible only if the developer has anticipated that such reasoning might be necessary and arranged to save the appropriate facts.

The ADS approach forces the developer to plan out exactly when and how the system will move from one context to another, and when specific facts will be used. On the other hand, it allows the developer to control the execution of an ADS consultation much more efficiently than is possible with ESE. It also means that ADS applications contain fewer rules, since ESE is forced to use rules to control events that are explicitly controlled by steps specified in ADS entry blocks. In addition, by eliminating all unspecified facts whenever the system leaves a context, ADS keeps the size of its working memory to a minimum.

If you are interested in developing a system to handle a vaguely defined structured analysis task, then ESE's approach may be more suitable. You can build your system without defining entry conditions or specifying data to be saved when a context is reinstantiated. Moreover, since ESE keeps all instantiations of a context in memory at the same time, you can write rules that apply across a set of context instantiations.

If, on the other hand, your problem is more procedural and you can define it precisely, or if you want to develop a system that you can embed within a conventional computer application and want very precise control over what happens and when, then the ADS approach has its advantages. Moreover, an application developed in ADS will usually require much less memory and execute faster than an ESE system as a result of the effort the developer must make to define the contexts and the flow of the consultation.

PHASE 2. CREATING AN INITIAL CONTEXT TREE

In essence, a context tree provides a hierarchically arranged overview of a problem-solving strategy. Each context contains rules to deal with one key aspect of the problem. Simply by examining a context tree, you can form an initial impression of how the developer analyzed the problem.

Normally, a developer uses a context-tree approach when she suspects that the resulting system is going to be large and complex. The first step in developing a context tree is to decide how to subdivide the overall problem. The developer represents each subdivision as a box on a context tree. Thus, the initial step in developing a structured rule system is to decide on the major components of the problem and what each context will represent.

Choosing an Overall Approach to Implementing a Context Tree

You can implement a context tree in one of three ways: all at once, one context at a time, or using a mixed strategy. Choosing which approach to take depends on the nature of your project.

Overview approach. The overview approach emphasizes implementing the entire system in a general way, without spending too much time on any part. This results in a comprehensive but shallow model. This approach is best when you need to give management the opportunity to confirm that the system fits the company's overall requirements. Although the demonstration won't show the system providing any meaningful advice, the overall flow and scope of a typical consultation should be clear.

The overview approach is easiest when your problem is procedural in nature. You can use your shallow model to demonstrate the steps the system will go through in coming to a solution, even though none of the steps will be anything significant at this point.

Narrow, detailed approach. In this approach, you concentrate on a single context, implementing it in detail. This gives you one functional piece of the system early on, although it addresses only a small part of the overall problem. This is the best approach to take when it is important to demonstrate the system's ability to reason. It provides a good way to allay the doubts of an expert who is skeptical that his knowledge can really be encoded.

The narrow approach is more typical of systems dealing with structural analysis tasks in which each branch of the context tree is concerned with a more or less independent aspect of the overall diagnosis.

A mixed development strategy. Some developers combine these two approaches. They develop all of the contexts at a superficial level of detail and then put a lot of work into implementing one of them. This results in an early version of the system that addresses the breadth of the problem, with at least one subproblem covered in depth. This approach allows the developer to demonstrate the overall flow of the system and then show how the system would work in considerable detail with one specific portion of the problem.

Sketching Out a Context Tree

No matter which approach you select, the next step is to come up with an initial context tree. You do this by conceptualizing the parts of the problem and examining how they are related. First, you need to identify the main problem addressed by the system, and then divide it into subproblems.

Whatever the nature of your specific problem, you need to ensure that the contexts are about the same size and that they divide the problem in a reasonable way so that further subdivisions are natural and efficient. The developer and the expert usually spend a good bit of time discussing the context until they reach agreement. In this sense, developing a context tree is just a variation of developing a network of objects in an object-oriented system. The developer needs to have a strong overview of the problem before actually beginning to write rules, and the development of a context tree is a good way for the developer and the expert(s) to agree on the nature and scope of knowledge that will be included in the expert system.

A structured analysis task. To develop a context tree, start by thinking about the overall problem you are addressing. Try to conceive of the root context that covers the entire scope of the system. In the automotive diagnostic system, the root context might be CAR-TROUBLE.

Once you've established the root context, the next step is to think of the subproblems. These might be ENGINE-TROUBLE, FUEL-TROUBLE, and ELECTRICAL-TROUBLE. Add these to your context tree as children of root context. If any of these children, in turn, can be broken into subproblems, add them on as children. Continue this process until you reach a level where the contexts represent small enough pieces that breaking them down further would serve no purpose.

A procedural task. If you are treating your contexts as steps in a process, you should make sure that steps on any one level of the hierarchy are more or less independent of each other.

A good example of a procedural context tree is that of Boole & Babbage's DASD Advisor. DASD Advisor is used for fine-tuning DASD units (direct-access storage devices) once they are sold. Before DASD Advisor, Boole & Babbage developed the DASD Monitor, which keeps data on how efficiently the storage devices are directing CPU jobs. If a company is not getting the productivity it needs from its mainframe, it may have to buy more DASD units, which are quite expensive. If the units can be fine-tuned to be more efficient and yield greater CPU production, the company can achieve substantial savings.

Interpretation of the output from the DASD Monitor requires a highly skilled performance analyst. Large companies usually have an in-house analyst available on a daily basis to do this job, while smaller companies often hire an outside consultant who may visit only once a month. Boole & Babbage decided the performance analyst's knowledge could be captured in an expert system and easily marketed to its existing clients as an add-on to the DASD Monitor. The company developed DASD Advisor to interpret the data from the Monitor and recommend how to reorder computer jobs to get the most efficiency from the DASD units. With DASD Advisor, companies get 24-hour access to monitoring of the storage units rather than having to rely on less frequent visits by a human expert.

Figure 10.4 shows the context tree for DASD Advisor. The root context is called BALANCE-MAIN. It represents the overall steps in analyzing an I/O device. BALANCE-MAIN's children represent two subproblems: CHECK-DEV-STATUS, which checks the status of devices, and BALANCE, which analyzes their usage. BALANCE, in turn, breaks down into two subtasks: QUERY-MAIN, and SELECT-LEVEL, in which the user chooses the level at which the system should be analyzed. Each context created in the hierarchy is large enough to be a distinct step, yet small enough to contain a manageable amount of knowledge.

PHASE 3. IMPLEMENTING THE CONTEXT TREE

Texas Instrument's Personal Consultant Plus, IBM's ESE (Version 2), and AION's ADS (Version 4.1) are all good examples of structured rule tools. Throughout our discussion of how you implement a context tree, we use an example from DASD Advisor, developed in ADS (Version 4.1). In ADS, the

196 PROGRAM DEVELOPMENT

Figure 10.4 The context tree for DASD Advisor.

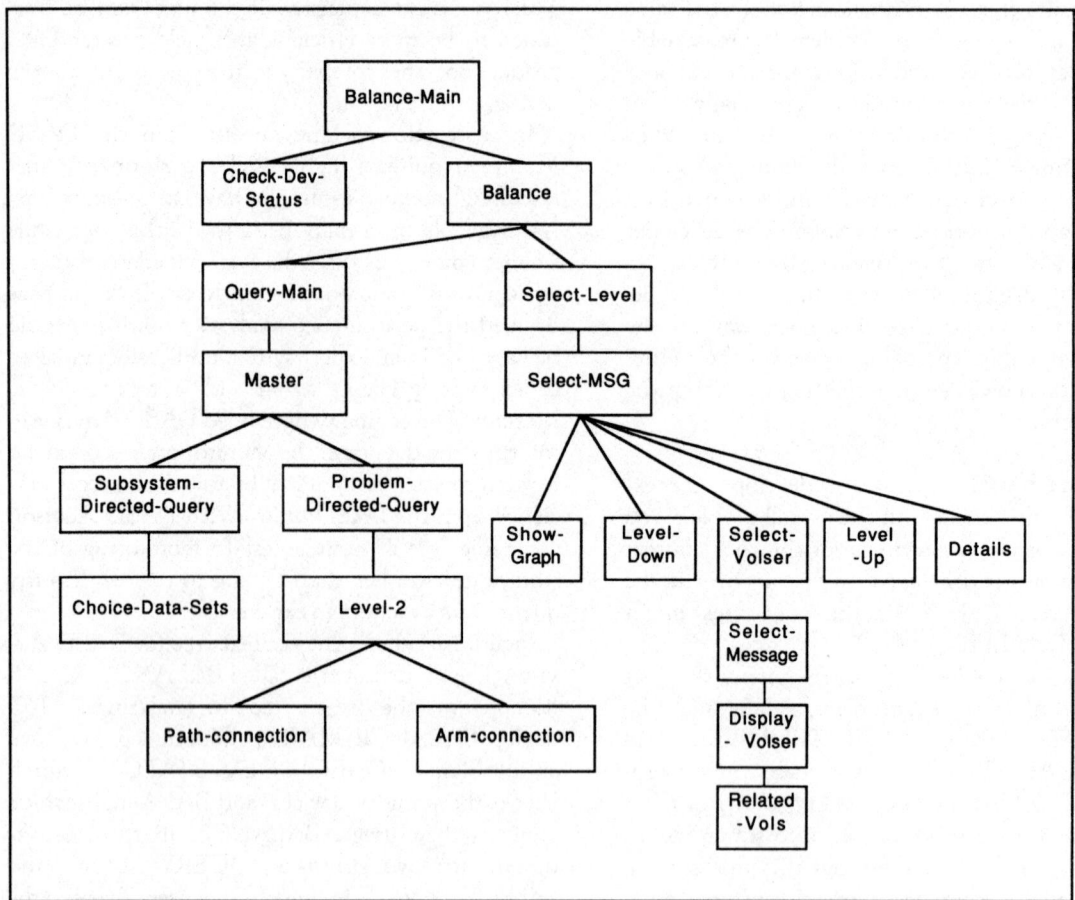

```
                        Balance-Main
                        /          \
              Check-Dev-            Balance
                Status                |
                  |               Select-Level
              Query-Main              |
                  |               Select-MSG
               Master           /  |   |   |   \
              /      \      Show- Level- Select- Level Details
    Subsystem-      Problem- Graph Down  Volser  -Up
    Directed-Query  Directed-Query          |
         |              |               Select-
    Choice-Data-Sets  Level-2           Message
                      /     \              |
              Path-connection            Display
                      Arm-connection     - Volser
                                            |
                                         Related
                                         -Vols
```

context tree is developed using the *state editor*. This is a menu-driven form with areas for filling in information about a context's definition—its entry conditions, goals, and so on. Even though the specifics of implementing a context tree vary from tool to tool, our examples from DASD Advisor illustrate concepts that apply to all structured rule systems.

Planning the Overall Flow from Context to Context

If you are building a nonprocedural system, you do not have to worry about this issue at all. In ADS, you would need to specify that any subcontext can be entered whenever a rule in a parent context needs a value for an attribute that was found in a rule in that subcontext.

If you are building a procedural system, however, you need to consider the conditions under which each context can be entered. A context cannot be entered until its entry conditions are true. Once entered, a context will reiterate only as long as its entry conditions remain true.

Figure 10.5 shows a sample screen from the state editor. The BALANCE context used in DASD Advisor is being edited here. Under the Entry Conditions heading, you can see the three conditions that must be true before the context can be entered:

MSG must be equal to DETAILS, LEVEL must not be equal to DRIVE, and STAY must be TRUE. For the purposes of our discussion, it is not necessary to understand the specific meaning of these terms, but rather the overall function of entry conditions. They have the same syntax as the premise of a rule, and they are evaluated in the same manner.

Now, let's consider how these entry conditions might be used during a consultation. The DASD Advisor begins executing with the BALANCE-MAIN context. When BALANCE-MAIN calls the BALANCE context, the entry conditions of the BALANCE context are evaluated. If they fail, then BALANCE can't be entered, and control returns to the parent context, BALANCE-MAIN. If the entry conditions pass, then control is passed on to the BALANCE context, and it begins to execute.

Iterative Contexts

When a context is defined in the state editor of ADS, you can specify whether or not the context is iterative. Notice the upper right-hand corner of the state editor screen shown in Figure 10.6. By entering TRUE under ITERATE, you've defined the context as iterative.

Once the system enters an iterative context, it is continuously re-executed until its entry conditions become false, after which control returns to its parent. Figure 10.7 shows how this occurs. First, the

Figure 10.5 Adding entry conditions in the state editor.

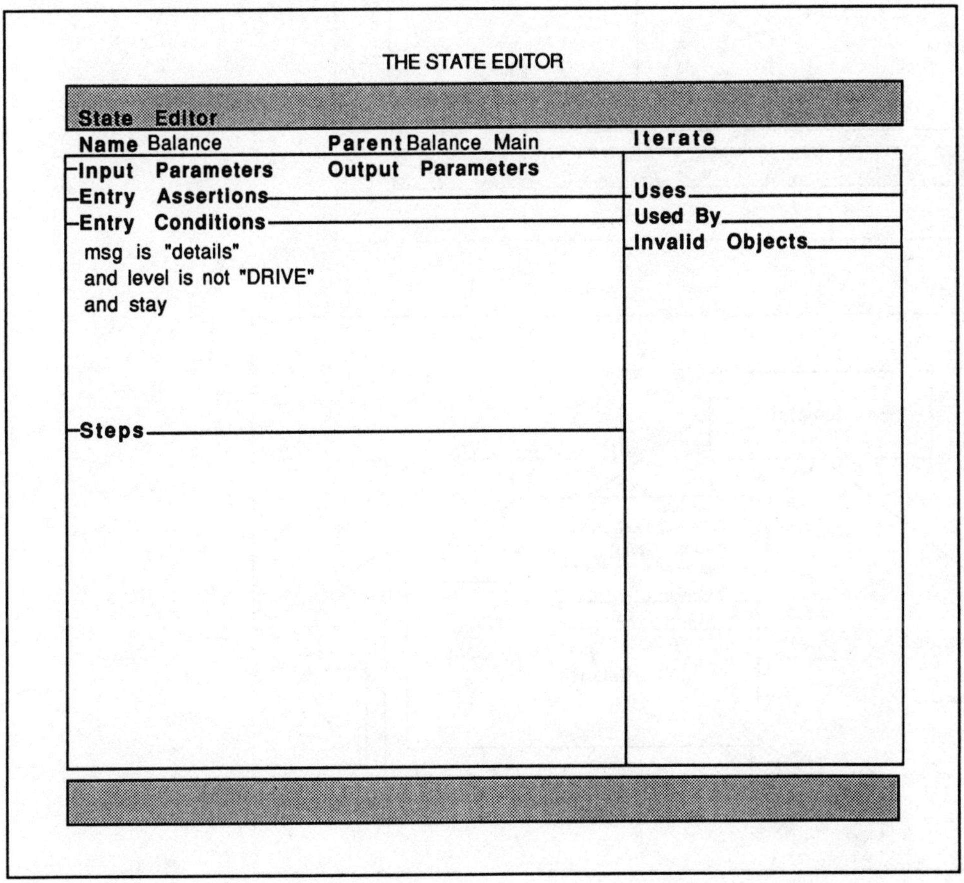

```
                    THE STATE EDITOR
┌──────────────────────────────────────────────────────────────┐
│ State  Editor                                                │
│   Name Balance        Parent Balance Main    Iterate         │
│  ─Input  Parameters    Output  Parameters                    │
│  ─Entry  Assertions──────────────────────── ─Uses─           │
│  ─Entry  Conditions─────────────────────     Used By─        │
│    msg is "details"                         ─Invalid  Objects│
│    and level is not "DRIVE"                                  │
│    and stay                                                  │
│                                                              │
│  ─Steps─                                                     │
│                                                              │
│                                                              │
│                                                              │
│                                                              │
│                                                              │
└──────────────────────────────────────────────────────────────┘
```

198 PROGRAM DEVELOPMENT

THE STATE EDITOR

State Editor
Name Balance **Parent** Balance_Main **Iterate** TRUE
─Input Parameters Output Parameters
─Entry Assertions─────────── ─Uses ────
 Used By ────
 Invalid Objects ────

─Entry Conditions───────
  msg is "details"
  and level is not "DRIVE"
  and stay

─Steps ──────────────

Figure 10.6 Defining an iterative state.

Figure 10.7 State iteration.

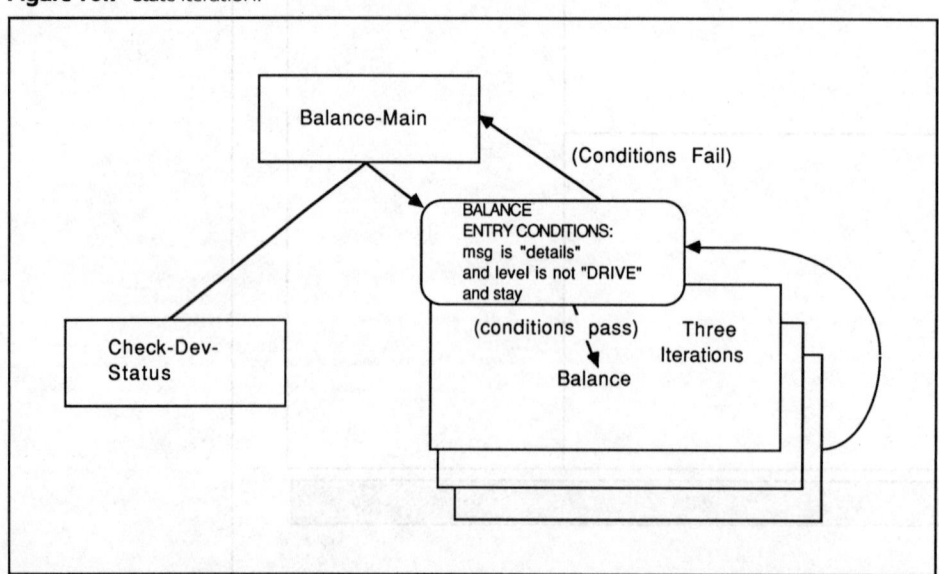

Balance-Main

(Conditions Fail)

BALANCE
ENTRY CONDITIONS:
msg is "details"
and level is not "DRIVE"
and stay

Check-Dev-Status

(conditions pass)   Three Iterations
Balance

system goes from the parent context, BALANCE-MAIN, to the child context BALANCE, initially checking to make sure its entry conditions are true. It then executes BALANCE three times, after which the entry conditions fail, and control is returned to BALANCE-MAIN.

By defining a context tree, specifying entry conditions for each context, and specifying when contexts should iterate, you can go a long way toward structuring the procedural flow of your consultation before you start to write any rules. This ability to sketch in the overall flow of a consultation is the great strength of a context-based approach.

Defining a Context's Attributes

In simple rule systems, attribute-value statements are defined when they are used as If- or Then-clauses of rules. If you create a rule and then want to tailor a question to it, you are forced to add ASK and CHOICES statements to your knowledge base. Likewise, if you want to specify that an attribute can take more than one value, you are forced to add a MULTIVALUED statement to your knowledge base.

Structured rule systems handle these issues in a much more elegant way. Each context has associated with it a set of attributes and a set of rules. If you define a rule without having defined one or more of the attributes that make up the rule, the system will prompt you to define the attribute. When you define the attribute, you not only name the attribute and all of the values it could take, you can also specify how those values are to be obtained (or sourced). If the values are to be obtained from a user, you can include one or more questions in the attribute definition. You can also specify if the attribute is multivalued, and so on. Some developers prefer to write rules and then describe the attributes, but most developers who work with context-based systems get into the habit of first defining the attributes that will go into a context and then writing the rules that will actually use specific attribute-value pairs to make inferences.

Thus, for most developers, the next step is to define the attributes that will be associated with each context. When you begin to consider how to place attributes within one or another context, you should think carefully about placing them so that any facts developed about that attribute in the course of a consultation will be available to the rules in other contexts that may need to know that fact. (Remember that an attribute-value pair is only a statement until it is recorded in working memory.) In order to place attributes and rules within the proper contexts of a context tree, you need to understand how facts are inherited throughout a context tree. In other words, you need to know the origin of the facts that are in working memory when a particular context is being used.

In most structured rule systems, contexts inherit information only from the contexts above them in a line to the root context. In other words, a context will have access only to the information placed in working memory by its parents, or the parents of its parents. For example, in the DASD Advisor context tree, facts in BALANCE are available to all of the contexts that lie below BALANCE in the tree.

Once the contexts in the BALANCE branch have executed, only facts stored in BALANCE-MAIN are saved in working memory. Thus, as the system begins using rules in CHECK-DEV-STATUS, those rules cannot access facts that may have been established when BALANCE rules were used. Figure 10.8 shows how rules residing within the SELECT-VOLSER context can access only facts established by rules in SELECT-MSG, SELECT-LEVEL, BALANCE, and BALANCE-MAIN; they cannot access facts established by rules in the MASTER or CHECK-DEV-STATUS contexts.

This narrow approach to inheritance increases the efficiency of a structured rule system by reducing the number of facts being accumulated in working memory. But it means that you must be sure to place rules and the attributes that comprise them in a context from which they will be available when rules in other contexts need them. Thus, if you had a rule that concluded a value for A, and a second rule that needed the value of A in one of its If-clauses, then you would have to be sure that the first rule was stored higher in the context tree so that A would be

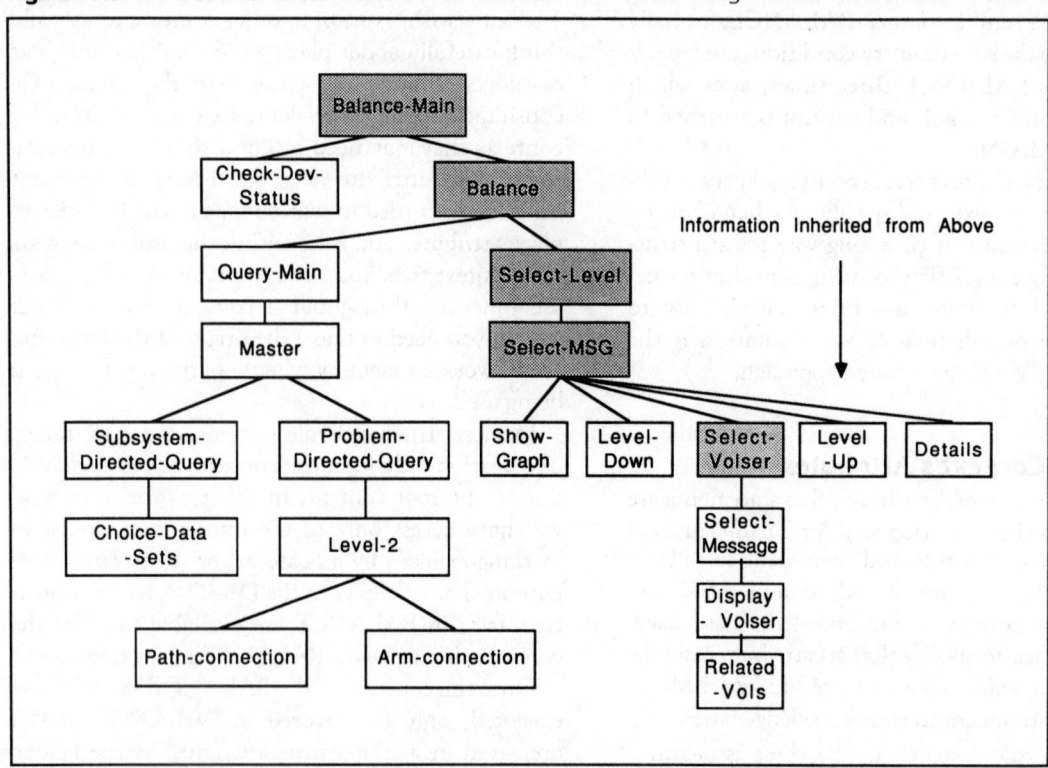

Figure 10.8 Information inherited in SELECT-VOLSER state in Boole & Babbage's DASD Advisor context tree.

inherited by the rule that needed it. If it were elsewhere in the context tree, the rule would not have the information it needed.

As you define the facts in your contexts, try to come up with a set of facts that will be relevant in every context of the problem. Pivotal information (such as the brand of car in a diagnostic system) may be needed everywhere in the system. Facts about the implementation of the system (like screen color) may be used frequently, and also be needed globally. You need to define these sorts of facts so that they are always available, no matter what context the system is currently in. Thus, you must define them in the root context, so that they can be inherited throughout all the contexts of the system.

If you find that you are having difficulty positioning information to be inherited into the proper parts of the context tree, it may be that your context tree has been poorly designed. You should consider revising its structure to make inheritance easier.

Providing Entry Assertions and Goals

In many context-tree systems, a list of goals to pursue follows immediately after the context is executed.

In the ADS state editor, there are two kinds of information about what happens when a context is entered: *entry assertions* and *steps*. Entry assertions establish attributes and initial values in working memory as soon as the context is entered. Steps are the goals for the system to pursue after the entry assertions are implemented. These steps are executed sequentially upon entering a context, providing the entry conditions are true. You can develop a variety of steps. They can cause the system to print a report, to call another context, or to go find the value of an attribute.

Figure 10.9 shows the definition of the BALANCE for the state editor. The Parameter command shown in the figure causes the system to backward chain to find a value for the attribute SIZE_CACHED (ADS calls attributes "parameters"). Next, it pursues the attribute DETAIL_LIST, followed by SELECT_DEVICE.

Adding Rules

One approach to filling in a context is to treat it like a small knowledge base development project, with its own goal, attributes, and rules. You can develop the first set of rules using the same approach we described in Chapter 8 for building a small system. First, decide what new attributes the rules in the context will be using. Some of these attributes may be unique to the context, others may be inherited from parent contexts. Using them, write a first set of "single-depth" rules that address the context's goal. Test and enhance these rules, adding abstraction, certainty factors, general rules, and so on, as you would in a small knowledge base project.

PHASE 4: EXPANDING AND REVISING THE CONTEXT TREE

While the initial context tree is created mainly for conceptual reasons, it will, over the course of development, be modified for programming reasons: to save memory, allow iteration, or ease maintenance.

Figure 10.9 Defining steps and entry assertions.

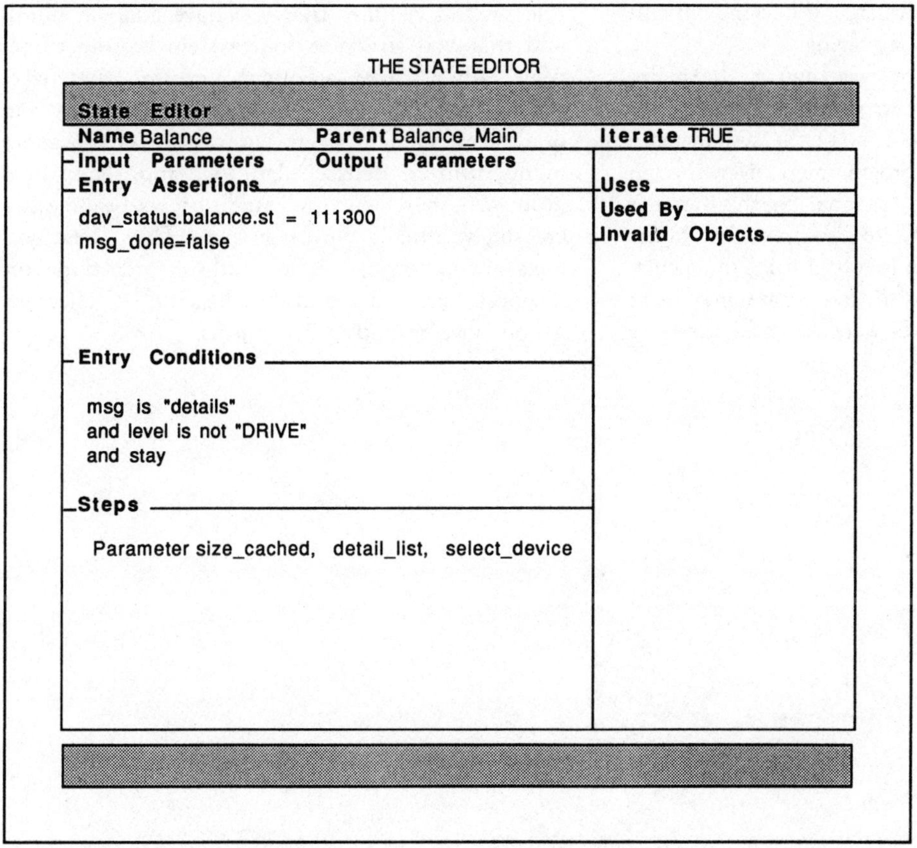

```
                        THE STATE EDITOR
┌─────────────────────────────────────────────────────────────────┐
│ State  Editor                                                   │
│ Name Balance      Parent Balance_Main      Iterate TRUE         │
│ ─Input  Parameters     Output  Parameters                       │
│ ─Entry  Assertions                          Uses                │
│                                             Used By             │
│   dav_status.balance.st = 111300            Invalid Objects     │
│   msg_done=false                                                │
│                                                                 │
│                                                                 │
│ ─Entry  Conditions ─────────────                                │
│                                                                 │
│   msg is "details"                                              │
│   and level is not "DRIVE"                                      │
│   and stay                                                      │
│                                                                 │
│ ─Steps ──────────────                                           │
│   Parameter size_cached,  detail_list,  select_device           │
│                                                                 │
│                                                                 │
│                                                                 │
└─────────────────────────────────────────────────────────────────┘
```

Where you cannot easily separate parts of a problem into discrete conceptual pieces, you can use other criteria to decide how to divide your problem. You should place parts of the problem requiring repeated execution into their own contexts. This allows them to be re-executed easily, without repeating other unnecessary steps.

You may also want to take time-intensive parts of the problem and place them into their own contexts. Later on, you can easily replace these time-consuming contexts with conventional code, while still leaving the rest of the context tree intact.

DASD Advisor is a good example of a system in which the context tree was modified for these reasons. When the contexts began to grow too large during development, they were broken down into smaller contexts. New contexts were also added to keep the tracing facilities comprehensible. When an individual context grew too large, it became difficult to use tracing facilities for debugging.

Because DASD Advisor was built to be maintained by more than one person, some contexts were added purely to make the flow of the system more understandable to other programmers, even though those contexts were not essential to the system's operation. New contexts were also created to house parts of the problem that involved a lot of calculation and hence consumed an inordinate amount of time. Later, these contexts were removed from the system altogether and were replaced by a call to a C program written to perform the calculations much faster than could be done using an inference engine.

SUMMARY

Developing a structured rule-based system is easier than developing a similar system in either OPS5 or in a hybrid system that depends on object-oriented programming. This is because so much is built into the structured rule systems to reduce the developer's task. The backward chaining approach used by most structured rule systems handles control issues that would have to be much more carefully considered if you wanted to develop a similar system in OPS5 or in a hybrid system.

On the other hand, the development of structured rule systems requires that you have goals in mind and that you structure your system around those goals. When you're faced with problems that have vague goals or a set of possible outcomes that you don't even want to try to enumerate—as you commonly find in design, planning, and scheduling problems—then structured rule systems become increasingly difficult to use effectively. Thus, these systems are most effective for mid-size procedural or diagnostic problems, and they become less effective as you move beyond such problems.

11.
Creating Hybrid Systems

INTRODUCTION

In the preceding chapters, we've looked at how to build small and mid-size rule-based systems that use forward chaining, backward chaining, and context trees. Now, we shift our focus to building mid-size to large systems, using high-end, hybrid tools like ART, GoldWorks, KEE, Knowledge Craft, and Nexpert Object. These tools vary, but in general, they combine the rules and contexts offered by smaller tools with the additional capabilities needed to build large systems—most notably, object hierarchies for storing facts and complex, "pattern-matching" rules that do the work of many standard rules. These tools also employ techniques from object-oriented programming, such as demons, message passing, and inheritance. Together, these features allow you to develop applications of greater complexity and flexibility than you can create using rule-based systems.

Object-Oriented Systems

Hybrid systems combine object-oriented techniques with rule-based techniques. You can use object-oriented techniques for knowledge representation or for building a user interface, and most of the hybrid tools use the same techniques for both purposes, resulting in some confusion. Figure 11.1 illustrates the two different purposes for which object-oriented techniques are used. In both cases, the objects in the system inherit their fundamental behavior from a single top-frame or "class of all classes"—the ultimate object that contains the code that defines how all objects should behave.

In this chapter, when we discuss objects used to represent knowledge, we often refer to them as *frames*. A frame is an object that contains knowledge about some subject matter. When we talk about using object-oriented techniques to create windows and other interface features, we simply refer to them as objects.

Modeling Knowledge in Hybrid Systems

In small systems, factual information usually lacks any explicit organization or structure. Instead, facts exist as isolated pieces scattered around the knowledge base. For example, in the VCR Advisor we introduced in Chapter 8, facts like "speed" and "search" were stored as separate, unrelated attributes. Related facts were linked implicitly, through rules. For instance, the following rule was used in the VCR Advisor to link the abstract concept "effects" to the concrete qualities "freeze_frame" and "search":

    IF   freeze_frame = yes AND
           search = yes
    THEN   effects = yes.

This rule could not be considered a heuristic, since it doesn't contain any expert knowledge about how the problem is solved. It contains declarative knowledge; it is used solely to express a relationship between facts.

Most large systems need to deal with an abundance of facts, and this makes it very difficult to store facts as unrelated attributes. To keep these systems manageable, you need a method to group facts together and define the relationships among them.

Figure 11.1 The two uses of objects in hybrid systems.

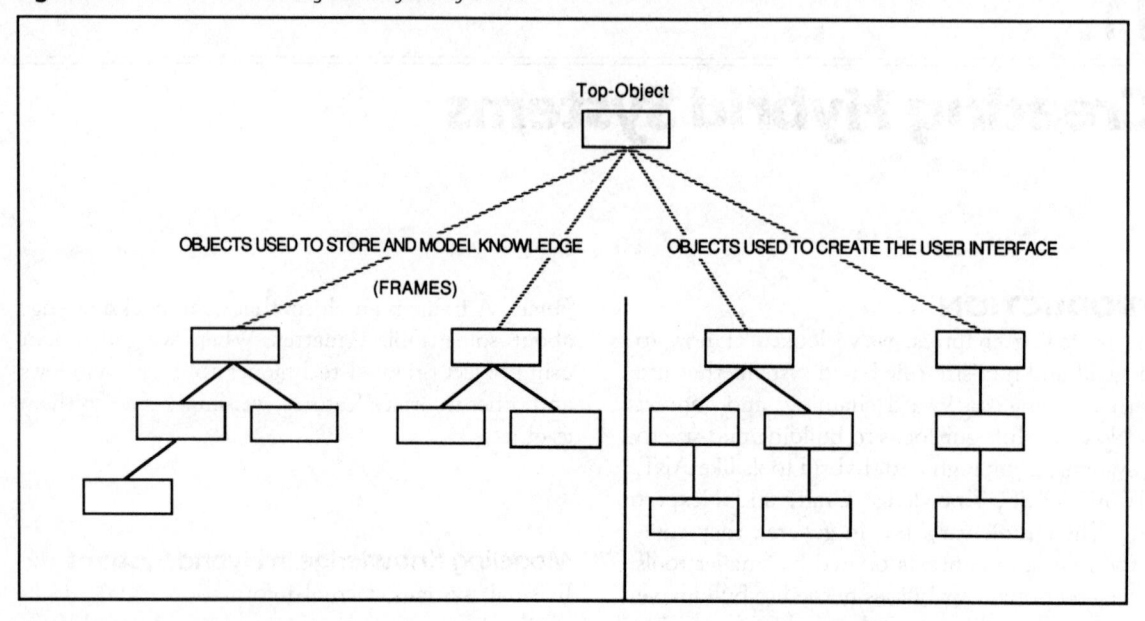

Working with a hybrid tool, you can define these relationships easily, without having to use rules at all. Using objects or frames to represent factual entities, you can build an explicit model of their relationships. This spares you from using rules like the one above to encode declarative information. Instead, you can limit the use of rules to pure heuristics.

Another benefit of object-oriented systems is their ability to keep information about an object's characteristics and behavior within the object, rather than have it scattered throughout the knowledge base. This makes the knowledge base more readable, since specific knowledge about objects doesn't have to be written into rules. Later in the chapter, we look at how this is done using demons and message passing.

Objects or frames are named for things or concepts in the real world. Thus, there is a correspondence between the frames and the concepts or things that the domain expert is concerned with. In addition, you can use the hierarchical nature of object-oriented systems to create object hierarchies or frame trees. Like all object hierarchies, the high-level frames represent very abstract concepts while the lower-level frames represent more specific entities. A frame tree allows you to organize domain knowledge in a hierarchical fashion, and that, in turn, makes it much easier to organize and modify the knowledge base as you acquire new information.

Creating the Initial Knowledge Base

As in the previous three chapters, we begin building a sample system by defining an initial set of facts and an initial set of rules. In later stages, we can give the knowledge base much more functionality as it takes advantage of the capabilities of a hybrid tool, but we will begin rather simply. We consider an example that we can build in Gold Hill Computers' hybrid tool, GoldWorks (Version 1).

Like a composer's decision to start writing a song with music or lyrics, the decision of where to start building a hybrid system can be a matter of personal taste. In some cases, the nature of the problem dictates the best place to start. Some problems are essentially rule-based by nature, and thus rules are the natural place to start. Other systems emphasize data over rules, making it better to begin by creating some frames. To figure out the nature of the problem, and therefore the best place to begin your work, it helps to listen to how the expert talks about solving problems.

If the expert describes the task largely in terms of making judgments, it suggests that rules should come first. This is commonly the case in diagnostic problems, where the expert's primary focus is on applying heuristics to pinpoint a problem. In an employee bonus system, for example, the expert discusses her task of picking bonuses mainly as applying rules of thumb. In early discussions, the expert might suggest "start by looking at the employee's sales figures. If they have improved from last year, that's a good sign." After hearing the expert rattle off a few more heuristics, it becomes clear that rules are the essence of the task.

On the other hand, if the expert's focus is on describing data, this suggests that the frames should be created first. This is commonly the case in planning and scheduling systems. The expert's emphasis in discussing the problem is on its resources and tasks. While rules are also mentioned, they are not the expert's principal concern.

You should also consider the attributes of the project's participants. As we mentioned earlier, experts are sometimes confused or doubtful about the expert system's ability to perform reasoning tasks. They need to be convinced at an early stage in order to be wholehearted contributors to the project. In these cases, it's very important to get the system to a stage where it is giving advice as soon as possible. This allows you to show off the system's reasoning at the outset of the project, which will help allay any lurking doubts your expert may have.

To come up with a working prototype quickly, you should put the emphasis on writing an initial set of working rules, instead of carefully structuring knowledge. These rules will undoubtedly have to be modified or even discarded in later stages as the system is refined. Even so, they will have served an important purpose.

Wherever you start, once you have written some initial rules and frames, you will undoubtedly have to revise them as you refine and expand your system. Since the rules reference the frames, when you change your rules, you have to change the frames to suit them. Likewise, when you change the frames, you have to modify the rules.

Phases in Building a Sample System

For the purposes of this chapter, we assume that you are faced with a complex problem and that you decide to begin by developing frames first. To illustrate how you might approach the development of such a system, we use the object worksheets that we introduced in Chapter 6. We assume that you have done an analysis using these worksheets and are now ready to actually create frames using GoldWorks. Using GoldWorks' menu-driven knowledge editor, we first show how to define frames, slots, and instances. We also create a simple user interface by creating screen objects, which handle the display of system results.

We consider how the initial frame hierarchy behaves during runtime, without any rules in the system. Then we proceed to add rules to the system and make them work in harmony with the frame tree. Finally, we see how techniques like demons and message passing can be used to enhance our frame-based system. If you begin by developing frames, you will progress through seven phases:

1. Define the problem
2. Define frames and slots
3. Define instances
4. Define screen objects (create an interface)
5. Add rules
6. Add demons
7. Add message passing

PHASE 1. DEFINING THE PROBLEM

In this example, you'll begin by creating a system to select prices for items sold by a supermarket distributor. You'll use frames to store information about each specific type of food the distributor sells, and then write rules to decide how much to discount orders made by special customers.

This simple example will demonstrate one of the strengths of hybrid systems—their ability to use frames for multiple purposes. You'll start by using a simple set of frames, or a frame tree, and some rules to help set discounts for orders. Later, you will use the same frame tree for an entirely different purpose: to calculate the expiration dates of various foods.

Currently, each item the distributor stocks has a price that has already been set. However, when large orders are negotiated, the stated prices are often discounted so as to give incentives to good customers, support old customers, or for other reasons. As the business grows, and more and more orders come in, an expert system is installed to help pick discounts automatically, ensuring that orders will be discounted consistently and correctly. See Figure 11.2 for a summary of this task analysis.

In your discussion with the expert, begin by focusing on the kinds of discounts given to faithful customers. The distributor has a group of customers with whom it has done business since the old days, when it was a small meat distributor. These customers are always given a 10 percent discount on meat items and milk, but pay the usual price for all other dairy products. Another group of preferred customers are more recent, but have distinguished themselves over the past year by large orders and prompt payment. These customers are given a 4 percent discount on orders of any products except fish, for which they get a 3 percent discount.

Another factor in calculating the discount has to do with how quickly the buyer needs delivery. Preferred buyers who place their orders for meat products 10 days in advance are given a 6 percent discount, while their early orders for dairy products receive a 7 percent discount.

PHASE 2. DEFINING FRAMES

From your initial discussions with the expert, it is clear that there are two different areas that your frame tree will have to address. It will have to (1) represent information about the kinds of foods that the distributor stocks, and (2) store information about the order at hand.

Assume you've already completed the object worksheets described in Chapter 6 for this problem. You can now start implementing these object worksheets as frames in GoldWorks. Begin with the most general frame on the worksheets, FOOD_ITEM. To create its definition, select FRAME from the DEFINE menu. This causes the system to open fields on the screen for information about the frame, such as its name and the name of its parent. (See Figure 11.3.) Since FOOD_ITEM is the most general category of food, it has no parent, so you do not have to fill in the Parent Frame field. If you simply leave the field empty, GoldWorks will assume that FOOD_ITEM is at the top of the frame tree and will automatically fill in the

Figure 11.2 The overall analysis of the discounting task.

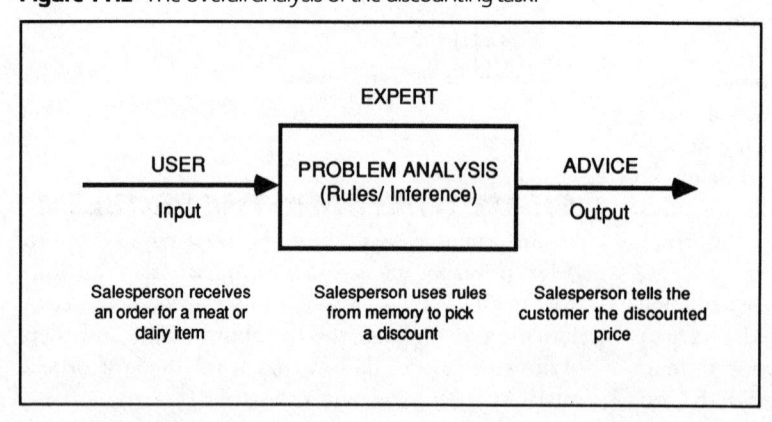

Figure 11.3 Defining the FOOD_ITEM frame using a GoldWorks menu screen.

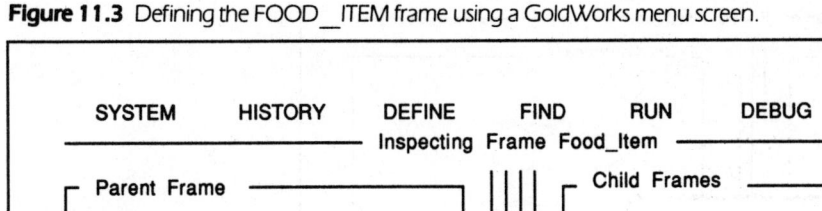

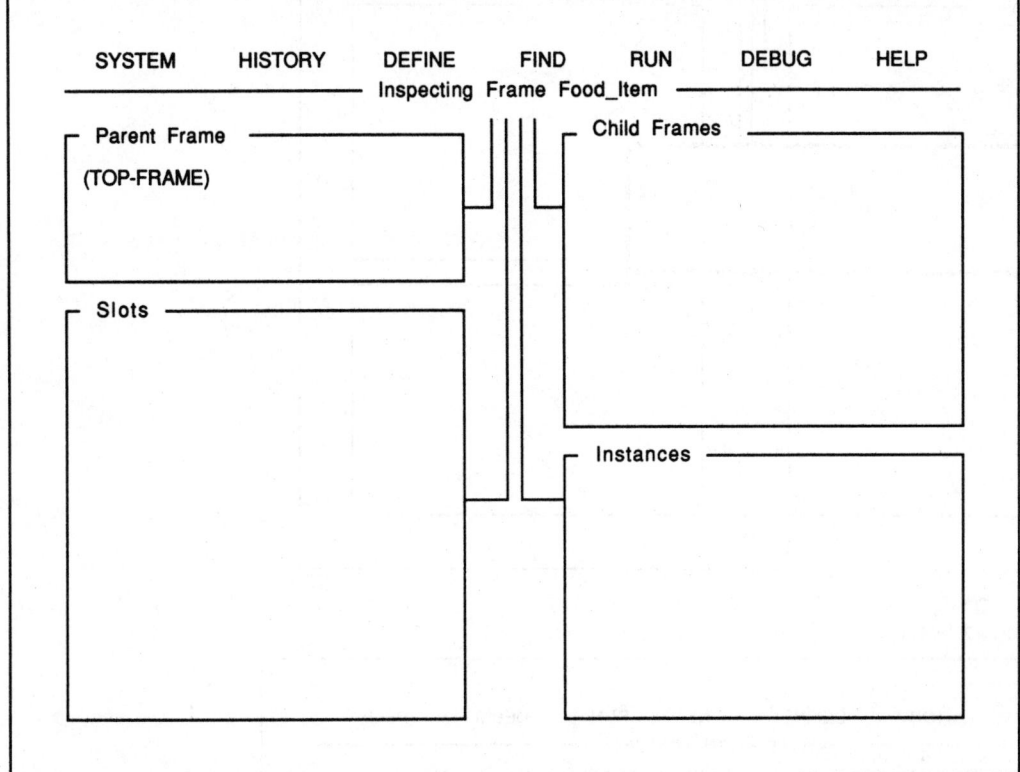

```
  SYSTEM     HISTORY     DEFINE     FIND     RUN     DEBUG     HELP
                         Inspecting Frame Food_Item
  ┌─ Parent Frame ─────────────────┐  ┌─ Child Frames ──────────────┐
  │  (TOP-FRAME)                   │  │                             │
  │                                │  │                             │
  │                                │  │                             │
  └────────────────────────────────┘  │                             │
  ┌─ Slots ────────────────────────┐  │                             │
  │                                │  └─────────────────────────────┘
  │                                │  ┌─ Instances ─────────────────┐
  │                                │  │                             │
  │                                │  │                             │
  │                                │  │                             │
  │                                │  │                             │
  │                                │  │                             │
  │                                │  │                             │
  └────────────────────────────────┘  └─────────────────────────────┘
```

field with the reserved word TOP_FRAME, signifying that FOOD_ITEM is at the top of the frame tree.

Next, you need to define some of the slots that make up FOOD_ITEM: the food's name, its price, and whether it has expired or not. When you select the slots option, the system asks for the name of the new slot. (See Figure 11.4.)

As you add each new slot to the frame, you must consult the object worksheet for its special characteristics. The PRICE slot, for example, can contain numbers only from 0 to 40. In order to include this information in the slot's definition, select the EDIT SLOT option. This brings up a screen containing all of the possible facets of the slot, such as constraints, multivalued definitions, and so on. (See Figure 11.5.) To restrict the value of the PRICE slot to the proper range, fill in the CONSTRAINT facet. You can constrain a slot in a number of ways: to a given set of legal values, to a certain type of data, or to a numerical range. In the case of PRICE, you should fill in the CONSTRAINT facet with the numerical range from 0 to 40. At later stages in development, you can fill in the slot facets in more detail to further define the slot.

You proceed next to the worksheet for MEAT_ITEM. Repeat the same steps you used for creating the definition for FOOD_ITEM, defining the frame's name and its parent frames. Since MEAT_ITEM is a special kind of FOOD_ITEM, you should fill in FOOD_ITEM as its parent. By doing so, you guarantee that each of the slots defined in FOOD_ITEM will be inherited by MEAT_ITEM. Indeed, in the frame definition shown in Figure 11.6, MEAT_ITEM already contains three slots automatically inherited

Figure 11.4 Adding a slot.

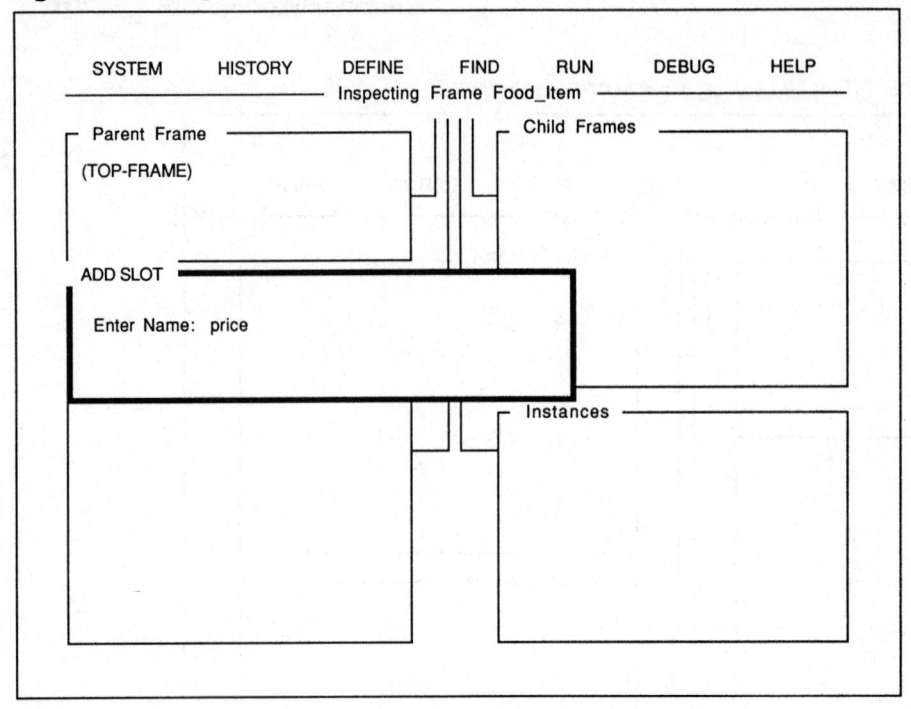

```
  SYSTEM     HISTORY     DEFINE     FIND     RUN     DEBUG     HELP
  ─────────────────────── Inspecting Frame Food_Item ───────────────────────

  ┌─ Parent Frame ──────────┐    ┌─ Child Frames ─────────────┐
  │  (TOP-FRAME)            │    │                            │
  │                         │    │                            │
  │                         │    │                            │
  │                         │    │                            │
  └─────────────────────────┘    │                            │
  ┌─ ADD SLOT ──────────────────────────────────┐             │
  │                                             │             │
  │   Enter Name:  price                        │             │
  │                                             │             │
  │                                             │             │
  └─────────────────────────────────────────────┘             │
                                 ┌─ Instances ────────────────┐
                                 │                            │
                                 │                            │
                                 │                            │
                                 │                            │
                                 │                            │
                                 └────────────────────────────┘
```

Figure 11.5 Editing slot facets.

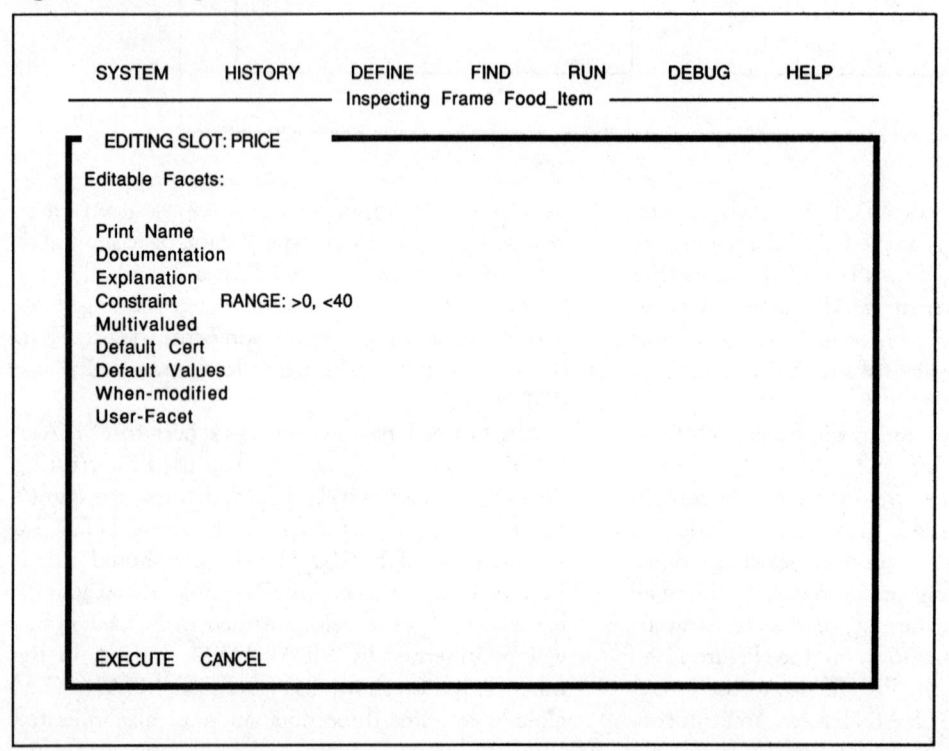

```
  SYSTEM     HISTORY     DEFINE     FIND     RUN     DEBUG     HELP
  ─────────────────────── Inspecting Frame Food_Item ───────────────────────

  ┌─ EDITING SLOT: PRICE ─────────────────────────────────────────────┐
  │                                                                   │
  │  Editable Facets:                                                 │
  │                                                                   │
  │    Print Name                                                     │
  │    Documentation                                                  │
  │    Explanation                                                    │
  │    Constraint      RANGE: >0, <40                                 │
  │    Multivalued                                                    │
  │    Default Cert                                                   │
  │    Default Values                                                 │
  │    When-modified                                                  │
  │    User-Facet                                                     │
  │                                                                   │
  │                                                                   │
  │                                                                   │
  │    EXECUTE    CANCEL                                              │
  └───────────────────────────────────────────────────────────────────┘
```

Figure 11.6 Inherited slots.

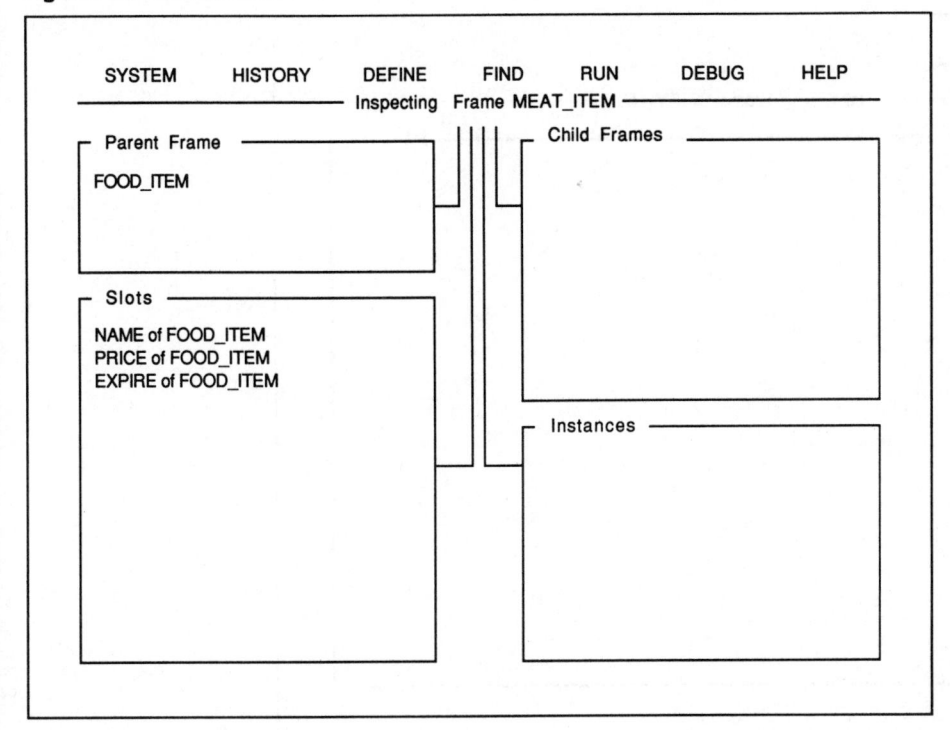

```
┌─────────────────────────────────────────────────────────────────────┐
│   SYSTEM    HISTORY    DEFINE    FIND    RUN    DEBUG    HELP       │
│   ─────────────────── Inspecting Frame MEAT_ITEM ───────────────    │
│   ┌─ Parent Frame ──────────────┐  ┌─ Child Frames ─────────────┐   │
│   │                             │  │                            │   │
│   │  FOOD_ITEM                  │  │                            │   │
│   │                             │  │                            │   │
│   │                             │  │                            │   │
│   └─────────────────────────────┘  │                            │   │
│   ┌─ Slots ─────────────────────┐  │                            │   │
│   │  NAME of FOOD_ITEM          │  │                            │   │
│   │  PRICE of FOOD_ITEM         │  └────────────────────────────┘   │
│   │  EXPIRE of FOOD_ITEM        │  ┌─ Instances ────────────────┐   │
│   │                             │  │                            │   │
│   │                             │  │                            │   │
│   │                             │  │                            │   │
│   │                             │  │                            │   │
│   │                             │  │                            │   │
│   │                             │  │                            │   │
│   │                             │  │                            │   │
│   └─────────────────────────────┘  └────────────────────────────┘   │
└─────────────────────────────────────────────────────────────────────┘
```

from FOOD_ITEM: NAME, PRICE, and EXPIRED.

If you examine the worksheets, you'll notice that FOOD_ITEMs and MEAT_ITEMs have different constraints on their prices. While the price of general FOOD_ITEMs ranges from 0 to 40, the price of MEAT_ITEMs ranges from 0 to 20. This means you have to override the inherited definition of PRICE so that it is constrained to the proper range for MEAT_ITEMS. You can do this simply by editing the constraints on the PRICE slot of the MEAT_ITEM frame and changing the range to 0 to 20.

In addition, the MEAT_ITEM worksheet contains some definitional information specific to meat, which is not present in FOOD_ITEM. An additional slot, QUALITY, defines the grade of a meat item. Meat qualities can be restricted to only three values: Prime, Choice, and Utility. You can restrict the QUALITY slot to these values using the CONSTRAINT facet. However, instead of constraining its value to a range, as you did for PRICE, you should constrain it to a set of legal values. You can do this by defining a ONE-OF constraint to a list of the three possible meat qualities.

Using the same approach you used to create the MEAT_ITEM frame and link it to its parent, you can create definitions for the frames described in the remaining worksheets. You can add a DAIRY_ITEM frame as a second child of the parent frame FOOD_ITEM, so that it inherits its slots, and you can add its own special slot called HAS_MILK.

When you create the definition for the HAS_MILK slot in the DAIRY_ITEM frame, you can also create a default value for it to assume in the absence of any direct assignment. Since it would be reasonable to assume that most of the dairy items contain milk, you should set the default value to YES. Later, as you create instances of DAIRY_ITEM for specific dairy items, the HAS_MILK slot will automatically be set to YES and will not have to be filled in

Figure 11.7 Setting default values.

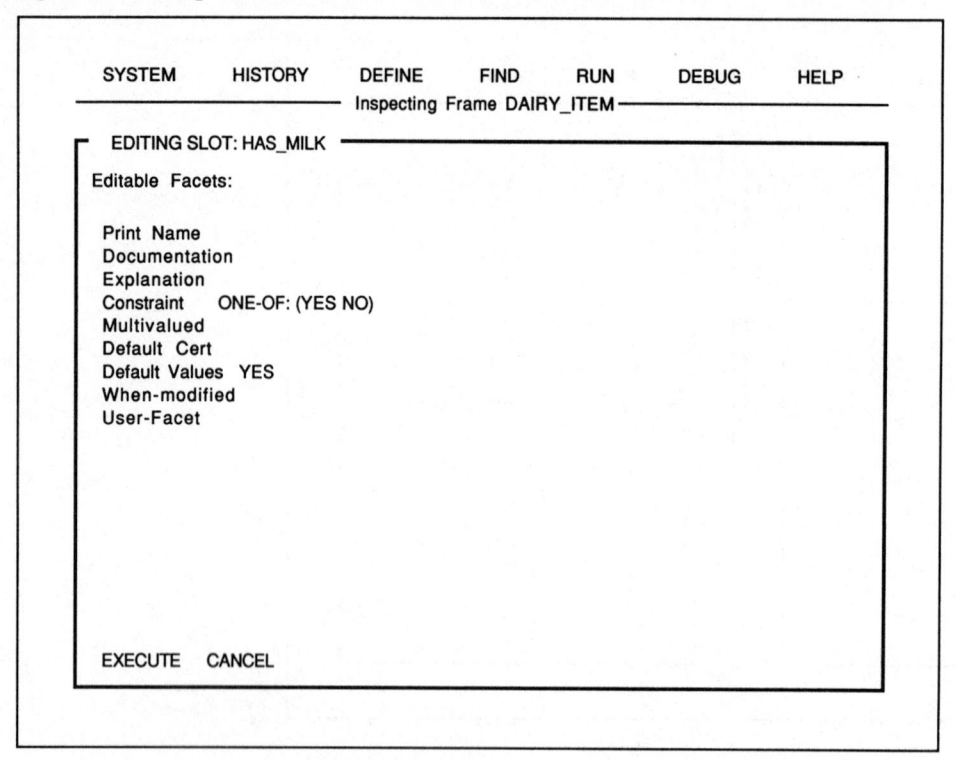

```
 SYSTEM     HISTORY    DEFINE    FIND    RUN    DEBUG    HELP
                     Inspecting Frame DAIRY_ITEM
   EDITING SLOT: HAS_MILK
  Editable Facets:

  Print Name
  Documentation
  Explanation
  Constraint    ONE-OF: (YES NO)
  Multivalued
  Default Cert
  Default Values   YES
  When-modified
  User-Facet




  EXECUTE   CANCEL
```

manually. You can define the default value by editing the DEFAULT VALUES facet for the HAS_MILK slot, as shown in Figure 11.7.

Next, you should define the ORDER frame, creating slots to represent the customer status (ORIGINAL_CUSTOMER, PREFERRED_CUSTOMER, or OTHER), how many days notice has been given for the order, and the name of the product that has been ordered. (See Figure 11.8.)

At this point, you have implemented all of the objects from the initial worksheets. Now you can put them aside and concentrate on the frame hierarchy that has been implemented in GoldWorks.

PHASE 3. DEFINING INSTANCES

The next step is to add instances of actual foods to the system. You can start by defining an instance of the DAIRY_ITEM frame to represent Swiss cheese. The Swiss cheese definition requires a name and a set of slot values. Figure 11.9 shows how these values are filled into the slots to make a Swiss cheese instance.

In a similar manner, you can define new instances for each specific food offered by the distributor. As you add instances, you will probably encounter various clues that the frame hierarchy may need some modification. For example, in adding instances of DAIRY_ITEM, you'll see that many instances of "dairy items" are not milk products at all—tofu, lard, pasta, and yeast. As you add these foods as instances, you'll keep having to override the default value of the HAS_MILK slot by setting it to NO.

It would be more efficient to modify the frame tree, creating a new child frame to DAIRY_ITEM called NON_MILK_DAIRY_ITEM. It would be exactly like DAIRY_ITEM, except that the default of the HAS_

Figure 11.8 Defining the ORDER frame.

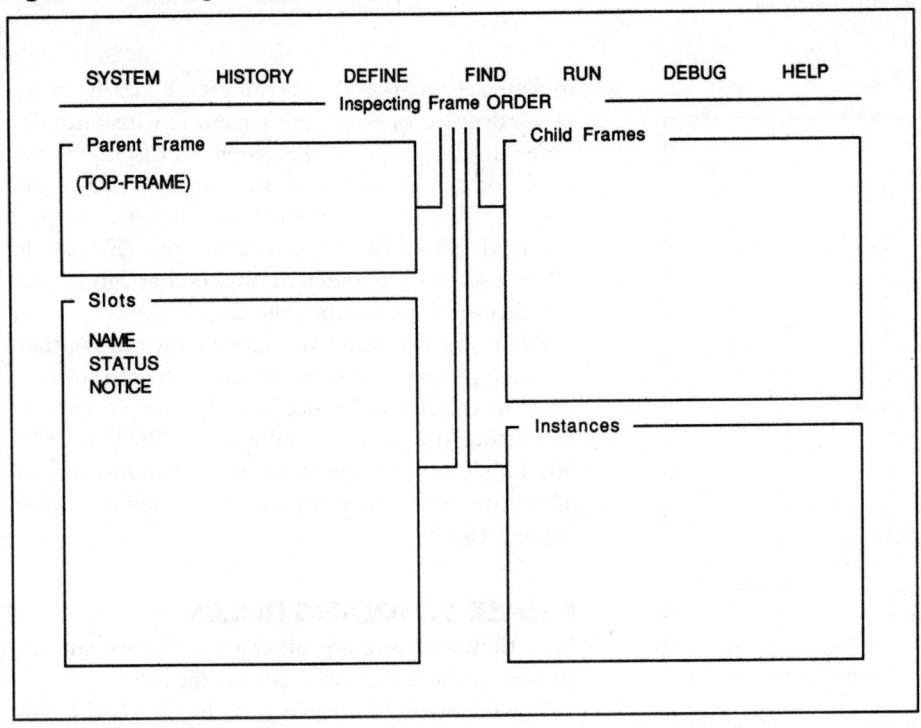

```
SYSTEM    HISTORY    DEFINE    FIND    RUN    DEBUG    HELP
                    Inspecting Frame ORDER
┌─ Parent Frame ─────────────┐   ┌─ Child Frames ──────────────────┐
│ (TOP-FRAME)                │   │                                 │
│                            │   │                                 │
└────────────────────────────┘   │                                 │
┌─ Slots ────────────────────┐   └─────────────────────────────────┘
│ NAME                       │   ┌─ Instances ─────────────────────┐
│ STATUS                     │   │                                 │
│ NOTICE                     │   │                                 │
│                            │   │                                 │
│                            │   │                                 │
└────────────────────────────┘   └─────────────────────────────────┘
```

Figure 11.9 Adding an instance of Swiss cheese.

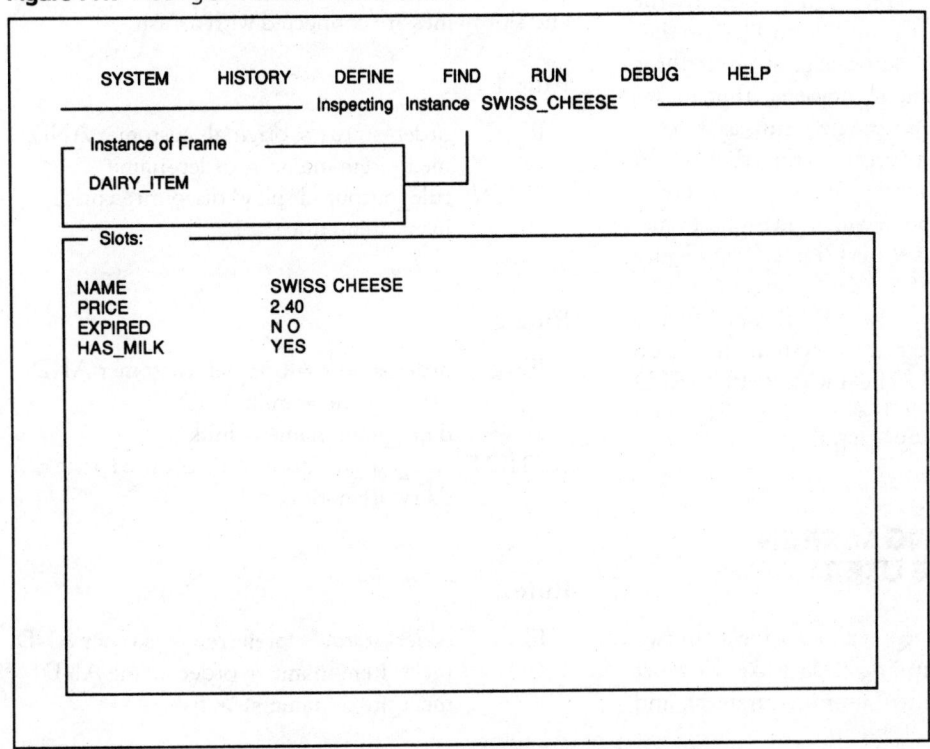

```
SYSTEM    HISTORY    DEFINE    FIND    RUN    DEBUG    HELP
                    Inspecting Instance SWISS_CHEESE
┌─ Instance of Frame ────────┐
│ DAIRY_ITEM                 │
└────────────────────────────┘
┌─ Slots: ───────────────────────────────────────────────────────┐
│ NAME          SWISS CHEESE                                     │
│ PRICE         2.40                                             │
│ EXPIRED       NO                                               │
│ HAS_MILK      YES                                              │
│                                                                │
└────────────────────────────────────────────────────────────────┘
```

Figure 11.10 Creating a new frame.

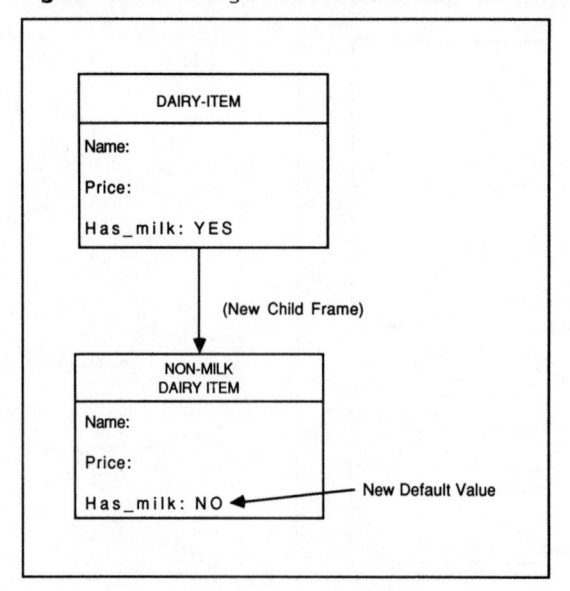

```
        DAIRY-ITEM
   Name:
   Price:
   Has_milk: YES
           │
           ▼  (New Child Frame)
       NON-MILK
       DAIRY ITEM
   Name:
   Price:
   Has_milk: NO ◄──── New Default Value
```

MILK slot would be set to NO. (See Figure 11.10.) This spares you from having to repeatedly override the default value of the HAS_MILK slot. In the context of the example, this may seem like a rather trivial improvement to the knowledge structure. It is this kind of small refinement, however, that makes development much easier in the long run, as it keeps your knowledge structure precise and efficient. In general, when you find that you are repeatedly creating similar overrides to the default values of a frame, you should probably add a new frame. (See Figure 11.11.)

Lastly, you can create a sample instance of the ORDER frame in order to test the system out. To do this, you fill in the STATUS field with PREFERRED_CUSTOMER, the NOTICE slot with EARLY, and the NAME slot with SWISS_CHEESE.

PHASE 4. DEFINING SCREEN OBJECTS (OR THE USER INTERFACE)

As we mentioned earlier, you can use objects in two ways: to represent domain knowledge, like the types of foods stocked by the distributor (i.e., frames), and to define elements of the user interface, like the types of windows to open on the screen. For instance, in order to allow this sample system to display its results, you need to define an instance of a *rule output window*. This is a predefined user interface object provided in GoldWorks' screen toolkit. The toolkit offers a selection of different objects that can be put together to create interface displays.

After you define an instance of the rule output window, you can change its default settings to customize it to the particular needs of the sample system. By setting the values of HEIGHT, WIDTH, TOP, and LEFT, you can specify where the window should appear on the screen and what its size should be. (See Figure 11.12.)

PHASE 5. ADDING RULES

Now that you have an initial set of frames and instances in place, you can begin writing rules.

The following rules are not in the standard GoldWorks' syntax. We have rewritten them in the syntax we used in previous chapters, in which frame names and slot names are connected with a dash.

Rule 1

IF   order-status = original_customer AND
         meat_item-name = order-name
THEN rule_output-display "discounted price = "
         meat_item-price * .1.

Rule 2

IF   order-status = original_customer AND
         order-name = milk AND
         dairy_item-name = milk
THEN rule_output-display "discounted price = "
         dairy_item-price * .1.

Rule 3

IF   order-status = preferred_customer AND
         meat_item-name = order-name AND
         meat_item-name < > fish

Creating Hybrid Systems 213

THEN rule_output-display "discounted price = "
meat_item–price * .4.

THEN rule_output-display "discounted price = "
meat_item–price * .6.

Rule 4
IF   order-status = preferred_customer AND
meat_item–name = order–name AND
meat_item–name = fish
THEN rule_output–display "discounted price = "
meat_item–price * .3.

Rule 6
IF   order-status = preferred_customer AND
order–notice = early AND
dairy_item–name = order–name
THEN rule_output–display "discounted price = "
dairy_item–price * .7.

Rule 5
IF   order-status = preferred_customer AND
order-notice = early AND
meat_item–name = order–name

Rule 7
IF   order-status = normal_customer
THEN rule_output–display "discounted price = "
meat_item–price.

Figure 11.11 Creating a new frame after frequent overrides.

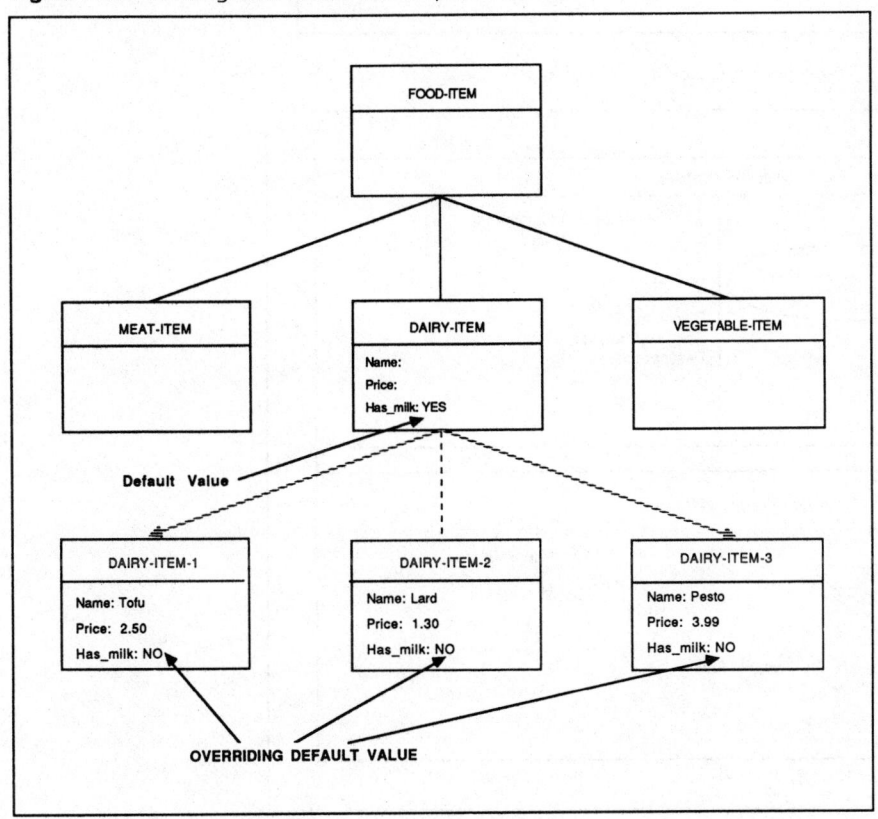

Figure 11.12 Customizing the rule output object.

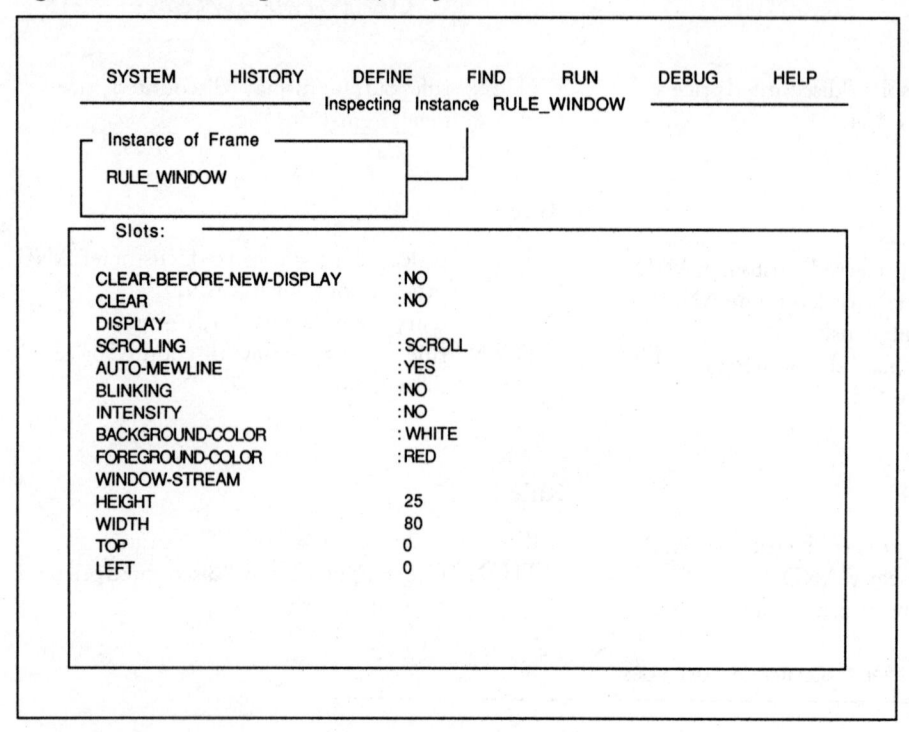

```
         SYSTEM     HISTORY     DEFINE      FIND      RUN      DEBUG      HELP
                             ──── Inspecting Instance RULE_WINDOW ────
   ┌─ Instance of Frame ──────────────────┐
   │  RULE_WINDOW                         │
   └──────────────────────────────────────┘

   ┌─ Slots: ──────────────────────────────────────────────────────────────┐
   │                                                                       │
   │   CLEAR-BEFORE-NEW-DISPLAY           : NO                             │
   │   CLEAR                              : NO                             │
   │   DISPLAY                                                             │
   │   SCROLLING                          : SCROLL                         │
   │   AUTO-MEWLINE                       : YES                            │
   │   BLINKING                           : NO                             │
   │   INTENSITY                          : NO                             │
   │   BACKGROUND-COLOR                   : WHITE                          │
   │   FOREGROUND-COLOR                   : RED                            │
   │   WINDOW-STREAM                                                       │
   │   HEIGHT                             25                               │
   │   WIDTH                              80                               │
   │   TOP                                0                                │
   │   LEFT                               0                                │
   │                                                                       │
   └───────────────────────────────────────────────────────────────────────┘
```

Figure 11.13 Demons monitoring user inputs in ATP.

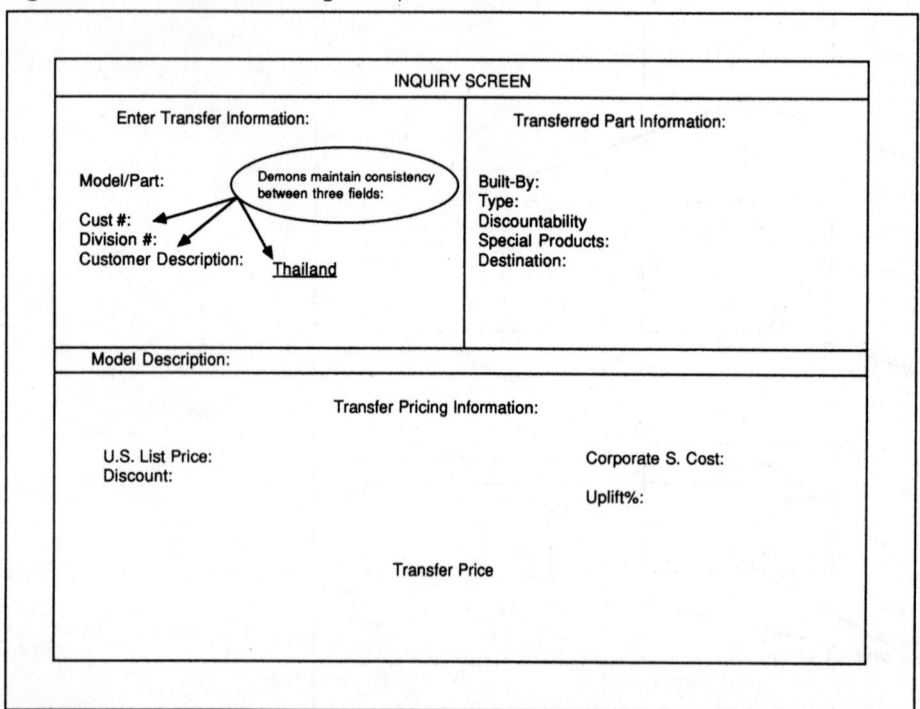

```
┌─────────────────────────────────────────────────────────────────┐
│                        INQUIRY SCREEN                           │
│  ┌───────────────────────────────┬───────────────────────────┐  │
│  │  Enter Transfer Information:  │ Transferred Part Information:│
│  │                               │                           │  │
│  │  Model/Part:    ╭─────────────╮ Built-By:                 │  │
│  │            ←── │Demons maintain│ Type:                    │  │
│  │  Cust #:   ←── │ consistency   │ Discountability          │  │
│  │  Division #: ← │between three  │ Special Products:        │  │
│  │  Customer Desc:│   fields:     │ Destination:             │  │
│  │                ╰─────────────╯                            │  │
│  │                     Thailand                              │  │
│  └───────────────────────────────┴───────────────────────────┘  │
│  ┌─────────────────────────────────────────────────────────┐    │
│  │  Model Description:                                      │   │
│  │                                                          │   │
│  │              Transfer Pricing Information:               │   │
│  │                                                          │   │
│  │   U.S. List Price:              Corporate S. Cost:       │   │
│  │   Discount:                                              │   │
│  │                                 Uplift%:                 │   │
│  │                                                          │   │
│  │                    Transfer Price                        │   │
│  │                                                          │   │
│  └──────────────────────────────────────────────────────────┘   │
└─────────────────────────────────────────────────────────────────┘
```

To start the system, you select RUN from the GoldWorks menu. The sample instance of the ORDER frame is then processed, causing Rule 6 to be fired and to succeed. The rule sets the value of the DISPLAY slot of the RULE_OUTPUT window, which causes a message to be printed in the output window indicating that the price of SWISS_CHEESE should be discounted 30 percent.

Obviously, you'll have to do much more work to make the interface truly useful. For example, by incorporating other user interface objects, you could enhance the system so that the user could fill in the order information in a screen input form and have the system's recommendation displayed in a second output window.

PHASE 6. ADDING DEMONS

Demons allow you to attach functions directly to a slot in a frame or screen object. Whenever the slot's value changes, the demon is invoked.

Demons are usually faster and more dependable than rules. They create an immediate cause-and-effect relationship between a value's change and a reaction by the system. Rules are less direct. Before a rule can fire, something needs to invoke it—another rule, a goal, or a fact entered into working memory. Demons are autonomous, always ready to spring into action no matter what else is going on.

Demons also have their disadvantages. Often, they are less readable than rules. While rules can be written in an English-like form, demons are usually encoded as functions in some computer language. In the case of GoldWorks, demons are written as LISP functions.

Another disadvantage of demons is their singular purpose. The knowledge contained in rules floats freely in the knowledge base, unattached to anything. Rules can be picked up at any time by the inference engine and pieced together to solve a problem. Demons, on the other hand, are anchored on specific slots. They can be used by that slot, but not by the rest of the knowledge base. This limits their applicability to a single function.

Another way to contrast rules and demons is to think of them in terms of early and late binding, a topic introduced in Chapter 2. Demons are a form of early binding—they made a commitment between two pieces of knowledge during compilation. Rules, on the other hand, are a form of late binding, since they are linked together dynamically, during runtime.

You could think of early binding as a kind of arranged marriage between two pieces of knowledge. Though it doesn't allow much flexibility, it avoids the time and expense of searching for the right relationship. Late binding, on the other hand, is a more adventurous approach. At best, late binding can link rules together during runtime to produce flexible, creative solutions. However, you also risk the poignant situation where rules aren't linked together in the best manner, and thus two otherwise compatible pieces of knowledge remain unbound forever.

Using Demons in ATP

In Data General's ATP, demons are used to monitor the information that users type onto the screen. When users want advice about a part shipment from ATP, they start by filling in input fields with information about the part to be shipped and the destination to ship it to. The user can provide the destination in any one of three ways: by typing its name (e.g., "Thailand"), by typing its customer number, or by typing its division number. The destination is displayed in each of these three conventions on the input screen. When the user gives the destination in one manner, a demon is triggered to automatically fill in the other two. So, for example, if the user changes the customer name from "Nippon Data General" to "Data General," the customer and division numbers are automatically updated on the screen to remain consistent with the new location.

Figure 11.13 shows how the demons are linked to the fields in the input screen. When the user clicks the mouse on a field in the entry screen and types in a value, a demon is triggered, which in turn triggers a LISP function to check its consistency with the other fields.

PHASE 7. ADDING MESSAGE PASSING

Message passing lets you hide procedures about an object's unique behavior within the object, rather than writing it elsewhere in the knowledge base. By sending a "message" to the object, you can trigger a procedure. For example, you might send a "check completeness" message to an Overseas-Order object. When the message arrived, the object would check certain slots to see if the order was complete, and return its findings to the message sender. In a sense, sending a message is like making a subroutine call in a conventional language, except the code is stored inside the object.

In GoldWorks, the procedures stored in objects are called *handlers*. To define a handler, you specify its name, the frame it links to, and the argument or arguments it will receive. By giving the command "send-msg" from any point in the knowledge base, you can trigger the handler. Along with the send-msg call, you also provide the object's name and the name of the handler to invoke.

Message passing is best used when your objects have diverse ways of accomplishing the same tasks. For instance, in the frame hierarchy of grocery items, each item might have its own way of calculating its expiration date. A beef product might expire six days after being put on display, while smoked fish might last a week. More elaborate calculations might need to be made to determine the expiration date of other items. The shelf life of milk, for instance, might vary according to the temperature of the grocer's refrigerator.

Suppose you had to check foods periodically to see if they should be discarded. Certainly, you could do this using rules. For example, the three following rules could be used to apply the appropriate formulas to compute the freshness of a type of food.

Rule 1

IF   fish_item–delivery_date + 3 > curr_date
THEN   expired = yes.

Rule 2

IF   meat_item–delivery_date + 3 > curr_date
THEN   expired = yes.

Rule 3

IF   milk_item–name = milk AND milk_item–delivery_date + ((temp-32)*.71) > curr_date
THEN   expired = yes.

Unfortunately, these rules would clutter the knowledge base. If there were 200 types of food, you might need hundreds of corresponding rules to check expirations. It would be better to store each formula within the object to which it applies. You could then

Figure 11.14 Slots with attached handlers.

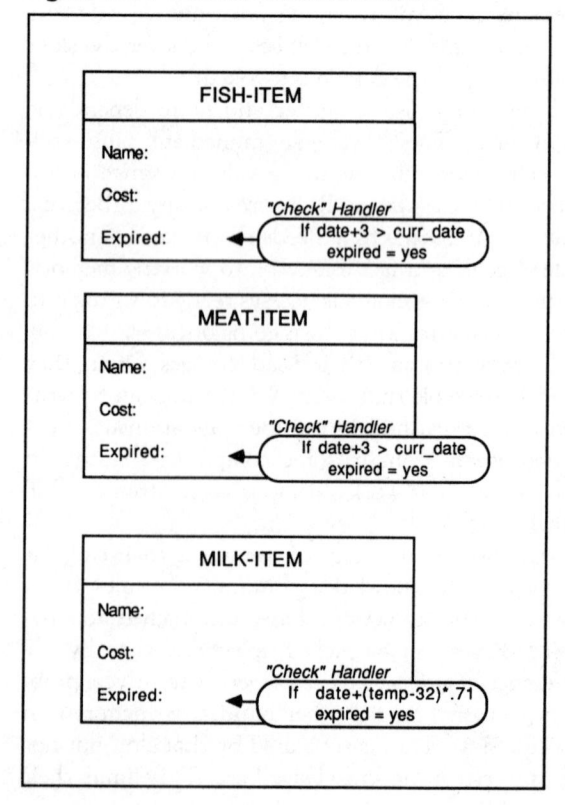

```
┌─────────────────────────────────────────┐
│  FISH-ITEM                              │
│  Name:                                  │
│  Cost:         "Check" Handler          │
│  Expired: ◄── If date+3 > curr_date     │
│               expired = yes             │
│                                         │
│  MEAT-ITEM                              │
│  Name:                                  │
│  Cost:         "Check" Handler          │
│  Expired: ◄── If date+3 > curr_date     │
│               expired = yes             │
│                                         │
│  MILK-ITEM                              │
│  Name:                                  │
│  Cost:         "Check" Handler          │
│  Expired: ◄── If date+(temp-32)*.71     │
│               expired = yes             │
└─────────────────────────────────────────┘
```

Figure 11.15 Sending a message

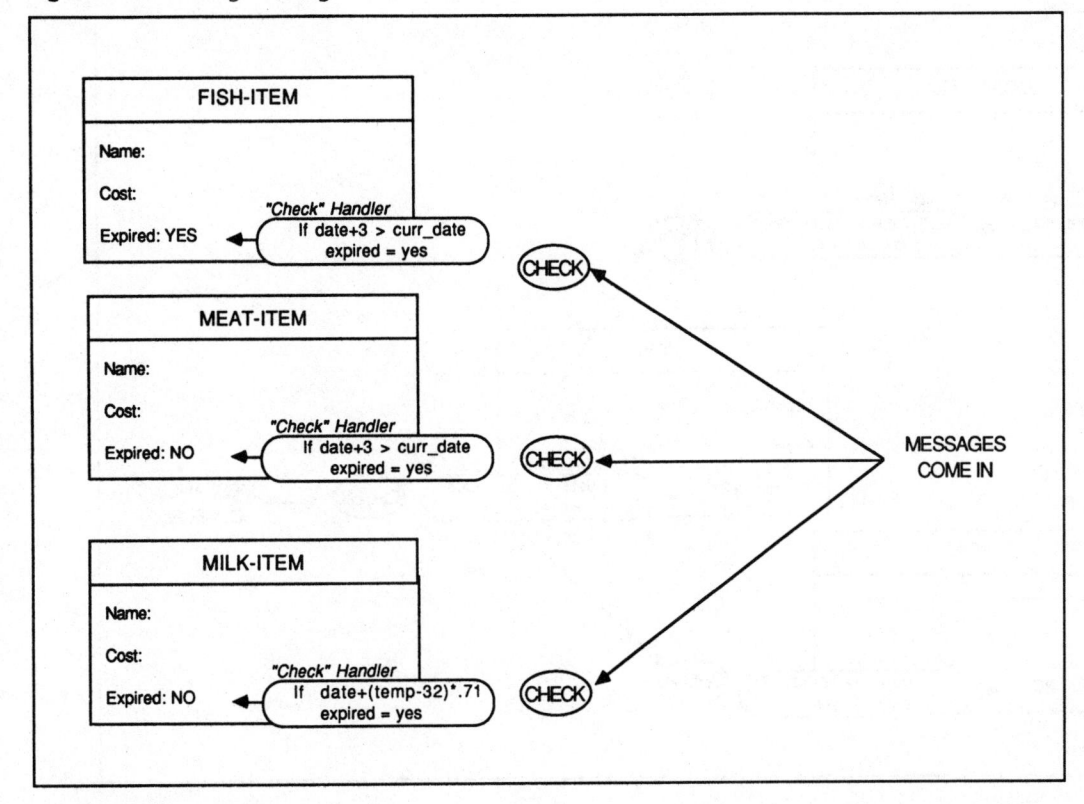

```
┌─────────────────────────────────────────────────────────────┐
│  ┌──────────────────┐                                       │
│  │    FISH-ITEM     │                                       │
│  ├──────────────────┤                                       │
│  │ Name:            │                                       │
│  │ Cost:            │   "Check" Handler                     │
│  │ Expired: YES ◄───┤ If date+3 > curr_date                 │
│  │                  │   expired = yes    (CHECK)◄─┐         │
│  └──────────────────┘                             │         │
│                                                   │         │
│  ┌──────────────────┐                             │         │
│  │    MEAT-ITEM     │                             │         │
│  ├──────────────────┤                             │         │
│  │ Name:            │                             │         │
│  │ Cost:            │   "Check" Handler           │         │
│  │ Expired: NO ◄────┤ If date+3 > curr_date       │         │
│  │                  │   expired = yes   (CHECK)◄──┤ MESSAGES│
│  └──────────────────┘                             │ COME IN │
│                                                   │         │
│  ┌──────────────────┐                             │         │
│  │    MILK-ITEM     │                             │         │
│  ├──────────────────┤                             │         │
│  │ Name:            │                             │         │
│  │ Cost:            │   "Check" Handler           │         │
│  │ Expired: NO ◄────┤ If date+(temp-32)*.71       │         │
│  │                  │   expired = yes   (CHECK)◄──┘         │
│  └──────────────────┘                                       │
└─────────────────────────────────────────────────────────────┘
```

send the object a message whenever you needed to check if it had expired. The actual formula would be hidden inside the object, and would be revealed only if you chose to inspect an object in detail.

Figure 11.14 shows how the three rules are now stored as handlers inside the Food objects. When a "check" message comes in, as shown in Figure 11.15, the handler performs a calculation and sets the value of the expired slot. Giving the command "send-Msg Fish_Item check" would cause the Fish object to invoke its formula to determine whether it had expired. If it had, then it would set its own EXPIRED slot to YES.

Note: Handlers are usually written in LISP. We show them here in a pseudocode, since we are interested in showing the principle at work and do not want to become involved in LISP details.

Should You Use Message Passing or Rules?

When your rules begin to include too much procedural code, they become unreadable and difficult to debug. Message passing solves this problem with encapsulation. It keeps the details of a frame's implementation neatly inside the frame, rather than strewn about the knowledge base. This is especially important in large systems, where encapsulation helps keep the knowledge base comprehensible.

You can also use message passing to propagate the effects of a localized event throughout an entire model. For example, suppose you send a message to a MILK frame to check its freshness, and discover that somehow it has expired on the shelf. This may be a warning sign—the grocer may have forgotten to check the freshness of all the dairy items. So, it would be a good idea to check the surrounding foods

Figure 11.16 Checking Neighbors using message passing.

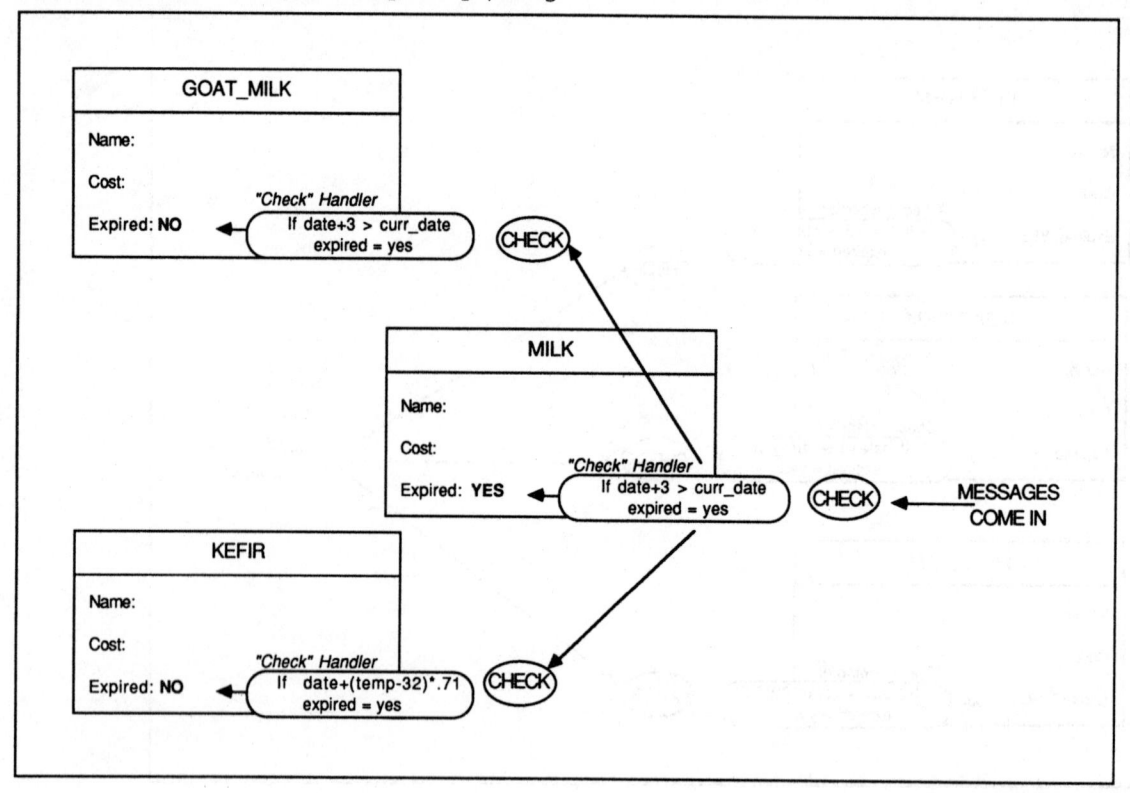

```
         GOAT_MILK
   Name:
   Cost:              "Check" Handler
   Expired: NO ◄──  If date+3 > curr_date     (CHECK)
                      expired = yes


                         MILK
                  Name:
                  Cost:           "Check" Handler
                  Expired: YES ◄── If date+3 > curr_date    (CHECK) ◄── MESSAGES
                                     expired = yes                        COME IN


         KEFIR
   Name:
   Cost:              "Check" Handler
   Expired: NO ◄──  If date+(temp-32)*.71     (CHECK)
                      expired = yes
```

to make sure they are still fresh. You could do this by having the MILK frame send messages to its neighbors so that they also check themselves for freshness. Figure 11.16 shows how the "check" handler in the MILK frame is modified to send messages to its neighbors.

If you are building a simulation, message passing is critical to propagate changes throughout your model. For example, in a simulation of an industrial process, you could use frames to represent connected pumps and chambers. Using message passing, you can propagate changes in pressure throughout the entire system. When one pump loses pressure, it causes a chain reaction. Each element in the system sends a message to its neighbors that a leak has occurred, until all affected components are notified. Pressure goes down throughout all the objects that make up the system's connected components.

INFERENCE AND CONTROL

Combining Inference and Control Strategies

Large systems often pursue a heterogeneous search strategy, combining backward and forward chaining. Such systems begin in one mode and then reverse when it is appropriate. Thus, a system might start with a goal and begin a backward search. Somewhere along the way, the inference engine might notice that it had facts in working memory that would allow it to fire some additional rules. It would then shift to a forward chaining strategy. If these rules established facts that reduced the subsequent backward search or eliminated questions that would have otherwise been asked of the user, you can see how it would be more efficient.

Sometimes, users cannot even state the problem that the expert system should solve. Instead, they are only able to make observations about various facts. By starting with forward chaining, the system can draw conclusions from the observations about problems that are occurring. Then the system can use backward chaining to pinpoint their causes and suggest solutions.

In some systems, each set of rules has a strategy associated with it. One group of rules might require backward chaining, while another set would require forward chaining. With such systems, you need to divide your rules based on a control strategy.

Other tools allow mixed control strategies within a single context. Rules are "tagged" with a label that says whether they should be used for backward chaining, forward chaining, or both. You can use a command to set the strategy used by the system and then change it at any time.

Truth Maintenance and Retraction

Once the user has answered a question, some tools allow the user to change that answer using *retraction*. Problems arise when the user takes back an assertion after the system has already drawn conclusions from it. These conclusions may no longer be valid, since they were based on the outdated information.

For instance, suppose a user tells an investment advisory system that he has $5,000 available to invest. The system uses this fact to determine the best type of account to open. Then, later, the user uses retraction to change the amount to be invested. The system must then retract any of its recommendations that were based on the user's willingness to spend $5,000.

If your system is subject to user retractions, you need to use a technique called *truth maintenance*, which helps keep the knowledge base valid. With truth maintenance, the system keeps a justification for every piece of knowledge, which is essentially a history of its derivation. Whenever the user retracts an answer, the system goes through all its assertions and retracts dependent information automatically.

Using Metarules

Sometimes your expert can give you hints about how to make the best use of rules. For example, an expert might tell you that it is always better to use a human expert's rule than a rule out of a manual. An expert for an industrial application might tell you that when in doubt, always pick a rule whose action uses less electricity. These are known as metarules—rules about how to use other rules. They give the system ways to make the best use of knowledge. There are three common types of metarules.

- Rules that say which rules are more reliable
- Rules that say which rules are less costly
- Rules that say which rules are safer

Metarules can also be very complex—saying, for example, always to pick rules that have the fewest clauses or rules that reference the variable X.

Let's consider a simple example of how a metarule could be used to guide the search process. Suppose you have a diagnosis system to pinpoint malfunctions in a piece of plant equipment. The system uses rules to find problems and to suggest corrective actions. Actions vary on how much disturbance they create for the rest of the plant. So you might have a metarule saying, given two courses of action, choose the corrective action that involves the least disturbance. For example, look at the following.

Rule 1

IF   vacuum_pump is malfunctioning AND pressure is low
THEN check to see if you hear a leak.

Rule 2

IF   vacuum_pump is malfunctioning AND pressure is low
THEN turn off power and examine the casing.

Rule 3

IF   vacuum_pump is malfunctioning AND pressure is low
THEN close off valves and look at pressures of each chamber.

Guided by the metarule, the system would select

Rule 1 in order to minimize the disturbance by keeping the power on and the valves open.

Using Metarules to Limit Search

Normally, in smaller systems, the built-in search strategy is sufficient to solve the problems that are developed in such tools. In larger systems, however, you need to give more detailed consideration to the search strategy. Unleashed on a large problem, a built-in inference engine may end up barking up the wrong tree. It may try to explore an impossibly large number of solutions and never come to a conclusion. The developer then needs to intervene, tailoring the inference engine's search for efficiency.

There are many techniques available to keep the inference engine from considering certain rules. You can use these techniques to direct the inference engine's search, focusing on fruitful paths while avoiding less promising ones.

By preventing the system from considering one rule, you may indirectly cut out scores of other rules from consideration. This has to do with how backward chaining works. While testing a rule, the system may set up subgoals, which bring more rules under consideration. These rules, in turn, can invoke still more rules. By pruning a rule from the system, you may prune thick branches of a decision tree. This can have a tremendous impact on the system's efficiency.

SUMMARY

Hybrid systems combine all of the techniques we have seen in simpler tools and allow (or force) the developer to make decisions about which techniques to use to solve each part of a problem. To find a value for a particular slot, the developer may decide to use backward chaining and a small set of rules. In another case, the developer may decide that forward chaining would be more efficient.

The large, LISP-based tools like ART, KEE, Knowledge Craft, and GoldWorks are among the most powerful programming environments available today. Hybrid tools written in conventional languages are not quite as powerful, but they are easier to use and integrate.

Most companies have decided to reduce the initial risks entailed with expert systems by focusing on smaller problems that can be tackled via rule-based systems. As programmers become more familiar with object-oriented techniques, however, and seek to handle more complex, knowledge-intensive tasks, more of them will turn to hybrid tools to gain the additional power and flexibility these tools offer.

12.
Procedural Considerations

INTRODUCTION

In earlier chapters, we considered how you can capture and encode knowledge in expert systems languages and tools. We have stressed capturing the heuristic verbal knowledge that is used to analyze and solve problems. There are, of course, other kinds of knowledge. The data stored in conventional databases is manipulated by numerical and algorithmic programs that conventional programmers have been using since people first started writing computer programs. Conventional programming techniques are very efficient in handling a wide variety of procedural problems. Though they lack the flexibility of inference based programs, they are much more efficient in manipulating numerical data in standard ways.

The earliest expert systems were written directly in LISP. LISP, like PROLOG, is a symbolic language with many features that make it a very good language to use when developing an expert system. Unfortunately, LISP does not run as well on commercial computers as the more conventional, procedural languages like C, BASIC, PASCAL, COBOL, and PL/1. Some expert systems developers have nevertheless elected to use LISP, and special computers have been designed to run LISP very effectively. (They are LISP machines—in effect, large workstations especially designed for LISP programming.)

Most expert systems developers have elected to develop expert systems by using one of the expert systems building tools. These tools make expert systems much easier and faster to develop. Some of these tools have been written in symbolic languages like LISP and PROLOG, and they allow the developer to incorporate code from these languages directly into the knowledge base. Most tools, however, have been written in conventional languages like C or PASCAL, and don't allow access to the underlying language.

Thus, expert systems applications have been written in four general ways:

1. Directly in a symbolic language, like LISP
2. Directly in a conventional language, like C
3. In a tool that was written in a symbolic language
4. In a tool that was written in a conventional language

When you consider incorporating procedural code into an expert systems application, the first thing you need to know is how the application was written. If it was written directly in a language like LISP, then you face a relatively easy task, since you can write and incorporate procedural code directly into a symbolic language. If you want to call another program from within your application, you will need to know what facilities are available to call other specific languages.

If the expert systems application was written in a tool, then you need to know about the features the developer of the tool has included to facilitate incorporating procedural commands or calls to other languages.

In the earliest expert systems, knowledge was always stored in either rules or declarative structures like frames. A system was built by dropping bits of knowledge into a knowledge base. This meant that the developer did not have to worry about such typical programmer concerns as writing loops, subroutines, and conditional branches. As developers tried to field systems, however, it became clear that AI techniques weren't enough. Some conventional programming was needed for things that were inconvenient, if not impossible, using AI. In some cases, parts of the system were so much better suited to conventional programming that they were implemented in languages like C and COBOL. Recognizing the need for conventional programming techniques, vendors added procedural features to their tools. Many now offer an assortment of commands to be included in a knowledge base.

In a wide variety of situations, the best solution results from a combination of symbolic and procedural programming. When Boole & Babbage developed DASD Advisor, for example, they combined heuristics, C code, and procedural code. This action reflects the new pragmatism in expert systems design. Instead of trying to squish everything into AI structures, people are now using them only when most effective. Often, parts of the problem are addressed with conventional code. This, in turn, means that knowledge engineers must analyze problems and decide how to distribute them between procedural code and expert systems techniques.

In this chapter, we discuss some of the ways in which you can combine procedural programming techniques with an expert system. We also consider some of the programming language issues and the problems involved in converting expert systems to a conventional language, or vice versa.

INCORPORATING SOME PROCEDURAL CODE INTO A KNOWLEDGE BASE

Before we consider more complex cases, let's look at how you might incorporate some procedural code into an existing knowledge base. These techniques are appropriate when you decide that most of your problem can be represented in rules or frames, but you want to make the knowledge base a little more efficient by introducing a small amount of procedural programming into it.

There are three common techniques that introduce procedural programming into knowledge bases:

1. You can put procedural commands into rule conclusions
2. You can arrange for iteration
3. You can create compound rules

We consider each technique in turn.

Procedural Commands in the Conclusions of Rules

Most expert systems applications need to do more than just ask questions and print recommendations on a screen. Most of them have to cause actions to occur; they need to print reports, put data on a worksheet, or show a table on the screen. In many cases, these actions must be done even before the system reaches its final goal. Your application may require a graphics display during the middle of a consultation, or you may need to enter data into a database. To accomplish this, you will probably have to embed procedural commands in your rules.

Most rule-based tools allow you to place commands in the conclusion of a rule. When a rule succeeds, commands in the rule conclusion fire sequentially. These commands resemble those of a conventional language, like C or PASCAL. Some perform screen operations, such as changing text color, printing a character, or drawing a line. Others can call external programs or read external data files. Constructs like FOR-NEXT or DO-WHILE loops are also available to cause other commands to be issued repeatedly. Using these commands, you can write simple procedures into a rule's conclusions to sort values, print reports, make calculations, and perform other tasks.

In the Oracle Credit Advisor, practically every rule includes procedural commands in its conclusion. Some are used to print messages when rules pass, others are used to make database calls.

For example, if the If-clauses of the following rule prove to be true, the rule will set the value of AGED_

INVOICES_RISK_WT to the value GET_FROM_TABLE. Next, the rule encounters a GET command, which makes a call to obtain database information:

Rule 1

IF   aged_invoices_risk_wt > = −45 AND
          aged_invoices_risk_wt < = 45
THEN aged_invoices_risk = get_from_risk_table
          GET aged_invoices_risk_wt = weight, risktbl, risk_assmt.

Note that in this situation, the value of AGED_INVOICES_RISK_WT (i.e., GET_FROM_RISK_TABLE) is unimportant. Any value will do; the value is there just to satisfy the syntax of the rule (i.e., a rule must assign some value to the attribute). The important thing, if the rule succeeds, is that a procedural side effect, initiated by the GET command, will occur.

Another rule from the Oracle Credit Advisor, shown below, illustrates how a command can be used to print a message when a rule fires. When this rule succeeds, the first clause in its conclusion: REV_COND_3_DISPLAY is given the value YES. Then the second clause, a DISPLAY command, is executed, which causes it to print the value of REV_COND_3 on the screen.

Rule 2

IF   rev_cond_3 < > NIL AND
          rev_cond_3 < > NA
THEN rev_cond_3_display = yes
          DISPLAY "{REV_COND_3}".

In effect, whenever you start introducing special commands like GET and DISPLAY into your rules, you are introducing procedural code into your knowledge base. To do this, you begin by writing rules, and then you attach procedural commands to the rules so that if the rules succeed, the procedural commands will be executed.

Iteration of Rules

Most small expert systems deal with only a few attributes. The VCR Advisor, for example, needed to deal with only eight attributes. Larger applications, however, often need to deal with information in long lists. This is commonly the case in mainframe data processing applications, where an expert system may have to process lists of records retrieved from a database. A case in point is Boole & Babbage's DASD Advisor. To reach useful conclusions, DASD Advisor sometimes has to consider over 1,000 I/O devices, connected by a web of paths. Deciding how to process this information efficiently while using inference and rules was a major hurdle in building the system.

Iteration simply refers to the fact that the same code is used more than once. The iteration of a rule means that the rule is fired more than once in the course of a consultation. There are two approaches to iteration, one is implicit and the other is explicit.

Implicit iteration. Implicit iteration is performed automatically by the system. Rather than writing commands in the rules to cause iteration, you simply write generalized rules. The system then automatically re-executes the general rule for each particular case it applies to.

We can illustrate each of the two approaches to iteration by considering the following example. Suppose you had to process 100 different part orders. The expert has said that if a part is a widget, and it has already been paid for, then you can ship it to the customer.

Using the implicit approach to iteration, which is used in most of the hybrid tools, you would encode each order as an instance of the frame ORDER, and write the following general rule:

Rule 3

IF   X−name = widget AND
          X−paid = yes
THEN X−status = send.

When you run the system, it would automatically

refire the rule for each instance of ORDER and set its STATUS slot to the appropriate value.

Explicit iteration. Explicit iteration is achieved by explicit FOR-NEXT or DO-WHILE loops written directly into rules. This causes the rule (or a part of the rule) to fire repeatedly.

To implement the part order system using explicit iteration, you would store each order as an element in a list, or array. You would then write the following rule, with an embedded FOR statement:

Rule 4

```
FOR order
IF      order[i].name is widget
        order[i].paid is yes
THEN    order[i].status is send.
```

When this system is executed, the counter variable [i] would begin with the value of 1. The rule would fire for the first order in the table, the value of i would be incremented, the next order would be processed, and so on. The iteration would stop when no orders remained. This approach is used in ADS and many other tools that are written in conventional languages.

Implicit and explicit iteration are logically equivalent—in our example, they go through a set of orders and flag the ones to be shipped. The difference is that GoldWorks' rule does not incorporate any explicit code to cause it to refire, while the ADS rule does contain explicit code (i.e., FOR) to make it refire. The implicit approach makes rules more readable and easier to maintain; the explicit approach often make rules more efficient.

A good example of explicit iteration can be found in the Oracle Credit Advisor. This system uses a number of different factors to rate a customer's credit level, which is stored in an array. A procedural WHILEKNOWN loop is used to go through the array, issuing a FIND command for each element. This command invokes rules to process the element, and continues until all elements are processed.

```
WHILEKNOWN kb_terms[x]
    . . .
    . . .
    RESET cred_recommend
    FIND cred_recommend
    x = (x + 1)
END
```

Rule 1

```
IF      recommend_wt[x] < -10
THEN    cred_recommend = yes
        recommend[x] = DENY.
```

You can find another example of explicit iteration in DASD Advisor, which contains many examples of procedural iteration. The DASD Advisor uses two different types of rules: *simple rules* and *complex rules*. The simple rules are the rules you expect to find in an expert system; they contain readable, declarative knowledge. A simple rule might read as follows.

Rule 2

```
IF      there is an arm contention AND
        a dual density problem OR
        a device contention
THEN    there is a pack contention.
```

DASD Advisor's complex rules, on the other hand, are long and cryptic, hardly resembling the readable heuristic of classic expert systems. Foremost in the mind of the developer was to get the system to function properly, and complex rules were a convenient programming construct to use. Largely procedural, they process lists of information, perform calculations, and set flags.

As noted above, ADS allows the developer to use a FOR loop to facilitate processing lists of information. You can write a loop into a rule to make it fire repeatedly, once for each element of a list. For example, the complex rule shown below has a FOR loop in it to go through each element in the list PATH_INFO to see which paths connect to the current device.

Rule 3

>FOR path_info
>>IF path_info[i].de is not d_rec.dev
>>> and (cu_sel includes path_info[i].cu
>>> or ch_sel includes path_info[i].ch)
>>
>>THEN add path_info[i].de to neighbors.

Though this rule has a procedural flavor, it is part of a knowledge base that makes use of declarative rules and backward chaining. The developer used procedural code for the parts of the problem where efficiency was critical, and used AI techniques where explicit judgment and inference were important. The emphasis was not so much on perfecting a knowledge model, as on getting a job done. Boole & Babbage uses AI techniques judiciously, rather than trying to use them for everything.

Compound Rules

Another popular procedural construct is the *compound rule*. A compound rule consists of a series of individual rules joined together by ELSEIF statements to form a single, large rule. The procedural nature of compound rules comes from the way in which the system evaluates them. When a compound rule is processed, each component in the premise is evaluated sequentially, just as a series of commands would be processed in a procedural language. Figure 12.1 shows a sample compound rule from DASD Advisor, along with the individual rules that compose it.

When a system processes a compound rule, it starts by testing the first set of IF conditions. If they pass, the system adds the rule's first set of conclusions to working memory. If one of the rule's first set of IF

Figure 12.1 Four simple rules combined into a single compound rule using ELSEIF.

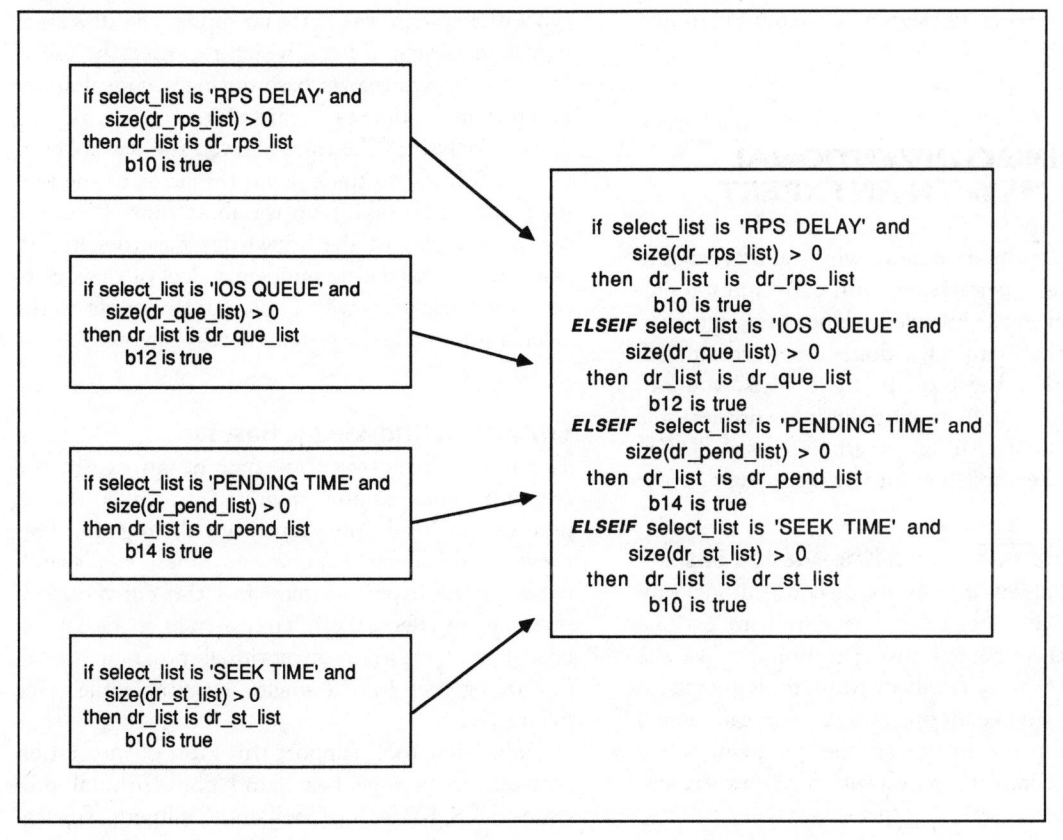

```
if select_list is 'RPS DELAY' and
   size(dr_rps_list) > 0
then dr_list is dr_rps_list
     b10 is true
```

```
if select_list is 'IOS QUEUE' and
   size(dr_que_list) > 0
then dr_list is dr_que_list
     b12 is true
```

```
if select_list is 'PENDING TIME' and
   size(dr_pend_list) > 0
then dr_list is dr_pend_list
     b14 is true
```

```
if select_list is 'SEEK TIME' and
   size(dr_st_list) > 0
then dr_list is dr_st_list
     b10 is true
```

```
        if select_list is 'RPS DELAY' and
           size(dr_rps_list) > 0
        then dr_list is dr_rps_list
             b10 is true
ELSEIF select_list is 'IOS QUEUE' and
           size(dr_que_list) > 0
        then dr_list is dr_que_list
             b12 is true
ELSEIF select_list is 'PENDING TIME' and
           size(dr_pend_list) > 0
        then dr_list is dr_pend_list
             b14 is true
ELSEIF select_list is 'SEEK TIME' and
           size(dr_st_list) > 0
        then dr_list is dr_st_list
             b10 is true
```

conditions fails, the system proceeds to the first set of ELSEIF conditions. If one set of IF conditions succeeds, the set of conclusions following that set of IF conditions is added to working memory. The effect is as if the system considered a set of rules, one after another, except that all of the rules are linked together into a single compound rule by ELSEIF operators.

There are advantages and disadvantages to compound rules. If you have a set of rules that will always be tested in a fixed sequence, consolidating them into a compound rule has advantages: They make the knowledge base more compact, and the rule is processed more efficiently.

Placing knowledge within a compound rule, however, can severely limit its flexibility. The system can use the rules only in the order they appear in the compound rule. This eliminates the possibility that individual pieces of the compound rule could be used independently when the system is attempting to find a novel solution.

COMBINING CONVENTIONAL PROGRAMS WITH AN EXPERT SYSTEM

There are two primary reasons why you may want to combine your expert system with conventional programs: to make your knowledge base run faster, or to do things that can't be done using commands provided within the tool. In these cases, you can implement your problem partially in a conventional language and partly in an expert systems shell. You can then tie them together into a single system.

Calling Programs from a Knowledge Base

The most rudimentary way to use conventional programs with knowledge bases is simply to execute them from the rule base using techniques like the ones we have just described. Most tools provide a command to invoke an operating system call, which can be a command to run another program. When the program completes its execution, the expert system resumes.

The disadvantage of this approach is that executing an external program can be rather slow, since it is loaded into memory, executed, and then removed from memory. The delay may be prohibitively long for certain real-time applications. If it takes 10 seconds to invoke a C program to read sensor data, and the expert system needs to analyze the data every 5 seconds, obviously, rule-based calls to programs are impractical.

Data is exchanged several different ways between the expert system and the program it calls. Some tools pass data on command line arguments. Others provide ways to write data to a file, and then call the external program that reads it in. Likewise, information returns to the expert system through a file created by the external program.

Portions of DASD Advisor were implemented in C for efficiency. Initially, the system was built entirely in the expert systems development tool ADS. Once the system was fairly far along, the developer used a *time-stamped trace*, which recorded the use of parts of the knowledge base during a consultation, and how much time each part took.

The analysis of the trace allowed the developer of DASD Advisor to track down the areas of the program that were taking up the most time. It turned out that a part of the knowledge base devoted to calculations was eating up a great deal of time. Supplanting these parts with C programs to perform the calculations made the system more efficient.

Embedded Knowledge Bases

The most efficient way to combine an expert system and a conventional program is to embed the expert system inside the conventional program. This prevents the delay experienced when you switch between the expert system and the conventional program. In effect, the inference engine, the knowledge base, and the conventional program are all linked together into a single, executable file. (See Figure 12.2.)

Only a few tools support this kind of integration between knowledge bases and conventional programs. KES, KnowledgeTool, and Cullinet's Applica-

Figure 12.2 Three ways expert systems interact with other programs.

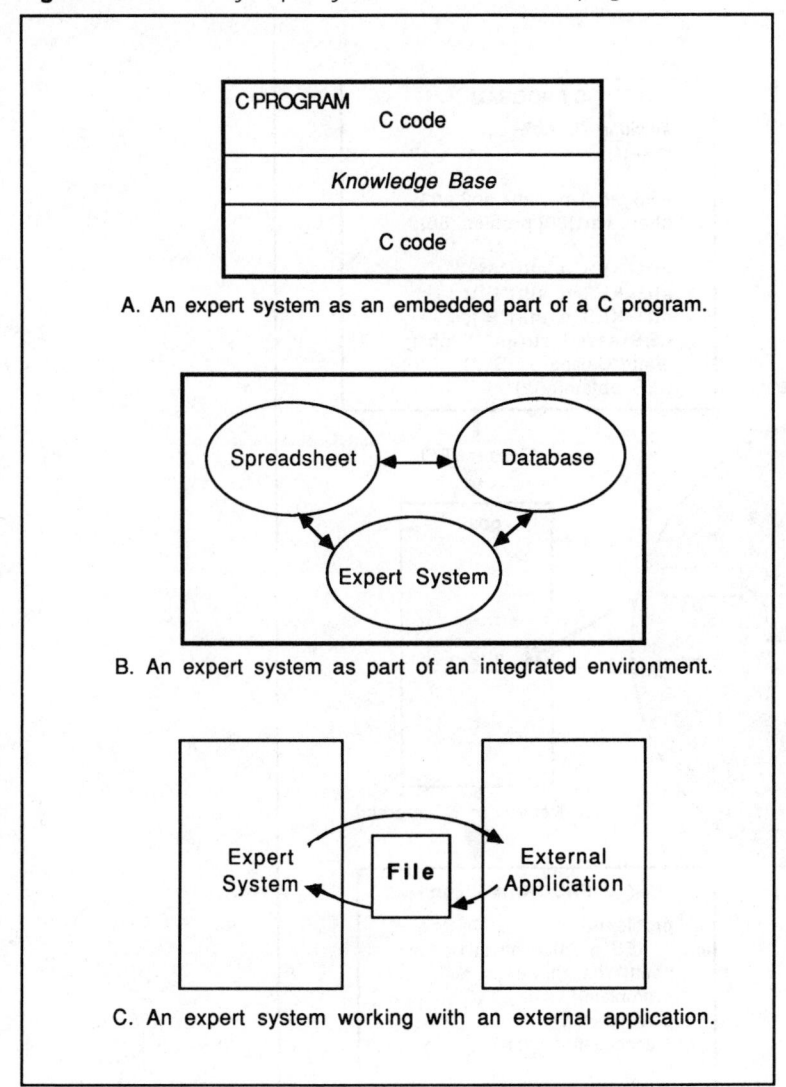

A. An expert system as an embedded part of a C program.

B. An expert system as part of an integrated environment.

C. An expert system working with an external application.

tion Expert are all good examples of tools that are designed to allow embedding within a language.

KES, for example, provides a library of C routines that you can use to interface C code directly with a knowledge base. Using these routines, you can make C calls to create new attributes, pursue goals, or even retrieve explanatory text from a knowledge base. Since information is exchanged with the knowledge base through memory, rather than through files, execution is very fast.

Figure 12.3 shows a sample C program working with a KES knowledge base. First, the C program calls the routines KES_g_attr() to initialize the attributes A, E, and F. Next, it calls KES_assert_str() to

Figure 12.3 Sample KES II knowledge base embedded in C.

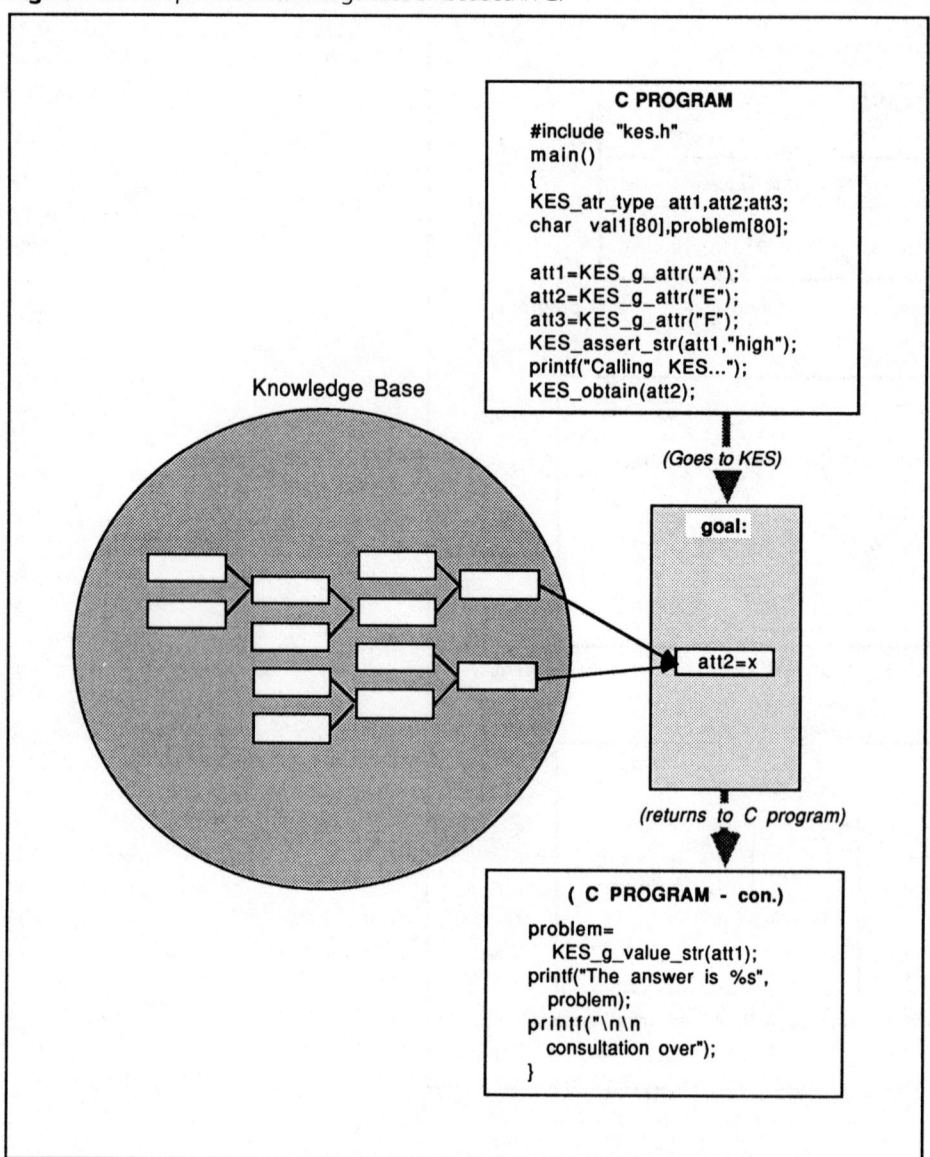

```
                C PROGRAM
#include "kes.h"
main()
{
KES_atr_type att1,att2;att3;
char    val1[80],problem[80];

att1=KES_g_attr("A");
att2=KES_g_attr("E");
att3=KES_g_attr("F");
KES_assert_str(att1,"high");
printf("Calling KES...");
KES_obtain(att2);
```

(Goes to KES)

goal:

att2=x

(returns to C program)

```
        ( C PROGRAM - con.)
problem=
    KES_g_value_str(att1);
printf("The answer is %s",
    problem);
printf("\n\n
    consultation over");
}
```

Knowledge Base

give attribute A a value of HIGH. Finally, the KES_obtain() function is invoked, which causes KES to backward chain to find the value of E.

Once a value is established for the goal, control returns back to the C program. The function KES_g_value_str() is called to return the value of the goal variable, which is then displayed with the C printf() function.

CONVERTING A SYMBOLIC LANGUAGE-BASED EXPERT SYSTEM TO A CONVENTIONAL LANGUAGE

Most expert systems are currently being developed in expert systems building tools that are written in conventional code. Some expert systems, however, are being written in languages like LISP or PROLOG and others are being written in tools that are written in LISP or PROLOG. In cases like these, the developers may eventually want to rewrite the application in a conventional language so that it can be more easily integrated into a conventional environment for delivery. Some of the LISP-based tool vendors have anticipated this need and developed utilities that will help developers port knowledge bases written in their tools to delivery systems coded in a conventional language. We consider both types of conversion.

Rewriting an Expert System in Conventional Code

The most common reason for porting an expert system to a conventional language is speed. Obviously, this discussion assumes that you have written the expert system directly in a symbolic language like LISP. If you have written the application in a tool, then you need only worry about porting the knowledge base from a symbolic-based tool to a tool written in a conventional language.

If an expert system is complete and thoroughly tested, you can port it to a conventional language. In many applications, however, if the knowledge keeps changing, the system will never be complete. In such situations, you should probably not port the application to a conventional language, since a conventional program will be much harder to change and maintain. Hence, we are talking here only about those rare situations in which a developer has written an expert system directly in LISP or PROLOG and the knowledge in the application is stable and likely to remain so.

Moving an application from a symbolic language to a conventional language normally results in an application that runs faster. The main reason is simply that code in the conventional language application is typically much more compact. This was the case in CATS-1, a system built by General Electric to diagnose locomotive malfunctions. The system was initially developed in LISP. Later, it was translated into FORTH to run efficiently in a real environment.

Another reason to port to a conventional language is to allow the system to be fielded on specific hardware. PUFF, a pulmonary diagnosis system used by The Pacific Medical Center in San Francisco, was originally written in LISP. Once the system had been thoroughly tested, it was ported to BASIC so that it could run on the hospital's PDP-11.

Porting a Knowledge Base to a Conventional Language

If you want to have the power of a symbolic language during the development phase of your expert systems project, but know that you will want to convert to a conventional language later, you should consider developing your expert system in a tool that supports automatic conversion from a symbolic language to a conventional language. This means, in effect, that the vendor has developed two inference engines, one in a symbolic language and another in a conventional language. In addition, the vendor has written a utility program that will convert a knowledge base written in LISP into a knowledge base that can be used by a conventional language inference engine.

If you develop an expert system using Personal Consultant Plus or TestBench, for example, conversion is a snap. Personal Consultant Plus is written in Scheme (a dialect of LISP) while TestBench is written in Common LISP. To make it easy for developers to field applications in conventional languages, Texas Instruments has created C versions of both inference engines and provided utilities that will automatically convert a LISP knowledge base into a C knowledge base. (There are usually some minor problems with converting graphics and calls to other programs that cannot be handled automatically, but must be hand coded.) Thus, if you create frames and rules in the LISP version of either Personal Consultant Plus or TestBench and anticipate conversion, you can accomplish it with about the same ease that you can convert files from one common word processing program to another.

CONVERTING A CONVENTIONAL APPLICATION INTO AN EXPERT SYSTEM

While some developers may consider converting a symbolically encoded expert systems application into a conventional language, many have faced just the opposite problem. They already have a conventional application and they want to convert it into an expert system. Typically, the conventional application has proved difficult to maintain, and maintenance problems are expected to continue in the future. Conventional programs that incorporate judgmental knowledge that keeps changing can quickly become tangled messes. It is often far easier to create and then maintain a knowledge base, where judgment is explicit and structured, than to unravel and reweave the lines of a conventional application. Almost everyone who decides to convert a conventional application to an expert system elects to use an expert systems building tool. Thus, their task becomes one of converting a conventional application into a knowledge base.

There are many other reasons to port a conventional application to an expert systems tool. It allows you to take advantage of the strengths of expert systems—their ability to justify reasoning to the user, to reason given uncertain or incomplete data, and to ask the user the minimal set of questions. In short, porting to an expert systems tool is worthwhile whenever the benefits of an expert systems implementation outweigh the effort to make the port.

How Programs Become Scrambled

Let's consider a small C program that gives advice about choosing paint. We will contrast it with a knowledge base that tackles the same problem, and show how they each are maintained. Since programs vary greatly in their implementation, the C program we present obviously could have been written many different ways.

The program, shown on page 231, recommends the best high-gloss enamel to use in a painting project. To do this, it considers three factors: how much rain the item will be exposed to, whether it is okay for the paint to be sticky, and how much sun the item will receive. The paints to choose from have the following characteristics:

- RustMaster is best for jobs where the furniture is exposed to heavy rain and open sunlight. The paint does not have a sticky feel.
- Solid Gloss is best for jobs exposed to heavy rain, but no sunlight. Like RustMaster, the paint does not have a sticky feel.
- RustKing can be used in projects that will be exposed to heavy rain, where a sticky surface is okay.
- Best Seal is appropriate in projects that are exposed to light rains and partial sunlight.

These rules are implemented in the following C program. You do not have to scrutinize the program's every detail, just understand its general approach. The program, in effect, hard-codes a decision tree. When the program is run, it calls procedures "askques1," "askques2," and "askques3," which ask the user to respond to questions. Using nested IF statements, the program is guided to the appropriate "printf" command to print the name of the best paint.

If you are a C programmer, you will note that, for simplicity, we have conveniently overlooked the issue of how user string inputs would be converted into numerical values used by the IF statements.

Now consider what happens when you want to add a new heuristic to the program. Suppose the painting expert remembers a new kind of paint to add to the system, called "SuperRust," which is best under conditions of light rain and no sunlight. Even after this paint dries, it remains slightly sticky to the touch. To add it to the knowledge base, you would have to make the following changes to the C program (changes shown in italics).

```c
main()

{
int answer;

askques1(answer);
if (answer = = HEAVY) {
    askques2(answer);
    if (answer = = NO_STICKINESS ) {
        askques3(answer);
        if (answer = = OPEN)
            printf("The Best Paint Is RustMaster");
        else printf("The Best Paint Is Solid Gloss");
        }
    else printf("The Best Paint Is RustKing");
    }
else {
    askques3(answer);
    if (answer = = PARTIAL)
        printf("The Best Paint Is Best Seal");
        }
    }
askanswer1(answer)
int answer;
{
printf("How much rain will it be exposed to?
1-heavy 2-light 3-none");
scanf("%d",&answer);
}

askanswer2(answer)
int answer;
{
printf("How much stickiness are you willing to tolerate?\n
(For example, chairs should not be sticky, while things
like stools can be slightly sticky)
1-no stickiness 2-some stickiness okay ");
scanf("%d",&answer)
}

askanswer3(answer)
int answer;
{
printf("How much sun will it be exposed to?
1-open sun 2-partial sun 3- no sun");
scanf("%d",&answer);
}
```

```
main()

{
int answer;
askques1(answer);
if (answer = = HEAVY) {
    askques2(answer);
    if (answer = = NO_STICKINESS ) {
        askques3(answer);
        if (answer = = CONSTANT)
            printf("The Best Paint Is RustMaster");
        else printf("The Best Paint Is Solid Gloss");
        }
    else printf("The Best Paint Is RustKing");
    }
else if (answer = = NONE) {
    askques3(answer);
    if (answer = = OCCASIONAL)
        printf("The Best Paint Is Best Seal");


    }
else {
    askques2(answer);
    if (answer = = SOME_STICKINESS_OK) {
        askques3(answer);
        if (answer = = NONE)
            printf("The Best Paint Is SuperRust");
        }

    }
```

You've had to change several IF statements and add function calls to ask additional questions. After a few more new rules come along, you can imagine what the C program would begin to look like, as you heaped together more and more nested conditional statements. Each time a change arises, you would have to consider rewriting the whole program to implement a more efficient decision tree. By the time you decided to add new factors to the decision process, the code would need a major overhaul.

At some point in this process, maintenance becomes so difficult that you might decide to port the system to an expert systems tool. You could convert the C program to the following knowledge base, which provides identical advice.

Rule 1

IF   rain_exposure = heavy AND
          stickiness = no_stickiness AND
          amount_of_sun = open
THEN paint = RustMaster.

Rule 2

IF   rain_exposure = heavy AND
          stickiness = no_stickiness AND
          amount_of_sun = none
THEN paint = Solid_Gloss.

Rule 3

IF   rain_exposure = heavy AND
           stickiness = okay
THEN paint = Rust_King.

Rule 4

IF   rain_exposure = none AND
           amount_of_sun = partial_sun
THEN paint = Best_Seal.

To add SuperRust paint into the system, you would add one new rule:

Rule 5

IF   rain_exposure = light AND
           stickiness = some_stickiness_ok AND
           amount_of_sun = none
THEN paint = SuperRust.

The expert systems tool will do the rest of the work. The inference engine uses the rules to dynamically construct an efficient decision tree every time the user runs the system. Rules are readable and independent, and maintenance is as easy as adding new rules to the knowledge base.

How to Accomplish a Port

Since programming in a conventional language is so radically different from developing a knowledge base, there is no general method to port code between them. Usually, the developer making the port will throw away all of the conventional code and start writing the expert system from scratch. In some cases, however, certain parts of the conventional program may have counterparts in the knowledge base.

Sometimes the developer can salvage parts of a conventional program when making a port. For example, COBOL programs for decision making will sometimes use COBOL tables to house a matrix of decisions. When the program is converted to a knowledge base, these tables may serve as a basis for an initial set of rules, or the initial structure for a frame. Also, restrictions on the values and types of variables in a conventional program can translate into the slot constraints in a knowledge base. Definitions of the database structures, text messages, and graphic images may also be useful.

Data General's ATP System is a good example of a conventional program that was ported to a knowledge base. Based on changing policies, what was originally a clean, table-driven COBOL program eventually became an unwieldy combination of overrides and special cases. In addition, as new parts came along or existing ones changed, these changes would become buried in the code. Finally, Data General decided to implement the system in an expert systems shell using GoldWorks.

The COBOL code was useless in the construction of the expert system, since GoldWorks uses a radically different way of representing knowledge and control. However, there were certain cases where elements of the COBOL program had counterparts in the GoldWorks code. For example, the COBOL program stored information about general kinds of transfer categories in tables. The structure of some of these tables corresponded to frames in GoldWorks.

Conventional programs contain knowledge, just as expert systems applications do, but they normally contain less knowledge and the knowledge is embedded in procedures or in database structures. When you are faced with the task of converting an existing program into an expert system, you should begin just as you would if you were planning a regular development effort—with an analysis phase. In this case, you would be analyzing an existing program to determine the knowledge contained in it. You can use all of the techniques we have discussed in earlier chapters. You can develop an object network and frame worksheets as you examine a conventional program and its associated databases. You don't need to worry about saving the procedural code, since the expert system's inference engine will handle control issues. What you do need to do is to identify the declarative knowledge contained in the conventional application and then encode that knowledge as either rules or frame structures.

SUMMARY

In general, procedural code is more efficient to run, while declarative approaches are more readable and maintainable. In most cases, when you evaluate your project, you will decide that some portions of the task should be represented as a knowledge base while other portions should be handled by code written in a conventional language. Once you have decided how to divide the task, you should decide which part of the task will predominate. If the knowledge-based portion of the task is the more important, you should develop the application in an expert systems building tool and call procedures from within your knowledge base, as needed. If the knowledge-based portion of the task is only a small part of the overall application, you should consider developing the application in a conventional language and developing the knowledge base in a tool that will interface with the application, or can be embedded within the application.

13.
Database Considerations

INTRODUCTION

In the early days of expert systems, expert systems development and database development were considered two independent technologies. Expert systems used inference and emphasized making judgment explicit. Database packages used query matching and emphasized performance and shared access to data. Recently, there has been a growing realization that these two technologies are really complementary—they can be used together to solve different parts of the same problem. Thus, in the past three years, there has been a gradual merging of the two; database management systems (DBMS) are beginning to provide AI functionality, and expert systems shells now provide links to databases.

Deciding how best to distribute a problem across knowledge bases and databases has become an important part of a knowledge engineer's job, and it will increasingly be considered an important aspect of the work performed by conventional database designers and software engineers: When should you take advantage of inference techniques and when should you use query matching?

The emergence of SQL (an IBM-supported database management language that facilitates access to DB2 and other relational databases) as a standard way to access data has greatly accelerated the merging of database and expert systems technology. By making use of SQL code libraries, vendors have been able to quickly add database access facilities to their tools. Usually, these tools don't require that the developer know SQL at all; the developer can simply specify the data item that is needed and leave it to the tool to construct the appropriate SQL query.

The current market reflects a wide variety of approaches to the challenge of bridging the gap between expert systems techniques and database techniques. (See Figure 13.1) We examine here two sides of the overall activity:

1. On the expert systems extreme, most expert systems tools are incorporating connections that make it easier for expert systems developers to design systems that acquire and manipulate data from databases. Some of these tools access data from PC programs, such as database files from dBASE and worksheet files from Lotus 1-2-3. Others offer links to mainframe databases, usually by way of SQL.
2. At the database extreme, several companies are experimenting with developing a whole new approach to database design: object-oriented databases. We consider some of the developments in each of these areas, paying special attention to the rationale and problems of connecting existing expert systems to existing databases.

INTEGRATING EXPERT SYSTEMS AND DATABASES

Whenever you are developing an expert system, you should consider what role, if any, there will be for a database in your application. The process of evaluating the role of a database and then creating a linkage, if appropriate, can be broken down into four steps.

Figure 13.1 The merging of expert systems and database technologies.

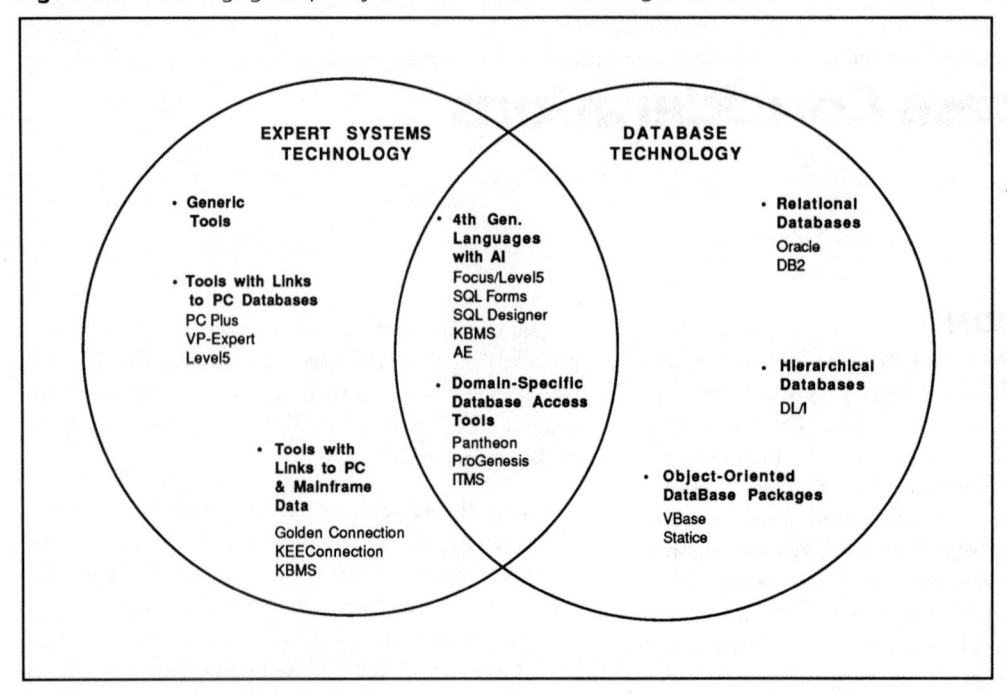

```
                    EXPERT SYSTEMS                 DATABASE
                    TECHNOLOGY                     TECHNOLOGY

         • Generic                                              • Relational
           Tools                  • 4th Gen.                      Databases
                                    Languages                     Oracle
                                    with AI                       DB2
         • Tools with Links         Focus/Level5
           to PC Databases          SQL Forms
           PC Plus                  SQL Designer
           VP-Expert                KBMS
           Level5                   AE
                                                                • Hierarchical
                                  • Domain-Specific               Databases
                                    Database Access               DL/1
                                    Tools
         • Tools with               Pantheon
           Links to PC              ProGenesis
           & Mainframe              ITMS                        • Object-Oriented
           Data                                                   DataBase Packages
                                                                  VBase
           Golden Connection                                      Statice
           KEEConnection
           KBMS
```

1. Decide whether database access is necessary
2. Decide on the role of the database
3. Prepare for data access
4. Make the database connection

Step 1. Deciding Whether Database Access Is Necessary

There are several reasons why people want to connect databases and expert systems.

- *Maintenance.* A database can be used to externalize the parts of the knowledge base that change frequently. This allows a clerk or other nonexpert to perform some kind of limited maintenance on the expert system using a database management system rather than requiring a knowledge engineer to edit the knowledge base. In general, separating data from knowledge makes the knowledge base easier to modify because it is easier to read. The system's rules are clearer since they are not cluttered by large amounts of declarative data.

- *Performance.* When a knowledge base becomes filled with excessive amounts of tabular data, you should consider whether that data can be externalized in a database file. This can improve the performance of the knowledge base in both its speed and memory consumption. A DBMS is often better suited to efficient search of large volumes of structured information than a knowledge base is. You can also preserve memory with this approach, since data that would normally take up memory as part of the knowledge base is kept separately in a data file and is never resident as a whole.

- *Sharing data with other applications.* Numerous applications can access information stored in a database file. For example, if a knowledge base logs the names and addresses of its users in a dBASE II file, the file might be used later by MailMerge to print out letters to each user.

- *Sharing data with other users and maintaining security.* Systems that are networked to other PCs or mainframes can allow database files to be accessed by multiple users. By working through a DBMS, multiple users can work on the same database at the same time, while the DBMS keeps the data consistent and secure.

Step 2. Deciding on the Role of the Database

There are a number of ways in which a database can work with an expert system, each appropriate under certain circumstances:

1. An expert system can be used as a front end for a database, asking questions and then initiating a database query.
2. An expert system can be used as a back end for a database, taking the results of a query and analyzing it with rules in order to make a recommendation.
3. The attributes and values of rules can be stored in a database.
4. A database can be used to store the cases that have been run through an expert system, in order to keep a record of its reasoning.

We consider each use in turn.

An expert system as a front end for a database. When you use an expert system as a front end for a database, you are normally using the expert system to construct database queries. The consultation with the expert system proceeds in the usual way, with the system asking the user questions and using rules to reach a final conclusion. But once the system reaches its conclusion, it then takes an extra step by going out to a database to find an even more specific recommendation to give. This approach is especially useful in systems where the set of actual recommendations changes frequently, while the rest of the underlying logic remains intact.

For example, consider an expert system designed to suggest the best restaurant to go to for dinner. Its decision is based on a number of factors—the restaurant's cost, proximity, and atmosphere. Once the system established (from rules) that a festive Japanese restaurant would be the best choice, it could go to a database and pick Kyoto Garden as the actual choice. In this approach, it's as if the lowest level of rules (i.e., those that recommend actual restaurants) are replaced by database records. This means that as some restaurants go out of business or new restaurants open, their names can be added or removed from the database using a database manager, while the knowledge base remains unchanged.

The database need not always store actual recommendations. Instead, information in a database can simply elaborate on the findings of the expert system. For instance, once a mechanical diagnostic system finds the defective part of an engine, it could access a database to find the part maker, its address, and its phone number.

Adding an expert systems front end to an existing database can be especially useful whenever users have trouble making effective database queries (e.g., they are constantly turning to an "expert user" to help them develop their database request). In some cases, the difficulty may lie in the unfriendliness of the database program, but more commonly it results from the complexity of the analysis and the judgments that the user must make in order to determine what kind of data to request.

This strategy is often followed when users find it hard to use a database because they don't understand the information the database requires. In effect, the expert system asks them for information they can more readily provide, applies rules to analyze the information, and then generates the actual database query.

The consultation begins with the expert system, although the user usually does not know that an expert system is involved. The system asks questions and uses rules to analyze the user's needs and to determine the final form of a database request that will obtain the information the user wants from the database. Once the system determines the correct form of the database query, it passes the query to the database program that then executes the command

and produces a response. The response could be a single data item (a person's social security number, for example), but more commonly the response will be a report of some kind.

For example, consider developing a system to help district insurance managers use a sales planning package. The planning package is, in effect, a database with zip codes and demographic information. If the sales managers can format their requests in the proper manner, the system will produce reports that help the sales managers plan sales campaigns. Unfortunately, the package asks the managers to analyze their sales needs in demographic jargon. Moreover, it assumes that the managers understand something about how database commands should be phrased to avoid long and expensive searches. The sales managers don't know about such things. The program is leased from an outside company that is not prepared to rewrite it to facilitate its use by the sales managers. A small expert systems front end could be added to ask the managers questions, offer them choices when appropriate, and then construct and execute the database query automatically, and return its results in a readable report.

An expert system as a back end for a database. When you use an expert system as a back end to a database, it takes the database output as its input, makes judgments based on it, and then presents specific suggestions to the end user.

Database information that is imported at the start of the consultation can be used to supplement or even totally replace information that would normally be given by the user. For example, a medical diagnostic system could go to a database to get information about a patient at the start of a consultation, thus sparing the user from having to type it in. The system still might need to ask for changing factors like the patient's current weight or age, but it could rely on existing database information to determine the patient's medical history—allergies, vaccinations, and so on.

Back end applications are usually created to take the raw data drawn from a database query, process it further, and convert it into specific action recommendations. This approach is very effective when you want to provide support to individuals who have difficulty interpreting the data output that the database was designed to produce.

A good example of an expert system serving as a back end to a database would be if the insurance sales planning system we considered earlier produced a report that analyzed a sales territory in demographic terms, but didn't make any recommendations about how to approach a specific sales campaign. Imagine that the sales program, and the database that comprises it, had been developed to support a senior sales planner. As time passed, and the sales districts and campaigns grew, someone decided that the sales demographic information should be sent directly to the field sales managers. Unfortunately, lacking the senior sales planner's knowledge about how to interpret the data contained in each report, the program wasn't much help to the field managers. An expert system, developed with the help of the senior sales planner, could take the database output, use rules to analyze the data, and then make specific action recommendations that the field sales managers could then implement.

Storing rules in a database. You can use a database to store information about attributes and values that generic rules can use in reasoning about a problem. In any large knowledge base, there will be rules with a similar structure. Many of the tools provide the ability to collapse these similar rules into a single, general rule. These general rules (some companies call them *variable rules*) are instantiated with values from a table, which is stored in a database.

In Oracle Electronics' Credit Advisor, some of the expert's knowledge is stored in *factor analysis tables*. These tables contain information about the factors that go into the decision of whether to grant a customer credit. For each factor in the decision, the tables contain a list of all its possible values. A numeric weight is stored with each value to denote its significance in the overall decision-making process. Although this information could have been stored as rules, it was stored in dBASE III database files to make the system more efficient and easier to maintain.

Using a database to store cases. You can also use a database to keep a record of all the consultations a system has been through. This information can be used during debugging sessions to evaluate the kind of advice the system has been giving.

Should you emphasize the database or the knowledge base? In the examples we have discussed so far, the database serves as a subordinate of the knowledge base. In fact, many applications require only a comparatively small expert systems element. For example, you can use small expert systems as front ends to databases for data entry: As the user adds new records to the database, the expert system can use a handful of rules to make sure that the data is kept valid and consistent. Or, consider a clerk taking product orders over the phone. As customers call in, the clerk adds information about each order to a database. A small expert systems front end could help the clerk with data entry, using a few rules to issue a warning if the customer has bad credit, and so on.

Step 3. Preparing for Data Access

It is uncommon that database data will be immediately useful to the rules in your system. In general, there are five areas that you must address first when you build an expert system that will use a database: file access, file format, data type, data abstraction, and data integrity.

File access. Database files are not always immediately accessible from the expert system—they may exist on other machines and need to be moved to a PC. This may require that the user copy files from one machine to another, or that the expert system access database files over a network.

Data General's ATP is a good example of an expert system that performs database access over a network. ATP runs on a PC, but it accesses data that is stored on a minicomputer, the MV 10000. By using Gold Hill's Golden Connection in conjunction with the GoldWorks expert systems tool, ATP has access to data files stored on the minicomputer.

With Golden Connection, the PC can trigger a wide variety of actions on the minicomputer by means of a *remote eval*. In a remote eval, a LISP expression is sent over the network from GCLISP running on the PC to MVLISP running on the MV. The LISP expression is then evaluated in MVLISP, which can cause a variety of actions, such as reading a record, opening a file, and so on.

You can access a database with Golden Connection without having to write a line of LISP code. You simply use an *INFOS action frame*. By setting the frame's slots to certain values, you can trigger actions on the minicomputer. To open a database file, for example, you create an instance of an INFOS action frame by setting the FILE-NAME slot to the name of the desired file to open, and setting the SERVER-NAME slot to the name of the server. Golden Connection automatically converts this frame into LISP code and sends it across the network to be evaluated on the minicomputer.

Figure 13.2 shows the linkage created by using Golden Connection. It also shows how creating an instance of an INFOS action frame enables you to access a database file on the minicomputer. First, you create an instance of an INFOS action frame in GoldWorks. Next, you give the slots of the action frame values that specify what kind of database call will be made. The LISP code is then sent over the network from Golden Common LISP to Data General's Common LISP running on the MV. The LISP code is evaluated, which causes commands to be issued to read the database file and return the result over the network.

File format. External data, especially when created by other applications, usually is not stored in a form directly readable by the expert system. The developer may need to write a conventional program to convert external data from a format that is unsup-

Figure 13.2 Using Golden Connection to link GoldWorks with a database on a minicomputer.

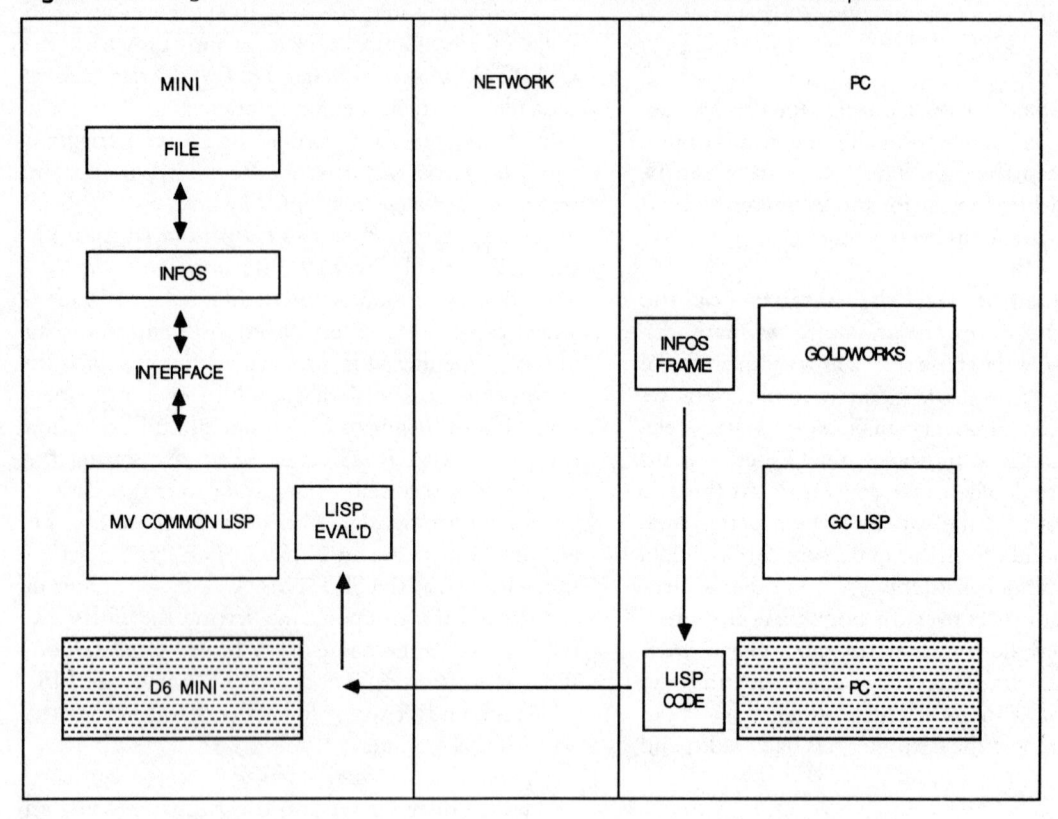

Figure 13.3 Flow of information in Boole & Babbage's DASD Advisor.

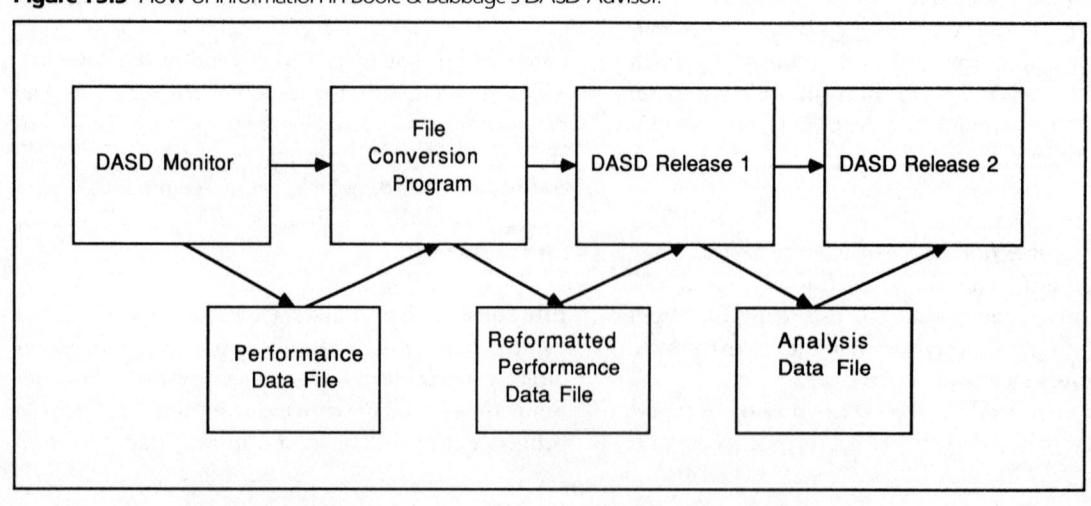

ported by the tool to a format that can be read by the expert system. The knowledge base then calls this program every time the system needs to read in new data. This was the approach taken by Boole & Babbage's DASD Advisor. DASD Advisor needed to read mainframe performance data that was output to a file by a separate program, DASD Monitor. A C program had to be written to convert the file into a format that could be read by DASD Advisor. Whenever DASD Advisor is executed with new data from DASD Monitor, the C program is invoked first. (See Figure 13.3.)

Data type. Once you've established the links between the expert system and the database and information can be read in, you may need various low-level transformations to convert the data into a format and type that the knowledge base can use. For example, you may have to remove leading spaces from a string, convert integers to floating point numbers, and so on.

Data abstraction. It is unlikely that external data will be expressed in a way that can be used by the rules in a knowledge base. Typically, the expert does not think in terms of the fields of the database records, so you need a way to translate the data into the higher levels of abstraction that the expert thinks in. This is almost always a problem when the database has been developed independently of the knowledge base.

For example, Data General's Automated Transfer Pricing System (ATP) reads a database on a minicomputer to get detailed information about parts. The parts database is comprised of esoteric codes like "family type" and "discount number." The pricing expert is not familiar with the specific part codes but rather with the idea represented by those codes (e.g., whether parts are manufactured or vendor-purchased.) *Recognition rules* (shown in Figure 13.4) are needed to translate the raw data in the database into the concepts the expert understands. For instance, there might be a rule that says "if the family code is 3 and the discount code is between 1 and 32, then the part type is manufactured."

Data integrity. When an expert system accesses a database, the desired data is copied from the database file into knowledge base structures. Occasionally, this duplication of data can cause problems. For example, if the database is modified immediately after the expert system accesses it, the expert system could be reasoning with outdated information. You can avoid this problem simply by "locking" the parts of the database that are used by the expert system for the duration of the consultation so that other users cannot modify it.

Figure 13.4 Data General's ATP System uses recognition rules to translate records into knowledge concepts.

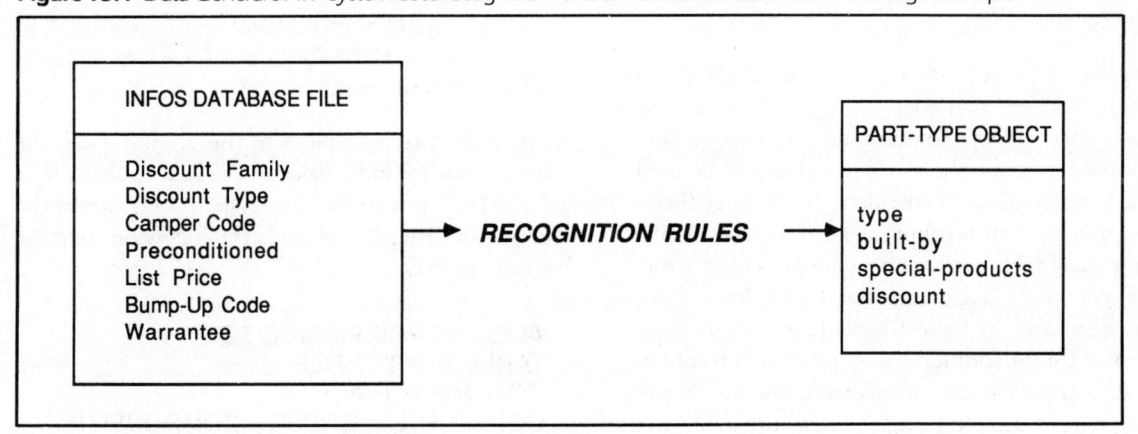

```
┌─────────────────────────┐                          ┌─────────────────────┐
│ INFOS DATABASE FILE     │                          │ PART-TYPE OBJECT    │
│                         │                          │                     │
│ Discount Family         │                          │ type                │
│ Discount Type           │      RECOGNITION RULES   │ built-by            │
│ Camper Code             │ ───▶                 ───▶│ special-products    │
│ Preconditioned          │                          │ discount            │
│ List Price              │                          │                     │
│ Bump-Up Code            │                          │                     │
│ Warrantee               │                          │                     │
└─────────────────────────┘                          └─────────────────────┘
```

Step 4. Making the Connection

There are two basic ways to establish a database connection: (1) by including database commands in a rule, or (2) by attaching a database *sourcing* to an attribute.

Using database commands. In some tools, the developer programs the database connection directly into the rules in a manner very similar to the various procedural calls we discussed in Chapter 12. In VP-Expert, for example, you can include a number of commands to read database files in the conclusions of rules. When a rule passes, the database commands in its conclusion are executed, causing the database to be accessed. The following rule is an example.

Rule 1

    IF   Payment = enclosed OR
               Credit = good
    THEN GET Order = Component, PriceFile, Price.

When Rule 1 fires, the database command GET is executed. It causes the dBASE file named PriceFile to be opened, and searches for a record that has a field named Component equal to the VP-Expert variable Order. If such a record is found, then the value of its Price field is loaded into the knowledge base. Using a different command, VP-Expert could get the entire record, but it can get only one record per call. Other systems allow you to load a whole set of records into memory with one call.

Sourcing. The second approach to accessing a database from a knowledge base is called *sourcing*. Systems that support sourcing usually require that the developer define the attributes that will be used by the various rules, independent of the rules themselves. Independent attribute definitions are missing in most small tools but are normally present in structured rule tools (e.g., Personal Consultant Plus, ADS, ESE) and in hybrid tools (e.g., GoldWorks, KEE, KBMS). In addition to defining such things as the values the attribute can take and the number of values an attribute can have, the attribute definition often includes information about a source from which the value of the attribute can be obtained. (If the source is "the user," then the attribute definition also includes a question the system can use when it asks the user for the value.)

Whenever the system needs the value of an attribute during a consultation, it checks the information stored with the attribute to determine where the value is to be obtained (the source of the value). If the value is to be obtained from a database, information about contacting the database is given as the source of the value.

Sourcing is usually a better approach than commands. It makes rules easier to read, since database access code is kept elsewhere. Sourcing may be essential for large, complex systems applications, where you can't anticipate all the points during the consultation where the system might need to draw on external data, and then write database commands in the appropriate places. Database commands are usually best when you know exactly where your system needs to access a database (e.g., at the very start or finish of a consultation).

In IBM's ESE, each attribute is sourced. If the system checks a given attribute and finds that its source is an external database, the system will make a database call to get the value if it is needed. Consider how ESE might evaluate the following rule.

Rule 2

    IF   Payment = enclosed OR
               Credit = good AND
               Price < 10000
    THEN Status = ship.

After the first two parts of the premise pass, the system needs to find a value for PRICE to check if its value is less than 10000. The system then checks the sourcing of PRICE, and finds the following sourcing has been provided:

```
ACQUIRE PRICE USING SQL
TABLE = PRICEFILE
COLUMN = PRICE
CONDITION = (ORDER = COMPONENT)
```

This ACQUIRE statement tells the system that whenever it needs to know the value of PRICE, it should search the file table PRICEFILE. It should get the value from the column in the table named "PRICE" from the record for the component that has been ordered. Given this sourcing, the tool automatically constructs the following SQL query:

"SELECT PRICE FROM PRICEFILE WHERE ORDER = COMPONENT"

The query is then sent out to the database, and the result that comes back is stored as the value of the attribute PRICE.

Many hybrid systems use a more sophisticated form of sourcing, in which you can connect objects to database records. In AI Corp's KBMS, for example, when you create an object hierarchy, there are two general types of objects you define—those that hold knowledge, and those that hold database information. Whenever a database object is referenced for its value, the system automatically retrieves it from a database.

Nexpert Object, GoldWorks, and KEE also enable you to connect objects in the knowledge base directly to database tables. When database records are brought into the knowledge base, they are automatically converted into instances of these objects. This makes it very easy to deal with database information, since it is automatically converted from the database representation to knowledge structures that can be used directly by rules.

You can see how this connection is actually established by looking at an example from KEEconnection. Using KEEconnection, the developer of a KEE application can tap data stored in relational databases that use SQL. Hence, KEEconnection hides LISP from the mainframe it is accessing by converting LISP requirements into SQL queries before accessing the mainframe. To achieve this, however, you must first craft a representation of the database that you want to access.

You build the connection between the database and the knowledge base graphically using a mouse. First, you identify which database tables need to be accessed from the knowledge base. Next, you specify a *mapping* between the database and the knowledge base. This tells the system how to translate the database information into a form that the knowledge base can use. The system then automatically creates a default mapping, in which each database table translates into a framelike KEE structure called a *class unit*. Figure 13.5 shows the default mapping of the database table "Machines" into a KEE class unit in the knowledge base. The class unit is automatically named "Machines," and each field of the database table becomes a slot in the class unit.

KEEconnection's graphic mapping editor allows you to modify the default mapping between the database and the knowledge base. You can change the names of slots or class units to be different from their database counterparts. The mapping editor also allows you to create new class units or modify existing ones. You can delete the slots in the class units or add new ones. You can also modify the connections between the database fields and these slots. You can easily change these links by using the mouse to draw a line between the database field and the slot to link it to.

Figure 13.6 shows a database mapping that has been changed substantially from the default mapping. A new class unit, called "Repairs," has been added to keep a log of the defects that were found in machines and the names of the service people who fixed them. The class unit "Machines," originally set up by the default mapping, now contains only three slots. It is now used to store the types of machines that have been sent back for repair, and the names of the customers who sent them. In addition, the slot that was named "Owner" by the default mapping has been changed to "Customer."

Once you've created the mapping, then applications developed in KEE can access that data. When the data is needed, KEEconnection automatically generates an SQL query and sends it off to the database. The developer need only be concerned with database tables and fields. He remains insulated from having to deal with file formats and query languages.

Each new generation of expert systems building

244 PROGRAM DEVELOPMENT

Figure 13.5 The default mapping between a database table and a KEE knowledge base.

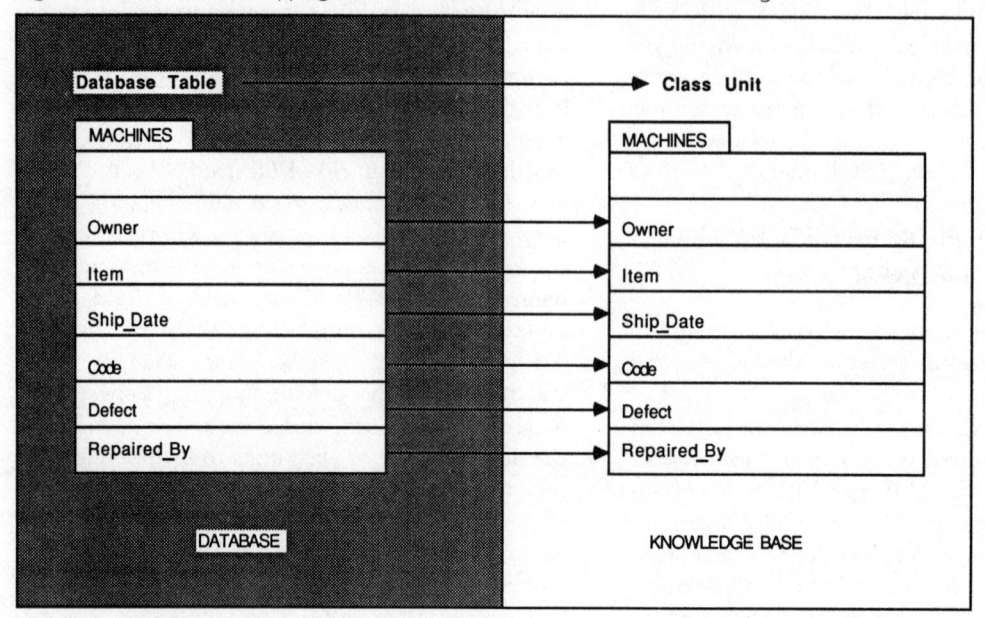

Figure 13.6 Changing the overall structure of the default mapping with KEEConnection.

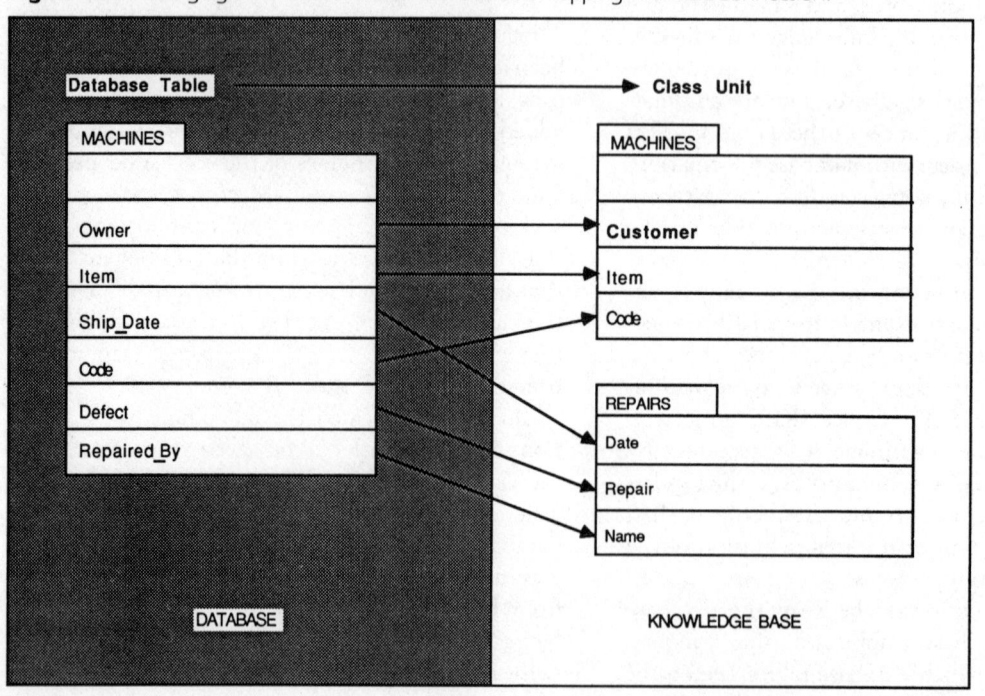

tools has featured more sophisticated ways of blending data from existing databases with the knowledge stored in the knowledge base of an expert system. This trend will certainly continue to accelerate.

OBJECT-ORIENTED DATABASES

Conventional database technology focuses on two general types of databases: hierarchical databases and relational databases. Hierarchical databases, like IBM's DL/I, store their data in tree structures. They provide a slightly richer representation of data and allow for a limited form of inheritance.

Relational databases, like INGRES, PC-Focus, Oracle, and DB2, store their data in unrelated tables and therefore lack the ability to represent complex data types and relationships. Relationships between pieces of data are expressed in procedural code written in the fourth-generation languages these packages provide.

Given all of the recent attention that SQL (a database query language for creating and accessing relational databases that is being promoted by IBM) has received, you might think that all databases will soon be relational databases and that all expert systems tools will soon use SQL to access any data they need. In fact, however, relational databases are rather limited in their ability to handle complex data or to support complex applications.

Relational databases like IBM's DB2 and Oracle Corp's Oracle may become increasingly popular for new and less sophisticated applications, but they are unlikely to replace hierarchical databases for more complex applications. Besides, many large companies maintain most of their data in IBM's DL/I hierarchical database and are not about to port it to DB2. Even hierarchical databases, however, have their limitations when it comes to really complex applications like those involved in CIM (computer integrated manufacturing), CASE (computer assisted software engineering), and the more complex applications that expert systems tools are being used to create.

Object-oriented database systems, at least in theory, have the power to handle the complex data used in complex applications. At least that is the conclusion of several vendors who have set out to market object-oriented databases to MIS/DP people.

Object-oriented database systems combine the characteristics of an object-oriented programming language like Smalltalk or C++ with a mechanism for data storage and access. In a way, object-oriented databases are very much like the large hybrid tools that also represent knowledge in object-oriented structures, except that the object-oriented tools focus directly on the database market rather than emphasizing the development of expert systems. Still, an object-oriented database allows you to analyze data at a conceptual level that emphasizes the natural relationships between objects. Abstraction is used to establish inheritance hierarchies, and object encapsulation allows the database designer to store both conventional data and procedural code within the same objects.

SPREADSHEET ACCESS

While much has been made of the potential benefits of connecting expert systems and spreadsheet software, there has been much more commercial activity in the area of intelligent databases than intelligent spreadsheets. About half of the currently available expert systems tools provide some form of spreadsheet access, most commonly access to Lotus 1-2-3.

Some tools don't read spreadsheet files in their native formats. You have to convert your worksheet to a form that can be read by the expert system. It is much easier to work with a tool that can read these files directly, without having to convert them. By far, the easiest approach is that of the GURU package. GURU provides a spreadsheet built right into its product. This enables you to combine a knowledge base and a spreadsheet within a single tool.

These tools allow you to write knowledge bases that can import data from a spreadsheet and use it to make decisions. Some tools also have the capability to modify spreadsheet data, and then write it back out to the spreadsheet file. Figure 13.7 illustrates how

246   PROGRAM DEVELOPMENT

an expert system can work with a spreadsheet program.

One of the best potential applications of an expert system connected to a spreadsheet is as an *intelligent critic*. By using a knowledge base to analyze spreadsheet data, such a system could offer expert advice to the users. The expert system could examine the data in a spreadsheet and offer help and suggestions.

Figure 13.8 shows an example of an expert system in this role. The spreadsheet contains information about employee sales figures for the year, and their salaries. The knowledge base reads this information in from the worksheet file and uses rules to find the appropriate bonus for each employee. As each bonus is selected, it is written back out to the spreadsheet.

An expert system could also be used as a front end to a spreadsheet. Instead of directly filling out cells, users could work through an interview with an expert system, which would then check the data for consistency and correctness.

SUMMARY

No one can be sure exactly where all this activity will lead. Clearly, expert systems developers will increasingly incorporate database technology in their applications. Likewise, the number of domain-specific tools that help programmers and users access databases and/or generate SQL code will grow. It may be that the different vendors will each carve off small niches and develop products for those niches, or it may be that there will be a major synthesis of AI techniques and database techniques into a really

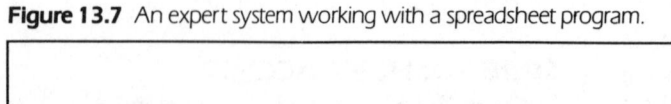

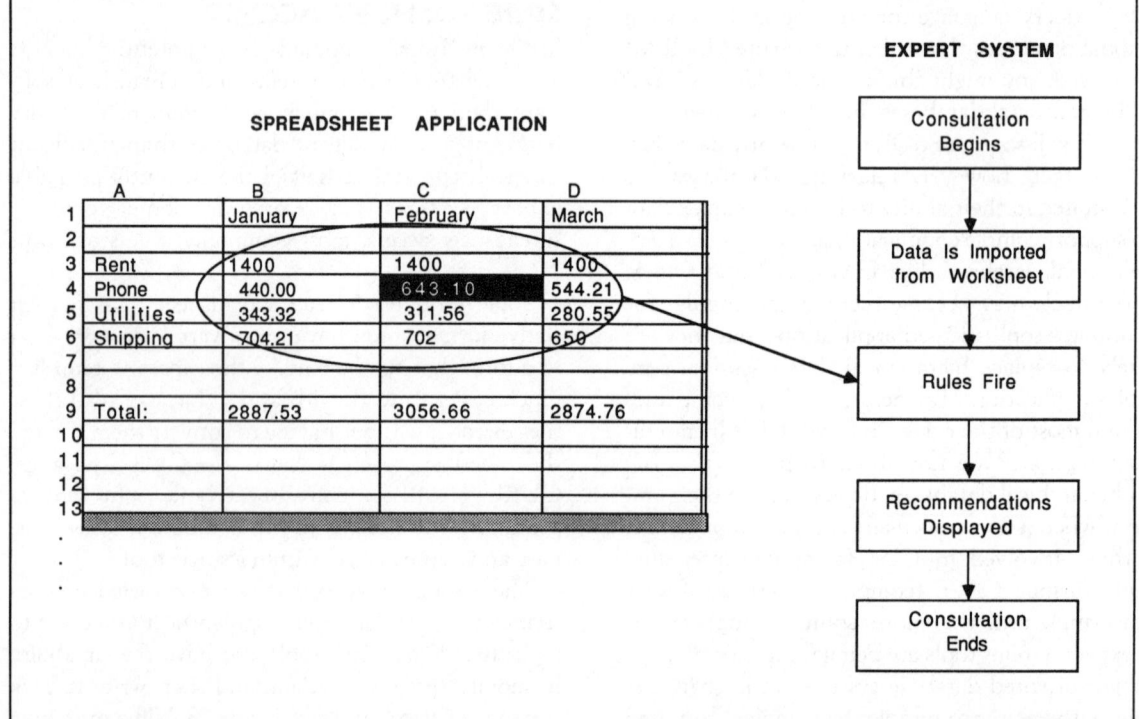

Figure 13.7 An expert system working with a spreadsheet program.

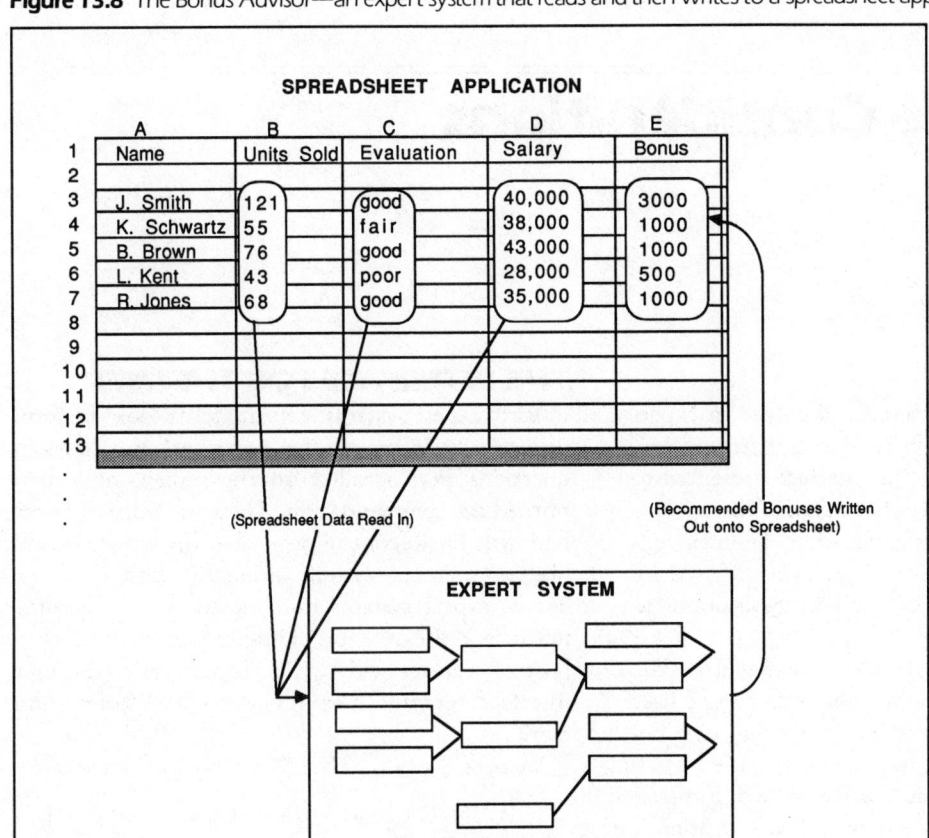

Figure 13.8 The Bonus Advisor—an expert system that reads and then writes to a spreadsheet application.

superior class of CASE products. Separately, object-oriented programming techniques are being used to design and develop a new class of databases that provide database developers with some of the representational power that is currently associated with the large hybrid object-oriented tools. The existence of object-oriented databases will undoubtedly inspire still more interesting expert systems tools and CASE products to take advantage of the new power of such databases, and so the technology evolves.

14.
Interface Considerations

INTRODUCTION

There are usually two interfaces involved in expert systems development. There is the interface presented by the tool itself—the interface presented to the knowledge engineers who will use the tool to develop an expert systems application. Then there is the interface the developer creates that is used by anyone who uses the expert systems applications to get advice.

This chapter examines interface issues from the point of view of the developer who is creating a user interface for an expert system. In general, the developer interface that the tool presents to the knowledge engineer is fixed. If it is well designed, it makes the development of an expert system much easier. It is important to consider the developer interface before you decide which tool to buy; once you've purchased a tool, the developer interface is simply something you have to live with.

The user interface, on the other hand, is created by means of the developer interface. Most tools provide you with many opportunities to tailor the user interface. You can usually control the appearance and flow of the consultation, and how it elicits information from the end user. If the tool lacks satisfactory support for user interface development, some knowledge engineers use other screen-building packages or graphics programs to create the exact screen they need for a particular application. In the long run, the development of the user interface contributes significantly to the success of the expert systems application. Thus, in this chapter, we give our attention only to user interface issues.

THE INTERFACE FOR THE USER

In early expert systems, consultations took the form of a *teletype interview*; the system asked a series of questions that scrolled up the screen, and then printed a recommendation. The knowledge engineer had little or no control over what the screen looked like, or how the system interacted with the user. Today, expert systems building tools have become much more flexible, providing the developer with a host of features with which to customize the user interface: graphics, windows, menus, forms, and more.

We consider how to build two kinds of systems:

1. *Advisory expert systems*. These systems ask a series of questions and then give a recommendation.
2. *Model world systems*. These systems show a graphic representation of a problem on the screen and allow the user to directly manipulate its elements.

We consider each in turn.

Building Advisory Systems

Most expert systems use an advisory format. The systems ask questions and evaluate the user's responses in order to provide a recommendation. These systems may use graphics in the process of asking questions, but the basic structure of the interaction is one of questions and answers.

There are six steps most developers follow when they build an advisory interface:

1. Evaluate interface needs
2. Provide an easy way to start the system
3. Design questions
4. Handle user inputs
5. Design explanations
6. Add graphics

We examine each of these steps in turn.

Step 1. Evaluating interface needs. In some systems, you need to give more consideration to an interface than with others. The Oracle Credit Advisor, for example, runs in batch mode and requires no user input at all. Consequently, no user interface was needed for it. Many small job aids need only a small amount of customizing of the default interface of a tool. Since they ask few questions and contain a small number of rules, a teletype interview may be sufficient.

Larger systems, on the other hand, may need to display information and elicit user information in much more complex ways. In these systems, the knowledge engineer needs to do a considerable amount of interface design.

Creating a primitive version of the user interface early on can speed development of a system. Sometimes called a *test interface*, it gives a way to test knowledge structures and rules as they are created, rather than after all the knowledge has been placed in the system. For example, a test interface might show graphic representations of three frames in the system and then let you experiment by putting values into them. This way you could make sure the frames behaved properly on their own before proceeding. You could use a test interface to make sure that the frames' constraints behaved properly, or that information was being inherited properly between related frames. This lets you actively test the functionality of different parts of the system instead of trying to suppose how they might behave by staring at their code.

In the AXLE training system, each of the sample knowledge base development projects covered make extensive use of test interfaces. In their canning plant diagnostic system, a test interface is built as soon as

the initial knowledge structure is in place. Figure 14.1 shows how it looks to the developer. It shows slots in some of the frames of the knowledge base. By pointing and clicking with the mouse, you can interact with the frames, changing slot values and executing rules. For example, if you put LOW into the box representing the OIL-AMOUNT slot in the WASH-PUMP frame, and then click on RUN SHUTDOWN RULES, rules begin to fire, setting the SHUTDOWN slots of frames WASHER-1 and WASH-PUMP to IMMEDIATELY. Figure 14.2 shows the modified screen after the rules have fired.

Many such test interfaces are created during the course of development of a system. Though they may build upon each other, test interfaces are usually not kept as part of the fielded system. Eventually, the test interface is thrown away and replaced by one tailored specifically to the end user.

Step 2. Providing an easy way to start the system. Many tools require users to give technical commands to begin a consultation. In some, the user gives a command to execute the tool, and then commands to load and run the knowledge base. Some even require the user to type in the goal for the knowledge base to pursue in order to get started. Ideally, a system should be started with the minimum amount of effort—a single command from the operating system.

Many tool vendors provide an efficient way to start an application when they compile systems into runtime versions. In effect, they eliminate all of the tool interface screens and provide the user with a single command that will immediately start the application.

Step 3. Designing Questions. The rules of the expert system are generally the property of the knowledge engineer and the expert, and can be in their language.

The part of the expert system with which the user interacts must be geared to the level of the user. If the user is a novice who knows nothing about the subject material, questions must be phrased using nontechnical language. In systems built by experts for

250 PROGRAM DEVELOPMENT

Figure 14.1 Changing a slot value in Albatheon's AXLE test interface.

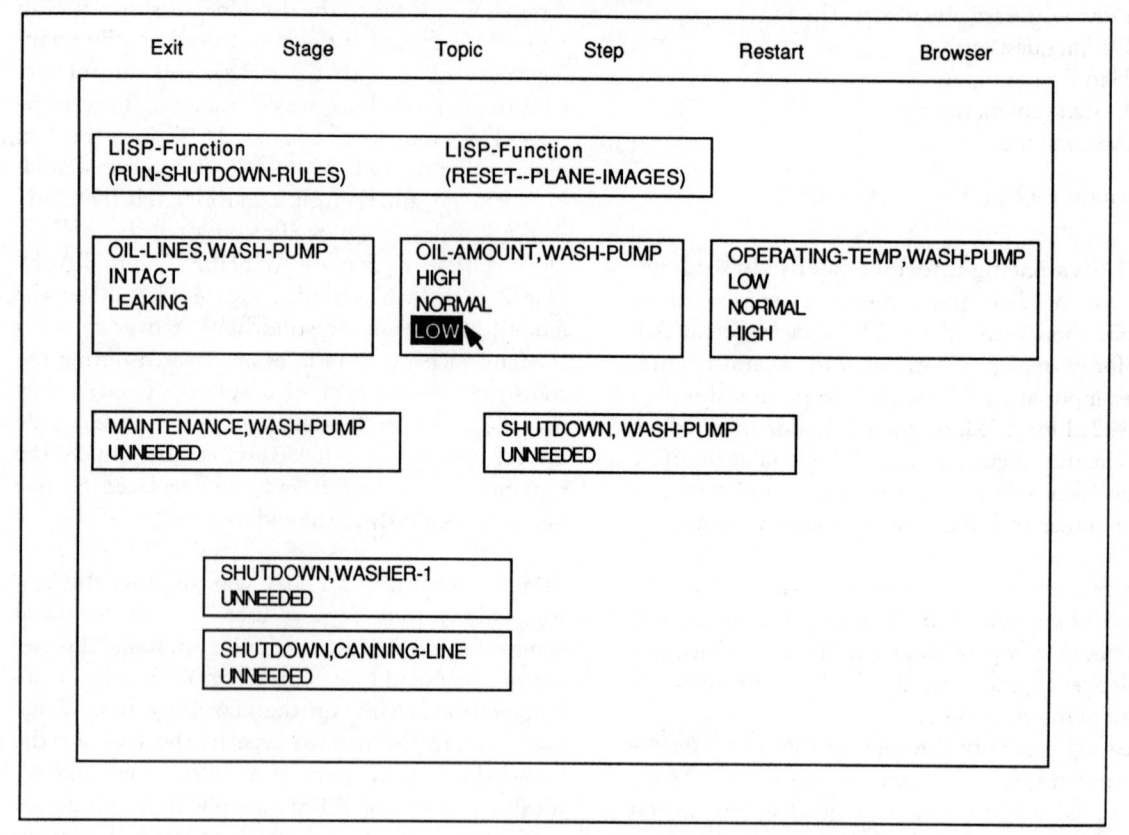

```
Exit      Stage      Topic      Step      Restart      Browser

   LISP-Function              LISP-Function
   (RUN-SHUTDOWN-RULES)       (RESET--PLANE-IMAGES)

   OIL-LINES,WASH-PUMP    OIL-AMOUNT,WASH-PUMP    OPERATING-TEMP,WASH-PUMP
   INTACT                 HIGH                    LOW
   LEAKING                NORMAL                  NORMAL
                          LOW                     HIGH

   MAINTENANCE,WASH-PUMP    SHUTDOWN, WASH-PUMP
   UNNEEDED                 UNNEEDED

        SHUTDOWN,WASHER-1
        UNNEEDED

        SHUTDOWN,CANNING-LINE
        UNNEEDED
```

others in their field, the questions may be phrased in the experts' terms.

In backward chaining systems, the questions generally follow a course from general to specific as the system zeros in on its recommendation. In most cases, the questions the system asks will be related to one another. For example, consider a system for finding faults in pipe equipment. As the system evaluates each condition in the rule below:

IF   leaking_part = pipe_a AND
           time = 10 days AND
           rust = yes
THEN suggest = replace_joint.

. . . it asks the following three questions:

Which part of the evaporator is leaking?

How long has this been occurring?

Is there rust on the joint?

These questions follow a trend from general to specific. If the tool clears the screen between each question, the questions need to be written so that they stand on their own and do not require the user to remember details from earlier questions. A fluid progression of questions helps give the impression of an underlying human intelligence at work.

Keep as many questions as possible on the screen, even after they have been answered by the user. This helps give the consultation more continuity by letting the user examine earlier responses while contemplating the question at hand.

Consider the first question above: "Which part of the evaporator is leaking?" By glancing at the rule, you know that an acceptable answer is "pipe." There could be many other names besides "pipe" that the user might type in to identify that part. Many systems arrange to put multiple choices on the screen. If they don't, the developer has to word the question in such a way that the user will know how to respond correctly. Thus, you might reword the question to read:

Which of the following evaporator parts are leaking: pipe, nozzle, or L-joint?

By the same token, you can tell from the rule that the second question requires information in terms of days, but the user may not make that same assumption. Thus, you should reword the question to read:

How many days has the evaporator been leaking?

Finally, to eliminate any ambiguity, and thus minimize the possibility of user frustration (that can kill otherwise useful expert systems applications), you can always add the user's options to the question:

Is there rust on the joint? (yes/no)

Ideally, you will have a tool that presents multiple choices. But if you don't, you should be certain that the correct answers are clearly presented to the user in the question itself.

Step 4. Handling User Inputs. There are two basic ways in which the user can answer a question: by making a menu selection or by typing something

Figure 14.2 Results of changes to slot values in Albatheon's AXLE test interface.

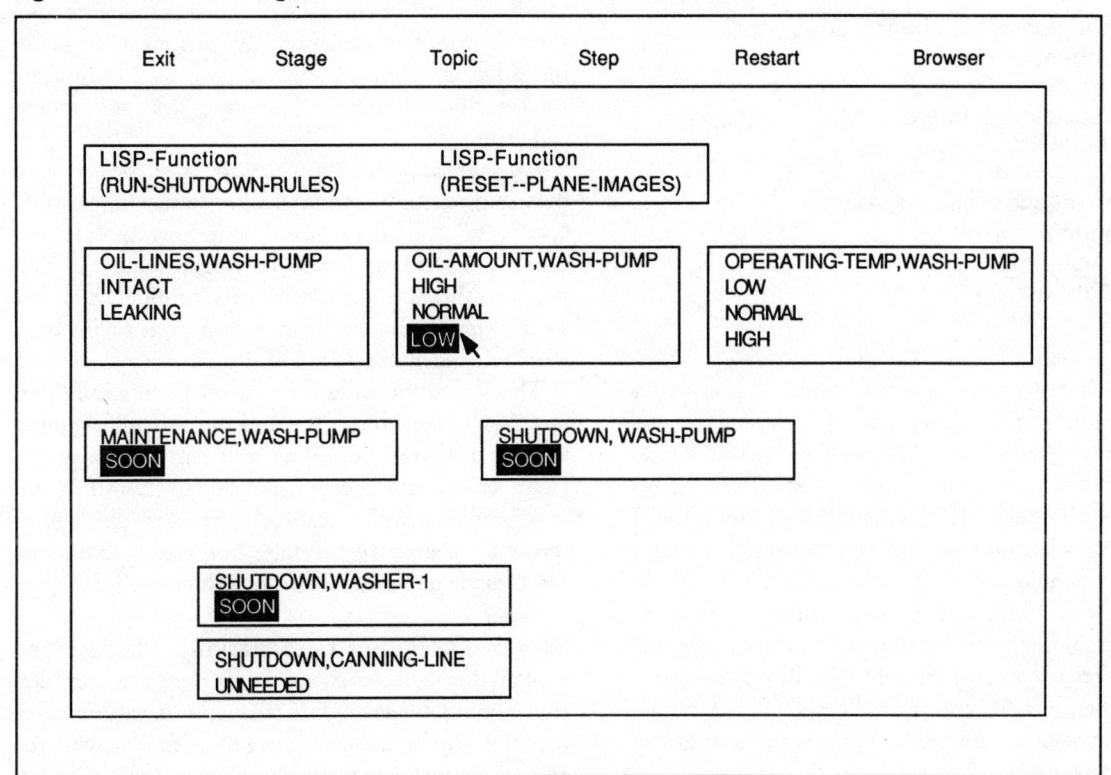

```
┌─────────────────────────────────────────────────────────────────────────┐
│   Exit        Stage         Topic        Step       Restart    Browser  │
│  ┌───────────────────────────────────────────────────────────────────┐  │
│  │ LISP-Function            LISP-Function                            │  │
│  │ (RUN-SHUTDOWN-RULES)     (RESET--PLANE-IMAGES)                    │  │
│  │                                                                   │  │
│  │ ┌──────────────────┐ ┌──────────────────┐ ┌────────────────────┐  │  │
│  │ │ OIL-LINES,WASH-  │ │ OIL-AMOUNT,WASH- │ │ OPERATING-TEMP,    │  │  │
│  │ │ PUMP             │ │ PUMP             │ │ WASH-PUMP          │  │  │
│  │ │ INTACT           │ │ HIGH             │ │ LOW                │  │  │
│  │ │ LEAKING          │ │ NORMAL           │ │ NORMAL             │  │  │
│  │ │                  │ │ ▐LOW▌            │ │ HIGH               │  │  │
│  │ └──────────────────┘ └──────────────────┘ └────────────────────┘  │  │
│  │                                                                   │  │
│  │ ┌──────────────────┐   ┌──────────────────────┐                   │  │
│  │ │ MAINTENANCE,     │   │ SHUTDOWN, WASH-PUMP  │                   │  │
│  │ │ WASH-PUMP        │   │ ▐SOON▌               │                   │  │
│  │ │ ▐SOON▌           │   └──────────────────────┘                   │  │
│  │ └──────────────────┘                                              │  │
│  │                                                                   │  │
│  │      ┌──────────────────────┐                                     │  │
│  │      │ SHUTDOWN,WASHER-1    │                                     │  │
│  │      │ ▐SOON▌               │                                     │  │
│  │      └──────────────────────┘                                     │  │
│  │      ┌──────────────────────┐                                     │  │
│  │      │ SHUTDOWN,CANNING-LINE│                                     │  │
│  │      │ UNNEEDED             │                                     │  │
│  │      └──────────────────────┘                                     │  │
│  └───────────────────────────────────────────────────────────────────┘  │
└─────────────────────────────────────────────────────────────────────────┘
```

on the keyboard. Menus are best when there is a predefined set of possible answers that the user can give. Typed inputs are necessary when you cannot anticipate the range of legal answers, or there are too many to fit in a reasonably sized menu. In the latter case, you can reduce the size of the menu by breaking the question into several subquestions. For example, the following question would need to present a menu of 50 choices:

>Which state does your dependent live in?
>>Alabama
>>Alaska
>>Arizona
>>. . .

A more sensible approach would be to break this into several questions. First, you could have the system ask the user for the general region she was interested in, followed by a second question that listed only the states within that area:

>What region of the country does your dependent live in?
>>South
>>Eastern Seaboard
>>Midwest
>>. . .
>
>Which southern state does your dependent live in?
>>Alabama
>>Georgia
>>. . .

These subquestions limit the menu of states to a manageable size. Another way of handling a large number of choices is to use *scrolling menus*. These allow menus to have more options than will fit on the screen at once. By moving to the extremities of the menu selection box, the user can scroll through additional choices.

If you are confident that users will enter information that is valid and complete, you need to make little effort to monitor their inputs. If, on the other hand, there is a likelihood that users will make mistakes, you should take measures to ensure that errors will be detected and handled properly.

Most tools offer features to help you determine whether the user inputs are valid. Using techniques like *type checking* and *range checking*, you can test the user's input and reject anything that is found to be invalid. Type checking checks whether input data is of the desired type. For example, if the system is looking for an integer, then any noninteger inputs will be rejected. Range checking makes sure inputs fall within a numerical range. For example, if the system asked for a patient's temperature, range checking could be used to restrict the answer to a range from 95 to 110 degrees.

Most tools also allow a certainty factor to be provided along with the user input. Some tools use graphics to make certainty factors seem less abstract to the user. Level5 shows a speedometerlike bar at the bottom of the screen. Its width indicates the certainty factor being selected. Texas Instrument's decision-support package, Arborist, uses a pie chart to show certainty. As the user increases the certainty factor, the size of the slice of pie grows. Figure 14.3 shows a sample screen from the Syntelligence Lending Advisor system. A shaded bar is used to indicate the certainty of factors in assessing risk for commercial insurance.

Another approach is to let the user pick a word describing certainty from a set of terms: "probably," "possibly," and so on. Each term corresponds to a numerical certainty factor. Although some precision is lost in this approach, users pick confidence factors so arbitrarily anyway that this may actually be a more reliable method.

This last point raises an issue common to all interface design. New hardware and software allow graphics that are very appealing and easy to construct. However, it is not always preferable to show information graphically. For example, graphic displays of certainty levels give the false impression that users can provide more information with greater precision.

Step 5. Designing Explanations. Messages and explanations presented to a user during a consultation should be geared to the appropriate level of expertise. If the user is a novice unfamiliar with the expert's terminology, then you must write messages

Figure 14.3 *Sample screen from Syntelligence's Lending Advisor.*

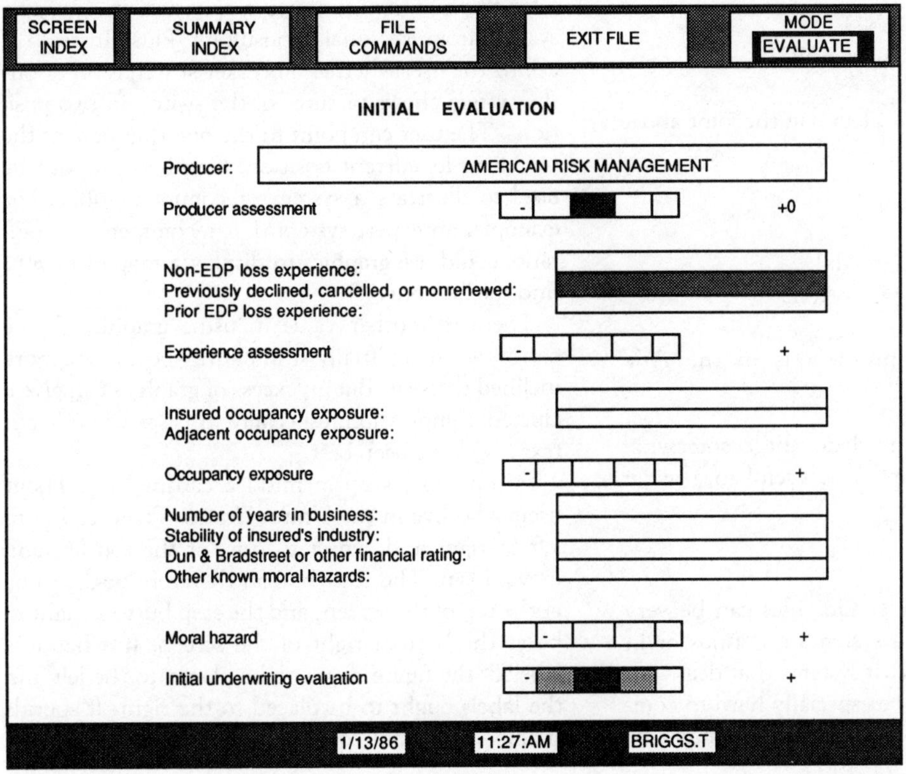

in a form that does not rely on the expert's terminology. If, on the other hand, the users are themselves skilled technicians, it is acceptable to have the system's text in technical terms.

If your system is intended to be used by audiences of varying levels of technical expertise, you may want it to have an adjustable level of explanation for the user, as was done with Boole & Babbage's DASD Advisor. Experts, technicians, and nontechnicians are all potential users of the product. However, each needs to see recommendations in a different way. A nontechnician could not understand the kind of advice that might be given to an expert. An expert would find advice geared to a novice obvious and verbose. Messages were therefore constructed to tailor advice to the level of the current user. This was done using the *conditional text* feature of ADS. The system uses flags embedded in the text to determine which parts need to be included or suppressed in printed messages. Figure 14.4 shows a portion of a message from DASD Advisor (written in AION's ADS tool), which includes embedded variables.

If you are using a tool that does not support conditional text in messages, there are other ways to give your system an adjustable level of explanations. One way is to create an attribute called LEVEL, which stores the level of the expert. At the beginning of the consultation, the system asks whether the user is a novice, a technician, or an expert. It then creates multiple versions of every rule that prints advice, each having text geared to different users of the system.

For example, during a consultation, one of the following rules would fire, depending on the value of LEVEL. It would print out a recommendation phrased for the appropriate audience:

Rule 335

IF   level = novice AND
           joint_problem = yes AND
           location = AV
THEN display "The problem is in the joint above the oil tank."

Rule 336

IF   level = technician AND
           joint_problem = yes AND
           location = AV
THEN display "The problem is in the A-V joint."

While this makes the knowledge base somewhat larger, it allows the system to be useful to a wider audience.

Step 6. Adding Graphics. Graphics can be very helpful in supplementing a system's questions or in showing its conclusions. With systems that deal with complex hardware, it can be especially hard to communicate in language those concepts that might be easily illustrated with a picture. Figure 14.5 shows how graphics can enhance a question in a sample system from Personal Consultant Plus. Instead of asking the user whether a breaker switch is on or off, the system shows pictures of the switch in two positions. The user can point to the one that depicts the switch in its current position. Graphics can also be used to illustrate a system's recommendations. For example, an expert system that recommends restaurants could use graphics to display a map of how to find the best one.

There is another value in using graphics: If the consultation is visually stimulating, people are more inclined to use it. But an excess of graphics can give a cluttered impression, especially in cases where plain text may have been best.

In any case, keep in mind a cardinal rule about users who live in the United States. They read from left to right and expect to start at the top left and move down. The start button therefore ought to be at the top of the screen, and the stop button ought to be at the bottom right of the screen. If a figure is labeled, the figure ought to be placed to the left and the labels ought to be placed to the right. It sounds simple, but many people lay out screens without

Figure 14.4 A sample message from AION's ADS.

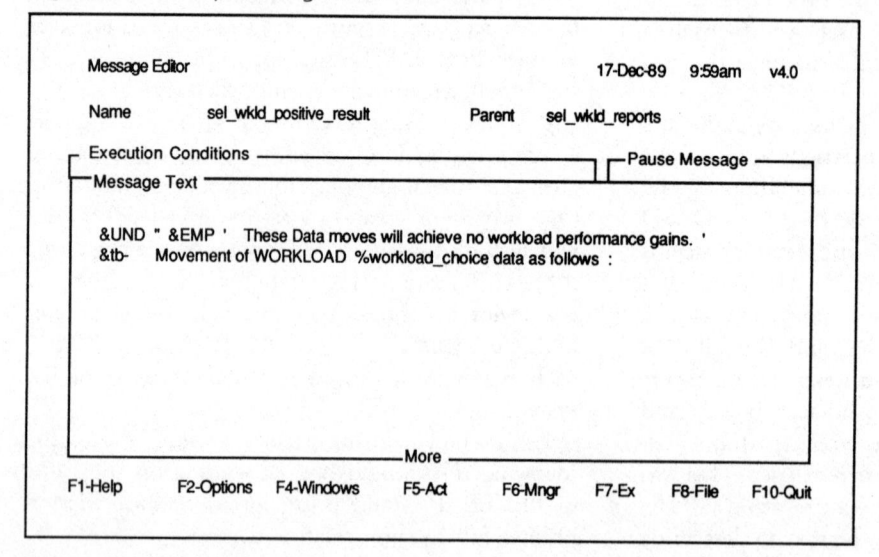

Figure 14.5 Graphics to enhance a question.

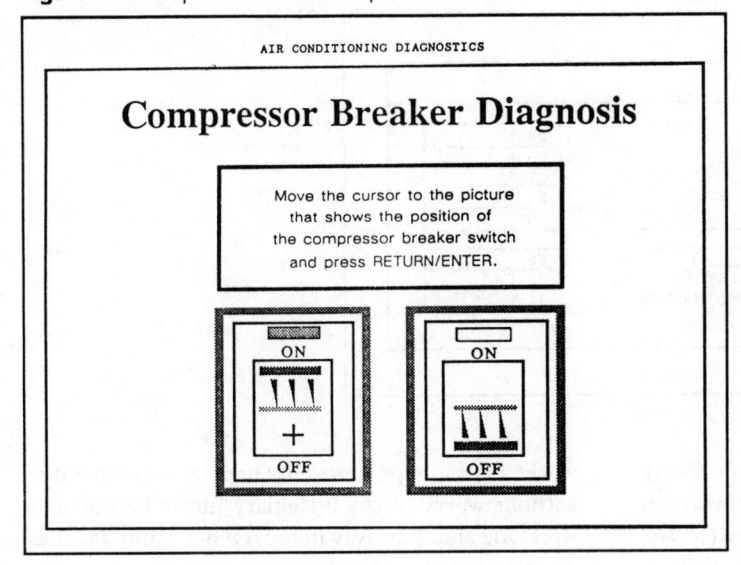

```
           AIR CONDITIONING DIAGNOSTICS

         Compressor Breaker Diagnosis

              Move the cursor to the picture
              that shows the position of
              the compressor breaker switch
              and press RETURN/ENTER.

                  ┌──────┐        ┌──────┐
                  │  ON  │        │  ON  │
                  │ ↓↓↓  │        │ ↓↓↓  │
                  │  +   │        │ ───  │
                  │ OFF  │        │ OFF  │
                  └──────┘        └──────┘
```

considering these elementary truths. People can usually still decode the screen, but it takes more time and is more frustrating.

The user interface developer ought to do everything he can to make the user interface easy and efficient to use. Consider an application that will be used by 10 users once a week for a year. That's about 500 uses per year. If the user interface is laid out in a way that takes the user 30 seconds longer to comprehend and respond than it would if it were laid out slightly better, that amounts to over 4 hours of wasted user time each year. If there are 100 users, it's 40 hours of wasted time. And that's a lot of accumulated frustration. If you can spend a half hour and clean up a screen design that will save all these people both the time and frustration of working with a poor screen design, it's worth much more than just the time that will be saved.

A good way to be sure that user interface screens are effectively designed is to test the screens with users. Ask the users what works and what doesn't. Ask them if the questions are worded in a readable and understandable way. Ask them if their eyes move smoothly across the screen from the top left to the bottom right, and so on. A few minutes of attention up front will save many complaints later, and it may make the difference between a system that is used and one that is never popular and hence never used.

Interfaces to Model World Systems

Students who doze through chemistry lectures may become much more interested when given the opportunity to explore the principles themselves in a lab experiment. It is a more participatory, more tactile, and usually a more stimulating experience. In a similar way, you can design the interface to an expert system to encourage users' experimentation, initiative, and continued use.

While advisory systems proceed like interviews, *model world systems* proceed like simulations. For example, while a tax advisory system might print 10 questions, a model world system would have the user fill out a replica of a tax form. (Such a form, created in TI's IMAGES package, is shown in Figure 14.6.) A model world system for diagnosing problems with an air conditioning system shows a diagram of the parts of the air conditioning system. (See Figure 14.7.) The user can open and close valves, read meters, and see the system in action.

Figure 14.6 Tax form replica from TI's Personal Consultant Plus.

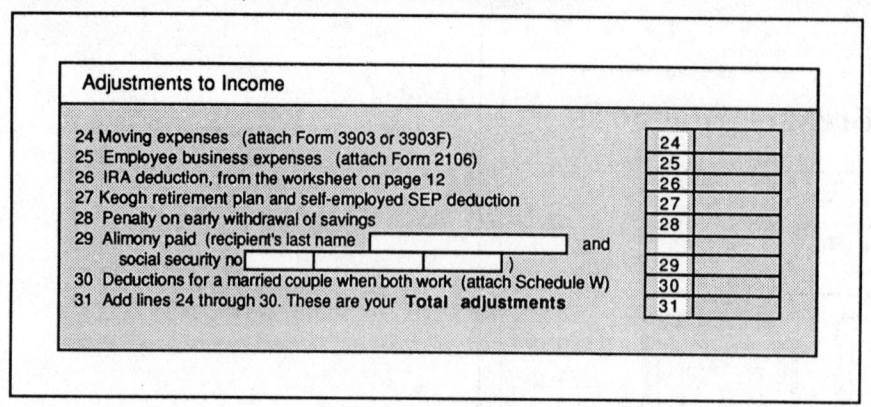

Adjustments to Income	
24 Moving expenses (attach Form 3903 or 3903F)	24
25 Employee business expenses (attach Form 2106)	25
26 IRA deduction, from the worksheet on page 12	26
27 Keogh retirement plan and self-employed SEP deduction	27
28 Penalty on early withdrawal of savings	28
29 Alimony paid (recipient's last name [ ] and social security no [ ])	29
30 Deductions for a married couple when both work (attach Schedule W)	30
31 Add lines 24 through 30. These are your **Total adjustments**	31

Once diagnostic systems grow to a point where they contain a detailed model of the domain, you can push them a step further to actually simulate the model at work. The user can feed in hypothetical situations and see what kind of advice the system will give. Such systems come close to being simulations of a process. They let the user set up scenarios that might be too dangerous, time-consuming, or costly to attempt in real life. The user can work in the safe world of the expert system, happily experimenting without worry of the imaginary havoc he might be wreaking along the way in broken parts and damaged plants.

The interface of a model world system may incorporate some of the features of advisory systems, but it gives much more consideration to graphics and knowledge modeling. The construction of a model world interface is divided into two primary areas:

Figure 14.7 Air conditioning system from TI's Personal Consultant Plus.

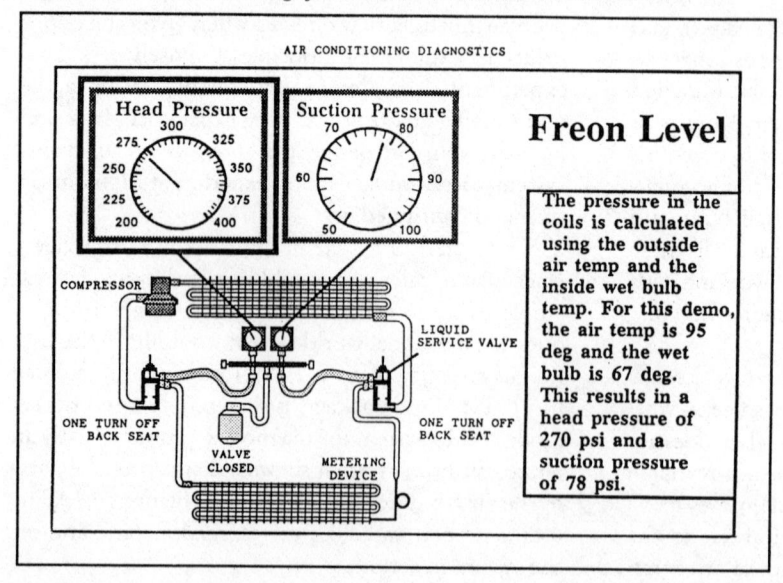

AIR CONDITIONING DIAGNOSTICS

Freon Level

The pressure in the coils is calculated using the outside air temp and the inside wet bulb temp. For this demo, the air temp is 95 deg and the wet bulb is 67 deg. This results in a head pressure of 270 psi and a suction pressure of 78 psi.

designing the elements of the screen, and inputting the knowledge to make it behave properly. The design of the visual element is largely an art—picking the right images and composing them to make the most informative, easy-to-use interface. Model world systems also have special hardware needs in order to display images and let the user interact with them.

The building block for a model world system is the *dynamic image*. These are predefined images you can use to piece together a screen display—dials, gauges, selection boxes, bar graphs, and so on. You can combine them to replicate real control panels, business forms, manufacturing plants, and much more. Some tools even allow you to construct your own images, or modify existing ones in cases where the predefined set of images is insufficient to build a model.

Each image is linked to a value in the knowledge base. This may be the value of a variable (as in VP-Expert), or the value of a slot in a frame (as in GoldWorks). Whenever this value changes, the image that it is linked to is automatically redrawn to reflect the change. For example, in Personal Consultant-Plus, a thermometer image could be linked to the parameter called TEMP. If the value of TEMP is 30 at the start of the consultation, a thermometer would be drawn on the screen with its mercury level shown at the level 30. If a rule later fired and set the value of TEMP to 110, the system would automatically redraw the thermometer with the temperature at the new level. Using images in this way, you can create animated objects that mirror the current state of knowledge base values.

In the temperature example, the thermometer worked as an *output image*, printing values from the knowledge base onto the screen. *Input images* work the opposite way: Whenever the user manipulates them on the screen, the values they are linked to in the knowledge base change. Using the mouse, the user can point to the dynamic image that corresponds to the variable she would like to supply. Figure 14.8 shows the thermometer image used for both input and output. It is used to display air temperature, as indicated by the length of the shaded region.

Figure 14.8 Thermometer image in TI's Personal Consultant Plus.

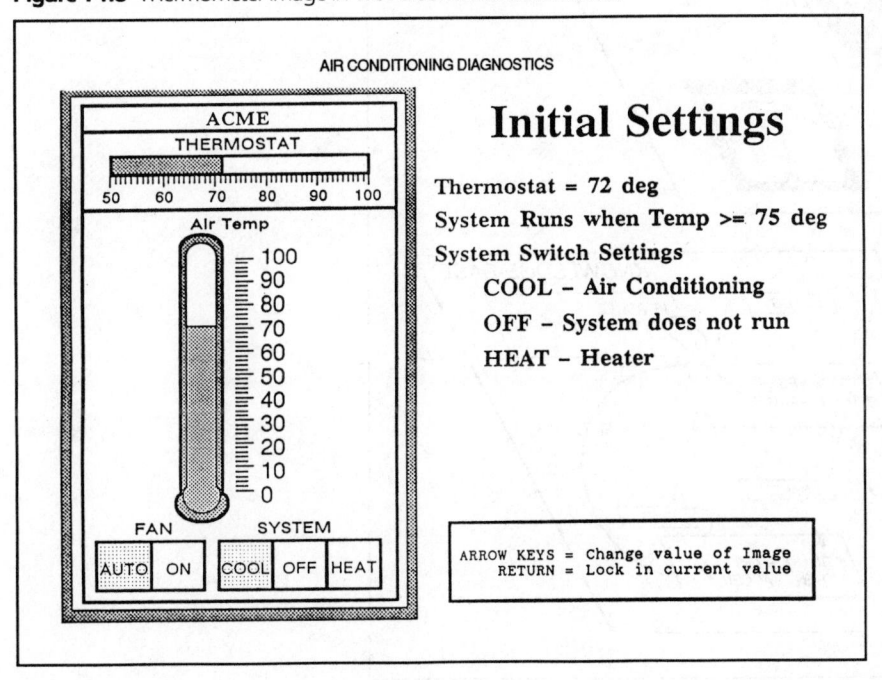

```
                    AIR CONDITIONING DIAGNOSTICS

         ACME                    Initial Settings
       THERMOSTAT
   |||||||||||||||||||        Thermostat = 72 deg
   50  60  70  80  90  100    System Runs when Temp >= 75 deg
         Air Temp             System Switch Settings
              ≡ 100              COOL - Air Conditioning
              ≡ 90               OFF - System does not run
              ≡ 80               HEAT - Heater
              ≡ 70
              ≡ 60
              ≡ 50
              ≡ 40
              ≡ 30
              ≡ 20
              ≡ 10
              ≡ 0
     FAN      SYSTEM          ARROW KEYS = Change value of Image
  |AUTO| ON |COOL|OFF|HEAT|    RETURN    = Lock in current value
```

The user can also use the arrow key to set its value; pressing RETURN will enter that value into the knowledge base.

When building a model world system, you need to find a balance between reality and ease of use. There are important advantages in literally representing a problem's domain on the screen. It is more quickly accepted by experts and users, who can readily recognize the display as the environment of the problem as they know it. However, it is not always best to be completely literal in a model; it may be better to sacrifice some realism in order to make information easier to understand. Elements of the model can be distorted and stylized to make the display more informative. For instance, a diagnostic system could enlarge malfunctioning plant components, or omit irrelevant plant components from the screen.

There are certain capabilities a tool must have if it is to allow you to build model world systems easily. Model world systems allow the user to feed in new information at arbitrary times, regardless of the system's current goal or state. When this occurs, the system needs to stop whatever it's doing, accept the new information, and propagate its effects throughout the rest of the knowledge base. For example, an industrial simulation could be modeling a plant behaving normally when the user unexpectedly simulates a loss of pressure in a pump. To maintain

Figure 14.9 VP-Expert car simulation.

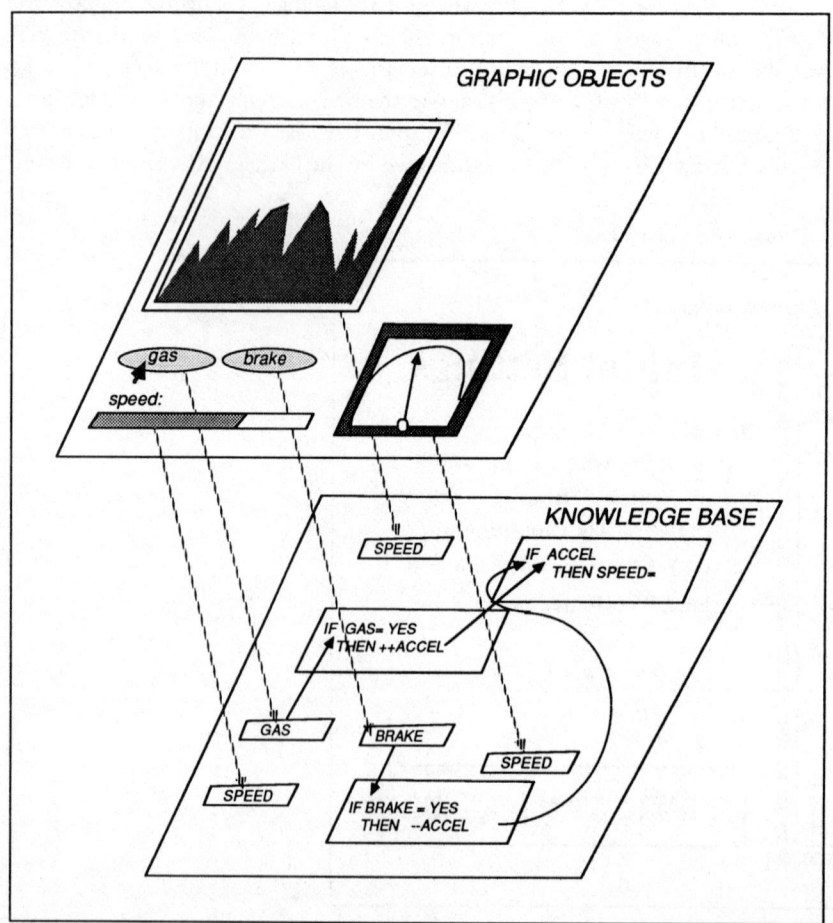

the realism of the simulation, the system would have to immediately lower the pressure of all of the components connected to the pump.

There is always a delay, however slight, between the time when the user selects an action and the time when its results show up on the screen. But in some cases, even a slight delay can break the illusion that the user is interacting with real components in the domain world. You need to keep this issue in mind while developing the expert system, since the way in which knowledge is modeled affects the speed with which the system reacts to user initiatives. Demons are usually faster than rules at triggering immediate actions when such a situation arises. This is because demons are linked directly to the objects and fire immediately when the objects take on certain values. Rules take longer, since the system has to seek out a rule and evaluate it before it can fire and have an effect.

A Car Simulation. Figure 14.9 shows the graphic objects used by a VP-Expert system that simulates a car's acceleration. The figure shows both the graphic objects that are displayed on the screen and the knowledge base rules and variables that they are linked to.

For example, the speedometer shown at the bottom right-hand part of the screen is an instance of the graphic object Meter. The speedometer is linked to the variable named SPEED. Note that the link is bidirectional: Whenever the user manually adjusts the speedometer, the value of SPEED is changed, and whenever the value of SPEED is set by a rule, the meter is redrawn on the screen.

Two other graphic objects are also linked to the SPEED variable: a Track object, and an Hgauge object. The Track graphic object (shown in the upper left of the display) creates a graph of the change in speed over time. The Hgauge (shown across the bottom of the screen) shows the current speed of the car as a horizontal bar. The two ovals above the Hgauge are Lbutton objects, which are used to create buttons to simulate the car's brake pedal and accelerator.

Figure 14.9 also shows the three forward chaining rules that the system uses. (VP-Expert calls forward chaining rules "whenever rules.") Each of these rules is linked to a variable's value. Whenever the value changes, the forward chaining that it is linked to is evaluated. When it passes, the rule can change the value of another variable which, in turn, may cause still more forward chaining rules to fire.

For example, consider the forward chaining rule "IF Brake = YES THEN Accel = Accel + 1." The rule fires when BRAKE is set to YES by the user pressing on the BRAKE button. After the rule fires, the value of ACCEL is increased by 1. This, in turn, causes "whenever Rule 3" to fire, which updates the car's speed depending on its acceleration. Lastly, all three graphic objects linked to SPEED are automatically redrawn to reflect the new value of SPEED.

The following is a listing of the car simulation knowledge base from VP-Expert.

ACTIONS
```
GMODE 14
done = NO
gas = NO
brake = NO
speed = 0
time = 0
whiletrue done = no then
     time = (time + 1)
end
tmode;

whenever 1
if gas = YES
then
accel = (accel + 1);

whenever 2
if brake = YES
then
accel = (accel − 1):

whenever 3
if accel < > unknown
then speed = (accel*time)
     time = 0;

meter speed: 250,120,0,100,1,7,1;
track speed: 10,10,0,100;
hgauge speed: 25,170,0,1,7,1;
lbutton brake: 5,17,7,1,Brakes;
lbutton gas: 17,17,7,10,Gas;
```

A form-based system. A promising new area of model world systems is that of forms—expert systems that imitate real business forms. The user uses the mouse to fill out the form while assisted by the system's advice. Forms can also be used as front ends to a database system. Instead of adding new records to a database with a database package, you could use a form-based expert system as a front end to a database to check to make sure that data is consistent and complete before adding it to the database.

The first step in creating a form-based system is to design a graphic model of the form on the screen. Its text, logos, boxes, and fields can all be modeled on the screen using dynamic images and graphics. Next, implement the images and the knowledge structures they are linked to. Lastly, add rules or demons to help the user fill out the form. You can use demons to trigger immediate action when the user fills in a certain value in the form. You can use rules in the same way as long as there is a method to get the system to evaluate them at the proper time. You can use rules or demons to accomplish three things in a form-based system:

1. *Modify the structure of the form.* You can use rules to remove irrelevant fields from the form, or to add newly relevant fields. For example, a rule could make sure that if the user has checked the "unemployed" box, the "business address" field is removed from the form. Another rule could say that if the user fills in that she has two dependents, the system should display two new fields on the form in which to enter their names.
2. *Maintain consistency between parts of the form.* You can use rules to alert the user to contradictory information supplied in the form. For example, they could alert the user if he supplies an area code that doesn't correspond to the given city.
3. *Offer guidance and advice.* For example, you can use rules to display a message about opening an IRA if a tax form does not have enough deductions. Figure 14.10 shows a sample screen from ENFORM, a domain-specific tool for creating form-based systems. As the user fills in the form, the system opens up a window to offer advice.

We will now illustrate the steps in building a form-based expert system. We start with a paper form, and convert it into a Personal Consultant Plus knowledge base using TI's add-in IMAGES graphics package. First, we analyze the paper form and convert it into a screen display composed of dynamic images linked to parameters (attributes in Personal Consultant Plus). We then supplement the system with rules that will help users fill out the form.

Our hypothetical case is the registration form for Ornville University. At Ornville, they have used paper registration forms for years. To make registration easier, the university has decided to give students the option to enroll for their classes on computer terminals in the Student Union. This is better for the students: They can register quickly and know that their registration forms are valid, since they have been verified by the computer. It is also better for the university, since it reduces the amount of data entry the clerical employees must do.

The existing registration form is shown in Figure 14.11. The back of the form contains the following instructions to the student: "First, check a box to indicate if you are a graduate or undergraduate. Undergraduates also need to check the box indicating standing: Freshman, Sophomore, Junior, or Senior, as well as a box to indicate the college you are enrolled in. Provide your complete name, address, and phone number. In the spaces at the bottom of the form, list the courses you want to take, followed by their departments, units, and the grading option you want. Fill in the total number of units of your course load in the space at the bottom of the page. Students are limited to a minimum of 8 units and a maximum of 20 units per semester. The Dean's approval is required to take a larger course load."

Examining the form, you should realize several things. There are various kinds of fields in the form—blank spaces where information is typed, and boxes that can be checked. These could translate into three kinds of dynamic images: *forms input, vertical selection box,* and *horizontal selection box.* Also notice that

Figure 14.10 A sample of Mind Path Technologies' ENFORM screen.

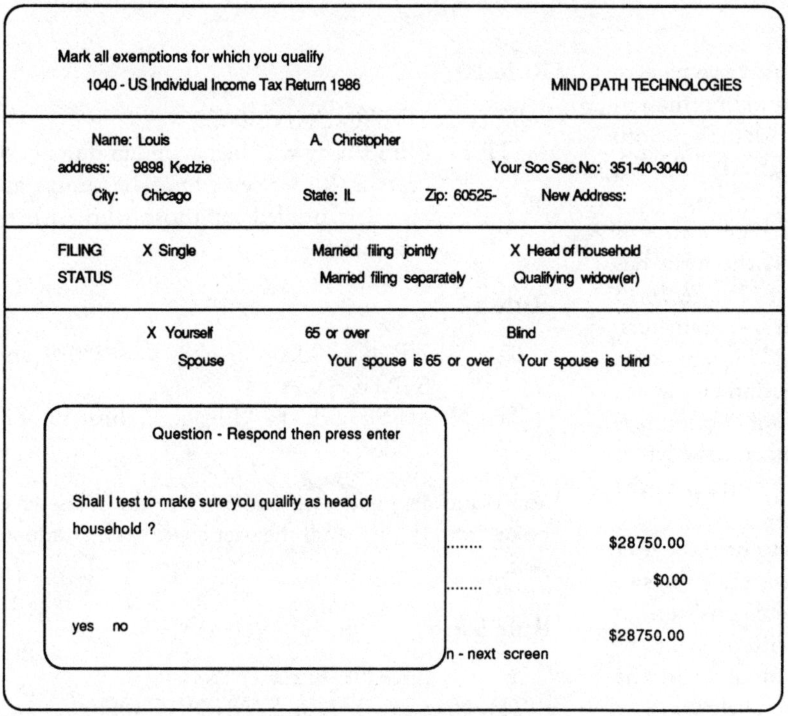

```
Mark all exemptions for which you qualify
    1040 - US Individual Income Tax Return 1986            MIND PATH TECHNOLOGIES

    Name:   Louis              A. Christopher
address:    9898 Kedzie                    Your Soc Sec No:  351-40-3040
    City:   Chicago        State: IL    Zip: 60525-    New Address:

FILING      X Single        Married filing jointly      X Head of household
STATUS                      Married filing separately    Qualifying widow(er)

            X Yourself      65 or over              Blind
              Spouse        Your spouse is 65 or over   Your spouse is blind

    ┌─────────────────────────────────────────┐
    │       Question - Respond then press enter│
    │                                         │
    │   Shall I test to make sure you qualify as head of
    │   household ?                           │
    │                                 ........    $28750.00
    │                                 ........        $0.00
    │   yes   no                                  $28750.00
    │                              n - next screen
    └─────────────────────────────────────────┘
```

Figure 14.11 The existing paper form.

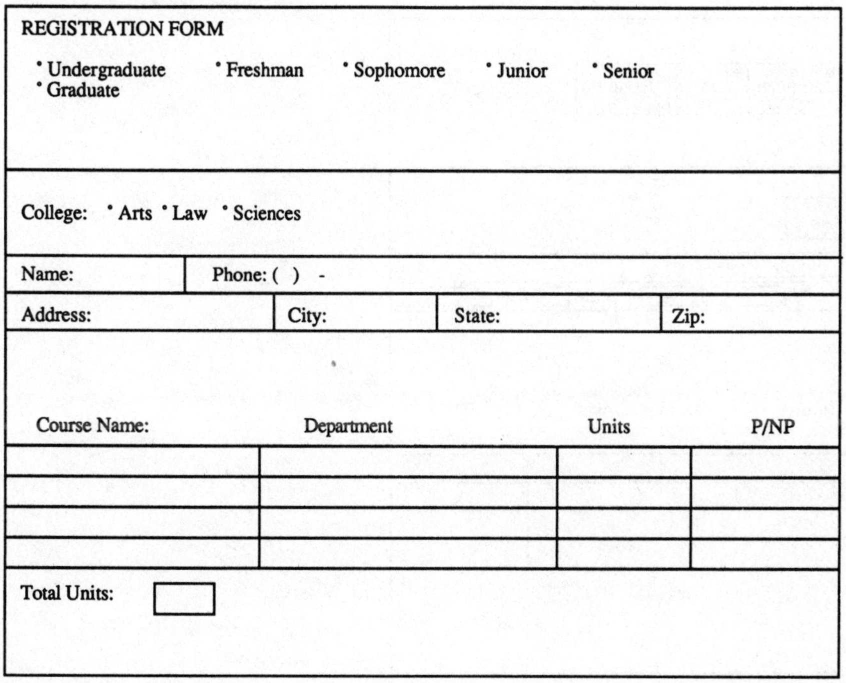

REGISTRATION FORM
• Undergraduate   • Freshman   • Sophomore   • Junior   • Senior • Graduate
College: • Arts • Law • Sciences

Name:	Phone: ( ) -			
Address:	City:	State:		Zip:

Course Name:	Department	Units	P/NP

Total Units: [   ]

information on the form is divided into two categories: information about the student, and information about the course load. You might translate these into various parameters like NAME, TOTAL_UNITS, and STATUS.

Our first implementation of a screen layout is shown in Figure 14.12. Each field in the form has been modeled with a dynamic image. Figure 14.13 shows how several images are linked to parameters: Class standing is stored in the STATUS parameter, which is linked to the horizontal selection box image at the top of the screen. The total number of units is stored in the TOTAL UNITS parameter, which is linked to a forms input image at the bottom of the screen.

Next, you can begin to write rules to help the user fill out the form. You could add consistency rules to make sure the State and Zip fields were consistent in the address. You could also use consistency rules to make sure that the total number of units in the course load do not surpass 20, as shown below.

Rule 10

IF   TOTAL-UNITS > 20
THEN MESSAGE = "The maximum number of units is 20 per semester. The dean's approval is needed for those who wish to take more."

Rule 12

IF   ZIP >= 90000 or ZIP <= 96099 and STATE = CA
THEN MESSAGE = "Illegal California Zip Code."

You could also add a rule to remove the Class level boxes from the screen if the user checks the Graduate box.

Rule 5

IF   GRADUATE = YES
THEN SET-IMAGE STANDING OFF.

Figure 14.12 The simulated form.

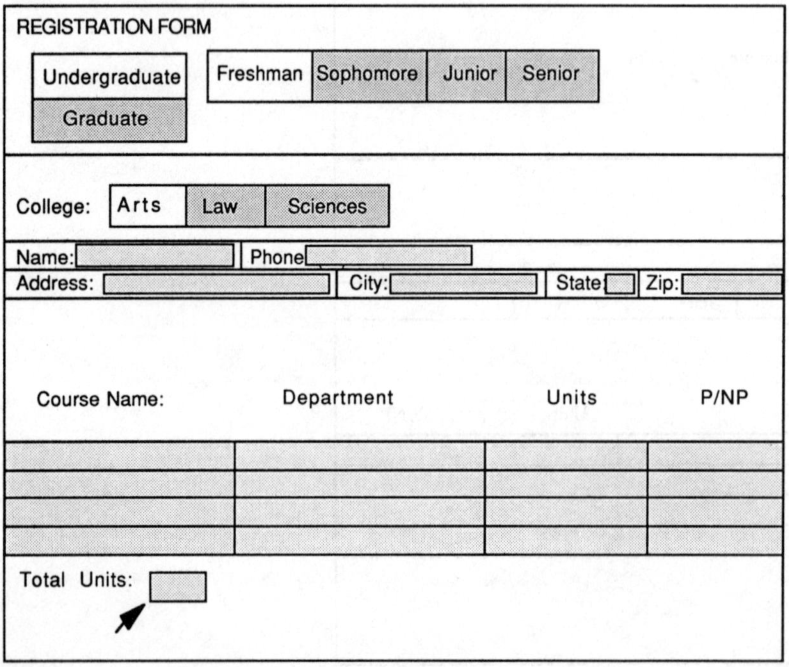

Interface Considerations 263

Figure 14.13 Images used by the simulated form.

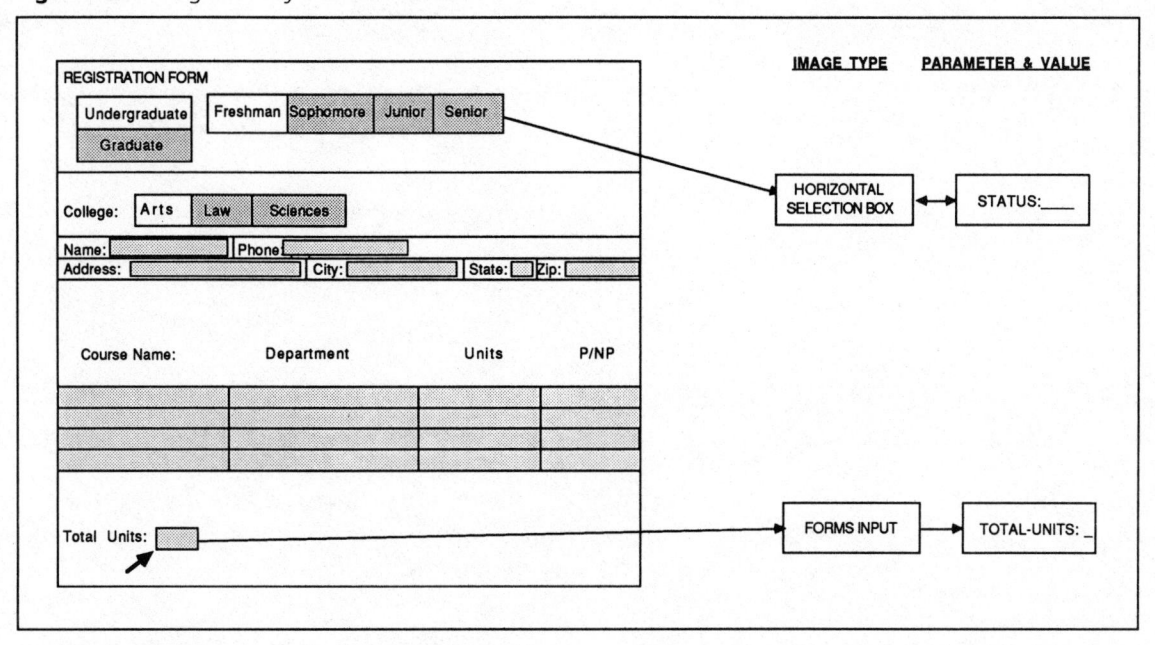

SUMMARY

Screen design is still more of an art than a science, but it's very important if you want to develop a successful expert systems application. It's not unusual for a developer to spend 30 to 40 percent of the total development time on the user interface alone. (Just as developers prefer to work with tools that provide good developer interfaces, users prefer to use applications that are fast, efficient, and intuitive to use.)

The primary rules are *never trick the user, test the interface with users,* and *always assume the user is right.* Don't ask questions that leave the user at a loss as to how to answer them. Test and retest the application with typical users. Ask for the users' opinions about what seems reasonable to them and what they find difficult—then follow that advice. A little extra care in designing the interface of your application will be more than rewarded by user acceptance and appreciation.

Section Five

MANAGING THE DEVELOPMENT OF EXPERT SYSTEMS

This section contains only one chapter. That chapter describes the development of an expert system from a manager's perspective. It considers what needs to happen when, and who needs to make it happen. In effect, this chapter is a summary of the entire book. In earlier chapters, we discussed basic concepts and techniques, how to analyze the behavioral and cognitive aspects of problems, and the specific problems associated with developing different types of expert systems. In this chapter, we pull it all together and try to describe how all of these techniques and skills must be orchestrated in order to create a successful application.

15.
Managing an Expert Systems Development Effort

INTRODUCTION

This chapter summarizes and integrates the concepts we have discussed throughout this book. It provides advice to someone who is asked to manage the development of an expert system. The chapter is structured around a schedule for the development effort. Along the way, we summarize some of the most important heuristics that we have introduced in previous chapters.

We consider here a generic procedure for managing the development of an expert system. Our overall procedure has six phases:

1. Front end analysis
2. Analysis and design
3. Prototype development
4. Systems development
5. Testing and implementation
6. Maintenance

Figure 15.1 provides an overview of the people and the phases involved in developing an expert system.

The overall schedule we have used to structure this chapter is derived from a planning program that we actually use to guide the development of expert systems. By filling in some concrete numbers in our planning software package, you could use this program to schedule and budget your own project.

In reality, of course, things are never as neat as our schedule assumes they are. Changes in any one phase often require that earlier phases be reconsidered. Moreover, depending on the size of the project, some steps that we describe sequentially may be done in parallel. Given that qualification, the sections that follow should help you organize in a systematic way the many different ideas we have discussed.

PHASE 1. FRONT END ANALYSIS

Overview

The first phase in the development of an expert system involves determining what kind of effort your organization wants to undertake, considering several potential applications, and then selecting an application to actually try. This phase usually ends with a report or presentation that identifies the application and formalizes some sort of consensus to proceed with the effort. Figure 15.2 provides an overview of the main tasks that need to be accomplished during this phase of the project.

Project Management

Assuming that this is your first project, you will be assembling your project team as you go. For the purposes of our discussion, we will assume that someone has already been hired to manage the project. We will also assume that the project manager will have the initial responsibility for selling management on an expert systems effort, selecting a specific project, and then hiring developers and programmers to work on the project.

Figure 15.1 Overview of the roles and phases of a mid-size expert systems development project.

PHASES / ROLES	1. Front End Analysis	2. Analysis & Design	3. Prototype Development	4. System Development	5. Testing & Implementation	6. Maintenance
Senior Management	Active		Active			
Project Management	Active	Active	Active	Active	Active	Active
E.S. Developers		Active	Active	Active	Active	
Expert		Active	Active	Active	Active	Active
Users		Active	Active	Active	Active	Active

The project manager should initially focus on two tasks: (1) determining what senior management wants, and (2) identifying potential projects.

In some cases, senior management will want a high visibility project that will make a large impact. In other cases, they will prefer a smaller project that will simply prove that expert systems techniques can be useful. Ideally, the project manager should have a good relationship with someone in senior management whom she can turn to for information, suggestions, and support. This person is often referred to as the *Project Champion*. The project manager and the project champion should consider the various options discussed in Chapters 3 and 4 and decide which strategy is most appropriate for their company.

At the same time, the project manager should be reviewing potential projects within the company to see which projects are viable candidates for expert systems development. Obviously, there is an interaction between the opportunities that the project manager has and the pressure from management to select a higher or lower risk strategy.

As the project manager explores various potential projects, she will be meeting experts and learning about the needs of various user groups within the company.

As a general rule, it's always best to choose a simple, easy project to try first. You can learn about the problems involved in expert systems development and the strengths and weaknesses of your project personnel without extreme pressure or dire consequences. Given the choice, take this conservative strategy.

The ideal first project is a small, PC-based stand-alone diagnostic project. As long as we are specifying an ideal situation, let's go further and suggest a project with only one expert. Moreover, let's pick an expert who enjoys explaining what he does and has a whole file cabinet full of information about all of the cases he has helped solve in the past several years. Let's also hope that the user group already has and uses PCs and is eager to have someone provide a system that can help them, since it's often hard to find the expert when he is needed.

A system to diagnose and recommend repair procedures for a relatively small piece of hardware or the selection of 1 of 10 products to satisfy a customer's needs are good, small projects. If you have the time and freedom to experiment, don't worry about the size of the project; even a seemingly small project will probably prove larger and more complex than you initially expect.

Keep in mind that it is always easier to work with people who want to work with you than it is to work with people who begrudge you the time. Try to find a user group that really needs help and an expert who is interested in learning about expert systems and will be happy if you develop a system that will relieve him of the need to answer the users' routine questions. There are many small projects like this in most companies. If you can tackle one of these projects first, and learn more about the whole process of expert systems development while simultaneously assuring yourself an early success, you'll have an ideal situation.

If your management wants you to tackle a larger project on a LISP machine or a mainframe and expects that the resulting system can be integrated with other existing software to solve a rather significant problem your company is facing, you have to be very careful to do everything you can to narrow the scope of the project and try to enlist the cooperation of experts and users.

Use the worksheet provided in Chapter 3 as you examine potential projects.

If you will be starting on a large, complex project, consider using outside consultants to help select and scope the initial project. If you already know the hardware that the system will be delivered on, consider what tools are available and what support each tool vendor offers. If a particular vendor's tool has been used in the development of similar projects, the vendor may be able to provide you with both informal and formal consulting. The vendor can probably also give you the names of people at other companies who have tried similar projects with the same tool. A

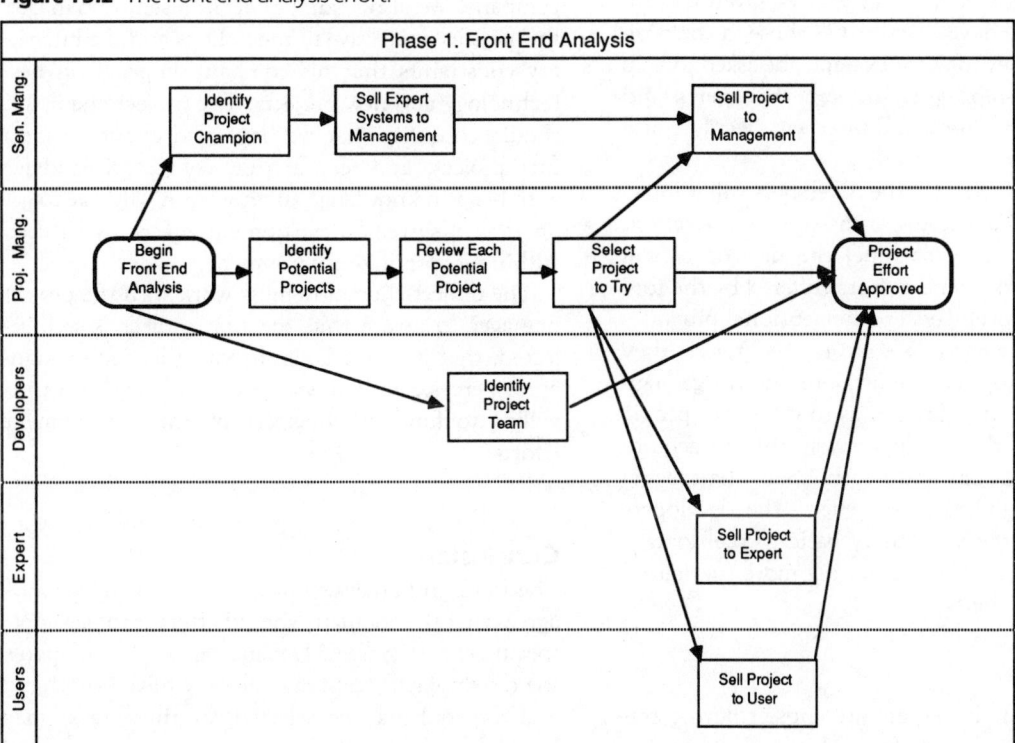

Figure 15.2 The front end analysis effort.

telephone call to someone at another company that has used a tool you are considering on a similar project can be a very cost-effective way to get a little informal consulting on the kinds of problems you may encounter.

Once the project manager has selected a project that seems appropriate, she should hire the developers required and purchase any hardware and software that will be needed. In addition, the project manager should check with each of the other groups that will be involved to be sure everyone understands what will be expected of them and what they will be getting out of the effort.

Expert Systems Development Staff

Depending on the company and the project, the actual people who will develop the expert system may be either transferred to the project or hired especially for the project. If the expert systems developers are already hired, or are hired during the front end analysis phase, they may be given responsibilities that we have described as those of the project manager. They may, for example, be asked to help review potential projects, meet with experts and users, help select a tool, and meet with vendors and consultants.

Once a tool is selected, the developers will want to learn to use it. If the tool runs on a workstation, mainframe, or LISP machine, the developers will probably want to attend a course offered by the tool vendor. If the developers are conventional programmers who are being transferred to the project, they may also want to take one or more knowledge engineering courses. In addition, as soon as the specific task is selected, the developers will want to acquire basic technical books and papers about the specific domain being addressed. In effect, the developers should acquire the vocabulary basic to the domain before they begin to try acquiring more specialized knowledge from the expert.

Expert

The project and the expert are chosen during the front end analysis (FEA) phase. Hence, the only role for experts during this phase is to meet with project personnel and discuss their jobs and the tasks they perform for users in order to help the project team identify a task that would be suitable for an expert systems development effort.

Users

Various user groups will be interviewed, and their contribution at this stage is simply to answer questions to help determine if they have a problem that could be ameliorated or solved by an expert system.

Senior Management

When we consider the role of senior management, we are normally talking about someone who is functioning as a project champion—someone who believes that expert systems technology can contribute to the future productivity, profitability, and success of the company. We also assume that, as a senior manager, this person is sensitive to the politics and the budgetary constraints that his company imposes on new technology and new projects. The project champion should consider what we have said about an ideal first project, and temper that conservative advice with his own knowledge about what it will take to get an expert systems development effort to succeed within his corporate environment.

The project champion must work with the project manager to assure that the first project is well selected, that it succeeds, and that other senior managers perceive that it was successful, and are thus willing to fund other expert systems development efforts.

Conclusion

The front end analysis phase is over when everyone agrees that the company should attempt to develop a specific expert system. Depending on the company, the development team may already have been hired and the tool may be selected, or those tasks may have been left until the next phase.

PHASE 2. ANALYSIS AND DESIGN

Overview

Once a project is selected, the project manager and the development team should analyze it in considerable detail. If they find things that they didn't discover during the FEA phase, it is hopefully not too late to drop the specific problem and look for another. By the same token, as they learn more about the project, they should be able to refine the scope of the system they plan to develop.

Different companies approach this process in different ways. Some combine the FEA and the analysis and design phases. Others keep them separate. Still others combine analysis and design with prototype development. How you divide the effort isn't important. What is important is that you consider several projects, select one, study that one in considerable detail, and then decide either to go on and develop a prototype or to look for a more suitable project. Figure 15.3 provides an overview of the tasks that must be accomplished during this phase of the project.

You should review Chapters 5 and 6 to get an overview of some of the analysis techniques you can use to identify all of the steps and components in the task and the various ways in which advice is delivered.

Project Management

During this phase, the project manager will be organizing for the remainder of the project. If staff, software, or hardware are needed, they must be acquired during this phase. In addition, the task itself should be studied in considerable detail. In general, the project manager will delegate the study of the task to the development team, but on smaller proj-

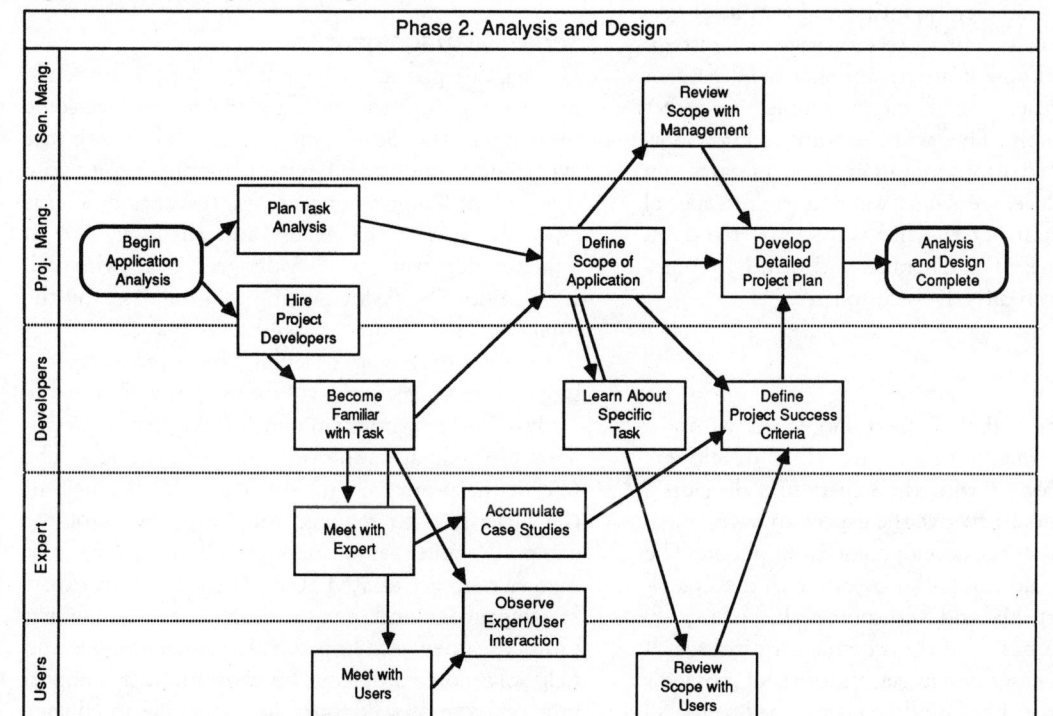

Figure 15.3 *The analysis and design effort.*

ects, the manager may become personally involved in analyzing the task. This is also the time when the project manager should become familiar with the experts and the user organization in order to assure smooth and efficient communications throughout the project.

Expert Systems Development Staff

The developers should learn everything they can about the specific task and about the cognitive knowledge involved in solving the problem. They will observe the expert and the users to acquire task knowledge. They will interview the expert and probably acquire books and articles to learn about the cognitive aspects of the task. If the project is complex, the developers may develop dataflow or entity relationship diagrams. If there is data to access that is on other systems, the developers should learn exactly where the data is and how it is formatted and stored.

The developers should also ask numerous questions about the quality, quantity, and format of output the users will want to receive from the system. They need to know if an answer that is 80 percent correct is sufficient, or if only a completely correct answer is valuable. They will also want to know how long the user can afford to wait at the terminal for an answer. The developers may want to explore special input and output options, like voice-generated questions or responses, or diagrams and printed reports that can be given directly to customers.

Expert

The developers and the expert should get to know one another during this phase. The developers should probably sit with the expert and develop a five-rule system just to give the expert an overview of what expert systems development is all about. The developers should obtain an overview of the knowledge the expert uses and find sources they can study to acquire the basics of the expert's terminology. If the expert has cases or can get cases of real problems faced in the past, he should be encouraged to round them up. If the expert lacks historical data, he should begin collecting it and also begin creating some sample cases to use during the initial stages of the development effort.

Users

Users should be interviewed to determine how they currently use the expert and what they will expect from the system. Typically, once they find they can get it, users will want more from the expert system than they get from the expert. For example, the expert may have made recommendations over the phone and left the end users to prepare a report for their customers. The expert system could generate recommendations already formatted as a report for the customer. Expansion of the current expert/user relationship should be negotiated. In general, since the expert system can always be expanded later, the project team should minimize their commitments until they actually have a prototype completed.

Senior Management

During this phase, senior management is normally just waiting until the project starts to produce some results. As the development team talks with the experts and the users, however, problems may arise that call for senior management intervention. This is especially true if the expert and the users are in separate departments and disagree over who will have responsibility for owning and maintaining the final system.

As the analysis and design phase proceeds, the scope of the project and its final output will probably evolve. The project champion should keep appropriate senior managers informed of these changes. The role of the project champion, here and throughout the project, is to manage the expectations of the company's other senior managers. It's easy for senior managers to get excited about the idea of an expert systems project and then be disappointed by the first prototype they see. Expert systems techniques can help solve some problems, but not others. It's important that the project champion continue to educate senior management about the limits of the technology, and what the first prototype will actually accomplish.

Conclusion

This phase should end when the project team has a specific, written proposal to develop a specific expert system. The proposal should include a clear statement of the scope of the effort, who will be involved, a budget, and a schedule. The report should also estimate the value of the completed system and thus, the return on investment (ROI) that the company can expect from the project.

If the project is small, the report may be an informal affair. But if it is large, then the report should be a formal document. Review Chapters 3 and 4 for some ideas about how to explain and justify an expert systems project. Many companies limit the initial formal approval of an expert systems project to the prototype phase and then wait until the prototype is done and better estimates can be made for the remainder of the effort before approving the budget for the systems development phase of the project.

When a formal report on a proposed expert system is developed and submitted usually depends on the size of the prototype effort. If the prototype effort is small, then it is considered part of the analysis and design phase and a formal proposal is made at the end of the prototype effort. If the project is large and the prototype will capture a significant portion of the task, then a formal proposal is usually submitted before the prototype phase, with a second, or modified, report submitted at the end of the prototype phase.

PHASE 3. PROTOTYPE DEVELOPMENT

Overview

The prototype phase serves three functions:

1. It determines if an expert system can be built.
2. If it is determined that an expert system can be built, it provides the developers with the experience needed to determine the final scope and design of the expert system.
3. It results in a small version of an expert system that can be used to explain and promote the project among experts, users, and other managers.

Most companies do not structure the prototype phase very tightly. In this sense, the prototype phase is really a part of the analysis and design effort. Time and budget constraints are established, but it is generally understood that the developers won't have a very precise idea of the scope of the project until they have worked with the expert and tried to model and encode his knowledge.

Most developers avoid database connections or other procedural programming when they are engaged in the prototype phase. They create "dummy" databases rather than worry about creating complex connections to real databases. In many cases, the project team is expanded at the beginning of the system development phase to include people who can develop conventional programs and database hooks or modify database records. By the same token, although some fancy graphics may be done during the prototype phase to illustrate to users and management how the final interface will look, extensive graphic development and interface work is usually put off until the systems development phase. In other words, the primary focus of the prototype phase is to explore the nature and scope of the knowledge the expert uses to solve the problem and what difficulties there are in representing that knowledge as rules and objects. Figure 15.4 provides an overview of the tasks that must be accomplished during this phase of the project.

Project Management

The main role of the project manager during the prototype phase is to monitor the effort, identify problems and needs, and, finally, assess what kind of team and effort will be required to develop a complete system.

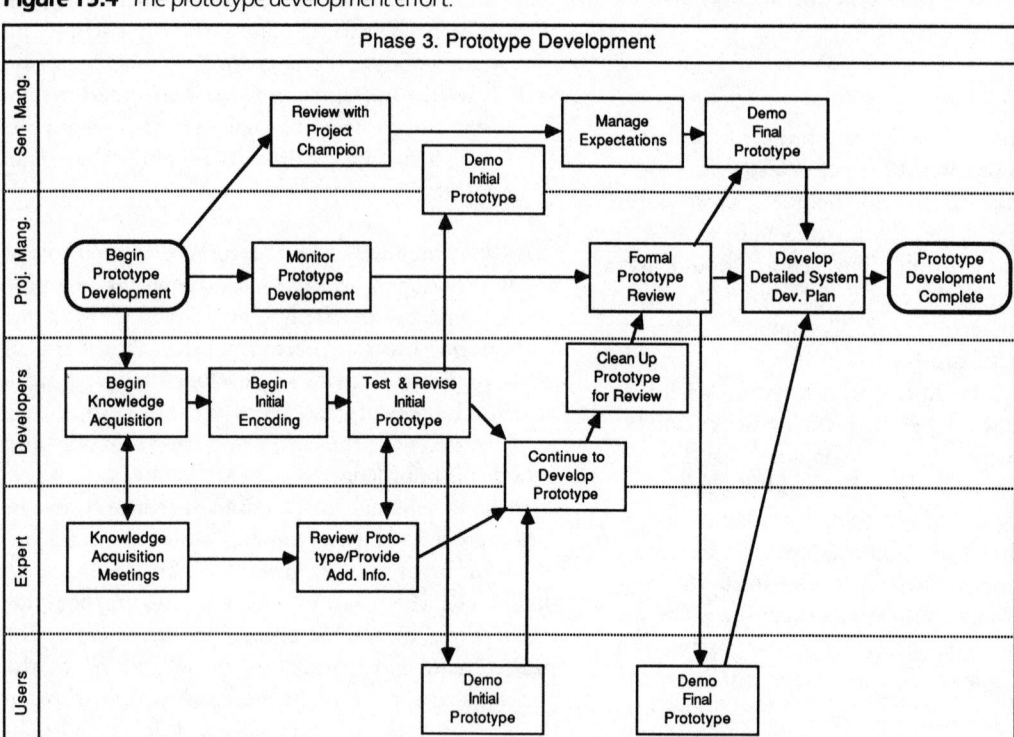

Figure 15.4 The prototype development effort.

The worst case is that it will turn out that the development of the expert system is too difficult or unwarranted. The expert may prove impossible to work with. The knowledge may prove too vast or too difficult to represent. The integration issues may prove to be too difficult to justify the effort. In such a case, the project manager has to arrange to cancel the project and find a better application to prototype. If it's a small project, this should not be difficult, but if it's a large, highly visible project, the project manager and the project champion may need to spend quite a bit of time to be sure that everyone understands that the failure has resulted not from a general deficiency of expert systems but from the specifics of the particular problem.

The best case is that the problem will prove easier than was anticipated and that a very significant part of the problem can be solved in the time allowed for the prototype phase. In this case, the project team will have to carefully evaluate what happened to determine if they overestimated the scope of the problem or underestimated the power of the technology. It's always nice to come in under budget and ahead of time; but in the long run, the project manager will want to understand the technology well enough so that future projects can be accurately budgeted and scheduled.

Expert Systems Development Staff

This is the first phase in which knowledge acquisition, knowledge mapping, and encoding occur. The developers should prepare for knowledge acquisition by studying the domain and the task vocabulary and any general principles that underlie the domain. They must also determine when and how they want to conduct interviews with the expert or experts. If there are two developers who will be working together, they may want to divide the subject matter they study. If there are multiple experts, the developers must decide if they will deal with all the experts at once, or work with them one at a time.

As a general rule, it's best to have short meetings with plenty of time in between to experiment with representing and encoding the knowledge that's been acquired. The expert's schedule may dictate the meeting times and the frequency, but an ideal schedule for a mid-size project is a few hours once every two weeks.

In the initial meetings, the developers should put considerable effort into teaching the expert about the technology and the methodology of expert systems development. They'll know they've done a good job of this if, after a few meetings, the expert can help edit knowledge base printouts or come to meetings with suggestions for how rules can be revised to be more effective. The expert has better access to his knowledge than the developers ever can. If the expert reaches the point at which he is actively looking for new knowledge to add to the system, or perhaps thinking about how a hierarchy of abstractions might be rearranged to be more effective, then any educational efforts will be fully justified.

The developers have four tasks:

1. Acquire knowledge
2. Create a formal map of that knowledge
3. Encode the knowledge
4. Work with the expert to assure that the knowledge can solve specific cases put to the system

If the task is small, the developers may pass rapidly from Step 1 to 3, but if the task is large or complex, then effort spent on Step 2 will be well rewarded. At the moment, the hardest thing for most knowledge engineers to do is to represent an expert's knowledge in such a way that they can then easily expand or modify the knowledge base. Too many developers simply dump the first batch of knowledge they get into a rule base and then go back for more. They do this a couple of times and then realize that the knowledge base isn't working very well—it needs better organization. Abstract terms need to be better defined. Rules pertaining to one aspect of the problem need to be written in such a way that they do not interfere with those written to handle another aspect of the problem.

If the task is complex, drawing an object-attribute-value network is worth the effort. The key is determining the right level of abstraction to use to organize the effort. If the developer focuses on too fine-grained a level, the details will overwhelm her. If she focuses on too abstract a level, the system will make recommendations that are too vague to be useful. The developer needs to experiment with representing knowledge and solving a few cases, but eventually, she must determine the basic set of objects or attributes to use to organize the core of the system.

Once the developers are satisfied that they have an approach that can not only handle the rules they are writing now, but can also be easily and logically expanded to handle the additional information they will get from the expert, they are ready to work up an initial prototype. In most cases, an initial prototype will solve only one or a few problems. An initial prototype is the first version of the system that the developers will show to the expert, to users, and perhaps, to selected executives.

Using the initial prototype, the developers and the expert can examine the system to see if it is, in fact, solving the initial case or cases in an accurate and efficient way. The same system can provide a starting point in a discussion with users about exactly how they would like to have the system question them and how they would like the results presented.

Once an initial prototype is available, then knowledge acquisition expands to include not only interviews, but sessions with the system. The developers consider additional cases and add knowledge to the system to handle those cases. If the system will be complex, the developers should choose the prototype cases carefully to be sure they gain experience in both the breadth and the depth of knowledge that the final system will require. If a wide variety of different types of cases will be handled by the system, they should choose very different cases for the prototype. If one or more cases will require extremely complex processing, they should choose one of the most complex to determine what is involved in acquiring and encoding the most complex of cases.

At the end of the prototype phase, the developers will be asked to estimate how long it will take to develop a complete system. To do this, the developers need to acquire a good overview of the entire task, and they need to have a concrete idea of what will be involved in developing each major portion of the overall knowledge base. Such an understanding requires that the knowledge engineers alternate between a top-down approach and a bottom-up approach.

When DEC was first developing XCON, the managers involved in the project were fooled because the first prototype could handle 80 percent of the test cases that they put to it. Observing it perform, the managers became convinced that a little additional effort would suffice to create a system that could handle all of DEC's configuration problems. In fact, it took much longer. Every expert knows how to solve the most common problems very effectively. They know just what questions to ask and what to do to eliminate the problem. If you build a prototype that captures the knowledge the expert uses to handle the two or three most common problems he deals with, you will probably seriously underestimate how long and difficult it will be to capture the knowledge the expert uses to solve the less common problems. Those are the problems the expert has to think about a little longer. A lot of knowledge can be brought to bear in a half hour of musing about a tricky problem. When developing a prototype, be sure you include some easy problems and that you also try to solve one of the most difficult tasks the expert system will be called upon to perform. If you do, you will develop a much better idea of how much effort it will take to expand the system to a fully functioning expert system.

Expert

The role of the expert or experts during prototype development is to explain to the development team what they do, answer questions, and review cases with the developers. Depending on the time available and the inclination of the expert, he can do the minimum required and leave the analysis and design to the development team, or the expert can become very involved in the process, drafting rules and experimenting with the object-attribute-value network in order to improve it.

The interviewing process can be painful for the expert. The expert normally receives a great deal of respect for being able to solve difficult problems. People are usually satisfied with the results and don't ask the expert to explain precisely how he arrived at his recommendations. Now, the expert will be asked to explain exactly how he thought when he solved the problem. In some cases, this will be straightforward, but in many others, the expert will not be sure what he did; and he may be embarrassed to admit to the developer that he just played a hunch or made a lucky guess.

When a mid-size to large expert system is completed, the experts involved commonly report that they learned a great deal and now understand what they do better than when the development effort began. However, most experts will also claim that it was difficult to keep thinking about the same problems over and over again, trying to explain precisely why one similar problem was actually quite different than another, and why they knew they were different.

If multiple experts are involved, and they commonly are, then the developers will have to manage the egos and negotiate a common vocabulary. Different, equally good experts use terms in slightly different ways. But since the system can use a term only in a single way, the experts will have to agree on what they will call different things or events, and they will have to remember to be consistent in following the definitions they agree upon. It's easy to say this, but over the course of several months, dozens of cases, and a few hundred rules and objects, there are many opportunities for ambiguities to slip in. The development team and the experts must work together, and that means that compromises and disciplined efforts must be forthcoming from everyone involved. It can be a challenge, and the responsibility for making it happen ultimately falls on the project manager, and secondarily on the developers.

Users

The users have a minimal, but important, role during the prototype phase. They must explain how they use expertise to solve problems in their work environment, and they must listen to questions and provide some reality checking on what the developers are learning from the experts.

An expert, for example, might say: "When I need that information, I simply ask the user to tell me what the average thermovariance for the kiln was for the previous day." Upon checking with the user, the developer may find that the user doesn't know what "average thermovariance" means at all. When the developer cross-checks with the expert, the expert may explain that, actually, he doesn't ask about "thermovariance," he asks for the readings on two dials. The user doesn't know it, but together, those dials add up to the average thermovariance. It's this kind of communication problem that can only be cleared up by checking with the users.

It's also important to involve users in the project as soon as possible so that they develop a sense of interest and ownership in the system that is being developed. Whenever there are noncritical interface issues, for example, it's always best to allow the users to say what they prefer. It's an easy way to get the users involved in the system.

Senior Management

The role of the project champion during this phase is to control the expectations of other managers. To do this, the project manager has to keep the project champion informed about how the system is developing, decisions that are made to limit its initial functionality, the look of the interface, and so on. The project champion should have a very good idea of what other senior managers will actually see when the prototype is demonstrated at the end of the prototype phase, and he should be sure that other managers also know what to expect.

Conclusion

The prototype phase ends when the project team is ready to demonstrate a prototype of the expert system. The prototype should be sufficient to convince management that further funding is desirable. It should also convince users that the system will be useful to them once it can handle more cases.

In most cases, the project team not only demonstrates the prototype system, but also submits a report detailing what has been done and what will be done through the remainder of the project. The report normally includes a detailed description of the architecture of the final system. In many cases, the prototype is initially conceived as a standalone system. As work progresses, however, the developers often see opportunities to obtain data from existing databases and other software applications, and perhaps, they also see the possibility of passing or storing output from the expert system in other places where such information can be useful. The fully integrated version of the expert system, along with an explanation of the effort required to achieve such integration, should be described in the report submitted at the end of the prototype phase. This report should also include a revised budget and schedule.

PHASE 4. SYSTEMS DEVELOPMENT

Overview

Early expert systems developers typically thought of the systems development phase as a natural extension of the prototype phase. More knowledge acquisition, more coding, more cases tested, and finally, when no more knowledge could be obtained from the expert, the system was done. In many cases, the simple extension of the prototype still describes the systems development phase.

Increasingly, however, companies are realizing that, in most cases, the systems development phase can be managed more like a conventional software development effort. If the resulting application is going to be integrated with other applications and databases, then the systems development effort is normally subdivided among several programmers, each with different and specific responsibilities. The entire effort may be guided by dataflow diagrams and something very close to a structured programming methodology. There may still be developers who work with experts to acquire, formalize, and encode knowledge. If the system is large, however, the prototype development phase has probably revealed ways in which the knowledge can be subdivided and mixed with conventional techniques. Whether you use object networks or databases, the ideal is to store as much definitional information as possible in a nonrule format. Inferencing is a powerful technique, but it can also be slow. Thus, inferencing should be used only where necessary, while conventional, better understood, and faster techniques should be used whenever possible.

Figure 15.5 provides an overview of the major tasks involved in the systems development phase of a project.

The goal of the systems development phase is to produce a computer software application that will be beneficial to the company. A beneficial application must perform some useful task, but it must do so efficiently, on appropriate hardware, and it must integrate with other applications whenever possible.

Project Management

The systems development phase of small projects may truly be a simple continuation of the prototype phase. In most cases, however, the systems development phase involves several developers each performing different tasks that must ultimately be integrated together in a complete application. In addition to knowledge acquisition, some programmers may be developing conventional programs to perform specific functions. Other programmers may be working on databases to rearrange their records into a format that the expert system can use, or they may be writing hooks to the database. Still others may be developing the final versions of the interface screens that the user will see. The expert systems project manager, like the manager of any software development project, needs to have a plan and a schedule. She should choose people and assign tasks in order to assure that everything is done in a logical and systematic manner.

If the expert system will interface with other applications or databases, then other managers will probably become involved, and the project manager needs to be sure that everyone understands what is happening and why. Communication may not assure cooperation, but lack of communication is almost certain to result in a lack of cooperation.

As the system nears completion, the project manager must make provisions for implementation and testing. Users must be trained to use the system, and supervisors must be told how the system will affect their operations.

Expert Systems Development Staff

The expert systems development staff may grow considerably during the systems development phase. Some staff members may focus only on database, communication, or interface problems, while others may be engaged in writing conventional programs to handle number-crunching tasks. For our purposes here, we consider only the staff members engaged in knowledge engineering.

As they were completing the prototype, the developers should have met with the project manager to decide how the final system should be designed. Having done this, they will probably have to begin the systems development phase by tearing down what they did during the prototype phase and restructuring the knowledge base. They will have to eliminate some rules because the information contained in them will now be obtained from other programs or from databases. The context or object hierarchy of the system will probably also have to be

Figure 15.5 The systems development effort.

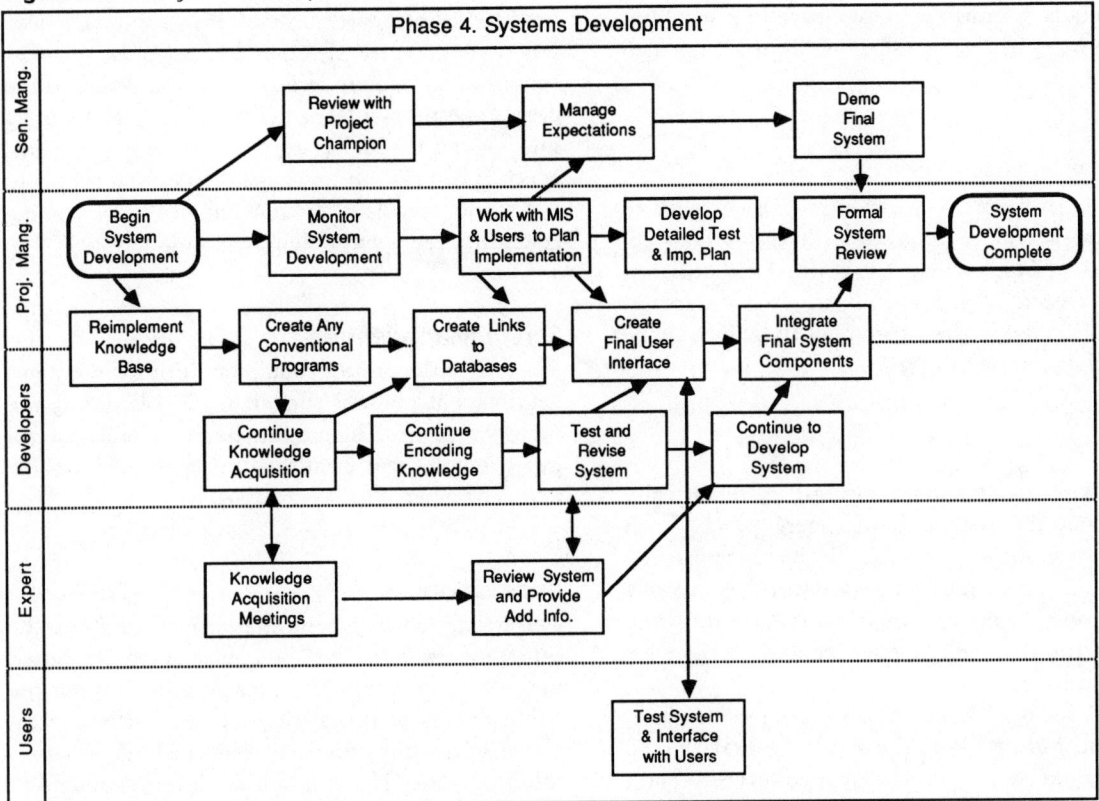

rearranged. The developers will probably introduce additional levels of abstraction to accommodate an increase in the amount of knowledge that is about to be added to the knowledge base. They may change object and attribute names to reflect changes in understanding that occurred during the prototype phase but were never incorporated into the knowledge base. The beginning of the systems development phase is the best time to rearrange everything so that the core system will be easy to expand.

Beyond rearranging the core knowledge base, the role of the knowledge engineers during the systems development phase is really very much like the role they played during the prototype phase. They need to work with experts to acquire, formalize, encode, test, and improve the knowledge in the system. If the system is large, experts and developers may be divided into teams, each assigned to a specific aspect of the knowledge base.

If the prototype was done quickly but the systems development phase is expected to run much longer, the knowledge engineers will need to take appropriate care to assure that the experts do not burn out before the system is completed. Pacing is critical. Typically, the experts have regular jobs to perform, and their work on the expert system is being squeezed in. That's acceptable for a month or two, but it can become quite unacceptable when they realize that the project is going to go on for another five to eighteen months. The scheduling of meetings and the intensity of the development effort should be carefully reconsidered at the beginning of the systems development phase. The developers must adjust the schedule to reflect a realistic pace to assure that the effort can be accomplished within the scheduled time.

Expert
Like the developers, experts must engage in more interviews and more case reviews during systems development. Experts may be assigned to work on specific aspects of the overall task, but otherwise, they will be doing the same thing they were doing during the prototype phase.

Users
User involvement should increase systematically throughout the systems development phase. Each new version of the system should be shown to the users, and they should be asked to work very closely with the developers creating the interface to assure that the interface will be effective and efficient for them to use.

The developers should review plans for the placement and integration of the system with the users. Users should get a chance to try a prototype version and suggest modifications. As appropriate, users should receive instruction in the design and development of an expert system so that they have a realistic idea about what to expect from the system.

There has been so much hype and science fiction about AI and "machine intelligence" and robotics that most users who hear that their company is experimenting with an expert system expect the worst. Maybe the system is being developed to replace them? Maybe the system will be impossible for them to understand? Maybe the system will totally restructure their work and they will no longer find their new tasks exciting or acceptable? The way to handle all these fears and many others is to explain the expert systems project to the users as soon as possible. Explain what an expert system is and what it will do. In almost all cases, an expert system will assist or support people, not replace people. In most cases, the expert system will make the users' jobs easier by providing them with the information they need to do their work in a faster and more efficient way than it is currently done. In most cases, the most complex and human decisions will still be left to the users. The project team needs to be sure the users know about the expert system and its implications, good or bad, as soon as possible. Leaving people to guess and speculate about what might be coming results in a tense and unhappy situation.

Senior Management
The role of the project champion during the systems development phase is similar to his role during the prototype phase: The project champion must control expectations about what the final system will be able to do and when it will be completed.

Conclusion
The systems development phase concludes when the expert system is ready to be implemented and tested in the work environment. This decision is as much a political as a technical decision. A partially completed system may be very useful to some group to solve a specific class of problems. It may be useful to implement it and obtain successful results in one area of the organization before the final system is ready to be used in other areas.

What is certain is that the expert system will not be complete when it is first used in the field. Expert systems are developed by capturing knowledge about specific cases. Like their human counterparts, they are no better than the cases they have solved. When the new expert system is fielded, it may quickly encounter many more cases during its first week than it was tested with during development. Moreover, some of the cases the system encounters during its first couple of weeks on the job are sure to have little twists that the expert didn't cover in the cases that he provided. All of this is quite normal and acceptable, as long as everyone is prepared for it. If, on the other hand, users or senior managers expect that the "completed system" will perform perfectly during its first week on the job, they will probably be disappointed and they may get upset. Again, it's a matter of explaining the technology, how it works, and of controlling expectations. Correctly positioned, the testing phase can be a chance for users to participate in the final development of the expert system.

PHASE 5. TESTING AND IMPLEMENTATION

Overview

The idea of the testing and implementation phase is to connect the expert system up, put it in the user environment, and see how it works. Thus, the "test" referred to is a pragmatic test and not a formal or logical test.

Many people who are involved in expert systems are concerned with the verification and validation of knowledge bases. They want to be assured that the completed expert system has all of the knowledge necessary to solve the problems it will encounter. They also want to be assured that there are no internal contradictions contained in the knowledge base. Neither kind of assurance can be satisfactorily given at this point in time. Small systems can be examined and certified, but this is just an alternative way of saying that small systems could have been developed using conventional programming techniques. If you can completely and formally define the search space, you can be sure that every possibility has been considered. With most mid- to large-size systems, though, the search space is too large to search. The systems are developed incrementally, and tested by having them solve cases. If you present the system with a new, complex case, you are no more certain that the system will be able to solve it than that a human expert will. This can be very frustrating, since people typically expect more accuracy from computers than they expect from people. Many people are working on the validation problem, but no one has yet advanced a good proposal for solving it (any more than anyone knows how to test human professionals to assure that they won't make any mistakes).

In the meantime, testing, relative to expert systems, simply means determining if the system can successfully solve all of the cases that you could reasonably expect the human expert to solve, and to do so in a manner and at a speed that is useful in the workplace. In most cases, companies are satisfied if the expert system can solve 75 to 85 percent of the cases it encounters. The rest of the cases, the really complex, tricky, or rare cases, can be referred to the human expert.

Thus, the goal of the testing and implementation phase is threefold:

1. To provide the developer with an opportunity to see how the system handles a normal stream of problems and to modify the system whenever it encounters cases that it isn't prepared to handle correctly
2. To allow the developers and users to see if the system can perform quickly and smoothly enough to be effective in the work environment
3. To give the users an opportunity to begin to learn how to use the system to help them perform their jobs

Figure 15.6 provides an overview of the major tasks that must be accomplished during the testing and implementation phase of an expert systems development project.

Project Management

The project manager should expect that the testing and implementation will involve a good bit of firefighting. The system will predictably fail to solve some cases. In most cases, the problem will be easy to fix, and the developers may want to fix most problems quickly to impress the users with how readily the system can be improved.

Whenever a system is integrated with other systems, there are problems to be worked out, and the project manager should try to anticipate these problems as well. Normally, the project manager should make a list of all of the things that have to happen to integrate the system and then support the system during the test period. Then, she should assume that

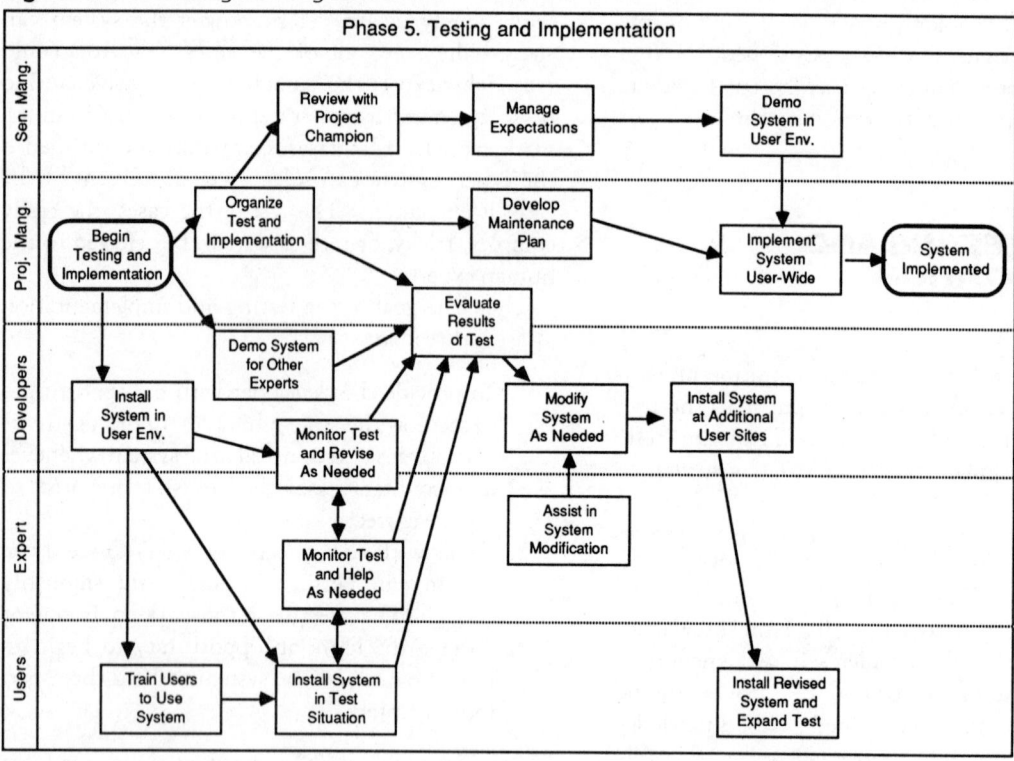

Figure 15.6 The testing and integration effort.

```
Phase 5. Testing and Implementation
```

Sen. Mang.: Review with Project Champion → Manage Expectations → Demo System in User Env.

Proj. Mang.: Begin Testing and Implementation → Organize Test and Implementation → Develop Maintenance Plan → Implement System User-Wide → System Implemented

Developers: Install System in User Env.; Demo System for Other Experts; Monitor Test and Revise As Needed; Evaluate Results of Test; Modify System As Needed; Install System at Additional User Sites

Expert: Assist in System Modification; Monitor Test and Help As Needed

Users: Train Users to Use System → Install System in Test Situation; Install Revised System and Expand Test

some things she hasn't anticipated will nevertheless occur, and try to provide some slack to handle those problems when they do occur.

Much of the manager's job during this period is coordinating and, once again, controlling expectations. Letting everyone know what to expect is the key. If they expect the worst and it turns out much better, the manager is usually a hero. If it happens the other way around, the manager isn't so highly regarded.

Expert Systems Development Staff

Part of the developer's job is to help implement and train. The other part is to wait until something goes wrong, figure out what happened, and fix it. Some fixes can only be effected after the testing period is over, but most can be done on a day-to-day basis, by adding or modifying rules already in the system.

Expert

Like the developer, the expert's role during this phase is to be available to provide an answer if the system fails, and then to help the developers figure out why the system failed and decide what knowledge to add in order to fix the problem.

Users

Hopefully, the users have been well prepared for the testing phase. Normally, the system is used only by a subset of the users who have been carefully trained and who expect the system to have difficulties during its first few weeks. Under these circumstances, the users can be thought of as part of the development team, presenting cases to the system and noting where it is deficient. Of course, the users also have their normal jobs to perform, so they need a way to handle problems when the system fails to provide the right answer.

Essentially, the users should use the system and complain when it doesn't perform correctly. If they do this, they will provide the developers with the information they need to improve the system.

Senior Management
Like the project manager, the project champion needs to work hard during this phase to control expectations and assure that senior management understands that the system will experience some problems and that they will be corrected.

Conclusion
Different companies handle the testing and implementation phase in different ways. Some make it a very elaborate test while others confine the test to a small group. Some run the test for a limited time while others run the test for a year and compare the results of the system with the results of users who do not rely on the system.

The important point of this phase is to find out how the system must be enhanced and modified in order to provide effective and timely assistance to the users who will use it once it is fielded.

At the end of the test and implementation phase, there is usually a period of reflection during which time the project team modifies the system and the users prepare for the final implementation of the system. In most cases, however, after some minor adjustments, the system is fielded and the users begin to use it on a full-time basis. This final fielding process may occur incrementally, with a few new users being trained and added to the system each month, or it may occur systemwide, after everyone has received appropriate training. Either way, the final result of this phase should be a system that is ready to be fielded and a plan for effectively implementing the system in its final configuration.

PHASE 6. MAINTENANCE

Overview
The final phase occurs when the system is fielded. However this occurs, the system begins to be used daily by the users and, hopefully, the performance of the users improves in one or more ways.

The development process is not yet over, though. Most expert systems contain knowledge that is changing and evolving over time. Thus, the systems need to be maintained. As the parts or policies or equipment the system considers when it analyzes and solves problems changes, someone has to change the knowledge in the system.

After a system is fielded, there are a variety of maintenance needs that can arise. Users can discover omissions, inconsistencies, or just plain bugs. Experts may want to add new rules if the system is based on changing judgment, or management may decide to broaden the system's scope. The data the knowledge base draws on may need to be modified or expanded. The knowledge base may have to be ported to other platforms, or translated into different languages. If a system is written with these possibilities in mind, it can be much easier to maintain over time.

Altering a knowledge base is a little like altering an elaborate dish. A kitchen worker could sprinkle a garnish on top, an assistant chef could double the ingredients, but only the head chef could be trusted to alter the recipe itself. Likewise, in expert systems development, maintenance is done by different players, each with a separate role. There is the clerk who knows nothing about rules but can reliably enter new data. There is the programmer or knowledge engineer who, although not involved in the development of the system, can make limited kinds of modifications to knowledge and interfaces. Finally, there are the primary system developers who are capable of modifying any facet of the system. We now consider the roles of each of these players in turn.

Maintenance by Users

Maintenance by a user is normally done at the data level, adding or changing the information the expert system uses in its reasoning. It's always easier to change data than to change structure. Therefore, where possible, you should always try to store volatile information in simple, fixed structures, like tables. Tables can be used to store all kinds of data—lists of names and addresses, lists of inventory, lists of prices, and so on. If your tool performs induction, you can even use tables to store examples of sample decisions, which can then be used to periodically induce a new set of rules.

Setting up a knowledge base to draw on tabular data permits a clerk to perform certain kinds of maintenance easily. By editing data stored in tables or adding new entries onto a table, a clerk can keep the system up to date. Of course, if the structure of the table changes (e.g., by the addition of a new attribute), the knowledge engineer must be called in.

There are three principal ways to store tabular information in an expert system: as rows in an induction table, as sets of frame instances, or as records in a database.

Induction tables can be used to store cases of sample decisions from which rules can be automatically reinduced. In certain problems, a clerk might be able to record new cases of a problem and its solution into an induction table. This table could then be periodically used to reinduce a new set of rules. It is likely, however, that the knowledge engineer or expert would have to review the new rules to confirm their validity before they could actually be used.

Another way to store tabular data is as a set of frame instances. Frame instances can be thought of as rows in a table, with slots as the table headings. However, the process of creating and editing frame instances must be done from inside an expert systems development tool, which may make it too difficult for a clerk.

The third way to represent tabular data, and usually the best, is to store it in a database. This allows a clerk to modify records from within a database manager, without ever having to touch the knowledge base at all.

Data General's ATP is a good example of a system whose use of a database makes it easy to maintain. A mainframe database is used to store information about the parts to ship. When new parts come into existence, or information about old parts needs to be modified, the appropriate changes can be made from within the database manager, without having to alter the knowledge base at all.

Boole & Babbage's DASD Advisor allows a maintenance of sorts to be done directly by the user. The knowledge base was built in a manner that allows the user to customize the program's behavior to fit changing needs. One of the options in DASD Advisor is to edit the values of a set of key variables that control the system's priorities, the hardware it deals with, and other information. By changing these values, the user can tailor the system's behavior, without having to actually change any rules.

Although this is not maintenance on the knowledge level, it does give the user a simple way to tailor DASD's behavior as hardware or priorities change. More significant changes to the behavior of DASD Advisor would have to be made by editing the knowledge base.

Maintenance by Developers

There is an idealized notion that rules in expert systems are maintained very easily, simply by throwing in a few more rules every time new knowledge comes along. In practice, however, it's hardly ever that simple. New knowledge entry must be tightly restricted if it is to become a useful part of the system. Often, this is done by way of a *maintenance interface*, which guides a developer through the process of adding new knowledge to the system. This allows certain limited types of knowledge to be entered into the system, checked for consistency, and automatically put into the proper place in the knowledge base. This guarantees that the new knowledge will be in harmony with the existing knowledge base.

The developers of Data General's ATP system plan to add such a maintenance interface to their system in the future. It will allow pricing experts to personally edit parts of the knowledge base. They will be able to inspect pricing rules and to make certain types of changes and additions to them.

Another example of a maintenance interface is one developed by DEC. DEC is currently involved in a major effort to revise its XCON expert system. As XCON has grown in size it has become increasingly difficult to maintain. With over 6,000 rules, it has become very difficult to modify XCON because too many different people have written rules. Only those with a good knowledge of the history of XCON know why certain rules are written as they are. Worse, developers have included clauses in individual rules that affect many different parts of the program.

DEC is in the process of reimplementing XCON in a higher-level language called RIME. (The new version of XCON is often called XCON-IN-RIME.) RIME is a domain-specific version of a research tool called SOAR, which was developed at Carnegie-Mellon to facilitate knowledge acquisition. RIME has been specifically designed to reflect what DEC has learned about writing and modifying a large knowledge base. RIME assumes that XCON is composed of some 40 sets of rules, each concerned with a different functional aspect of the system. It further assumes that within each of these sets, a specific series of steps should occur. Finally, it assumes that all rules used in XCON will take one of six forms: (1) establish purpose, (2) reject, (3) evaluate, (4) apply, (5) recognize success, or (6) recognize failure.

RIME allows the developer to specify the set of rules to be modified, the step in the sequence to be modified, and the type of rule to be entered or changed. Once the developer has provided this information, RIME provides a template into which the developer enters necessary information. Since RIME knows quite a bit about the nature and working of the different kinds of rules, as well as the contexts in which the rules will operate, RIME is able to fill in much of the information without bothering to ask the developer.

Once RIME knows what the user wants to enter, it generates OPS5 code. A few lines of RIME code generates a great many lines of OPS5 code. Moreover, RIME provides users with a very good explanation facility, something that is notoriously lacking in OPS5 and is desired by DEC users of XCON. (RIME's explanations are keyed to the intermediate representation that is created by RIME during its interaction with the developer, and not with the OPS5 rules.) Some 200 rules have been entered in XCON-IN-RIME, and thus far the developers have been happy with the better organization and the ease of entry and modification that RIME provides.

Each company and perhaps each system will call for different arrangements. In many cases, especially with small systems, the user organization can handle routine maintenance. More complex maintenance and efforts to significantly expand or further integrate the system, however, will probably require an individual or group of programmers or knowledge engineers to make the modifications. Large, strategic systems like DEC's XCON may justify and require a full-time maintenance team, just as important corporate databases require daily maintenance.

Conclusion

A systematic maintenance procedure needs to be established for every system. Users need to report errors they encounter, and experts need to report changes in the knowledge they provided during knowledge acquisition sessions. Developers need to be available to modify and expand the knowledge base to accommodate this feedback. And, of course, someone needs to manage this whole process to assure that it is accomplished in an efficient and effective manner.

APPENDICES

Appendix I
A List of Expert Systems Building Tools

The charts on the following pages list the expert systems building tools that were being sold in the United States in the early summer of 1989.

As new tools are constantly being introduced and the current tools are being improved and ported to new hardware, this list should not be considered definitive. We have provided it simply to give you an overview of how the tool market stands in 1989.

Several of these tools run on many different platforms, but we have only listed each tool once. We have classified the tools according to how we believe they are perceived by the market.

Small, PC/Mac-Based Tools

TOOL (Knowledge Representation) (Vendor)	Price Range	Hardware (Operating System/Language)	Generates SQL	Databases that system can access without writing hook	Memory Requirements RAM/Harddisk
1st-CLASS FUSION (Inductive) (1st-CLASS Expert Systems, Inc)	$1495-2495	IBM PC's and compatibles, VAX under VMS (Pascal)	No	Lotus 1-2-3, dBASE III, HyperText, ASCII files	Dev.: 512 K HT: 640 K
Crystal (Simple Rule) (Intelligent Environments Ltd.)	$995-1995	IBM PC's and compatibles (MS-DOS); OS/2, (C)	No	dBASE, Lotus 1-2-3, Lotus Symphony, Presentation Graphics, Business Graphics	PC: 350 K OS/2: 2 mb RAM Hard Disck recom.
CxPERT (Software Plus)	$395	MS-DOS	–	–	C Compiler
Easy Expert (Simple Rule) (Park Row Software Inc.)	$49.95	MS-DOS	No	–	256K
EST (Simple Rule) (Mind Path Technologies)	$495	IBM PC's and compatibles (Pascal)	No	Lotus 1-2-3	256 K
ExperCommonOPS5 (OPS) (Expertelligence)	$625	MAC (Requires ExperCommonLisp) (Lisp)	No	–	1 mb
Experfacts (Simple Rule) (Expertelligence)	$495	MAC (Requires ExperLisp) (Lisp)	No	–	512 K
ExperOPS5+ (Simple Rule) (Expertelligence)	$495	MAC (Requires ExperLisp) (Lisp)	No	–	512 K
Expert Edge (Simple Rule) (Helix Expert Systems Ltd.)	$795	IBM PC's and compatibles (C)	–	Lotus 1-2-3, Multiplan, dBASE	256 K 512 K recom.

Small, PC/Mac-Based Tools (Continued)

TOOL (Knowledge Representation) (Vendor)	Price Range	Hardware (Operating System/Language)	Generates SQL	Databases that system can access without writing hook	Memory Requirements RAM/Harddisk
Exsys (Simple Rule) (Exsys Inc.)	$395-8 K	IBM PC/AT and compatibles (MS-DOS), VAX (VMS or Altrex), Unix, SUN 3 & 4, (C)	No	dBASE III, Lotus 1-2-3	640 K Hard Drive recom.
flex (Hybrid) (Programmming Logic Associates Ltd)	$295-495	IBM PCs (MS-DOS), MAC (Multi_Finder) Prolog required ($595)	No	—	512 K 640 K and Hard Drive recom.
Instant Expert (Simple Rule) (Human Intellect Systems)	$69.95-99.95	IBM PC's and compatibles (MS-DOS), MAC, (Modula II)	No	—	PC:640 K MAC: 512 K
Instant Expert+ (Simple Rule) (Human Intellect Systems)	$498	IBM PC's and compatibles (MS-DOS), MAC, (Modula II)	Yes	HyperCard	PC:640 K MAC: 512 K
Intelligent Developer (Simple Rule) (Hyperpress Publishing Corp.)	$295	MAC +, SE or II	No	HyperCard, HyperText	1 mb
KDS 2 & 3 (Inductive) (KDS Corp.)	$970-1,495	IBM PC's and compatibles (MS-DOS), (Assembler)	No	Lotus 1-2-3, dBASE	640 K Hard Drive recom.
KnowledgePro (Simple Rule) (Knowledge Garden Inc.)	$495	IBM PC/AT and compatibles (MS-DOS), OS/2, (Turbo Pascal)	No	dBASE III, Lotus 1-2-3	640 K Hard Drive recom.
MacSmarts/MacSmarts Professional (Simple Rule) (Cognition Technology)	$195-495	MAC (Prolog, C)	No	HyperCard, HyperText, SuperCard, Excel	512 K 1mb & Hard Drive recommended
Micro Expert (Simple Rule) (McGraw-Hill Book Co.)	$54.95-64.95	IBM PC/AT and compatibles (MS-DOS), Apple Computers, (Pascal)	No	—	256 K

Small, PC/Mac-Based Tools (Continued)

TOOL (Knowledge Representation) (Vendor)	Price Range	Hardware (Operating System/Language)	Generates SQL	Databases that system can access without writing hook	Memory Requirements RAM/Harddisk
Magellan (Simple Rule) (Emerald Intelligence)	$195	Commodore Amiga (Amiga DOS),(C, Assembly)	No	—	528 K
Mahogony Professional (Hybrid) (Emerald Intelligence)	$495	MAC	No	Lotus 1-2-3, dBASE III, Hypercard	1 mb memory
OPS-2000 (OPS) (Intellipro)	$45-295	MS-DOS	No	Lotus -1-2-3, dBASE III	1 mb memory
PC Expert 2.0 (Simple Rule) (Software Artistry)	$199.95	MS-DOS (C, Pascal, Modula 2, Ada)	No	—	
PC Expert Professional (Hybrid) (Software Artistry)	$495	MS-DOS (C, Pascal, Modula 2, Ada)	No	Lotus 1-2-3, dBASE III	512 K, 5mb Hard Disk space
Personal Consultant Easy (Simple Rule) (Texas Instruments)	$495	IBM /XT/AT or compatibles, PS/2, Explorer or MicroExplorer (PC or MS-DOS), (Scheme, C)	No	dBASE, Lotus 1-2-3	640 K; expaned or extended mem., Hard Drive recom.
Procedure Consultant (Decision Tree) (Texas Instrument)	$495	IBM /XT/AT or compatibles, PS/2, Explorer or MicroExplorer (PC or MS-DOS), (Scheme, C)	No	DOS files only	640 K; expaned or extended mem., Hard Drive recom.
SuperExpert (Inductive) (Softsync Inc.)	$199.95	IBM PC's and compatibles (MS-DOS), MAC, PS/2, (Pascal)	No	—	256 K
Sierra OPS5 (OPS) (Inference engine Technologies)	$795	IBM PC/XT/AT or compatibles (DOS 2.0 or later)	No	—	384 K

Small, PC/Mac-Based Tools (Continued)

TOOL (Knowledge Representation) (Vendor)	Price Range	Hardware (Operating System/Language)	Generates SQL	Databases that system can access without writing hook	Memory Requirements RAM/Harddisk
SuperExpert (Inductive) (Softsync Inc.)	$199.95	IBM PC's and compatibles (MS-DOS), MAC, PS/2, (Pascal)	No		256 K
VP Expert (Simple Rule/Inductive) (Paperback Software)	$249	IBM PC's and compatibles (MS-DOS), (C)	No	dBASE 1-4, Lotus 1-2-3, VP-Info	384 K
XI Plus (Simple Rule) (Expertech Ltd.)	$1,995-17 K	IBM /XT/AT or compatibles (MS-DOS), All MicroVAX workstations, (MicroProlog/ Assembler)	No	dBASE, Oracle	640 K Hard Drive recom.

Midsize PC/Workstation-Based Tools

TOOL (Knowledge Representation) (Vendor)	Price Range	Hardware (Operating System/Language)	Generates SQL	Databases that system can access without writing hook	Memory Requirements RAM/Harddisk
Application Software Expert (Software Artistry)	$5,000-36 K	OS/400 (Pascal)	No	Any Database on the AS/400	—
ART-IM (Hybrid) (Inference Corp.)	$8000-100 K	IBM PC/AT, PS/2 and compatibles (MS-DOS) IBM Mainframes (MVS), SUN 3 & 4 (Unix), DEC (VMS), Apollo (Unix), TI Explorer I & II, Symbolics 3600 series. (C)	No	IMS, DB2, VSAM, Flat files	PC: 640 K 1-2 mb extended memory; 8 mb Hard Disk M/F: 3 mb address space for develop.
CLIPS (OPS) (COSMIC)	$312	IBM PC and compatibles (DOS & Xenix), MAC, VAX, Sun, Apollo, HP9000, CDC Cyber, CRAY (C)	No	—	—
Enterprise Expert (Simple Rule) (Cullinet Software)	$19 -60 K	IBM Mainframes(OSV2, MV2, MVS/XA, MVS/SP, DOS-VSE ORVM/CMS), VAX/VMS (CICS, IDMS/DC,VCF, (Cobol)	No	DBMS, IDMS,V/SAM, IMS,DB2,Oracle, RDB, RMS, Enterprise DB	1mb 25mb Hard Drive recom.
Exsys Prfessional (Simple Rule) (Exsys Inc.)	$795-12 K	IBM PC/AT and compatibles (MS-DOS), VAX (VMS or Altrex), Unix, SUN 3 & 4, (C)	No	dBASE III, Lotus 1-2-3	640 K Hard Drive recom.
GURU (Structured Rule) (MDBS Inc.)	$6,500	IBM PC's and compatibles (MS 0r PC-DOS), MicroVAX (VMS), (C)	Yes	dBASE III	PC: 640 K Hard Drive required
KES II/KES/VE (Structured Rule) (Software A&E, Prime Comp., Unisys, Control Data)	$4,000-60 K	IBM PC's and compatibles (MS-DOS), Workstations, Minis, Mainframes (NOS/VE, MVS/TSO, CICS, IMS andVM/CMS)	Yes	dBASE, Oracle	PC: 640 K Hard Drive recom.
Laser (Bell Atlantic KnowledgeSystems)	$900-25 K	PS/2 (OS/2, MAC II, SUN, microVAX (Unix), (C) IBM Mainframe (MVS,VM)	No	—	2 mb
Level5 (Simple Rule) (Information Builders Inc.)	$685 - $48-57.6 K - $1,200-58.4 K	IBM PC's and compatibles, PS/2 (MS-DOS), MAC+ IBM Mainframes (VM/CMS, MVS) Digital VAX (VMS)	No	PC: dBASE II & III MAC: HyperCard, Excel Mainframe: Focus, DB2, SQL/DS VAX: Focus, Rdb, RS1, RMS - CDD	PC:512 K MAC: 512 K Hard Drive recom.

Midsize PC/Workstation-Based Tools (Continued)

TOOL (Knowledge Representation) (Vendor)	Price Range	Hardware (Operating System/Language)	Generates SQL	Databases that system can access without writing hook	Memory Requirements RAM/Harddisk
Nexpert Object (Hybrid) (Neuron Data)	$5,000-8,000	IBM PC/AT, PS/2 and 386 and compatibles (MS-DOS), MAC +, SE and II, Dec VAXstations /Dec-stations (VMS and Ultrix), IBM RT, Sun Apollo, HP, VAX (Unix), Mainframe (delivery) - (VM), (C)	Yes	Oracle, Sybase, Ingres, Informix, Lotus 1-2-3, dBASE III, SQL, RDB	IBM: 1mb and 1 mb expanded memory. MAC: 2 mb
Nexus (Hybrid) (Human Intellect Systems)	$698	IBM PC/AT and compatibles (MS-DOS), MAC, (Modula II)	Yes	dBASE	640 K Hard Disk recom.
OPS/83 (Simple Rule) (Production Systems Technologies Inc.)	$1,900-25 K	IBM PC's and compatibles (MS-DOS), Apollo, AT&T 3B & 386, Unix 386 (Unix), HP 9000's, VAX, MicroVAX, Sun 3&4, OS/2 or compatible, (C)	No	dBASE III	PC: 640 K; Hard Drive recom.
Personal Consultant Plus (Struct. Rule) (Texas Instruments)	$2,950	IBM /XT/AT or compatibles, PS/2, Explorer or MicroExplorer (PC or MS-DOS), (Scheme, C)	No	dBASE, Lotus 1-2-3, External Lang. Interface to Cobol, Pascal, C	2 mb expanded or extended mem.; KB occupies 640 K
RuleMaster (Inductive) (Radian Corp.)	$7,500-28 K	IBM PC's and compatibles (MS-DOS, XENIX), VAX and Unix work stations (Unix, VMS)	Yes	–	–
TIMM (Inductive) (General Research)	$1,900-19 K	IBM PC/AT and compatibles (MS-DOS), IBM Mainframes,(MVS/VM, VMS) Digital VAX, Unix, Primos (Unix), (Fortran)	No	–	640 K 10 mb Hard Disk recom.
VAX Decision Expert (Digital Equipment Corp.)	$6,000-28 K	Any Dec VAX workstation (VMS), (VAX C)	No	–	16 mb and RD54 Hard Drive Recom.
VaxOPS5 (3.0) (Digital Equipment Corp.)	$6,000-28 K	All VAXstations, MicroVAX (VMS) (Bliss)	No	RDB	User: 8 mb Develop.: 16 mb

Mainframe-Based Tools

TOOL (Knowledge Representation) (Vendor)	Price Range	Hardware (Operating System/Language)	Generates SQL	Databases that system can access without writing hook	Memory Requirements RAM/Harddisk
Aion Development System (ADS)(5.1) (Hybrid) (Aion Corp.)	$7000-85 K	IBM PC's and Mainframes S/370 (MVS/TSO, CICS, IMS, DB/DC, VM/CMS, MS-DOS) (Pascal,COBOL,C)	Yes	DL/I, DB2, SQL/DS, QSAM, VSAM	PC: 640 K OS/2: 1.5 mb/RAM Hard Disk recom.
Expert System Environment (ESE) (Struct. Rule) (IBM)	$23,410- $60,440	IBM PC's - delivery, Mainframes (MVS/XA, MVS/TSO, VM/CMS, MVS/CICS, MVS/IMS) (Pascal)	Yes	DB2, SQL/DS, VSAM	–
KBMS (Hybrid) (AI Corp., Inc.)	$9,500 - $90-225K	IBM PC's 286 &386 or compatibles (MS-DOS & OS/2) IBM Mainframes (MVS/XA, MVS, VM, CICS, TSO, IMS/DC, CMS), (C)	Yes	DB2, SQL/DS, IDMS, VSAM, ADABAS, IMS	4 mb
Knowledge Tool (OPS) (IBM)	$950/mo.	IBM Mainframes (MVS/XA/TSO, MVS/ESA/ TSO, IMS/VS, CICS/OS/VS, VM/SP/CMS, VM/SP/HPO), (PL/I)	Yes	DB2, D/I, VSAM, SQLDS, PL/I Supp. Struct.	–
TOP-ONE (Simple Rule) (Telecomputing)	$145 K	Mainframe (MVS/XA, CICS, DOS/VSE) (Transaction Oriented Prolog [TOP])	–	SQL/DS, DB2, DL/I	–

Lisp-Based Tools

TOOL (Knowledge Representation) (Vendor)	Price Range	Hardware (Operating System/Language)	Generates SQL	Databases that system can access without writing hook	Memory Requirements RAM/Harddisk
ART (Hybrid) (Inference Corp.)	$22.5-30 K	Symbolics (Genera), TI Explorer, DEC workstations ((VMS), Sun, Apollo & HP workstations (Unix), (Lisp)	No	Flat files, Call Facilities	12 mb minimum, 16 mb recom.
Eloquent (Hybrid) (Eloquent Systems Corp.)	$50-150 K	TI Explorer (Co-processor equiped) (Lisp), Mac - using Explorer as main file server, (C)	No	–	512 K, 1 mb recom.
G2 Real Time Expert System (Gensym Corp.)	$18,000	MAC II, Compaq 386, DEC workstations, Symbolics 3260, TI Explorer, Sun, DecVAX, (Lisp)	No	–	8-16 mb
GEST (Generic Expert System Tool) (Georgia Tech. Reserarch Institute)	$15-45 K	VAX workstations, Sum Micro, Symbolics, Explorer, (Lisp)	No	No	–
GoldWorks II (Hybrid) (Gold Hill Computers)	$7,500	286 PC (Golden Common Lisp)	No	dBASE	6 mb
Joshua (Hybrid) (Symbolics)	$10,000	Symbolics (Lisp)	–	–	–
KEE (Hybrid) and IBM/KEE (Hybrid) (Intellicorp) (IBM & Intellicorp)	$9,000-$98 K or $4,900 mo.	VAX, Apollo, Sun, Symbolics, Explorer, Micro-Explorer, 386 PC (Lisp) IBM/KEE: Mainframe (MVS), access via PC	Yes	DB2, IMS/DB	10 mb 100 mb Hard Drive recom.
Keystone (Technology Applications Inc.)	$4,000	IBM 286 and 386 or compatibles (MS-DOS) (Golden Common Lisp)	No	–	6-8 mb, Hard Drive recom.
KnowledgeCraft (Hybrid) (Carnegie Group)	$10-70 K	386 PC (Unix), Sun MicroVAX (VAX), Symbolics, Explorer, Mainframe (VAX)	Yes	Oracle, dBASE	8-16 mb recom.
Mercury KBE (Hybrid) A I Technologies	$21 K	VAX workstations	Yes	Rdb, Sybase, Oracle, DB2, RMS	–
OPS5E ((OPS) (Ball Systems Engineering Division)	$3,000 - 10 K	Symbolics 3600, TI Explorer (Lisp)	–	–	–

Problem-Based Tools

TOOL (Knowledge Representation) (Vendor)	Price Range	Hardware (Operating System/Language)	Problem	Memory Requirements RAM/Harddisk
Diagnostic Reasoning Template (Coherent Thought)	$19-100 K	Mainframe (MVS/XA/TSO, CICS), IBM PC's, various workstations, (C)	Equipment Diagnosis	–
Genesis V (help/systems Inc.)	$14,950	System/38	Develops expert frontends for relational databases	–
Intelliform (Mind Path Technologies)	$495	IBM PC's and compatibles (C)	Intelligent Forms Entry	512 k
ProGenisis (Quantum inKNOWvations)	$895-4,995	IBM PC's and compatibles, (MS-DOS), (C)	Develops expert frontends for SQL releational databases	–
TestBench (Texas Instruments/Carnegie Group)	$35-40 K	TI Explorer, Sun, MicroVAX (Lisp) Delivery via PC (C)	Equipment Diagnosis	8 mb, 2 Hard Disks of 140 mb recom.
Service/Maintenance Planner (Carnegie Group)	$295 K	Sun-4, TI Explorer, Symboliics (Lisp)	Develops service and maintenance plans and schedules	–

Application-Specific Tools

TOOL (Knowledge Representation) (Vendor)	Price Range	Hardware (Operating System/Language)	Domain	Memory Requirements RAM/Harddisk
CAIS (Rosh Intelligent Systems Inc.)	$100-200 K	Unix-based or MS-DOS (Prolog)	Troubleshooting for service technicians	PC/AT or higher 640K
Cogensys Judgement Software (Cogensys Corp.)	$200,000	PC AT, PS/2 or compatibles (DOS) (C, Pascal)	For developing financial applications	512 K memory 20 mb Harddisk recom..,
Expert Controller (Umecorp)	$10,000	Development: IBM Pc's and compatibles (DOS), Runtime on Expert Controller	Automation of process controller programming	PC: 640 K, 10 mb Harddisk recom.
Flexis ToolSet (Savoir Systems Group)	$35,000	Sun 3 & 4, Sparcstation Xerox 1185 & 1186	Manufacturing control	8 mb
ICAD (ICAD Inc.)	$40-95 K	Sun 4/110, 4/260, Sparcstation, T I Explorer, Apple microExplorer (Lisp)	Engineering design automation	8 mb
I-CAT (Automated Reasoning Corp.)	$10,000	IBM PC/AT (DOS), MAC II, Apollo, Unix, Sun, DecVAX, (Lisp)	Diagnostic testing of electrical equipment	—
Intelligen (CIMTelligence Corp.)	$35,000	Digital VAc 2000 or larger (VMS), (Fortran 77)	Generates process plans	2-4 mb
Maingen (OXKO Corp.)	$195	IBM PC's and compatibles (Level5)	Maintenance Application Systems	512 K
Operations Planner (Carnegie Group)	$39,000	IBM PC's and compatibles, (MS-DOS), (Fortran)	Create and compare alternative scenarios of plant operations	640 K Harddisk recom.

LIST OF VENDORS AND PRODUCTS MENTIONED IN TABLES

1st-Class Expert Systems, Inc.
1st-CLASS FUSION
One Longfellow Center
526 Boston Post Road, Suite 150 East
Wayland, MA 01778
Phone: (508)358-7722

Aion Corp.
ADS (Aion Development System)
101 University Ave.
Palo Alto, CA 94301
Phone: (415)328-9595

AI Corp Inc.
KBMS
100 Fifth Ave.
Waltham, MA 02254
Phone: (617)890-8400

Artificial Intelligence Technologies, Inc.
MERCURY KBE
1 Skyline Drive
Hawthorne, NY 10532
Phone: (914)347-6860

A List of Expert Systems Building Tools

Automated Reasoning Corp.
I-CAT (Formerly IN-ATE)
1800 Northern Blvd.
Roslyn, NY 11576
Phone: (516)484-6254

Ball Systems Engineering Div. (Formerly Verac)
OPS5e
9605 Scranton Road
San Diego, CA 92121
Phone: (619)457-5550

Bell Atlantic Knowledge Systems, Inc.
LASER
P.O. Box 3528
Princeton, NJ 08543-3528
Phone: (609)275-4545

Carnegie Group, Inc.
KNOWLEDGE CRAFT
TESTBENCH
SERVICE/MAINTENANCE PLANNER
OPERATIONS PLANNER
Five PPG Place
Pittsburgh, PA 15222
Phone: (412)642-6900

CIMTelligence Corp.
INTELLIGEN
One Forbes Road
Lexington, MA 02173
Phone: (617)861-1996

Cognition Technology
MACSMARTS
MACSMARTS PROFESSIONAL
55 Wheeler Street
Cambridge, MA 02138
Phone: (617)492-0246

Cogensys Corp.
COGENSYS JUDGEMENT SOFTWARE
11077 N. Torrey Pines Road
La Jolla, CA 92037
Phone: (619)458-1500

Coherent Thought
DIAGNOSTIC REASONING TEMPLATE
3350 West Bayshore Road, Suite 205
Palo Alto, CA 94303
Phone: (415)493-8805

Cosmic
CLIPS
The University of Georgia
382 E. Broad Street
Athens, GA 30602
Phone: (404)542-3265

Cullinet Software Inc.
ENTERPRISE EXPERT
400 Blue Hill Drive
Westwood, MA 02090
Phone: (617)329-7700

DEC
VAX DECISION EXPERT
VAS OPS5
AI Technology Center
290 Donald Lynch Blvd.
Marlborough, MA 01752
Phone: (508)493-5111

Eloquent Systems Corp.
ELOQUENT
Technology Park Building 2
Londonderry, NH 03053
Phone: (603)627-9494

Emerald Intelligence
MAGELLAN
MAHOGANY PROFESSIONAL
3915-AI Research Park Drive
Ann Arbor, MI 48108
Phone: (313)663-8757

Expertech Inc.
XI PLUS
P.O. Box AF
Incline Village, NV 89450
Phone: (702)831-0136

ExperTelligence, Inc.
EXPERCOMMONOPS5
EXPERFACTS
EXPEROPS5+
5638 Hollister Ave., Suite 303
Goleta, CA 93117
Phone: (805)967-1797

Exsys Inc.
EXSYS
EXSYS PROFESSIONAL
P.O. Box 11247
Albuquerque, NM 87192-0247
Phone: (505)256-8356

General Research
TIMM
7655 Old Springhouse Road
McLean, VA 22102
Phone: (703)893-5915

Gensym Corp.
G2
125 Cambridge Park Drive
Cambridge, MA 02140
Phone: (617)547-9606

Georgia Tech. Research Inst.
GEST
AI Branch
Georgia Institute of Technology
Atlanta, GA 30332
Phone: (404)894-3559

Gold Hill Computers
GOLDWORKS II
26 Lansdowne St.
Cambridge, MA 02139
Phone: (800)242-5477

Helix Expert Systems Ltd.
EXPERT EDGE
190 Strand
London, WC2R 1DT, England
Phone: (01) 836 7788

Help/Systems, Inc.
GENESIS V
210 Baker Technology Plaza
6101 Baker Road
Minnetonka, MN 55345
Phone: (612)933-0609

Human Intellect Systems
INSTANT EXPERT
INSTANT EXPERT+
NEXUS
1670 S. Amphlett Blvd., Suite 326
San Mateo, CA 94402
Phone: (415)571-5939

Hyperpress Publishing Corp.
INTELLIGENT DEVELOPER
P.O. Box 8243
Foster City, CA 94404
Phone: (415)345-4620

IBM Inc.
IBM/KEE
ESE
KNOWLEDGETOOL
P.O. Box 10
Princeton, NJ 08543
Phone: (201)329-7000

ICAD Inc.
ICAD
1000 Massachusetts Ave.
Cambridge, MA 02138
Phone: (617)868-2800

Inference Corp.
ART
ART-IM
5300 West Century Blvd.
Los Angeles, CA 94005
Phone: (213)417-7997

Inference Engine Technologies
SIERRA OPS5
1430 Massachusetts Ave., Suite 306-I
Cambridge, MA 02138
Phone: (800)255-0625

Information Builders Inc.
LEVEL5
1250 Broadway
New York, NY 10001
Phone: (212)736-4433

Intellicorp
KEE
1975 El Camino Real West
Mountain View, CA 94040
Phone: (415)965-5650

Intelligent Environments Ltd.
CRYSTAL
One Village Square
P.O. Box 388
Chelmsford, MA 01824
Phone: (508)256-6412

Intellipro
OPS-2000
10 Park Place
Morristown, NJ 07960
Phone: (201)605-5131

KDS Corp.
KDS 2 & 3
934 Hunter Road
Wilmette, IL 60091
Phone: (312)251-2621

Keystone Technologies Inc.
KEYSTONE
7400 Bay Meadows Way
Jacksonville, FL 32217
Phone: (904)737-1685

Knowledge Garden Inc.
KNOWLEDGEPRO
473A Malden Bridge Road, RD2
Nassau, NY 12123
Phone: (518)766-3000

McGraw-Hill Book Co.
MICRO EXPERT
11 West 19th St., 4th Floor
New York, NY 10011
Phone: (212)337-5962

MDBS Inc.
GURU
P.O. Box 248
Lafayette, IN 47902
Phone: (800)344-5832

Mind Path Technologies
EST
INTELLIFORM
12700 Park Central Drive, Suite 1801
Dallas, TX 75251
Phone: (214)233-9296

Neuron Data
NEXPERT OBJECT
444 High Street
Palo Alto, CA 94301
Phone: (415)321-4488

OXKO Corp.
MAINGEN
P.O. Box 6674
Annapolis, MD 21401
Phone: (301)266-1671

Paperback Software
VP-EXPERT
2830 Ninth Street
Berkeley, CA 94710
Phone: (415)644-2116

Park Row Software Inc.
EASY EXPERT
4640 Jewell Street #232
San Diego, CA 92109
Phone: (619)581-6778

Production Systems Technologies Inc.
OPS/83
5001 Baum Blvd.
Pittsburgh, PA 15213
Phone: (412)683-4000

Programming Logic Associates
FLEX
31 Crescent Drive
Milford, CT 06460
Phone: (203)877-7988

Quantum inKNOWvations Corp.
PROGENSIS
2953 Bunker Hill Lane, Suite 200
Santa Clara, CA 95054
Phone: (408)496-6933

Radian Corp.
RULEMASTER
P.O. Box 201088
Austin, TX 78720
Phone: (512)454-4797

ROSH Intelligent Systems Ltd.
CAIS
850 Boylston Street, Suite 316
Chestnut Hill, MA 02167
Phone: (617)734-4445

Savoir Systems Group
FLEXIS TOOLSET
3102 Diablo
Hayward, CA 94545
Phone: (415)732-9800

Softsync Inc.
SUPEREXPERT
162 Madison Ave.
New York, NY 10016
Phone: (212)685-2080

Software A & E
KES II
KES/VE
1600 Wilson Blvd., Suite 500
Arlington, VA 22209
Phone: (703)276-7910

Software Artistry, Inc.
PC EXPERT
PC EXPERT PROFESSIONAL
APPLICATION SOFTWARE EXPERT
3500 De Pauw Blvd., Suite 2021
Indianapolis, IN 46268
Phone: (317)876-3042

Software Plus
CxPERT
1652 Albermarle Dr.
Crofton, MD 21114
Phone: (301)261-0264

Symbolics Inc.
JOSHUA
11 Cambridge Center
Cambridge, MA 02142
Phone: (617)621-7500

Telecomputing
TOP-ONE
244 Barn's Road
Oxford OX4 3RW, England
Phone: (0865)777-755

Texas Instruments
PERSONAL CONSULTANT EASY
PERSONAL CONSULTANT PLUS
PROCEDURAL CONSULTANT
TESTBENCH
12501 Research Blvd., MS 2244
P.O. Box 2909
Austin, TX 78769
Phone: (800)527-3500

Umecorp
EXPERT CONTROLLER
45 San Clemente, D-200
Corte Madera, CA 94925
Phone: (415)924-6700

Appendix II
Glossary

Active value. A special type of method that allows the user to trigger rules in a system simply by changing a graphic image on the screen.

Agenda. An ordered list of actions. Some systems maintain or develop lists of possible actions. An agenda is used to control the reasoning during a consultation.

Algorithm. A step-by-step procedure that guarantees a correct outcome. To develop a conventional computer program, the programmer specifies the algorithm that the program will follow.

Artificial intelligence. "A subfield of computer science concerned with the concepts and methods of symbolic inference by a computer and the symbolic representation of the knowledge to be used in making inferences. A field aimed at pursuing the possibility that a computer can be made to behave in ways that humans recognize as 'intelligent' behavior in each other." (Feigenbaum and McCorduck, 1983) Artificial intelligence is an academic discipline, like physics; it isn't a product, it's a broad research program aimed at improving what computers can do.

Attribute. A property of an object. For example, *tire* is an attribute of a car. Attributes can have various values. They have specific values in particular situations. Thus, a 1985 Saab came equipped with four Pirelli 185/65 tires.

Back end. An expert system that acquires facts from a database at the start of a consultation, and then incorporates these facts into its reasoning process.

Backtracking. The process of backing up through a sequence of inferences, in order to try a different path. Planning problems typically require backtracking strategies that allow a system to try one plan after another until the system finds a path that has no unacceptable outcomes.

Backward chaining. (Back chaining.) A control strategy that regulates the order in which inferences are drawn. In a rule-based system, backward chaining is initiated by a goal. The system attempts to determine a value for the goal. The system identifies rules that conclude a value for the goal, then backs up and attempts to determine if the If-clauses of the rule are true. Thus, the attributes of the If-clause of the rule become secondary goals, and the system backs up again to find rules that would determine the value of those attributes. This, in turn, leads the system to consider other rules that would confirm the If-clauses. In this way, the system backs into its rules. Eventually, the backward chaining sequence ends when a question is asked or a previously stored result is found.

Blackboard architecture. (HEARSAY architecture.) An expert systems design in which several independent knowledge bases each examine a common working memory, called a "blackboard." An agenda-based control system continually examines all of the possible pending actions and chooses the one to try next.

Breadth-first search. A control strategy that examines all of the rules or objects on the same level of the hierarchy before examining any of the rules or objects on the next lower level.

Certainty. The degree of confidence a person has in a fact or relationship. As used in AI, this contrasts with probability, which is the likelihood that an event will occur. There are two types of certainty: the certainty that the expert has in a relationship expressed in a particular rule or relationship, and the certainty that the user has when providing information during a consultation.

Certainty factor. (Confidence factors.) A numerical weight given to a fact or relationship to indicate the confidence a person has in the fact or relationship. The most common kind of certainty factors are sometimes called "EMYCIN certainty factors" to indicate that they are calculated by the formula developed during the development of MYCIN. In general, methods for manipulating EMYCIN certainty factors are more informal than approaches to combining probabilities. Most rule-based systems use EMYCIN certainty factors rather than probabilities.

Common LISP. The standard dialect of LISP that is used in commercial AI.

Compound rule. A large rule composed of a number of smaller rules, grouped together with ELSEIF statements.

Conflict set. The set of rules in a forward chaining system that contains the current candidates for execution.

Consultation paradigm. A paradigm that describes a generic problem-solving scenario. Most expert systems building tools are good for one or a few consultation paradigms but not for others. Most of the smaller rule-based tools are designed to facilitate rapid development of expert systems that utilize the Diagnostic paradigm.

Context-parameter-value triples. (Object-attribute-value triples, or frame-parameter-value triples.) This is the way that facts are described in EMYCIN. A context is an actual or conceptual entity in the domain of the consultant (e.g., a patient, an aircraft, an oil well). Parameters are properties or attributes associated with each context (e.g., age and sex of a patient or location and depth of an oil well). Each parameter (or attribute) can take on values (e.g., the parameter "sex" could take the value "male").

Context tree. (Object tree or frame tree.) A context tree arranges rules into sets (or contexts) and determines, in a hierarchical manner, which set is used in what order. Most context tree systems have several contexts. A context tree provides the structure in a structured rule system. A static context tree describes the structure of the knowledge base when it is not being used. When the system is being used, a dynamic context tree is created. The dynamic tree may omit unnecessary static contexts or may use a single static context several times (i.e. multiple instantiation).

Control (of a knowledge system). The methods used by the inference engine to determine the order in which reasoning occurs. Backward chaining and depth-first search are both examples of control methods.

Dataflow analysis. A technique to divide a problem into discrete activities, processes, or computations and show the data that is passed from one activity to another. A dataflow diagram represents processes as circles and the data that is passed between one process and another (a dataflow) as an arrow. In effect, the processes are the verbs and the data are the nouns of a dataflow diagram.

Deep knowledge. Knowledge of basic theories, first principles, axioms, and facts about a domain. This contrasts with domain models and surface knowledge.

Default or **Default values**. Computer programs often have prespecified values that they use if they are not given alternative values. These assumed values are called default values. Object-oriented systems typically have higher-level objects with default values that lower-level objects inherit.

Definitional rule. A rule that is used to define relationships among objects in the knowledge base, but doesn't contain any expert knowledge about how to solve a problem. Definitional rules are usually found in systems that are built using small tools. Mid-size and large tools offer rich enough knowledge structures that definitional rules become unnecessary.

Demon. A procedure attached to a slot. Whenever the slot's value changes, the demon is invoked.

Depth-first search. A control strategy in which one rule or object on the highest level is examined and then the rules or objects immediately below that one are examined. Proceeding in this manner, the system searches down a single branch of a tree until it reaches the end. It then backs up to the first unsearched branch and goes down that branch, and so on. This contrasts with breadth-first search.

Diagnosis. A consultation paradigm that assumes you know the possible outcomes or recommendations that a system can make and that you search for evidence that will confirm or deny each of the possible recommendations.

Domain. A subject matter area or problem-solving task. Finance and factory automation are very broad domains. Existing systems provide good advice only when they are used to assist users in solving problems that lie within very narrowly defined domains. Analyzing auto loans, or diagnosing what could be wrong with a particular type of robotic device are examples of narrow domains or tasks.

Domain-specific tool. An expert systems development tool that is tailored to a specific domain or subject area. Some of these tools are specialized for a generic type of problem, like diagnosis problems, while others are specialized for specific domains or vertical markets, like process control or financial risk analysis.

Dynamic images. (Also known as "active images," or "graphic objects.") These are predefined graphic images that developers can incorporate into their own applications. By choosing images and specifying how they should be displayed, the developer can design screens with meters, gauges, buttons, and other elements. These images can be linked to values in the knowledge base that control their appearance.

Early binding. The process of establishing the links between pieces of knowledge prior to the start of a consultation, as opposed to constructing these links during a consultation as a result of inference (late binding). Early binding is generally more efficient than late binding, but less flexible.

EMYCIN. The first expert systems building tool. EMYCIN was derived from the expert system MYCIN. After the developers of MYCIN completed that system, they decided that they could remove the specific medical knowledge in MYCIN (hence *Empty MYCIN*). The resulting shell consists of a backward chaining inference engine, a context tree system, confidence factors, a consultation driver, and several knowledge acquisition aids. By adding new rules about some new task to this shell or tool you can produce a new expert system.

Environment. See *Programming environment*.

Example-driven system. See *Induction system*.

Exhaustive search. A search strategy that systematically examines every possible path through a decision tree or network. Exhaustive search is costly or impossible for many problems. Small expert systems typically search exhaustively through all of the rules in their knowledge bases.

Experiential knowledge. Knowledge gained from hands-on experience. This typically consists of specific facts and rules of thumb (surface knowledge). This is in contrast to deep knowledge of formal principles or theories.

Expert system. As originally used, it referred to a computer system that could perform at, or near, the level of a human expert. Evaluations of MYCIN place its competence at or near that of highly specialized physicians. Configuration systems like XCON (R1) probably exceed human competence. As the term is currently being used, it refers to any computer system that is developed by means of a loose collection of techniques associated with AI research. Thus, any computer system developed by means of an expert systems building tool would qualify as an expert system even if the system were so narrowly constrained that it could never be said to rival a human expert. The popular press and various software entrepreneurs have already used the term "expert system" in so many ways, however, that it now defies any precise meaning.

Expertise. The skill and knowledge that some humans possess that result in performance that is far above the norm. Expertise often consists of massive amounts of factual information coupled with rules of thumb, simplifications, rare facts, and wise procedures, all compiled in a way that allows the expert to analyze specific types of problems in an efficient manner.

Explanation. Broadly, this refers to information that is presented to justify a particular course of reasoning or action. In expert systems, explanation normally refers to a number of techniques that help a user understand what a system is doing. Many knowledge systems allow a user to ask "Why," "How," or "Explain." In each case, the system responds by telling the user something about its assumptions or its inner reasoning.

Explicit iteration. The re-execution of a rule caused by explicit looping commands (such as FOR-NEXT or DO-WHILE) written directly into the rule.

Facet. One aspect of a slot's definition. Possible slot facets include the slot name, the slot's default value, the slot's constraints, the certainty factor of the slot's value, and so on.

Fact. Broadly, a statement whose validity is accepted. In most expert systems, a fact consists of an attribute and one or more values that are associated with the attribute.

Forward chaining. A control strategy that regulates the order in which inferences are drawn. In a rule-based system, forward chaining begins by reviewing the known facts and then firing all of the rules whose If-clauses are true. The system then begins another cycle and checks to determine what additional rules might be true, given the facts established during the first cycle, and so on. This process is repeated until the program reaches a goal or runs out of new possibilities.

Frame. (Object or Unit.) A knowledge representation scheme that associates an object with a collection of features (e.g., facts, rules, defaults, active values). Each feature is stored in a slot. A frame is the set of slots related to a specific object. A frame is similar to a property list, schema, or record, as these terms are used in conventional programming.

Front end. An expert system that uses its recommendations as the basis for a database search.

Heuristic. A rule of thumb, or other device or simplification that allows its user to draw conclusions without being certain. Unlike algorithms, heuristics do not guarantee correct solutions.

Heuristic rules. Rules written to capture the heuristics an expert uses to solve a problem. The expert's original heuristics may not have taken the form of If–Then rules, and one of the problems involved in building a knowledge system is converting an expert's heuristic knowledge into rules. The power of an expert system reflects the heuristic rules in the knowledge base.

Hierarchy. An ordered network of concepts or objects in which some are subordinate to others. Hierarchies normally imply that subordinate concepts or objects inherit some or all of the properties of the superordinate or parent objects, in the sense that Fords and Hondas are both cars and inherit the generic properties of Car. "Tangled hierarchies" occur when a lower-level entity inherits properties from more than one higher-level entity.

If–Then rule. A rule that establishes a relationship among a set of facts in an If-clause and one or more facts in a Then-clause. Rules may be definitional (e.g., if female and married, then wife) or heuristic (e.g., if cloudy, then take umbrella).

Implicit iteration. The automatic re-execution of a rule that refers to a broad range of instances. The system automatically retrieves each instance and plugs it into the rule.

Induction system. (Example-driven system.) A knowledge system that generates a decision tree or rule from a set of examples.

Inference. The process by which new facts are derived from established facts.

Inference engine. That portion of an expert system that contains the inference and control strategies. More broadly, the inference engine also includes various knowledge acquisition, explanation, and user interface subsystems. When an inference engine is separated from a knowledge base, it is, in effect, an expert systems building tool.

Inheritance. A process by which characteristics of one object are assumed to be characteristics of another. In effect, inheritance is the inference strategy used by object-oriented systems. Thus, if you determine that a company is a bank, then you automatically assume that the company sells checking and savings accounts to customers.

Inheritance hierarchies. When knowledge is represented in a hierarchy, the characteristics of superordinate (parent) objects are inherited by subordinate objects (children).

Instantiation. The process by which a static rule or object is used during a consultation and is assigned specific values.

Interface. The link between a computer program and the outside world. A single program may have several interfaces. Expert systems typically have a developer interface, a user interface, and a systems interface through which they relate with other software and with hardware.

Iterative rules. Rules that are repeatedly fired during a consultation in order to process multiple frame instances, or multiple elements of an array.

Job aids. (Performance aids.) Job aids are devices that individuals use when they perform tasks. Well-constructed job aids allow the performer to avoid memorization. Thus, they allow individuals to perform jobs more quickly and more accurately than they would if they had been trained in any conventional manner. Moreover, performers memorize frequently used responses while using job aids; hence, they serve as structured on-the-job training. Whenever they are appropriate, job aids are the current medium of choice among instructional designers. Small knowledge systems are ideal job aids for a wide variety of tasks and will rapidly replace most of the checklists, procedures manuals, and other common job aids currently in use.

Knowledge. An integrated collection of facts and relationships which, when exercised, produces competent performance. The quantity and quality of knowledge possessed by a person or a computer can be judged by the variety of situations in which the person or program can obtain successful results.

Knowledge acquisition. The process of locating, collecting, and refining knowledge. This may require interviews with experts, research in a library, or introspection. The person undertaking the knowledge acquisition must convert the acquired knowledge into a form that can be used by a computer program. Knowledge is derived from current sources, especially from experts.

Knowledge base. The portion of an expert system that consists of the facts and heuristics about a domain. The knowledge may be in the form of examples, facts, rules, or objects.

Knowledge bottlenecks. These are situations in which many tasks or too much information converge on one person at one time. Knowledge bottlenecks typically occur when people wait for someone else to make a decision, when people have to stop what they are doing to go look up or search for information needed to make a decision, or when items pile up because decisions "can't be made" regarding them (e.g., the decision is complex and it takes several different people to consider it to be sure all of the angles are covered).

Knowledge engineer. (Knowledge engineering). An individual whose specialty is assessing problems, acquiring knowledge, and building knowledge systems. Ordinarily, this implies training in cognitive science, computer science, and artificial intelligence. It also suggests experience in the actual development of one or more expert systems.

Knowledge representation. The method used to encode and store facts and relationships in a knowledge base. Semantic networks, facts, rules, objects, and frames are all ways to represent knowledge.

Knowledge system. A computer program that uses knowledge and inference procedures to solve difficult problems. The knowledge necessary to perform at such a level, plus the inference procedures used, can be thought of as a model of the expertise of skilled practitioners.

Language-system spectrum. A continuum along which various software products can be placed. At one extreme are expert systems. In the middle are the narrowly defined tools that are optimized to help developers build systems to perform specific tasks. At the other extreme are general purpose languages that can be used for many different applications.

Large, hybrid expert systems building tools. A class of knowledge engineering tools that emphasizes flexibility. The systems are designed for building large knowledge bases. They usually include a hybrid collection of different inference and control strategies. Most commercial hybrid tools incorporate frames and facilitate object-oriented programming.

Large, rule-based expert systems building tools. A class of knowledge engineering tools that sacrifices flexibility to facilitate the efficient development of more narrowly defined expert systems.

Late binding. The process by which links are established between pieces of knowledge at the time when the system is actually being used for a consultation.

LISP. A programming language based on List Processing. LISP is the AI language of choice for American AI researchers.

Machine learning. A research effort that seeks to create computer programs that can learn from experience. There are no commercial systems that can currently be said to learn from experience.

Maintenance of an expert system. Unlike conventional computer software that is only infrequently updated, expert systems by their nature are very easy to modify. Unlike conventional systems that are "completed," most expert systems that are currently in use are constantly being improved by the addition of new rules. In most applications, the user organization will want to establish a regular routine to capture and incorporate new knowledge into the system. For example, an application processing advisor system would be maintained by the senior application processing clerk. That clerk would be responsible for entering new rules whenever data or procedures changed or whenever questions arose that the current system could not answer.

Mental models or **Domain models** (of human experts). The symbolic networks and patterns of relationships that experts use when they are trying to understand a problem. Mental models often take the form of simplified analogies or metaphors that experts use when first examining a problem. Mental models can sometimes be converted into rules or context trees. They are easier to represent via object-oriented techniques, but in many cases the models that experts use still defy commercial AI techniques and are the object of considerable research in cognitive psychology.

Message passing. A technique used in object-oriented programming, in which an object can be sent a "message" from another object, triggering a procedure stored within it. Message passing is best used when objects have unique methods of accomplishing common tasks.

Metaknowledge. Knowledge about how to use knowledge.

Mid-run explanation. The ability of a computer program to stop upon request, and explain where it currently is, what it is doing, and what it will seek to accomplish next. Expert systems tend to have features that facilitate mid-run explanation while conventional programs do not.

Model world systems. Model world systems show a graphic simulation of a problem on the screen and allow the user to directly manipulate its elements. For example, while a tax advisory system might ask the user 10 questions, a model world system would have the user fill out an actual replica of the tax form.

Monotonic reasoning. A reasoning system based on the assumption that once a fact is determined, it cannot be altered during the course of the reasoning process.

Multivalued attribute. This refers to a knowledge system that allows the designer to specify that the system will seek all possible values that could apply to a particular attribute. If you developed a system to recommend an appropriate restaurant and the system did not allow for multivalued attributes, the system would determine the first restaurant that satisfied all the criteria and recommend it. If you could specify that restaurant was a multivalued attribute, however, the system would identify every restaurant that could satisfy all of the criteria.

MYCIN. An expert system developed at Stanford University in the mid-1970s. It is a research system designed to aid physicians in the diagnosis and treatment of meningitis and bacteremia infections. MYCIN is often spoken of as the first expert system. There were other systems that used many of the AI techniques associated with expert systems, but MYCIN was the first to combine all of the major features with the clear separation of the knowledge base and the inference engine. This separation, in turn, led to the subsequent development of the first expert systems building tool, EMYCIN.

Natural language. The branch of AI research that studies techniques that allow computer systems to accept inputs and produce outputs in a conventional language like English. At the moment, systems can be built that will accept typed input in narrowly constrained domains (e.g., database inquiries). Several expert systems incorporate some primitive form of natural language in their user interface to facilitate rapid development of new knowledge bases.

Nonmonotonic reasoning. Reasoning that can be revised if some value changes during a session. In other words, nonmonotonic reasoning can deal with problems that involve rapid changes in values in short periods of time. If you were developing an on-line expert system that monitored the stock market and recommended stocks to purchase, you would want a system that used nonmonotonic reasoning and was thus able to continually revise its recommendations as the prices and volumes of stock changed.

Object. (Context or Frame.) Broadly, this refers to physical or conceptual entities that have many attributes. When a collection of attributes or rules are divided into groups, each of the groups is organized around an object. When a knowledge base is divided into objects, it is often represented by an object tree that shows how the different objects relate to each other. When you use object-oriented programming, each object is called a frame or schema, and the attributes and values associated with it are stored in slots. An object is said to be "static" if it simply describes the generic relationship of a collection of attributes and possible values. It is said to be "dynamic" when an expert systems consultation is being run and particular values have been associated with a specific example of the object.

Object-attribute-value triples. (O-A-V triples or triplets.) One method of representing factual knowledge. This is the more general and common set of terms used to describe the relationships referred to as context-parameter-value triples in EMYCIN.

Operating system. The computer software system that does the "housekeeping" and communication chores for the more specialized systems. Most conventional computers have standard operating systems that software is designed to utilize. Thus, for example, the IBM personal computer uses MS-DOS. AI languages can be used to write operating systems so that the expert system and the operating system are written in the same language. LISP workstations, like the Symbolics LISP machines and the Texas Instruments Explorer, are computers that use a LISP operating system to improve their efficiency and flexibility when running expert systems written in LISP. In a similar manner, a Macintosh uses an operating system especially designed for object-oriented programming.

OPS5. An AI programming language commonly used for developing rule-based forward chaining systems. It has been used to develop large, complex systems, including DEC's XCON. OPS5 is probably the most popular development environment for building rule-based forward chaining systems. Though OPS5 is not limited to forward chaining, it is well suited for it.

Pattern-matching rule. A rule that applies not just to a single instance of an object, but across many instances of multiple objects. When a pattern-matching rule is evaluated by the system, it is automatically reinstantiated with every instance to which it applies.

Porting. The process of moving an application from one language to another, or from one platform to another.

Probability. Various approaches to statistical inference that can be used to determine the likelihood of a particular relationship. Expert systems have generally avoided probability and used confidence factors instead. Some systems, however, use a modified version of Bayesian probability theory to calculate the likelihood of various outcomes.

Problem solving. Problem solving is a process in which you start from an initial state and proceed to search through a problem space in order to identify the sequence of operations or actions that will lead to a desired goal. Successful problem solving depends upon knowing the initial state, knowing what an acceptable outcome would be, and knowing the elements and operations that define the problem space. If the elements or operators are very large in number, or if they are poorly defined, you are faced with a huge or unbounded problem space and an exhaustive search can become impossible. Methods are domain independent strategies like "generate and test." Strong methods exploit domain knowledge to achieve greater performance, usually by avoiding an exhaustive search in favor of exploring a few likely solutions.

Problem space. A conceptual or formal area defined by all of the possible states that could occur as a result of interactions between the elements and operators that are considered when a particular problem is being studied.

Procedures versus declarations. Procedures tell a system what to do (e.g., multiply A times B and then add C). Declarations tell a system what to know (e.g., $V = IR$).

Programming environment. (Environment.) A programming environment is about halfway between a language and a tool. A language allows the user complete flexibility. A tool constrains the user in many ways. A programming environment, like OPS5, provides a number of established routines that can facilitate the quick development of rule-based programs.

PROLOG. A symbolic or AI programming language based on Predicate Calculus. PROLOG is the most popular language for AI research outside of North America.

Prototype. In expert systems development, a prototype is an initial version of an expert system that is developed to test the effectiveness of the overall knowledge representation and inference strategies being employed to solve a particular problem.

Pruning. In expert systems, this refers to the process whereby one or more branches of a decision tree are "cut off" or ignored. In effect, when an expert systems consultation is underway, heuristic rules reduce the search space by determining that certain branches (or subsets of rules) can be ignored.

Reasoning. The process of drawing inferences or conclusions.

Recency. A measure of the length of time that a particular fact has existed in working memory. This is used by the OPS5 inference engine as one of its criteria in selecting rules to fire.

Repertory grid. The graphic representation of a psychological model called Personal Construct Theory, used to quantify a person's conceptual structures. A typical repertory grid contains three components: elements, constructs, and linking mechanisms. The conceptual structures are normally expressed in terms of bipolar dimensions (or constructs) like hot–cold or organized–disorganized.

Representation. The way in which a system stores knowledge about a domain. Knowledge consists of facts and the relationships among facts. Facts, rules, objects, and networks are all formats for representing knowledge.

Rete algorithm. An algorithm used by forward chaining systems to improve their performance. Executed before runtime, the Rete algorithm creates a data structure that the system uses during runtime to quickly locate rules that need to be evaluated.

Robotics. The branch of AI research that is concerned with enabling computers to "see" and "manipulate" objects in their surrounding environment. AI is not concerned with robotics, as such, but it is concerned with developing the techniques necessary to develop robots that can use heuristics to function in a highly flexible manner while interacting with a constantly changing environment.

Rule. (If–Then rule.) A conditional statement of two parts. The first part, comprised of one or more If-clauses, establishes conditions that must apply if a second part, comprised of one or more Then-clauses, is to be acted upon. The clauses of rules are usually A-V pairs or O-A-V triples.

Rule-based program. A computer program that represents knowledge by means of rules.

Rule network. A diagram that shows the general relationships among the rules in the knowledge base. A rule network is usually a more powerful debugging aid than a rule trace, since it is independent of any particular case.

Rule trace. A graphic diagram that shows how rules were invoked during a particular consultation. It is used primarily as a debugging aid while developing a system, in order to examine the system's reasoning for specific cases.

Runtime version or system. Knowledge systems building tools allow the user to create and run various knowledge bases. Using a single tool, a user might create a dozen knowledge bases. Depending on the problem the user was facing, she would load an appropriate knowledge base and undertake a consultation. With such a tool, the user can easily modify a knowledge base. Some companies may want to develop a specific knowledge base and then produce copies of the tool and that specific knowledge base. Under these circumstances, the organization will not want the user to have to "load" the knowledge base, nor will it want the user to be able to modify the knowledge base. When an expert systems building tool is modified to incorporate a specific knowledge base and to deactivate certain programming features, the resulting system is called a runtime system or a runtime version.

Screen frame. An object that exists solely for the purpose of constructing a system's user interface, and contains no knowledge about the problem domain. Some tools, like GoldWorks and KEE, offer developers a set of predefined screen frames to integrate into their own systems.

Screening clause. A set of clauses in a rule that dictates when the rule should be invoked. Screening clauses are usually added to heuristic rules to ensure that they are considered only at specific times.

Search and **Search space**. See *Problem solving* and *Problem space*.

Semantic. Refers to the meaning of an expression. It is often contrasted with syntactic, which refers to the formal pattern of the expression. Computers are good at establishing that the correct syntax is being used; they have a great deal of trouble establishing the semantic content of an expression. For example, look at the sentence, "Mary had a little lamb." It is a grammatically correct sentence; its syntax is in order. But its semantic content—its meaning—is very ambiguous. As you alter the context in which the sentence occurs, the meaning will change.

Semantic networks. A type of knowledge representation that formalizes objects and values as nodes and connects the nodes with arcs or links that indicate the relationships between the various nodes.

Slot. A component of an object. Slots can contain intrinsic features such as the object's name, attributes, and values, attributes with default values, rules to determine values, pointers to related objects, and information about the frame's creator.

Small expert systems. In general, small expert systems contain under 500 rules. They are designed to help individuals solve difficult analysis and decision-making tasks without aspiring to be the equivalent of any human expert. They are usually developed by nonprogrammers and thus represent a significant extension of who is involved in software development.

Small expert systems building tools. As used in this book, small tools are tools that can run on personal computers and that lack either variable rules or any way of structuring rules into sets (i.e., context trees). The line between small and mid-size tools is rapidly being obscured as the newer small tools add more powerful features.

Software, levels of. A continuum that begins at the lowest level with computer assembly language and extends up through low-level languages, high-level languages, tools, and finally to systems that users can use to actually solve problems.

Software engineer. An individual who designs conventional computer software. This individual serves a role similar to a knowledge engineer in the development of a conventional software program.

Sourcing. Storing a procedure in an attribute's definition that specifies how the attribute's value can be obtained. Sourcing can be used to link a database query to a slot's value. The query is then invoked anytime the value is referenced by the system.

Surface knowledge. (Experiential or heuristic knowledge.) Knowledge that is acquired from experience and is used to solve practical problems. Surface knowledge usually involves specific facts and theories about a particular domain or task and a large number of rules of thumb.

Symbol. An arbitrary sign used to represent objects, concepts, operations, relationships, or qualities.

Symbolic versus numeric programming. A contrast between the two primary uses of computers. Data reduction, database management, and word processing are examples of conventional or numerical programming. Knowledge systems depend on symbolic programming to manipulate strings of symbols with logical rather than numerical operators.

Syntactic. Refers to the formal pattern of an expression. (Contrast *Semantic*.)

Technology transfer. In the context of expert systems, this is the process by which knowledge engineers turn over an expert system to a user group. Since expert systems need to be continually updated, the knowledge engineers need to train the users to maintain a system before it arrives in the user environment. In effect, some users must learn how to do some knowledge engineering.

Tools. As used in this book, tools are computer software packages that simplify the effort involved in building an expert system. Most tools contain an inference engine and various user interface and knowledge acquisition aids and lack a knowledge base. Expert systems building tools tend to incorporate restrictions that make them easy to use for certain purposes and hard to impossible to use for other purposes. In acquiring a tool, you must be careful to select one that is appropriate for the type of expert system you want to build. More broadly, a tool is a shell that allows the user to rapidly develop a system that contains specific data. In this sense, an electronic spreadsheet program is a tool. When the user enters financial data, he creates a system that will do specific financial projections just as the knowledge engineer uses a tool to create an expert system that will offer advice about a specific type of problem.

Truth maintenance system. A system that automatically takes back all dependent information once a fact is removed from memory. Using truth maintenance, the system keeps a justification for every piece of knowledge, which is essentially a history of its derivation. Whenever the user retracts an answer, the system goes through all its assertions, retracting all dependent information as well.

Uncertainty. In the context of expert systems, uncertainty refers to a value that cannot be determined during a consultation. Most expert systems can accommodate uncertainty. That is, they allow the user to indicate that she does not know the answer. In this case, the system uses its other rules to try to establish the value by other means, or it relies on default values.

User interface. See *Interface*.

Value. A quantity or quality that can be used to describe an attribute. If you are considering the attribute "color," then the possible values of color are all of the names of colors that you might use. If you are considering a particular object, you observe it and assign a specific value to the attribute by saying, for example, "That paint is colored bright red."

Windows. Conventional computer terminals use the entire screen to present information drawn from one database. Computer terminals that can utilize window software can divide the screen into several different sections (or windows). Information drawn from different databases can be displayed in different windows. Thus, for example, with a Macintosh computer, you can have a word processing program going in one window and a graphics program going on simultaneously in a second window. Most current expert systems research is being conducted on computers that allow the user to display different views of the systems activity simultaneously. Windows are an example of a technique originally developed by AI researchers that has now become a part of conventional programming technology.

Workflow analysis. A technique to identify the people or jobs (when several people perform the same job) involved in a task and then track the flows of materials, paper, information, and feedback between each person or job. This allows you to see which people are analyzing and making decisions and helps to identify knowledge bottlenecks that exist.

Workstation. (Professional workstation, Intelligent workstation.) In this book, workstations generally refer to LISP machines or 32-bit computer systems that are used by expert systems developers or professionals (e.g., engineers) or to field expert systems. The coming generation of PCs will be 32-bit machines and thus, workstations will soon be a synonym for PCs.

References and Notes

The following list of references is not intended to be comprehensive. Instead, we have tried to indicate the most important and most readily available sources that you should consider if you wish to learn more about the topics discussed in any chapter of this book. In most cases, we have cited books because, even though they tend to be less current than magazine articles, they tend to be more readily available. Except in rare cases, we have avoided journal articles and monographs because they are often difficult to obtain.

We acquired most of the material in this book in the course of talking with people who are actively engaged in developing expert systems. In a few cases, some of the information has already been published in *Expert Systems Strategies*, the monthly newsletter edited by Paul Harmon. *Expert Systems Strategies* is published in the United States by Cutter Information Publications, 1100 Massachusetts Ave., Arlington, MA 02174. (617) 648-8700.

Section One. Basic Concepts

Chapter 1. Expert Systems Today

Feigenbaum, Edward, Pamela McCorduck, and H. Penny Nii. *The Rise of the Expert Company*. New York: Times Books, 1988.

Harmon, Paul, and David King. *Expert Systems: Artificial Intelligence in Business*. New York: John Wiley, 1985.

Harris, Larry R., and Dwight B. Davis. *Artificial Intelligence Enters the Marketplace*. New York: Bantam Books, 1986.

Chapter 2. Basic Expert Systems Techniques

Harmon, Paul, Rex Maus, and William Morrissey. *Expert Systems: Tools and Applications*. New York: John Wiley, 1988.

Shapiro, Alen D. *Structured Induction in Expert Systems*. New York: Addison-Wesley, 1987.

Walters, John, and Norman R. Nielsen. *Crafting Knowledge-Based Systems*. New York: John Wiley, 1988.

Section Two. Identifying Opportunities

Chapter 3. Identifying and Scoping Potential Applications—Part 1

Feigenbaum, Edward, Pamela McCorduck, and H. Penny Nii. *The Rise of the Expert Company*. New York: Times Books, 1988.

Harmon, Paul, Rex Maus, and William Morrissey. *Expert Systems: Tools and Applications*. New York: John Wiley, 1988.

Schoen, Sy, and Wendell Sykes. *Putting Artificial Intelligence to Work: Evaluating and Implementing Business Applications*. New York: John Wiley, 1987.

Chapter 4. Identifying and Scoping Potential Applications—Part 2

Kline, Paul J., and Steven B. Dolins. *Designing Expert Systems*. New York: John Wiley, 1989.

Section Three. Knowledge Acquisition and System Design

Chapter 5. Analyzing a Consultation

Bailey, Robert W. *Human Performance Engineering: A Guide for System Designers*. Englewood Cliffs, NJ: Prentice-Hall, 1982.

Gilbert, Thomas F. *Human Competence: Engineering Worthy Performance*. New York: McGraw-Hill, 1978. (Dr. Gilbert is the human performance analysts' performance analyst and this book is his best statement of the technology involved in understanding how and why people do things.)

Keller, Robert. *Expert System Technology: Development and Application.* Englewood Cliffs, NJ: Yourdon Press, 1987.

Yourdon, Edward. *Managing the Structured Techniques* (3rd Ed.) Englewood Cliffs, NJ: Yourdon Press, 1976.

Zemke, Ron, and T. Kramlinger. *Figuring Things Out: A Trainer's Guide to Needs and Task Analysis.* Reading, MA: Addison-Wesley, 1982. (This is probably the best general introduction to the various approaches to analyzing human task performance.)

For detailed training in how to analyze the flow of information within your organization, consider taking a Rummler-Brache Group workshop. For more information, contact The Rummler-Brache Group, 50 Mount Bethel Road, P.O. Box 4537, Warren, NJ 07060. (201) 757-5700.

Chapter 6. Cognitive Analysis

Holland, John H., et al. *Induction: Processes of Inference, Learning, and Discovery.* Cambridge, MA: MIT Press, 1986.

Holtzman, Samuel. *Intelligent Decision Systems.* Reading, MA: Addison-Wesley, 1989.

Newell, Allen, and Herbert A. Simon. *Human Problem Solving.* Englewood Cliffs, NJ: Prentice-Hall, 1972. (Newell and Simon are among the founders of AI, and this book is still the best general introduction to the cognitive analysis of human problem solving.)

Rasmussen, Jens. *Information Processing and Human-Machine Interaction: An Approach to Cognitive Engineering.* New York: North-Holland, 1986.

Stillings, Neil A., et al. *Cognitive Science: An Introduction.* Cambridge, MA: The MIT Press, 1987.

For a hands-on approach to learning object-oriented analysis and programming, consider buying the Object Vision software. For information, contact Object Vision, Inc., 2124 Kittredge Street, Suite 118, Berkeley, CA 94704. (415) 548-6935.

Chapter 7. Knowledge Acquisition

Boose, John H. *Expertise Transfer for Expert System Design.* New York: Elsevier, 1986.

Boose, John H. and Brian Gaines. *Knowledge Acquisition Tools for Expert Systems.* New York: Academic Press, 1988.

Hart, Anna. *Knowledge Acquisition for Expert Systems.* New York: McGraw-Hill, 1986.

Kidd, Alison L. *Knowledge Acquisition for Expert Systems.* New York: Plenum Press, 1987.

Section Four. Program Development

Chapter 8. Creating Small Rule-Based Systems

Hicks, Richard, and Ronald Lee. *VP-Expert for Business Applications.* Oakland, CA: Holden-Day Inc., 1989.

Holsapple, Clyde W., and A.B. Whinston. *Manager's Guide to Expert Systems Using GURU.* Homewood, IL: Dow Jones-Irwin, 1986.

Pedersen, Ken. *Expert Systems Programming.* New York: John Wiley, 1989.

Weiss, Sholom M. and C.A. Kulikowski. *A Practical Guide to Designing Expert Systems.* Totowa, NJ: Rowman & Allanheld, 1984.

For detailed training in the development of a small expert system using VP-Expert, consider taking the Harmon Associates workshop. For information, contact Harmon Associates, 151 Collingwood, San Francisco, CA 94114. (415) 861-1660.

Chapter 9. Creating Forward Chaining Systems

Brownston, Lee, et al. *Programming Expert Systems in OPS5: An Introduction to Rule-Based Programming.* Reading, MA: Addison-Wesley, 1985.

Cooper, Thomas A., and Nancy Wogrin. *Rule-Based Programming with OPS5.* Palo Alto, CA: Morgan Kaufmann Pub. Inc., 1988.

Stock, Michael. *AI Theory and Application in the VAX Environment.* New York: McGraw-Hill, 1989.

For detailed training in the use of OPS5, consider taking training in the use of VAX OPS5 or KnowledgeTool from DEC or IBM, respectively.

Chapter 10. Creating Systems with Context Trees

Most of the context-tree-based tools were derived from the work at Stanford on MYCIN and EMYCIN. The following book provides the best summary of all of the original research.

Buchanan, Bruce G., and E.H. Shortliffe. *Rule-Based Expert Systems: The MYCIN Experiments of the Stanford Heuristic Programming Project*. Reading, MA: Addison-Wesley, 1984.

Murray, Jerome T., and Marilyn J. Murray. *Expert Systems in Data Processing: A Professional's Guide*. New York: McGraw-Hill, 1988.

For detailed training in the development of a mainframe-based expert system using AION's ADS, consider taking the Harmon Associates workshop. For information, contact Harmon Associates, 151 Collingwood, San Francisco, CA 94114. (415) 861-1660.

Chapter 11. Creating Hybrid Systems

Charniak, E., C.K. Riesbeck, and D.V. McDermott, *Artificial Intelligence Programming*. Hillsdale, NJ: Lawrence Erlbaum Associates, 1980.

Cox, Brad J. *Object-Oriented Programming: An Evolutionary Approach*. Reading, MA: Addison-Wesley, 1986.

Kunz, J.C., T.P. Kehler, and M.D. Williams. "Applications Development Using a Hybrid AI Development System." *AI Magazine*, 5 (3), 1984.

Schmucker, Kurt J. *Object-Oriented Programming for the Macintosh*. Indianapolis, IN: Hayden Books, 1986.

Stroustrup, Bjarne. *The C++ Programming Language*. Reading, MA: Addison-Wesley, 1986.

The best way to learn about LISP is to buy Gold Hill Computer's Golden Common LISP software (which runs on a PC) and study the excellent tutorial that is included with the LISP package. Gold Hill Computers, 163 Harvard Street, Cambridge, MA 02139. (617) 492-2071. With the Gold Hill package, you will also get the two most important books on LISP:

Steele, G.L., Jr. *Common LISP: The Language (Reference Manual)*. Maynard, MA: Digital Press, 1984.

Winston, P.H. and B.K.P. Horn. *LISP (2nd Ed.)*. Reading MA: Addison-Wesley, 1984.

If you are considering developing an application in a hybrid LISP tool, then you should also consider acquiring AXLE, a tutorial in hybrid system development that is sold by Albathion Software. The tutorial sits on top of Gold Hill's GoldWorks, but it can also be purchased in a standalone version ($1,995). For more information, contact Albathion Software, 186½ Hampshire St., Cambridge MA 02138. (AXLE is also available from Gold Hill Computers.)

Chapter 12. Procedural Considerations

Kowalik, J.S., ed. *Coupling Symbolic and Numerical Computing in Expert Systems*. (Papers from a workshop.) New York: Elsevier Science, 1986.

Chapter 13. Database Considerations

Addis, T.R. *Designing Knowledge-Based Systems*. Englewood Cliffs, NJ: Prentice-Hall, 1985.

Parsaye, Kamran, et al. *Intelligent Databases: Object Oriented, Deductive Hypermedia Technologies*. New York: John Wiley, 1989.

Zdonik, Stanley B. and David Maier. *Readings in Object-Oriented Databases*. San Mateo, CA: Morgan Kaufmann, 1989.

Chapter 14. Interface Considerations

Hendler, James A., ed. *Expert Systems: The User Interface*. Norwood, NJ: Ablex Pub. Corp., 1988.

Margolis, Neal. "Expert System Interfaces and Domain Modeling" in *Expert Systems Strategies* newsletter. Vol. 4, No. 6, 1988.

Shneiderman, Ben. *Designing the User Interface: Strategies for Effective Human-Computer Interaction*. Reading, MA: Addison-Wesley, 1987.

Section Five. Managing the Development of Expert Systems

Chapter 15. Managing an Expert Systems Development Effort

Bachant, J., and J. McDermott. "R1 Revisited: Four Years in the Trenches." *AI Magazine*, 5 (3), 1984. (This is a magazine article, but it is the best account of the problems of expanding and maintaining a very large expert system. R1 is another name for DEC's XCON system, which was fielded in 1981, has over 12,000 rules, and is maintained by a staff of several people.)

Schoen, Sy, and Wendell Sykes. *Putting Artificial Intelligence to Work: Evaluating and Implementing Business Applications*. New York: John Wiley, 1987.

Appendices

Feigenbaum, Edward, and Pamela McCorduck. *The Fifth Generation: Artificial Intelligence and Japan's Computer Challenge to the World*. Reading, MA: Addison-Wesley, 1983.

Additional Notes

The following is the best general handbook on artificial intelligence and a good supplement to our Glossary:

Shapiro, Stuart C., ed. *The Encyclopedia of Artificial Intelligence*. (2 vols.). New York: John Wiley, 1987.

The field is changing too fast for any general magazine to keep up. If you are serious about developing commercial expert systems, you should consider subscribing to one or more newsletters and to the following journals and magazines:

AI Expert. Miller Freeman Publications, 500 Howard St., San Francisco, CA 94105. ($37/yr)

AI Magazine. American Association for Artificial Intelligence, 445 Burgess Dr., Menlo Park, CA 94025-3496. ($25/yr for membership in AAAI, which includes this magazine.)

Data & Knowledge Engineering. Elsevier Science Pub. Journal Information Center, 655 Avenue of the Americas, New York, NY 10010. ($149.75/yr)

Expert Systems: The International Journal of Knowledge Engineering. Learned Information Inc., 143 Old Marlton Pike, Metford, NJ 08055. ($79/yr)

Expert Systems Strategies Newsletter (Paul Harmon, Editor). Cutter Information Corp., 1100 Massachusetts Ave., Arlington MA 02174. (617) 648-8700. ($327/yr)

Expert Systems With Applications. Pergamon Press, Inc., Maxwell House, Fairview Park, Elmsford, NY 10523.

IEEE Expert. IEEE Computer Society, 345 E. 47th St., New York, NY 10017. ($12 for IEEE members. IEEE membership is separate. Nonmember subscriptions are available.)

Knowledge Acquisition. Academic Press, Journal Dept. 1250 Sixth Ave., San Diego, CA 92101 ($49/yr)

PC AI. Knowledge Technology Inc., 3310 West Bell Rd., Suite 119, Phoenix, AZ 85023. ($28/yr)

Index

Page references in boldface type indicate the location of key definitions or examples.

Page references in italic indicate the location of a figure or table that illustrates the concept or the relation of the concept to other concepts.

A

Abstraction, 115–116
   adding, small rule-based systems, *156*
   levels of, *44*, *122*
   replacing recurring rules, 165, *165*
Accuracy, user concerns, 84
ACTIONS block, **167**
ADS. *See* AION Development System (ADS)
Advisory systems, user interface, 248–255
AI Corp., KBMS, 242, 243
AION Development System (ADS), 193–194, 195–197, 200, 224, 226, 242, 253, 254
   conditional text feature, **253**
   see also Boole & Babbage, DASD Advisor
Albatheon, AXLE, 249, *250*, *251*
Algorithm, **12**
Alphabetic rule
   base, *186*
   decision tree, *187*
Analogy, reasoning-by-, avoid, 72
Analysis and design, managing expert systems development, 271–272, *271*; *see also* Cognitive structure of problem, analyzing; Consultation, analyzing
Apple, 8
   Knowledge Navigator, 8
   Macintosh, 45, 54
      intelligent job aids, 51, **52–54**, 59

Application selection
   cognitive structure, identifying, 50, 75–83
   corporate strategy, 49, 51–58
      common strategies, listed, 51, *52*
   cost issues, 50, 85–89
   key expert systems criteria, 50, 66–74
      case data, 67–68
      human expert, 66–67
      need for narrow, well-defined task, 68–70
   management issues, 50, 85–89
   potential applications, developing list, 49, 58–66
      bottlenecks, knowledge, 59
      task definition, 62–66
      top-down vs. bottom-up approach, 58
      worksheet, *64–65*, 66
   steps, 49–50
   user issues, 50, 83–85
Arborist (TI), 252
Architecture
   hybrid systems, *47*
   induction systems, *24*
ART, 213, 220
Artificial intelligence, **3**
ASEA Advisor System (Ford Motor), 191–193, *192*
   Maintenance Assistant, 69, *70*
Attribute(s), **13**, *14*, *21*
   context trees, 199–200
   multivalued, small rule-based systems, **161–162**
   names, knowledge mapping notation, 129–130

319

Availability, user concerns, 84
AXLE, Albatheon, 249, *250, 251*

B

Backward chaining systems, 76, 80–81, *81, 172*, 174, 181
   context trees, 189–190, 193, 201
   hybrid systems, 218, 219
   rule-based systems, **30–36**, *30, 32, 33*
BASIC, 75
Bonus Advisor, *247*
Boole & Babbage, DASD Advisor, 195–197, 199, *200*, 202, *240, 241*, 253, 284
   context tree, *196*, 222–226
Bottlenecks, knowledge
   application selection, 59
   identification, 91

C

C, 153, 202, 221, 222, 226, 229–230, 241
   converting conventional to expert systems, 230–232
   library, KES, 227–228, *228*
   procedural consideration, 230–232
C++, 41, 245
Career enhancement, management concerns, 85–86
Carnegie-Mellon, SOAR, 285
Car simulation (VP-Expert), user interface, *258, 259*
CASE, 8, 56–58, 61, 245, 247
Case data
   application selection, 67–68
   storing in database, database integration with expert systems, 239
Case-driven theorists, **67**
Case Review Interviews, knowledge acquisition, 142, 147–149
CATS-1 (GE), 229
Causal or temporal relationships, complex, avoid, 74
Certainty factors, adding, small rule-based systems, 162–164, *162*
Chunking, conceptual, 114–120
   limits on, 116–120
   unchunking, 119

Chess, heuristics, 18–19
Classification hierarchies, cognitive analysis of problem, 121–122, *123*
Class-object description, knowledge mapping notation, 128–130
Class unit, **243**
COBOL, 56, 57, 75, 133, 221, 222, 233
Cognitive structure of problem, 50, 75–83
   application selection, 50, 75–83
   configuration/design problems, **77–78**, *78*, 79
   diagnostic problems, **76, 77**
   implications of different types, 81–83
   inference and control, 80–81
   monitoring problems, **76–77**
   planning/scheduling problems, 79–80, *79*
   procedural problems, 75–76
Cognitive structure of problem, analysis, 90, 109–136
   classification hierarchies, 121–122, *123*
   complex relation hierarchies, 122–124, *124*
   conceptual chunking and problem-solving space, 114–120
      limits on, 116–120
      unchunking, 119
   knowledge map development, 133–135
   knowledge-mapping notation, 124–133
      class-object, description, 128–130
      hierarchy description, 124–128
      rule description and procedural model specification, 130–133, *132*
   knowledge, types, 110–113
   memory, hierarchical structure, 113–114, *113*
   object-attribute-value model, **120–124**, *126*
Collins and Quillian, 113–114
Common-sense tasks, avoid, 71–72
Complex causal or temporal relationships, avoid, 74
Complex relation hierarchies, cognitive analysis of problem, 122–124, *124*
Complex rules, **224**
Complicated geometric or spatial reasoning, avoid, 74
Compound rules, procedural consideration, **225–226**
Computer-assisted software engineering (CASE), 8, 56–58, 61, 245, 247
Computer-integrated manufacturing, 245

Conceptual chunking and problem-solving space, cognitive analysis of problem, 114–120
 limits on, 116–120
 unchunking, 119
Conditional text feature (AION ADS), **253**
Confidence
 expert, **37**
 factor(s)
  MYCIN, 38, *39, 40,* 41
  rule-based systems, 36–41
 user, **37–38**
Configuration/design problems, cognitive structure, **77–78,** *78,* 79
Conflict resolution problem, **78**
Conflict set, **173**
Constraints, 78, *125,* 130, *184*
Construct trees
 dynamic, *29*
 static, *28*
Consultation, analyzing, 91–108, *106*
 creating scenario/summary, 105–108
 dataflow analysis, 99–105, *100, 101, 102, 103, 104*
 human performance analysis, 92–99, *93*
Context, **189**
Context trees, 189–202
 deciding what contexts signify, 191–194
  traversing tree, 193–194
 expansion/revision, 201–202
 how system works, 189–190
  backward-chaining, 189–190, 193, 201
 implementing, 195–201
  adding rules, 201
  attributes, 199–200
  entry assertions and goals, **200–201,** *201*
  iterative contexts, 197–199, *198*
  planning flow, context-to-context, 196–197
 initial, creating, 194–195
  overview vs. detailed approach, 194
 procedural taks, *192,* 195
 static cf. dynamic, **190–191**
 structured analysis task, 195
Control knowledge, writing into rules, forward chaining systems, 180–181
Conventional programs, combining with expert system, 226–228, *227*

Conversions, adding rules for, small rule-based systems, 166
Coopers & Lybrand, ExperTax, 140, 141, 148
Corporate strategy, application selection, 49, 51–58
 common strategies, listed, 51, *52*
Cost/benefit analysis, management concerns, 87–88
Cost issues, application selection, 50, 85–89
Cullinet, Application Expert, 226–227
Cultural impact, management concerns, 86–87
Customizing inference, small rule-based systems, 167–169

D

DASD Advisor (Boole & Babbage), 195–197, 199, 200, 202, 240, 241
 context tree, *196,* 222–226
Data cf. knowledge, **12**
Database, 235, 245–247
 object-oriented, 245
 relational, 245
 rule, **166,** 238–239
Database integration with expert systems, 235–245, *236*
 cases, storing in database, 239
 data type, 241
 expert system as
  back end, 238
  front end, 237–238
 file format and access, 239–241
 making connection, 242–245
  database commands, 242
  sourcing, 242–245
 rationale, 236–237
 rules, storing in database, 238–239
Database management systems, 235–237
Dataflow analysis, 99–105, *100–104*
Data General, Automated Transfer Pricing System, 183–184, 233, 239, 241, *241*
 demons, 215
 priority use, *185,* 284, 285, 133
Data type, database integration with expert systems, 241
Data-typing, dynamic, **48**
DB2, 235, 245

dBASE, 235, 236, 239, 242
Decision table, **157–159,** *158*
Decision tree, alphabetic rule, *187*
Deep knowledge, 111–113
Definitional relationships, **13**
Definitional rules, **25–26**
Demarco, Tom, 99
Demons
　adding, hybrid systems, *214,* 215
　Data General ATP, 215
Dependencies, forward chaining systems, 180
Depth first and breadth first search, OPS5, **186,** *187*
Development. *See* Managing expert systems development
Diagnostic problems, cognitive structure, **76, 77**
Digital Equipment Corp. (DEC), 8
　RISC-based UNIX machine, 4
　VAX, 59, 60, 80, 88
　　VMS system, 4
　　workstation, 54
　XCON, 4, 60, 73, 173, 276, 285
　XCON-IN-RIME, 285
Distribution-Type Object (Data General), *134,* 135
DL/I, 245
Domain, knowledge, 111–113
Duda, Richard, 100
Du Pont
　MIS group, 53, 54
　PC-based system, ROI, 88
Dynamic data-typing, **48**
Dynamic image, **257,** 260

E

ELSEIF statements, 225–226, *225*
Embedded expert systems, prototype/maintenance aid, 51, 56–58, 60–62
Embedded knowledge bases, procedural consideration, 226–228
EMYCIN, 190, 191, 193
Enabling/disabling conditions, forward chaining systems, **181–182**
Encapsulation, **42**
ENFORM (Mind Path Technologies), 260, *261*

Entry assertions and goals, context trees, **200–201,** *201*
Expansion/revision, context trees, 201–202
Expert(s), human
　application selection, 66–67
　confidence, **37**
　consultation with, forward chaining systems, *178–179*
　disagreement among, 73–74
　managing expert systems development, 270, 272, 276–277, 280, 282
　see also Knowledge acqusition
ExperTax (Coopers & Lybrand), 140, 141, 148
Expert knowledge
　recommendations and user actions, 107
　source, 107
Expert system(s), **3**
　architecture, 20
　design, 89–90
　embedded, prototype/maintenance aid, 51, 56–58, 60–62
　fielded applications, total, 6
　history, 4–7, *5*
　integration, 10
　management and pitfalls, 9–10
　market for, 3–4
　problems in widening use, 8–10
　strategies for 1990s, 7, 7–8
　see also Managing expert system development; Techniques, basic
Expert System Environment (IBM), 193–195
　Focus Control Blocks, **193**
Explanation design, user interface, 84–85, 252–254
Explorer (TI), 7

F

Factor analysis tables, **238**
Feedback, human performance analysis, 92, 94–95
Fielded applications, total, expert system, 6
File format/access, database integration with expert systems, 239–241
FIND statements, **167**
1st Class, 23, 24

Focus, PC-, 245
Ford Motor, 54
    ASEA Advisor System, 191–193, *192*
    ASEA Maintenance Assistant, 69, *70*
Form-based system, user interface, 260–262, *261, 262, 263*
FORTH, 229
Fortran, 57
Fortune 500 companies, 55, 56
Forward chaining systems, 76, 80–81, *81*
    hybrid, 218, 219
    rule-based, *31*, **36**, *37*
Forward chaining systems, creating, 171–188, *172*
    expert, consultation with, *178–179*
    giving system a way to stop, 179–180
    knowledge acquisition, *175*
    object-attribute-value characteristics, *176*
    phases, 174
    problem definition, 174–176
    rule execution, controlling, 180–185
    rule set, initial, 177–179
        control knowledge, writing into rules, 180–181
        dependencies, 180
        enabling/disabling conditions, **181–182**
        rule priorities, **183–185**, *185*
    writing code to obtain facts, 176–177
Fourth-generation language tools, 57–58
Frames, **203**, 204
    creation, *212, 213*
    definition, hybrid systems, 206–210, *207, 211*
Front-end analysis, **89**
    managing expert systems development, 267–270, *269, 271*

G

Garbage collection, **48**
General Electric, CATS-1, 229
General Motors, 54
Geometric or spatial reasoning, complicated, avoid, 74
Gilbert, Thomas F., 95
Glossary, 305–313
Goal statement, writing, small rule-based systems, 159
Gold Hill Computers
    Golden Connection, 239, *240*
    GoldWorks, 203, 204, 205, 207, 212, 215, 216, 220, 224, 233, 239, *240*, 242, 243, 257; *see also* Hybrid systems
Graphics, user interface, 254–255, *255*
GURU, 245

H

Handlers, **216**, *216*, 217
Hardware, user concerns, 83–84
Heuristic(s), **13**, 14
    chess, 18–19
    knowledge, 111–113
    rules, **25–26**
Hewlett-Packard workstations, 54
Hierarchy. *See under* Cognitive structure of problem, analysis
History, expert systems, 4–7, *5*
Human expert. *See* Experts, human
Human performance analysis, 92–99, *93*
Hybrid systems, 203–220
    adding demons, *214*, 215
    adding rules, 212–215
    architecture, *47*
    combining rules and objects, 41, 45–46
    frame definition, 206–210, *207, 211*
        slots, *208, 209*
    inference and control, 218–220
    instance definition, 210–212, *211*
        backward chaining, 218, 219
        forward chaining, 218, 219
    knowledge base, initial, 204–205
    message passing, adding, 216–218, *217, 218*
        cf. rules, 217–218
    metarules, 219–220
    modeling knowledge, 203–204
    object-oriented programming, **41–45**, 203, 204, 220
    phases, 205
    problem definition, 205–206, *206*
    screen object, 212
    techniques, basic, 20, **41–47**

324 INDEX

Hybrid Systems (Continued)
    truth maintenance/restraction, **219**
    user interface, 212
    see also Gold Hill Computers, GoldWorks

I

IBM, 4, 8, 55, 57
    DL/I, 245
    Expert System Environment, 193–195, 242
        Focus Control Blocks, **193**
    Knowledge Processing Environment, 8
    PCs, intelligent job aids, 51, **52–54,** 59
If-then construct, 25
Image
    dynamic, **257**, 260
    input, **257**
    output, **257**
Implementation, 281–283, *282*
Induction systems
    architecture, *24*
    techniques, basic, **20–24**
        architecture, *24*
Inference, **14**
    and control
        hybrid systems, 218–220
        problem, cognitive structure, 80–81
        rule-based systems, 29–36
Inference engine, **19**, *34–35*
    OPS5, 173
INFOS action frame, **239**
INGRES, 245
Inheritance, **42–43**, *43*
Input image, **257**
Instance definition, hybrid systems, 210–212, *211*
Instantiation, **167**, *167*
Intelligence, basic techniques, **14–17**, 121
Intelligent critic, **246**
Intelligent job aids, 51, **52–54,** 59
    vs. memorization, 96–99, *98*
Interface
    maintenance, **284**
    test, **249**, *250*, *251*
Interviewing, knowledge acquisition, 142–149
Iterative contexts, context trees, 197–199, *198*

J

Job aids
    intelligent, 51, **52–54,** 59
    memorization vs., 96–99, *98*

K

KBMS, AI Corp., 242, 243
KEE, 131, 213, 220, 242, 243
    default mapping, *244*
KES, 226, 227–228
    C library, 227–228, *228*
Knowledge, **12–14**
    bottleneck
        application selection, 59
        identification, 91
    cf. data, **12**
    domain, 111–113
    heuristic, 111–113
    procedural vs. delcarative, **12–13**
    representation, OPS5, 173–174
    separation from inference, techniques, basic, 19–20
    techniques, basic, **12–14**
    types, cognitive analysis of problem, 110–113
    see also Expert(s), human
Knowledge acquisition, 10, 89–90, 137–149, **137**, *143*
    forward chaining systems, creating, *175*
    interviewing, 142–149
        Case Review Interviews, 142, 147–149
        initial, 142, 144–147
        preparing for, 142–144
        task analysis, initial, 142–143
        test case use, *145*, 146–147
        time and case need estimates, *146*
    as own expert, 138
    working with expert, 138–142
        choosing expert, 138–139
        human communication problems, 141–142
        scheduling and management support, 139–140
        single vs. multiple, 141
        users, 140–141
Knowledge base, initial, hybrid systems, 204–205

Knowledge Craft, 213, 220
Knowledge engineering, process, *137*
Knowledge map development, cognitive analysis of problem, 133–135
Knowledge-mapping notation, 124–133
  class-object, description, 128–130
  hierarchy description, 124–128
  rule description and procedural model specification, 130–133, *132*
Knowledge Navigator (Apple), 8
Knowledge Processing Environment (IBM), 8

L

Language tools, fourth-generation, 57–58
Late binding, **48**
Levels of abstraction, *44*
LISP, 5, 7, 8, 41, **47–48**, 215, 217, 220, 221, 229, 239, 243
LISP-based tools, 82–83
LISP machines, 5, 51, 56, 60
Loan analysis, 19; *see also* Oracle Credit Advisor
Lotus 1-2-3, 235, 245

M

Macintosh. *See* Apple
Mahler, Ed, 53
Mainframes, mid-size advisors, 51, 55–56, 60
Maintenance
  embedded expert systems, 51, 56–58, 60–62
  interface, **284**
  managing expert systems development, 283–285
Management issues, application selection, 50, 85–89
Managing expert systems development, 9–10, 265, 267–285, *268*
  analysis and design, 271–272, *271*
    return on investment, 273
  expert, 270, 272, 276–277, 280, 282
  front-end analysis, 267–270, *269, 271*
  implementation, 281–283, *282*
  maintenance, 283–285
  pitfalls, 9–10
  Project Champion, 268
  prototype development, 273–277, *274*
  senior management and, 270, 272–273, 277, 280, 283
  staffing, 270, 272, 274–276, 278–280
  systems development, 277–281, *279*
  testing, 281–283, *282*
  users, 270, 272, 277, 280, 282–283
Manufacturing, computer-integrated, 245
Market for expert systems, 3–4
Memorization vs. job aids, 96–99, *98*
Memory, hierarchical structure, 113–114, *113*
Menus, scrolling, **252**
Message passing, **43**
  adding, hybrid systems, 216–218, *217, 218*
  cf. rules, 217–218
Metarules, hybrid systems, 219–220
MicroExplorer, 7
Mid-size advisors
  mainframes, 51, 55–56, 60
  PCs or workstations, 51, 54–55, 59–60
Miller, G.A., 116, 117
Mind Path Technologies, ENFORM, 260, *261*
MIS groups, 4, 6, 9
Modus ponens, 14, 29
Monitoring problems, cognitive structure, **76–77**
Motivation, user concerns, 85–86
MV 1000, 239
MYCIN, 56, 133, 190, 191
  confidence factors, 38, *39, 40,* 41

N

Needs, user
  evaluation, user interface, 249
  perceived, 83
Networks, **122,** *124, 127*
Nexpert Object, 213, 220, 243
Nickel and dime problem, *15–16*

O

Object(s), **13,** *14, 21*
  rule output, customizing, *214*
Object-attribute-value characteristics
  cognitive analysis of problem, **120–124,** *126*
  forward chaining systems, creating, *176*
  rule-based systems, small, creating, *155*

Object Description Worksheets, *129*, 130, *134*
Object-oriented programming/systems, 8
  databases, 245
  hybrid systems, **41–45**, 203, *204*, 220
OPS5, 82, 171–174, 180, 186–188, 190, 285
  depth first and breadth first search, **186**, *187*
  inference engine, 173
  knowledge representation, 173–174
  Rete algorithm, 186, 188
  rule food, 174
Oracle Credit Advisor, 59, *61*, 68, 69, *100*, 101, *103*, *104*, 222–224, 238, 245, 249
Organization diagram, Rummler-Brache, 97
Output
  human performance analysis, 92, 95
  image, **257**

P

Pacific Bell, 54
Pascal, 75, 153, 221
PC-Focus, 245
PCs, mid-size advisors, 51, 54–55, 59–60
Perceived need, user concerns, 83
Perceptual expertise tasks, avoid, 72
Performer, human performance analysis, 92–94
Personal Consultant Easy (TI), 7, 189, *190*
Personal Consultant Plus (TI), 7, 189, *190*, 195, 229, 230, 242, 254, *256*, *257*, 260
PL/1, 221
Planning/scheduling problems, cognitive structure, 79–80, *79*
Porting
  conventional to expert systems, 233
  knowledge base to conventional language, 229–230
Problem
  cognitive content, 90
  definition
    forward chaining systems, creating, 174–176
    hybrid systems, 205–206, *206*
    rule-based systems, small, creating, 153–155, *154*
  recognition, users, 105–107
  scoping, **89**
  see also Cognitive structure of problem *entries*
Procedural considerations, 221–234
  conventional programs, combining with expert system, 226–228, *227*
    calling programs from knowledge base, 226
    embedded knowledge bases, 226–228
  converting conventional to expert systems, 230–233
    C, 230–232
  converting symbolic language based expert system to conventional language, 229–230
    porting knowledge base to conventional language, 229–230
    rewriting, 229
  incorporating procedural code into knowledge base, 222–226
    compound rules, **225–226**
    inconclusiveness of rules, 222–223
    iterations of rules, 223–225
Procedural vs. declarative knowledge, **12–13**
Procedural model specification, knowledge mapping notation, 130–133, *132*
Procedural problems, cognitive structure, 75–76
Procedural tasks, 68
  context trees, *192*, 195
Project Champion, 268
PROLOG, 47, 221, 229
Protocol analysis, **146**
Prototype
  development, 273–277, *274*
  embedded expert systems, 51, 56–58, 60–62

Q

Question
  design, user interface, 249–252
  development, specific, small rule-based systems, 160–161

R

Range checking, **252**
Reasoning-by-analogy tasks, avoid, 72

Recognition rules, **241**
Recurring clauses in rules, small rule-based systems, 164–166
Recursion, **47–48**
Relational databases, 245
Remote evaluation, **239**
Results, human performance analysis, 92, 95–96
Rete algorithm, OPS5, 186, 188
Return on investment analysis
  Du Pont PC-based system, 88
  managing expert systems development, 273
RIME, 285
RIME-based UNIX
  DEC, 4
  TI, 7
The Rise of the Expert Company, 87
Rule(s), 25–26
  adding
    context trees, 201
    hybrid systems, 212–215
  complex, **224**
  definitional, **25–26**
  description, knowledge mapping notation, 130–133, *132*
  execution, controlling, forward chaining systems, 180–185
  food, OPS5, 174
  heuristic, **25–26**
  ordering, small rule-based systems, 168
  output
    object, customizing, *214*
    window, **212**
  priorities, forward chaining systems, **183–185**, *185*
  recognition, **241**
  simple, **224**
  storing in database, database integration with expert systems, 238–239
Rule-based systems, 26–27, 28–29
  backward-chaining, **30–36**, *30, 32, 33*
  confidence factors, 36–41
  forward-chaining, 31, **36**, **37**
  inference and control, 29–36
  simple cf. structured, 26–29
  techniques, basic, 20, **24–40**

Rule-based systems, small, creating, 153–170
  customizing inference, 167–169
    expanding system with multiple goals, 169
    rule ordering, 168
    truth thresholds, 168, *169*
  enhancing rules, 159–167
    adding rules, 160
    attributes, multivalued, **161–162**
    certainty factors, adding, 162–164, *162*
    consolidating repetitive rules, 166–167
    conversions, adding rules for, 166
    question development, specific, 160–161
    recurring clauses in rules, 164–166
  initial rule set, 155–159
    abstractions, adding, *156*
    adding new rules, *157*
    decision table, developing from, 157–159
    goal statement, writing, 159
  problem definition, 153–155, *154*
    object-attribute-value characteristics, *155*
Rule set, initial, forward chaining systems, creating, 177–179
Rule systems, structured, **189**, *191*
Rummler, Geary, 96, 97
Rummler-Brache organization diagram, 97

S

Scheme (LISP dialect), 229
Schon, Donald, 67
Scoping problem, **89**
Screening clause, **181**
Screen object, hybrid systems, 212
Scrolling menus, **252**
Search spaces and decision trees, basic techniques, **16**, **17–19**, *17, 18*
Senior management role, expert systems development, 270, 272–273, 277, 280, 283
Significance, scientific meaning, 115–116
Simple rules, **224**
Simulation or modeling, user interface, 255–262
Situation, human performance analysis, 92–93
Slots, **173**
  hybrid systems, *208, 209*
Smalltalk, 41, 245

SOAR, 285
SPARC chip, Sun Microsystems, 7
Spatial or geometric reasoning, complex, avoid, 74
Speed, user concerns, 84
Sponsor, 85, 87
Spreadsheet access, expert systems, 245–246, *246*, *247*
SQL, 235, 243, 245, 246
Staffing, managing expert systems development, 270, 272, 274–276, 278–280
State, 16
    editor, **196**, *197*
Statement, **13**
Static cf. dynamic context trees, **190–191**
Steps, **200**, *201*
Structured analysis tasks, 68–70
    context trees, 195
Structured rule systems, **189**, *191*
Sun Microsystems, 54
    SPARC chip, 7
Symbolic language, 47–48
Syntelligence, 100
    Lending Advisor, 252, *253*

T

Tasks
    analysis, initial, knowledge acquisition, 142–143
    definition, application selection, 62–66
    procedural, 68
    structured analysis, 68–70
    things to avoid, 71–74
    verbal knowledge in, 70–71
        telephone test, 71
Techniques, basic, 12–48
    hybrid systems, 20, **41–47**
    induction systems, **20–24**
        architecture, *24*
    intelligence, **14–17**, 121
    knowledge, **12–14**
        separation from inference, 19–20
    rule-based systems, 20, **24–40**
    search spaces and decision trees, **16**, **17–19**, *17*, *18*
    symbolic language, 47–48

Telephone test, 71
Teletype interview, **248**
Temporal relationships, complex, avoid, 74
TestBench, 229, 230
Test case use, knowledge acquisition, 145, 146–147
Testing, managing expert systems development, 281–283, *282*
Test interface, **249**, *250*, *251*
Texas Instruments, 54
    Arborist, 252
    Data Systems Group, 7
    Personal Consultant Easy, 7, 189, *190*
    Personal Consultant Plus, 7, 189, *190*, 195, 229, 230, 242, 254, *256*, *257*, 260
    strategies for 1990s, 7–8, *7*
Text feature, conditional, (AION ADS), **253**
Theorists, **67**
Time and case need estimates, knowledge acquisition, *146*
Time-stamped trace, **226**
Top-down vs. bottom-up approach, application selection, 58
Trace, time-stamped, **226**
Training, user concerns, 86
Truth
    maintenance/restraction, hybrid systems, **219**
    thresholds, small rule-based systems, 168, *169*
Type checking, **252**

U

UNIX, 4
    RISC-based
        DEC, 4
        TI, 7
U.S.
    Department of Defense, 56
    NASA, 56
User(s)
    confidence, **37–38**
    interaction, 107
    issues in application selection, 50, 83–85
    managing expert systems development, 270, 272, 277, 280, 282–283
    problem recognition, 105–107

User interface, 248–263
   advisory systems, 248–255
      easy start for system, 249
      explanation design, 252–254
      graphics, 254–255, *255*
      need evaluation, 249
      question design, 249–252
   hybrid systems, 212
   simulation or modeling, 255–262
      car simulation (VP-Expert), *258*, 259
      form-based system, 260–262, *261*, *262*, *263*

V

Values, **13**, *14*, 21
   knowledge mapping notation, 130
Van Cuylenberg, Peter, 7
Variable rules, **238**
VAX (DEC), 59, 60, 80, 88
   VMS, 4
   workstation, 54

Verbal knowledge in tasks, 70–71
VMS system, DEC, 4
Volatile expertise tasks, avoid, 72–73
VP-Expert, 242, 257, *258*, 259

W

Window, rule output, **212**
Work environment, human performance analysis, 92, 94
Worksheet, application selection, *64–65*, 66
Workstations, 51, 56, 60

X

XCON (DEC), 4, 60, 73, 173, 276, 285
   -IN-RIME, 285
Xerox Star, 45